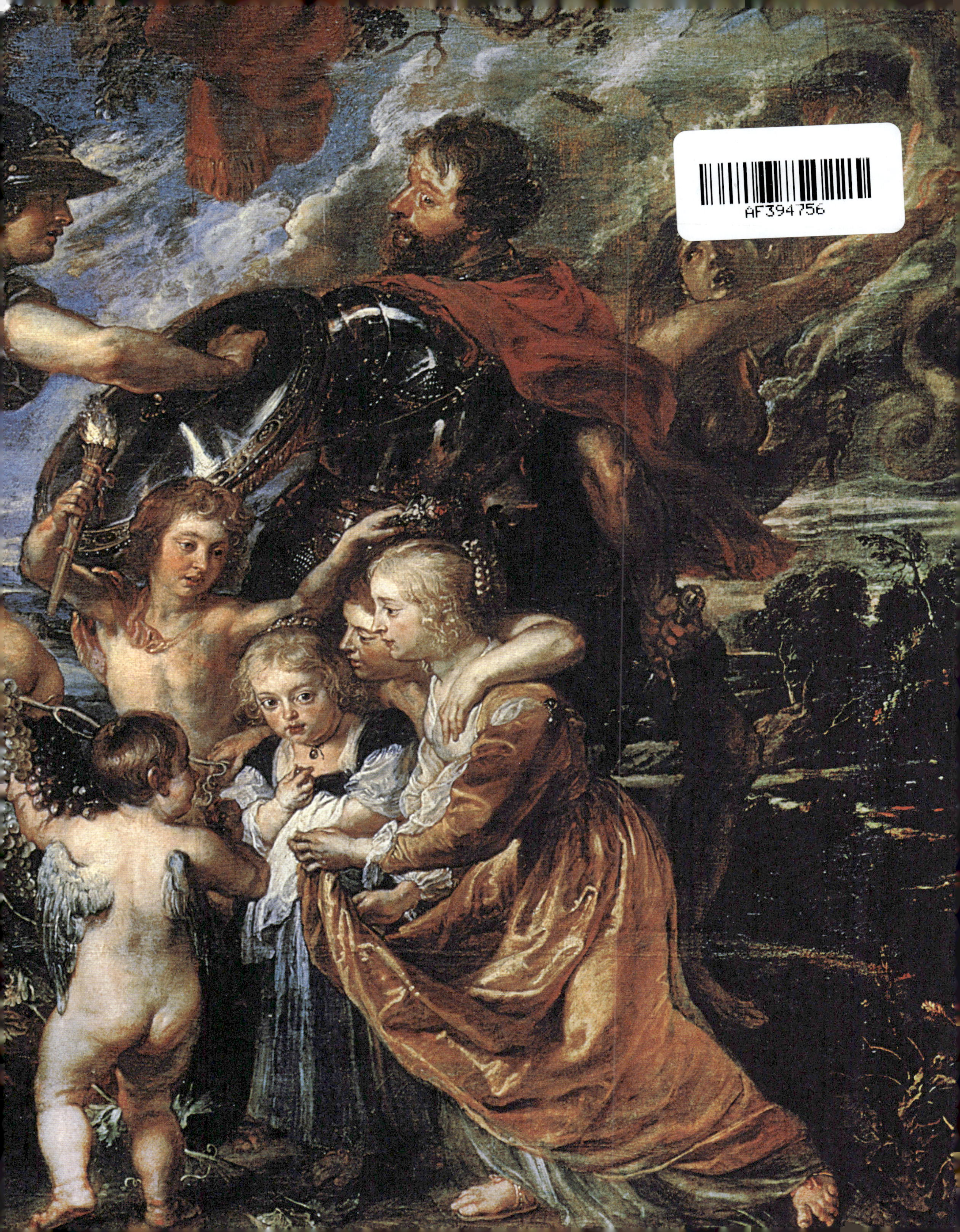
AF394756

RUBENS

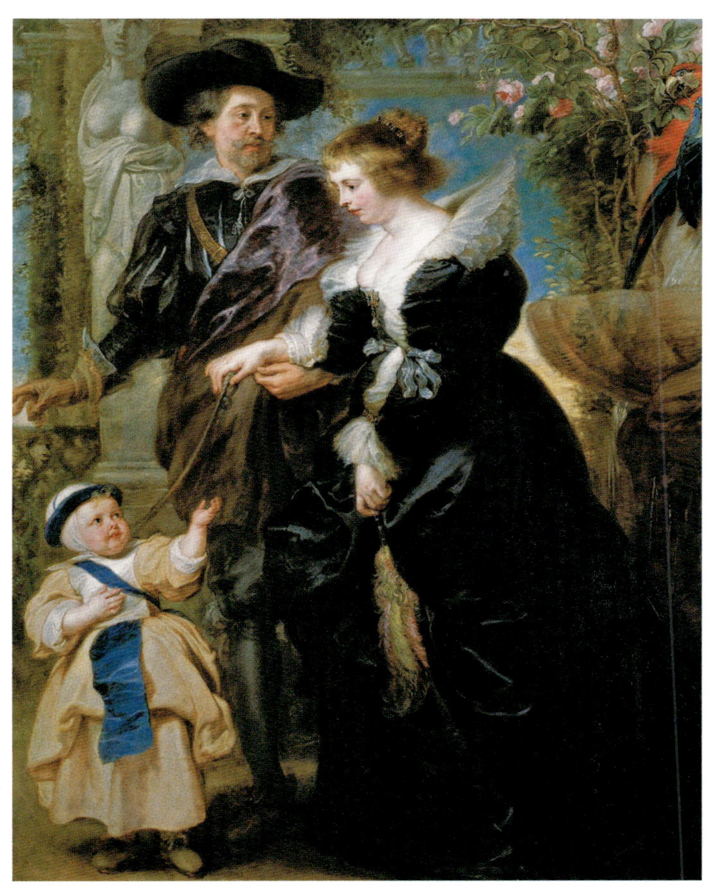

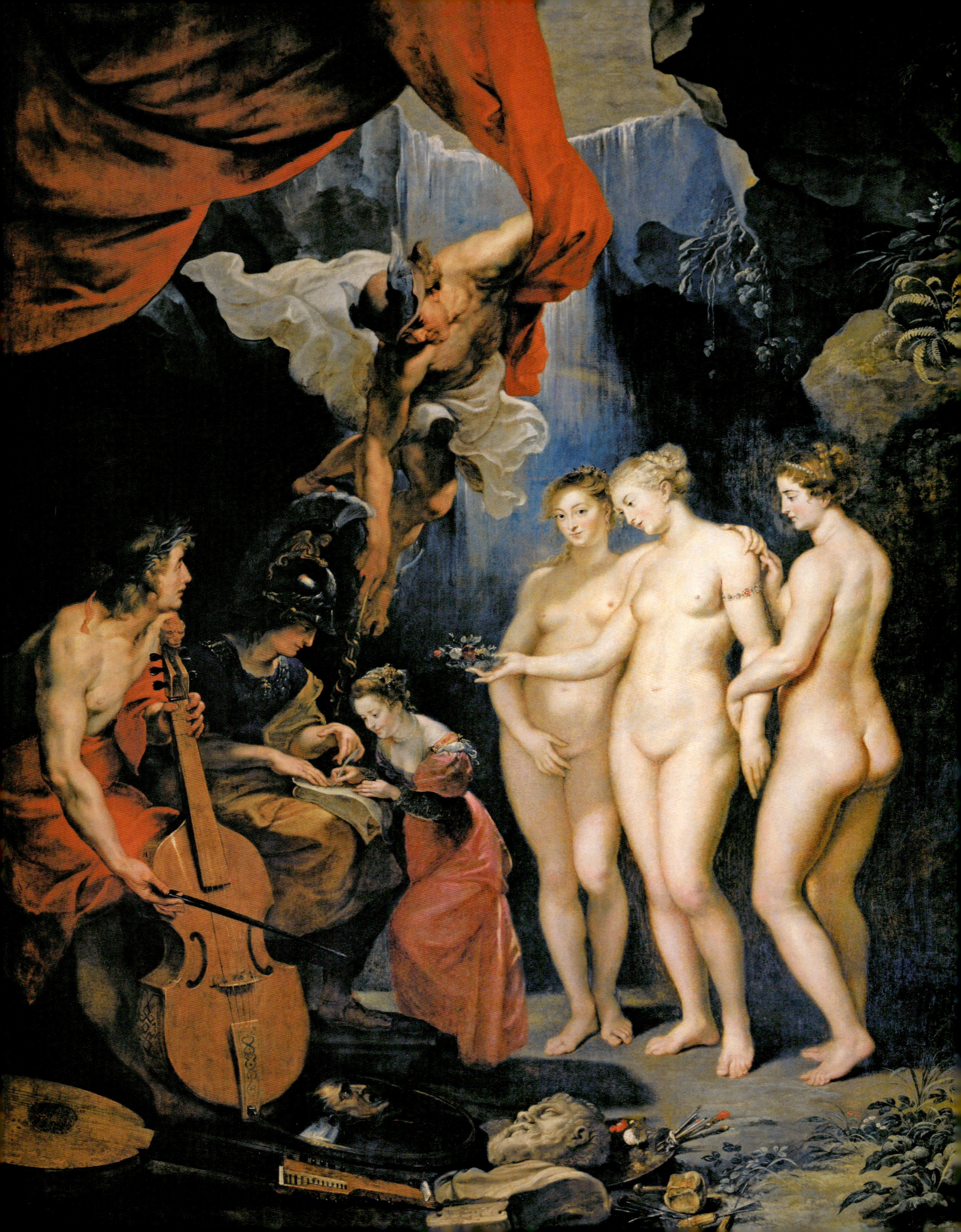

RUBENS

HIS LIFE AND WORKS IN 500 IMAGES

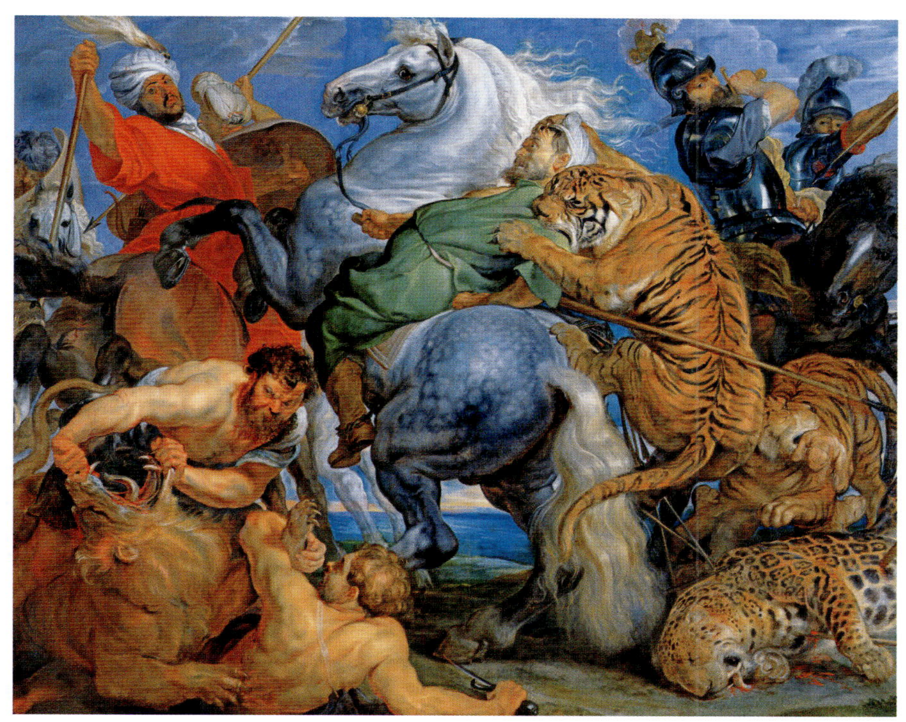

AN ILLUSTRATED EXPLORATION OF THE ARTIST, HIS LIFE AND
CONTEXT, WITH A GALLERY OF 300 PAINTINGS AND DRAWINGS

SUSIE HODGE

LORENZ BOOKS

Page 1: *Rubens, his Wife Hélène Fourment and
their son Frans*, c.1635. Page 2: *The Medici Cycle:
Education of the Princess*, 1622–25. Page 3: *Tiger
Hunt*, 1615–16. Below: *Self-portrait*, c.1615–34.
Opposite left: *Portrait of Susanna Fourment*,
c.1625. Opposite middle: *King David Playing
the Harp*, 1616, Rubens and Jan Boeckhorst.
Opposite right: *Clara Serena*, 1616.

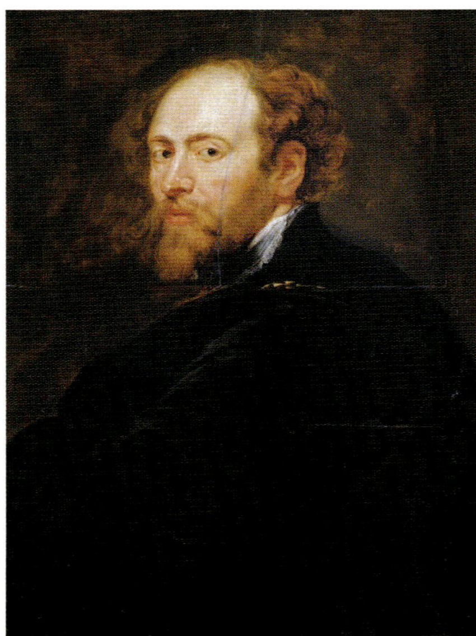

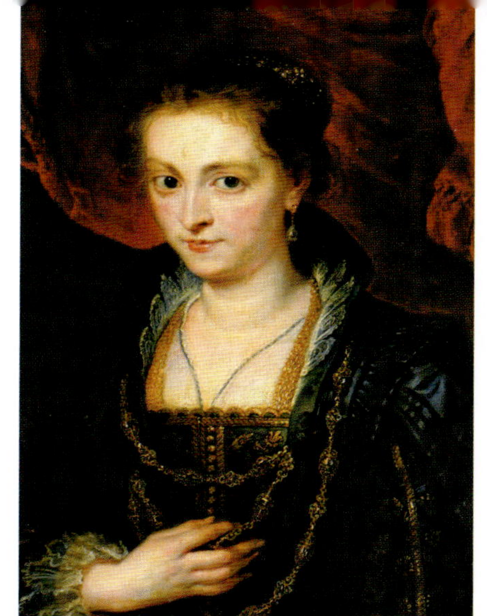 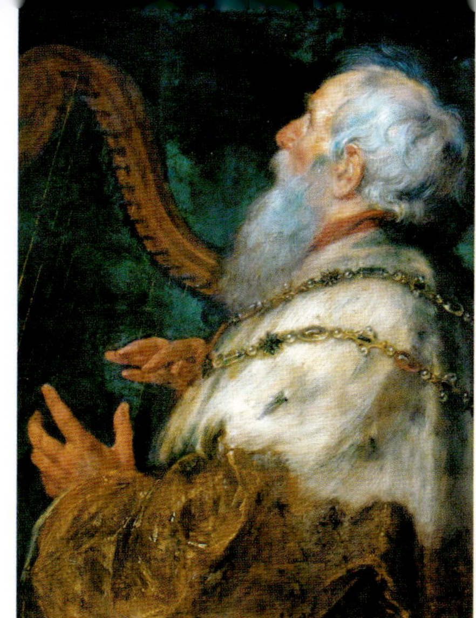 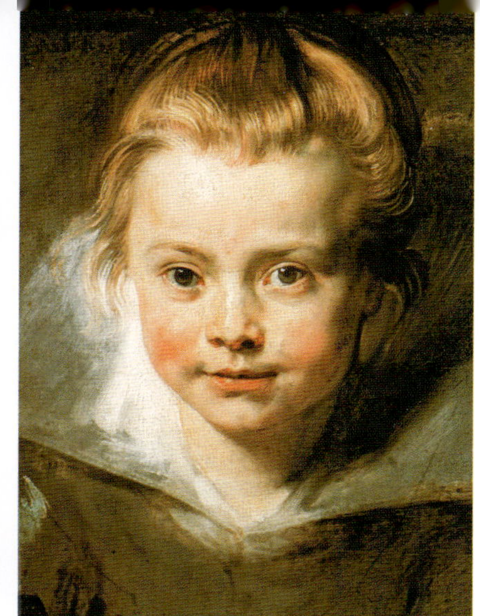

CONTENTS

INTRODUCTION

One of the most influential and versatile artists of the 17th century, Peter Paul Rubens (1577–1640) painted dynamic, passionate and compelling portraits, allegories, altarpieces and landscapes. He also designed sculpture, tapestries, book illustrations, processional floats, and even his own house.

Rubens's expressive, emotive and sensual paintings are now instantly recognizable, while the word 'Rubenesque' has become a universal term to describe particularly voluptuous female figures in acknowledgement of the curvaceous women he portrayed. Rubens was the leading Baroque and most prolific painter in northern Europe, the ideal artist for the period. A devout Catholic, he preferred to paint vast works that perfectly suited the demands of the Counter-Reformation; for art to impress viewers with the power and vigour of the Catholic Church.

Having started as a young apprentice in Antwerp, by the time he was 35 years old Rubens was the most successful international artist of his time, sought after and commissioned by both the Church and European monarchs. Although he was from northern Europe, the kings of Spain and England

Below: The Hermit and the Sleeping Angelica, *Rubens, 1626–28, depicting part of the poem* Orlando Furioso *by Italian author Ludovico Ariosto (1474–1533).*

bestowed knighthoods on him. Called 'the prince of painters and painter of princes', his accomplishments were unparalleled. He was a celebrated artist, international diplomat, classical scholar, linguist, successful businessman, admired teacher, avid art collector, and devoted family man. Through his skilful diplomatic negotiations, he was as closely involved in the political issues of 17th century Europe as he was in the development of its culture and the history of art.

DISCORD AND CONFLICT

Throughout Rubens's life, Europe was affected by huge religious, social, political and cultural upheavals, provoked by the Protestant Reformation which had started in 1517 and had splintered the Catholic Church. It had incited wars, persecutions and the Counter-Reformation. Although the Catholic Church had regained authority and wealth by the time Rubens was born, religious discord continued. Against this conflicting backdrop, across Europe there was also great competition for wealth and power as the Dutch,

French, Spanish, Portuguese and English struggled to maintain and expand colonies and trading posts around the world. At the same time, Europe saw the emergence of absolute monarchies: in France with Louis XIV (1638–1715); in Spain with Philip IV (1605–65); and in England with Charles I (1600–49).

INFLUENCED AND INFLUENTIAL

For most of his life, Rubens managed a large studio in Antwerp, training many apprentices and employing assistants

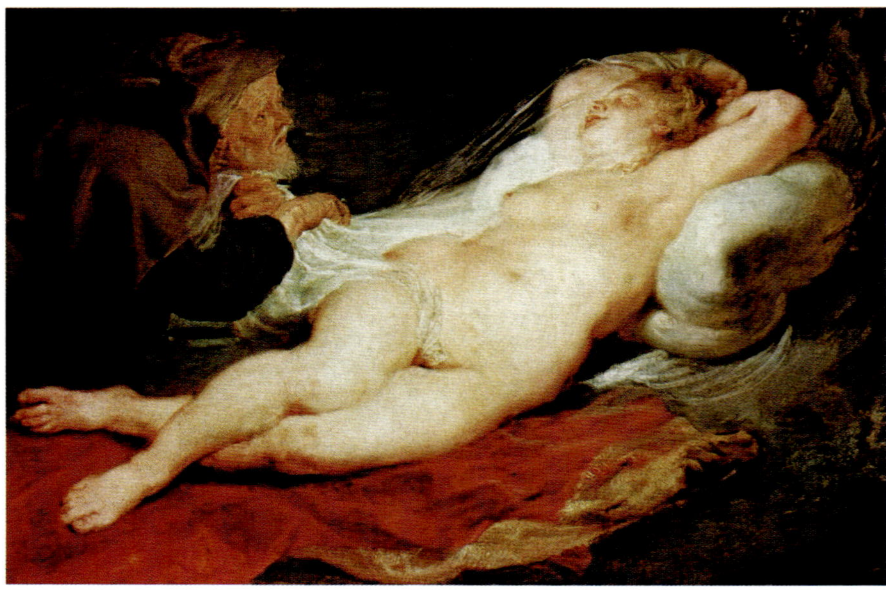

THE BAROQUE

After the Catholic Church regained its confidence and control, encouraged by new evangelizing orders such as the Jesuits, vast rebuilding and refurbishing programmes occurred in many parts of Europe. Between 1545 and 1563 the Council of Trent decreed that a new kind of religious imagery should express this fervent mood, appeal to the senses and engage and educate followers in the teachings of the Catholic Church. The ensuing art was dramatic, colourful, exuberant and realistic, as it attempted to strengthen the image of the Catholic Church, to show Protestants its power, and to encourage the return of the faithful. It began in Rome directly from the Council of Trent, and spread across Europe. In the north, Rubens played a significant role in the development of the style that later became called the Baroque. Derived from the Portuguese word *barroco*, Spanish *barroco*, or French *baroque*, it refers to a 'rough or imperfect pearl', and has become associated with extravagant ornament.

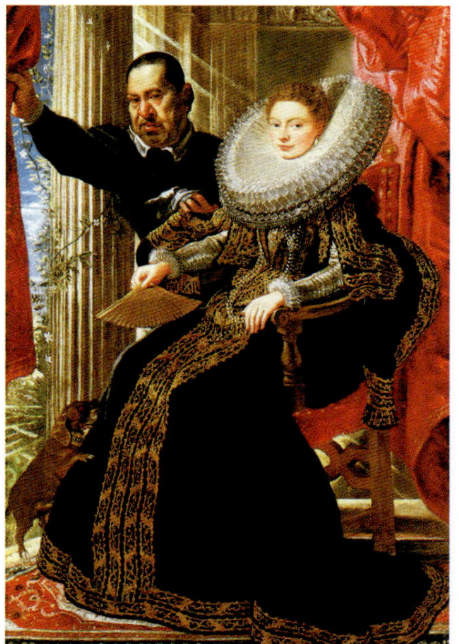

Above: This elaborately dressed, regal woman with her dwarf is probably Marchesa Maria Grimaldi and her dwarf, painted by Rubens in c.1607.

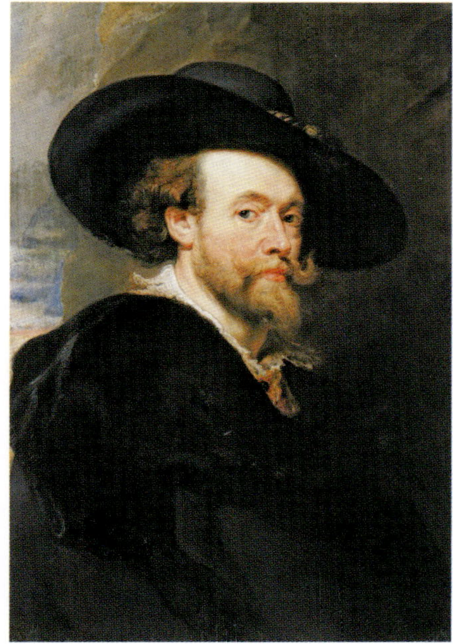

Above: Rubens painted a few self-portraits over his career. He painted this in 1623 when he was 46, emphasizing his ability to portray luminous light effects on the face.

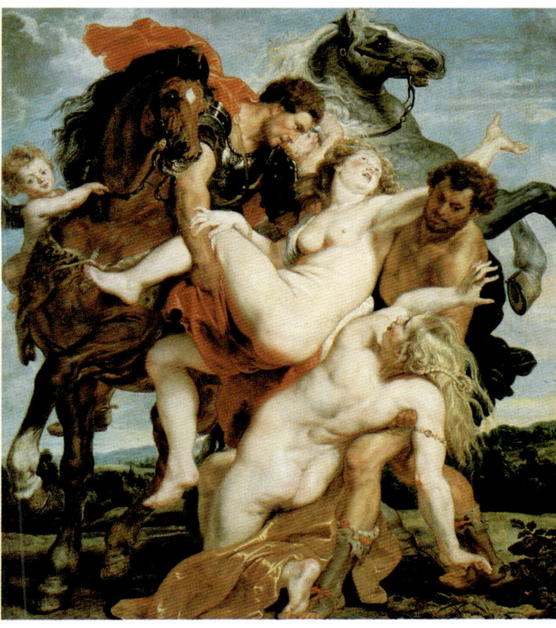

Above: Over his career, Rubens became renowned for his dynamic, dramatic and impactful paintings, seen here in his 1618 Rape of the Daughters of Leucippus.

and colleagues to help execute vast projects. He also worked in Italy, Spain and England, and gained the respect of patrons and other artists alike. Known for his religious and mythological compositions, portraits, landscapes and allegories, he amalgamated and assimilated a broad variety of influences, including some of the greatest artists of the High Renaissance and Mannerism, ancient Greek and Roman artefacts, classical literature and mythology. His powers of invention enabled him to use all these inspirations to create a painting style that was entirely new and original, blending his northern European sense of realism and personal sensuality and exuberance with the grandeur and monumentality he admired in the art he saw in Italy and Spain. His free, expressive and vigorous style was in turn hugely influential to generations of artists who came after him.

TIMELINE

1577: Peter Paul Rubens born on June 28 in Siegen, Westphalia (now Germany).

1587: Family moves to Antwerp in the Spanish Netherlands (now Belgium).

1598: Admitted to Antwerp's professional guild for painters.

1600: Travels to Italy and Spain, creating works such as *The Raising of the Cross* (1602) and *Self-Portrait in a Circle of Friends from Mantua* (c.1602–4).

1605: Spends most of the next three years in Genoa or Rome.

1608: Returns to Antwerp.

1609: Marries Isabella Brant and paints *Self-portrait with Isabella Brant*, or *The Honeysuckle Bower*.

1610: Paints *Samson and Delilah*.

1610–14: Paints triptychs of *The Raising of the Cross* and *Descent from the Cross*, making him the most celebrated artist in Europe.

1611: First child Clara born.

1614: Second child Albert born.

1618: Third child Nicholaas born.

1622–25: Produces a tapestry cycle for Louis XIII of France, the *Medici* cycle, and portraits of the French royal family, becoming known as 'the prince of painters and the painter of princes'.

1624: Paints *Adoration of the Magi*.

1625: Jan Bruegel dies and Rubens becomes guardian of his children.

1626: Wife Isabella Brant dies. Rubens begins suffering with gout.

1629: Paints the ceiling of Whitehall in London.

1629–30: Paints *Allegory of Peace and War*, or *Minerva Protects Pax from Mars*.

1630: Marries Hélène Fourment. She and Rubens go on to have five children, the last of whom is born five months after Rubens's death.

1630–32: Completes monumental commissions such as *The Ildefonso Altarpiece*.

1635–40: Paints mythological works such as *Hercules Slays the Dragon in the Garden of Hesperides*.

1640: Dies from heart failure in Antwerp on May 30, aged 62.

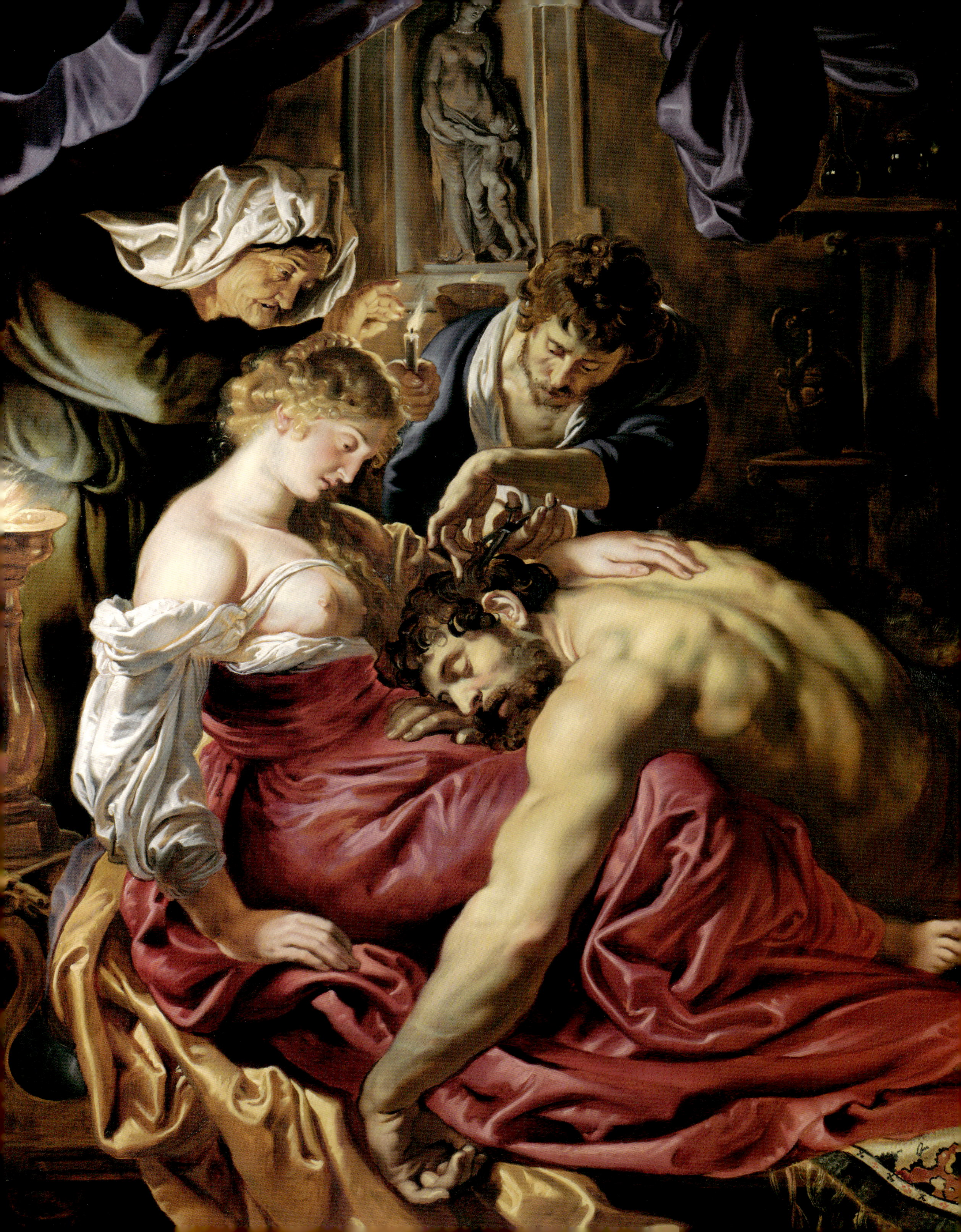

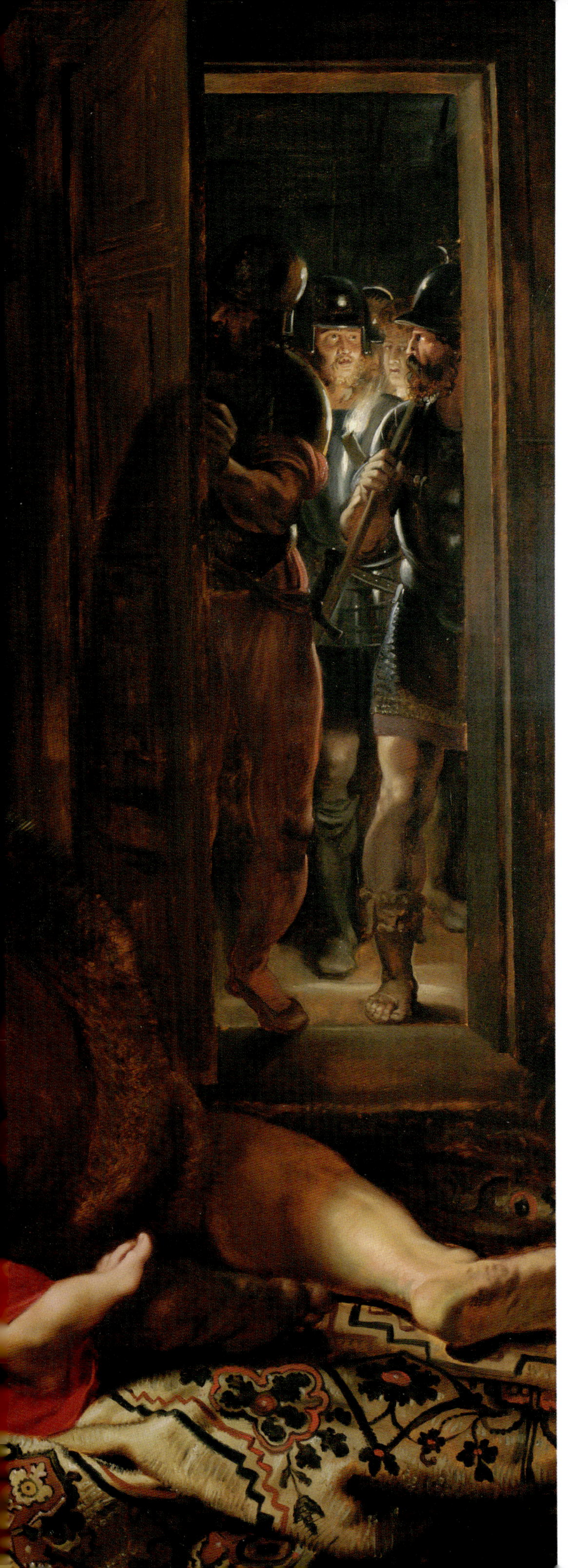

GENIUS OF THE BAROQUE

Encompassing most painting genres, Rubens's prodigious output included dramatic altarpieces, grand portraits, atmospheric landscapes and complex historical and mythological scenes. Usually classed as the supreme Baroque painter of northern Europe, the unparalleled brilliance of his career changed perceptions about artists and painting. His outstanding creative talents were combined with an engaging personality, great intellect and energy, and he socialized with scholars, artists, merchants and kings. Renowned for his art, his business acuity and his vast art collection, his command of Flemish, German, Latin, Spanish, English, Italian and French aided his negotiations at the greatest courts of Europe.

Left: Samson and Delilah, *c.1609, oil on wood. Commissioned by Rubens's friend, alderman Nicolaas Rockox for his house in Antwerp, this was a uniquely dramatic portrayal of the Old Testament story of Samson, the Jewish strongman hero, who had fallen in love with Delilah. Bribed by the Philistines, she allowed them to cut his hair while he slept, which sapped his strength, and enabled the Philistines to capture him.*

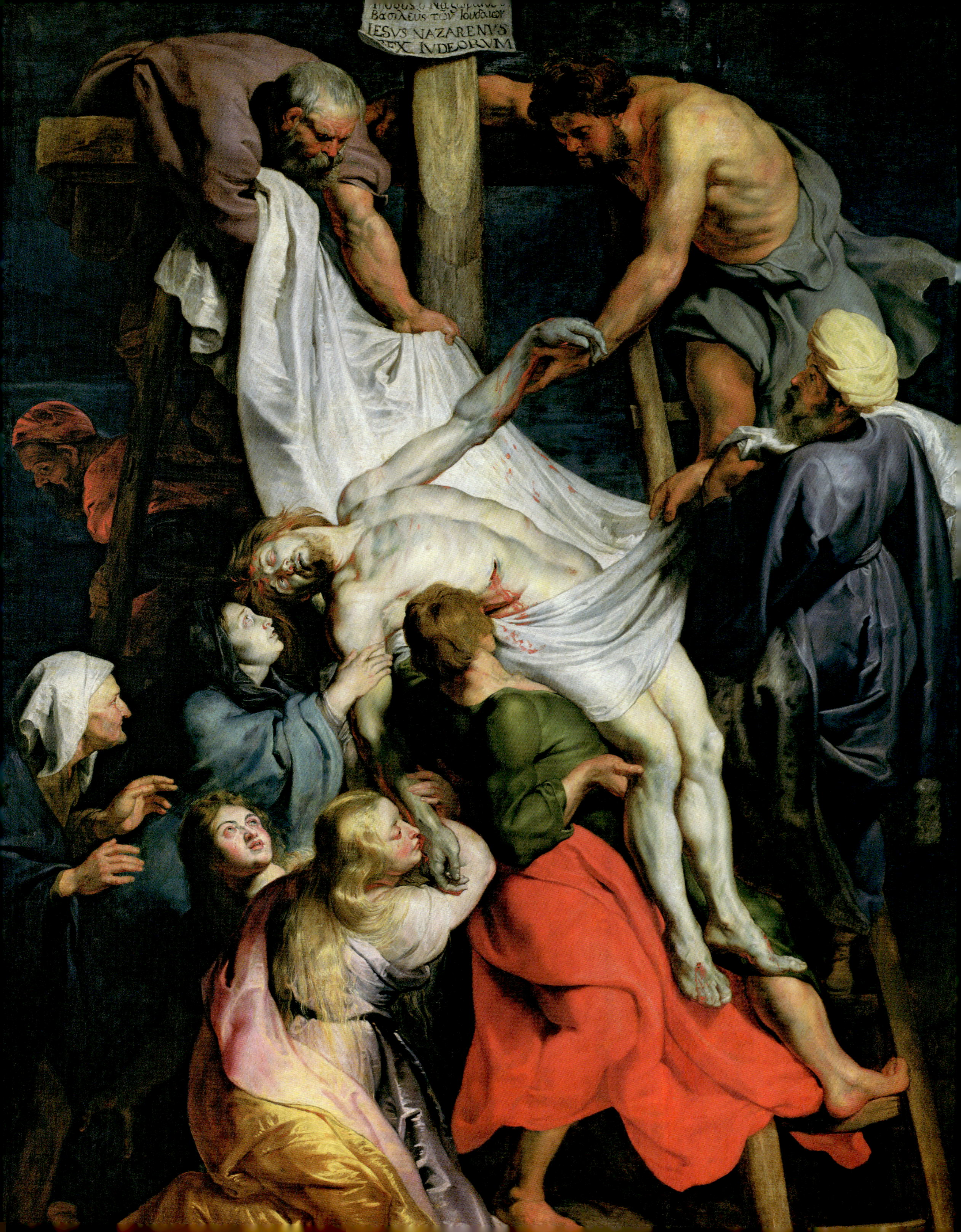
Ἰησοῦς ὁ Ναζωραῖος ὁ
Βασιλεὺς τῶν Ἰουδαίων
IESVS NAZARENVS
REX IVDEORVM

WONDER OF THE WORLD

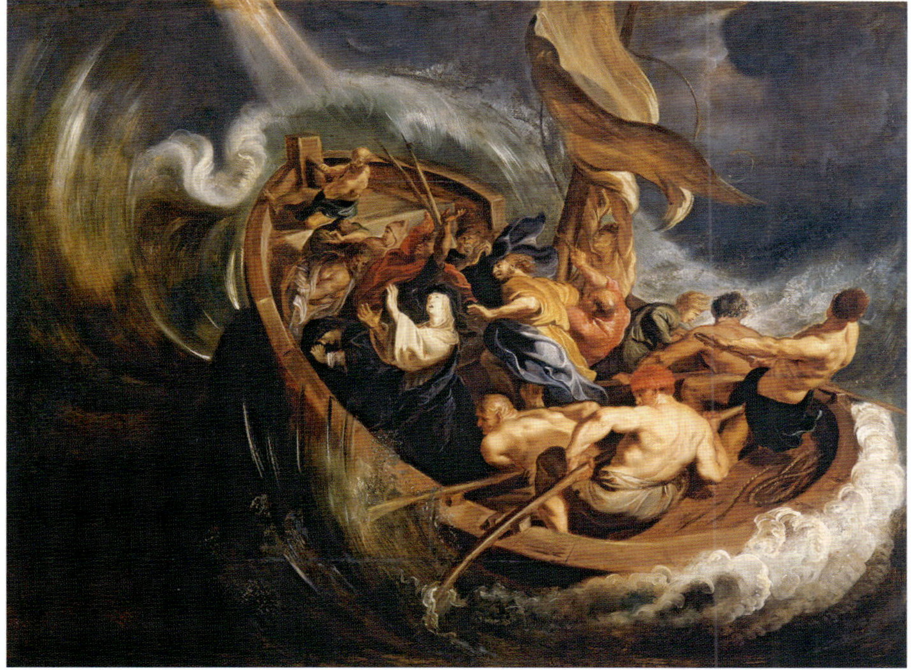

One of the 17th century's most versatile, original and prolific artists, Rubens was praised almost universally during his lifetime. Often called the modern Apelles after the famed 4th-century BCE painter of ancient Greece, he was also described as 'one of the wonders of the world' by the Dutch poet and composer Constantijn Huygens (1596–1687). From the Neoclassical period to the end of the 20th century his popularity lessened – abundant flesh became unfashionable, and his colour and blatant eroticism seemed too excessive for the period. However, he is now once again acknowledged as one of the greatest masters in the history of art.

Above: The Miracle of Saint Walburga, c.1610–11, oil on panel. Saint Walburga – or Walpurga – is the patroness of Antwerp, and is also seen as a protector against hydrophobia and storms, and of sailors. Rubens painted one of her miracles for the altarpiece for the church of St Walpurgis in Antwerp.

Left: Descent from the Cross, 1617, oil on canvas. After the success of his huge altarpiece for Antwerp Cathedral in 1614, Rubens received a number of commissions to produce variations of this theme. Following tenets from the Council of Trent, Rubens only included people who were directly mentioned in the Bible.

TURBULENT TIMES

Peter Paul Rubens was born on June 28, 1577, in Siegen, Westphalia in Germany, the sixth and youngest child of Jan Rubens (1530–87) and his wife Maria Pypelinckx (1538–1608). Originally from Antwerp in Flanders, Jan and Maria had fled to Germany in 1568 to escape religious persecution.

Jan had grown up in Antwerp, and he studied in Italy, gaining a doctorate in civil and canon law. He and Maria married in 1561, and the following year he became an alderman. He also joined the growing number of converts in Antwerp to Calvinism, following the teachings of the Protestant reformer John Calvin (1509–64). At that time, the Low Countries (present-day Belgium, Luxembourg, the Netherlands and parts of northern France) were ruled by Catholic Spain, and while the Emperor Charles V (1500–58) was tolerant, his son King Philip II (1527–98) was rigidly Catholic. Determined to eradicate both Protestant heresy and prevent political independence in the Netherlands (heavy taxes there helped the Spanish economy), he filled all positions of power with only Spaniards, and persecuted all those he viewed as heretics. In the Netherlands, hundreds of Protestants were sentenced to death, and thousands were banished with their properties confiscated.

DUTCH WAR OF INDEPENDENCE

Philip's actions provoked a rebellion in Spanish-controlled northern Europe. Calvinist preachers held public meetings, criticizing Catholicism and demanding Protestant places of worship. In 1566, a wave of iconoclasm swept through Antwerp, with thousands of works of art destroyed or looted from churches and monasteries. Philip sent in a Spanish army under Fernando Alvarez de

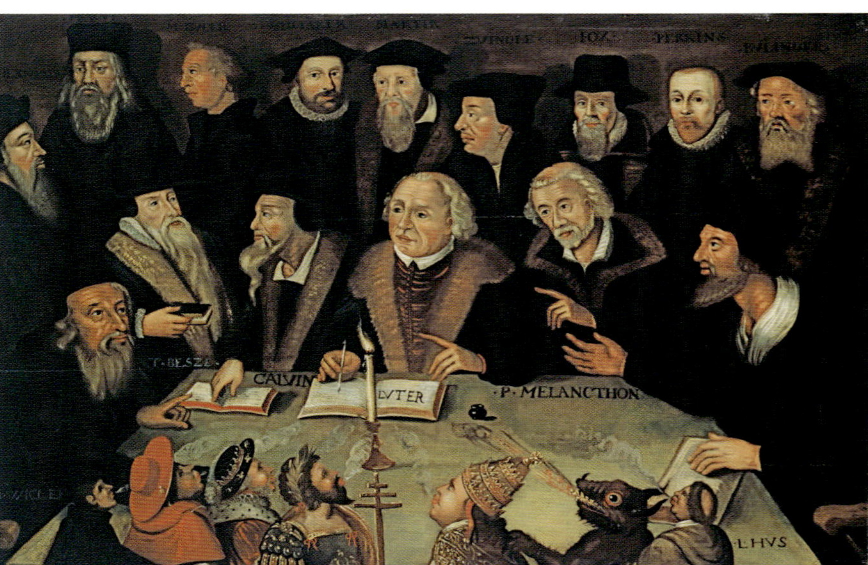

Left: Martin Luther in the Circle of Reformers. *German School, c.1625–50. Here, Martin Luther is surrounded by other theologians and Christian reformers.*

Below left: Allegory of the Tyranny of the Duke of Alba. *In September 1567, on the orders of Philip II of Spain, the third Duke of Alba, 'punished' citizens of the Netherlands. The tribunal became known as the 'Council of Blood'.*

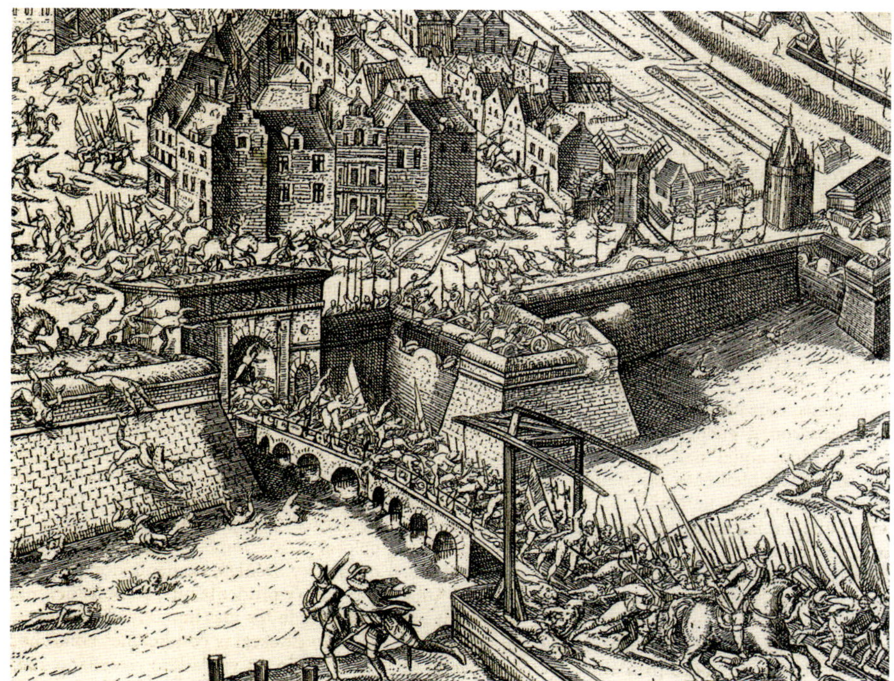

Toledo, the Duke of Alba (1507–82), who became Governor-general of the Netherlands from 1567–73. Resistance to Spanish dominance became even stronger. In 1559, Philip had made William I, Prince of Orange (1533–84), known as William the Silent, governor of Holland, Zeeland and Utrecht. Believing in freedom of religion for all, he was disturbed about the persecution of Protestants, and raised an army. Within four years, Holland and Zeeland were liberated from Spanish rule, but the war continued, and several other European countries became embroiled in it. Lasting from 1568–1648, it became known as the Dutch War of Independence, or the Eighty Years' War.

SIEGE OF ANTWERP

The Duke of Parma, Alexander Farnese (1545–92) was appointed governor of the Netherlands in 1578, and through him, Spanish forces recaptured the main cities in the south (now Belgium). As the cultural, economic and financial centre of north-western Europe, Antwerp

Right: The Spanish Fury, attributed to Daniel van Heil (1604–62). The Siege of Antwerp was also called the Spanish Fury. Occurring during the Eighty Years' War, it caused Antwerp's decline from which it never regained its prominence.

became the capital of the Dutch Revolt. From July 1584 during the Eighty Years' War, it was put under siege. After a year, the citizens surrendered and Antwerp was returned to the control of Catholic Spain. From this point, the Northern Netherlands became an independent republic, while the Southern Netherlands remained under Spanish rule.

After Antwerp surrendered, the Duke of Parma issued his troops with strict orders not to sack the city. The return to Spanish control was handled with tact. Antwerp's Protestants were given four years to settle their affairs before leaving. Some returned to Roman Catholicism, but many moved north. The pre-siege population of 80,000 people dwindled to 42,000. Many skilled craftsmen left, and as the numbers declined, the economy also diminished.

FLEEING FROM ANTWERP

In 1568, at the start of the Dutch War of Independence, Jan and Maria, along with many of their friends and neighbours, were accused of heresy in Antwerp. To escape the problems, they fled with their four young children to Cologne in Germany. Despite being a Catholic city, Cologne showed tolerance to Protestant refugees, and Jan's profession and a certain amount of religious dissembling made them feel relatively safe in their new community for the time.

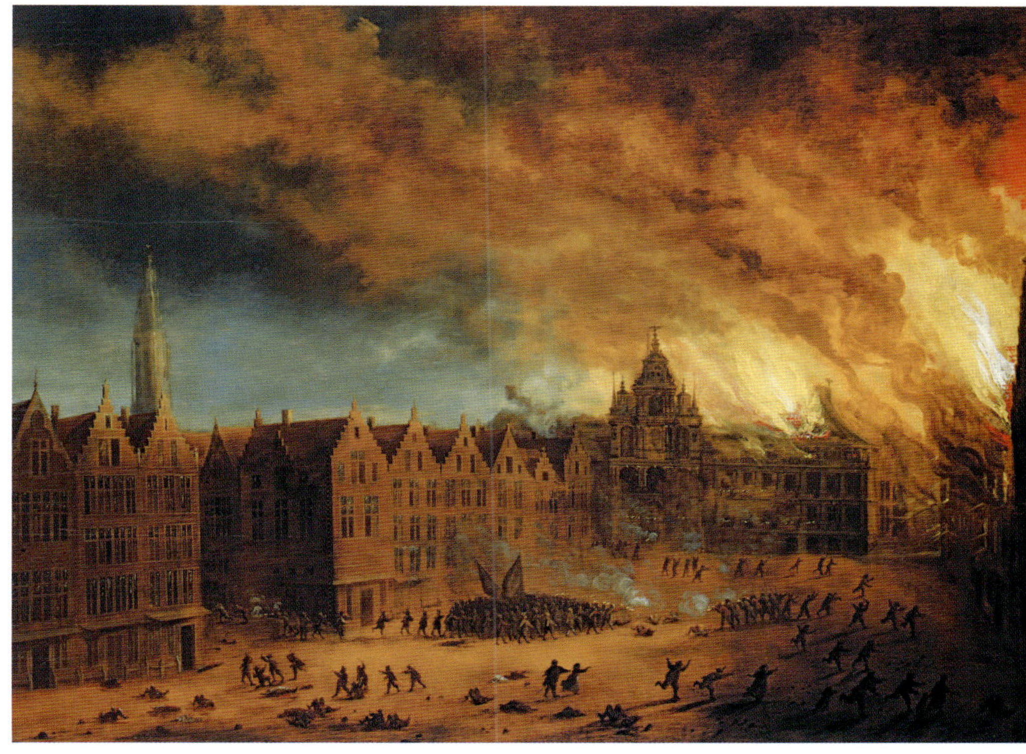

GROWING UP

In Cologne, through an introduction by a compatriot, Jan was appointed secretary and legal advisor to the second wife of William the Silent. Anna of Saxony (1544–77) and William had married in the same year as Jan's own marriage to Maria, but the union was not a happy one.

While William raised reinforcements for his battle against Spain, in 1568 he left Anna in Cologne. In 1570 she moved west to Siegen, and her legal advisor and his family followed. Described by contemporaries as 'self-absorbed, weak, assertive and cruel', Anna was demanding and difficult, as well as frequently drunk and violent. Fourteen years younger than Jan, she made excessive demands on his time – and on his fidelity to his wife. In March 1571, she was pregnant.

After numerous pleading letters from Anna to Jan had been intercepted by William's brother, Jan was arrested and confessed to his part in the affair. For adultery between a commoner (albeit a middle-class one) and a princess, the penalty could have been death, but with great generosity of spirit, Maria offered her husband forgiveness and began a series of petitions to the authorities, pleading for his life. William divorced Anna (who, despite those letters, denied the affair), while Maria's persistence and

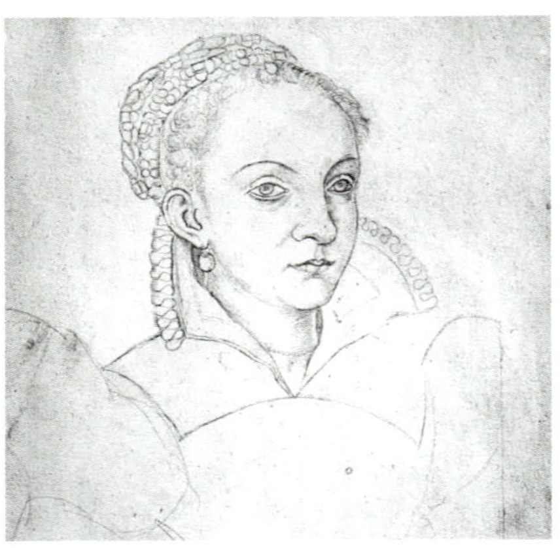

Above: A drawing of Anna of Saxony, Princess of Orange, by an unknown 16th-century German artist.

an enormous payment in bail earned Jan an eventual pardon. He was kept under house arrest in Siegen, and with Maria's payment of another large fine, after two years he was released.

SIBLINGS AND SHAME

Little is known of Rubens's four elder siblings who were born before Jan's infidelity. There were two sons and two daughters, the eldest of whom was Jan-Baptist (1562–1600), 15 years Peter Paul's senior and who also became an artist, but died at just 38. The others were Blandina (1564–1606), Clara (1565–80), and Hendrik (1567–83). After Jan's release from prison, the couple had three further children: Philip Rubens (1574–1611), then Peter Paul, and finally another son, Bartholamaus, who was born in 1581 but lived for just two years. Philip grew up to become a scholar and lawyer like his father, and he and Peter Paul were especially close. When Peter Paul was born, the family

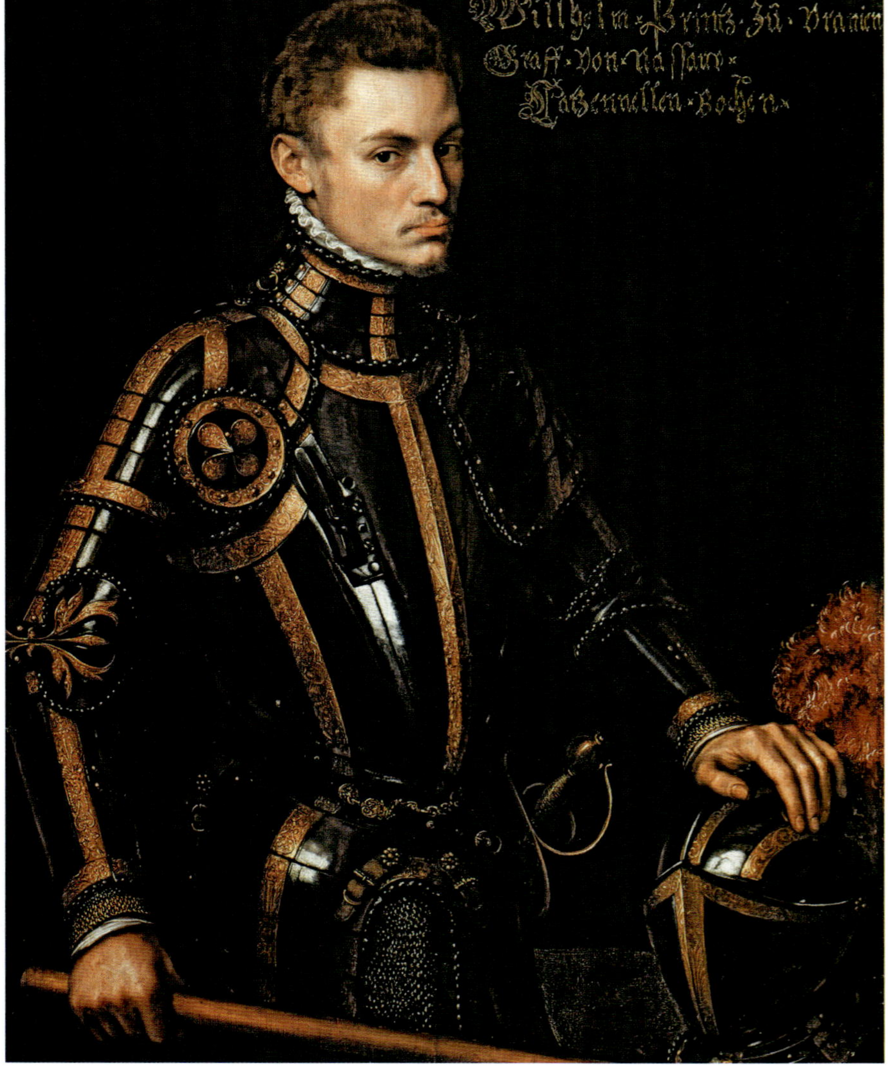

Left: William the Silent, Anthonis Mor c.1552. William I, Prince of Orange led the Dutch revolt against the Spanish Habsburgs that set off the Eighty Years' War.

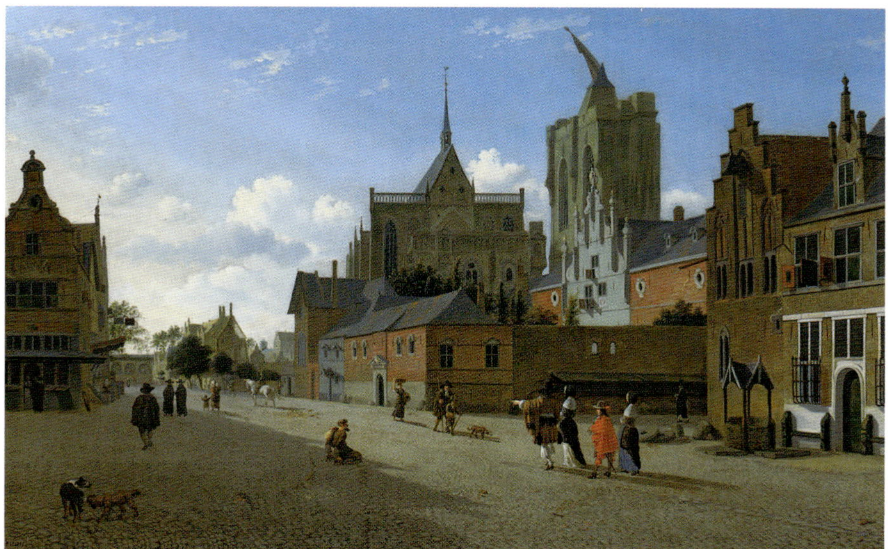

Maria Rubens buried her husband in the Church of St Peter in Cologne. His tombstone declared that they had lived in Cologne for 19 years and all their married life had been happy. Clearly not all of this is true, but she sought to expunge all memory of the distressing and humiliating events in Siegen. Later, even Rubens's birth was often described as being in Cologne. Not long after, she took her children back to Antwerp where her family still owned property.

Below: Philip II of Spain, Titian, *c.1550–51. Philip ruled Spain, Portugal, Naples, Sicily and Milan, and with his wife Mary he was also King of England and Ireland.*

was cloaked in shame, ostracized by society and scorned by neighbours. Jan was not allowed to earn money and provide for his family, nor to enter churches. To survive, Maria had started taking paying guests into their home.

BACK IN COLOGNE

The Dutch War of Independence changed the priorities of the authorities, and Jan's crime was eventually disregarded. A few months after Peter Paul's birth, the family was allowed to move back to Cologne, Jan was allowed

to resume his practice, and by 1583 he and Maria returned to the Catholic faith. To survive, Jan worked night and day, but the strains of work and the past few years affected his health adversely. Clara had died at 15 in 1580, and their second-born son Hendrik died in the same year as their youngest Bartholamaus. Hendrick was just 16.

Although details of their education is vague, the two youngest Rubens boys were probably initially instructed at home by their highly educated father. It was also probably from him that the boys gained a love of learning, and when they were admitted to the local parish school run by Jesuits, they surpassed most other pupils academically. Early in 1587, succumbing to fatigue as well as illness, shortly before his youngest son's 10th birthday, Jan died.

Below: St Bartholomew's Day Massacre, François Dubois, c.1572–84. Unrest stretched across Europe, and in 1572 a massacre of Huguenots occurred across Paris in a wave of Catholic violence.

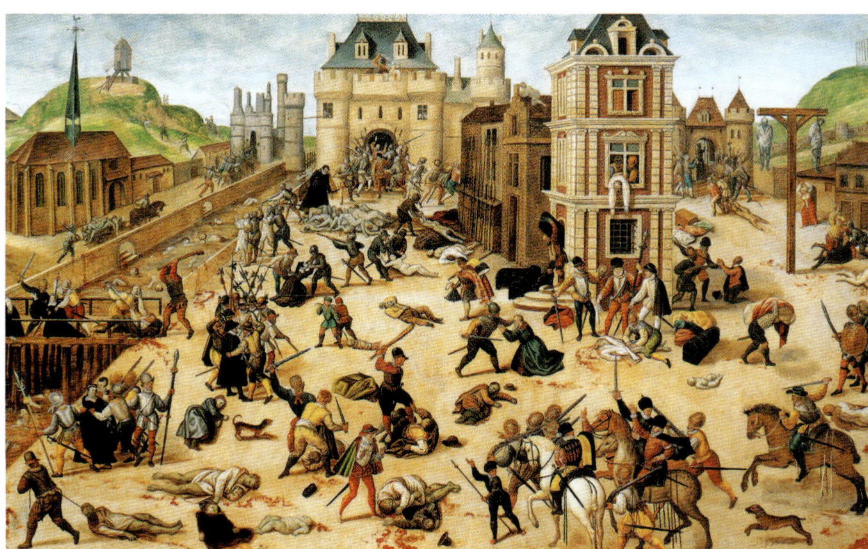

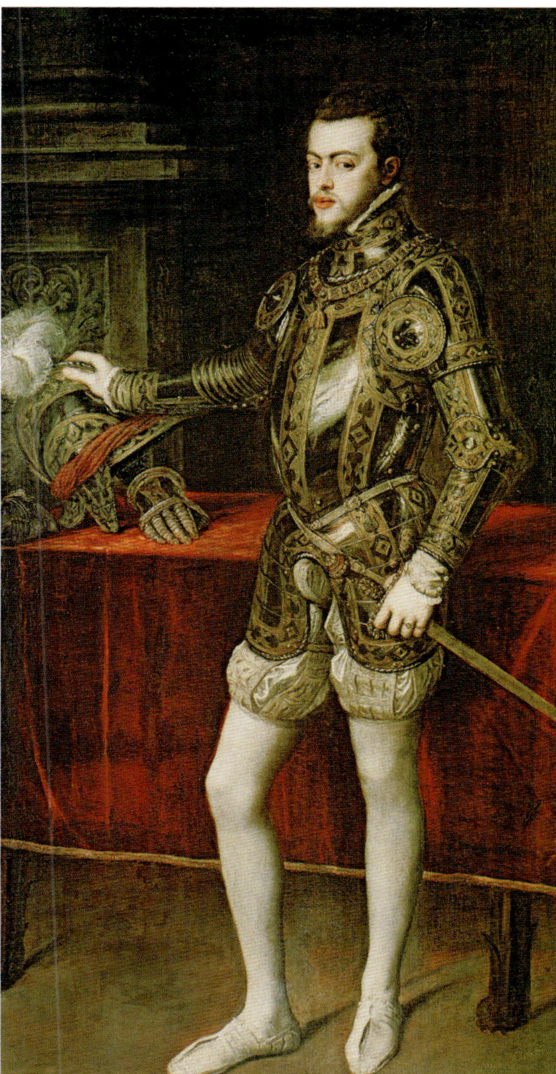

FORMATIVE YEARS

With little money but excellent social connections, Maria and the children settled in Antwerp in 1589. They lived in a family-owned house in one of the city's most elegant districts. The house was on the Meir, the main shopping street, so much life could be seen passing them by.

At age 16, Philip Rubens secured a position as secretary to the magistrate, diplomat and statesman Jean Richardot (1540–1609) in Brussels. He had a passion for scholarship and followed his father as a student of philosophy and law. In 1590, Blandina also moved away when she married a Flemish nobleman, Siméon du Parcq (1565–1625).

CLASSICAL EDUCATION

Peter Paul Rubens attended the exclusive Papenschool, behind Our Lady's Cathedral on Melkmarkt Street, five minutes' walk from his home. Run by the Humanist Rombaut Verdonck (1541–1620), the school held 30 boys who were given a grounding in the liberal education of the time, which was mainly grammar, literature and analysis of Latin and Greek classics. Rubens's intellect and capacity for learning once again impressed his teachers and friends. With his wife, Verdonck ran the school strictly. Classes began at seven or eight in the morning, with a break for lunch when the boys either ate what they had brought with them or went home. Then classes resumed until four in the afternoon. The boys recited a prayer before each class, and the first class was followed by a morning mass. Lessons were shaped by pupils studying at their desks, and in turn each boy was called up to recite an assigned passage, usually from a classical text, and then to answer individual questions about it. These questions could be about grammar and syntax, or analysis and understanding. If the questions were not answered promptly or politely, the particular boy would be caned. Despite this seemingly restrictive manner of learning, it produced a flow of brilliant thinkers in all fields. Rubens thrived on this classical education, made friends – and left after two years.

PAGE TO A PRINCESS

Rubens was 13 when he left school. Most boys at that time left their full-time education when they were 14. It may be that with his precocity, the earlier grounding he had received from his father and the Jesuits in Cologne that he had reached the capacity for learning at that particular institution. Or perhaps his mother could no longer afford to keep him there, as with great difficulty she had managed to give Blandina 200 florins for her dowry. Whatever the reason, by August 1590, Rubens had taken a job as

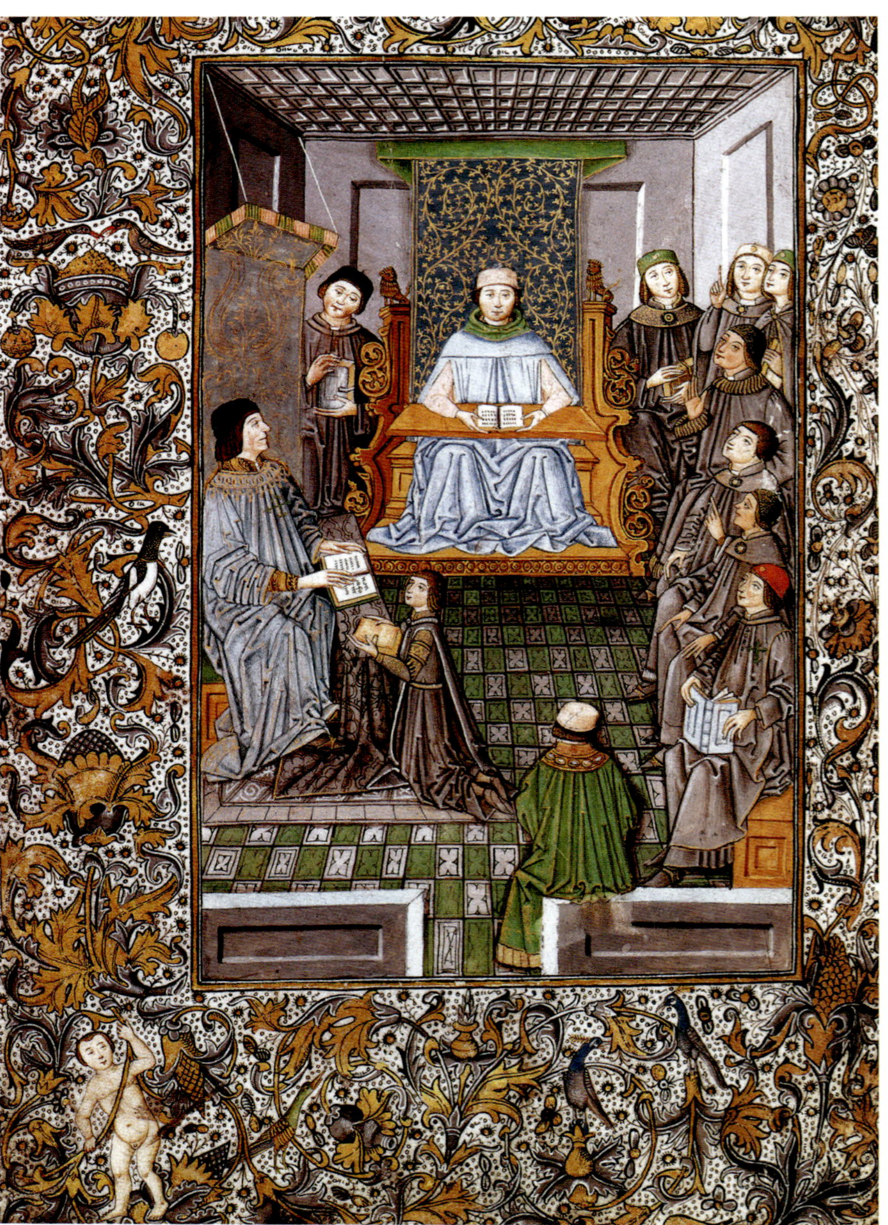

Left: Humanist school, 16th-century Spain. The Council of Trent made things difficult for other religions, but Humanism still flourished, and Rubens did well at his Humanist school.

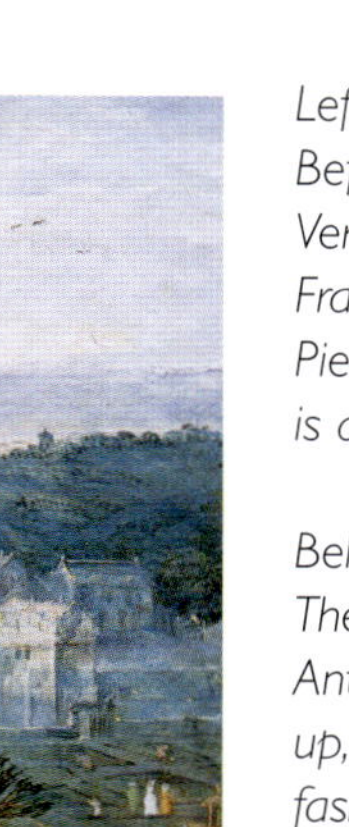

Left: Landscape Scene, *Tobias Verhaecht.*
Before working successfully in Antwerp,
Verhaecht worked in Florence for
Francesco I de' Medici. The influence of
Pieter Bruegel the Elder (c.1525–69)
is also apparent in this painting.

Below: Procession along the Meir.
The Meir was the busiest street in
Antwerp, and this is where Rubens grew
up, amid the hustle and bustle of daily,
fashionable life. From his window, his
sharp gaze took in movement, interaction,
the flow and drape of garments, and
individual social interaction.

a pageboy with the Princess Marguerite
de Ligne-Arenberg (1532–1611), widow
of Count Philip de Lalaing of Oudenarde.
With her great wealth, Marguerite
maintained an independent court at her
lavish Castle Escornaix that was crammed
with galleries full of paintings.

For the next eight months, Rubens
worked for Marguerite and lived in her
palace, lifting the burden of his upkeep
from his mother. All Marguerite's pages
received a modicum of academic
instruction and learned courtly etiquette,
and Rubens also improved his French
conversation and learned to ride. This
was probably Maria's motivation when
she sent her youngest son there. Almost

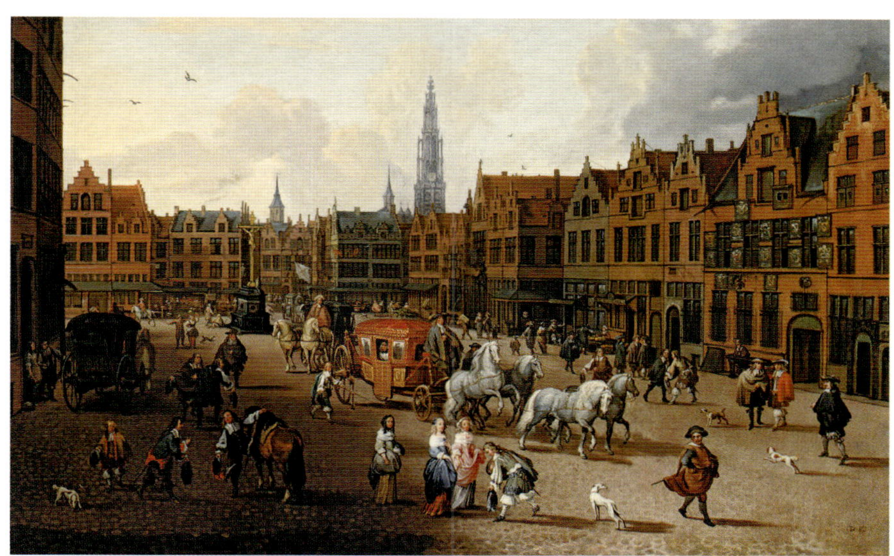

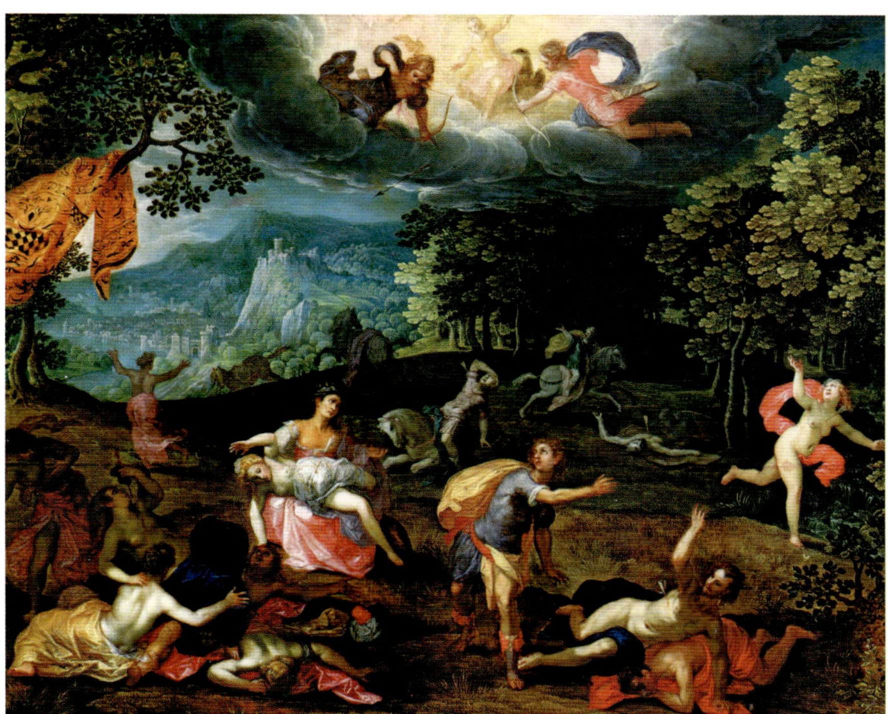

like a finishing school, this was the perfect
grounding for a diplomatic career. Yet it
did not take long for Rubens to become
disillusioned with the small-mindedness,
frivolity and tedium of courtly life. At
some point, even at just 13 years old,
he decided to commit himself to art,
and told his mother that he wished to
become an apprentice painter. At first
she objected, but as a compassionate
woman she was persuaded by her son's
earnestness to let him move back to
Antwerp and become apprenticed to
Tobias Verhaecht (1561–1631). Related
to Rubens through marriage, Verhaecht
had lived and worked in Florence and
Rome. His landscapes generally expressed
religious or mythological themes.

Left: The Punishment of Niobe, *Tobias*
Verhaecht. At the age of 13, Rubens was
apprenticed to local artist Verhaecht.

THE APPRENTICE

Although Antwerp in particular and other cities in northern Europe in general were suffering through war, Antwerp had been a thriving artistic community at the end of the 16th and start of the 17th centuries, and it remained an established location for Rubens to undertake an artistic apprenticeship.

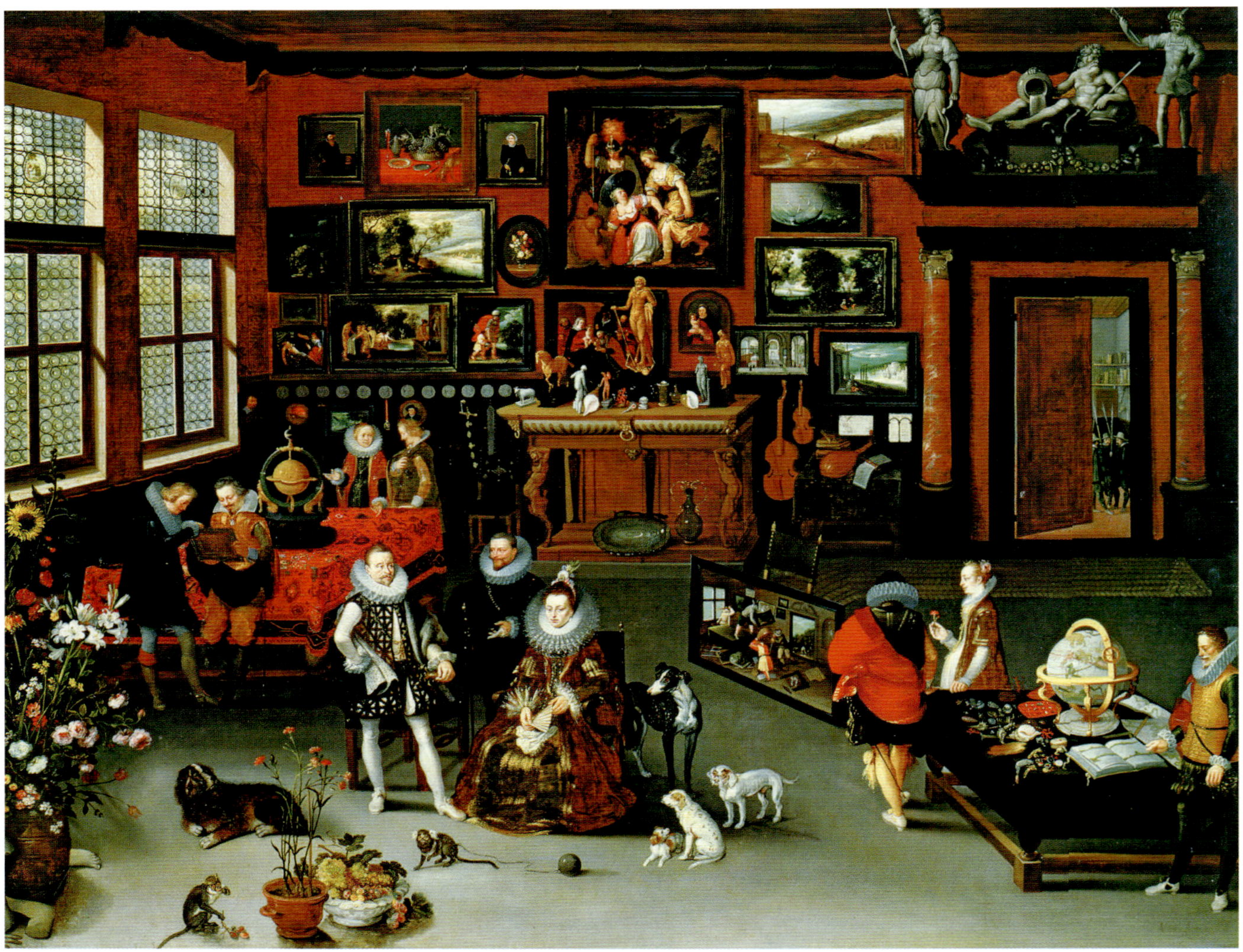

From 1591, for eight years, Rubens trained as an apprentice in artists' workshops. First, he entered the studio of Verhaecht, who was a distant relative by marriage, although not a particularly outstanding artist. After a year, he transferred to Adam van Noort (1561–1641) who was a figure painter, meaning he created history paintings, allegories, portraits and other works featuring human figures. Like Verhaecht, however, Noort was not an especially distinguished artist, but he was a popular teacher and attracted many pupils, including his future son-in-law Jacob Jordaens (1593–1678). Rubens spent three or four years with Van Noort, and it was during this apprenticeship that he produced his earliest firmly attributed works. In 1594 or 1595, he changed studios once more, this time to study with his most eminent teacher so far. Intellectual and talented, Otto van Veen (1556–1629) was one of the most admired artists in Antwerp. Originally from Leiden in the Northern Netherlands, he had moved to Antwerp as a child. A devout Roman Catholic and pro-Spanish rule, he introduced Rubens to new ideas and ways of thinking.

Above: Archduke Albert and Archduchess Isabella Visiting a Collector's Cabinet, *Hieronymus Francken II and Jan Brueghel the Elder, 1621–23.*

INTELLECT AND AMBITION

After studying with Verhaecht and Van Noort, Rubens knew what he wanted in an art teacher. As well as being a skilful artist, Van Veen was a sophisticated and cultured gentleman with a keen interest in ancient art and literature, and knowledge of the Italian Renaissance. He even often used a Latin version of his name – Octavius Vaenius –

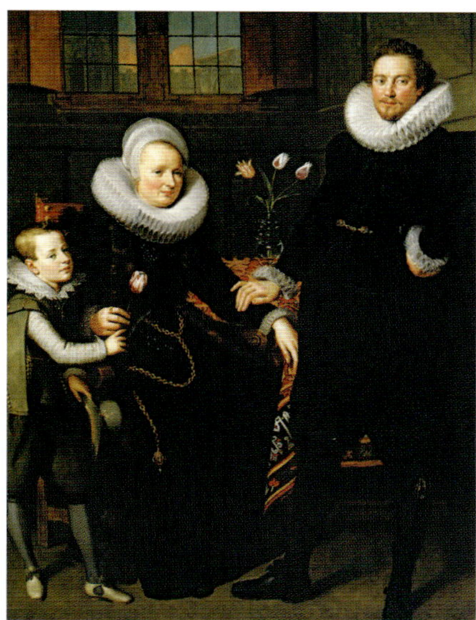

Above: Portrait of a Family in an Interior, *Adam van Noort. A competent painter, Van Noort is most famous for teaching Rubens and Jacob Jordaens.*

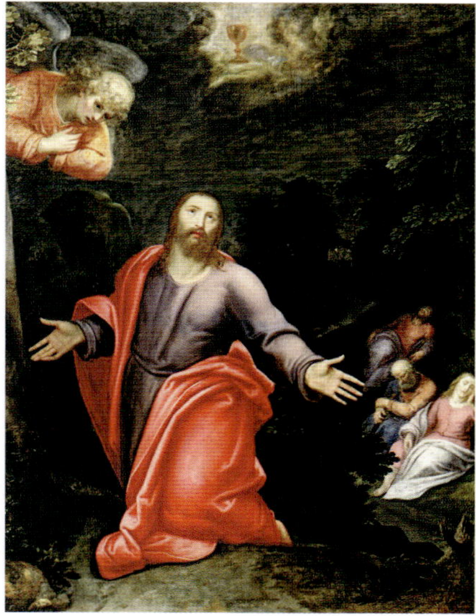

Above: Jesus in the Garden of Olives, *Otto van Veen, c.1590–95. Draughtsman and humanist, Van Veen taught Rubens at the time he was painting this work.*

GUILD OF ROMANISTS

The Guild of Romanists or *Confrérie van Romanisten* was a society in Antwerp from the 16th to 18th centuries. Members had to be notables and artists from Antwerp who had visited Rome. Romanist works evolved from the study of ancient Greek and Roman literature that balanced the Christian outlook with a more human-centred focus. Otto van Veen was a member, as he had studied in Italy and his work was suffused with the Humanist expression of the Renaissance.

in the Humanist fashion, and perceived art as a cultivated, scholarly pursuit. By the time Rubens joined his studio, he demonstrated outstanding artistic skills, and his intellect and ambition meant that he and Van Veen became good friends. From each of his teachers, Rubens learned essential skills. Among other things, from Verhaecht he learned how to draw precisely using the tip of his brush. Van Noort furnished him with the rudiments of portrait painting, and Van Veen taught him even more. By 1598, at the age of 22, he had surpassed his teachers and qualified as a master himself.

ALBERT AND ISABELLA

In 1595, Philip II appointed his nephew Archduke Albert VII of Austria (1559–1621) as Governor General of the Netherlands. Three years later, Philip betrothed his daughter Isabella Clara Eugenia (1566–1633) to Albert, with the Southern Netherlands as her dowry. In 1599, the compassionate, erudite couple settled in Brussels, and for a third of a century they ruled with fairness and devotion. From the

Right: Portrait of a Man, *c.1597–99. One of Rubens's earliest portraits shows that he had already surpassed his teachers.*

earliest days, their royal court at Brussels set new artistic standards. Early in the new century, they summoned the artist, architect, engineer and economist Wenzel Cobergher (1560–1634) to work for them, and in 1609, Rubens became one of their most favoured employees.

As the strains of the past years dispersed, a massive campaign of restoration and new building of churches occurred in Antwerp. The works of art that had been destroyed in the iconoclastic episodes were replaced by images designed to inspire the faithful by their beauty, and enlighten and encourage them by example. Even though many artists, craftspeople and scholars had left the city, many others remained, and some new specialists moved in.

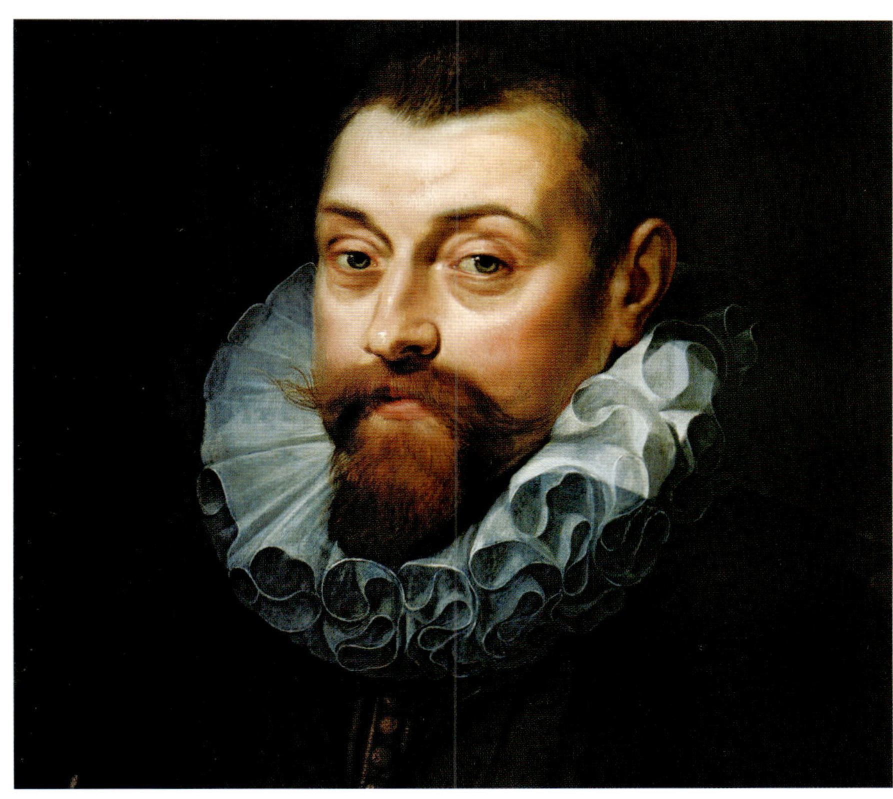

THE YOUNG ARTIST

As a courtier, Van Veen had introduced Rubens to a wide range of interests. He knew Spanish royalty and Italian dukes and princes, and had painted royal portraits. He probably also convinced Rubens of the merits of travelling around Europe.

With all his teachers, Rubens had followed conventional methods of artistic training by copying works by great masters. Many of his copies remain, including some following Hans Holbein the Younger (1497/8–1543), Albrecht Dürer (1471–1528), and prints by Marcantonio Raimondi (c.1480–c.1534) after Raphael (1483–1520). Even from early on, Rubens imbued new life into his versions of these images. Rather than careful, exact imitations, his interpretations are individual and expressive. His figures are more muscular, and overall, his style is lively and sensuous.

Right: St Luke Painting the Virgin, Maarten de Vos, 1602. Saint Luke was said to be a fine painter, and legend tells that he painted the Virgin Mary's portrait, which is why he was later made the patron saint of artists.

Below: Dance of Death, Rubens. A great admirer of Hans Holbein the Younger, Rubens copied his celebrated series of woodcuts in c.1590.

THE GUILD OF SAINT LUKE

Identified by John of Damascus as having painted the Virgin Mary's portrait, Luke the Evangelist became the patron saint of artists, and the Guild of Saint Luke was the most common name for a city guild of artists in Europe during the 16th century. One of the first and most famous of these guilds was founded in Antwerp in c.1382, and the local government gave it power to regulate certain types of trade in the city. To belong, artists had to take on apprentices or sell works of art to the public. The Guild of Saint Luke made judgements on disputes between artists and other artists or their clients, and had rules and the power to fine members. Members were also allowed to sell their works at the guild-owned market stall in front of Antwerp Cathedral.

STARTING OUT

Rubens's character had been shaped predominantly by his father, and then after 1587 by his mother, who was praised by contemporaries as being intelligent and devoted to her children.

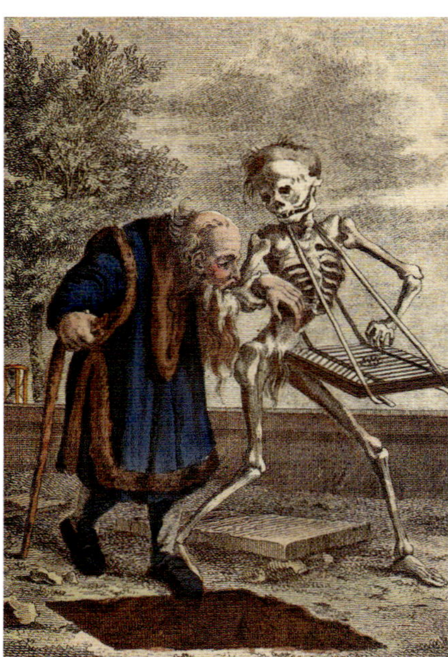

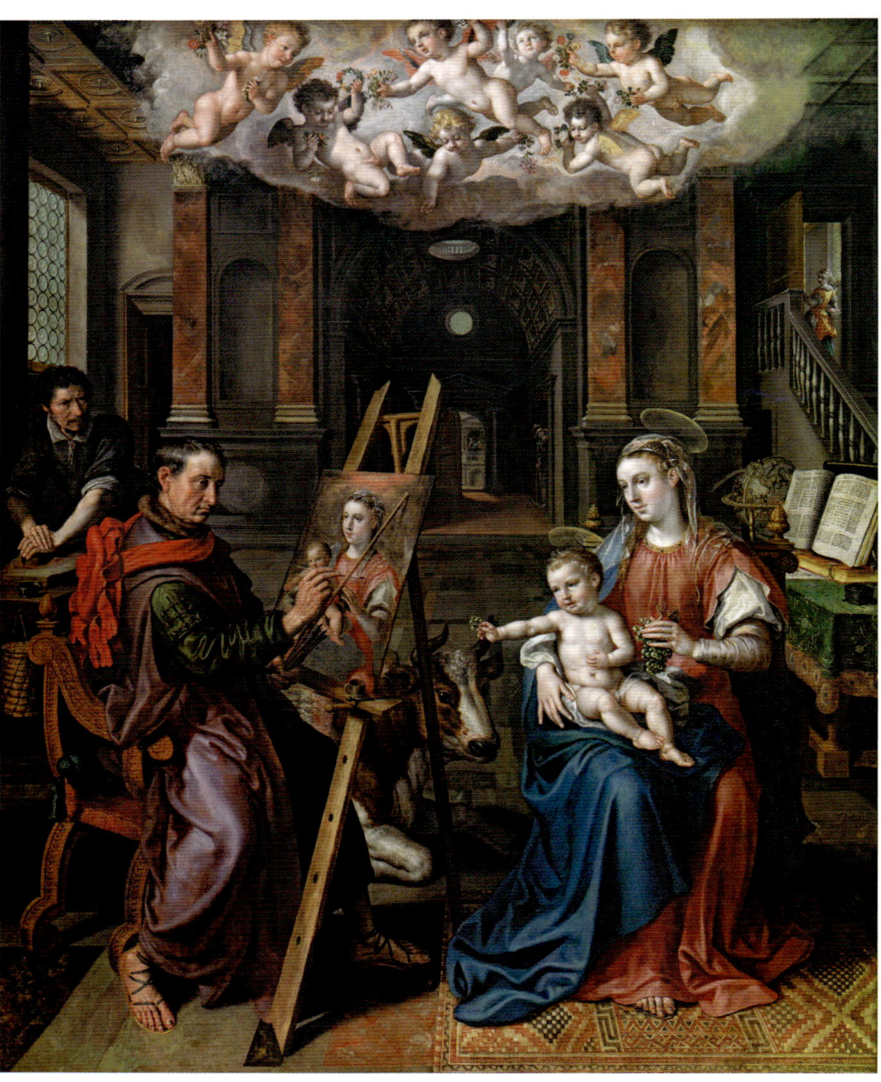

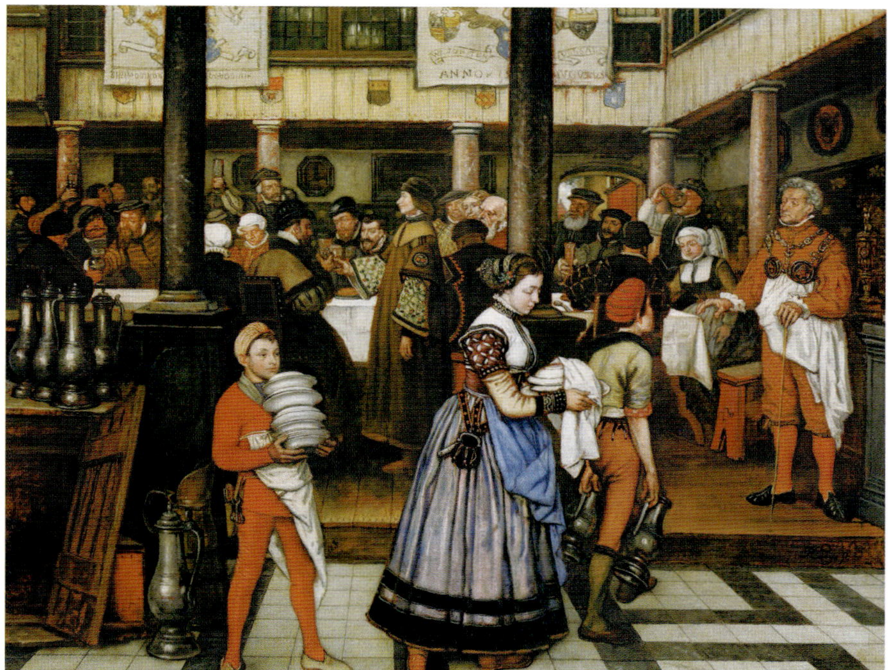

Above Frans Floris Attending a Banquet of the Guild of Saint Luke, *Jan Leys. Antwerp was probably the first city to found a Guild of Saint Luke.*

BOOK PRODUCTION

In the 15th century, Antwerp had become a centre of printing. Thousands of books were produced there, and the most prolific printer was Christophe Plantin (*c.*1520–89), who was also an influential Humanist. From 1555–89, Plantin produced approximately 2,450 books. The quality of his work was so high that scholars from all over Europe asked him to print their writings. Hans Ruckers (*c.*1550–98) also had a similar-sized printing workshop, and through this many learned men were attracted to the city of Antwerp. By that time, Rubens was living there too, and although much of Antwerp's cultural life had reduced, book production continued to thrive, spreading the word that it was a city of culture.

She had an excellent collection of books, which she had taken from Antwerp to Cologne when they fled in 1568 after the increased religious turmoil.

After 1599, Rubens was officially an artist. He became a master of the Antwerp Painters' Guild (Van Veen was the dean), and was allowed to work independently and receive pupils. He enrolled at least one apprentice, Deodat del Monte (1582–1644) who, according to contemporary witnesses, was also his best friend. From the start, Rubens was busy and produced a number of paintings, some of which found their way to his mother's house, where she proudly displayed them on her walls. It is difficult to verify many of these early works, however, as he rarely signed them. It is also probable that he worked in collaboration with Van Veen on numerous commissions, as his early style owes much to his teacher, and it is often difficult to differentiate their works. Several paintings from that period have been verified as being by him, however. They include a portrait, two biblical scenes and a scene from ancient Greek mythology. One biblical

Right: The Judgement of Paris, *Rubens, c.1579–99. Paris, seated with his back to the viewer, gives the prize of a golden apple to Venus, the central standing goddess.*

scene is *Adam and Eve*, *c.*1599 (see page 103), based on an engraving by Raimondi, which in turn follows a (lost) painting by Raphael. In Rubens's work, Eden has become a north European forest, with a hare sitting on a path. Adam is muscular and Eve voluptuous.

They both look somewhat confused, while a large snake wraps itself around a nearby tree. The other biblical painting is *The Holy Trinity* (see page 71). These two paintings show his bold, vigorous handling, virtuosity and understanding of the human temperament.

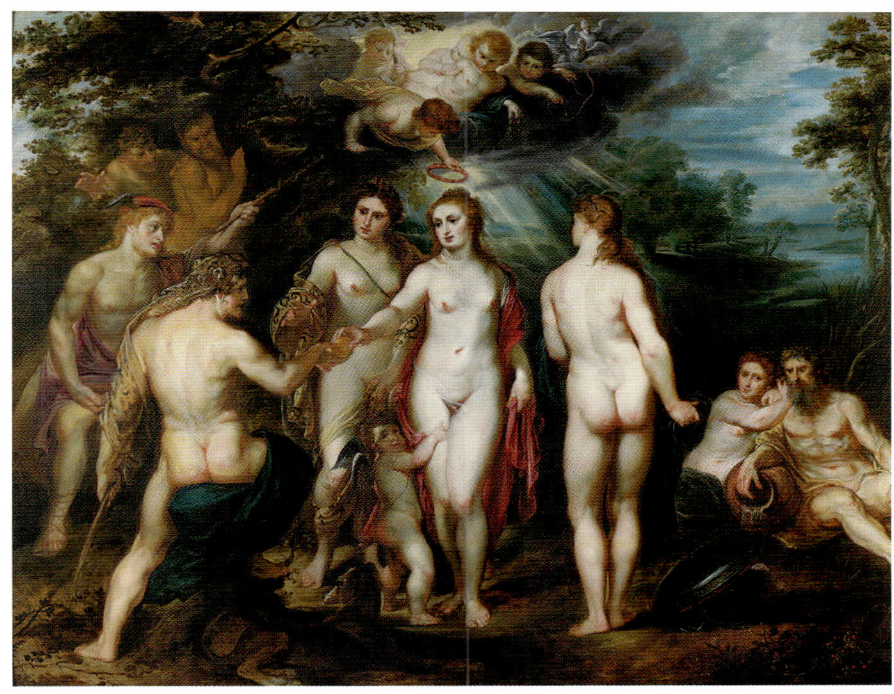

TRAVELLING TO ITALY

The goal of all young northern European artists was to go to Italy and see the Renaissance and Classical works of art that they knew from prints. The trip had become an established tradition, and on May 9, 1600, Rubens and his friend and pupil del Monte set off.

Before he left, Rubens had obtained the necessary traveller's certificate from Antwerp City Council, declaring that he was in good health and the city was free from plague or disease. He had been inspired to travel to Italy through tradition, and to emulate artists such as Albrecht Dürer (1471–1528), as well as his eldest brother Jan-Baptist and Van Veen, but also, of course, because his own father had studied law there, and had probably told Rubens many alluring stories about the country.

So it was with great excitement that he set off, despite the rather onerous journey. At this time, the 'Grand Tour' was becoming established as a custom, with many young European aristocrats concluding their education with extended visits to Paris, Venice, Florence and Rome. The Grand Tour was most fashionable from c.1660, but it was beginning to become popular when Rubens was travelling.

REACHING VENICE

Rubens almost certainly rode for most of the journey, and probably travelled through Paris and Lyon and then around the Alps. He reached Venice in June. From the moment he arrived, he was enchanted by the palaces that emerged from the turquoise lagoon and canals; the alleyways and bridges; the light on the water; the hustle and bustle of people dressed in their finery; the abundance of brilliantly coloured fruits and vegetables in the market; the busy waterways filled with gondolas and other boats; and the lavish paintings by artists such as Titian (c.1488/90–1576), Tintoretto (1518–94) and Veronese (1528–88).

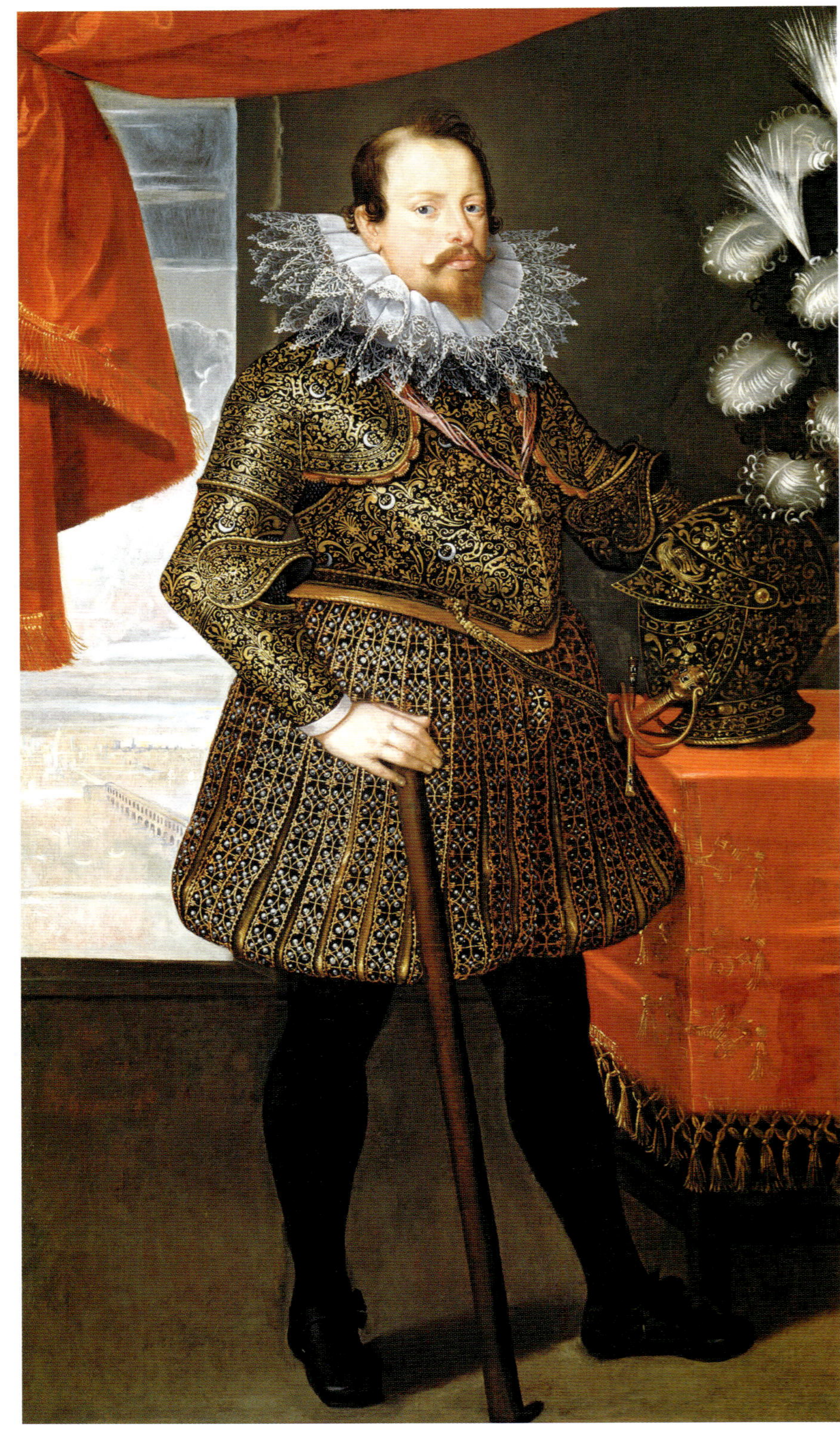

Right: Portrait of Vincenzo Gonzaga by Frans Pourbus. Gonzaga was Duke of Mantua and ruler of the Duchy of Mantua and the Duchy of Montferrat from 1587 to 1612.

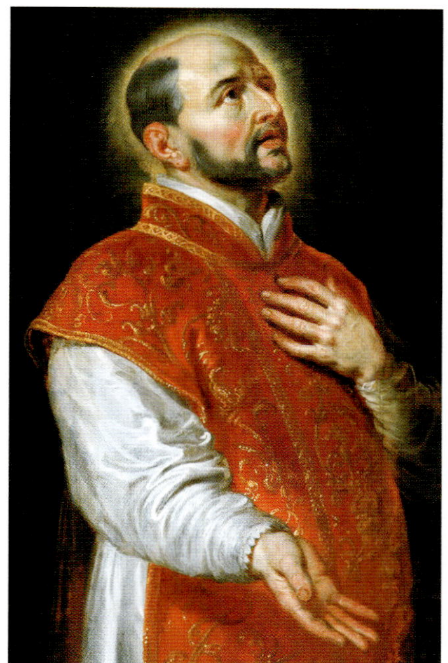

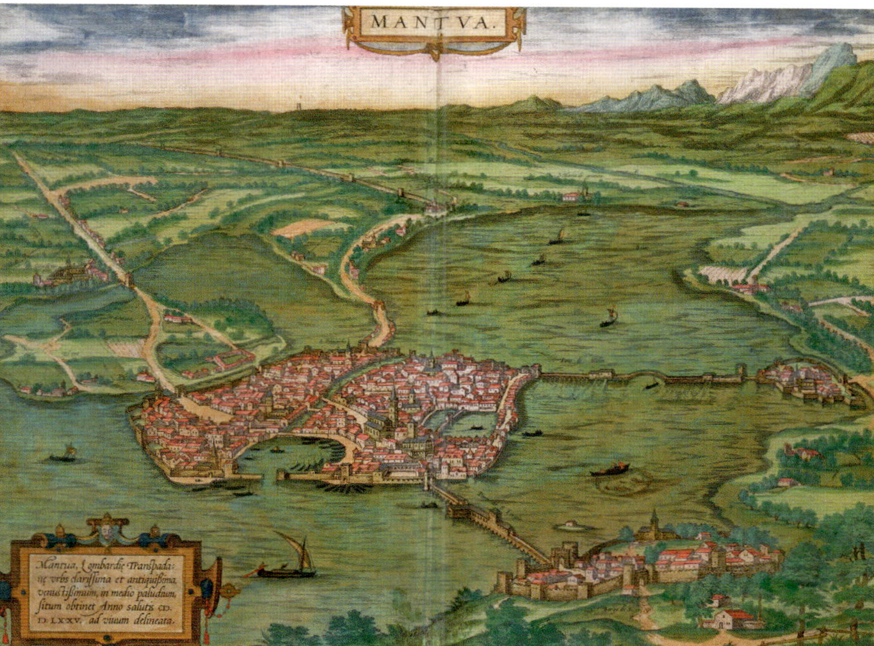

Above left: Saint Ignatius, Rubens, 1600. Ignatius of Loyola (1491–1556) was a Spanish knight, priest and theologian who founded the Jesuit Society.

Above: Map of Mantua. From 1327, the small, damp town of Mantua was under the control of the Gonzaga family, who transformed it into a centre of culture.

Without patrons or commissions, Rubens stayed in Venice with a nobleman from Mantua, who was probably introduced to him by Van Veen or the Archduke Albert. This nobleman was in the service of Vincenzo Gonzaga, the Duke of Mantua (1562–1612), and he showed some of Rubens's paintings to his employer, who immediately offered Rubens a position as one of his palace artists. In September Rubens agreed to work in Mantua, one of the leading courts of Europe, and in October he accompanied his new employer to Florence for the proxy marriage of Gonzaga's sister-in-law Marie de' Medici to King Henri IV of France.

DISCOVERING THE ART OF MANTUA

For Rubens, Mantua was a rich location for both study and inspiration. The Duke's museum of ancient Greek and Roman artefacts fascinated him, and he learned how to date and identify them and how to decipher underlying meanings, which since Raphael's time had become a craze among intellectuals. He was also especially intrigued by paintings filled with numerous figures and animals, less so by portraits and medieval art, and he was particularly inspired by the work of Andrea Mantegna (1431–1506).

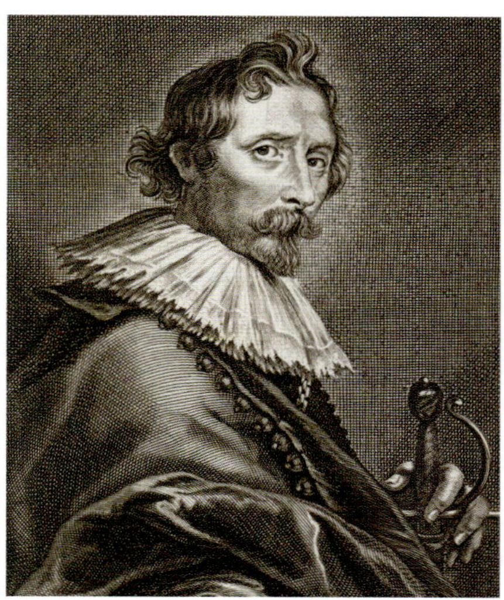

Above: An engraving by an unknown artist. Deodat del Monte (1582–1644) was Rubens's friend. He was a Flemish Baroque painter, architect, engineer, astronomer and art dealer.

He made copies of paintings by Giulio Romano (c.1499–1546), who had been one of Raphael's pupils, and at least one of Mantegna's nine large canvases depicting *The Triumphs of Caesar*, which are filled with figures, colour and action. Overall, Mantua became an important part of his education.

NEW SIGHTS AND EXPERIENCES

Besides acting as a courtier in Mantua, Rubens's duties included painting portraits of the Duke's family and of beautiful court ladies, making copies of famous artworks, learning from the art and artefacts that surrounded him, and sending money home to his mother.

It was a great honour to attend the proxy wedding of Marie de' Medici to Henri IV of France in Florence on October 5, 1600. Rubens was at the ceremony and at the royal banquet and ball in the evening as one of the Duke of Mantua's party. Fascinated by the proliferation of taffeta, silk, gemstones, pomaded hair, food and music, he recalled years later that he was struck by the beauty of a woman who sang, dressed as Iris the goddess of purity and the rainbow, and of another woman dressed as Minerva, who dined with her. The next day, he probably attended the world's first opera at the Pitti Palace with the Mantuan party. *Euridice* was described as a musical extravaganza; the lyrics were written by Ottavio Rinuccini (1562–1621) and the music was by Jacopo Peri (1561–1633). The innovation instigated many possibilities for artists of all kinds, and its significance would not have been lost on Rubens. The following day, he went to view the works of art by the Renaissance artists he had longed to see, especially those by Michelangelo. He copied at least one of Michelangelo's sculptures and his relief *The Battle of the Lapiths and Centaurs*, a small, unfinished work in marble that Michelangelo created when he was in his teens. It depicts an ancient Greek myth about a wedding feast that went horribly wrong. Michelangelo's interpretation is a tangle of figures all trying to kill each other. Rubens reversed the image and attempted to create something new from it. From then on, he developed a more sculptural approach to drawing.

LIFE IN ITALY

Back in Mantua, Rubens made frequent excursions to nearby towns and cities on one of Gonzaga's many horses. He also spent time studying the techniques of Titian, Raphael and Antonio da Correggio (1489–1534), and he painted two sketches in black and red chalk of Gonzaga's sons, 14-year-old Francesco (1586–1612) and 13-year-old Ferdinando (1587–1626), in preparation for a family portrait. In the spring of 1601, he received a letter from his brother Philip, who was still in the service of Richardot in Brussels, while also studying philosophy. It demonstrates the closeness between the brothers and how much Philip missed him: 'It has now been one year, my dear brother, since Italy took you away, one year that for me has been

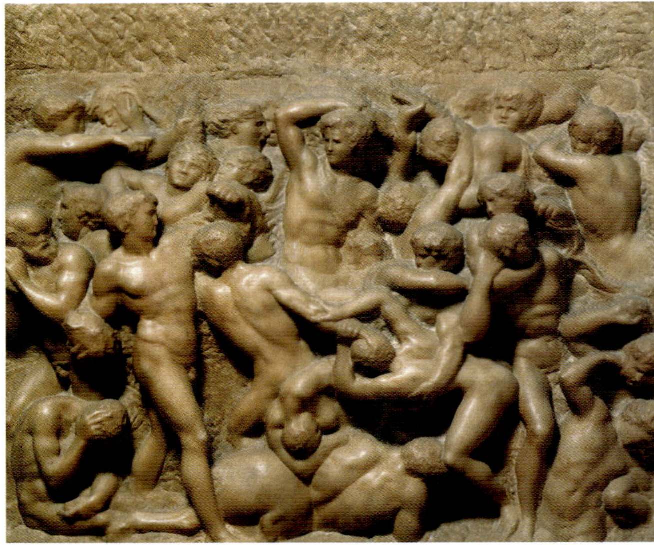

Left: The Battle of the Lapiths and Centaurs, *Michelangelo, c.1492. Inspired by a classical relief created by Bertoldo di Giovanni, Michelangelo created this unfinished relief depicting the mythical battle, and Rubens made a copy of it while he was in Florence.*

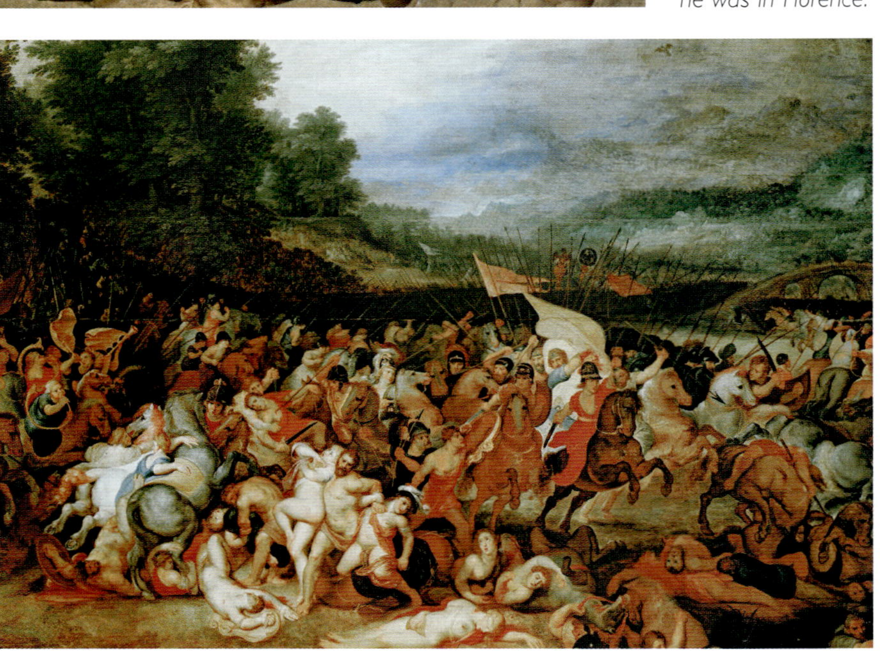

Left: The Battle of the Amazons, *Rubens. The first of three versions of this subject painted by Rubens, this one was completed before he left for Italy.*

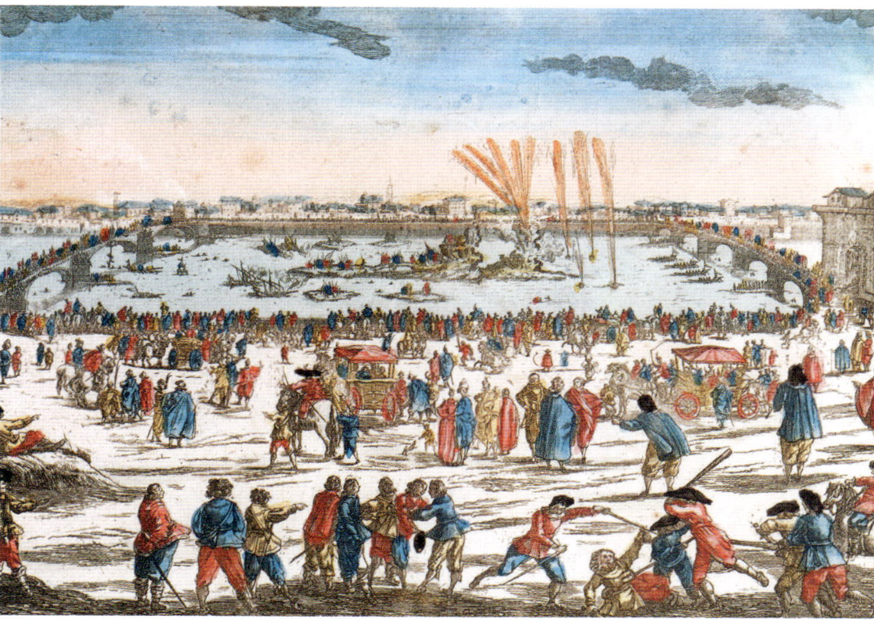

Right: A contemporary illustration of the marriage by proxy of Henri IV of France with Maria de' Medici in Florence that Rubens attended with the Duke of Mantua.

longer than that of Eudoxus...When you were in our homeland, fate often kept us from being together and we rarely had the consolation of seeing each other. Still, the feeling of separation was greatly alleviated by the idea that we were living only a short distance from each other and we could get together again quickly...' The letter continues full of affection, respect and love, and ends with: 'Farewell, to you whom I miss!'

By the end of that year, unable to bear the separation any longer, Philip found a reason to travel to Padua, and the following June the two brothers arranged to meet in Verona.

TO ROME

Meanwhile, Rubens's life was filled with new opportunities. In mid-August 1601, Gonzaga sent him to Rome to paint copies of great works of art for the Mantuan court, while he rode to Croatia via Graz, to help fight invading Turks. On July 8, 1601, Gonzaga wrote to the pope's nephew, Cardinal Alessandro di Montalto (1571–1623), to request protection for 'my Flemish painter... in all that he may require for my service'. This meant that he wanted Rubens to be allowed to enter certain sacred places in order to copy the great works of art held there. On August 15, Montalto wrote back to the Duke, confirming Rubens's arrival and wishing him success in Croatia.

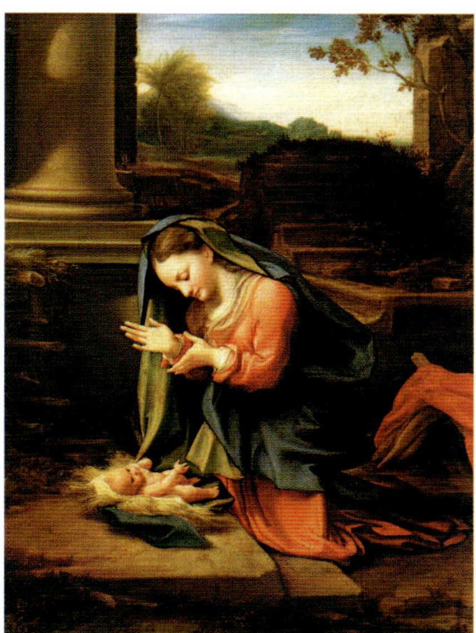

Above: Our Lady Worshipping the Child, *Antonio da Correggio. This was another Italian artist who amazed Rubens. Rubens absorbed a great deal from studying Correggio's works.*

Right: Bacchus and Ariadne, *Titian. From his earliest encounter, Rubens admired Titian enormously, and learned a lot from the Venetian master's style and palette.*

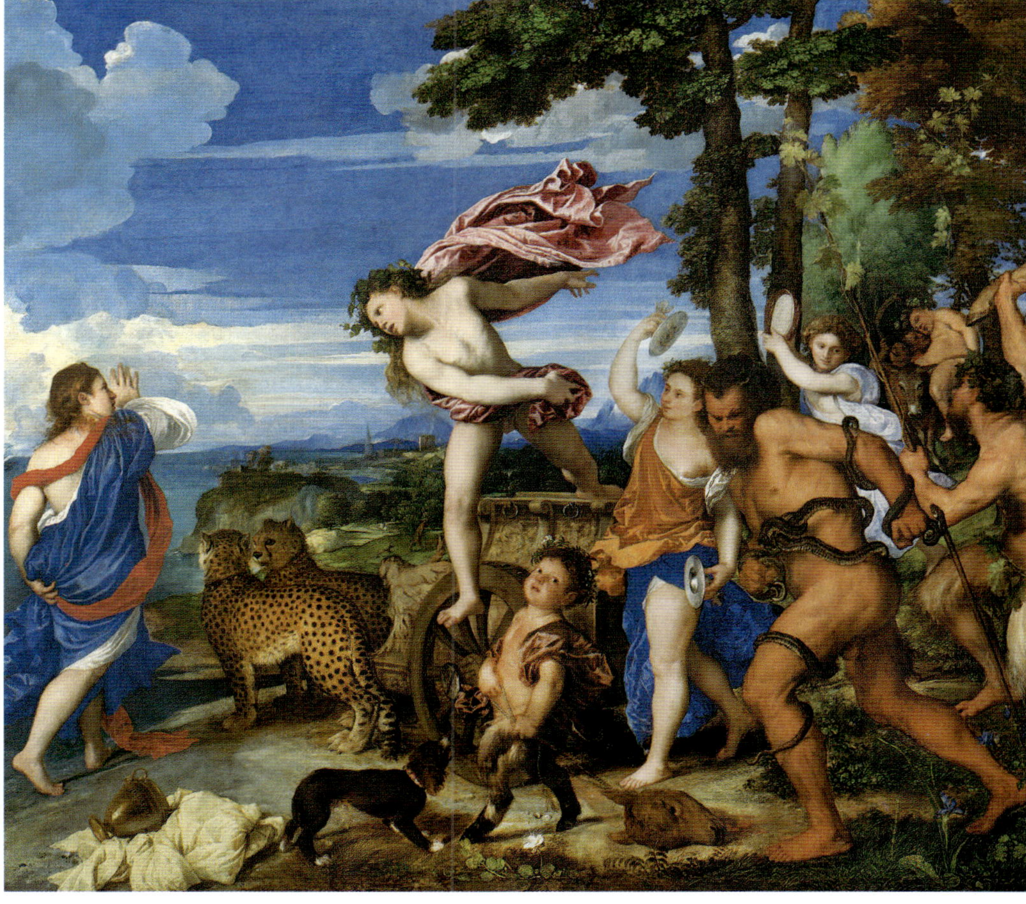

RUBENS IN ROME

When Rubens was in Rome, it had a population of under 110,000, which was less than Venice. It was also less commercially important than both Venice and Florence. Yet to Rubens it was a city of wonder – from the ancient art and artefacts of Greece and Rome, to the paintings of living masters such as Caravaggio.

During the ancient Roman period, many Greek sculptures were looted from temples and bought by wealthy Romans to adorn their homes. Most of these works were lost during the fall of Rome, but were rediscovered in the Renaissance period when they were excavated from beneath ancient Roman ruins.

Below: Saint Sebastian Tended by Angels *is thought to have been painted by Rubens in 1602–03, although the two angels at the top were probably added later, in about 1610.*

COPYING ANCIENT SCULPTURE

Many of the ancient Greek artefacts discovered by later generations were actually Roman copies, but this did not concern artists of the time. In the 16th century, collections of these works were made, and Rome became both the centre of classical studies and the artistic capital of Europe. The impact of seeing these ancient works at first hand on Rubens was profound. He wrote: 'I am convinced that in order to achieve the highest perfection, one needs a full understanding of the statues, indeed a

Below: Laocoön and his Sons. *This ancient sculpture was excavated in Rome in 1506 and placed on display in the Vatican. Rubens made numerous drawings of it during his stay.*

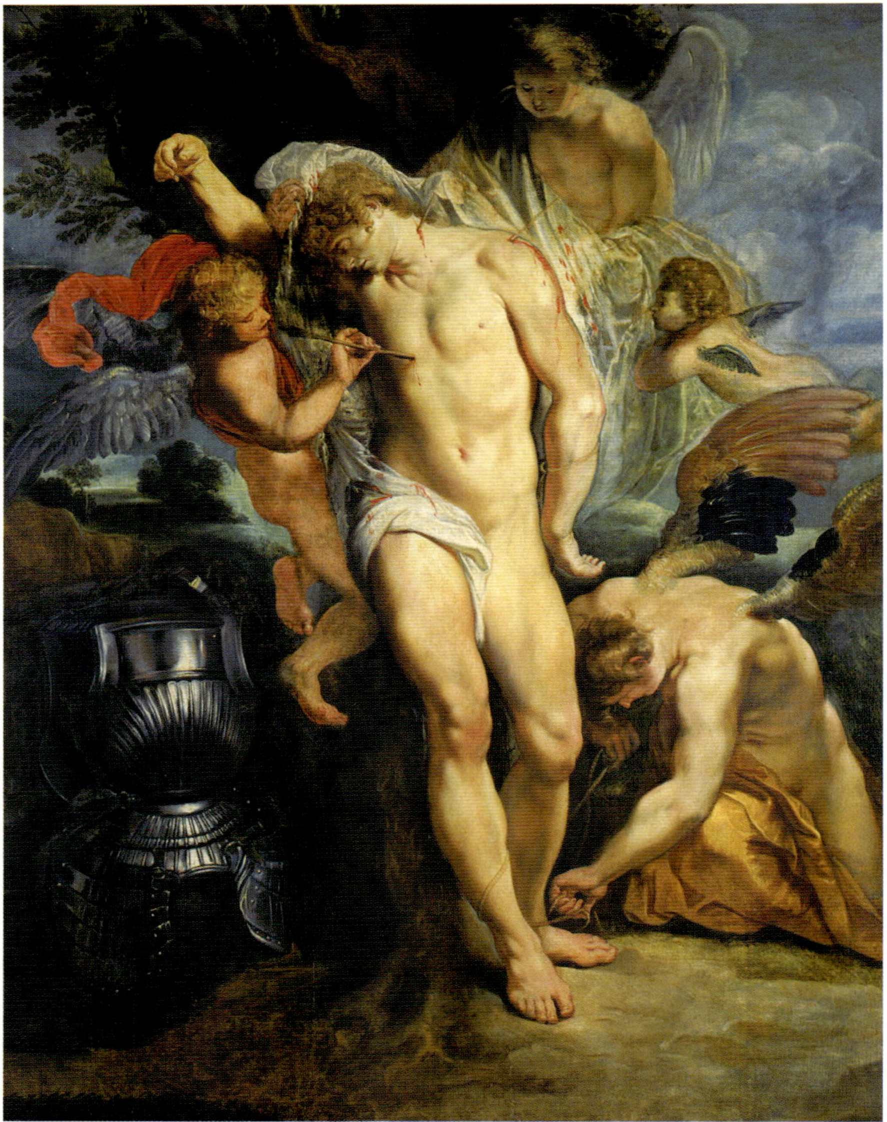

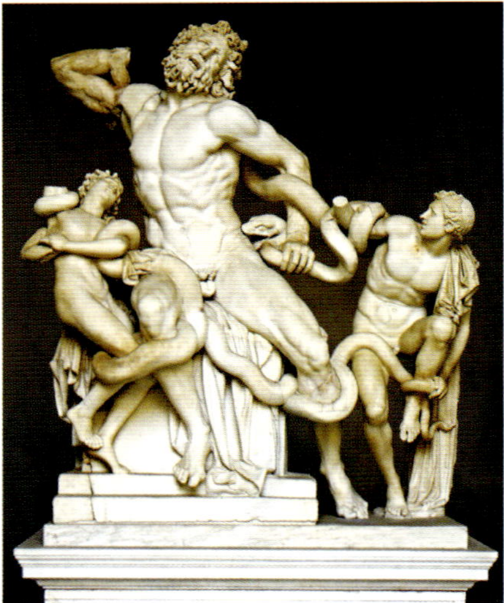

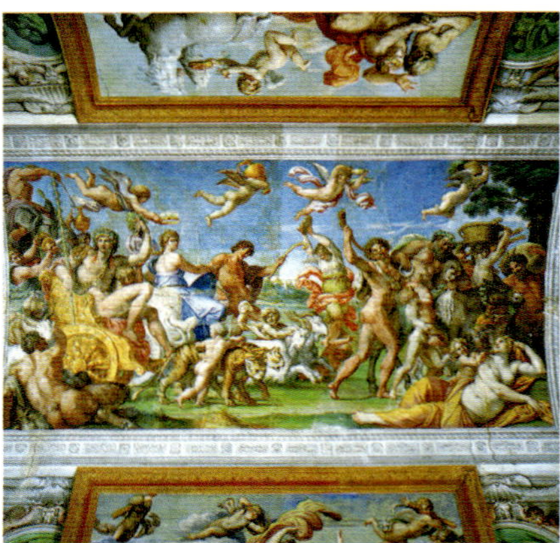

Above: Rubens was captivated by this monumental fresco cycle, completed by the Bolognese artist Annibale Carracci and his studio in the Palazzo Farnese from 1597–1602.

DISCOVERING CARAVAGGIO

By 1600, Michelangelo Merisi da Caravaggio (1571–1610) had been famous for about a decade, and by 1601, when Rubens arrived, he had been painting in Rome for nine years. His paintings *The Martyrdom of Saint Matthew* and *The Calling of Saint Matthew* hang opposite each other in the Contarelli Chapel of the church of San Luigi dei Francesi. At the time when Rubens was there, Caravaggio was still working on the altarpiece for the Contarelli Chapel, *The Inspiration of Saint Matthew*. Caravaggio's paintings were perceived as both shocking and amazing. His dramatic tonal contrasts – known as *chiaroscuro* and *tenebrism* – have the effect of making his paintings appear to be happening at that moment in the shadowy, flickering candlelit recesses of the churches they hang in. The flesh looks real, unwashed and warm, and the figures seem to be thrust forward in the powerful compositions. Caravaggio had been condemned for his irreverence and rebelliousness, but by the 1590s he was increasingly admired. Rubens studied his works intently, including his just-completed painting *The Conversion of Saint Paul on the Road to Damascus* in the Cerasi Chapel of the church of Santa Maria del Popolo.

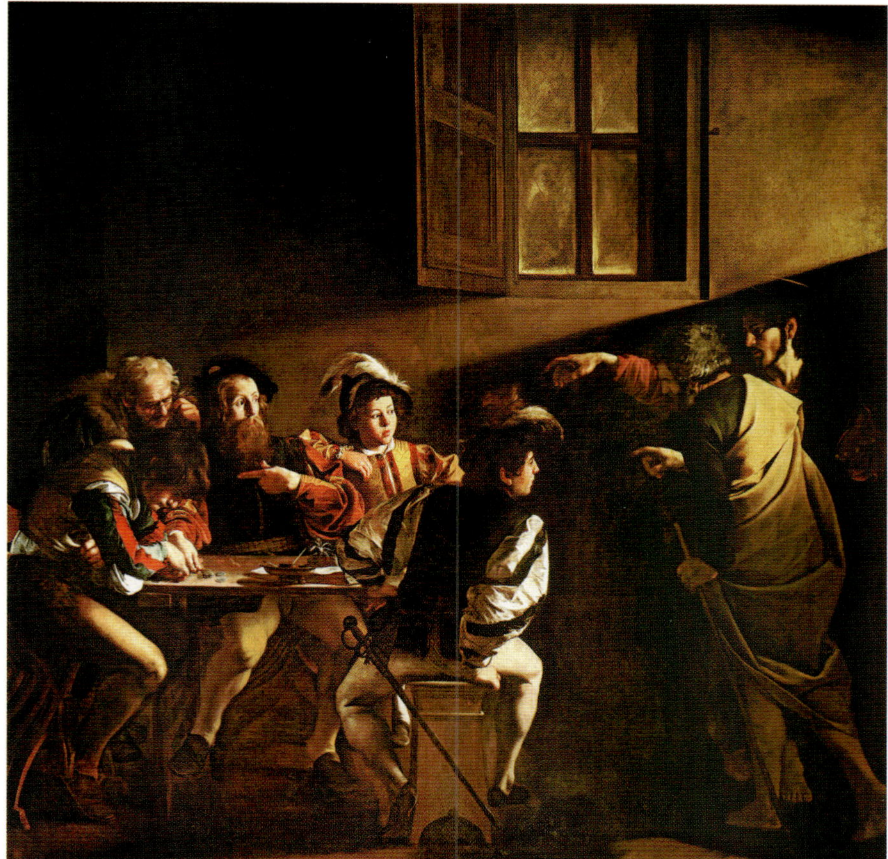

Above: The Calling of Saint Matthew, *Caravaggio, painted in 1599–1600. Rubens was instantly inspired by the dramatic style of Caravaggio's works.*

complete absorption in them: but one must make judicious use of them and before all, avoid the effect of stone.'

His copies, usually in chalk and made from various viewpoints, do indeed appear to have been drawn from live models, as he makes the hard stone look like flesh. Following tradition, his copies of sculptural works are drawn from the front, side and back. One of his copies of this period is from the Laocoön that had been discovered in 1506 and had created a sensation among artists since that time. An ancient Roman copy of a Greek sculpture from c.150 BCE, it was marvelled at for its dynamism and sophistication. Rubens made several careful and sensitive drawings from it.

ASSIMILATING IDEAS

While Rubens was in Rome, as well as Caravaggio, the Bolognese painter Annibale Carracci (1560–1609) was also working there. From 1597–1604 Carracci and his assistants were painting frescoes in the Palazzo Farnese. These were a resplendent cycle of decorative paintings on the theme *The Loves of the Gods*, and were filled with colour and light. From the moment they were completed, the paintings became hugely influential, and Rubens was one of the first artists to see them. In Rome, he also copied more works by Michelangelo, and all these works of art he studied in Rome had a marked effect on him. With his extraordinary ability to remember images and visual effects,

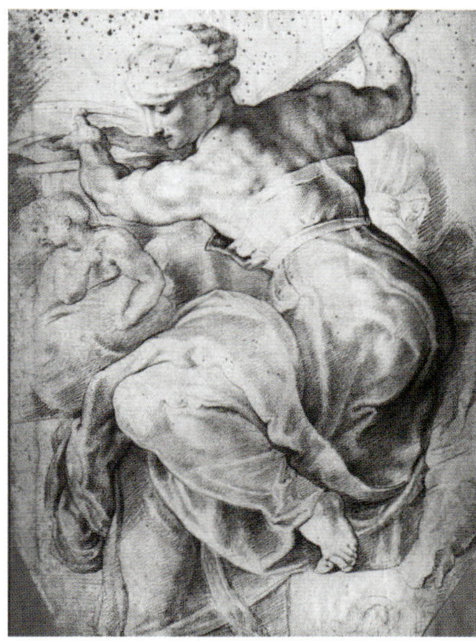

Below: While in Rome, Rubens made this copy of Michelangelo's Libyan Sibyl *in pencil and red chalk on paper.*

he later assimilated many of the ideas, along with techniques he had studied in the Venetian masters' paintings, resulting in original complex compositions filled with figures, colour, light, life, movement and loose brushwork.

FIRST PRESTIGIOUS COMMISSION

After Rubens had returned to Mantua, in about mid-December 1601, he received his first major public commission. Interestingly, it was for a church in Rome, and it arose through two Flemish connections: the Archduke Albert and Philip's employer, Jean Richardot.

Long before his marriage, the Archduke Albert had been a cardinal, archbishop and Grand Inquisitor of Toledo, and at that time an alleged relic of Christ's cross had been entrusted to him. Subsequently, he had donated it to the church of Santa Croce in Gerusalemme in Rome. According to tradition, the church was consecrated in c.325 to accommodate the relics of Christ's Passion brought to Rome from the Holy Land by the Empress Helena, mother of the Roman Emperor Constantine I.

Soon after Albert had donated his relic to the Santa Croce, it had been stolen, but it had recently been recovered, and to celebrate this and also to honour the church where he had been made a cardinal, he decided to have an altarpiece painted for the small underground Saint Helena chapel. He wrote to his diplomat Richardot who was in Rome on business, asking

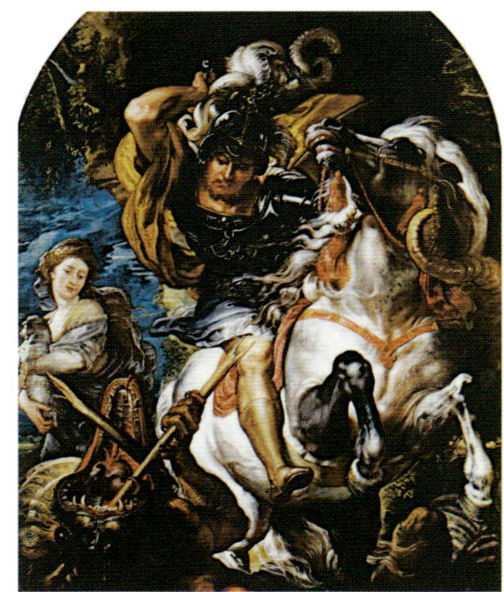

Below: Saint George and the Dragon. This is a copy of a lost painting by Rubens, dated c.1602–03, and painted during the first years of his stay in Mantua.

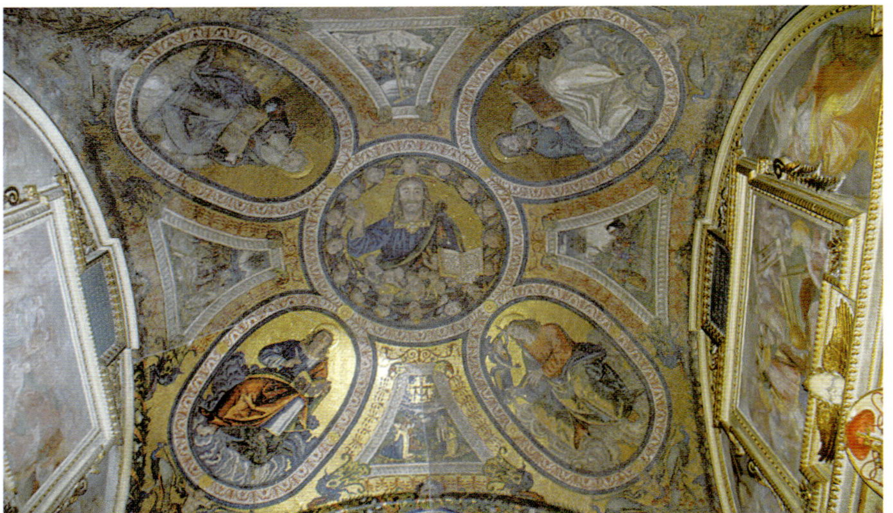

Below: Rubens was inspired by so many sights in Rome, including the stunning mosaics on the ceiling of the Santa Croce in Gerusalemme.

Bottom: The Discovery of the True Cross, Tintoretto, 1562. Tintoretto profoundly influenced Rubens, as can be seen in this clever composition with numerous figures carefully placed.

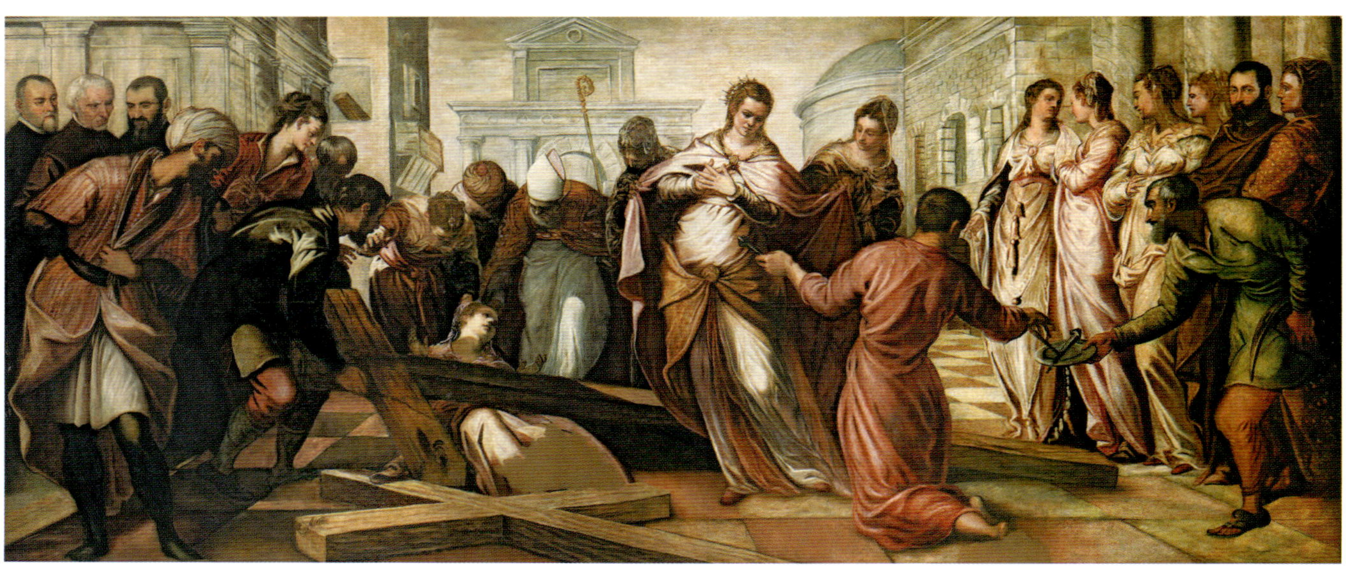

THE FATE OF THE PANELS

The three Santa Croce paintings were on arch-shaped wooden panels, and after some time they began to deteriorate through dampness in the chapel. Eventually, in the early 19th century they were moved. The two panels of *Saint Helena with the True Cross* and *The Crowning with Thorns* were taken to the Notre Dame Cathedral in Grasse, France. In 1811, *The Raising of the Cross* was sold to an English art dealer and imported to England. It was subsequently auctioned at the Squibb's sale in London in 1812, sold to a private collector and, after 1820, was lost at sea.

him to find a suitable artist, and stated how much he was prepared to pay for a well-executed painting. At the time, Rubens's brother Philip was touring Italy with Richardot's son Guillaume (1579–1640) and heard of the commission. He immediately suggested his brother, and Richardot duly wrote to the Duke of Mantua, asking for the services of his 'young Flemish painter called Peter Paul'. Although usually possessive with his own artists, Gonzaga was quite relieved to release Rubens for a time, as he was experiencing financial problems. Overstretched, he was finding it difficult to pay those in his service, and the 400 ducats a year he had promised to Rubens were going to be hard to find. So he agreed, and sent Rubens back to Rome.

SEIZING THE OPPORTUNITY

Rubens had been amassing a huge amount of research – he took his sketchbooks with him everywhere – and so felt ready for the commission. Prestigious, ambitious and exactly the sort of thing he was eager to undertake after seeing the works of so many great artists in Rome, the painting was the

chance he had been waiting for. He set off for Rome immediately, and completed the central panel in a matter of weeks by the end of January 1602. The painting was of a young *Saint Helena with the True Cross* looking up to heaven, surrounded by cherubs. The next two panels took longer, and he had to write to Gonzaga to beg leave to be allowed to stay in Rome for a lengthier period. The Duke was irked, as although he was saving money without Rubens, he liked his courtiers around him, and as well as being an accomplished artist, Rubens was

good company. However, Gonzaga recognized the reflected prestige of the commission for his own court painter, and as it was still saving him money, he gave his consent. The two final panels were *Christ Mocked* or *The Crowning with Thorns* and *The Raising of the Cross*. Rubens completed both by April 1602, and unlike his later works they were slightly self-conscious, painted smoothly and with strong chiaroscuro. The colours are bright, the figures sensuous and the compositions fairly complex, but his later, looser, bolder style was yet to appear.

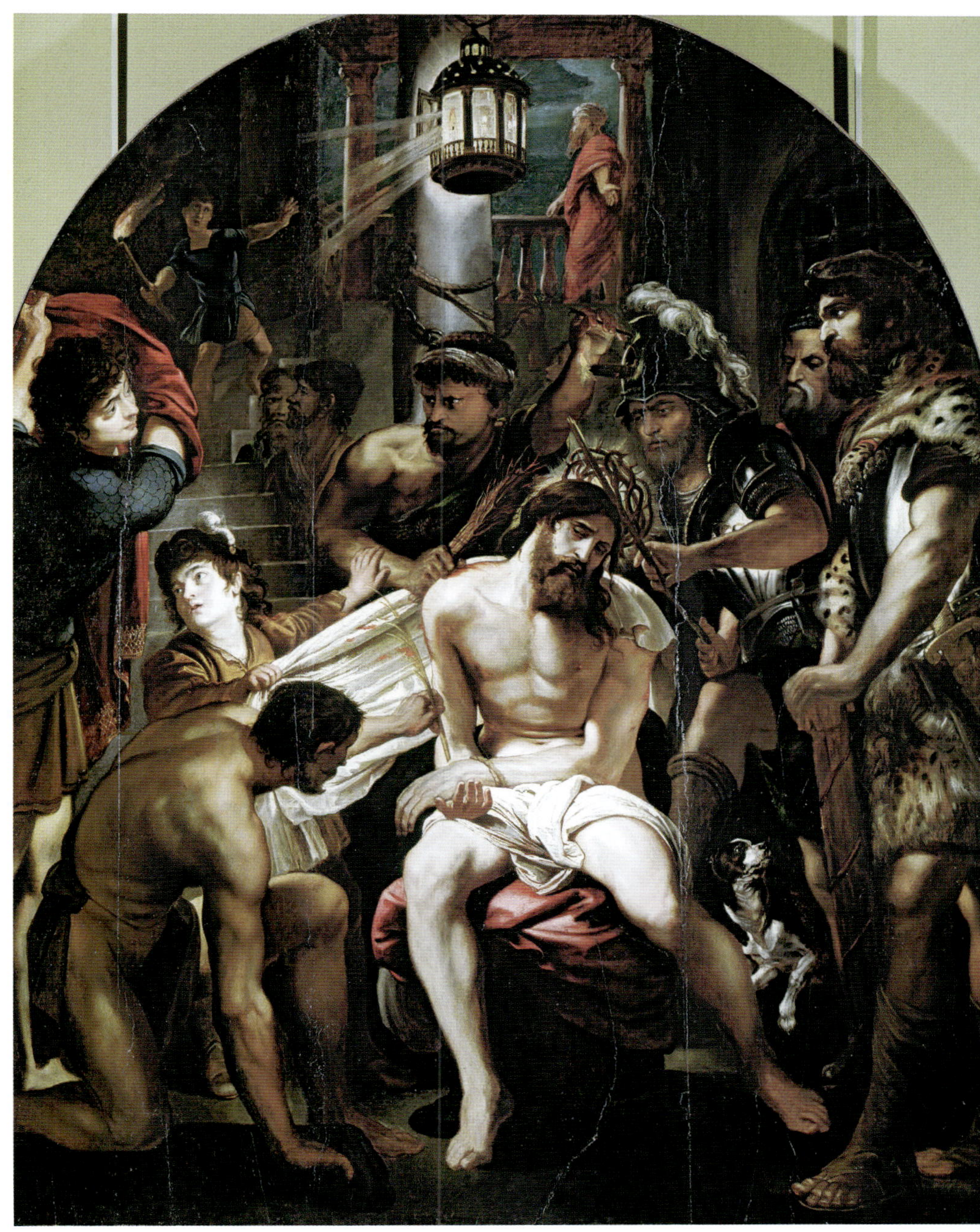

Right: Painted by Rubens in 1602, The Crowning with Thorns *shows his early, smooth painting style, albeit influenced by the chiaroscuro of Caravaggio.*

FRIENDS AND RIVALS

By the end of April 1602, the commission completed, Rubens had once again returned to Mantua, but back
at Gonzaga's court, he discovered that he had a rival. In the month before he had been appointed by
Gonzaga in 1600, another artist from Antwerp had accepted a similar role from the Duke.

Frans Pourbus the Younger (1569–1622)
was the son and grandson of two
accomplished painters, and had
completed his apprenticeship in
Antwerp in 1591. Soon after this, he
had started working for Albert and
Isabella in Brussels, and in the summer
of 1600 he accepted the position of
court painter to the Duke of Gonzaga.
His official duties were predominantly
to paint portraits, but despite the clash
of interests, there is no evidence of
hostility between him and Rubens. In
fact, given their relaxed and amiable
personalities and their divergent
ambitions, they seem to have been
dignified and fairly friendly in a situation
that could have been troublesome.
Pourbus was also in the party of the
guests at the proxy wedding in
Florence, which had consequences
for his later career – from 1609, he
became Marie de' Medici's court
painter. As well, Claudio Monteverdi
(1567–1643), the greatest composer of
the day who perfected the developing
musical format of opera, was at the
Mantuan court at that time.

Yet Mantua was not fulfilling
Rubens's lofty ambitions and so he
was considering his next step, looking
forward to new experiences. At
around that time, he began creating
a large, expressive painting of *Aeneas
Prepares to Lead the Trojans into Exile*.
Commissioned by Gonzaga, the painting
developed as a dramatic mythological
image of refugees escaping, with the
heroic figure of Aeneas in a lion skin.
Although his earlier images had shown
a strong influence of Van Veen, in this
work the greater influence appears to
have been Titian, with its rich colours
and lively sense of movement.

MEETING IN VERONA
That summer, Rubens rode to Verona
to meet his brother, who had ridden
from Padua. Philip had previously
written: 'My first desire was to see Italy,
my second to meet you there again.
The first is fulfilled and the second will, I
hope, soon be fulfilled.' Philip introduced
Rubens to Guillaume Richardot and
Nicolas-Claude Fabri de Peiresc
(1580–1637), a French astronomer,
scholar, historian and bibliographer,
who was also friends with the Italian
physicist, mathematician, astronomer

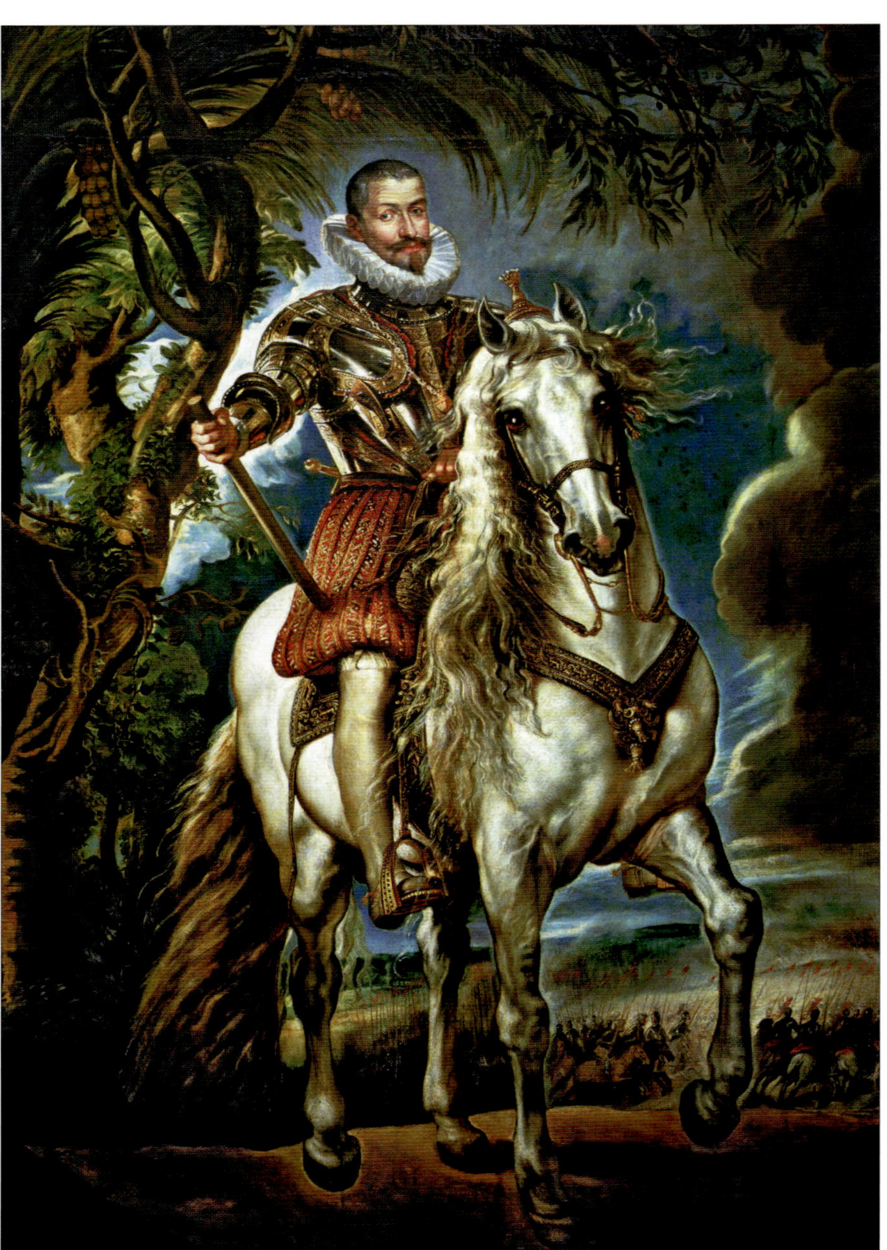

*Left: Painted by Rubens in 1603, this is
Philip III's favourite courtier, Francisco de
Sandoval y Rojas, Marquis of Denia and
the First Duke of Lerma.*

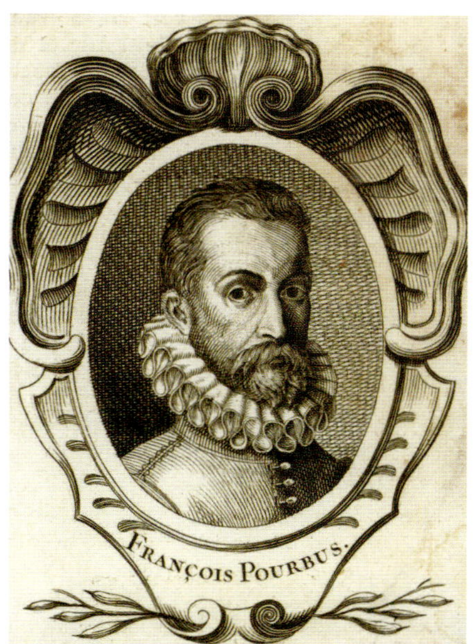

Above: Portrait of Frans Pourbus the Younger. *Although there was no rivalry between Pourbus and Rubens, neither did they become particular friends.*

and philosopher Galileo (1564–1642). With Philip was Jan van der Wouwer, or Jan Woverius (1576–1636), a friend of both brothers, who was the financial counsellor to the Archduke Albert. The meeting must have been exceptionally congenial. They were all highly intelligent, vital young men, eager to learn and extremely ambitious (Guillaume was Philip's pupil).

It was probably during that time that Rubens painted a group portrait that has come to be known as *Self-portrait in a Circle of Friends from Mantua*. Depicting himself, his brother and their friends, the most prominent figure on the right (facing the viewer) is thought to be Rubens's first self-portrait, and Philip is on his right, just behind Rubens, almost in the centre of the painting. Justus Lipsius (1547–1606), a Flemish philosopher, Latin scholar and Humanist who had been Philip's teacher at the University of Louvain, is on the extreme right of the painting, and the others are possibly Pourbus, Richardot and

Right: Self-portrait in a Circle of Friends from Mantua, c.1602–4, Rubens. *This shows (from left to right) Frans Pourbus, Caspar Schoppe, William Richardot, Philip Rubens, Peter Paul Rubens and Justus Lipsius.*

the German philologist, Caspar Schoppe (1576–1649). It is not an exact rendition of the meeting in Verona because Lipsius was not there, but it appears to be a representation of friendship and conviviality. These were all educated and accomplished men, on the cusp of great achievements.

SENSUOUS STYLE

The convivial meeting of friends and brothers in Verona did not last long, as all the men returned to their busy lives.

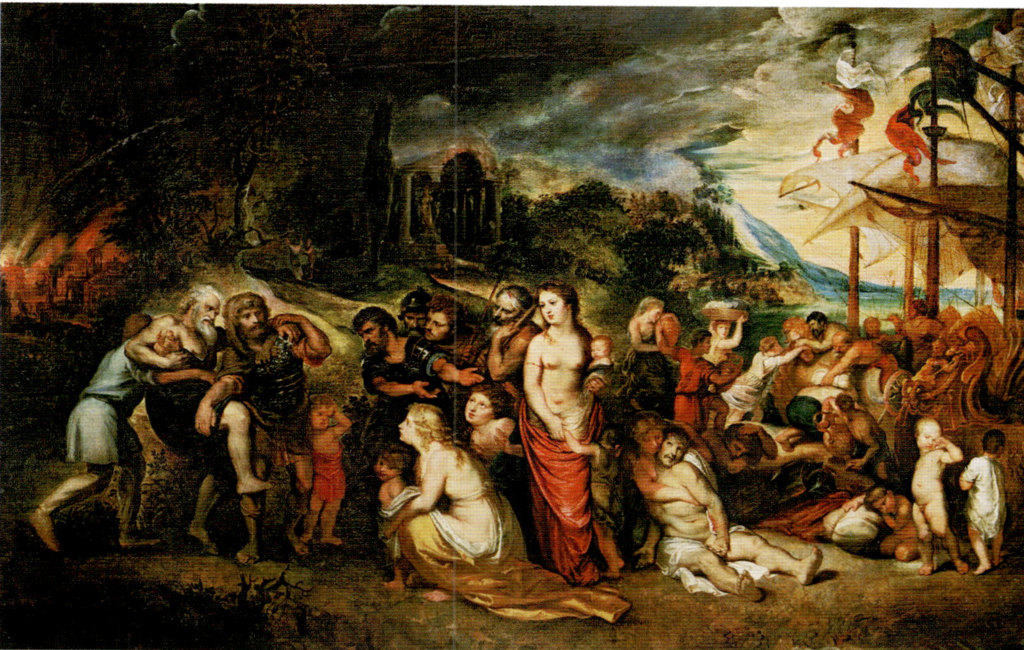

Above: Aeneas Prepares to Lead the Trojans into Exile, Rubens, c.1602. *From early on in his career, Rubens had a great ability in painting complex, densely populated compositions.*

By the end of July, Rubens was back in Mantua, and Philip was in Padua. On his return to Mantua, Rubens painted a monumental work, another episode from Greek mythology. *Assembly of Olympian Gods* shows further development toward his sensuous style.

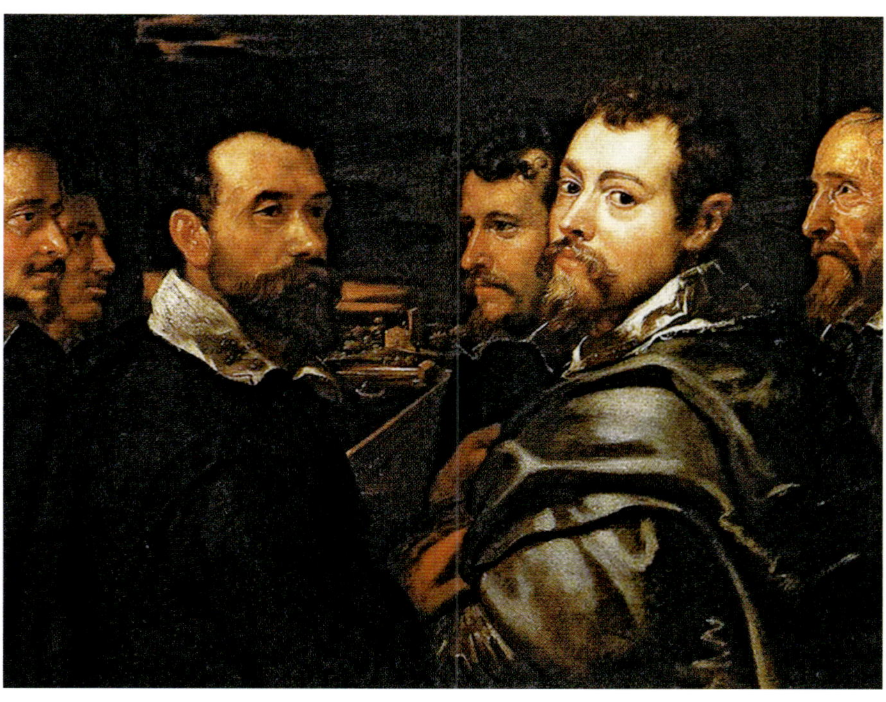

THE DIPLOMAT

The Duke of Mantua had long wanted to strengthen his relations with the King of Spain, to increase his prestige and wealth. King Philip III (1578–1621) had inherited the thrones of Spain and Portugal in 1598, and Gonzaga had ambitions to be appointed as admiral of the Spanish fleet.

So far, the Duke had not been sure how to win the King's favour, but in February 1603 he came up with a plan. He sent Rubens on a diplomatic mission to Madrid, bearing gifts for King Philip and his family. It was not completely unusual to send a mere artist on such a mission – artists were not questioned too much as their presence in all sorts of places was common, and they were often sent by rulers to copy works from various collections. They were also fairly apolitical. Yet why did Gonzaga send Rubens? Pourbus was a more prominent artist at the Mantuan court and had been commissioned with a greater number of portraits, plus his family credentials singled him out as an established artist, whereas Rubens was an unknown. Alternatively,

Mantuan-born Pietro Facchetti (1539–1613) might have been chosen as he was currently acting as Gonzaga's agent in Rome. It was probably because Rubens's charm, intellect, wit and tact had already become apparent, along with the courtly manners he had learned as a pageboy to Princess Marguerite de Ligne-Arenberg.

THE ARDUOUS JOURNEY

Whatever the reasons for sending Rubens, in March 1603 he left Mantua with a startling array of gifts for the King of Spain and his favourite and most influential minister, Don Francisco Gómez de Sandoval, First Duke of Lerma (1552/3–1625). The gifts included a rock crystal vase of perfume, ornate firearms, gold and silver vessels, copies of works by Raphael painted by

Facchetti, and a gilt coach with six of the Duke's best horses (which, according to detailed instructions, were to be pampered in particular ways, including being bathed in wine).

Following the route he had been told to take, Rubens's journey was particularly challenging. With his wagon-loads of goods, ox-drivers and other burdens, it took ten days to reach Florence. The weather was bad, he was short of money and he was not even sure why he was being sent to Spain. In a letter of 18 March to Annibale Chieppio (1563–1623), Gonzaga's Secretary of State, he wrote: '... Well, I finally arrived in Florence on 15 March (not without the greatest expense, as I will tell you later, in transporting the baggage across the Alps – especially the little coach) ... When [important Florentine merchants] heard of the undertaking, they were amazed; they almost crossed themselves in astonishment at such a mistake, saying

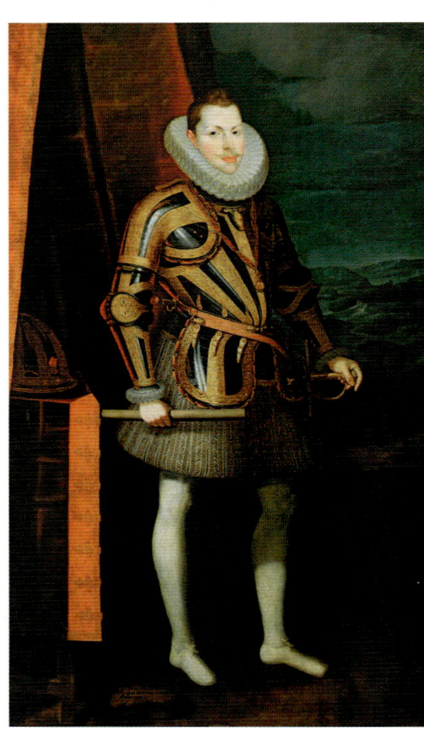

Below: Portrait of Philip III of Spain, *Juan Pantoja de la Cruz, 1606. De la Cruz worked for both Philip II and Philip III.*

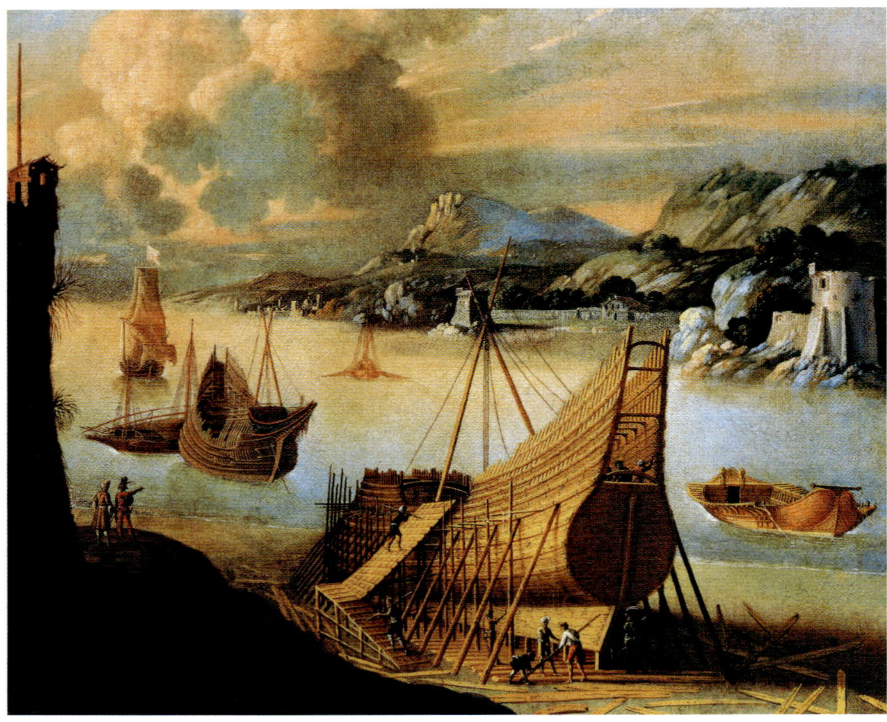

Below: Port of Livorno, *17th century. The city of Livorno was one of the most important Mediterranean ports.*

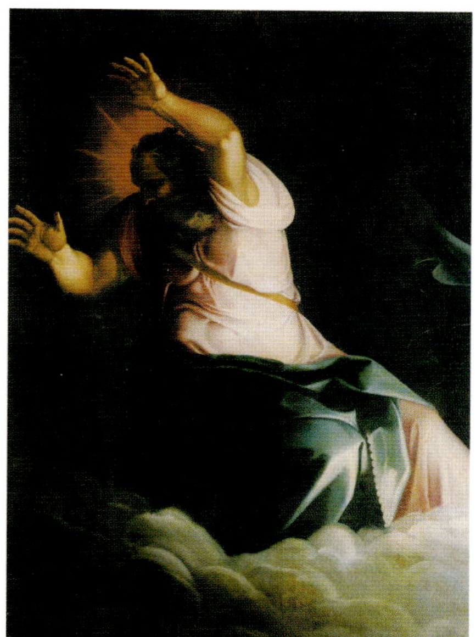

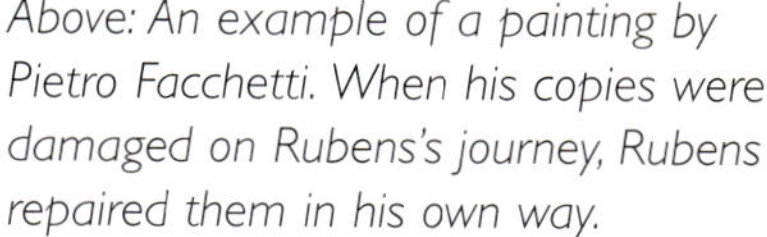

Above: An example of a painting by Pietro Facchetti. When his copies were damaged on Rubens's journey, Rubens repaired them in his own way.

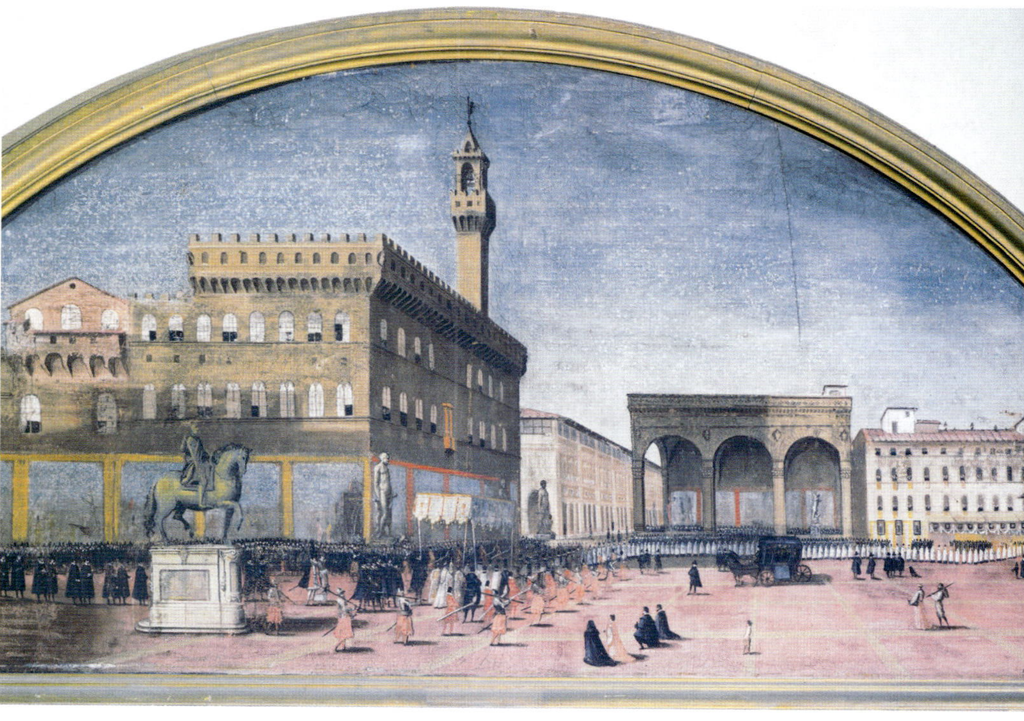

Above: Procession in Florence. Pageantry and processions in Florence were common during the time when Rubens travelled there, and he enjoyed the spectacle.

that we should have gone to Genoa to embark, instead of risking the roundabout route to Livorno without being first assured of a passage. And everyone asserts that I might perhaps wait there three or four months in vain . . .'

Rubens continued in his polite and ironic manner, explaining to Chieppio the trials he had suffered so far and the problems he envisaged for the rest of the journey. Another letter, written on 29 March, explained how he discovered that the Grand Duke of Florence had been spying on him: '. . . this prince astonished me by showing how minutely he was informed in every detail as to the quantity and quality of the gifts destined for this person or that. He told me . . . who I was, my country, my profession and the rank which I held. I stood there like a dunce.'

RESTORATION AND RENEWAL

Continuing on his trying and uncomfortable journey, Rubens eventually embarked on a ship that took him from Livorno to Alicante, and reached Spain at the end of April 1603. On May 24, he wrote to Chieppio that the horses had arrived in good health, but the paintings had been damaged: '. . . The deterioration is probably due to the continuous rains which lasted for twenty-five days – an incredible thing in Spain.' However, he skilfully managed to restore some, and also quickly painted some new pictures to replace those that were beyond repair.

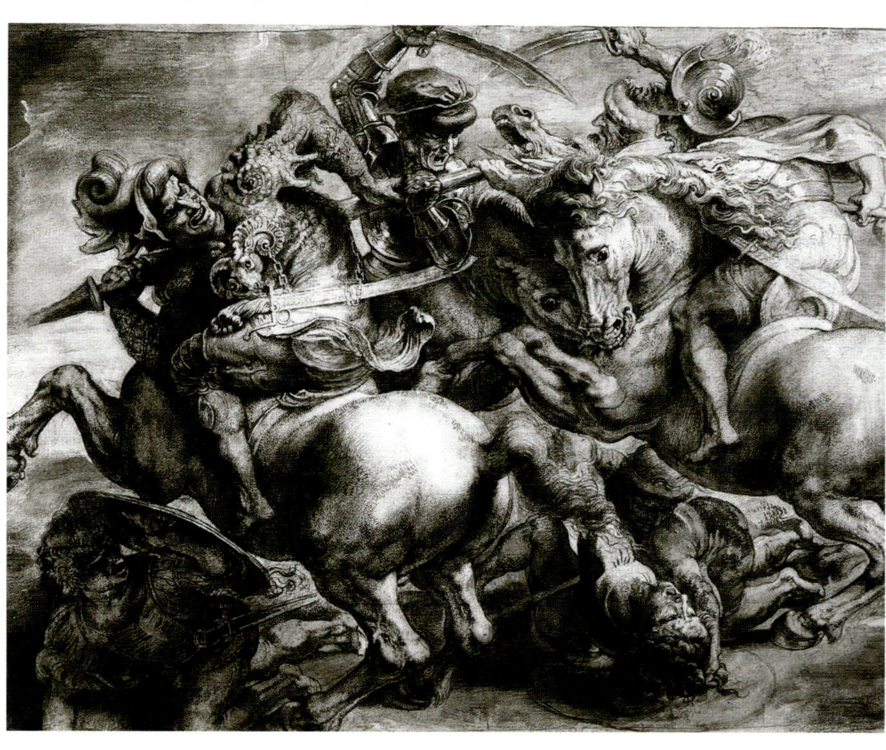

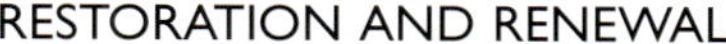

Left: In 1505, Leonardo da Vinci painted The Battle of Anghiari, *recalling a real battle of 1440. However, the painting has been lost and Rubens's copy here, c.1603, was taken from an engraving of Leonardo's painting in 1553 by Lorenzo Zacchia (1524–87).*

THE SPANISH MISSION

On his arrival in Alicante, Rubens found that his problems were not over. He continued with his party through further torrential rain and violent storms, eventually reaching the Escorial Palace in Madrid. However, the Spanish court was not there; the King had left Madrid and gone north-west to Valladolid.

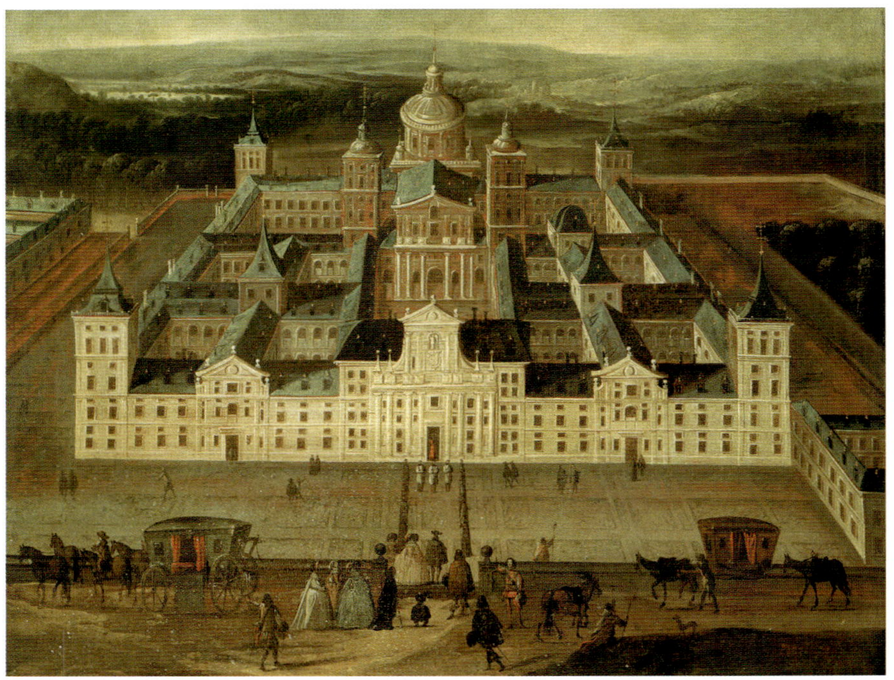

Above: The Palace of the Escorial. *Construction of the vast palace of El Escorial in Madrid began in 1563 and ended in 1584.*

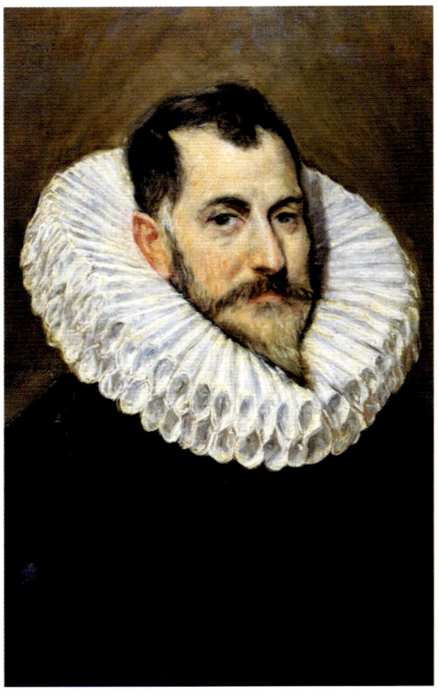

Above: A Spanish Nobleman, *El Greco,* c.1603. *The haunting, elongated style of El Greco fascinated Rubens when he saw the work in Spain.*

When he reached Madrid, Rubens was told of further delays. The royal party had left Valladolid, but rather than return, they had headed south-east to Aranjuez. Although this was another setback, it had some compensations for Rubens. He no longer had to rush to meet the royal party; instead, Gonzaga's representative in Spain, Annibale Iberti, journeyed there to give the king some of the presents from Mantua, leaving Rubens in Madrid, where he had time to study the royal collection. It included works by the contemporary master, El Greco (1541–1614) and numerous other great painters. He wrote to Chieppio of his joy at seeing 'so many splendid works of Titian, of Raphael and others which have astonished me, both by their quality and quantity, in the King's Palace, in the Escorial, and elsewhere.'

FIRST COMMISSION IN SPAIN

Iberti was Gonzaga's ambassador at the Spanish court, and one of the few people who did not succumb to Rubens's charms, but remained exceptionally jealous of him, doing all he could to hinder his reception in Spain. Iberti declared that he had not been expecting Rubens. However, the Duke of Lerma, Philip III's favourite minister and the richest man in Spain, was struck by Rubens's skill on seeing the paintings that he had replaced from the damaged gifts, particularly his *Heraclitus Crying and Democritus Laughing*. The men liked each other instantly, and Lerma immediately commissioned Rubens to paint his portrait.

Prior to his arrival in Spain, Rubens had been commissioned by Gonzaga to paint a number of portraits of beautiful women at the Spanish court, but he resented the task and wrote to Chieppio: '. . . I beg him earnestly to employ me, at home or abroad, in works more appropriate to my talent'. Rather than follow his patron's instructions, he began work on the portrait of the Duke of Lerma, placing him on a horse.

The completed painting astonished all who saw it. With an atmospheric sky and framed by branches of olive and palm, symbolizing victory, Lerma is seen from a low viewpoint. His powerful horse tosses its plume and canters forward, while the Duke in full armour sits upright, noble and commanding.

The original style of the work, with its implications of importance, began a fashion for equestrian portraits throughout Europe. Next, also for Lerma, Rubens painted a series of *Christ and the Twelve Apostles*, and was soon occupied painting portraits of nobles at the Spanish court.

FROM SPAIN TO GENOA

In October, Rubens was a guest at Lerma's country estate in Ventosilla near Valladolid, and then spent time in Valladolid, which Lerma was trying to make the capital over Madrid. By then, Rubens was celebrated for his equestrian portrait and his confidence was growing. Beyond this, there is little documented evidence about his time in Spain, except that Gonzaga began to request his return to Mantua, asking him to travel via France in order to paint yet more portraits of beautiful women at the French court for his gallery. Rubens remained reluctant to undertake more of such work that he considered demeaning, so he lingered in Spain where he was well received. By February 1604, however, he had started his return journey to Italy, but instead of making the detour through France, he stopped at the port of Genoa in north-west Italy — an independent and wealthy republic, a centre of banking and commerce. He met with Gonzaga's banker Nicolò Pallavicini, who reimbursed him on Gonzaga's behalf for the expenses he had incurred on the Spanish mission. Although Rubens only passed through Genoa on that occasion, he and Pallavicini instantly got along.

Right: Study for an Equestrian Portrait of the Duke of Lerma, *Rubens. This work, when completed (see page 30), was admired by many at the Spanish court.*

Below: Genoa, 17th century. From the late 16th century onwards, Genoa entered 'the gold age of Genoese bankers.'

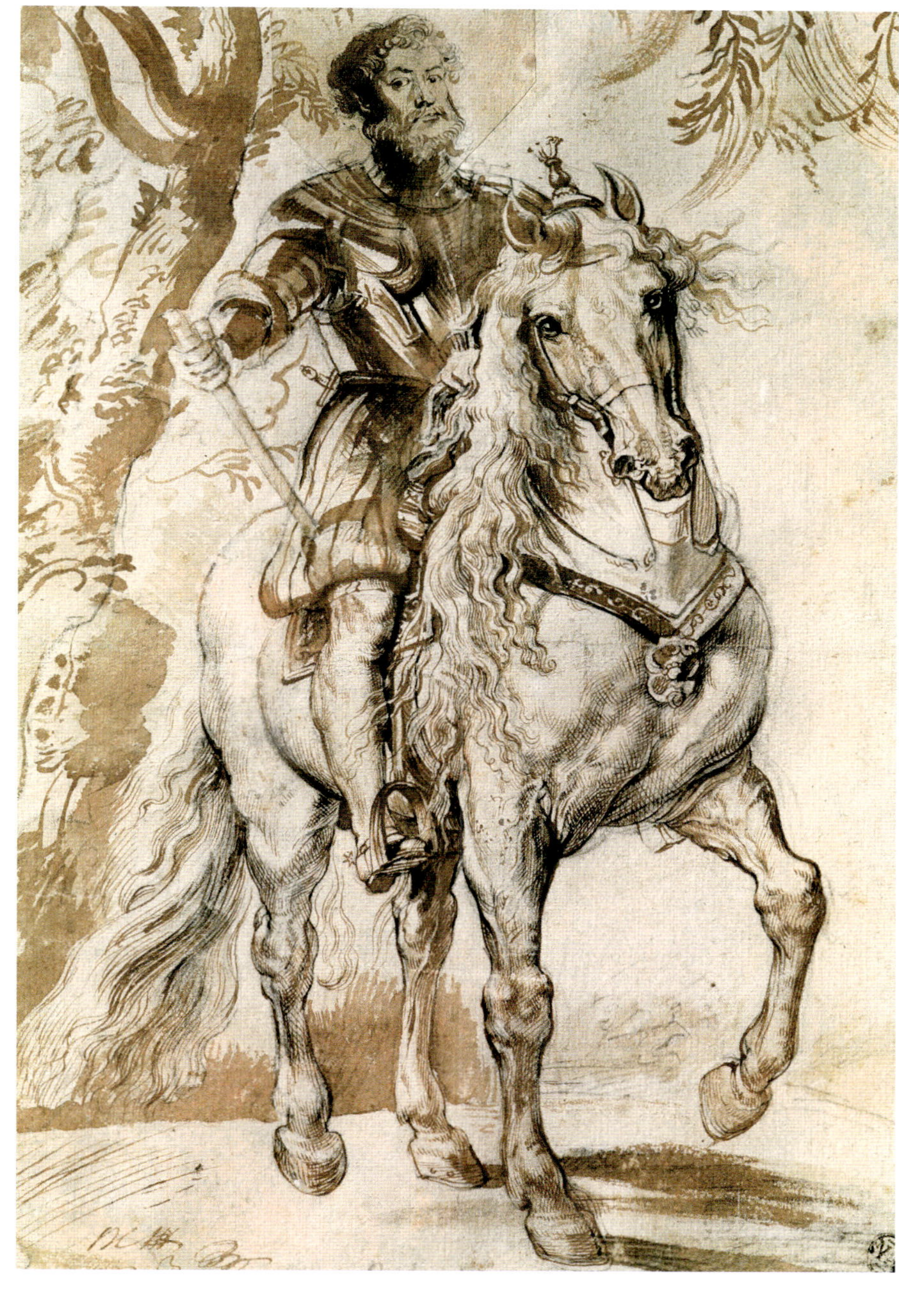

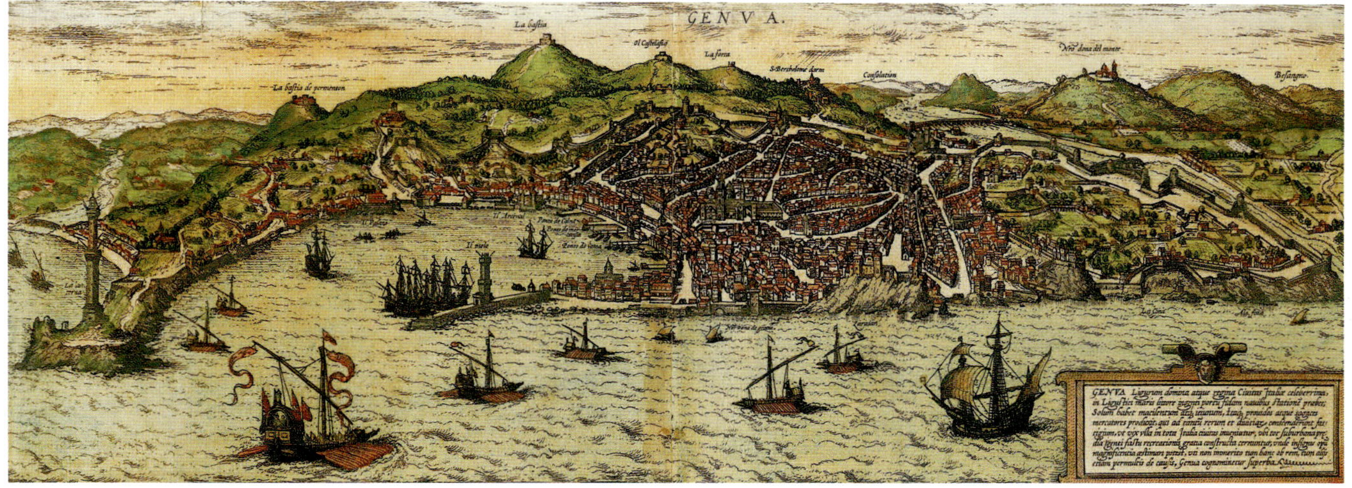

ASCENDANCY IN MANTUA

Before returning to Mantua, Rubens travelled on to Venice once more, to examine the artists' work he had so admired. Once he had returned to Mantua, he was buoyed with confidence and determination to work on more ambitious projects. Soon after his arrival, in March 1604, he was visited by his brother Philip.

When Philip arrived in Mantua, he was accompanied by Richardot and Juan Batiste Perez de Baron, the son of a Portuguese businessman living in Antwerp. Galileo also arrived there at that time. Gonzaga was fascinated by Galileo's invention of a military compass, and had invited him to negotiate terms for a possible appointment there as a resident scientist, but in the end they could not agree. However, the visit was not wasted – Galileo and the Rubens brothers had some lively discussions and established a firm friendship. In addition to all his interests, Galileo was a keen amateur painter, and some time before 1610, he wrote a treatise on colour: *De Visu et Coloribus*. Significantly, this was written after his meeting with Rubens in Mantua. Rubens and Galileo had much in common, and they respected each other greatly. *The Mantuan Friendship Portrait*, also called *Self-portrait in a Circle of Friends from Mantua* (see page 31), is Rubens's tribute to the older man.

Right: Portrait of Galileo. *Rubens found Galileo fascinating for his artistic as well as scientific ideas, and the two men became good friends.*

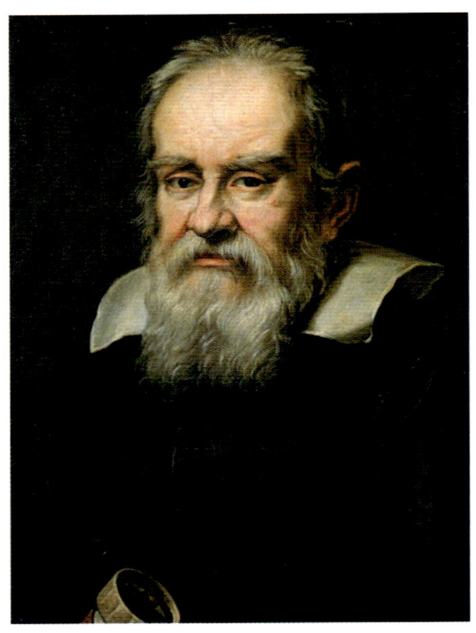

Below: Deposition, *Rubens. This is the earliest version of the subject of Christ's downfall, painted in 1602.*

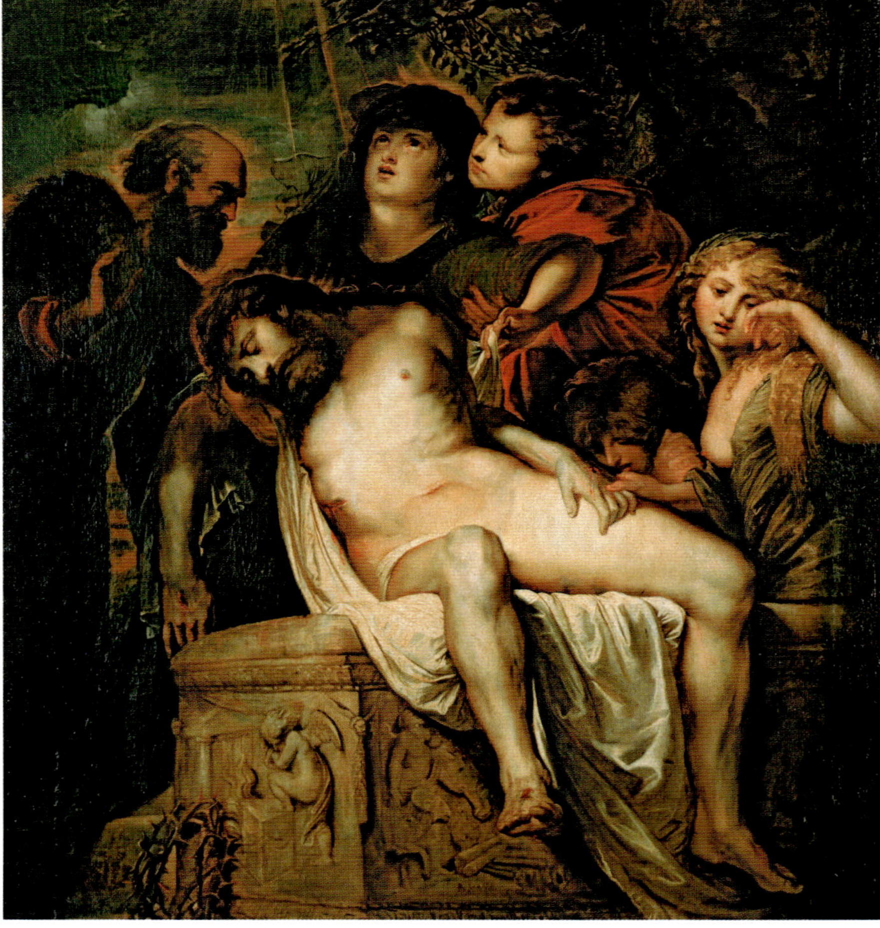

INFLUENCE OF GALILEO

Often called the Father of Modern Science, Galileo made contributions to physics, astronomy, cosmology, mathematics and philosophy. He improved the telescope, enabling him to observe Jupiter' moons, the rings of Saturn, phases of Venus, sunspots, and the surface of the Earth's moon. He also invented a military compass. He had powerful friends among Italy's ruling élite, and enemies among the leaders of the Catholic Church. His belief in a heliocentric universe brought him before religious authorities in both 1616 and 1633, when he was 'suspected of heresy' and forced to renounce his beliefs. He spent the last nine years of his life under house arrest. During that time, he wrote one of his finest works, *Two New Sciences*, which summarized some of his earlier work. He had been a professor of mathematics at Padua University where Philip Rubens had been studying.

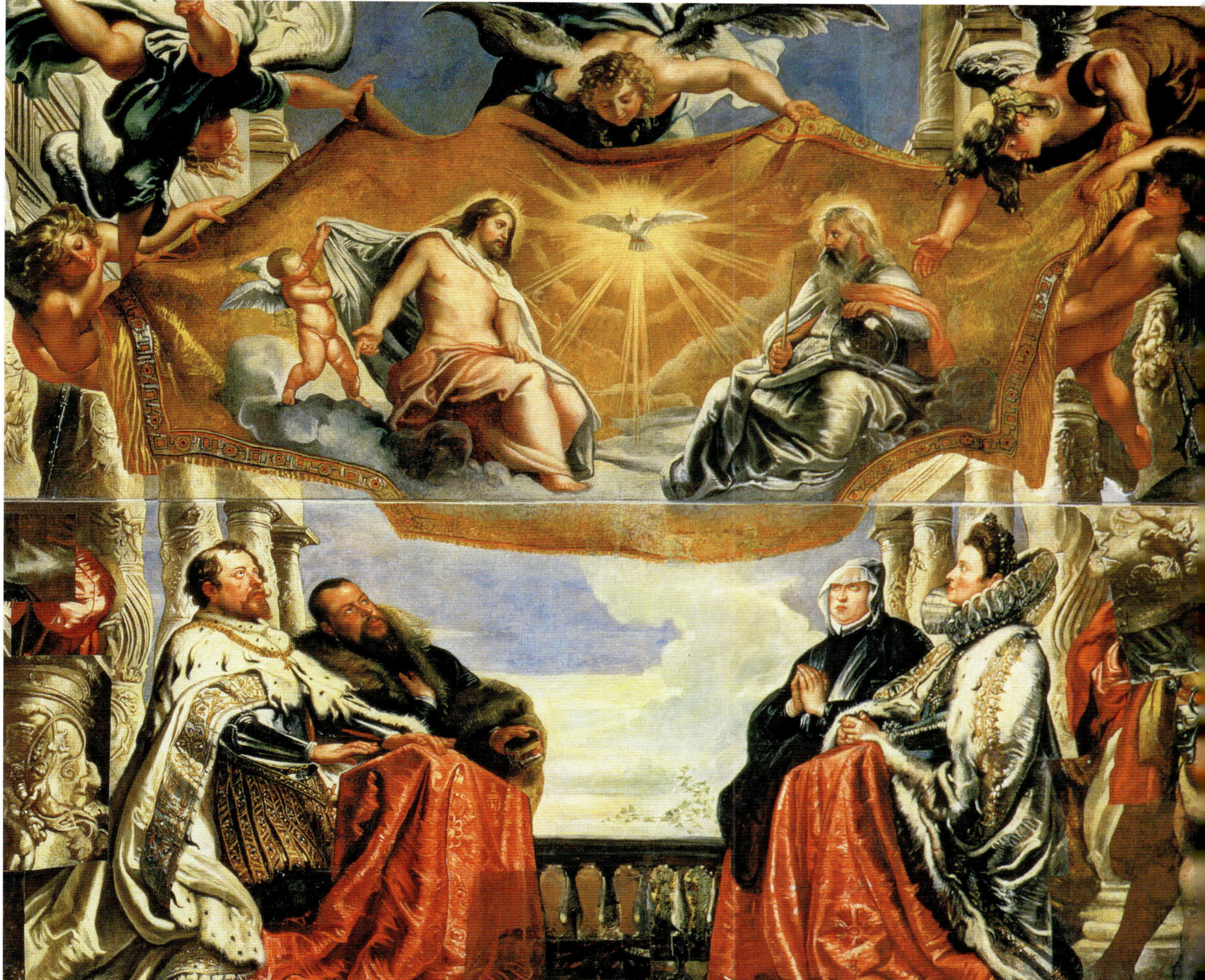

ALTARPIECE IN JESUIT CHURCH

At last, Rubens received from the Duke of Mantua the commission he had hoped for. Early in 1604, Gonzaga asked him for three large paintings to decorate the main chapel in Mantua's Jesuit church, dedicated to the Holy Trinity. Completed by the summer, the central canvas was *The Gonzaga Family in Adoration of the Holy Trinity*, and the two side canvases were *The Baptism of Christ* and *The Transfiguration*. Predominantly in a palette of white, blue, red and ochre, the paintings were sculptural and architectural, an accolade of all Rubens admired in Venetian painting, and particularly paintings by Veronese. In the main part of the altarpiece, Rubens depicts the Gonzaga family on a marble balustraded terrace. The family includes the current Duke and the previous one, his father Gugliemo, with their wives Eleonora de' Medici (Marie's sister) and Eleonora of Austria. It is believed that they were also flanked by their children, but these fragments have disappeared. Unfortunately, during the Napoleonic wars in 1796 the paintings were removed. *The Transfiguration* was taken to Paris, *The Baptism of Christ* was sold and is now in Antwerp, and *The Adoration of the Holy Trinity* was cut up. The main fragment was left in Mantua, but other parts were distributed elsewhere.

Above: The Gonzaga Family in Adoration of the Holy Trinity, *Rubens. Commissioned by the Duke of Gonzaga for the Jesuit church in Mantua, this is the central part of a triptych.*

ROME REVISITED

After he had completed the altarpiece, Rubens returned to Rome to study the art there once more. The visit was undertaken at his request, and although the Duke encouraged it for the prestige of having a court painter accomplished in the methods of the greatest artists, the pay he owed Rubens while he was away was not forthcoming, causing difficulties and embarrassment for Rubens.

RETURN TO ROME

In December 1605, Philip arrived in Rome after a visit to Flanders, to his old university at Louvain. As Rubens and his brother were both living in the same city once more, they decided to move in together. They established themselves with a couple of servants in a house on Via della Croce near the Piazza di Spagna.

Philip had taken a job in Rome as librarian for Cardinal Ascanio Colonna (1560–1608), a member of one of Rome's most wealthy and powerful families. At first, the siblings began to work together on a book on ancient Roman costumes, but then Rubens contracted pleurisy. Johann Faber (1574–1629) was a German doctor, botanist and art collector, physician to Pope Paul V, curator of the Vatican botanical garden and had several friends in common with Rubens, including Galileo, the German painter Adam Elsheimer (1578–1610) and Caspar Schoppe. He was duly called in to treat Rubens, and within weeks had cured him of what was a potentially fatal illness at the time. In gratitude, Rubens painted Faber's portrait, now lost. Later, Rubens recalled that period of time

Below: The Stoning of Saint Stephen, *Adam Elsheimer. It is possible that Rubens's friend, the Flemish artist Paul Brill, owned this painting of the first Christian martyr.*

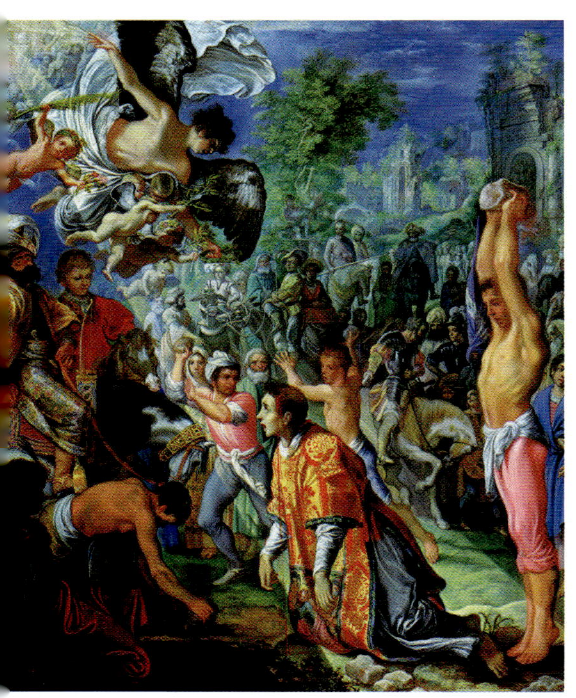

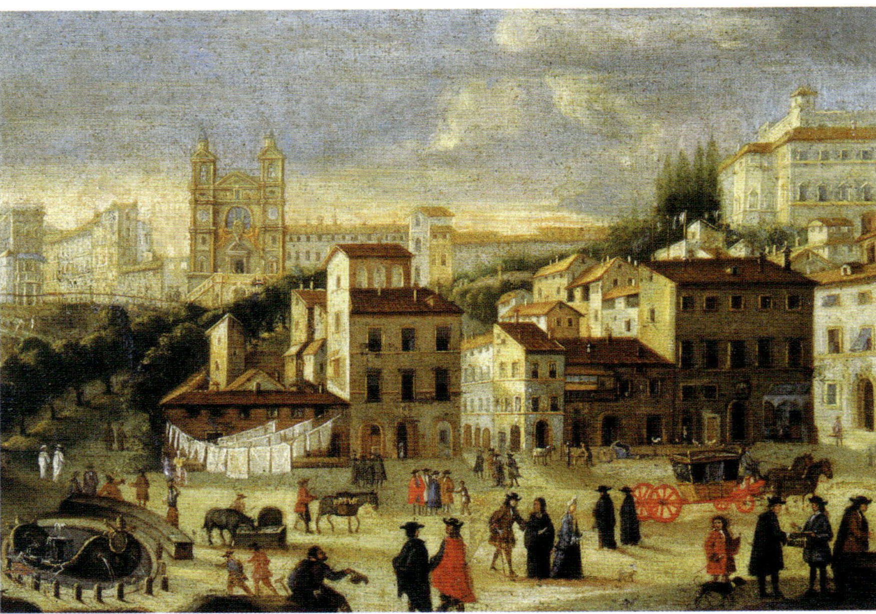

Above: Piazza di Spagna e Trinita dei Monti. *This is a contemporary painting of the centre of Rome during the period that Rubens was there.*

spent with such a strong circle of fascinating friends with nostalgia: 'friends whose good conversation makes one often long for Rome.'

THE CHIESA NUOVA

However, Rubens was constantly short of money because the Duke of Mantua frequently failed to pay him. He wrote to Chieppio asking him to intercede with the Duke on his behalf, and threatened that he would have to find more appreciative patrons to supplement his income if the Duke continued to leave him short. Gonzaga, meanwhile, was paying for his eldest son's wedding and could not fulfil his obligations to Rubens. Frustrated and disappointed, in 1605 Rubens entered a competition held by the Priests of the Oratory, one of the most important new orders of the Counter-Reformation, to paint an altarpiece for

their newly built church, the Chiesa Nuova, or the church of Santa Maria in Vallicella in the centre of Rome. On winning the commission, he wrote to Chieppio that he could not return to Mantua for some time as he was busy working on an important work that he had to accept out of necessity.

The new commission was full of stipulations, however. Rubens had to submit several preliminary drawings to the priests before embarking on the final painting, he had to incorporate a small fresco of the Virgin Mary brought from the previous church into his painting, and finally, the entire work had to be completed in less than nine months. *The Ecstasy of Saint Gregory the Great* was the result. It a majestic image of saints and martyrs before a Roman triumphal arch, with putti holding up a painting of the Virgin Mary and Child. Clearly inspired by Federico Barocci (1523–1612), Carracci and Correggio, the painting is sumptuous and commanding, with strong tonal contrasts in predominantly blue, white, cream and gold.

CARAVAGGIO'S DEATH OF THE VIRGIN

When he painted *Death of the Virgin* in about 1601–06, Caravaggio had been working in Rome for 15 years. By then, he and Rubens had become friends, and Rubens admired this latest work greatly, but it caused a completely different reaction among others, and was rejected as being inappropriate for the church of Santa Maria della Scala. The Virgin Mary was barefooted, in a bright scarlet dress, bloated and looking like a common woman rather than the Mother of God. There was no sense of the spiritual in the image; it was all too realistic. Several said that the model was a prostitute with whom Caravaggio was having an affair. No one confirmed this, however, because by then Caravaggio was on the run. The Pope had issued a death warrant for him for killing a young man, possibly unintentionally, at the end of May 1606. Although Caravaggio would not receive the payment for the work (this would go to the papal lawyer Laerzio Cherubini (*c.*1556–1626) who commissioned it), Rubens encouraged Gonzaga to buy it. Rubens wrapped the painting himself and organized its shipment to Mantua.

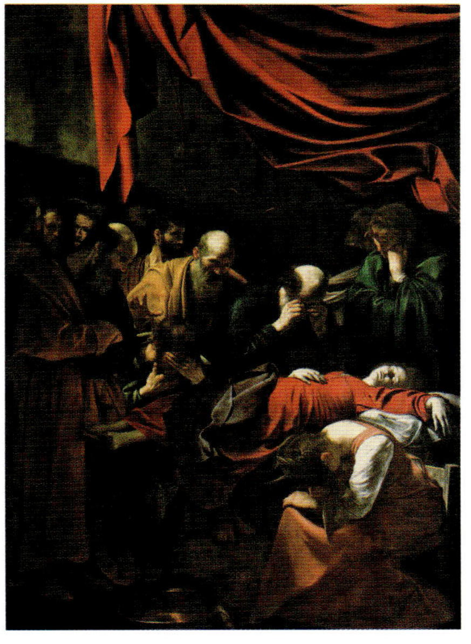

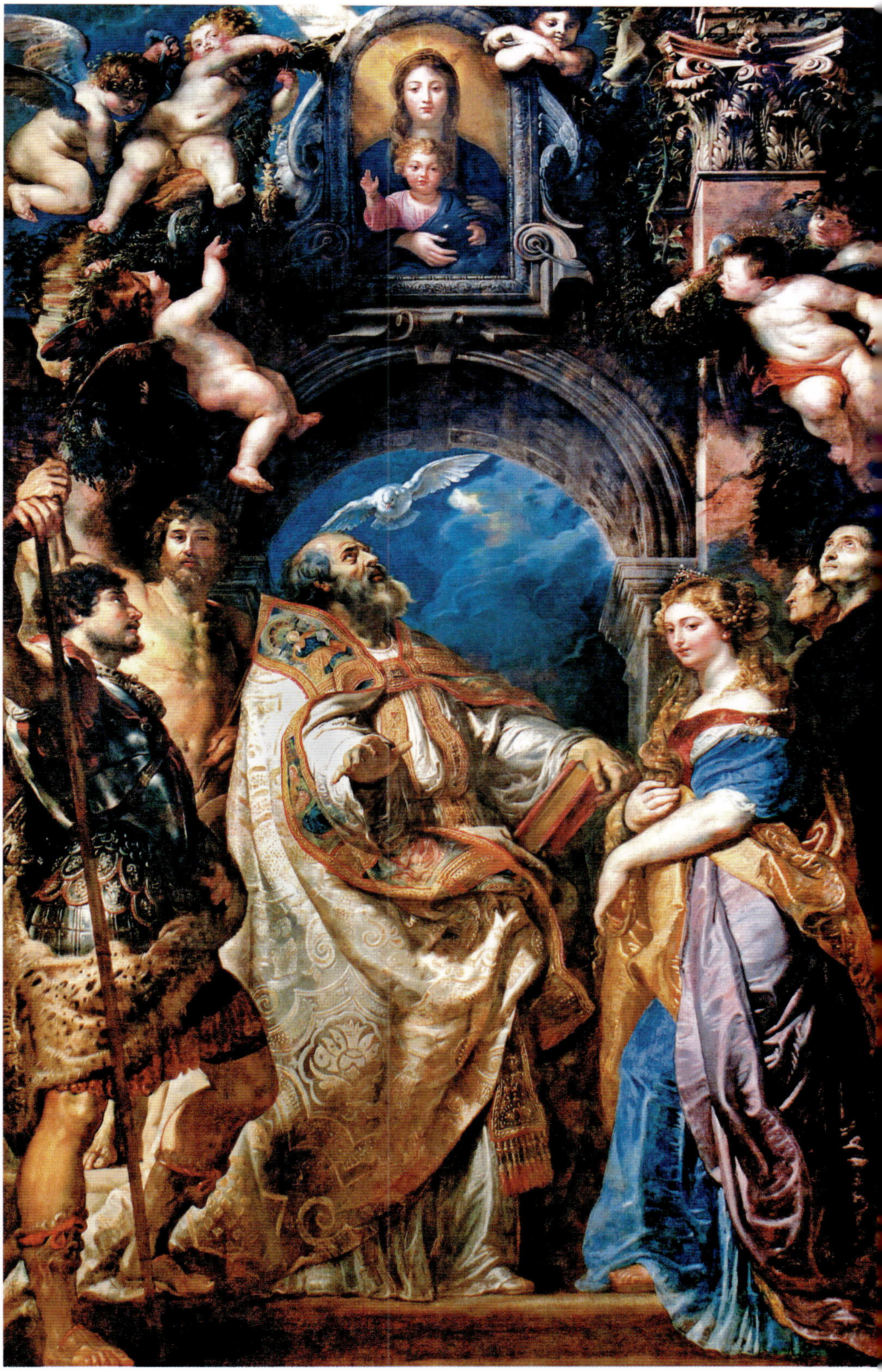

Left: Death of the Virgin, *Caravaggio, c.1605–06, Considered too realistic, not sacred enough and with Mary too swollen and not ethereal, this was the last work Caravaggio undertook before leaving Rome.*

Above: The Ecstasy of Saint Gregory the Great, *Rubens, 1605. This painting was moved from its original location in Rome and placed above Rubens's mother's tomb in Antwerp.*

POWERFUL CONNECTIONS

Rubens's success in obtaining the commission for the Chiesa Nuova was largely due to powerful connections and influences beyond the Priests of the Oratory. His greatest advocate for the work was Cardinal Giacomo Serra (1570–1623), Treasurer to Pope Paul V.

Serra was from Genoa, and had seen examples of Rubens's work there when Rubens stopped over on his return to Mantua in 1604, whereas the Oratorian brothers were not familiar with his style and wanted to commission another artist. However, Serra was insistent on the commission going to Rubens, and threatened that he would give his substantial donation elsewhere if they did not employ the artist of his choice.

PAINTING FOR THE ARISTOCRACY

Serra's high opinion of Rubens arose from the reputation he had gained in Genoa. Since Rubens's first visit there,

he had returned and was welcomed by the aristocratic families who governed it, including the Pallavicinis, Durazzos, Grimaldis, Imperiales and Spinolas. These families controlled the banking, economy and politics of the republic, and several of them commissioned Rubens, mostly for portraits. Informal for the period, relaxed and expressive, with bold brushwork and a high degree of realism, many of these portraits are of beautiful, confident women who were members of the aristocratic Genoese families. Genoa was often described as *aparadiso delle donne* (a paradise of women), partly because

women there were given greater freedom and respect than in most other parts of Europe. The influences of Titian and Veronese can be seen in Rubens's treatment of colour and light and his depiction of costly silks and satins the women wore.

In 1605, the year after his first visit to Genoa, members of the Pallavicini family commissioned him to paint an altarpiece. The resulting richly coloured *Circumcision of Christ* is energetic, radiant, and recalls Tintoretto's dramatic foreshortening. Also in Genoa, Rubens painted a dynamic image of Saint George fighting the dragon (see page 112).

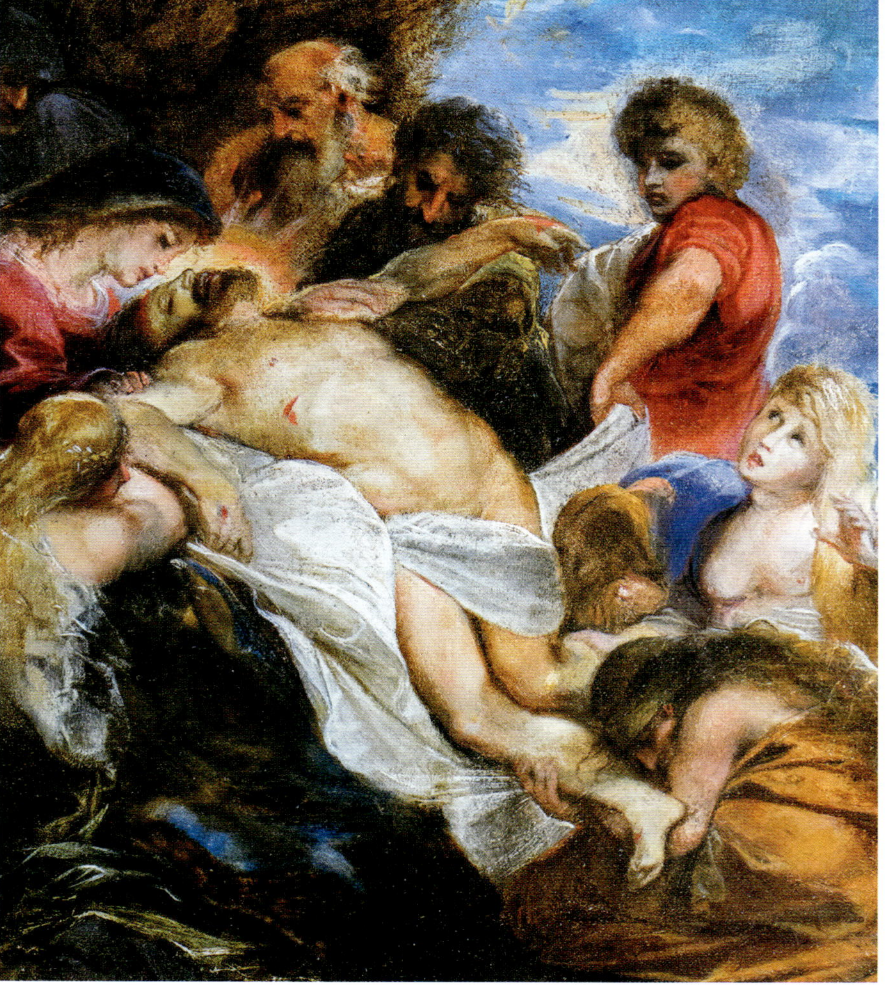

Left: The Lamentation of Christ, *Rubens, c.1605. This painting depicts the scene after Christ's descent from the cross. The Virgin leans over his body, while Mary Magdalene kneels at his feet.*

Below: Marchesa Pallavicino, *Rubens, 1606. This shows a beautiful 22-year-old newlywed from a prominent family in Genoa. Rubens excelled in his depiction of textures and inner personality.*

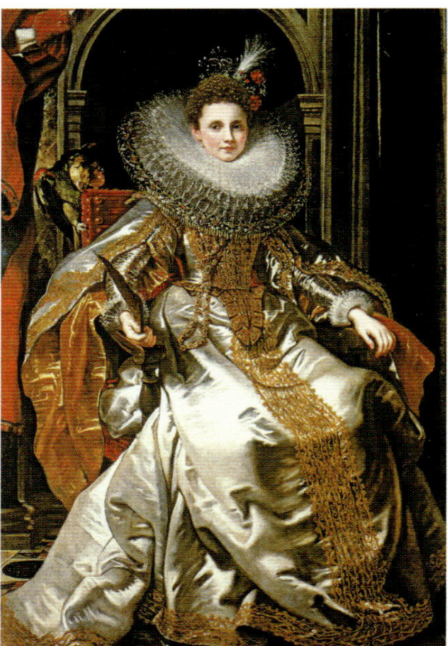

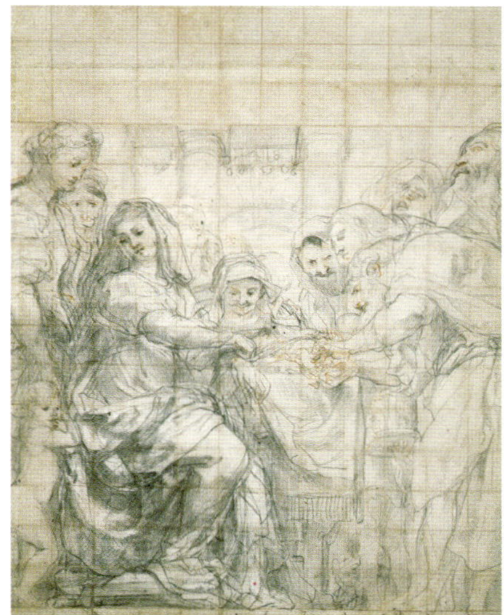

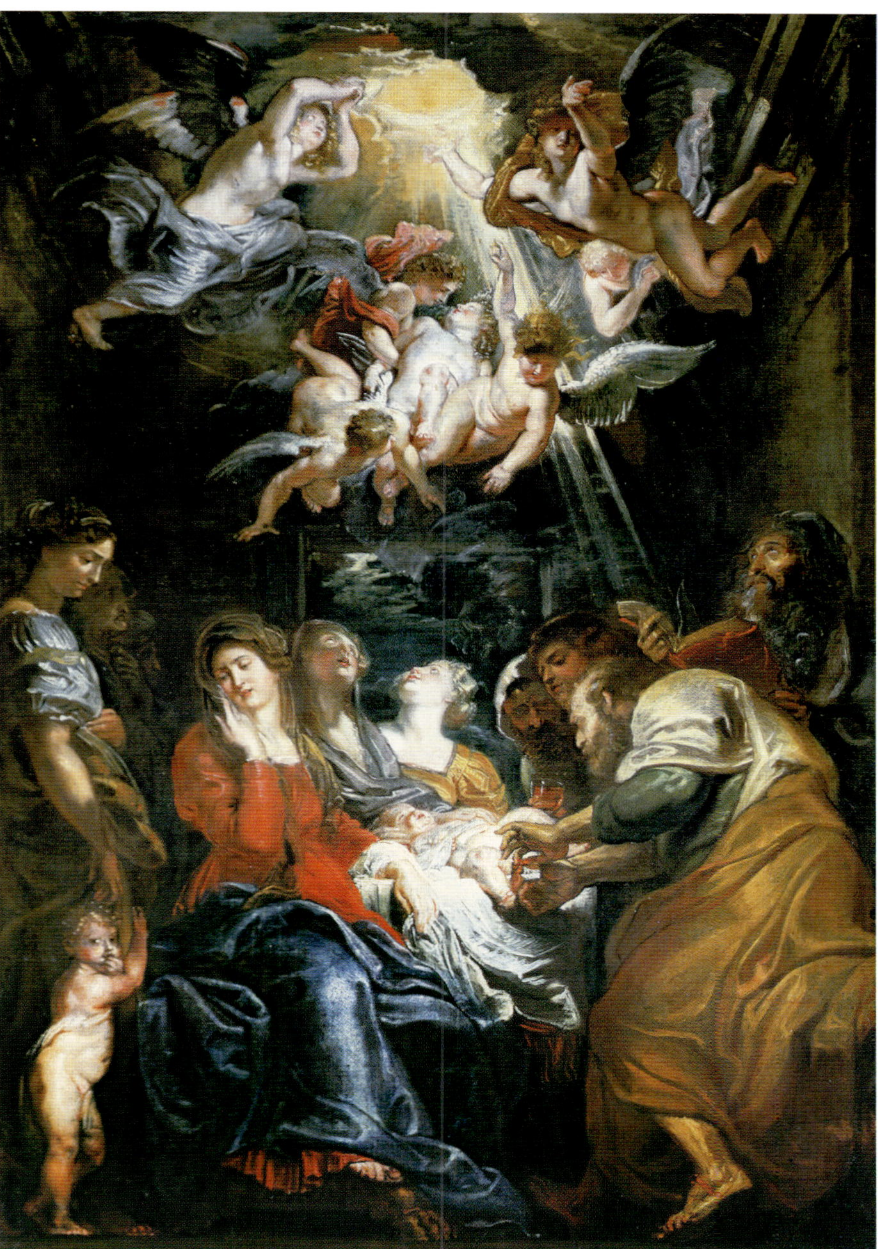

George, the patron saint of Genoa, sits on a rearing horse, its mane and tale swishing as the dragon removes a broken lance from its jaws. George courageously continues to fight the dragon, while watching from behind is the beautiful princess he has saved. This commission was probably for the church of San Ambrogio in Genoa, but for some reason Rubens kept it. Between 1605 and 1608, he returned to paint in Genoa at least four times. Back in Rome, Cardinal Colonna also commissioned Rubens, and his reputation continued to soar in privileged Italian circles.

SAN PIER D'ARENA

After he had completed *The Ecstasy of Saint Gregory the Great* (see page 39) in the Chiesa Nuova in Rome, but before

Above left: Sketch for Circumcision, Rubens. *This is a sensitive pencil-on-paper sketch for an emotive painting.*

its unveiling, Gonzaga invited Rubens to San Pier d'Arena, a seaside resort near Genoa, where he stayed regularly to take the waters for his health. It was July 1607, and Gonzaga invited Rubens at this time not for his artistic skills nor for his diplomacy, but for his personal charm, companionship and conversation. Rubens duly travelled to meet Gonzaga and his party at San Pier d'Arena, spent some time with them and then journeyed on to Genoa, where he was still greatly

Above: Circumcision, Rubens, 1605. *The pencil composition has changed, but this colourful work is just as emotive and full of life and colour as the original sketch.*

in demand. It may seem surprising that he did not wait in Rome to see the unveiling of his altarpiece, especially as he was so pleased with it, but Serra was on a diplomatic mission in Venice and the church was not completed, so the event was delayed until the autumn. The following September, however, Rubens made preparation to return to Rome, where he was greatly celebrated for his latest masterpiece.

RETURNING HOME

The following May, Philip Rubens resigned his position of librarian and returned to Antwerp by November 1606. He had heard that their 71-year-old mother was seriously ill. Once back in Antwerp, he was employed by the local government in local public offices.

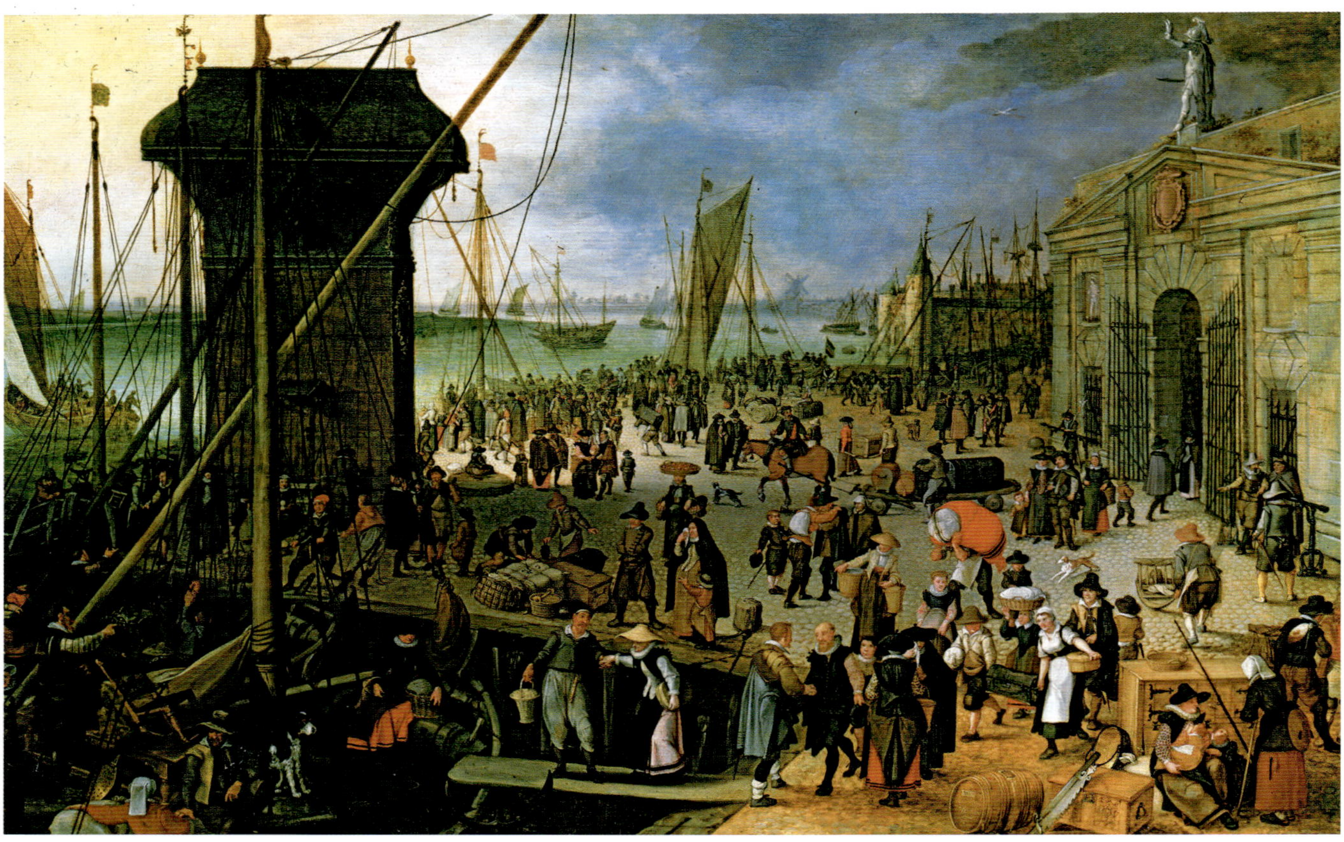

Above: View of Antwerp Harbour, Sebastian Vrancx, 1608. This was the port that Rubens returned to from Italy.

It is not clear why Rubens, who was especially close to his mother, did not return to Antwerp at the same time as Philip, but he remained in Italy, continuing to paint – mainly his popular portraits in Genoa, and also to make sketches of Genoese buildings.

THE ALTARPIECE UNVEILED

In September 1607, Rubens returned to Rome to witness the unveiling of *The Ecstasy of Saint Gregory the Great* (see page 39) in the Chiesa Nuova. However, rather than being congratulated on his skill, when the painting was revealed a massive problem became apparent. Through the unusual angle of light entering the apse, the colours on his canvas seemed to vanish. The Priests of the Oratory rejected the work, saying that although it was a remarkable painting, their venerated icon of the Madonna and Child was not prominent enough, and the painting itself could not be seen. Rubens was dismayed, but knowing that his work was not at fault, he made sure that the picture went on public display to be admired by all who saw it, while he embarked on a replacement, this time on slate.

More elaborate than the first, the new painting, *Madonna della Vallicella*, shows a continuing development of his creative skills. The colours are lighter than in the previous painting, and the figures are more dynamic and human. By now, he was assimilating all his influences, and with growing confidence he was beginning to create a unique and powerful style of his own. In addition, this time he made the icon of the Madonna and Child that the Priests of the Oratory revered as miraculous, even more prominent. Surrounded by lighter colours, he placed the painting above the saints, held by several adoring putti, while the saints below all look up, carrying palm branches, acknowledged symbols of Christian martyrdom. The lively imagery enhanced and augmented the spirituality of the entire image.

He tried to sell *The Ecstasy of Saint Gregory the Great* to Gonzaga, and was hurt when the Duke rejected it. But Gonzaga was also peeved at the time because Rubens had stayed away from Mantua for a considerable period, and he had heard that the Archduke Albert was making moves to recall him back to

Right: Garden of Royal Palace in Genoa, 17th century. Rubens spent a great deal of time in the homes of the wealthy Genoese.

Far right: Adoration of the Shepherds, Rubens, 1608. Painted in about three months for the Church of Saint Philip Neri in Ferma, this follows the tenebrism (dark tones and dramatic light effects) of Caravaggio, whom Rubens had befriended in Rome.

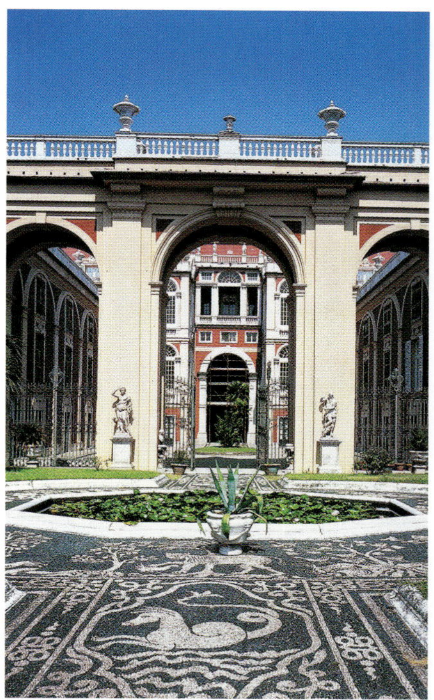

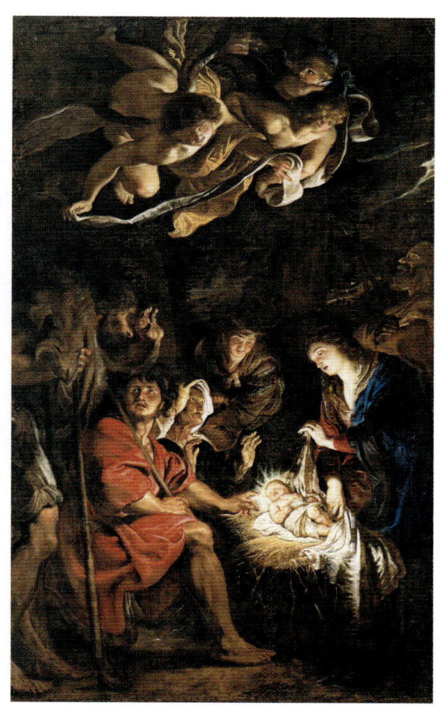

Flanders. Rubens, meanwhile, struggled to live on arbitrary and insufficient payments from Gonzaga, and carried on painting his replacement for the Chiesa Nuova, creating an uplifting composition to assist worshippers to concentrate. But in the event, however, he could not attend the new work's unveiling. He received news that the asthma his mother had suffered with for years had worsened, and he hurried back to his homeland.

DEATH OF HIS MOTHER

After 44 days of riding, Rubens arrived in Antwerp in December 1608. But he was too late. His mother Maria had died nine days before he had left Rome. When he met Philip, he discovered that Maria had already been buried in the nearby Abbey of Saint Michael. Her will, which had been drawn up in December 1606, returned to him the paintings he had given her in 1599; works of his apprenticeship and when he had recently qualified as a master. As their sister Blandina had also died two years earlier, the brothers were now the last two left of what had been a large family.

Rubens was 31 years old. When he had left Antwerp in 1600, he had been a young man of 23, freshly trained and eager to learn. He returned from Italy, having studied some of the greatest artists' work, and had assimilated many of skills and approaches he admired. He was now a respected courtier and diplomat, with influential connections in Italy and Spain. Most of all, he had become a celebrated artist.

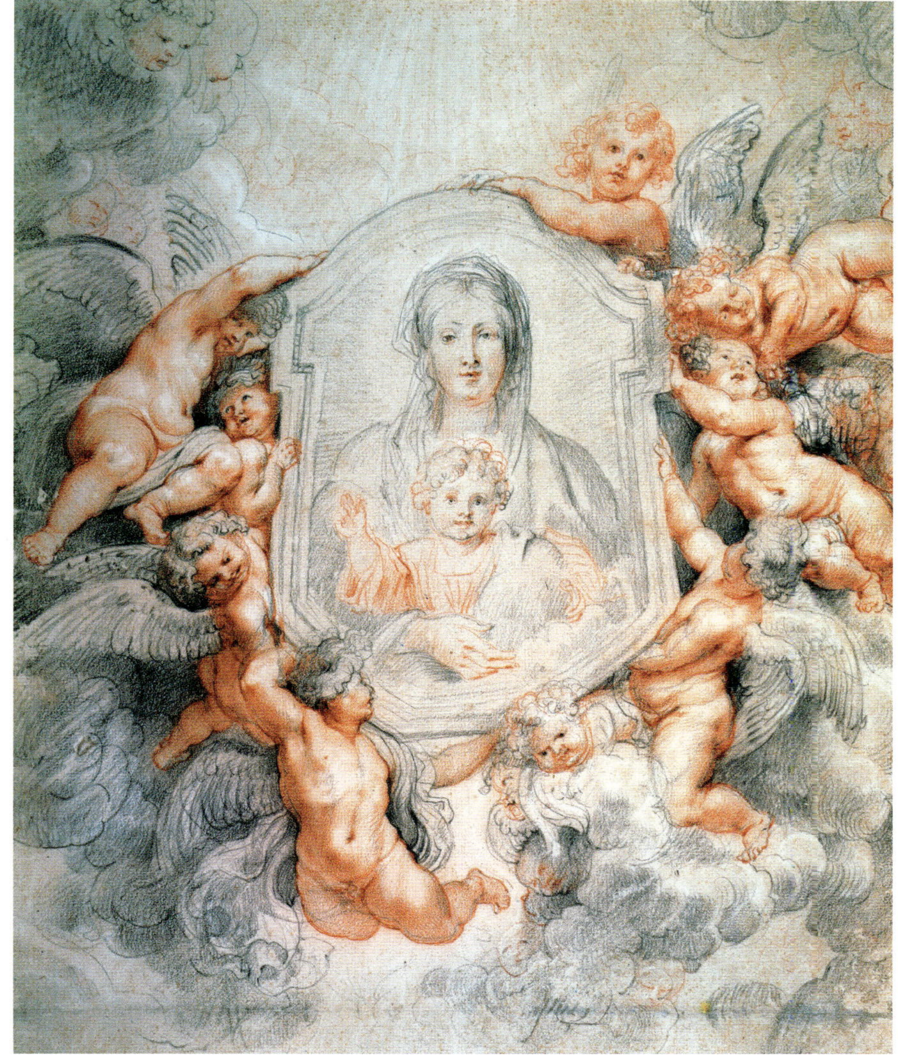

Right: Sketch for Madonna della Vallicella, Rubens, 1608. In pencil and pastel on paper, here Rubens captures the reverent image of the Virgin Mary encircled by putti.

LIVING IN ANTWERP

On leaving Italy for Antwerp, Rubens had written to Gonzaga that he was looking forward to returning to Italy soon. Although he did not intend to stay there long, from the beginning of 1609, once again he and Philip shared a house in Antwerp, and both enjoyed it.

There is no written record their grief, but the brothers must have felt the loss of their mother keenly; she had been an intelligent woman who had encouraged their ambitions. Yet once back in Antwerp, despite his earlier determination to return to Italy, Rubens became indecisive. Early in 1609, he wrote to his friend Faber: 'I have not yet made up my mind whether to remain in my own country or to return to Rome, where I am invited on the most favourable terms. Here also, they do not fail to make every effort to keep me, by every sort of compliment.'

A DAMAGED CITY

Since the Spanish Fury over 30 years earlier, Antwerp had been neglected. Damaged buildings remained, many still scorched; those inhabitants who had left had not returned; and the once bustling

Below: The Disputation of the Holy Sacrament, *Rubens, 1608. This richly coloured painting illustrates one of the central issues of the Reformation and Counter Reformation.*

port was empty due to the Dutch naval blockade enforced since 1585 a mile up the River Scheldt as part of the economic warfare against the Spanish Netherlands. Antwerp had been a major commercial centre, but was in crisis due to this Dutch blockade. The War of Independence had incited atrocities on both sides, and most citizens of Antwerp simply longed for peace. The blockade was lifted in 1609.

PHILIP'S MARRIAGE

Amid this changing yet still volatile situation, where hope for the future was now glimmering, Rubens became settled. He renewed his acquaintance with old friends and made some new ones, including his former teacher Otto van Veen, as well as Balthasar Moretus (1574–1641), who was now head of the Plantin Printing Press, Nicolaas

Below: Interior of Antwerp Cathedral, *Pieter Neefs the Elder (1573–1661), c.1640, oil on oak panel. The figures in this work were probably painted by Frans Francken the Younger (1581–1642).*

THE TWELVE YEARS' TRUCE

On April 9, 1609, the Treaty of Antwerp was signed, initiating the Twelve Years' Truce. Hostilities between Spain, the Southern Netherlands and the Dutch Republic (or the Independent United Provinces) ceased. It was a breakthrough in a war that had already continued for almost 40 years. Under the Treaty's terms, the blockade of the River Scheldt was lifted, and for the first time the United Provinces received official recognition from foreign powers. The suspension of hostilities raised the twin prospects of peace and economic recovery for Flanders. Robustly advocated by both the Archduke Albert and the Archduchess Isabella, the period of the Truce was welcomed, and they used it to implement the Counter-Reformation in the territories under their rule.

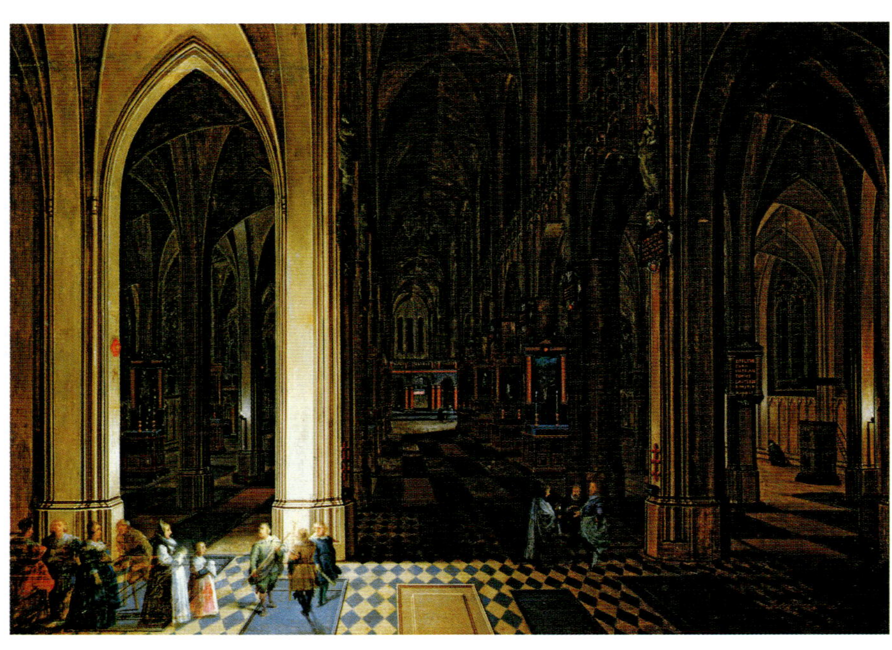

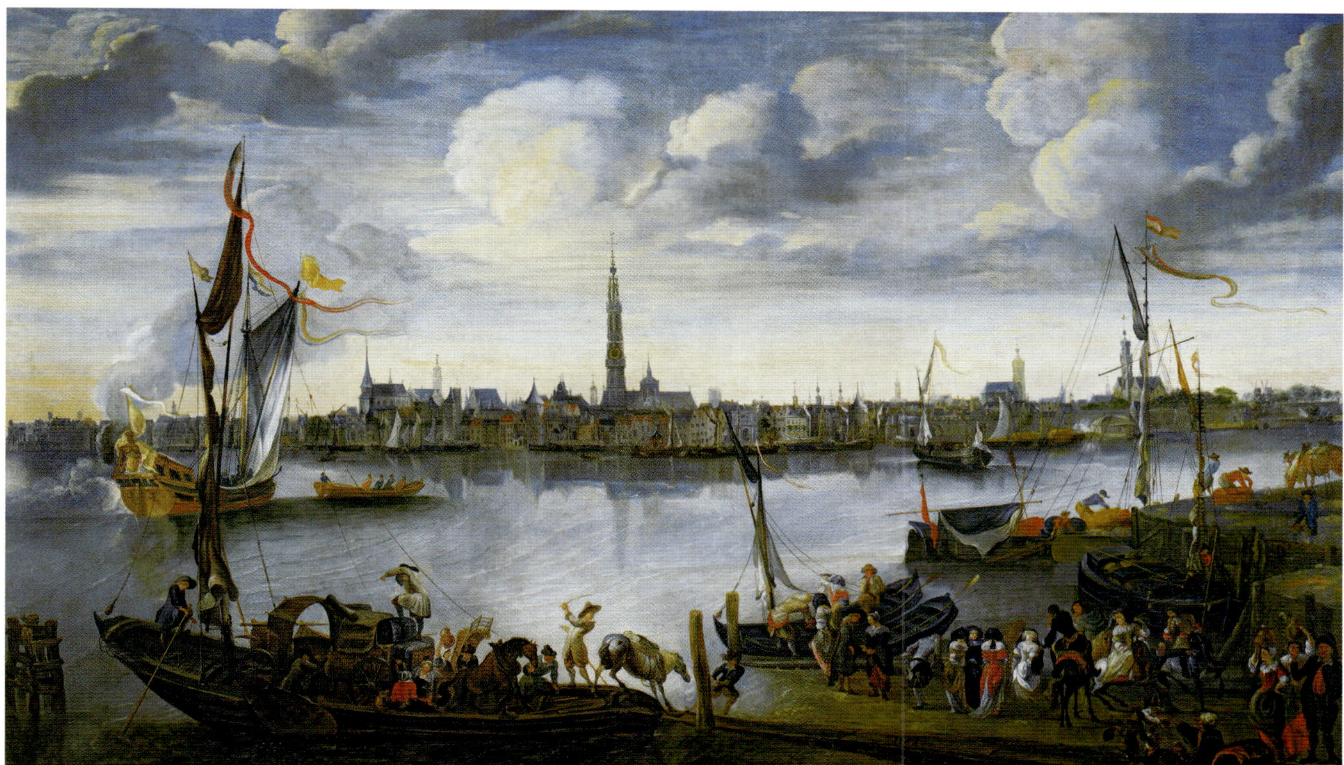

Rockox (1560–1640), a Humanist, antiquary and art collector; and the art collector Philips van Valckenisse (1554–1614). Life in Antwerp contrasted with life in Italy, but with his outgoing personality, Rubens adapted well. Philip, a more contemplative character, had not left the country for so long and settled quickly.

By January 1609, Philip had been appointed one of Antwerp's municipal secretaries – a prestigious post that had also previously been held by their father. Then, in March 1609, Philip married a beautiful and intelligent young woman. Maria de Moy (1586–date of death unknown) was the daughter of another municipal secretary. Rubens was best man at their wedding, and referred to it in a letter to Faber in April: 'We have been so involved in the marriage of my brother that we have been unable to attend to anything but serving the ladies – he as bridegroom and I as best man . . . I myself will not dare to follow him, for he has made such a good choice that it seems inimitable.'

Right: Twelve Years' Truce. *This is a contemporary illustration of the excitement and hope created by the Truce.*

Above: Antwerp from the River Scheldt. *The Treaty of Antwerp meant that the naval blockade of the River Scheldt was lifted, enabling trade to resume.*

OFFER FROM BRUSSELS

The Archduke Albert had given Rubens his first major commission in the church of Santa Croce in Gerusalemme in Rome in 1601, and soon after his return to Antwerp, Albert and Isabella offered him extremely generous terms to work as a court painter. He wrote to Faber: 'The Archduke and the Most Serene Infanta have had letters written urging me to remain in their service. Their offers are very generous, but I have little desire to become a courtier again.'

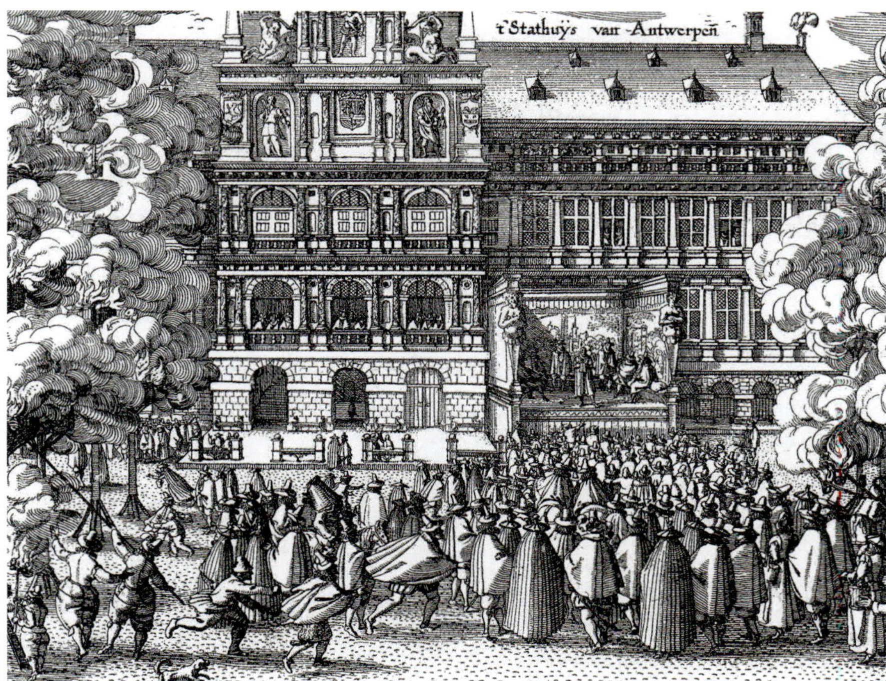

NEW BEGINNINGS

Despite his initial misgivings, Rubens soon succumbed to Albert and Isabella's generous offers. When he told them that he did not want to be a courtier, their generosity extended to allowing him to remain in Antwerp instead of moving to their palace in Brussels.

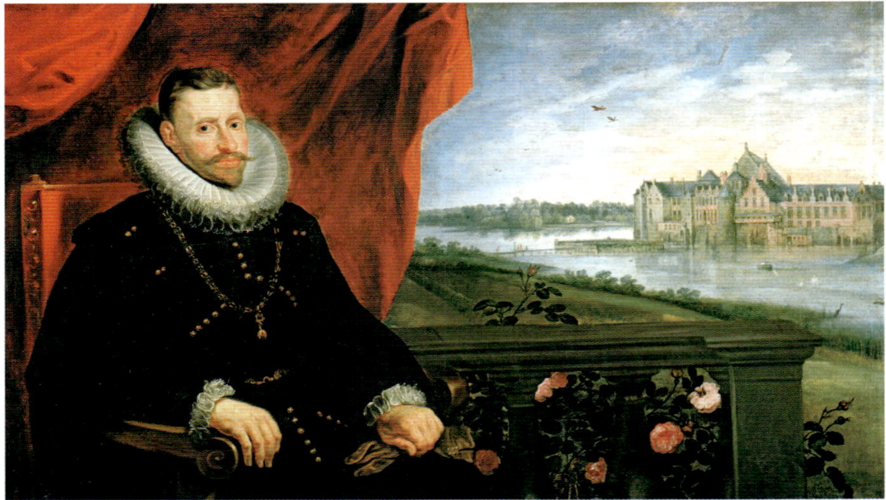

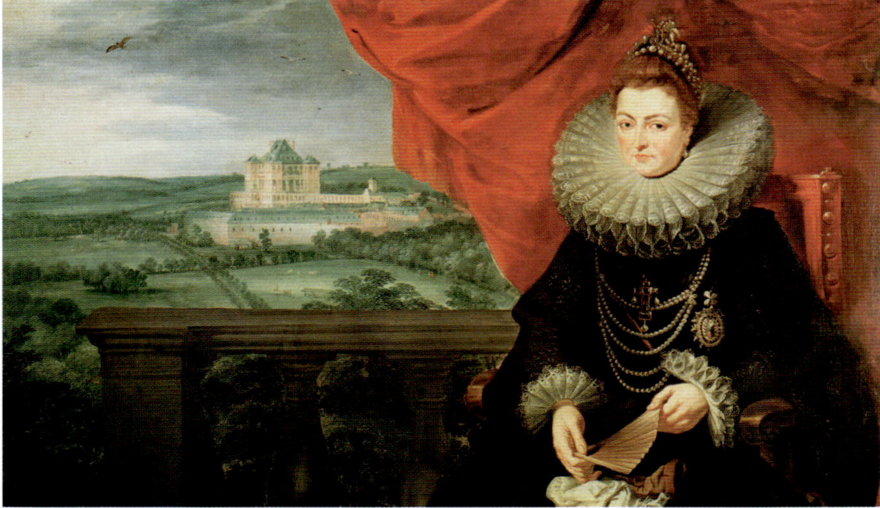

The special dispensation given to him by Albert and Isabella suited Rubens extremely well. He could receive their salary, mainta n the high status of court painter, but remain in Antwerp, close to his brothe and his wife and their friends. He could also teach while being exempt from paying both painters' guild fees and taxes, and also being allowed to accept commissions from other patrons. In September 1609, after painting large portraits of the couple that they were delighted with, he accepted the position. They presented him with a gold chain and medal bearing their likenesses.

MARRIAGE

Having declared in his letter to Faber that he would not be able to imitate his brother in marriage as Philip had made such a good choice of bride, it was not long before Rubens changed his mind. Isabella Brant (1591–1626) was the 18-year-old n ece of Maria, Philip's new wife. She was the daughter of Maria's sister and Jan Brant (1559–1639), a leading Antwerp citizen and Humanist, and, like Philip with whom he went to school, a lawyer and one of the municipal sec etaries. An extremely wealthy and cultured man, Brant published a n mber of studies and

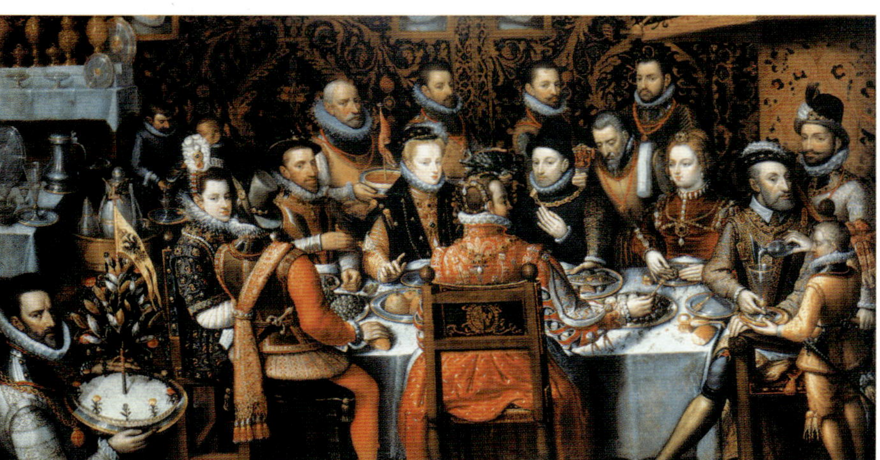

Top left: Archduke Albert, *Rubens, c.1616– 17. Albert VII was Archduke of Austria for a few months in 1619, then sovereign of the Habsburg Netherlands from 1598–1621.*

Middle left: Archduchess Isabella, *Rubens, c.1616–17. Isabella Clara Eugenia was sovereign of the Spanish Netherlands and an infanta of Spain and Portugal.*

Left: The Banquet of the Monarchs, *c.1579 by Alonso Sanchez Coello, showing Albert and Isabella at a banquet with the Spanish monarchs.*

formed a close friendship with Rubens that lasted for the rest of his life.

At the beginning of October 1609, Rubens married Isabella in Saint Michael's Abbey, where his mother Maria was buried. Soon, the abbey also housed his painting of *The Ecstasy of Saint Gregory the Great*. The wedding was a somewhat sumptuous affair, with many guests, hired carriages and a huge feast. To celebrate, Rubens painted a full-length self-portrait with his new wife, sitting hand-in-hand in a honeysuckle bower. Honeysuckle symbolizes love. Both figures are richly and fashionably dressed and appear as a wealthy young couple, not as an artist and his wife. Most wedding portraits were not full-length and were on a small scale. Rubens broke with tradition in this, even portraying himself with a sword, which was usually only worn by the aristocracy. It echoes several of his Genoese portraits of the nobility, and it shows his skill in depicting the sumptuous textures of the silks, lace, brocade and velvet they wore. He and Isabella began their married life living in her father's large house.

Below: Self-portrait with Isabella Brant, *or* The Honeysuckle Bower *was painted by Rubens to commemorate his marriage on October 3, 1609.*

THE ARCHDUKES ALBERT AND ISABELLA

The rule of the Archdukes Albert of Austria and Isabella of Spain in the Spanish Netherlands brought peace and a rebirth of the economy to the region. The Twelve Years' Truce was accomplished mainly through their patient and determined negotiations. Albert was the son of the Holy Roman emperor Maximilian II and Maria, the daughter of Charles V. As a young man, he had been appointed archbishop and cardinal of Toledo in Spain. He also served his uncle, King Philip II, as a soldier and diplomat, and he governed Portugal as Philip's viceroy from 1581–1595. In 1595, he was appointed Governor-general of the Spanish Netherlands by Philip, with instructions to subdue the rebellious Protestants in the north. To do this, at Philip's insistence, Albert reluctantly obtained a papal release from holy orders and married the Infanta Isabella, Philip's favourite daughter. After so many years of war, their level-headed, sympathetic and conscientious management established a strong, independent country, and helped to disperse a great deal of anti-Spanish sentiment. In using the visual arts as a means of communication, they patronized the greatest Flemish artists of the time, and helped to instigate a Golden Age of art in the Southern Netherlands, stimulating the development of Flemish Baroque painting.

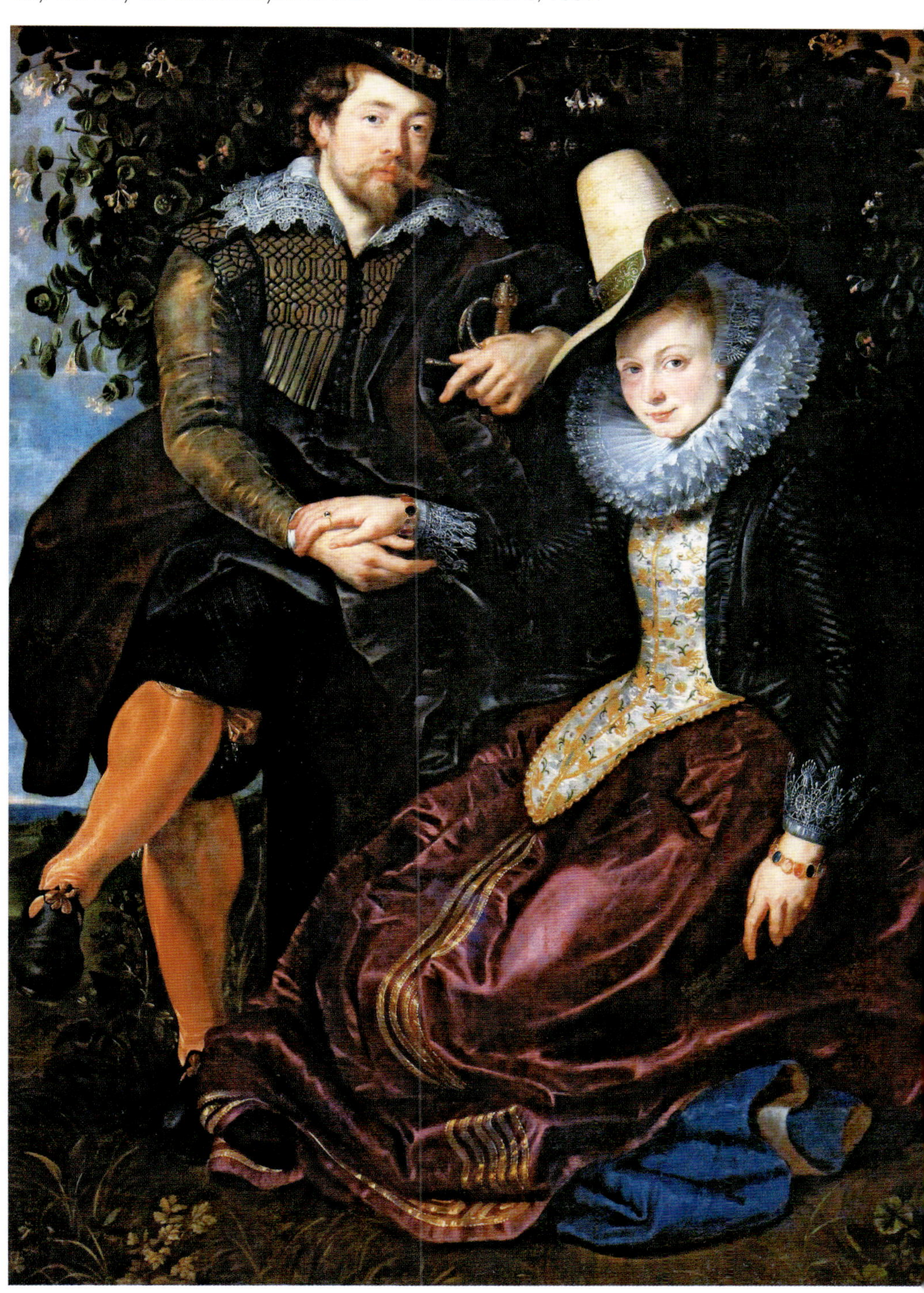

DEVELOPING ASSURANCE

Through the artist Jan Brueghel the Elder (1568–1625), Rubens was elected into Antwerp's prestigious Society of Romanists. Active from the 16th to the 18th centuries, the Romanist Society, or Guild, was comprised of selected distinguished figures and artists from Antwerp who had studied in Italy.

The Romanist Society of Antwerp included Rubens's former teacher Otto van Veen, Frans Snyders (1579–1657), Jan Wildens (1586–1653) and Jacob Jordaens. This circle of talented fellow artists, plus his other intellectual friends and the breadth of interests in Antwerp satisfied Rubens that he had made the right choice in not returning to Italy. His enlightened friends were at the hub of a city that encouraged religious tolerance and embraced new scientific and technological ideas. They were hopeful that Antwerp would prosper again with the Truce, and although the population was not noticeably increasing, they believed that the city's dominance in banking and trade would indeed soon be restored. Rubens found the atmosphere stimulating, and despite his Catholic beliefs, particularly enjoyed discussing Humanist ideas.

GRAND COMMISSIONS

Even before he had accepted the appointment as court painter to Albert and Isabella, Rubens had been commissioned by others to produce numerous significant works in Antwerp, Malines, Brussels and Ghent. Working

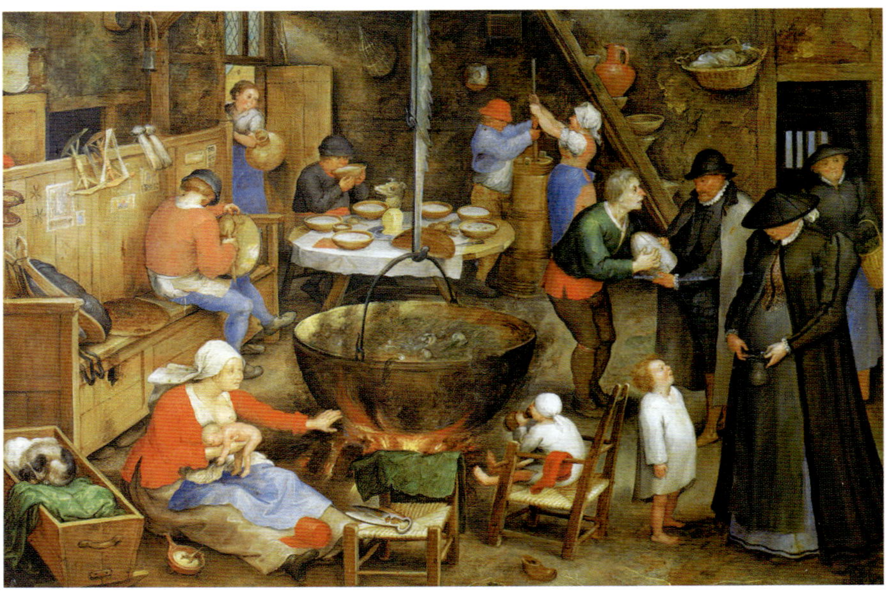

Above: Visit to a Farm *by Rubens's friend, Jan Brueghel the Elder (also known as 'Velvet Brueghel') in 1597.*

with his customary alacrity, he completed some of his greatest works to date, clearly gaining assurance and outstanding skills. Although not regaining its former glory, Antwerp nonetheless attracted many foreign visitors who marvelled at the bravura of Rubens's work and his

reputation as the foremost artist of the Southern Netherlands became established. His main paintings of that time included *Self-portrait with Isabella Brant*, *The Four Philosophers*, *Samson and Delilah*, and *Descent from the Cross*.

Below: View of Antwerp from the River Schelde, *Jan Wildens. Antwerp's inhabitants had great hopes for their city's economic revival.*

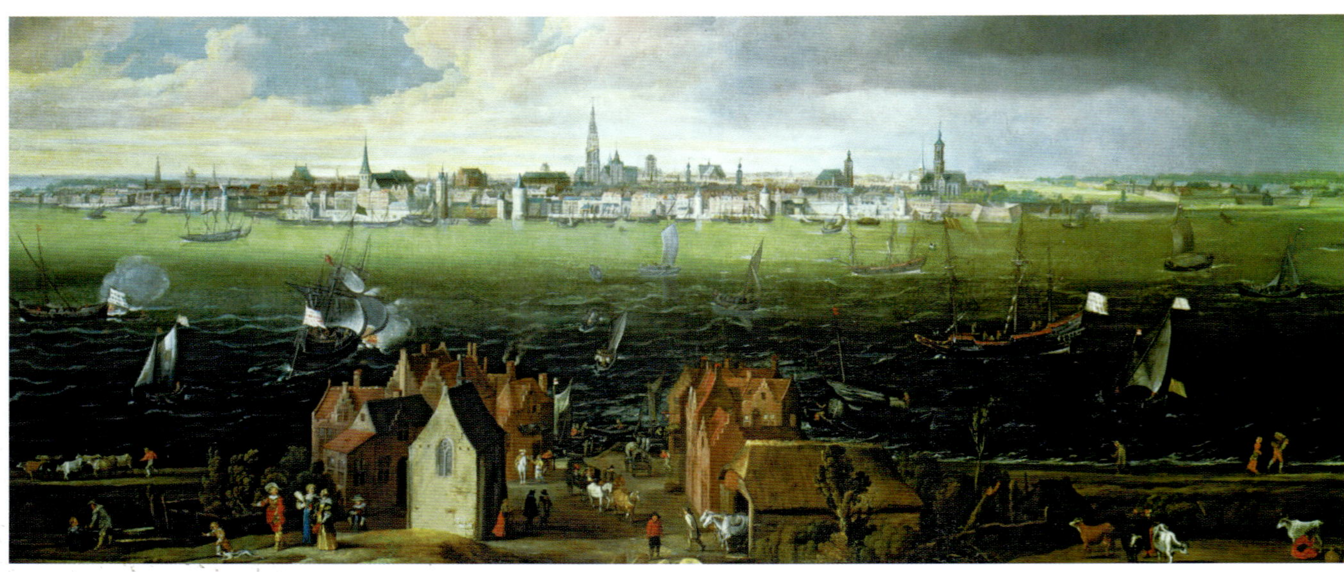

Descent from the Cross was commissioned through the influence of his friend Nicolaas Rockox, who was also mayor of Antwerp and president of the Arquebusiers' Guild (Antwerp's civic guard). Three years later, he painted Rockox as a bystander in his painting *The Presentation in the Temple*. *The Four Philosophers* celebrates his relationship with some of the most intellectual men of contemporary Flanders. It includes a self-portrait with three prominent Humanists: his brother Philip, Woverius and Lipsius. In it, he also suggests the importance of Stoicism – one of the four main schools of philosophy in ancient Greece that flourished for approximately 250 years alongside Plato's Academy, Aristotle's Lyceum and Epicurus's Garden. Stoicism was particularly popular with the ancient Romans, especially the statesman Seneca. Rubens also pays homage to classical culture in the painting, with the ruins of ancient Rome in the background.

ADORATION OF THE MAGI

At the end of 1608, Antwerp prepared to receive the peace delegates who would try to end the war between

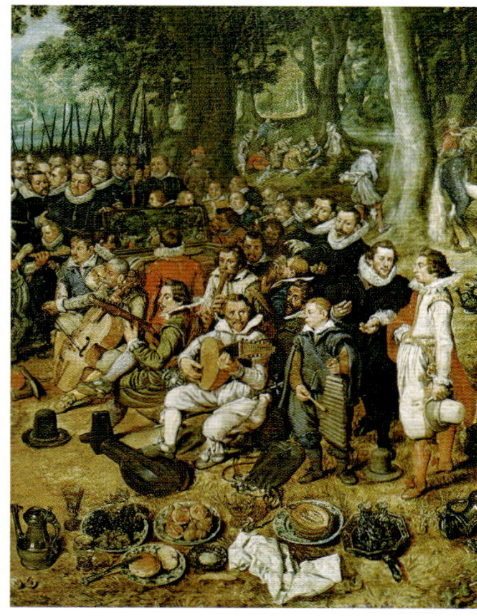

Right: Detail of Celebration of the Truce of 1609 *by Adriaen van de Venne, showing a band of musicians. This illustration demonstrates the optimism in Antwerp over the Twelve Years' Truce.*

Spain and the Dutch Republic. Negotiations (that resulted in the Twelve Years' Truce) were to be held in Antwerp City Hall (Statenkamer) between March 28 and April 9, 1609. Hopes were high for a positive outcome and for the renewed economic prosperity of the city that peace would bring. In early 1609, the city council commissioned Rubens to produce a painting for the Hall where the negotiations would be held. *Adoration of the Magi* was the result, for which he was paid 1,800 florins or guilders (at that time, a master carpenter earned just over 450 guilders per year). The huge, crowded painting demonstrates his increasing technical facility, with lighting effects that evoke Caravaggio, and colouring and grandeur that recall Titian and Tintoretto.

In spring 1612, Rodrigo Calderón, Count of Oliva (1576–1621), adviser to the Duke of Lerma, visited the Spanish

Netherlands as ambassador of the King of Spain. His aim (although unsuccessful), was to try to extend the Twelve Years' Truce. To obtain his good opinion, the municipality of Antwerp presented him with Rubens's *Adoration of the Magi*, but in 1621, Calderón fell into disgrace and was executed. Philip IV of Spain bought the painting from Calderón's collection and installed it in the Alcázar in Madrid. Later, Rubens went to Spain and enlarged it, adding horsemen and a self-portrait.

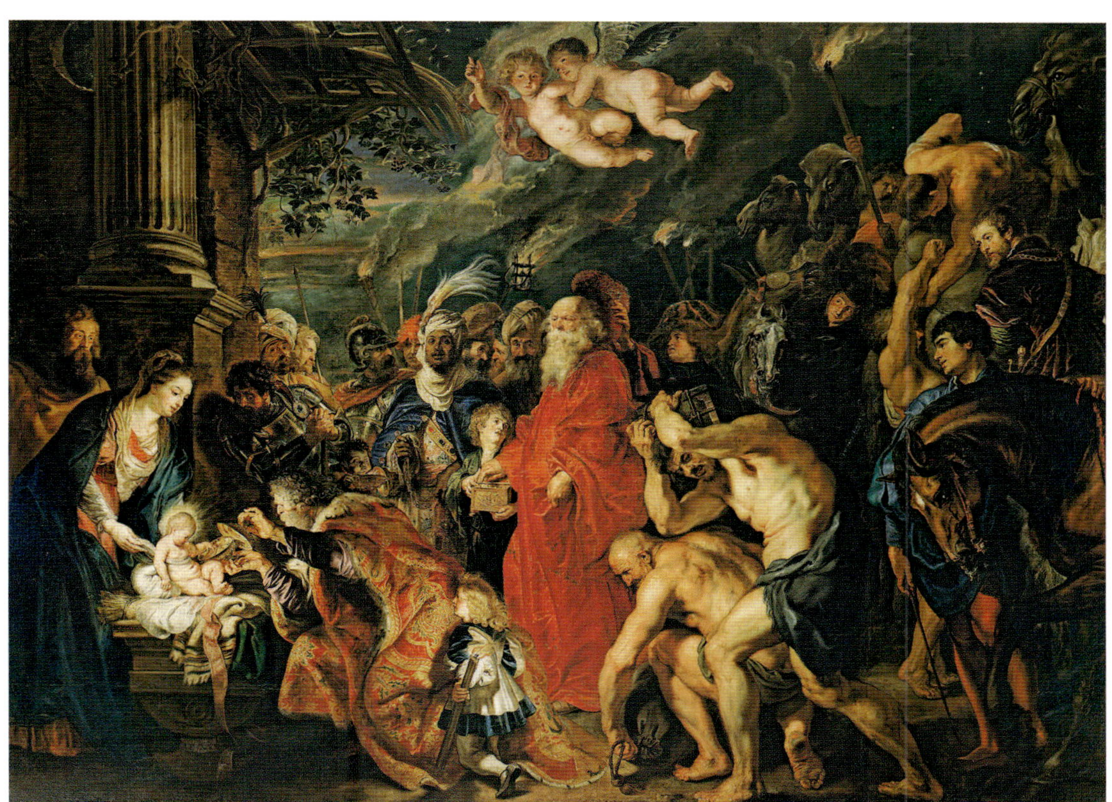

Left: Adoration of the Magi. *Rubens first painted this in 1609, then gave it a major reworking during 1628 and 1629 on his second trip to Spain. The scene takes place at night, with moonlight radiating on all the figures. The complex composition features many figures arranged in a dynamic, diagonal composition pointing to Jesus, the focal point of the work.*

THE RAISING OF THE CROSS

One of the fundamental problems facing Albert and Isabella in governing the large and disconnected region (that became called variously the Southern Netherlands, the Catholic Netherlands and the Spanish Netherlands) was that there was no sense of national identity.

Separated from their northern neighbours, inhabitants of the Southern Netherlands felt quite isolated. Also, three main languages were spoken across the country: Dutch, French and German; which added to a feeling of disengagement.

PASSIONATE INTENSITY

In accordance with the Counter-Reformation, Albert and Isabella avidly supported the arts, which also helped to build a sense of unity across the Southern Netherlands. Although not always commissioned by them, Rubens produced numerous important religious works of passionate intensity. In 1610, he was commissioned to paint the

Right: Cornelis van der Geest, by Van Dyck c.1620. A wealthy and powerful spice merchant from Antwerp, Van der Geest held Rubens in high esteem.

Below: The Council of Trent, 1563 was one of the Roman Catholic Church's most important ecumenical councils that reinforced the Counter-Reformation.

altarpiece of the Church of Saint Walburga (or Walpurgis). Cornelis van der Geest (1577–1638), a wealthy local spice merchant, Dean of the Haberdashers' Guild, Warden of the Church of Saint Walburga and art collector, supported artists in Antwerp and arranged for Rubens to receive the commission, which resulted in his huge triptych representing *The Raising (or Elevation) of the Cross.*

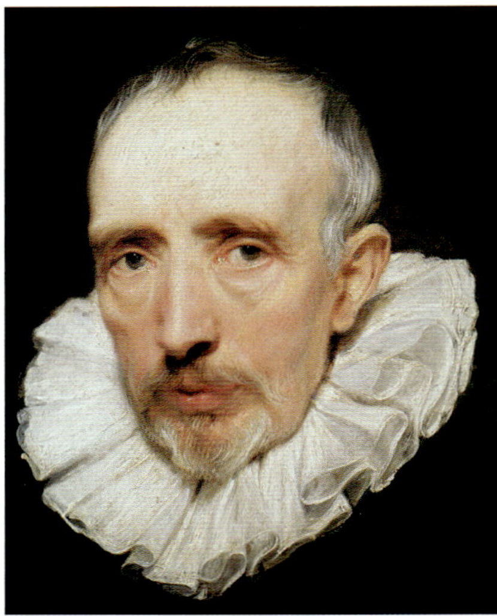

COMMANDING ATTENTION

The central panel portrays a dramatically foreshortened, diagonal figure of Christ being raised on the cross, with the might of the executioners emphasized in their powerful, muscular bodies. The two movable wings of the triptych create a continuation of the picture. On the left, the Virgin, Saint John, plus some women and children watch events, while on the right, the two thieves are also prepared to be crucified, with a Roman officer watching on a foreshortened horse.

COUNTER-REFORMATION

Until the Reformation, the Roman Catholic Church had dominated Western Europe for 1000 years. Then, starting in Germany in 1517, the ideas of Protestantism had spread quickly throughout Europe, and traditions of Roman Catholic art were rejected as idolatry. In response to this, the Council of Trent prompted the Counter-Reformation, with artists across Europe being challenged to create imagery that aroused greater religious intensity in Catholics and instigated the conversion of Protestants. The Counter-Reformation achieved its aims rapidly. In 1600, approximately half of Europe was Protestant, but within 50 years, 80 per cent of the population had either returned or converted to Catholicism. This was achieved largely through compelling art that instructed and captivated, working as propaganda and helping the illiterate to understand Catholic teachings. With his own Catholic beliefs, knowledge of Italian art, expressive, fluid style and dynamic compositions, Rubens was the perfect Counter-Reformation artist.

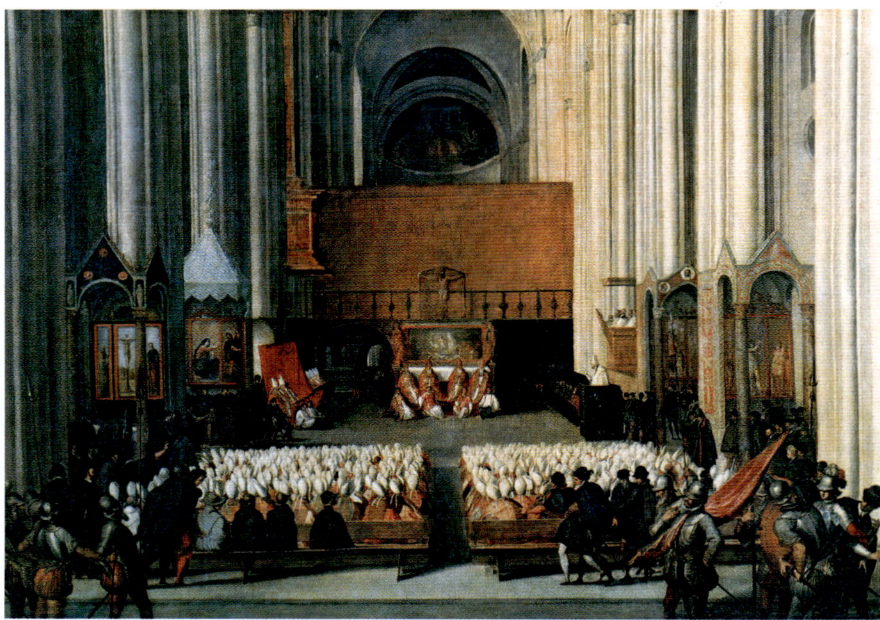

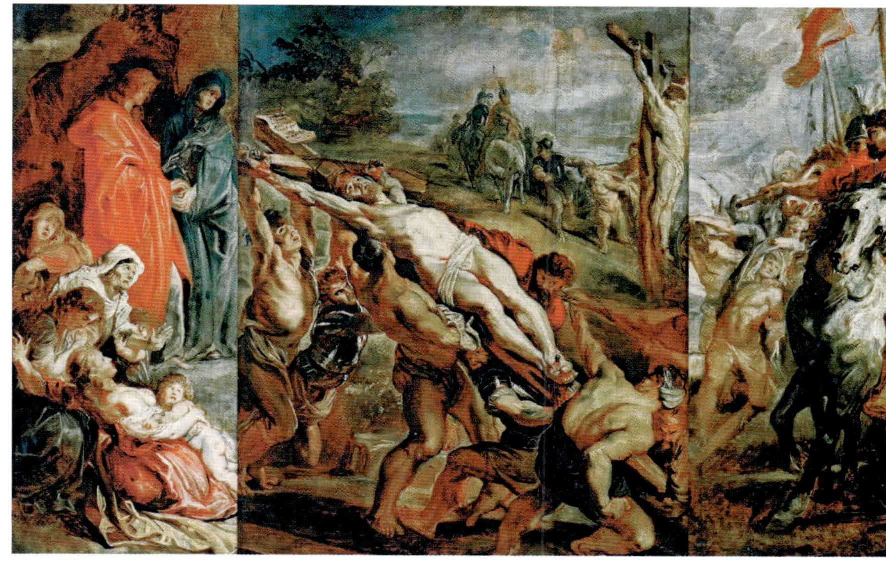

Right: This sketch for The Raising of the Cross *was painted by Rubens in c.1609 in preparation for the triptych in the Church of St Walburga in Antwerp.*

The work shows clear influences of Italian Renaissance and Baroque artists such as Caravaggio, Tintoretto and Michelangelo, of Greek and Roman sculpture, and also of traditional northern art. Rubens's northern roots are apparent in close details and textural qualities, such as on the leaves of the tree, the shining armour and the dog's fur. In Flemish art, dogs symbolize fidelity. Christ's body – simultaneously graceful and powerful – appears solid and heavy, a strong physical presence evoking Michelangelo's figures on the Sistine Chapel ceiling, while the nine executioners with their bulging muscles emphasize the brutality of the struggle. Christ's body cuts across the composition, dominating the image

Below: Showing a clear influence of the Italian Renaissance, The Raising (or Elevation) of the Cross *was completed by Rubens in 1610–1611.*

and recalling Caravaggio's *Entombment.* Motion, space and time are all illustrated, while the dynamic colour and chiaroscuro command attention. Pronounced physicality was an important aspect of Counter-Reformation art, as was the representation of Mary as a resilient, strong woman. Rubens shows her looking sad but not broken, accepting her son's fate and suffering with

decorum. On the backs of the triptych's wings are images of the saints Amandus, Walburga, Eligius and Catherine – all particularly revered in Antwerp. With its rich palette, strong tonal contrasts, foreshortening and expressive gestures, the monumental work instantly captures viewers' emotions, stressing Christ's humanity and marking it out as Baroque.

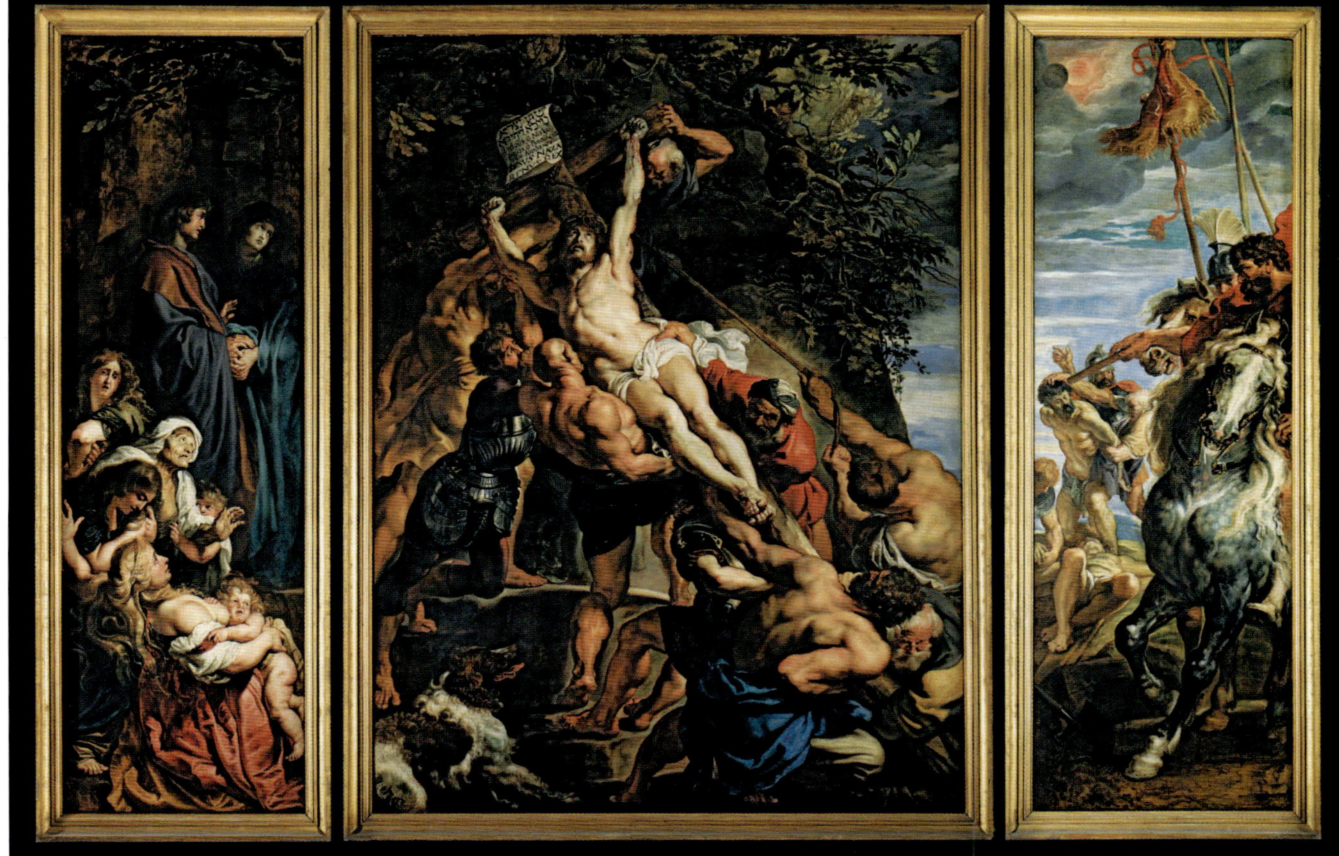

A QUEST FOR BEAUTY

While painting the triptych for the Church of St Walburga, Rubens bought a house with land on the Wapper canal, which supplied fresh water to Antwerp. He designed an extension to the house, creating an imposing and richly ornamented building inspired by Genoese architecture and classical antiquity.

At the end of September 1610, Rubens and Isabella were proud to witness the unveiling of his *Ecstasy of Saint Gregory the Great* in a new chapel dedicated to his mother in Saint Michael's Abbey in Antwerp. But Rubens's emotions were to be sorely tested. Less than two months later, his friend and fellow artist Elsheimer died in Rome at just 32 years old. On March 21, 1611, he and Isabella became parents to their first child, Clara Serena (1611–23). Five months later, on August 28, 1611, Rubens's beloved brother Philip died suddenly after a short illness. He was just 37 years old, and left his pregnant wife and their young daughter Claire (1610–78). Their second child, named Philip (1611–78) after his father, was born two weeks later. Philip had been Rubens's closest ally, friend, advisor and counsellor. Just as after his mother's death, there is no record of Rubens's emotions at this time, but his grief must have been acute.

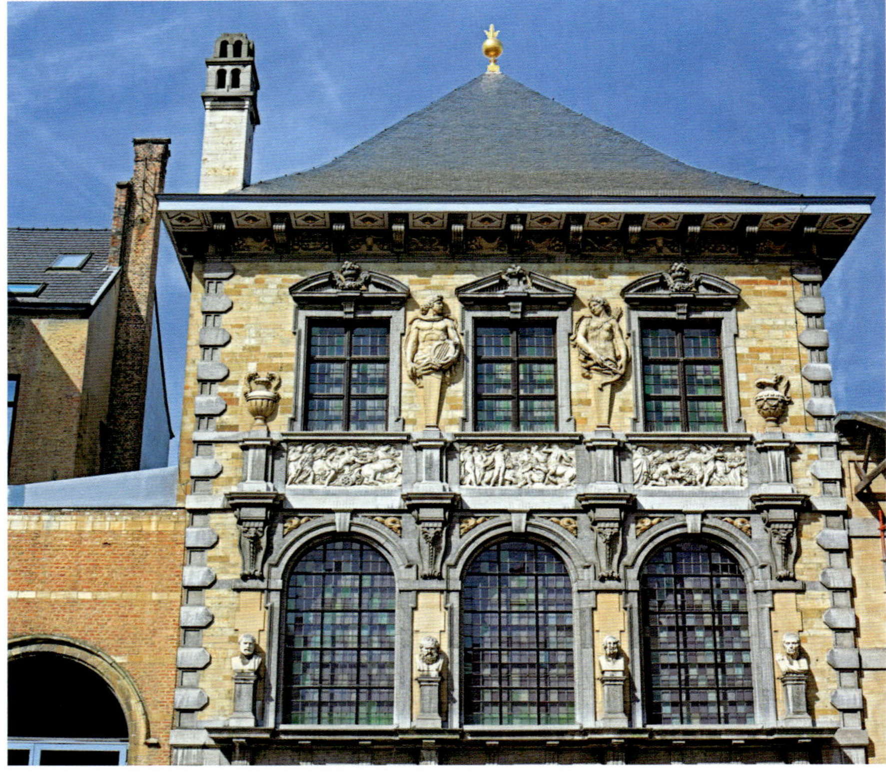

DESCENT FROM THE CROSS

Stunned by the magnificence of *The Raising of the Cross*, in 1611 the Arquebusiers' Guild commissioned Rubens to paint a *Descent from the Cross* for the altar in Antwerp cathedral, for 2400 florins. The commission was instigated by the Guild's president at the time, Rubens's friend Rockox. *Descent from the Cross* is perhaps even more powerful than *The Raising of the Cross*, and effectively changed the history of art. From its unveiling, Rubens became internationally recognized as one of the greatest living artists, and students and assistants applied to work with him from far and wide. Once again, he utilized the dramatic effects of a diagonal composition on the main central panel. He also emphasized

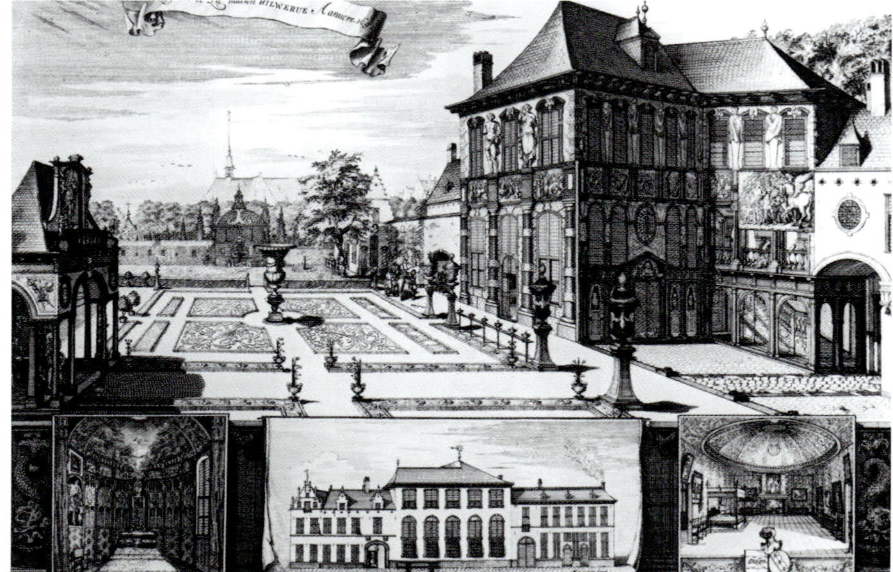

Top: Rubens based his new house on the buildings he had studied in Genoa. This announced to the world that he was now a noteworthy figure.

Left: Rubenshuis, Antwerp. A year after marrying Isabella Brant in 1609, Rubens began redesigning and constructing his Italian-style villa. It took him seven years to complete the ambitious project.

chiaroscuro and bold coloration to attract viewers' attention, while forcefully depicting human physicality.

Seemingly thrusting forward from the picture plane, the dead Christ is lowered from the cross with the aid of a shroud. His apostles and friends show tremendous physical and emotional strength as they lean and struggle to support his body, while simultaneously trying to suppress their overwhelming emotions. Voluptuous, blonde Mary Magdalene stands at his feet, and the Virgin, distraught but composed, extends her arms to her son. Conforming to Council of Trent guidelines, on the outer panels of this triptych Rubens portrayed two other important stories from the New Testament: *The Visitation* and *Presentation in the Temple.*

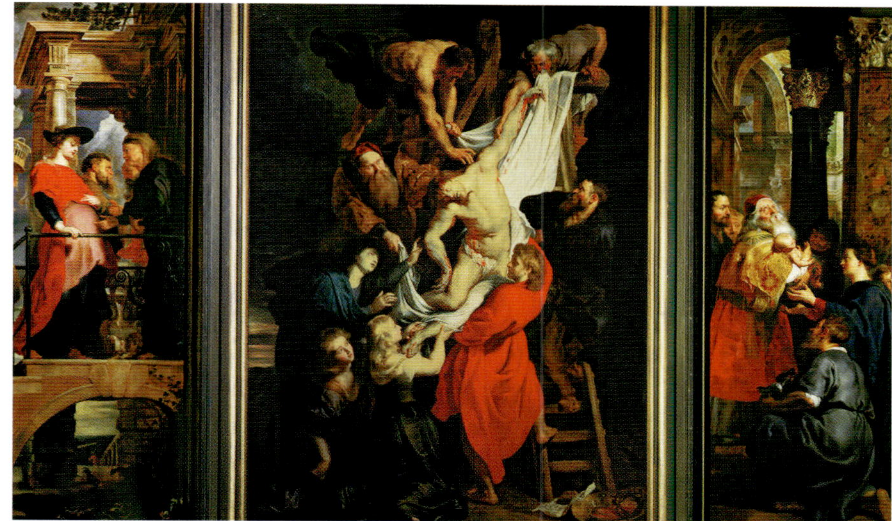

Above: Triptych of Descent from the Cross, *Rubens, 1611–14. This powerful depiction is of a theme that Rubens returned to repeatedly.*

Below: Descent from the Cross, *Rubens. The rich colours and paint application includes elements of Venetian painting and the drama of Caravaggio.*

RUBENSHUIS

In November 1610, Rubens bought a house from the Arquebusiers' Guild for 10,000 guilders. It was expensive, but it was a handsome house in the traditional Flemish style, with three storeys in red brick, white stone trim and a steep roof, plus an adjacent laundry house that, once demolished, made space for Rubens to build a new wing and two small houses that he let. In the back, he created a large formal garden. Basing the house on the architecture he admired, he redesigned and rebuilt it. By c.1617, it was complete. He added a semi-circular sculpture gallery for his collection of art and antiquities, plus a huge portico and an interior courtyard that opened on to his Baroque-style garden. Opulent and imposing, it announced his success and importance, and he filled it with the large collection of Renaissance and ancient Roman treasures he had amassed, including a real Egyptian mummy and paintings by Titian, Veronese, Tintoretto, Pieter Bruegel the Elder, Quentin Massys (1465–1530), Holbein and Dürer.

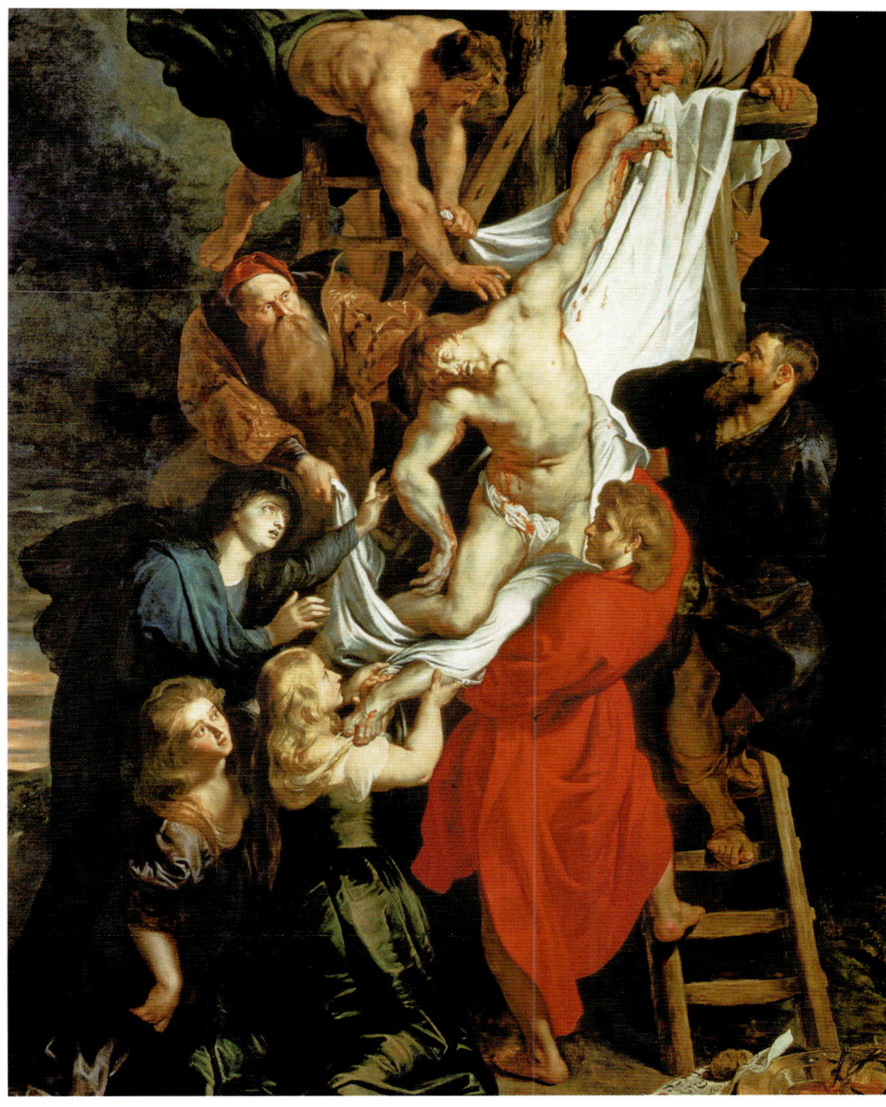

STUDENTS AND COLLABORATIONS

With his burgeoning reputation, Rubens's workload soared. His large studio produced vast numbers of paintings for numerous clients, and although always responsible for the ideas and compositions, he gave his students and assistants responsible tasks for their completion, and charged according to how much of each work he personally painted.

Along with paintings that he produced aided by his students and assistants, Rubens also painted several works in collaboration with other professional artists. His studio was necessarily extremely organized. Following long-established traditions, apprentices and assistants were allowed to perform different tasks according to their abilities. Novice students prepared his pigments, panels and canvases, while those more advanced in their training were allowed to make copies of their master's work, which were in great demand. Assistants, who were generally apprentices who had completed their main years of training but had not yet become professional artists, were usually allowed to help prepare and execute paintings with the master, following his drawings and oil sketches, and mixing paints in his selected colour palette. However, Rubens always oversaw the work in progress and made the final and most important touches to each painting. No work could leave the studio without his approval, and he always created the initial idea, planned the compositions and chose the exact palette for each painting.

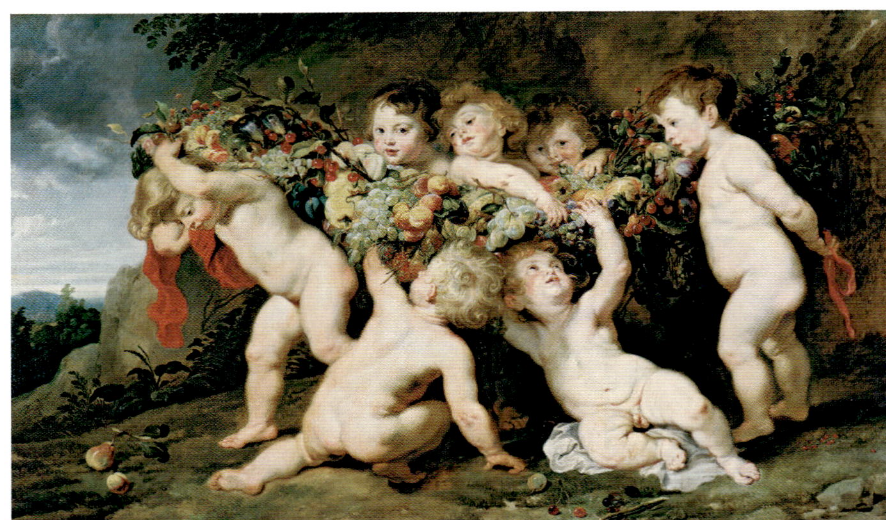

Above: Garland of Fruit, *Rubens and Snyders, c.1615–17. This type of gentle, sensitive work was extremely admired.*

EQUAL CONTRIBUTIONS

For several paintings, Rubens collaborated with other established artists. As an equal partnership, these works were executed entirely differently from the way he worked with his students and assistants. Utilizing each artists' strengths or specific skills, the practice of two professional artists producing work together became somewhat of a fashion in Antwerp at that time. The works became particularly sought after, and the artists could charge highly for them. Frans Snyders, who specialized in still life and animal paintings, became a regular

Below: The Garden of Eden, *Rubens and Brueghel. With Rubens's skills in painting human figures and Jan Breughel's in depicting nature, their collaborations were in great demand.*

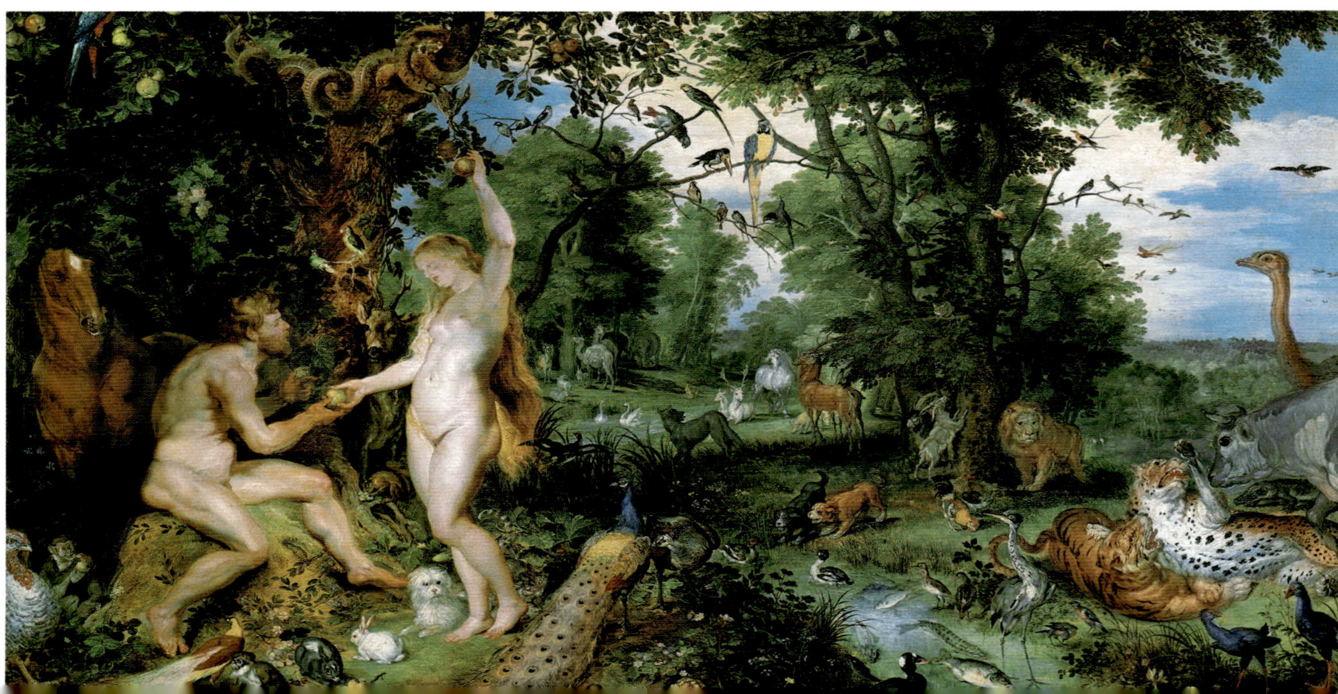

'THE BEST OF MY PUPILS'

By 1618, Antwerp-born 19-year-old Anthony van Dyck (1599–1641) was working as an assistant in Rubens's studio. In February of that year, he had been admitted as a free master into the Antwerp Painters' Guild, and previously – from the age of 10 – he had trained with the painter Hendrick van Balen (1575–1632). However, it is not completely clear when he entered Rubens's studio. It has been speculated that he began training there as a student from about 1613, but this has not been substantiated. What is known is that during 1618, Rubens made Van Dyck his chief assistant, and in a letter to Sir Dudley Carleton (1573–1632), an English art collector and ambassador to the Netherlands from 1616–20, Rubens described him as 'the best of my pupils'. In 1620, when Rubens was commissioned to paint in the Church of St Carolus Borromeus in Antwerp, Van Dyck was his main assistant.

collaborator. He painted animals, fruits and flowers in Rubens's pictures, and Rubens painted figures in his.

Another frequent partnership was with his friend Jan Brueghel the Elder. In these works, Brueghel executed the backgrounds, usually of landscapes or flowers, while Rubens painted the rest of each image. Enjoying their working partnership, the two artists produced several paintings of the Madonna and Child encircled by flower garlands, which were extremely popular in Catholic Antwerp, as well as various other, mainly religious works. Both

Right: Interior of Church of St Carolus Borromeus. Built by the Jesuits between 1615 and 1621, Rubens contributed to much of the interior.

Far right: St Carolus Borromeus. With its spectacular façade, based on Il Gesu in Rome, this is an opulent Baroque church that was nicknamed 'the marble temple'.

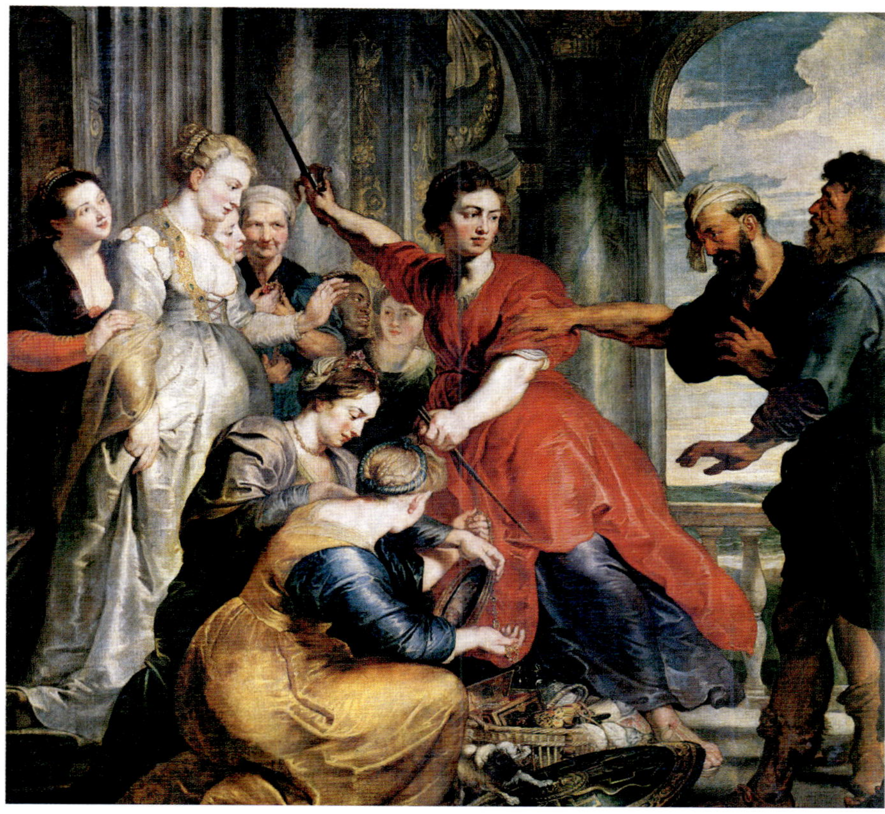

Above: Achilles Discovered by Odysseus, Rubens and Van Dyck, 1617–18. This is a rich and theatrical painting of a dramatic Greek myth, by Rubens and his best pupil.

artists were held in high esteem and their shared works were in demand. Even though Rubens and Brueghel charged highly for these joint paintings, they were eagerly bought by some of the wealthiest collectors in Europe.

ST CAROLUS BORROMEUS

In 1615, a new Jesuit church began to be built in Antwerp. Five years later, Rubens was commissioned to prepare designs and sketches for three altarpieces and 39 ceiling pieces for

it (now the Church of St Carolus Borromeus). It was agreed that the bulk of the project would be executed by his pupils and assistants, although he would retouch anything necessary at the end. The huge project was completed within a year, in time for the church's consecration in 1621.

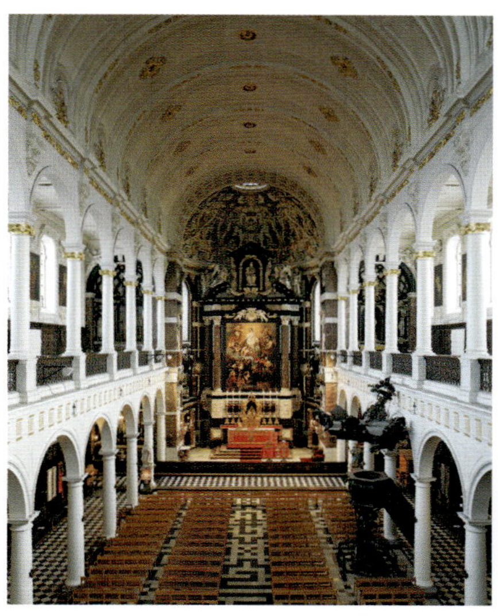

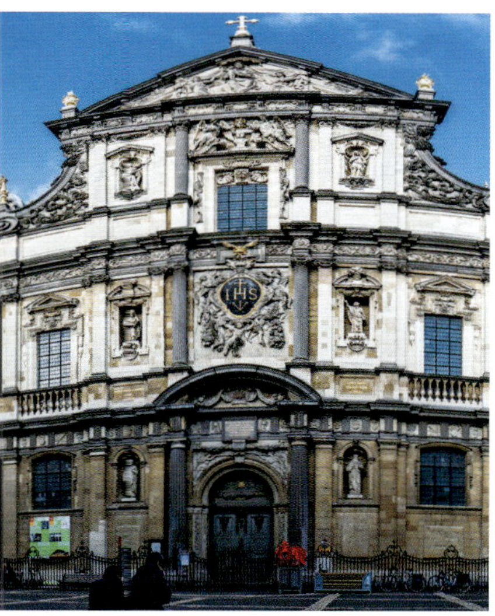

PROMINENT PATRONS

While the Archdukes Albert and Isabella continued to employ him, one of the main factors in Rubens's decision to stay in Antwerp was the flow of patronage from others. With such a steady stream of prominent commissions, he soon became prosperous and highly respected.

As soon as Rubens had arrived back in Antwerp in 1609, his circle of professional and personal contacts expanded, and through several of these, commissions poured in. Rather than royalty or the nobility, most of these early commissions came from wealthy burghers. Rockox, a highly respected citizen who played a significant political role in Antwerp during the first half of the 17th century, became one of his major patrons. A lawyer and Humanist, Rockox also cultivated an international reputation as a great art and antiques collector. He had been the main instigator in the commissioning of *Adoration of the Magi* to be hung in the Hall of State in Antwerp's Statenkamer in 1609. Within a few months, he also commissioned Rubens to paint a smaller work, *Samson and Delilah*, which he hung on the chimney breast of the parlour in his own house. By 1611, together with other members of the Arquebusiers' Guild, he also commissioned Rubens to paint *Descent from the Cross*. Rubens later acknowledged Rockox's patronage by including his portrait in *The Presentation in the Temple* on the right-hand wing of *Descent from the Cross*.

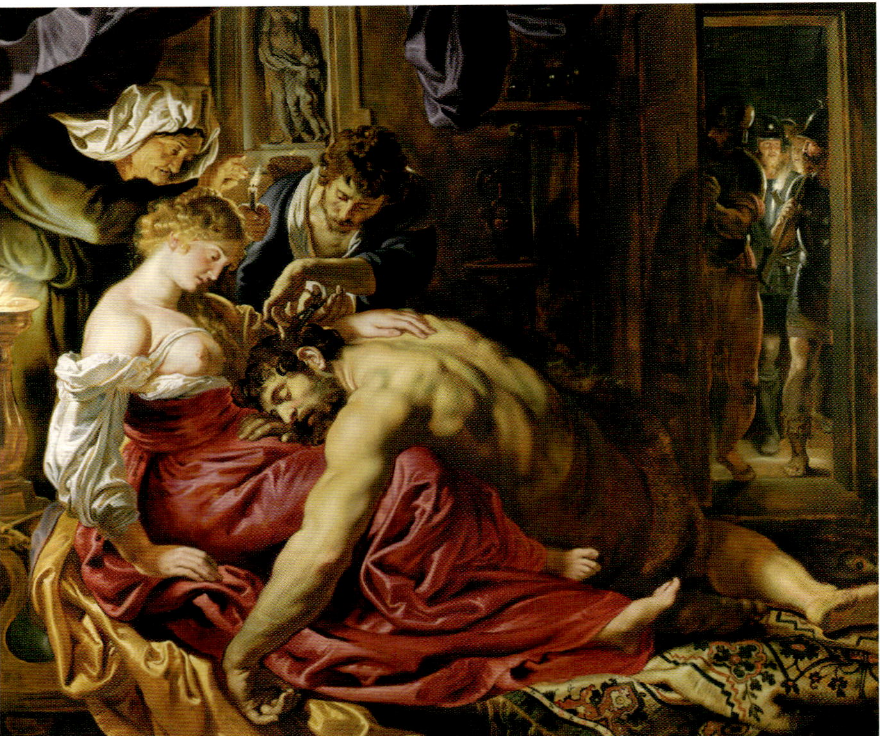

SAMSON AND DELILAH

Created to hang in Rockox's home, this work is deliberately richly coloured and sensuous. Strong tonal contrasts create drama even before the action is closely viewed. The sumptuous but restricted palette depicts a subtly lit interior. Flesh and drapery are lavishly portrayed. Illustrating the biblical story of Samson's betrayal by Delilah, the work was unique, erotic and extravagant. Samson's massive, muscular, sleeping figure is slumped across Delilah's lap, while she looks down at him. Blonde, voluptuous beauties seemed to be

Above: Samson and Delilah, *Rubens, 1610. From the Old Testament story, Samson tells Delilah the secret of his strength – and she betrays him.*

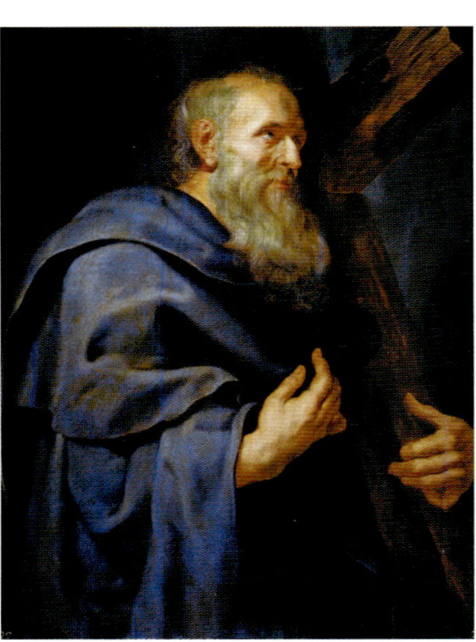

Far left: Saint Philip, *Rubens, 1610–12. From his* Twelve Apostles *series, this is Rubens's depiction of the apostle who preached in Greece, Syria and Phrygia.*

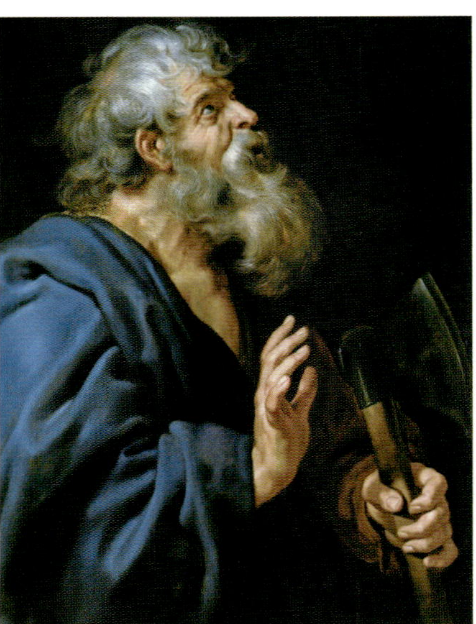

Left: Saint Matthias, *Rubens, 1610–12. Not much is known of Matthias, but the axe that he is holding in his left hand refers to his death.*

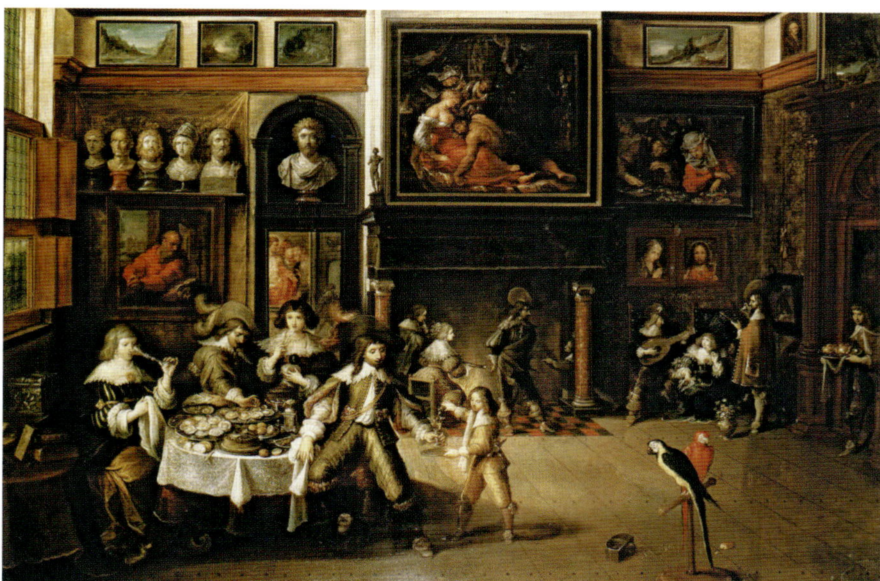

Above: A painting of the interior of Nicolaas Rockox's house, including Rubens's painting of Samson and Delilah *hanging on the wall.*

Rubens's favourite type of female, even though his own wife Isabella was dark. With her breasts bursting from her chemise, Delilah looks down at her victim as a barber cuts his hair — the source of his strength. Her seduction of Samson has led to his downfall, and this suggestion of woman's power over man was popular with contemporary viewers. Rubens emphasized it with a statuette of Venus in the background. An open door reveals guards ready to capture Samson. Although a biblical story, this was clearly intended for a private residence and not suitable for a religious institution. In 1610–12, Rubens painted a series of the 12 apostles against dark backgrounds in similarly powerful chiaroscuro, and like Samson and Delilah, they show a strong influence of Italian painting.

UPPER AND MIDDLE CLASSES

Another of Rubens's patrons, Van der Geest, enabled him to produce some of his greatest works, specifically *The Raising of the Cross*, and in 1630, the *Ildefonso* altarpiece. Some years later,

Right: The Gallery of Cornelis van der Geest, Willem van Haecht, 1628, featuring various contemporary portraits.

in dedicating a print made after *The Raising of the Cross* to Van der Geest, Rubens acknowledged his help in securing the original commission. Sir Dudley Carleton also bought several of his paintings, including a collaborative work with Snyders: *Prometheus Bound*. Rubens also worked for several anonymous patrons, generally members of Antwerp's wealthy middle class.

THE PLANTIN-MORETUS PRESS

Soon after his return to Antwerp, Rubens began working with his childhood friend Moretus, who was head of the Plantin Press. Initially they collaborated on Philip Rubens's book on ancient Roman customs, which Rubens had illustrated throughout. For the next 30 years, Moretus employed Rubens to illustrate the title pages of a broad range and vast number of books published by the Plantin Press. His drawings for these were complex, detailed and harmonious. As his days were spent painting, Rubens produced these illustrations in his rare leisure time, so each design took him six months to complete. Moretus paid him according to the sizes of each book: 20 florins for folios (the largest size), 12 for quartos (a slightly smaller size), eight for octavos (still smaller) and five for even smaller-sized books.

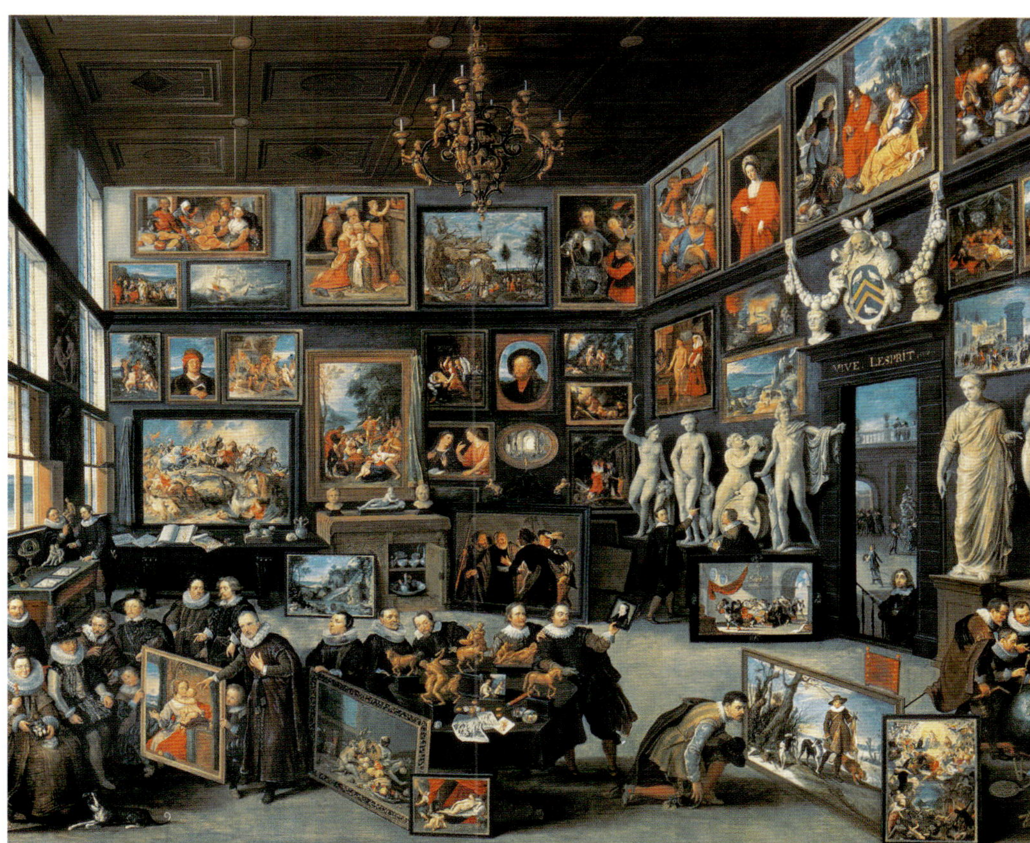

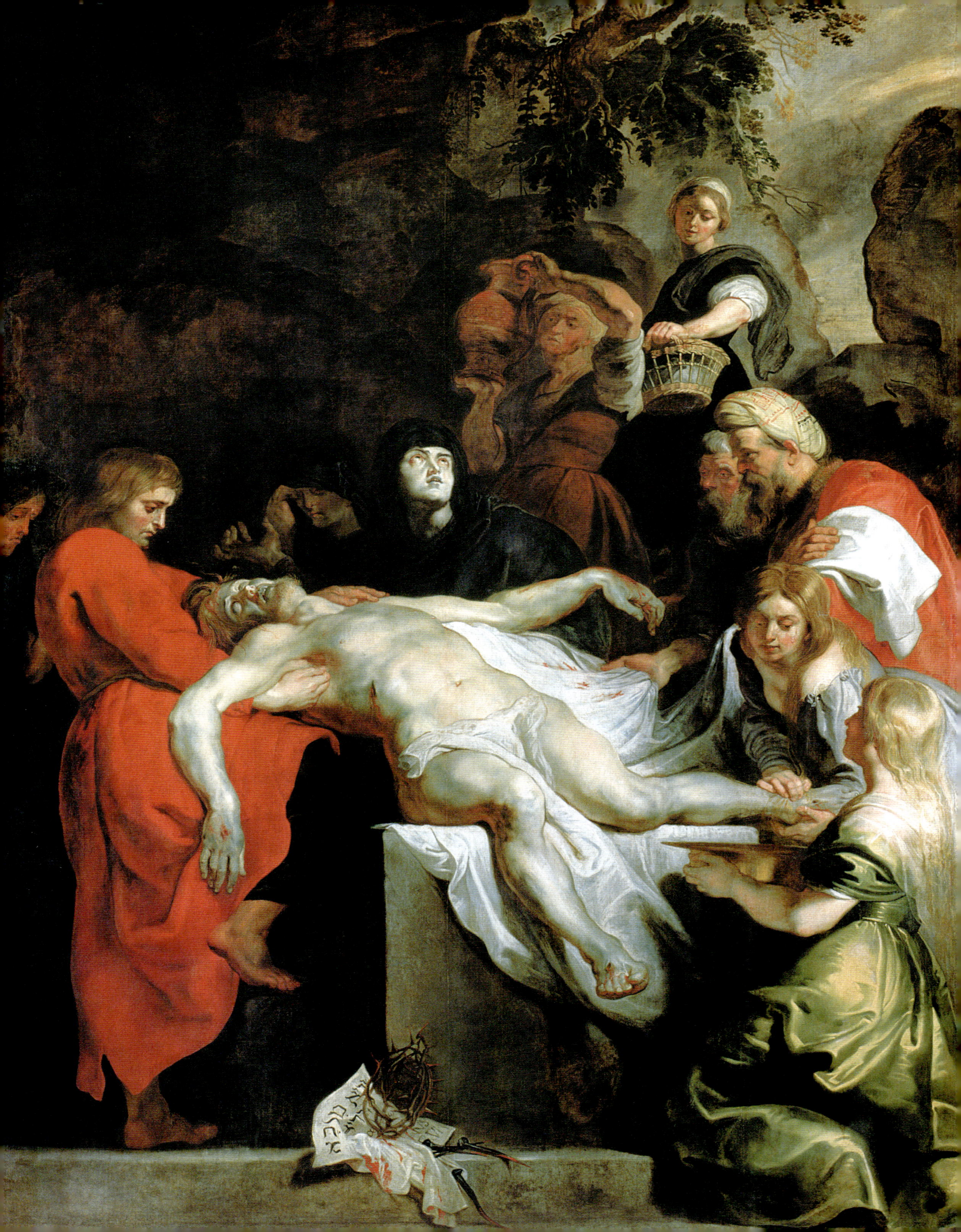

DIPLOMAT AND ARTIST

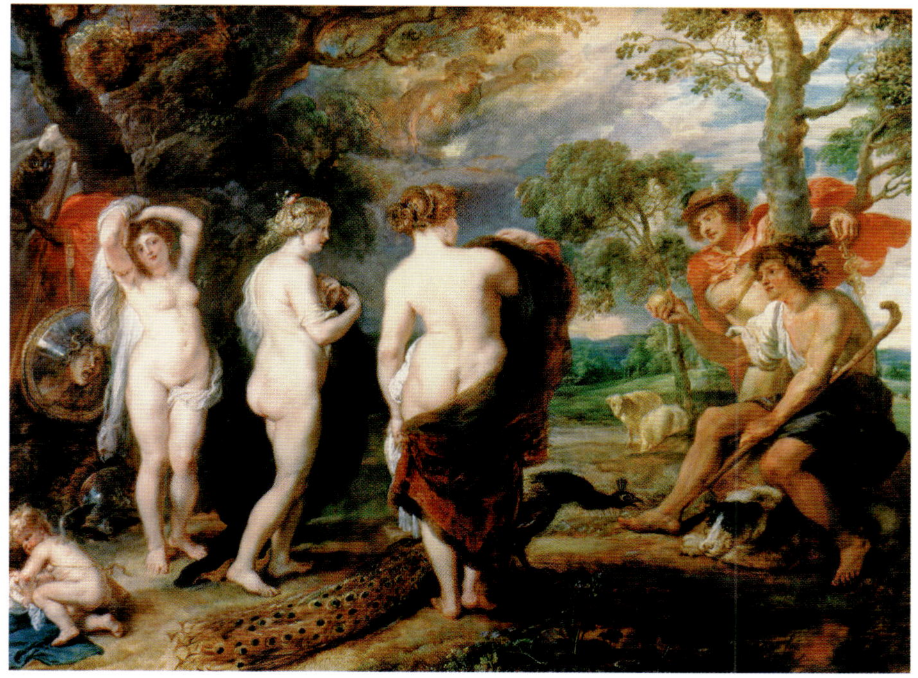

From the moment *Descent from the Cross* was unveiled, Rubens became inundated with requests for more paintings. His magnificent house helped to reinforce his position of first painter of Flanders and the most celebrated artist in Europe, and his reputation continued to expand. His creativity, thoughtfulness, intellect, energy and graciousness were recognized, and the diplomatic roles he had previously undertaken in Italy and Spain were called upon with further missions for the Habsburg rulers. A knowledgeable art collector and astute businessman with seemingly unlimited energy, he became hailed as 'the prince of painters and the painter of princes'.

Above: The Judgement of Paris, *1639, oil on panel. A favoured subject, this painting shows Rubens's idealized idea of femininity; this idea was fashionable, but made even more so by his paintings.*

Left: The Entombment, *c.1616, oil on canvas. This altarpiece demonstrates Rubens's sensitivity and understanding of emotion and pathos. While those around Christ's body lift him into his tomb, his mother remains pale and isolated, her eyes looking up to heaven.*

EXPRESSION AND INVENTION

Rubens's financial success enabled him to collect more of the art and antiquities he loved. With his inventive imagination, he used many object and paintings from his collection as references – incorporating elements such as shapes, colours and figure positions and techniques in his own work.

By 1618, Rubens's family had grown. After Clara, Isabella and Rubens had two sons: Albert (1614–57) and Nicolaas (1618–55). It was a happy time and their lives were comfortable – they were living in their newly refurbished house and Rubens also worked there in his studio, spending evenings with his family or studying his collections. He had become what he called a 'lover of antiquities', and had developed a keen talent for bargaining. From 1616, he became good friends with Sir Carleton, the English ambassador to the Netherlands, and he exchanged some of his paintings for a vast number of ancient sculptures from Carleton's collection. In a letter to Carleton on the topic, he wrote: 'Your Excellency may be assured that I shall put prices on my pictures, just as if I were negotiating to sell them for cash ... and in this I beg you to rely upon the word of an honest man.' As well as showing his earnestness, this demonstrates the charm and courtesy that made him such an effective diplomat. Carleton subsequently replied, saying he had selected six of Rubens's paintings, and invited Rubens to visit him at the Hague so that he could inspect the marbles (statues) that Rubens wanted in exchange.

Below: Nicolaas Rubens Wearing a Red Felt Cap, *Rubens, 1625–27. This is a sensitive chalk portrait of Rubens's second son and third child Nicolaas.*

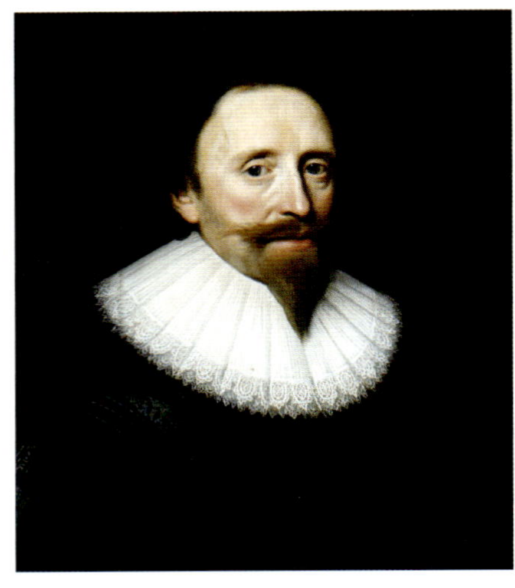

Above: Sir Dudley Carleton, Rubens, *1628. The first Viscount Dorchester (1573–1632) was an English art collector, diplomat and Secretary of State.*

CLASSICAL PERIOD

Since first going to Italy, Rubens had used the work of other artists and the art of antiquity to inform his own work. In his new house, he increasingly also used his own collection for this, and from 1611, his style became even more inventive and expressive, but was clearly informed by art of the past. It became called by many his 'Classical' period.

On September 7, 1611, he had been invited to a meeting of the Arquebusiers' Guild by Rockox, to discuss requirements for the altarpiece they were commissioning. His execution of the huge triptych took over two and a half years, with the altar being ceremoniously dedicated on July 22, 1614, the feast day of Mary Magdalene. Although all his paintings in Antwerp were greeted with increasing acclaim, *Descent from the Cross* was the first to show his latest evolution and to comprehensively establish his artistic eminence. In the central panel, Christ's dead body is directly inspired by the main figure in the Hellenistic Laocoön group that he had copied in 1601.

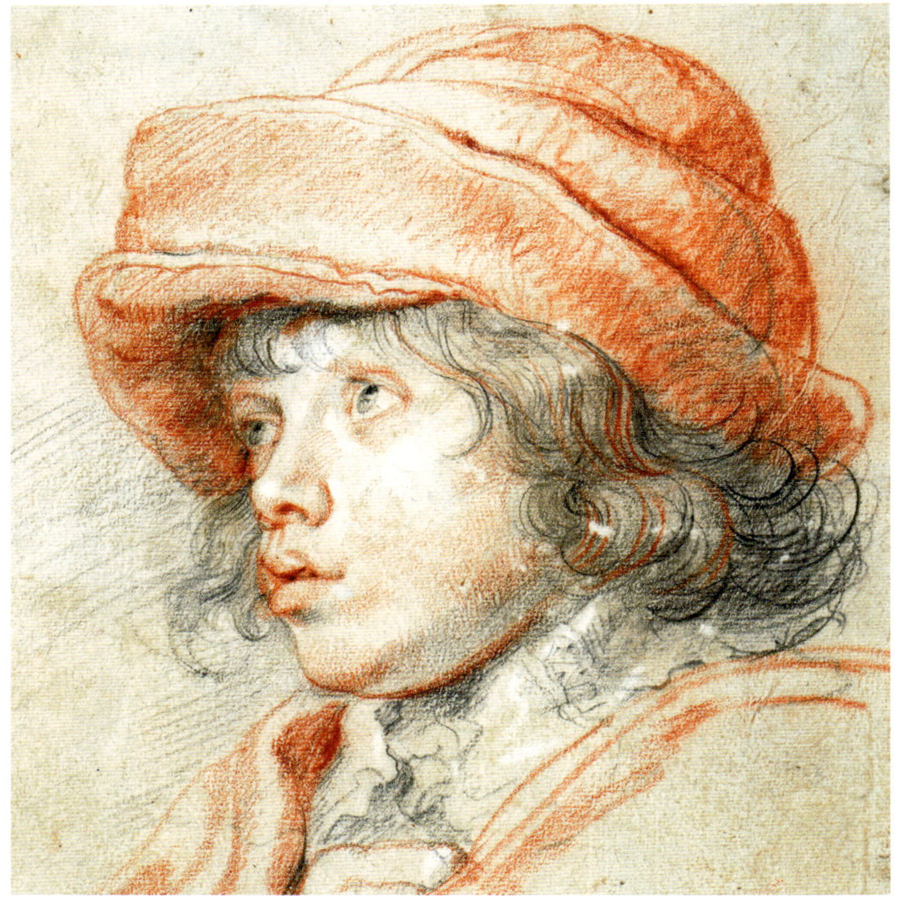

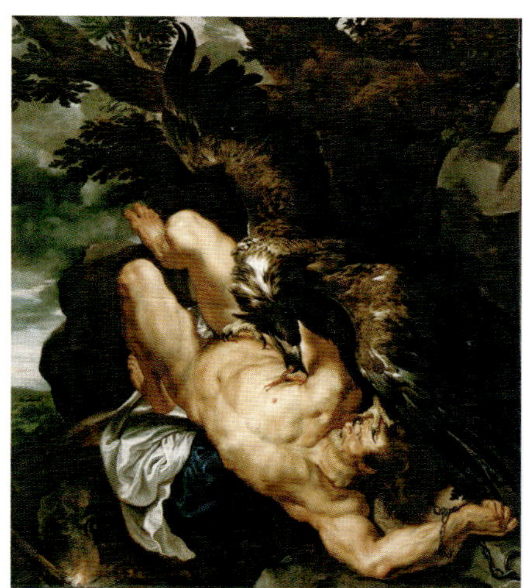

Above: Prometheus Bound, *Rubens, 1611–18. This depicts the punishment of Prometheus in the Greek myth, and was painted by Rubens, with the eagle painted by Frans Snyders.*

The other figures in the work rely on each other to create tension and a strong sense of movement, weight and passion. The rich tones and colours also intensify the sense of unity and fluidity.

His innovative new style seems to have been the result of Rubens's confidence and decision to create a completely independent approach, amalgamating others' ideas but expressing himself with both courage and originality.

PRIVATE MUSEUM

Rubens's house became a great attraction. Public museums did not exist until the later 17th century. Prior to that, certain individuals in different countries created specialized collections, normally called a *cabinet, kabinett* or *Kunstkammer,* that they made accessible to certain members of the public by special arrangement. Many of these collections were symbols of social prestige, or concerned with enjoyment and the advancement of knowledge. Rubens showed his art and artefacts to illustrious personages such as the Archduchess Isabella and Marie de' Medici.

LEGENDARY OUTPUT

As court painter to Albert and Isabella, Rubens was exempted from the usual requirements imposed by the Antwerp Painters' Guild, including the paying of taxes and restrictions on numbers of students he was allowed to teach. The freedom and financial benefits resulted in his building his large studio in his new house, and as demand for his work kept increasing, his extraordinary intellectual and physical stamina became apparent. He rarely stopped working, which resulted in an astonishing output.

Below: Crucifixion, *Rubens, 1614. The strong chiaroscuro and focus of this work recalls the work of several Spanish Baroque artists, including Velázquez and Francisco de Zurbarán.*

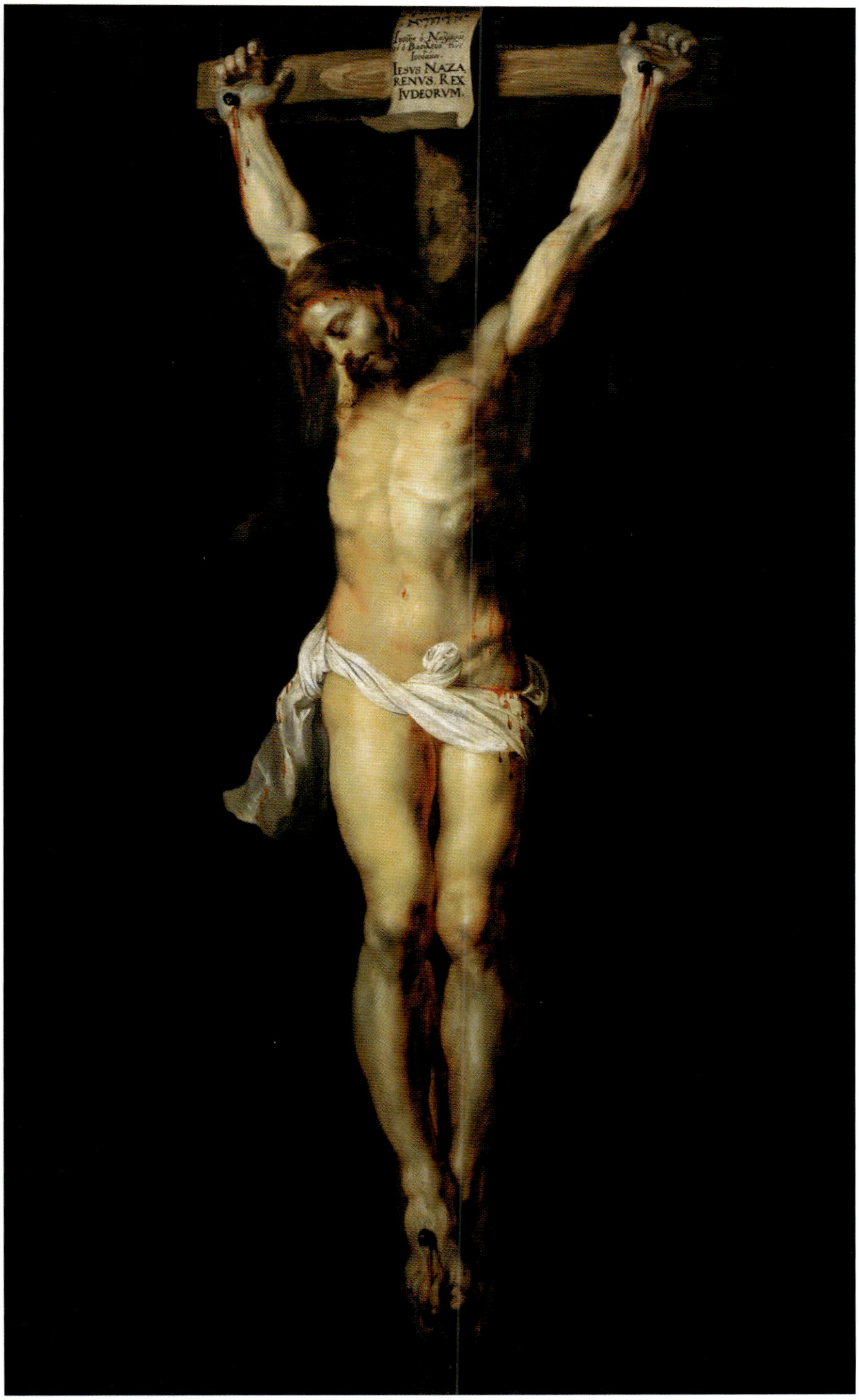

RELIGIOUS AND SECULAR WORKS

Rubens's art had become seen as an affirmation of the new, unified identity of Flanders. Although most of his religious paintings were staunchly Catholic, they were distinctively northern European interpretations of traditional ideas. His fluid style helped to create a unique image and boost the confidence of his fellow citizens.

Rubens was in an unusual position: he was a Flemish artist with extensive familiarity and understanding of Italian art; a Roman Catholic with knowledge and sympathies for Humanism; and an intellectual with a fascination for both new developments and inventions, and events and beliefs of the past. Although he continued to incorporate all that he had learned in Italy, after his return to Flanders he began using more elements in his work that were the legacy of his Flemish ancestors. For instance, he stopped painting on canvas using dark underpainting, and instead began painting on wooden panels against light coloured backgrounds. This light underpainting made his work resonate with radiant colour, contrasting with other Counter-Reformation paintings. While he assimilated the legacy of Italian art, he also followed his own heritage in expressing worldly sentiments and rendering conspicuously realistic material qualities.

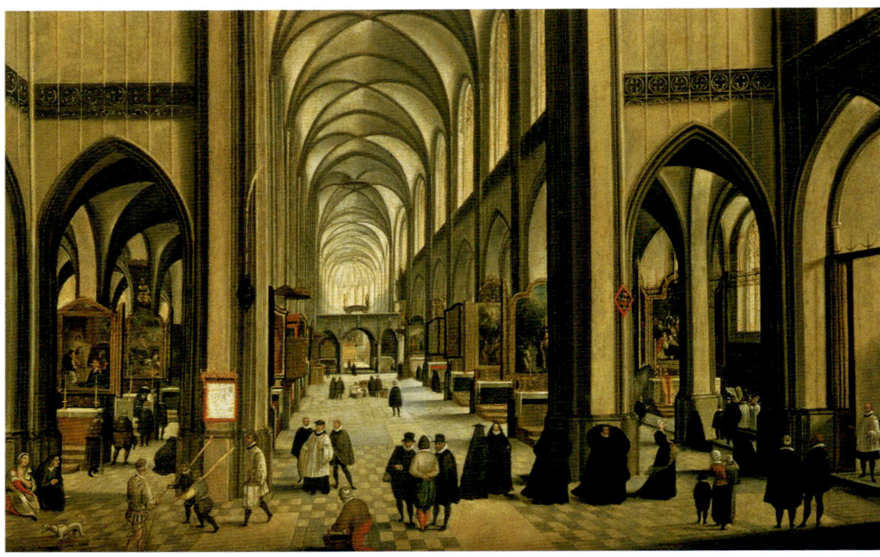

Above: A View of the Interior of Antwerp Cathedral with the Seven Sacraments, *Hendrik van Steenwyck (1550–1603). Steenwyck was a Baroque painter who followed his father in painting architectural interiors. He painted this view of Antwerp Cathedral in 1590.*

HUMAN VIRTUES

To express himself and his fellow citizens, whether he was depicting religious or secular subjects, Rubens sought to depict human virtues in all his paintings, such as endurance, selflessness, courage, self-sacrifice – and youth and beauty.

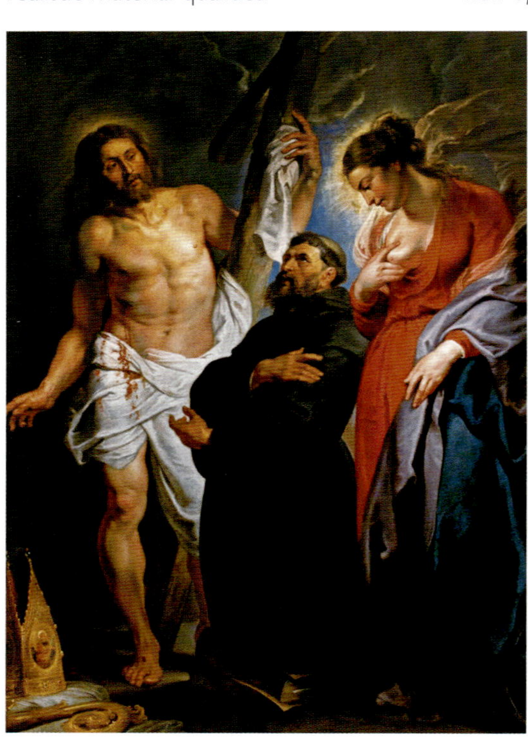

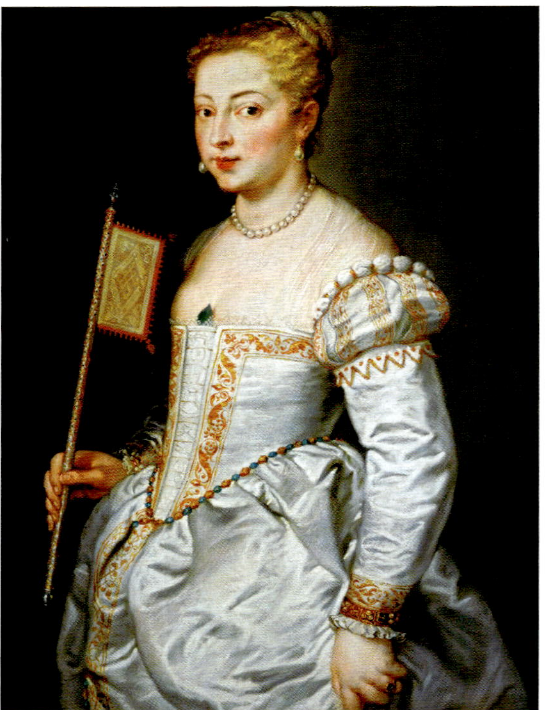

Far left: Saint Augustine between Christ and Mary, *Rubens, 1615. Powerful and full of dynamism, this shows Rubens's originality in portraying Catholic subjects.*

Left: Girl with Fan, *Rubens, 1612–14. This formal portrait reveals Rubens's remarkable ability to depict texture.*

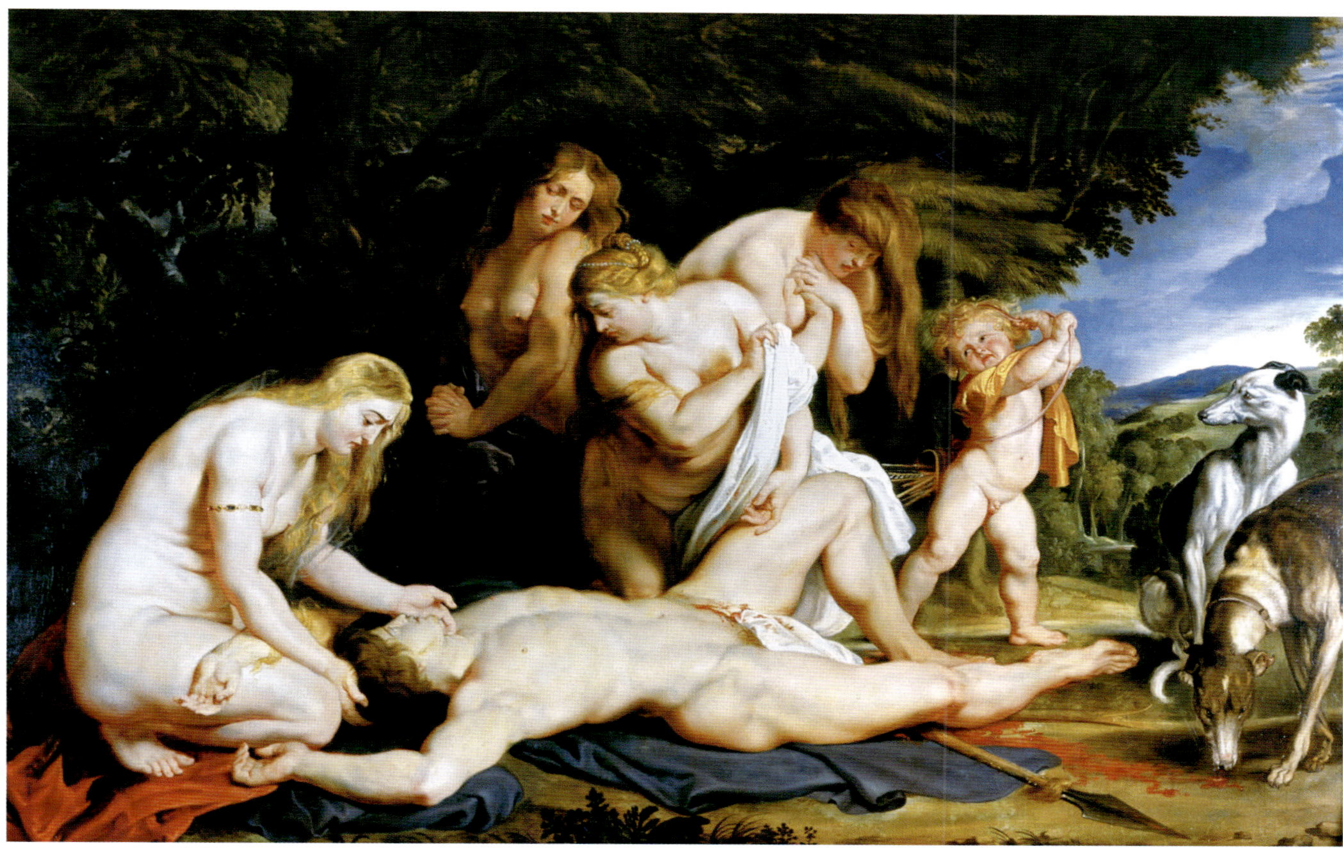

Above: Death of Adonis (with Venus, Cupid and the Three Graces), *Rubens, c.1614, from Ovid's* Metamorphoses.

He became celebrated for his ability to convey hidden dramas and inner tensions in both religious and secular subjects. By the 1620s, his spectacular paintings of battles, wild animals, rampages, orgies and celebrations were awaited with anticipation. He continued amalgamating aspects of ancient and contemporary art in all his themes, from biblical to mythological, from portraits to history, and in stories from literature or the Gospels. For the time and place he lived, there was no contradiction in painting religious images such as Christ on the Cross or the Assumption, as in representing mythologies such as Perseus and Andromeda or the Union of Earth and Water. Whatever he portrayed, be it spiritual or worldly, violent or peaceful, the real, underlying theme of every painting was human nature in all its manifestations and of individual, human endeavour against adverse forces. In this way, whether he represented classical mythology, the Old Testament, teachings of Christ, actions of the saints, or representations of nature, it was all a vehicle for his articulation of human nature when faced with adversity. Even in his portraits, he captured the characteristic features of individual personalities, while also expressing his sitters' gestures and reactions to outer influences.

FREEDOM OF EXPRESSION

While Rubens was kept busy producing both large-scale, spiritual works for grand Catholic churches and other public places, he also produced smaller works for wealthy citizens' homes and private collections. These smaller works continued to show human endeavour, struggles and qualities, and were often erotic or sensual in nature. It is a mark of his nationality that he could explore these ideas freely. Although the oppression of the Spanish Inquisition had diminished by the 17th century, artists there and also in other Roman Catholic countries continued to be far more repressed than those in northern Europe. Rubens exploited this freedom to the full.

CONTRAPPOSTO AND SERPENTINATA

Another example of Rubens's independent approach can be seen in his figure poses. Ignoring contemporary preferences for rather rigid, strong poses, he made use of the ancient *contrapposto* and *Figura Serpentinata*. *Contrapposto* is an Italian term meaning counter-pose, and describes a standing person with most weight on one foot, shoulders and arms twisting in the opposite direction from the hips and legs. It was used extensively by Italian artists during the Renaissance, who in turn had learned it from ancient Greek art. *Figura Serpentinata*, Latin for serpentine figure, is similar to *contrapposto*, but more twisted. Leonardo, Michelangelo and Raphael used these poses frequently, and Rubens also made great use of them in his work to express dynamic movement and powerful emotion.

ENGRAVINGS AND PRINTS

As an adroit businessman, Rubens became extremely dissatisfied with the unauthorized reproductions of his work that frequently appeared. By 1619, he obtained legal authority to copyright his images, and he hired printmakers to produce official, authorized engravings and woodcuts of his paintings.

Rubens had a pronounced business sense, and even after he was able to copyright his images, he closely supervised the printmaking of his work. He then directed a concerted campaign to disseminate the prints throughout Europe, which hugely extended and consolidated his fame. He had a clear notion of the styles he wanted, and encouraged all printmakers he worked with to copy his painterly effects, usually producing modellos for them to follow.

WORKING RELATIONSHIPS

Although all the printmakers that Rubens worked with were highly skilled, he often corrected or retouched their reproductions of his work with pen and ink or gouache. He also closely supervised every aspect of their printmaking, avoiding those printmakers

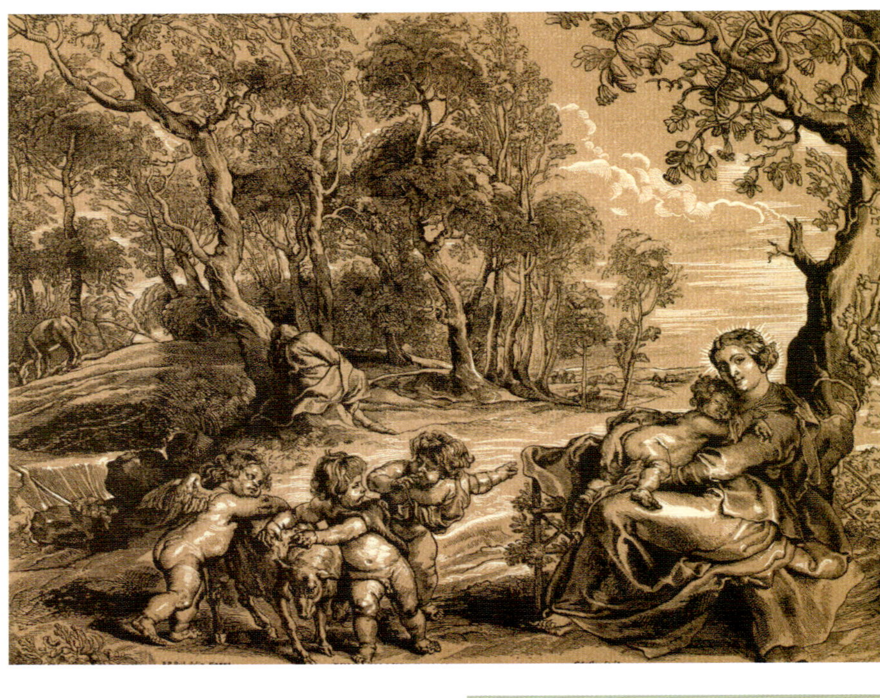

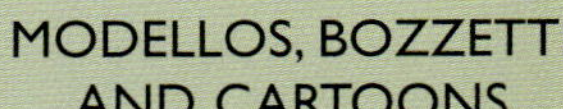

Above: The Flight from Egypt, *1635. This is one of Rubens's successful engravings that helped to publicize his work.*

who tried to impose their own ideas and styles on his work. The first engraver to work for him regularly from 1619 onwards was Lucas Vorsterman (1595–1675). Vorsterman worked well, until a violent dispute occurred between them in 1621. It is not clear whether there was a physical altercation, but the situation was sufficiently serious for Rubens's lawyers to successfully petition the authorities for a protection order. The causes of the dispute have never been substantiated, but it is generally believed to be over the issue of ownership of the rights to the prints engraved by Vorsterman of Rubens's paintings. They never worked together again.

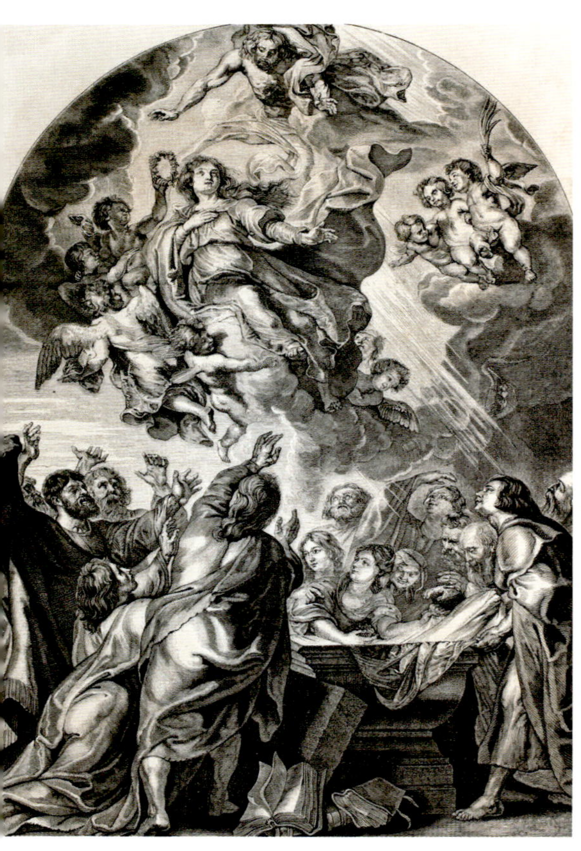

Left: The Assumption of Mary. *Rubens made great efforts in the reproduction and dissemination of his paintings, drawings and tapestry designs in prints.*

MODELLOS, BOZZETTI AND CARTOONS

A modello (from the Italian word *modelli* meaning 'models') describes a preparatory sketch for a work of art. Modellos were made to show patrons what their completed painting would look like, to help artists work out their ideas and to guide assistants – or printmakers. Cartoons (from the Italian word *cartone* meaning strong, heavy paper or pasteboard) are full-sized, detailed drawings on strong paper of artworks before they are made. Modellos are not as finished as cartoons, but more complete than rough, preliminary drawings that are known as bozzetti (Italian for 'sketches'). Rubens usually first produced bozzetti, followed by modellos, and then finally painted detailed cartoons, which are almost exact versions of his final works.

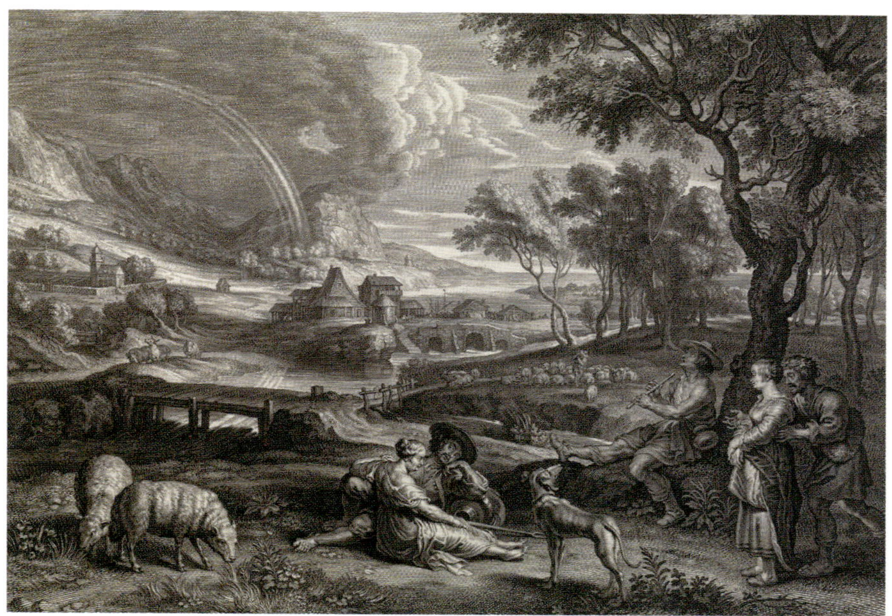

Other engravers who worked with Rubens included one of Vorsterman's pupils, Paulus Pontius (1603–58), who specialized in portrait engravings. In 1624, Pontius prepared an engraving after Rubens's monumental altarpiece *The Assumption of the Virgin*. First, he drew a copy of the painting in black chalk, and Rubens reworked it with ink, wash, gouache and oil paint, adding a figure of Christ, which demonstrates their close working relationship. Boetius à Bolswert (c.1585–1633) and his brother Schelte à Bolswert (1586–1659) both became renowned for their copper-plate engravings of Rubens's landscapes. For the last five years of his life, Boetius worked on engravings for Rubens, and after his death in 1633, Schelte was employed by Rubens in his place. During the mid-1630s, Christoffel Jegher (1596–1652) made woodcuts of some of Rubens's paintings, such as *The Garden of Love* (see page 235). Two drawings by Rubens, finished by Jegher, served as models for this, and together, Rubens and Jegher revived the art of the woodcut, a printmaking technique that had been largely relegated to cheap book illustrations by the 1620s. Rubens drew complex marks directly on to the woodblocks and Jegher carefully carved them. These prints capture the energy and rich tonality of Rubens's paintings during the 1630s. Jonas Suyderhoef (1613–86) was a

Above: Made in 1638 by Schelte à Bolswert of Rubens's Landscape with a Rainbow *of 1632–35 (see page 244), this engraving shows precise details and atmospheric tones.*

draughtsman and etcher who skilfully reproduced the textures and qualities of light and shade that Rubens so sensitively depicted in his paintings.

PAINTING VIOLENCE
Having grown up during endless conflict, it is perhaps not surprising that Rubens created some paintings at the end of the Twelve Years' Truce in 1621 that show ferocity and barbarism. In 1615–16, Prince Maximilian of Bavaria (1573–1651) commissioned him to paint four hunting scenes for his Castle Schleissheim. The paintings comply with contemporary attitudes about hunting wild animals – the violence and cruelty was expected, but, following the art of ancient Greece and Rome, there is no blood.

Below: Diana's Return from the Hunt, 1616. The details, tones and careful attention to detail made Rubens's prints achieve bestseller status during his lifetime.

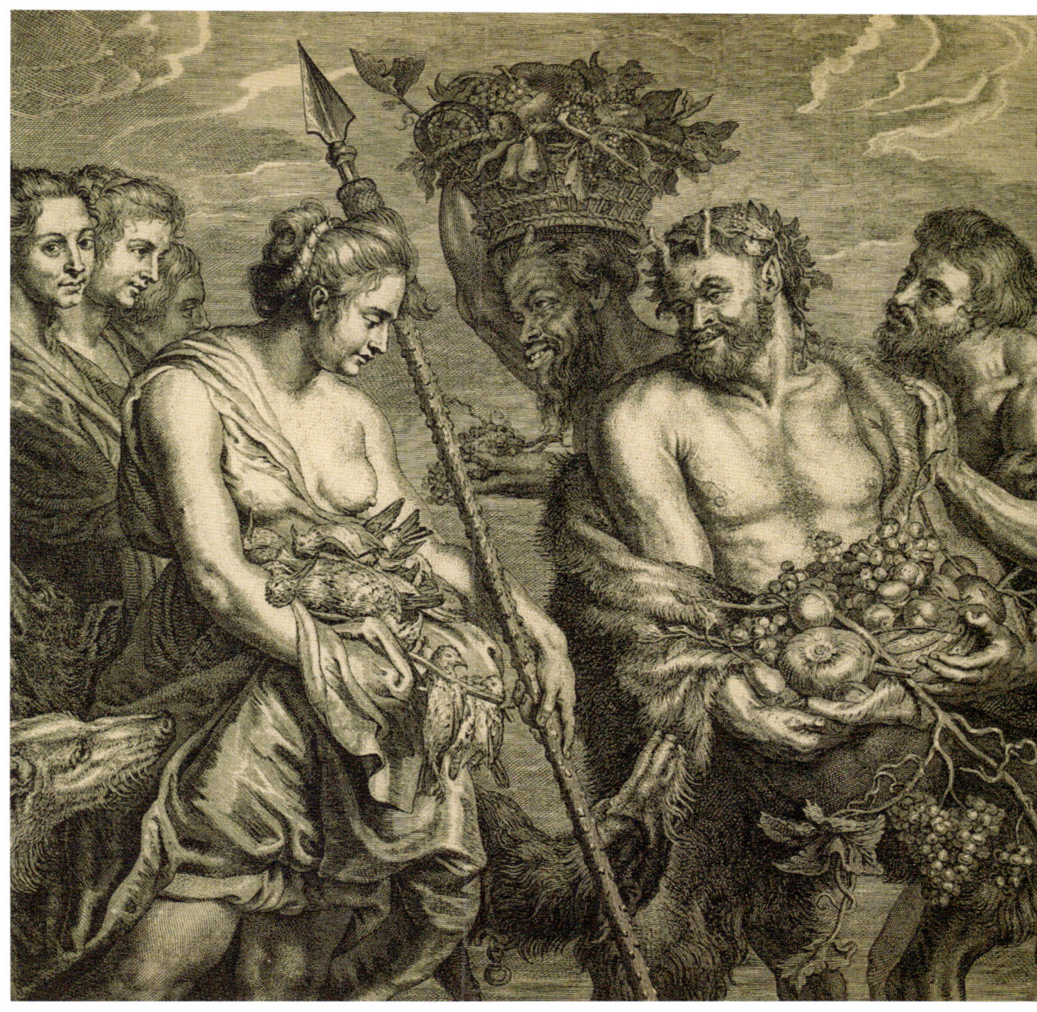

TAPESTRIES AND ARCHITECTURE

As Rubens's art became increasingly renowned through paintings and prints, he also became recognized for his book designs, knowledge of antiquities, gifts as a statesman, and for his monumental tapestry, sculpture and architectural designs. His complex compositions made particular advances in tapestry production.

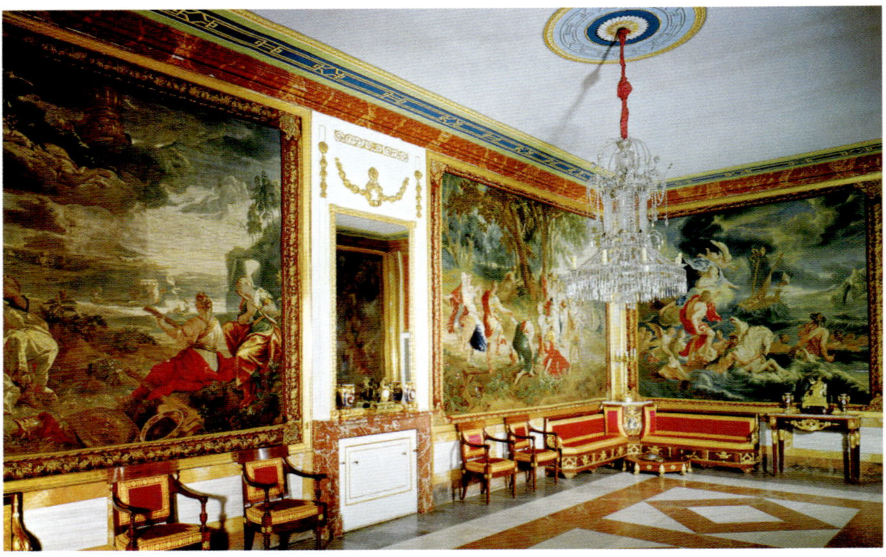

Above: Rubens's tapestries created a sumptuous effect where they were hung, and changed the course of tapestry design.

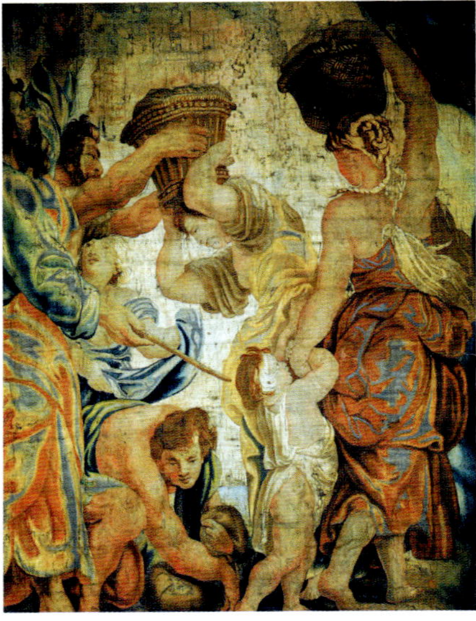

Above: Rubens's tapestry The Fall of Manna *is one of his designs for the Monasterio de las Descalzas Reales in Mardrid.*

In November 1616, Rubens was commissioned by some (currently unidentified) Genoese noblemen to create designs for a series of tapestries on *The History of the Consul Decius Mus.* Publius Decius Mus was a legendary Roman consul who sacrificed himself in the Battle of Vesuvius in 340 BCE, between the Romans and the Samnites. Rubens's lively interpretations of this laid the foundations for more demanding tapestry designs. For each scene, he drew an initial sketch, then painted a modello and then a full-scale cartoon, which served as a reference for weavers to copy as tapestries. After his in-depth research into ancient Roman history for this series, he became inspired to create some of his most important paintings based on similar themes.

CONVENT TAPESTRIES

Soon after the *Decius Mus* tapestry series, the Infanta Isabella commissioned Rubens to design another series of monumental tapestries for the

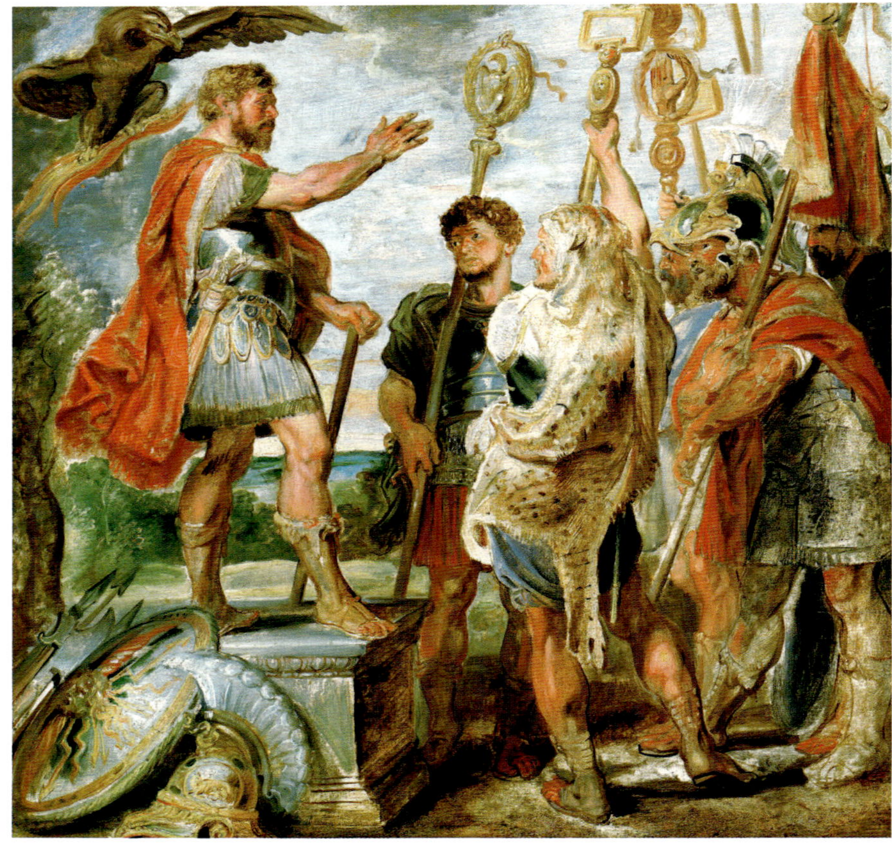

Right: Decius Mus Addressing the Legions, *1616. This is the first in the series of eight tapestry designs created by Rubens.*

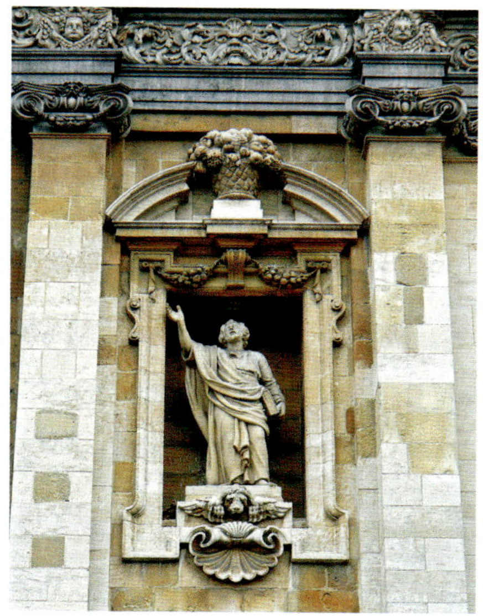

Above: Rubens played an important part in the decoration of the façade and sculpture of Church of Saint Carolus Borromeus.

Monasterio de las Descalzas Reales (Convent of the Barefoot Royals) in Madrid. The convent was founded by Isabella's aunt, Dona Juana of Austria, and became a retreat for females of the Spanish royal family. Each year, the nuns of the convent borrowed tapestries from the Spanish royal collection to decorate their chapel on special feast days, so Isabella's commission provided the nuns with hangings of their own. After Albert's death in 1621, Isabella began wearing the habit of the Convent of the Barefoot Royals, while remaining in Brussels as Governor-general.

Once again, Rubens devised the tapestries far away from their intended location, in his studio in Antwerp. There were 20, and they expressed *The Triumph of the Eucharist*. Projecting Rubens's outstanding powers of invention, the compositions are vivid and dynamic, drawing on a wide range of classical and Christian iconography and traditional allegories of good versus evil. In all, they portray the spiritual victory of the Catholic Church over its enemies. The complex scenes are innovative and comparable to his large-scale paintings, and challenged weavers to create a sense of volume using gradations of different coloured wools and silks. The tapestries were woven in Brussels by two of the most prominent

tapestry workshops, headed by Jan Raes I (1574–1651) and Jacob Geubels II (1599–c.1633).

In 1622, while Rubens was in Paris discussing a commission for Marie de' Medici, he was also commissioned to produce a third series of tapestry designs. The patron was probably Louis XIII (1601–43), although this has not been verified. Depicting the life of the first Christian emperor of ancient Rome, Constantine I, Rubens's dynamic designs were made into tapestries in Paris at the workshop of Marc Comans (1563–1644) and François de la Planche (1573–1627).

ARCHITECTURAL DESIGNS

Rubens's architectural appreciation is apparent in many of his paintings, but he also designed altar frames and statues, including the façade and high altar of the Saint Carolus Borromeus church, and, of course, much of his own home in Antwerp. Inspired by the elegant Mantuan homes of Mantegna and Romano just as much as by Genoese architecture and classical

PALAZZI DI GENOVA

In 1622, Rubens published *Palazzi di Genova*, his collection of 72 plates of engravings of 'plans, façades and cross-sections' based on his drawings of Genoese architecture. As a direct result, the Genoese style of architecture became popular in northern Europe.

antiquity, he created several *trompe l'oeil* ('fool the eye') paintings that seem like additional architectural and sculptural details on certain walls. For instance, on the façade of his studio, what appeared to be low sculptural reliefs were actually *trompe l'oeil* depictions painted in grisaille, a technique using monochrome pigments to imitate the effects of stone. He even added what looks like one of his paintings stretched out to dry – as a joke.

Below: Temple of Janus, Rubens, 1630s. This dynamic, detailed and lavish image demonstrates Rubens's clear understanding and appreciation of architecture.

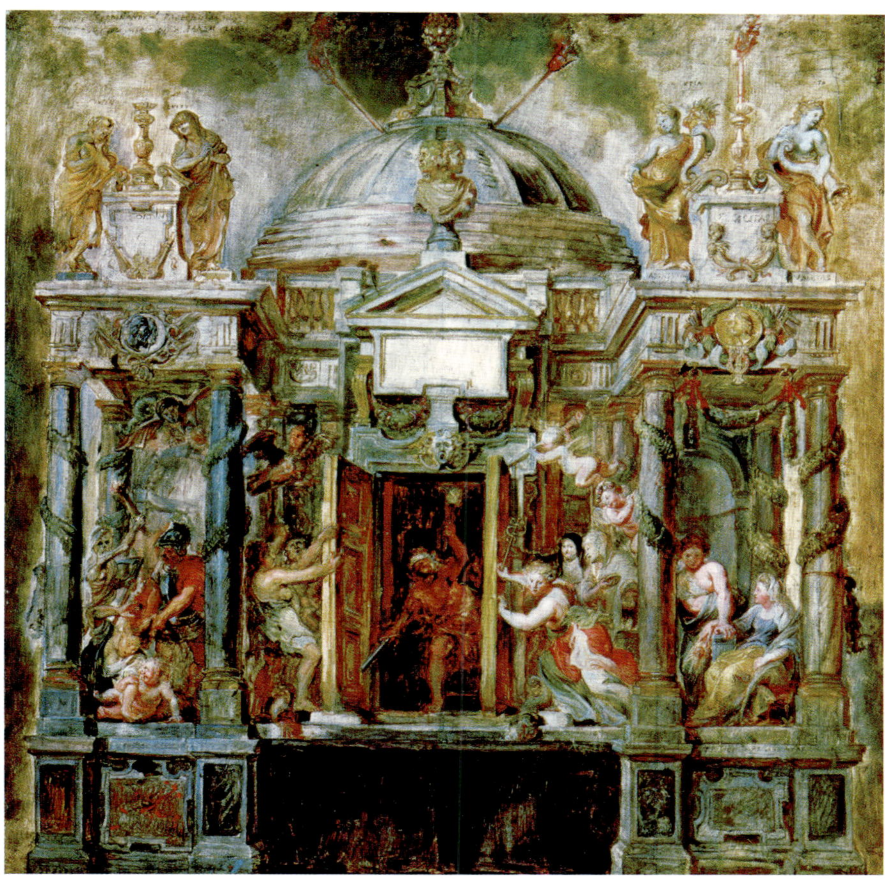

CEILING PAINTINGS

'I confess that I am, by natural instinct, better fitted to execute very large works than small curiosities,' wrote Rubens in 1621. He was referring to a huge commission for ceiling paintings that King James I of England was intending to give him. Throughout his life, he preferred monumental commissions to small-scale works.

Rubens had a thorough understanding and appreciation of architecture. In 1615, building had commenced on the Antwerp Jesuit Church, and six years later it was dedicated to St Ignatius Loyola, founder of the Society of Jesus, in anticipation of his canonization in 1622. Designed by François d'Aguilon (1567–1617) and Pieter Huyssens (1577–1637), both Flemish Jesuits and architects, the building also includes elements designed by Rubens, including sculpture for the façade, the marble high altar and all the decoration of the Lady Chapel.

On March 29, 1620, Rubens had also signed a contract for an even greater undertaking in the church, his largest decorative cycle yet. With the help of assistants, he was to provide, in less than a year, 39 large ceiling paintings. Despite his students' considerable contribution, he conceived, planned and organized the whole series by himself. Unfortunately, a fire destroyed much of it in 1718, although some sketches for it remain.

WHITEHALL CEILING

In 1629, eight years after it had first been discussed and four years after James I's death, his son Charles I commissioned Rubens to decorate the ceiling of Whitehall in London. After King James had originally suggested the project, it had been stalled for various reasons. But when Rubens was in England on a diplomatic mission for King Philip of Spain, Charles I commissioned him. Undaunted by the immense scale of the project, Rubens wrote: 'Everyone according to his gifts. My talent is such that no undertaking, however vast in size or diversified in subject, has ever surpassed my courage.'

After discussing the commission in England, he returned to Antwerp and painted the canvases there. In October 1635 they were shipped to London, and by March 1636 they were in place. Rubens never saw them in their intended location, and he had to wait two years to be paid the £3,000 he was owed for them (at a time when

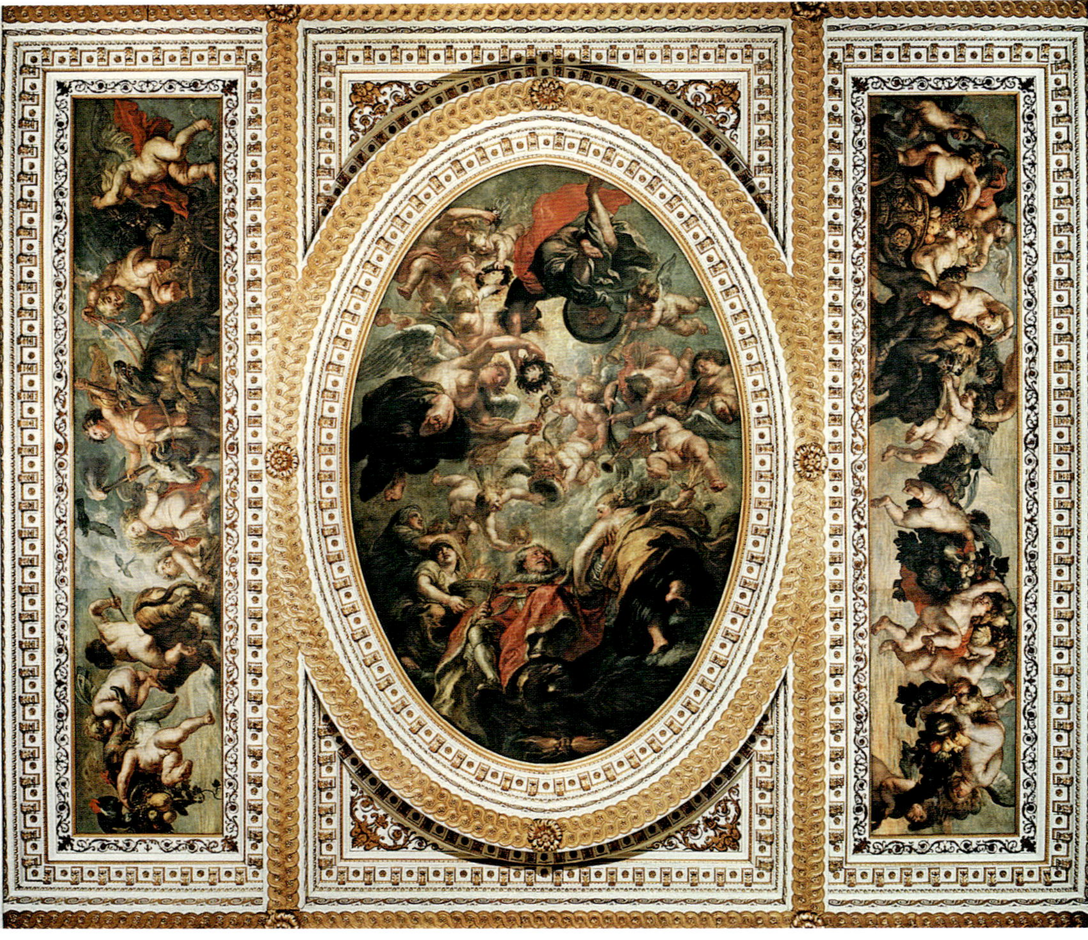

Left: Whitehall Ceiling: The Apotheosis of James I, *Rubens, commissioned in c.1621 and c.1629, completed in c.1632–34. These paintings ensured that the English king was perceived as having sophisticated artistic tastes.*

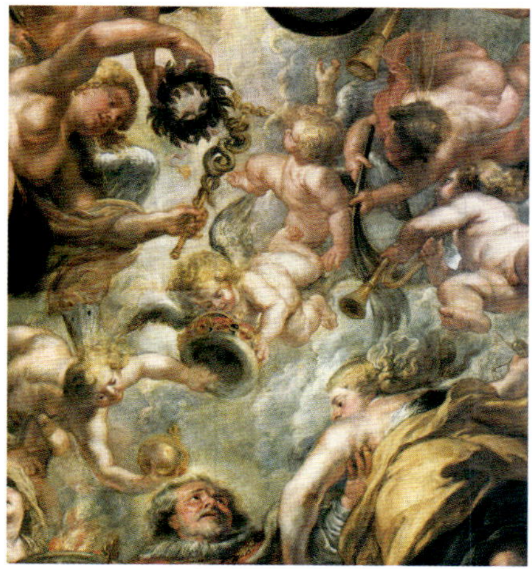 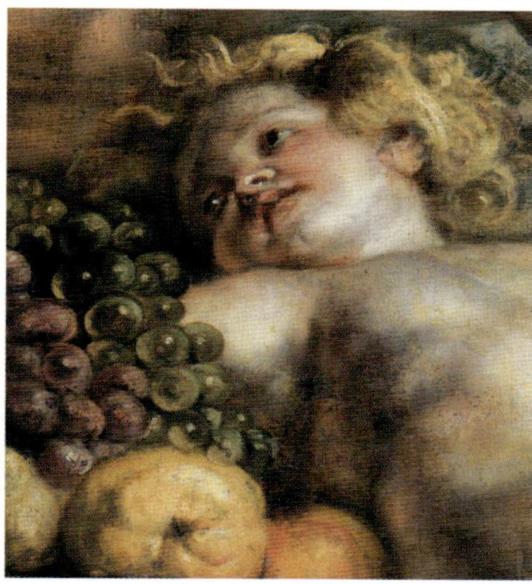

Above: The three main Whitehall ceiling paintings depict The Union of the Crowns, The Apotheosis of James I *and* The Peaceful Reign of James I. *Commissioned by Charles I to honour his father, these images show (from left to right) details of* The Union of the Crowns, *or* The Union of England and Scotland, *and a cherub carrying luscious ripe fruit, which represents the 'peace and plenty' of King James's reign.*

servants earned approximately £3–5 per year). Although the king was delighted with the paintings, tragically they were one of his last sights before he was executed on a scaffold outside Whitehall in 1649.

Initially, however, there was a problem. When the paintings arrived at Whitehall, the illustrious architect

Below: The Sacrifice of Isaac, *sketch for ceiling in the Jesuit Church, Rubens, 1620–21. Foreshortening is used to prominent effect as this work was viewed from below.*

Inigo Jones (1573–1652) discovered that their dimensions were incorrect. Although both Belgium and England measured in feet and inches, each country used a different length for a foot, and drastic and judicious moderations had to be made in order to make them fit.

Even so, the vast works demonstrate Rubens's great powers of invention and organization. The three main canvases adorning the enormous Banqueting Hall glorify the life and times of James I, and also exalt King Charles's birth.

CHARLES I AND RUBENS

In 1629, Charles I had dispatched his warship *Adventure* to Brabant to meet and convey Rubens safely to England. The king also went to Greenwich to greet Rubens on his arrival. These were huge honours, and indicated the high esteem with which Rubens was held. Charles and Rubens had already met in Madrid in 1623, when Charles (then the Prince of Wales) had commissioned Rubens to paint his portrait and a self-portrait. Ultimately, largely through Rubens's magnificent Whitehall paintings, Charles I became renowned as a discerning patron of the arts. However, his plans of convincing Rubens to remain in England as his court painter were dashed when, nine months after his arrival, Rubens returned to Antwerp.

The Union of Crowns celebrates the joining of the Scottish and English crowns on James's ascension to the English throne in 1603. *The Apotheosis of James I* expresses the notion held by both James and Charles of the 'Divine Right of Kings', and *The Peaceful Reign of James I* honours King James's reign.

Below: Charles I in Three Positions, *Van Dyck, 1635. Depicted with a less painterly approach than is usual with Van Dyck, this noble portrait of King Charles I is richly coloured, demonstrating Rubens's influence.*

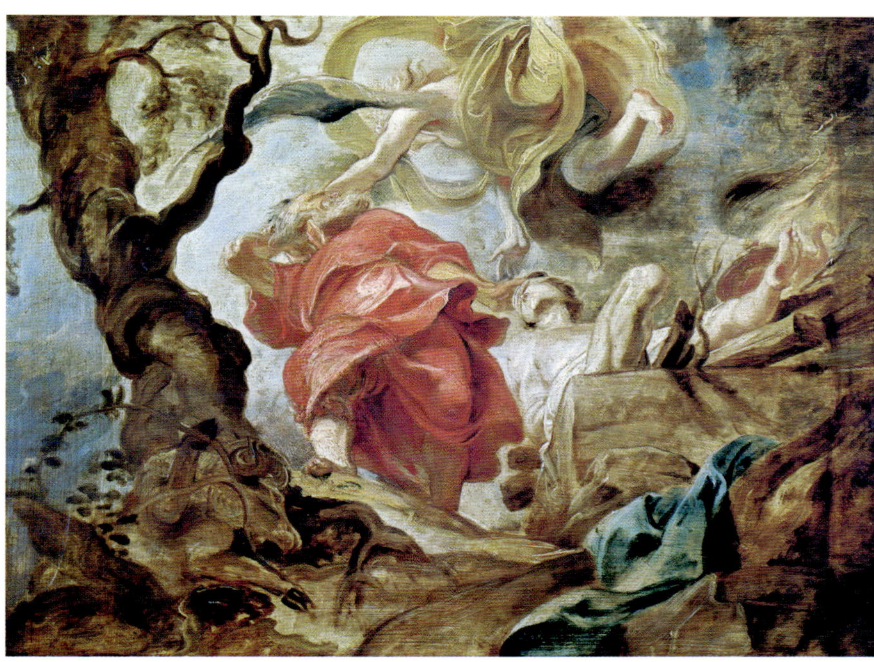

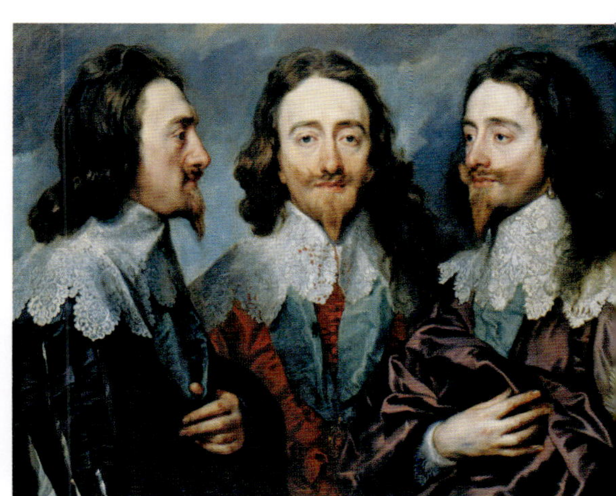

CONFIDENTIAL AGENT

The Twelve Years' Truce expired in April 1621, and Archduke Albert died three months later. As his and Isabella's marriage was childless, control of the Habsburg Netherlands adhered to the wishes of Philip II, and reverted to the charge of the Spanish sovereign.

At the end of March 1621, just before the Twelve Years' Truce ended, Philip III of Spain had died, leaving his rather ineffectual teenage son Philip IV as king. Four years later, the Duke of Lerma, Philip III's favourite who had been particularly supportive of Rubens, also died, leaving Philip IV, now 20 years old, to promote his own favourite, Gaspar de Guzmán, Count of Olivares (1587–1645) to the position of Prime Minister. Obsessed with gaining power for himself and Spain, Olivares tried to enforce national unity across the Spanish-controlled world, which eventually provoked rebellion and ultimately his own downfall. All these events had significant consequences on Spain and the Spanish Netherlands, and on Rubens.

SEARCH FOR PEACE

Rubens was not against Olivares's ambitions. He simply wanted peace and independence for his own country, and the Infanta Isabella fought assiduously for the same thing. In 1623, she engaged Rubens as her confidential agent to assist her efforts to try to end the war.

By that time, Rubens's fame as an artist meant that he was able to travel freely, and he was welcomed in royal courts everywhere to paint for monarchs and their ministers. While sitting for their portraits, these important figures were charmed and encouraged by his beguiling personality, and they frequently if discreetly discussed matters of state with him. In addition, Rubens paid close attention to what was happening around him, and his astuteness and intelligence meant that his diplomatic services became extremely valuable to the Spanish Habsburg rulers. He regularly advised Isabella, who added a monthly allowance for his strategic assignments on top of his court painter's salary. The two jobs constantly overlapped. For example, in 1622 he was called to Paris by Marie de' Medici to undertake a huge commission for her (see pages 72–3). While there, he was involved in secret meetings and other information-gathering activities for Isabella.

HELPFUL FRIENDS

One of his good friends, Ambrogio Spinola (1569–1630), a Genoese aristocrat who served as a Spanish general, expressed the impressiveness of Rubens's diplomatic skills when he said: 'of all his talents, painting is the least'. Anther good friend, Nicolas-Claude Fabri de Peiresc (1580–1637), a French astronomer, intellectual, collector and politician, helped him with his diplomatic missions. Highly respected, Peiresc had connections across Europe and beyond, his broad range of interests attracting friends and acquaintances from many different areas, enabling him to introduce Rubens to some of the most important people of the day.

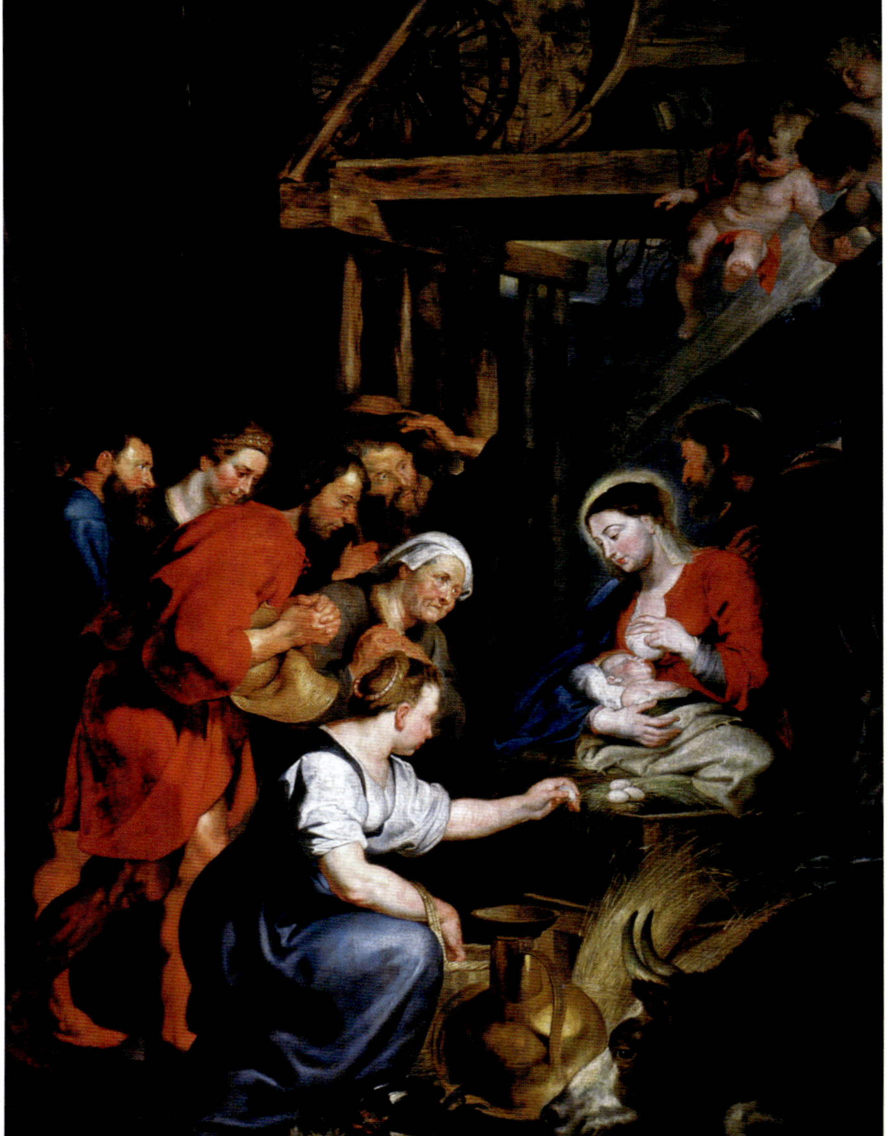

Left: Adoration of the Shepherds, *Rubens, 1620. One of several versions of this biblical story, Rubens depicts Mary wearing deep red and holding the baby, which was unconventional and naturalistic.*

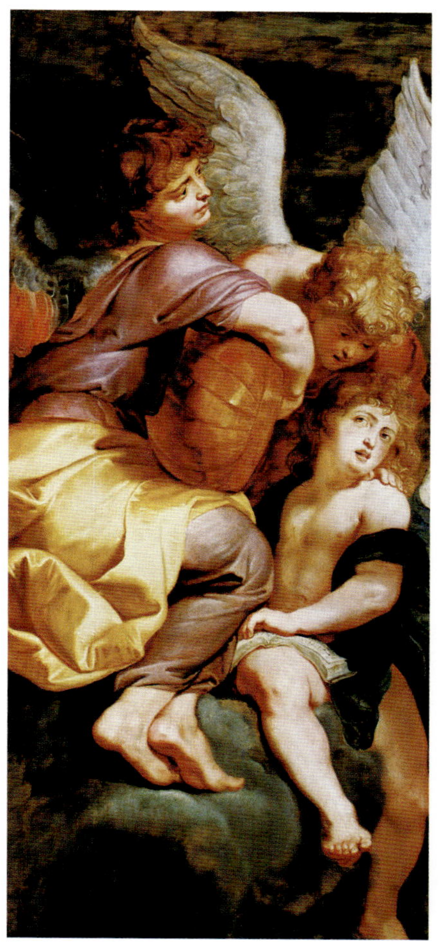

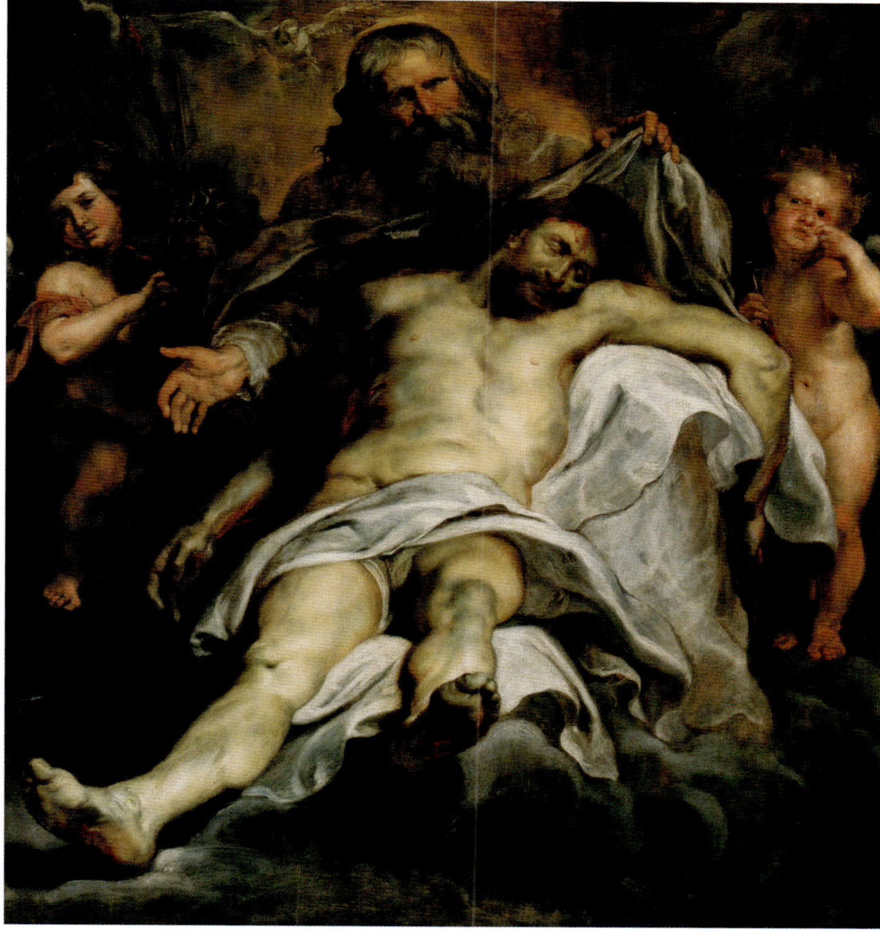

RECEIVED AS A GENTLEMAN

Contradicting the widespread opinion that those who worked with their hands were common labourers, Rubens was received as a gentleman across Europe. Between 1627 and 1630, his diplomatic career was particularly active. He spent eight months in Spain from 1628 to 1629, where he negotiated for peace between Spain and England and executed several important works for Philip IV and other

Above left: Three Angels Making Music, *Rubens, 1620. This was probably painted as part of an unfinished project for an alterpiece representing the Coronation of the Virgin for Antwerp Cathedral.*

Above: The Holy Trinity, 1620. At this time, Rubens's style softened and became more painterly and expressive.

private Spanish patrons. In 1629, Philip IV sent him to Charles I in England, and it is largely through Rubens's personal efforts that the peace treaty of 1630 between England and Spain can be attributed. While in Spain, he also befriended Philip's court painter, Diego Velázquez (1599–1660). They planned to travel to Italy together the following year, but in the event Rubens returned to Antwerp and Velázquez made the journey without him.

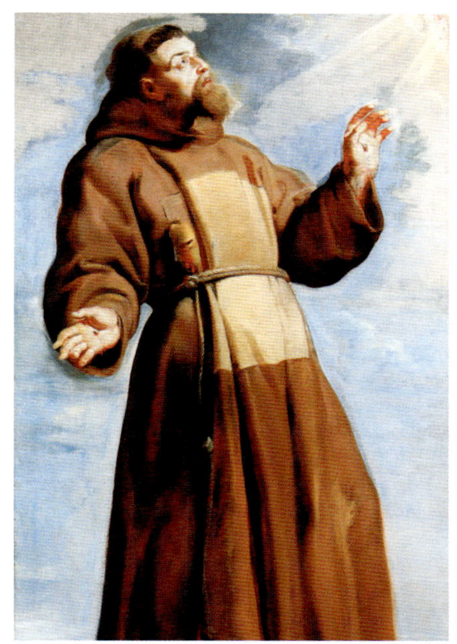

Left: Saint Francis, *1620. At this time, Rubens was earning a substantial amount from his depictions of saints.*

THIRTY YEARS' WAR

Even before the Truce was over, from 1618 fighting resumed, and later became called the Thirty Years' War. Affecting most of Europe, it began when the future Holy Roman Emperor, Ferdinand II, attempted to impose Roman Catholic absolutism on his domains, and it became a Europe-wide conflict between the Habsburg Catholics and Protestants, fuelled by political ambitions, as religious beliefs were significant to those who ruled. The war ended in 1648 with the Treaty of Westphalia, and Spain finally recognized Dutch independence.

THE MEDICI CYCLE

Early in 1622, Rubens was summoned to Paris by Marie de' Medici, now the widow of Henri IV and mother of the king of France, Louis XIII. Marie, whose wedding by proxy Rubens had attended in Florence in 1600, commissioned him to paint a large number of paintings for two galleries in the Palace of Luxembourg.

Lodging near the Pont Neuf on the Quai Saint-Germain l'Auxerrois, Rubens spent six weeks in Paris discussing a new commission. Marie's advisor, Claude Maugis, Abbé de Saint-Ambroise (1600–58) led the negotiations and enthusiastically supported Rubens's ability to accomplish the enormous task. He declared that 'two painters of Italy could not carry out in ten years what Rubens would do in four'. Originally intended to be a brief sojourn, Rubens's stay in Paris extended as he continued his diplomatic activities, discussed the king's tapestry cycle, *The Life of Constantine I*, and painted portraits of Marie and Louis XIII's wife, Anne of Austria.

INNOVATIVE AND MONUMENTAL

The first cycle of paintings for Marie was to be dedicated to her eventful life and decorate the gallery of her newly

Right: Marie de' Medici, Rubens, 1622, a member of the powerful House of Medici. Following the assassination of her husband in 1610, Marie acted as regent for her son the day after her coronation.

Below: Luxembourg Palace and Gardens. On the positive recommendation of her sister, Marie de' Medici called Rubens to her French palace where she commissioned him on a grand scale.

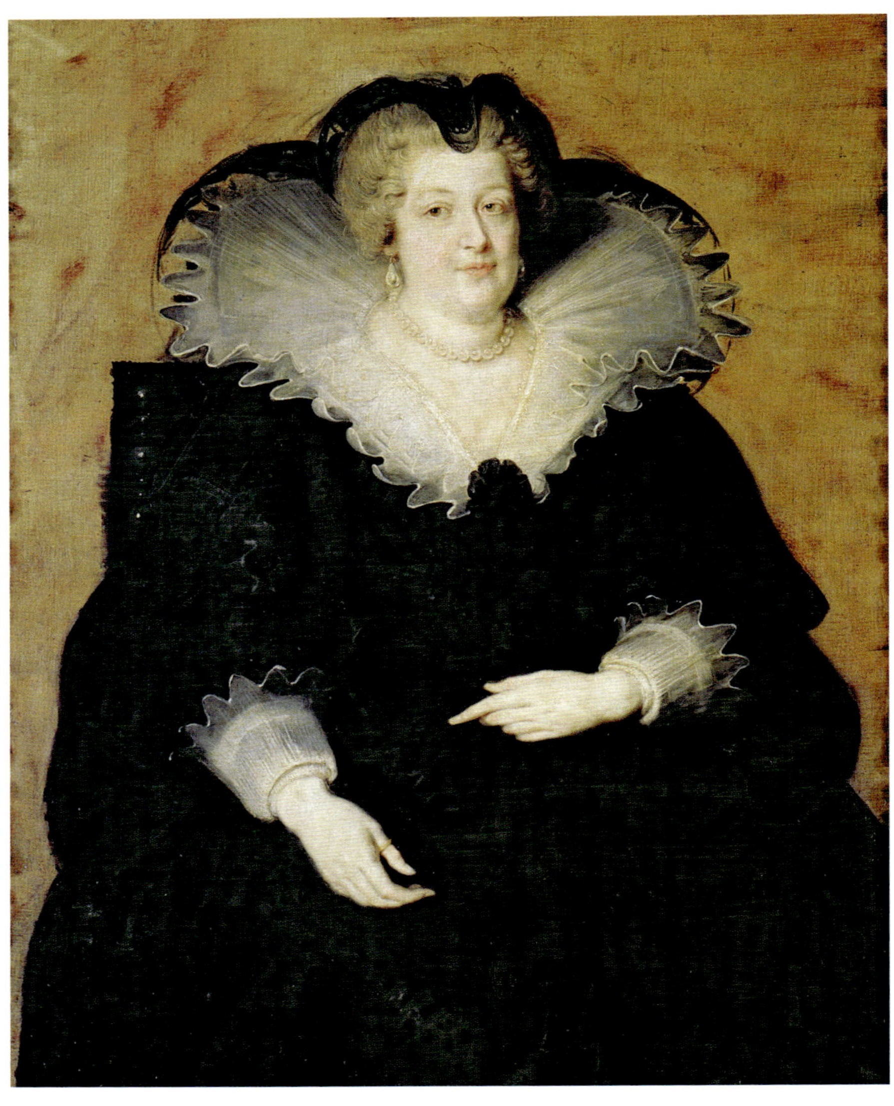

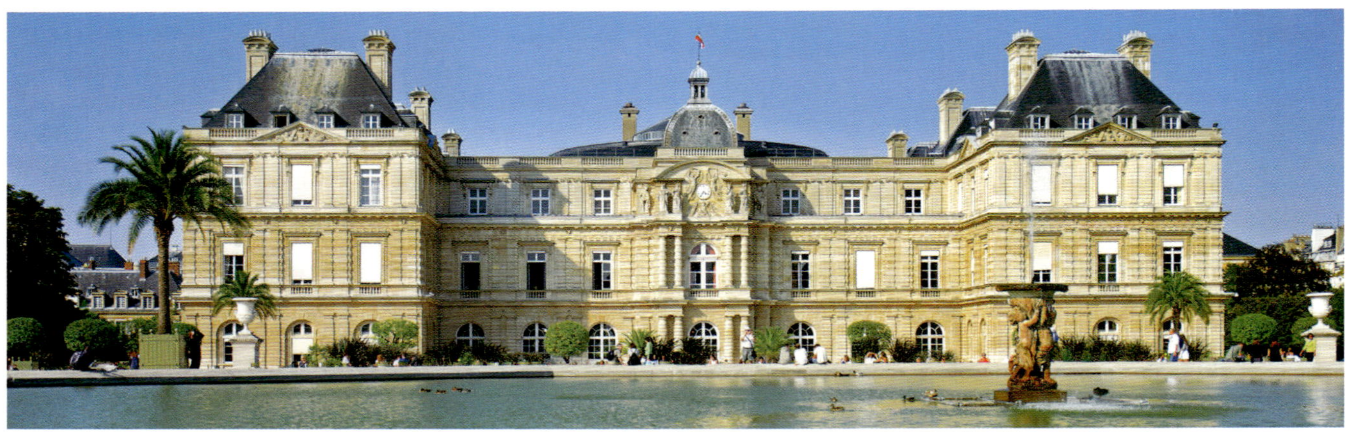

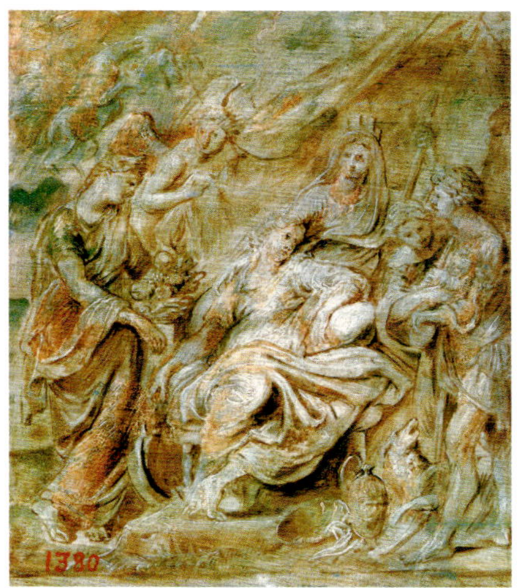

built Luxembourg Palace. Composed of three portraits – Marie; her father Francesco I Grand Duke of Tuscany; and her mother Joanna of Austria – plus 21 narrative scenes, the work became one of Rubens's most celebrated masterpieces, highly innovative for its style, content and scale.

The contract stated that the first 24 paintings were to be completed within two years, to coincide with the marriage of Marie's daughter, Princess Henrietta Maria, to Charles, the heir to the throne of England. (In the event, they married and he ascended the throne of England in the same year, 1625.) This first series was to depict Marie's 'heroic deeds,' or the struggles and triumphs she had experienced in her life. So Rubens included images of her childhood in Italy, her marriage and coronation, her husband's assassination, and the disagreement and reconciliation with her son Louis XIII.

Rubens not only had to conform to extravagant spatial requirements, but he also had to introduce the controversial images into a tense and troubled political situation. Not wishing to offend the French, he romanticized the truth with elaborate, mythological allusions, symbols and religious metaphors. For both cycles, he was to receive 20,000 crowns – at the time, a qualified knight earned approximately 200 crowns a year.

Right: The Birth of Marie de' Medici. *Here, Rubens depicts the birth of the woman who became noted for her political intrigues at the French court.*

Left: Birth of the Dauphin, *1622. Rubens was commissioned to portray important moments in the queen's life. This is his sketch for the birth of her first son, Louis.*

THE FINEST PAINTER OF WOMEN

Marie had chosen Rubens to undertake the project partly because she knew of and admired his work, partly because her sister Eleonora, the Duchess of Mantua, had recommended him, and partly because in his wall and ceiling decorations he followed the approaches of some of the most revered Italian artists, including Michelangelo, Tintoretto and Veronese. As a Florentine, Marie favoured the Italian style of painting. Furthermore, Rubens was celebrated across Europe as the finest painter of women since Titian.

Rubens returned to Antwerp and worked on the first cycle of paintings for two years. In 1625, he was back in Paris, installing the paintings in the west gallery of the Palace of Luxembourg. His contract also asserted that he was to paint all the figures, which meant that his assistants could complete the backgrounds and other details, but when the canvases were being installed, he spent a lot of time improving areas that he had not painted.

RICHELIEU'S OPPOSITION

Apart from the challenges of the work, the commission was fraught with problems. Marie was difficult and capricious, and her principal advisor, Cardinal Richelieu (1585–1642), saw Rubens as a political threat. The second cycle was intended to celebrate the life of Henri IV, featuring scenes from his military career, but it was never finished. First, the gallery was not completed until the summer of 1629, and second, Marie was banished from Paris in 1631, while Richelieu became the king's principal advisor. Because he opposed Rubens's peace missions between Spain and England, Richelieu tried to replace him with another artist, but in the end the project was simply abandoned.

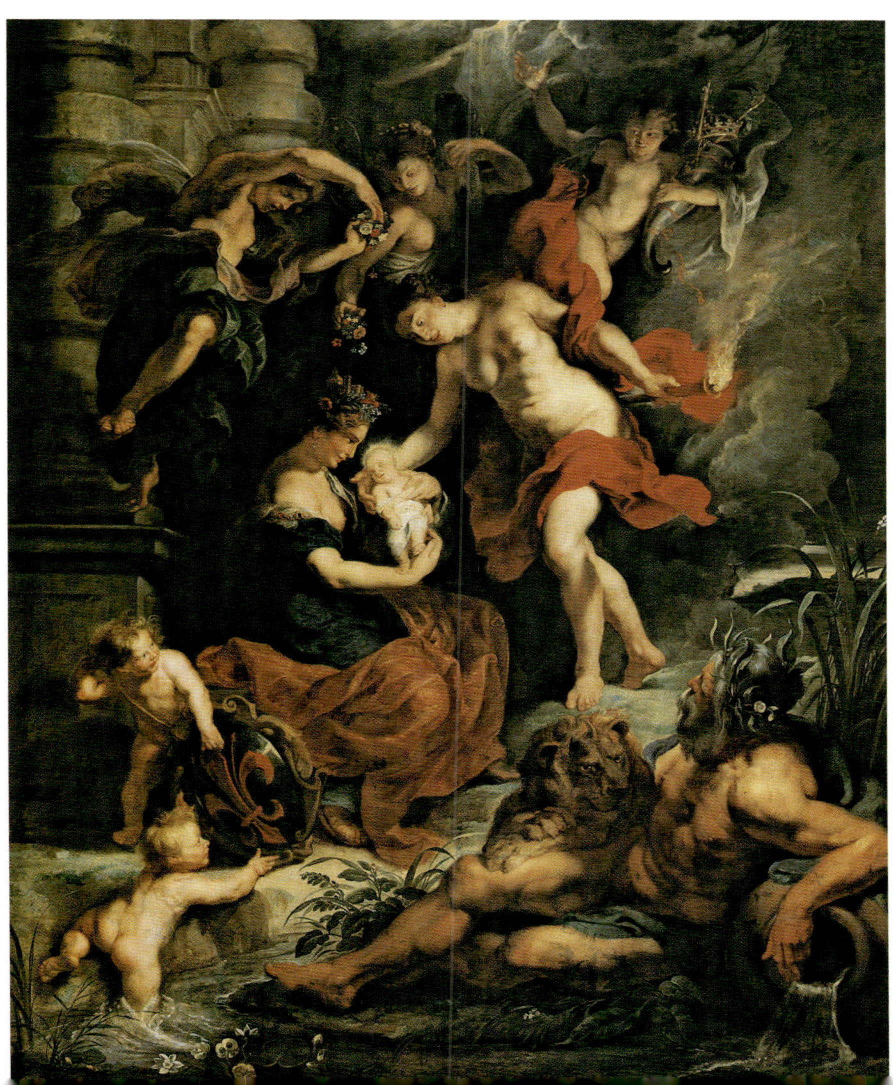

PAINTER OF PRINCES

Although in 1609 Rubens had accepted his appointment to become court painter to Albert and Isabella, surprisingly they commissioned only a few portraits. This was not through a lack of admiration for his work, however; in common with most other European rulers, they held Rubens in extremely high regard.

Rubens's special position as both painter and diplomat brought him numerous commissions from royalty and high-ranking statesmen. In 1621, after both her husband Albert and brother Philip III had died, Isabella gave him one of his most demanding commissions to date: the tapestry designs for the Monasterio de las Descalzas. By then, he was also working as her most trusted counsellor, advising her either in person, or in long letters written while he was away on diplomatic missions. For this unceasing devotion to his aunt, in 1624 Philip IV granted him a patent of nobility. In support of Rubens for the accolade, the Bishop of Segovia, Iñigo de Brizuela

and Arteaga (1599–1629) wrote to Philip: 'Many sovereigns have tried to induce him to leave Antwerp by promises of great honours and large sums of money. He . . . unites to his rare talent as a painter, literary gifts and a knowledge of history and languages; he has always lived in great style and has the means of supporting his rank.' In 1627, Isabella advanced him even further, promoting him from court painter to 'gentleman of the household of Her Most Serene Highness'.

Rubens's discretion, linguistic abilities, gentlemanly demeanour, insight and charm made even august members of European royal families feel comfortable in his presence. They visited his house

to sit for him, admire his art collection, observe the activities of his studio and buy his paintings. The large garden at the back of his house was also excellent for

Below left: Portrait of Don Rodrigo Caldéron on Horseback, *Rubens, c.1612–15. This equestrian portrait is of one of the Duke of Lerma's favourite ministers. At this time, Rubens was sought after internationally for his portraits.*

Below: Portrait of Louis XIII, King of France, *Rubens, c.1622–25. After becoming king at the age of nine, Louis was dominated by others throughout his reign, but became one of the most powerful rulers in Europe.*

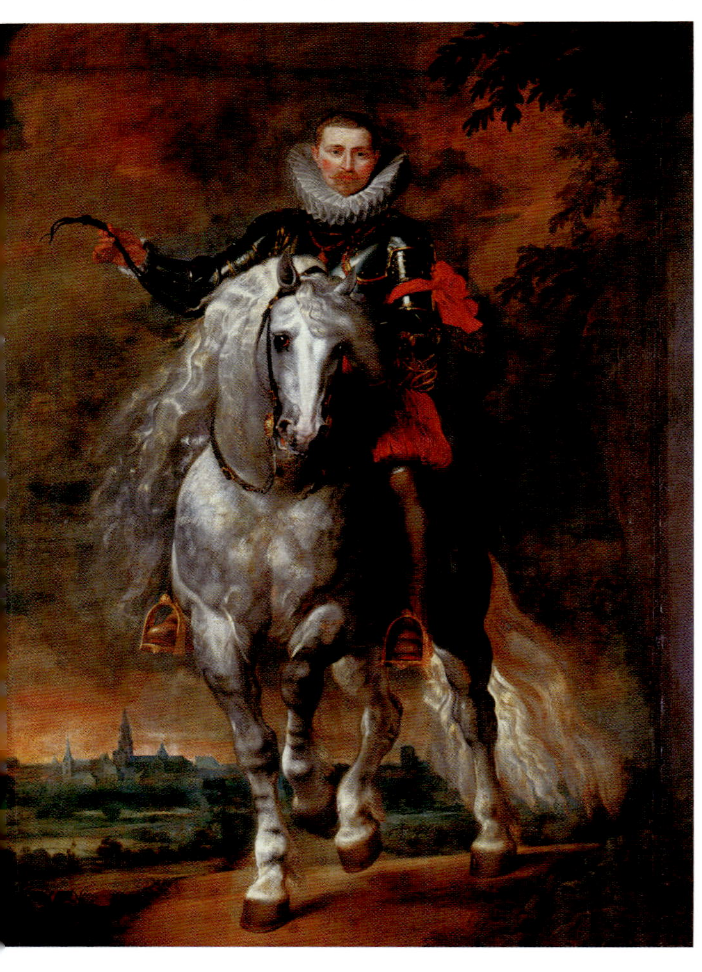

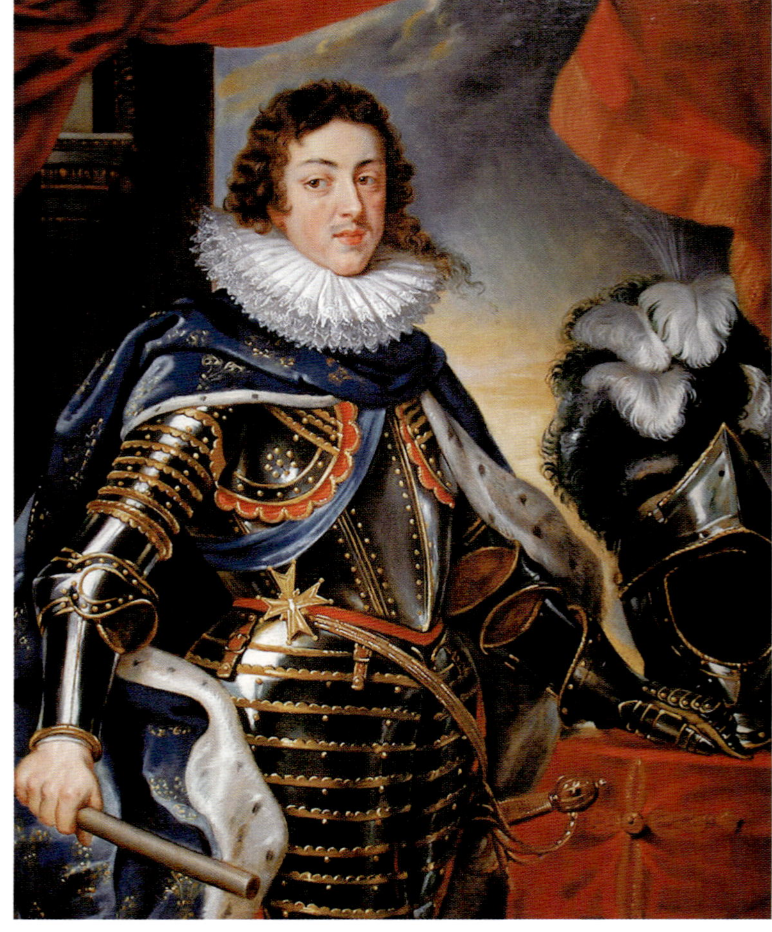

THE DUKE OF BUCKINGHAM

Some of Rubens's portrait commissions were for high-ranking individuals who were often close to the monarch they served. Rubens met George Villiers, 1st Duke of Buckingham (1592–1628) in Paris in 1625. A favourite of King Charles I and a major art collector, Buckingham commissioned Rubens to paint him in a grand equestrian portrait. The elegance and bravura of this work later inspired writer Alexander Dumas (1802–70) in *The Three Musketeers* in 1844. Privately, however, Rubens noted Buckingham's 'arrogance and caprice' and predicted that he was 'heading for the precipice.' By 1628, Buckingham had become resented for his unsuccessful military campaigns against Spain and France, and was assassinated by a discontented army officer.

Right: Equestrian Portrait of Philip IV, *c.1645. Rubens became known not only for his skills with a brush, but also for his discretion, lively conversation and ability to mix comfortably with kings.*

In a letter to Peiresc, Rubens wrote of the most significant of these: '. . . Already I have done an equestrian portrait of His Majesty to his great pleasure and satisfaction. He really takes an extreme delight in painting . . . I know him already by personal contact, for since I have rooms in the palace, he comes to see me almost every day. I have also done the heads of all the royal family.' The portrait was displayed in the prestigious Royal Alcázar Palace, where it was probably destroyed in a fire of 1734. It is known today from a copy by Juan Bautista Martinez del Mazo (c.1612–67) and possibly Velázquez, and shows the king performing the levade – a classical dressage movement, with several religious figures symbolizing his role as the defender of the True Faith.

private conversations, where delicate political matters could be discussed, and his closeness to the Habsburg rulers made him useful to many.

PORTRAITS OF KINGS

While in Paris working on the Medici cycle, Rubens also painted portraits of the French royal family. Louis XIII had begun his reign as a child of nine, with his dominating mother acting as regent. Even when he came of age, he was bullied by his ministers and never learned to rule his kingdom effectively. Yet in his portrait of the young French king, Rubens portrayed attributes of strength and valour.

Until Rubens's diplomatic visit to Madrid from 1628–29, only Velázquez, Philip IV's court painter, had been permitted to paint the Spanish sovereign. Yet Philip commissioned Rubens to paint five portraits of him.

Right: Equestrian Portrait of the Duke of Buckingham, *1625. This is the sketch for the grand equestrian portrait that George Villiers, 1st Duke of Buckingham, commissioned Rubens to paint.*

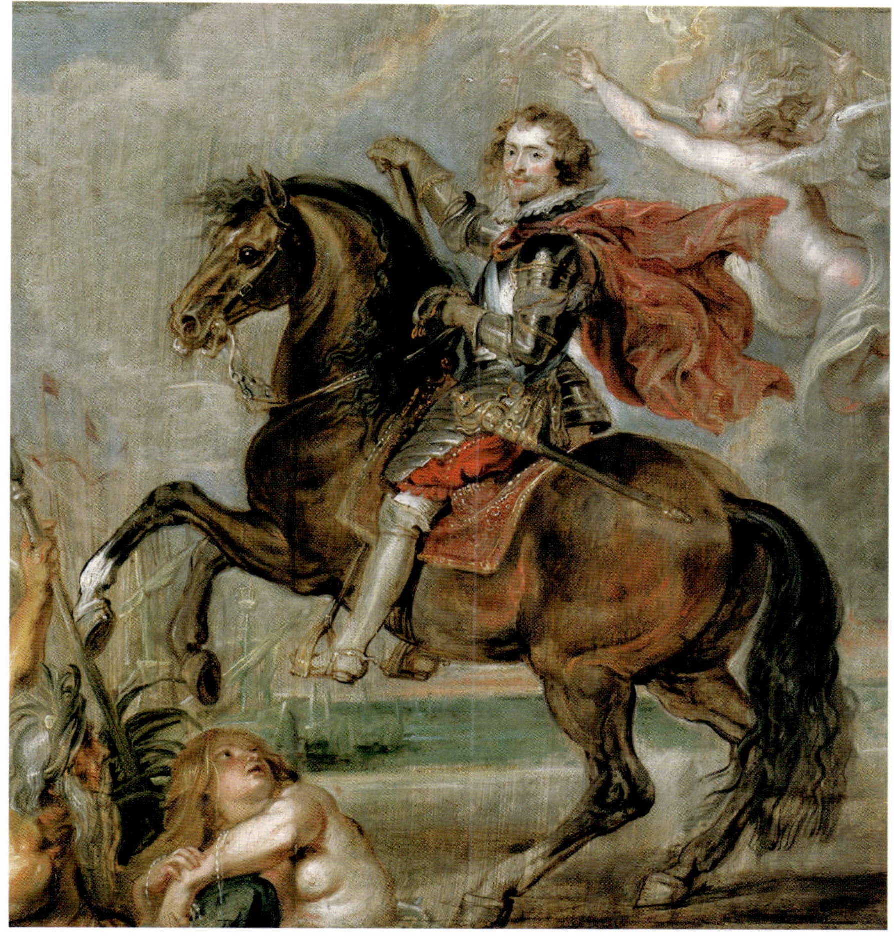

IMPORTANT ALTARPIECES

Although Rubens complained that he was the 'busiest and most harassed man in the world', he continued to accept important commissions, particularly monumental and challenging altarpieces. Through these works, he augmented the power of sacred art, and became known throughout Europe as a 'Catholic painter.'

By now, renowned as 'the most famous [painter] in Europe', Rubens was commissioned by the most important religious orders as well as royalty and the aristocracy. Among his most powerful ecclesiastical patrons were the Jesuits in Antwerp, who commissioned altarpieces depicting the miraculous deeds of two of their pre-eminent members – Ignatius of Loyola and Francis Xavier – shortly before both were canonized. *The Miracles of Saint Ignatius of Loyola* and *The Miracles of Saint Francis Xavier* extol Jesuit missionary work, and convincingly portray both saints' abilities to perform miracles.

Many of Rubens's altarpieces reference and adapt the poses of classical sculptures. In this way, he turned mythological figures into Christian saints and martyrs, captivating worshippers and inspiring all who saw them, and so meeting the criteria decreed at the Council of Trent.

GLORIFYING CATHOLICISM

In 1623, Rubens was commissioned to create an altarpiece for Freising Cathedral in Bavaria, which he completed the following year. Like many of his altarpieces, the work, *The Virgin as the Woman of the Apocalypse* (see page 212), served both religious and political functions. Portraying a victory achieved by the archangel Michael which was blessed by the Virgin and Child, it simultaneously exalts a Catholic triumph over Protestants in Bohemia in 1620. With its dramatic, twisting composition, vibrant colours and figures that suggest pagan deities and classical heroes, the image helped to stimulate the notion of Catholic superiority over Protestantism. As well as his references to antique

Left: Adoration of the Magi, *1624. With so much happening in this work, it becomes apparent why Rubens was one of the most sought-after artists in the world during his life. Few other artists could paint such crowded compositions with this skill.*

Below: Christ as Redeemer, *Rubens, 1624. This is softly painted, passionate and bathed in what appears to be a divine light.*

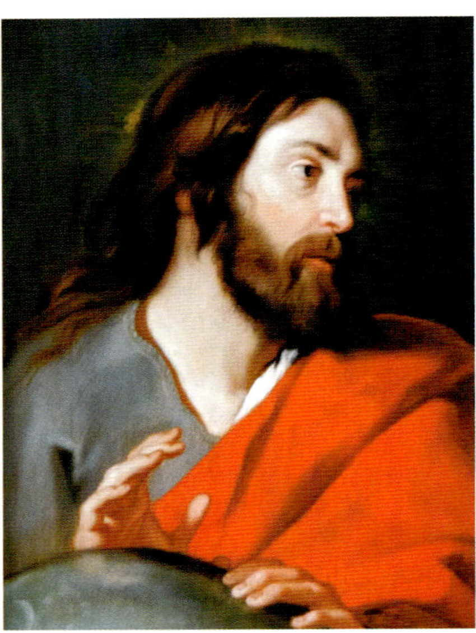

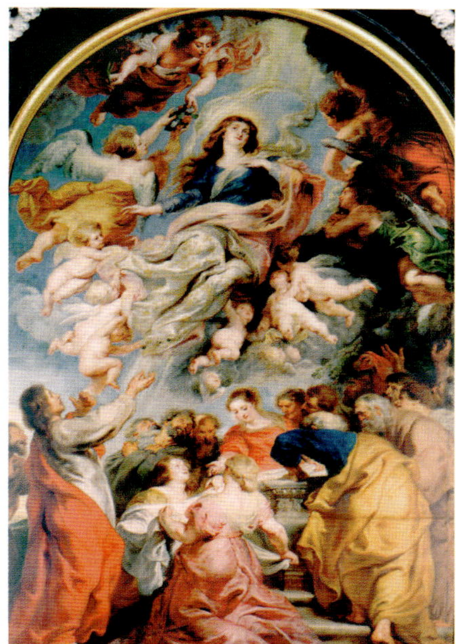

statuary, Rubens's rich painterly technique also incorporates elements of Venetian art, specifically the colour and brushwork of artists including Titian, Tintoretto and Veronese, and also the composition and lighting of Caravaggio. However, his interpretation and synthesis of all these elements are unique and original.

A SENSE OF WONDER

Rubens's blend of rich colour, serpentine figures and dramatic compositions created a unique visual and universally understood language. His violence, passion and dynamism demanded attention and helped to invigorate Catholic beliefs, inspiring a sense of wonder. The two altarpieces he painted when he first returned to Antwerp in 1610–14 – the triptychs of *The Raising of the Cross* and *Descent from the Cross* – initiated his popularity in painting Catholic images. In 1611–12, shortly after completing *The Raising of the Cross*, and at the same time as he was painting the centre panel of *Descent from the Cross*, he also painted the *Moretus* triptych. Martina Plantin (1550–1616), widow of the printer Jan Moretus (1543–1610) of the Plantin Press, commissioned this.

Right: Almost shockingly, Christ's body falls forward from the cross – seen clearly here in this detail from Descent from the Cross *by Rubens in c.1612.*

Left: Rubens's The Assumption of the Virgin *in Antwerp Cathedral is imposing, dramatic and compelling – ideal for the Counter-Reformation.*

It shows Christ leaving his rocky tomb with stunned soldiers watching in the shadows. The panels show John the Baptist, Jan Moretus's patron saint, and Saint Martina, the patron saint of Moretus's widow.

Rubens's output of altarpieces was astonishing. Among many others, in 1624 he painted *Adoration of the Magi* for Saint Michael's Abbey in Antwerp, and designed three accompanying monumental sculptures. In 1626, he completed *The Assumption of the Virgin* for the marble high altar of Antwerp Cathedral – a commission he had won in a competition eight years earlier. In the lively work, a choir of angels lifts Mary in a spiralling motion, while the apostles gather around her tomb below.

DEPICTING LOCAL SAINTS

To augment the sense of pride inspired by his religious works, Rubens was often commissioned by priests and brothers to depict local saints in their churches. For example, his monumental *The Martyrdom of Saint Livinus*, 1633, was commissioned by Jesuits in Ghent, to decorate their high altar. According to the legend, Livinus, the Scottish bishop of Ghent, had his tongue torn out. Rubens's depiction of this is gory and vivid. Strong gestures, rhythmical brushstrokes, shimmering light and a vivid palette enhance the shocking realism of the painting. These images of local saints helped to inspire sentimentality and pride within the parish.

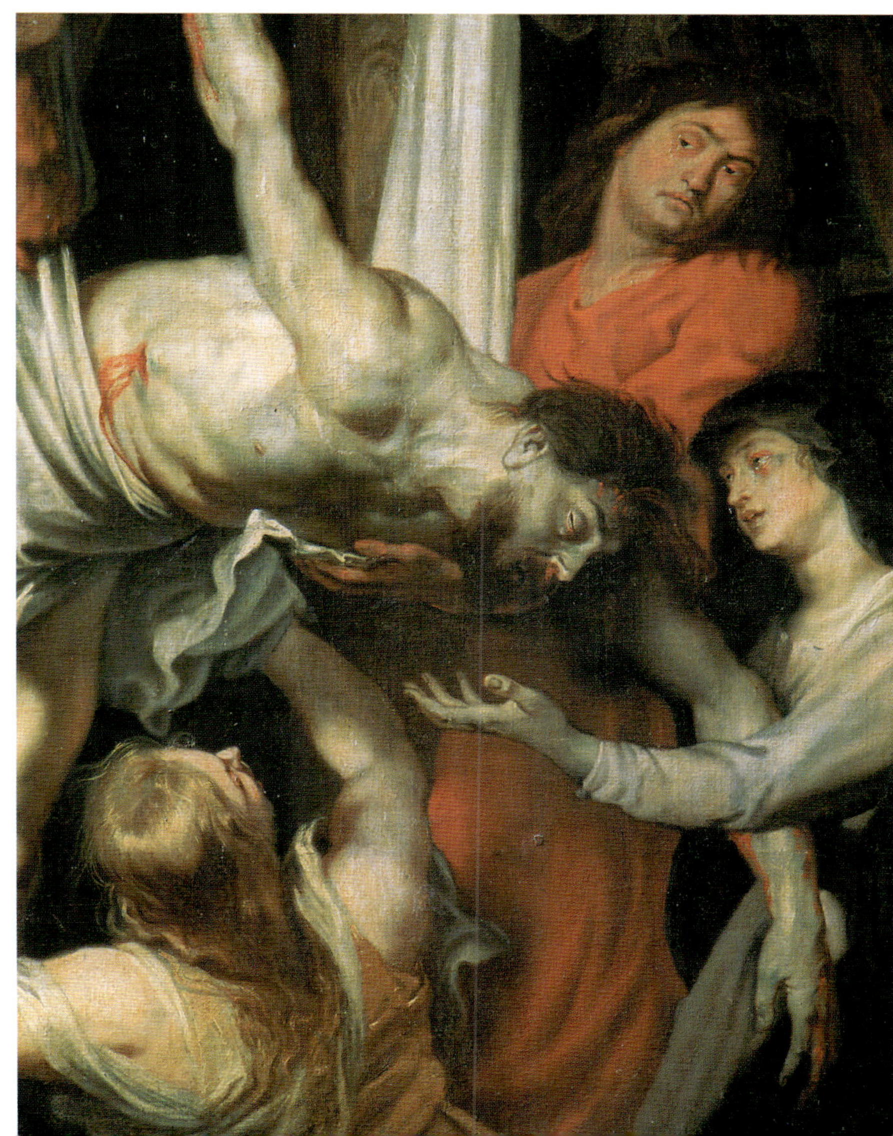

PORTRAITURE

Despite being one of the greatest portraitists of his time, and having been employed constantly since the start of his career to paint them, Rubens found painting portraits to be quite tedious. They were essential for his fame, but he could survive financially without them.

Because of his outstanding abilities in so many painting genres, as well as his skills in diplomacy, Rubens was never compelled to have to earn his living solely from portraits, and was able to choose which commissions he accepted, but he was famed for his portraits.

From his early appointment in Mantua to his diplomatic travels and his role as court painter to Albert and Isabella, he painted the portraits of many auspicious personages, including royalty, aristocrats and clerics, as well as friends and relatives, to great acclaim. They all reveal the sitters' intellectual roles and significance in society, such as his friend Ludovicus Nonnius (1553–1645), a doctor and antiquarian of Portuguese descent who worked in Antwerp, with a bust of Hippocrates behind him. In common with usual portraiture, he reveals not only his subjects' physical features, but also elements of their underlying personalities, and he accentuated or minimized physical, psychological

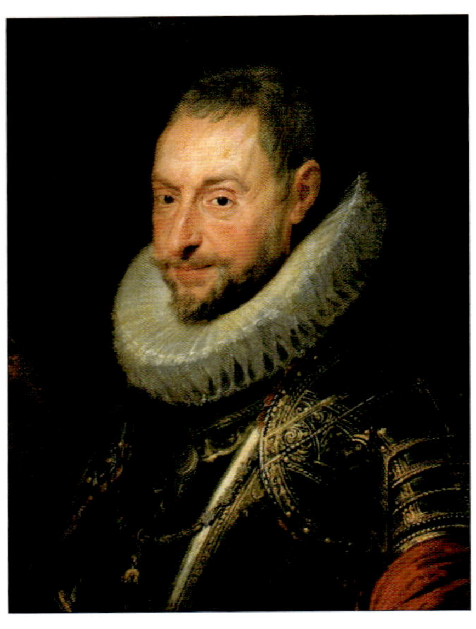

Above: Portrait of Ambrogio Spinola, *Rubens, c.1625. Don Ambrogio Spinola Doria, marqués de los Balbases (1569–1630), was an Italian general at the service of Spain.*

Below: Portrait of Susanna Lunden (Le Chapeau de Paille), *Rubens, c.1622–25. This is probably a portrait of Susanna Lunden, née Susanna Fourment, third daughter of Daniel Fourment, an Antwerp tapestry and silk merchant.*

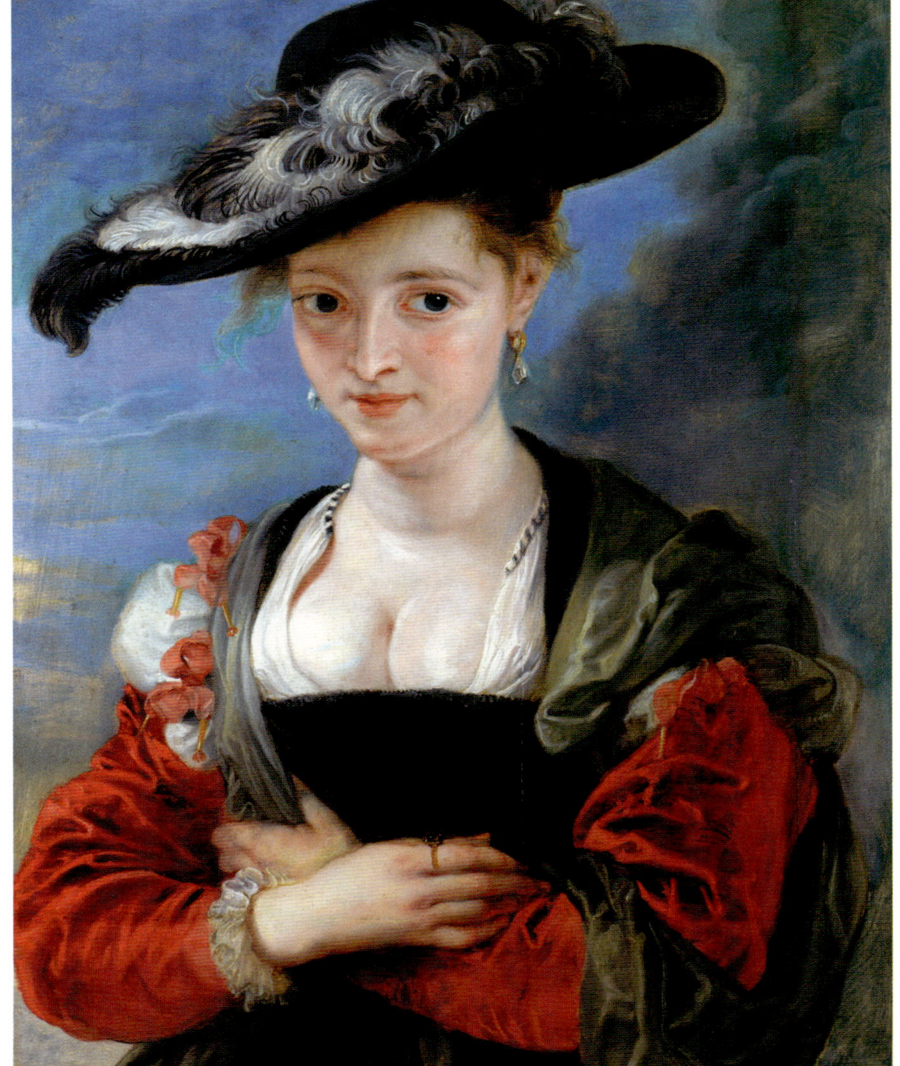

or social traits. Unconventionally, he also made his portraits appear as if his sitters were involved in life beyond the frames; all seem involved, individual and alive. He understood how posture, hands and eyes inform viewers subconsciously and immediately of many unspoken aspects of a person, so these are always important elements in his portraits.

Additionally, Rubens changed traditions in group portraiture. For instance, in both *Self-Portrait in a Circle of Friends from Mantua* and *The Four Philosophers*, he painted his friends as if they are in a frieze, while he looks out of the picture, directly at the viewer.

SUPPLE AND LIFELIKE

When painting his earliest portraits in Italy, Rubens took inspiration from 16th-century Venetian artists. His large equestrian portraits and full-length paintings of ladies from the highest social circles in Genoa have none of the

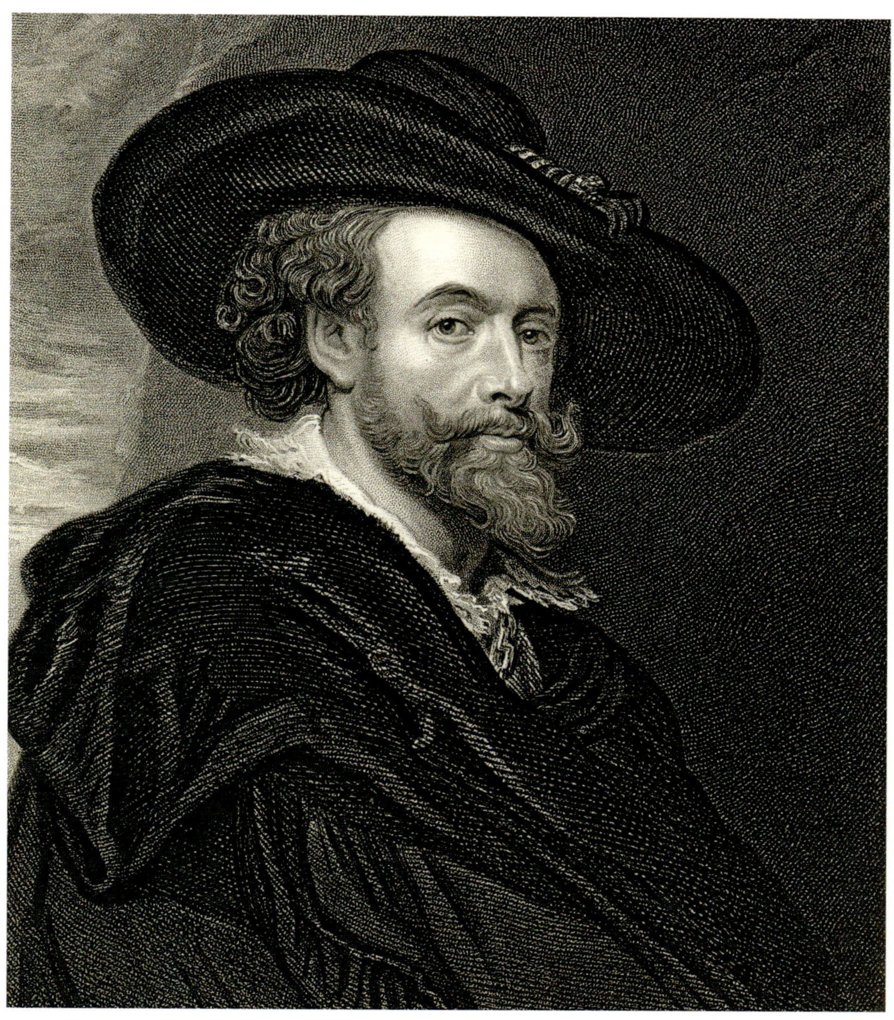

Above: Engraving of Self-portrait, Rubens, 1623. By the 1620s, Rubens was such a celebrity that even his own likenesses were sought after. This is based on a self-portrait, translated skilfully in an engraving.

courtly formality that was characteristic of Flemish portraiture traditions, but use colour and fluid brushmarks to convey activity and a sense of spontaneity. Once back in Antwerp in 1608, Rubens began adopting elements of Netherlandish portrait styles, with more severe compositions and closer details. From that time until about 1620, all his work was characterized by a smooth execution and sense of pliancy, with clearly defined textures in skin and

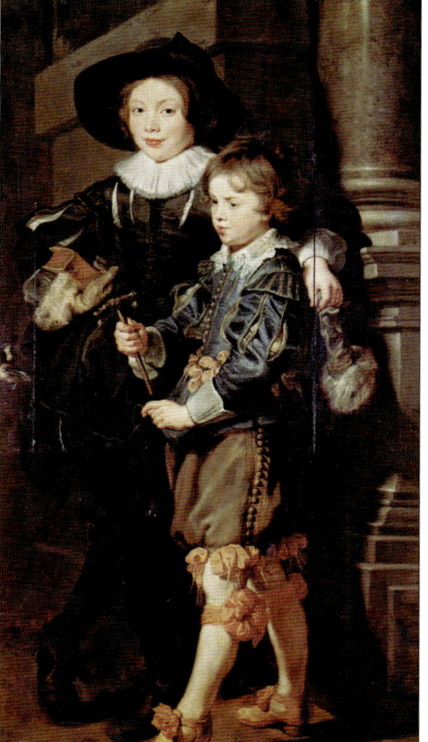

Left: The Artist's Sons, Rubens, 1626–27. An informal portrait of his beloved boys, Albert and Nicolaas, every stroke of this work was painted by the doting father. No assistants were involved.

clothing. During the 1620s his portraits became more lifelike, supple and direct.

When painting close friends and family, his portraits were more natural and instinctive, such as the relaxed, personable image of Susanna Fourment (or Lunden), c.1622–25, which is probably a marriage portrait, and his sons Albert and Nicolaas, 1626–27. Both paintings appear particularly sensitive, relaxed and empathetic. Others that also express informality yet retain a sense of grandeur include portraits of two of his friends: Don Ambrogio Spinola Doria, an Italian general who served Spain and became one of the greatest military commanders of his time, and Ludovicus Nonnius (1553–1645) (see page 222). Both portraits convey important, influential figures with a sense of humility.

PAINTING NATURE

In contrast to Rubens's many commissioned portraits, his landscapes were usually painted for his own private pleasure. It was not until the final decade of his life that he found time to paint these works, and he rarely sold them. As with the rest of his work, these landscapes are gestural, lively and colourful. They reflect a period in his life when he was financially comfortable and domestically contented, when he began to withdraw from public duties. His landscapes are complex creations, painted in the studio, of what he had seen, expressing his perceptions of the natural world. Landscapes at the time were undervalued and not considered serious themes for painting, yet Rubens enjoyed painting them, omitting the detailed figures and action that dominated his other work. His landscapes were personal expressions with an influence of both classical and contemporary ideas about nature. In them, he actually pre-empted early landscape painting of the late 18th and early 19th centuries.

SPANISH EXPERIENCES

While in Paris completing his Medici cycle in 1625, Rubens attended the wedding by proxy of Princess Henrietta Maria of France to Charles I of England. He also renewed his acquaintance with Frans Pourbus, now Marie de' Medici's chief portraitist, and with Peiresc, with whom he had been corresponding for several years.

At the wedding of Princess Henrietta Maria to Charles I, the Duke of Buckingham stood in as Charles's proxy bridegroom, and was introduced to Rubens. While painting Buckingham's portrait (see page 75), Rubens had an idea. Soon after his return to Antwerp, the Archduchess Isabella told him about renewed problems between Spain and the Northern Provinces. Rather than retaining peace after the Twelve Years' Truce, the Spanish kings (first Philip III and then his son) wanted to resume warfare against the Dutch Republic in an effort to unite the Northern and Southern Netherlands once again under Spanish sovereignty. As Philip IV's subject, Isabella should have been supportive of these proposals, but she longed for peace, and when her own secret

negotiations with the Northern Provinces failed, Rubens mentioned his plan. The hostilities between Spain and the Dutch Republic had engulfed all of Europe. Rubens believed he could resolve this by arranging peace between Spain and England, hoping that England would then force its Dutch ally to compromise with Spain. The idea would only work if Rubens could convince England and Spain – traditional enemies – to come to terms. Peace was vital to him; after the Twelve Years' Truce, the port of Antwerp had once again been closed and the city was in decline.

COMPROMISING SPAIN'S DIGNITY

At first, Philip ignored Isabella's suggestions for peace negotiations. Then the situation changed. Spain had formed

an alliance with the Catholic French monarchy to help subdue French Protestants in 1627, but the collaboration soon broke down, and Philip IV and his ministers began assessing alternatives to strengthen their position in Europe. They reconsidered Isabella's peace plans, and in August 1628 she sent Rubens to Madrid. Yet this was not favourably received. Two months before Rubens's departure, Philip wrote to Isabella: 'I am displeased at your mixing up a painter in affairs of such importance. You can easily understand how gravely it compromises the dignity of my kingdom, for our prestige must necessarily be lessened if we make so mean a person the representative with whom foreign envoys are to discuss affairs of such great importance.'

However, within a short time of his arrival, Rubens's magnetism, sagacity and wit overcame Philip's reservations. As an enthusiastic patron of the arts, Philip greatly admired Rubens's work, and already owned his monumental *Adoration of the Magi* of 1609. During his eight months in Madrid, Rubens charmed the king and his First Minister Olivares, and painted numerous paintings, as well as enlarging his *Adoration of the Magi*.

DIEGO VELÁZQUEZ

While in Spain, plans for the peace negotiations with England were stalled when news came of Buckingham's assassination. Since painting his portrait in Paris, Rubens had been corresponding with him about the proposed Spanish–English negotiations. Urgent meetings ensued in the Spanish court, and while letters and messengers

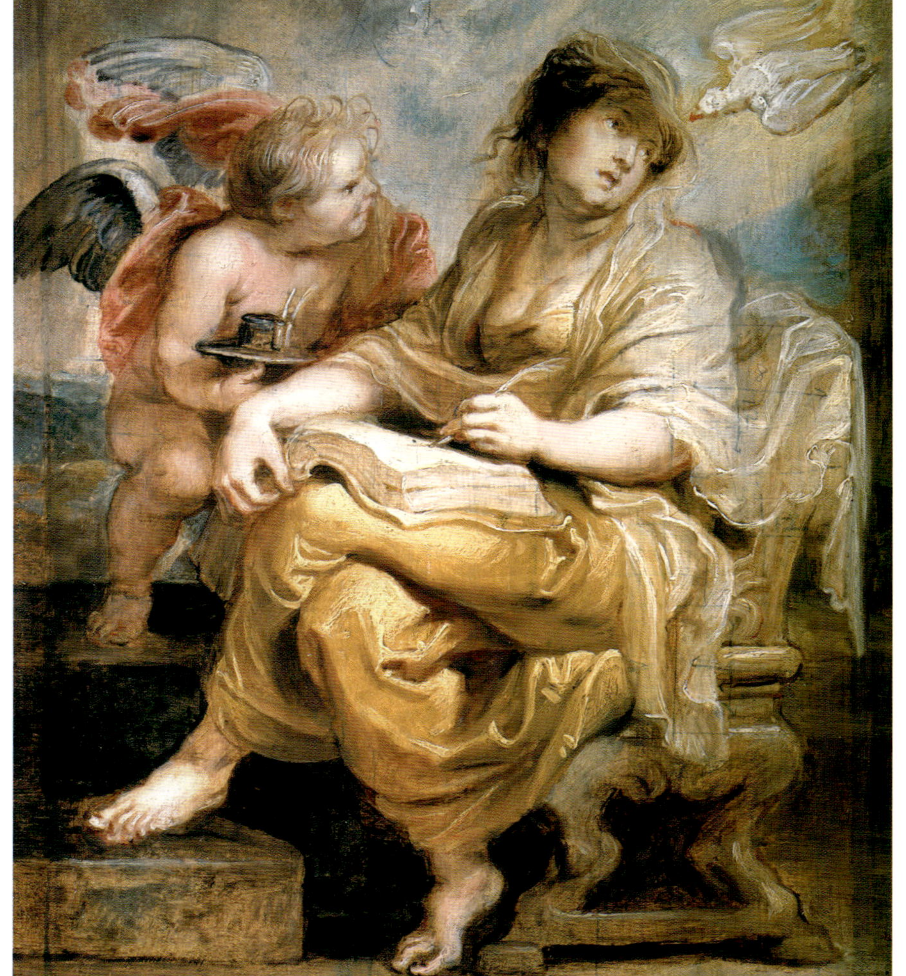

Left: Allegory of Sacred Wisdom, Rubens, 1625–30. The dove represents the Holy Spirit, and the cherub with the inkstand are both imparting divine inspiration to the writer.

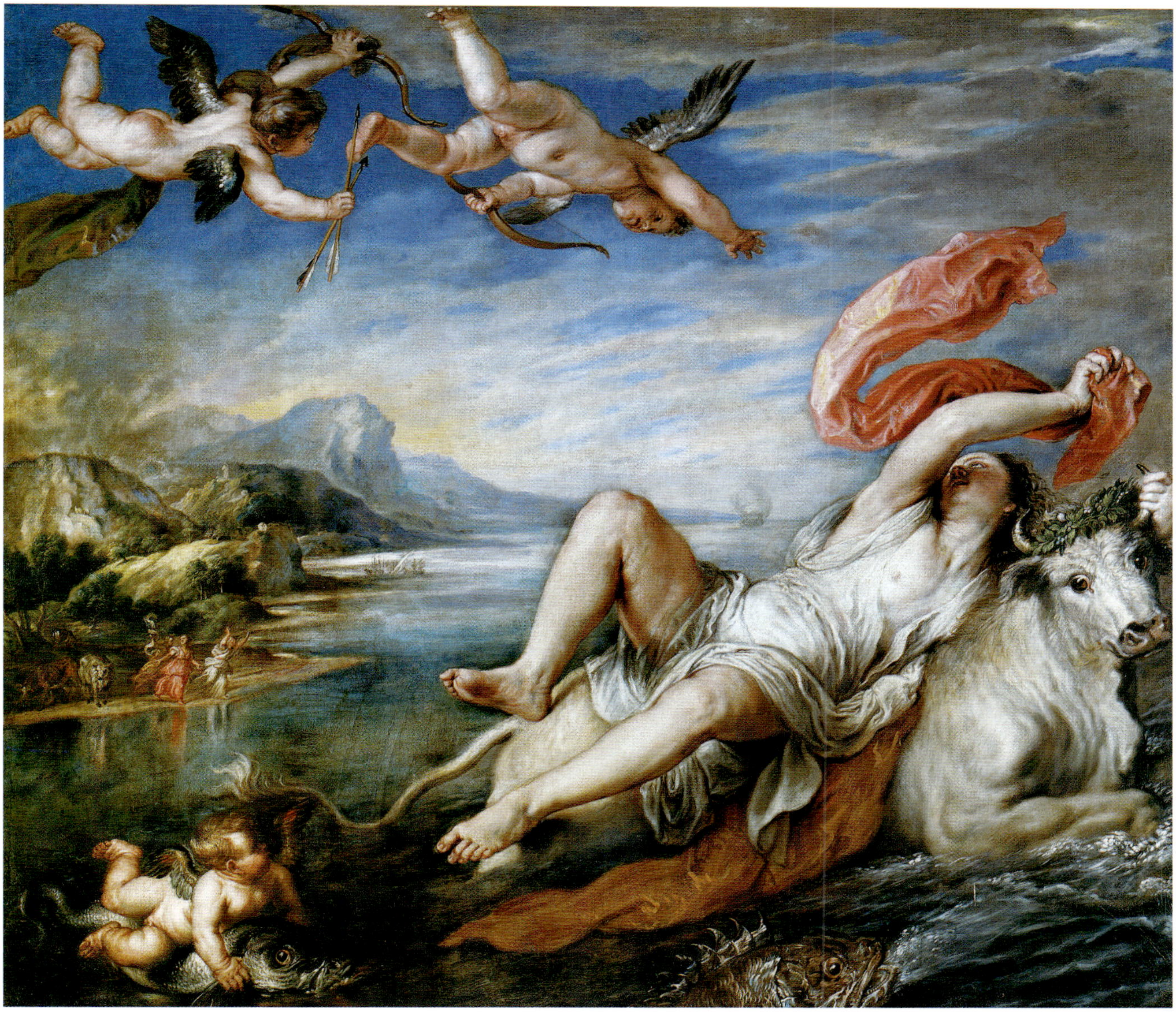

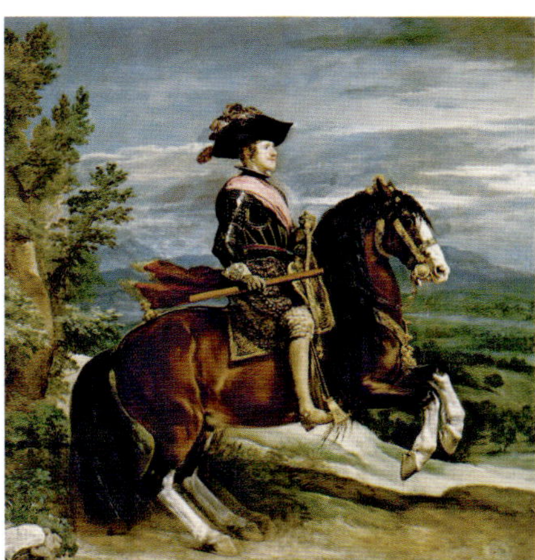

Above: The Rape of Europa, *Rubens, 1628–29. This is a copy of a painting by Titian of 1562. It depicts a story from Ovid's* Metamorphoses. *Unusually for Rubens, he copied this painting directly, with no personal interpretation.*

travelled back and forth between the two countries, all Rubens could do was wait, complete commissions, study the art in the royal collection, and befriend Velázquez. Despite being the one artist who broke the king's promise to Velázquez that no one else would ever paint his portrait again, Rubens neither angered nor irritated Velázquez. On the contrary, Velázquez greatly admired Rubens, and the two men felt an immediate strong bond of friendship.

Above: Equestrian Portrait of Philip IV of Spain, *1634–35, Velázquez. This is one of five equestrian portraits by Velázquez of the Spanish royal family that particularly inspired Rubens and influenced his style.*

COPYING TITIAN

While waiting for renewed negotiations with England, Rubens copied many works in the Spanish royal collection. In particular, he systematically copied all of Titian's works there. For a mature and established artist, this was quite unprecedented, yet the fluent brushwork, vibrant colours and luminous modelling of these copies greatly affected Rubens's subsequent painting style. From that time onwards, his own work became looser and freer, and he always maintained that Titian was the artist he revered above all.

SORROW AND SUCCESS

As well as the international importance of his mission, there was a personal reason that made Rubens wish to travel at that time. In the summer of 1626, his beloved wife Isabella had died, probably of the plague. Just three years earlier, their adored daughter Clara Serena had also died at just 12 years old.

In October 1625, Rubens's close friend Jan Bruegel had died of cholera, not long after Rubens had agreed to be the guardian of his children. It was a particularly grief-stricken period. Although there is no record of his feelings after the deaths of other close members of his family, letters remain that express Rubens's sorrow after Isabella's. Pierre Dupuy (1582–1651),

Below: Portrait of Isabella Brant, c.1620–25. Fourteen years younger than her husband, Isabella died in 1626, at just 35 years old. Rubens was heartbroken.

a French scholar and royal librarian, had been introduced to Rubens by Peiresc in Paris in 1623. Since that time, he and Rubens had become regular correspondents. In response to Dupuy's letter of condolence about Isabella's death, Rubens wrote: '[Fate] does not comply with our passions...It has the absolute dominion over all things, and we have only to serve and obey. There is nothing to do in my opinion, but to make this servitude more honourable and less painful by submitting willingly; but at present such a duty seems neither easy, nor even possible. You are very

prudent in commending me to Time, and I hope this will do for me what Reason ought to do....Truly I have lost an excellent companion...she was loved during her lifetime, and mourned by all at her death...since the true remedy for ills is Forgetfulness, daughter of Time, I must look to her for help. But I find it very hard to separate grief for this loss from the memory of a person whom I must love and cherish as long as I live. I should think a journey would be opportune to take me away from so many things which again and again seem to renew my grief...I shall have to travel in the society of my own lonely self, and with no company but my own sad thoughts.'

ROYAL ACCOLADES

Balthazar Gerbier (1592–1663) was a Dutch painter, courtier, diplomat and the Duke of Buckingham's Master of Horse. He acted as Buckingham's agent in the negotiations over Rubens's

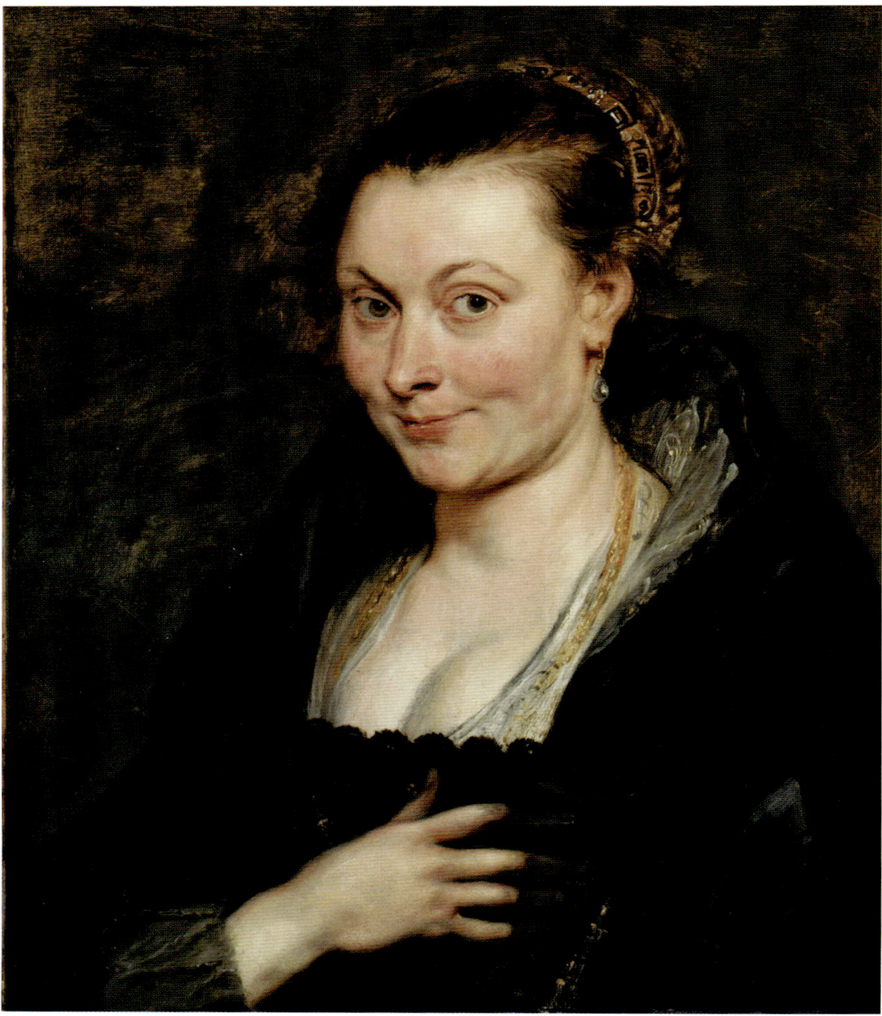

SELLING HIS COLLECTION

After having Isabella's body interred with his mother's in the Abbey of Saint Michael, where their wedding had taken place in 1609, Rubens felt desolate. His house, studio and collection became painful reminders of his happy life with Isabella. Six months after her death, he decided to sell his collection of gems, coins and statues. The buyer was George Villiers, the Duke of Buckingham, whom he had met in Paris and with whom he was planning an alliance between England and Spain. His only reason for selling his antiquities was because they exacerbated his grief; he certainly did not need the money.

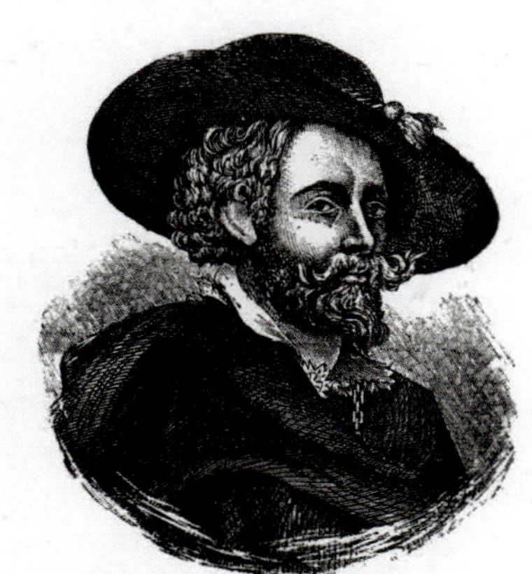

PETER PAUL RUBENS.

Above: An excerpt from one of Rubens's letters that he wrote from Antwerp to Peiresc in Italian. The letter discusses the defeat of the English navy at the Siege of La Rochelle in December 1627.

collection of antiquities, and while he and Rubens negotiated this, they also secretly discussed peace possibilities between their countries and Spain. After Buckingham's murder, Gerbier took over the peace negotiations on England's behalf, and in April 1629 Charles I sent directly for Rubens. By then, Rubens had travelled to Brussels to update the Infanta on his progress.

Before he had left Spain, Philip IV had been so pleased with his diplomacy (and art) that he bestowed him with the title 'Secretary of the King's Privy Council of the Netherlands'.

After nine months' stay in England, Rubens left with a peace treaty, a knighthood, an honorary degree from Cambridge University and a stash of royal gifts, including a jewelled sword, a diamond-studded hat band, and a ring from the king's own finger. In 1631, Philip IV also knighted him. Everyone concerned recognized Rubens's pivotal role in securing the peace treaty of 1630 between England and Spain.

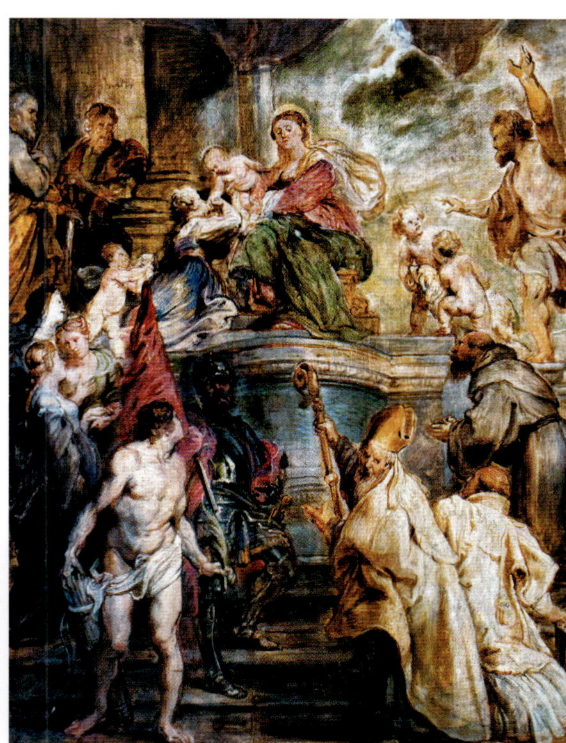

Above: The Mystic Marriage of Saint Catherine, Rubens, 1628. Two years after the death of his beloved Isabella, Rubens painted this oil sketch as a plan for the high altar of the Church of Saint Augustine in Antwerp. Absorbing himself in work such as this helped him to assuage his grief.

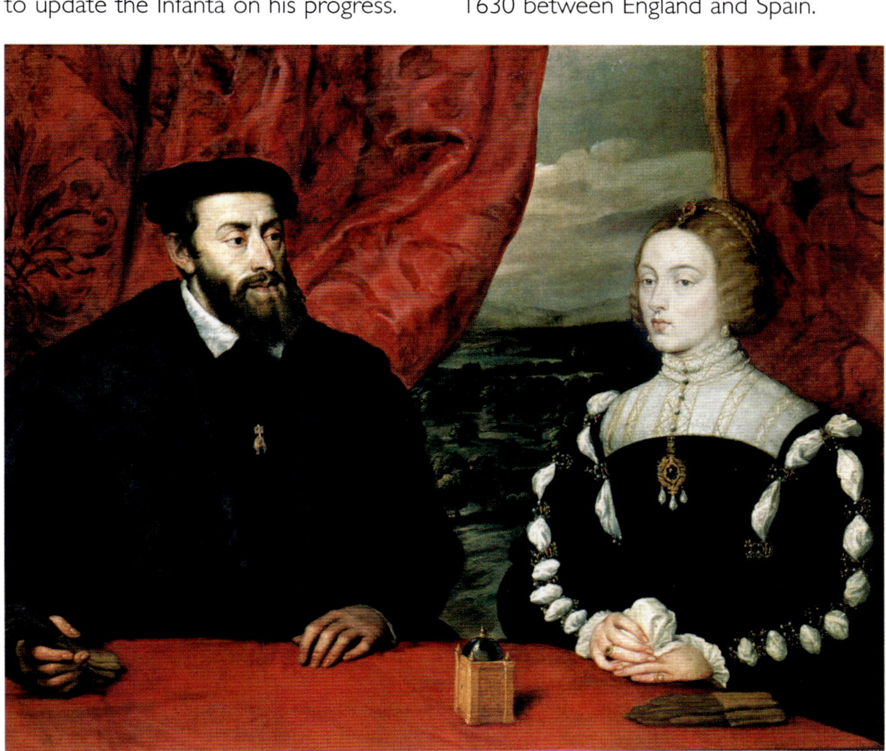

Left: Charles V and Empress Isabel, Rubens, c.1628. This is a copy of a lost painting by Titian from 1548. The image is static and uncharacteristic of both Titian and Rubens, but Rubens was perfecting his tonal modelling and contrasts of landscapes and figures.

PEACE AND WAR

During the nine months that Rubens spent at the English court, he had been commissioned to paint various portraits and other works for the king and his nobles, as he had in Spain. Of everyone he met there, he formed the closest relationship with King Charles himself.

Charles gave Rubens gifts and accolades, and in turn, most historians believe that Rubens executed *The Allegory of Peace and War*, or *Minerva Protects Pax from Mars* as a diplomatic gift for Charles in celebration of his efforts in securing peace with Spain. The treaty was signed on November 15, 1630, and Rubens's exuberant painting extols the benefits of peace in a powerful allegory. Created with fluid impasto paint and transparent glazes, it shows Pax (Peace) as one of his voluptuous nudes, giving milk to the infant Plutus, the god of wealth. At her feet, a satyr holds the horn of plenty, while an attendant brings her gold and jewels – implying that peace brings happiness and wealth. Following

Below: Allegory of Peace and War, *or* Minerva Protects Pax from Mars, *Rubens, 1629–30. This painting is believed by many to have been a diplomatic gift from Rubens to King Charles.*

tradition, Bacchus is accompanied by leopards and women with tambourines. In the foreground are children – a reminder of war's most vulnerable victims. Minerva, the goddess of wisdom and the arts restrains Mars, the god of war. The painting delighted Charles for its sentiments and for the skill in its execution. He was a great collector of art, and especially admired Rubens's work. The painting also served to convince him that Rubens should be commissioned to paint the Whitehall Banqueting House ceiling.

HÉLÈNE FOURMENT

On his return to Antwerp, Rubens and his studio were engaged on many large undertakings, including the vast commission for the Whitehall ceiling, a new cycle of tapestry designs portraying the life of Achilles, and the Henri IV series for Marie de' Medici that he believed was still wanted. Yet despite his hectic schedule, he was lonely. Later,

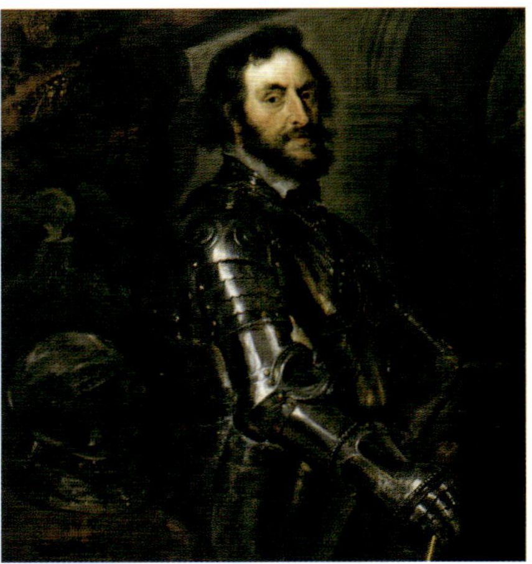

Above: Thomas Howard, 2nd Earl of Arundel, *Rubens, 1629–30. This prominent English courtier was also an avid art collector, and often called affectionately 'the collector Earl'.*

in 1635, he wrote to Peiresc about how he had felt at that time: 'I made up my mind to marry again, since I was not yet inclined to live the abstinent life of a

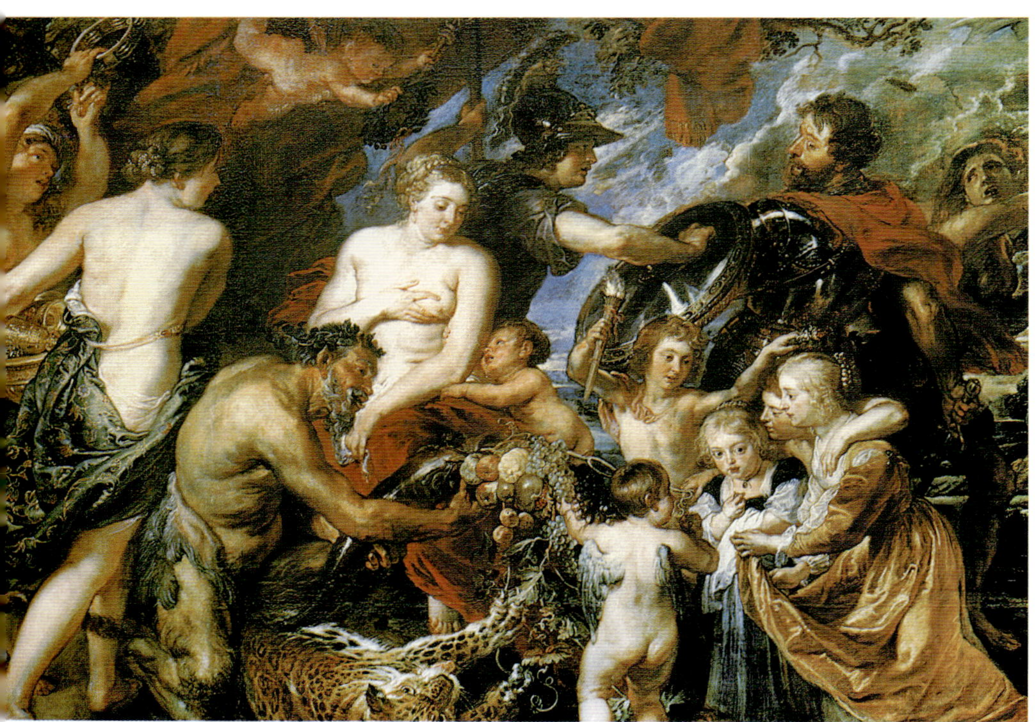

THE END OF A DIPLOMATIC CAREER

Early in 1631, Rubens wrote to his friend Jan Woverius that, although he was delighted with the (fragile) peace between Spain and England, he had: '. . . occasion to lament my misfortune in ever having become involved in that affair. For I cannot obtain any reimbursement for what I spent in the service of His Majesty on the journeys to Spain and England.' While he awaited to be reimbursed by the Spanish king for his most recent diplomatic services, he felt marginalized and resolved to resign from the role. So when the Infanta died in 1633, he asked to be and was exempted from further diplomatic missions.

celibate . . . I chose one who would not blush to see me take my brushes in hand. And to tell the truth, it would have been hard for me to exchange the priceless treasures of liberty for the embraces of an old woman.'

The wife he had chosen was from a middle-class family whom Rubens knew well. Her father was his friend, the silk and tapestry merchant Daniel Fourment (c.1565–1643), and he had painted several portraits of her elder sister Susanna. Beautiful and demure, Hélène Fourment (1614–73) was just 16 years old. Rubens was 53. They married on December 6, 1630.

Rubens was completely infatuated with Hélène. For the next ten years she became his muse in a way that Isabella had never been. He painted her in loving portraits with their children (they eventually had five), and he also depicted her as goddesses and temptresses. She became his universal beauty. Despite the nearly 40-year age gap between them, there was genuine fondness on both sides of the marriage. Rubens was by then highly respected and extremely wealthy. His celebrity

Below: Portrait of Susanna Fourment, *c.1625. This is a sensitive portrait of the sister of Rubens's second wife.*

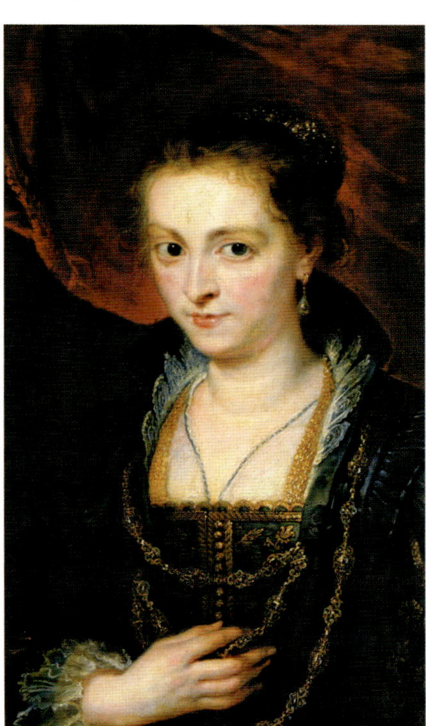

status was considerably raised when Philip IV knighted him in 1631, and he became the only painter so honoured by the kings of both England and Spain.

Below: Hélène Fourment, *c.1630–32. Showing skill in rendering textures and smooth flesh tones, this is Hélène as herself, not a goddess.*

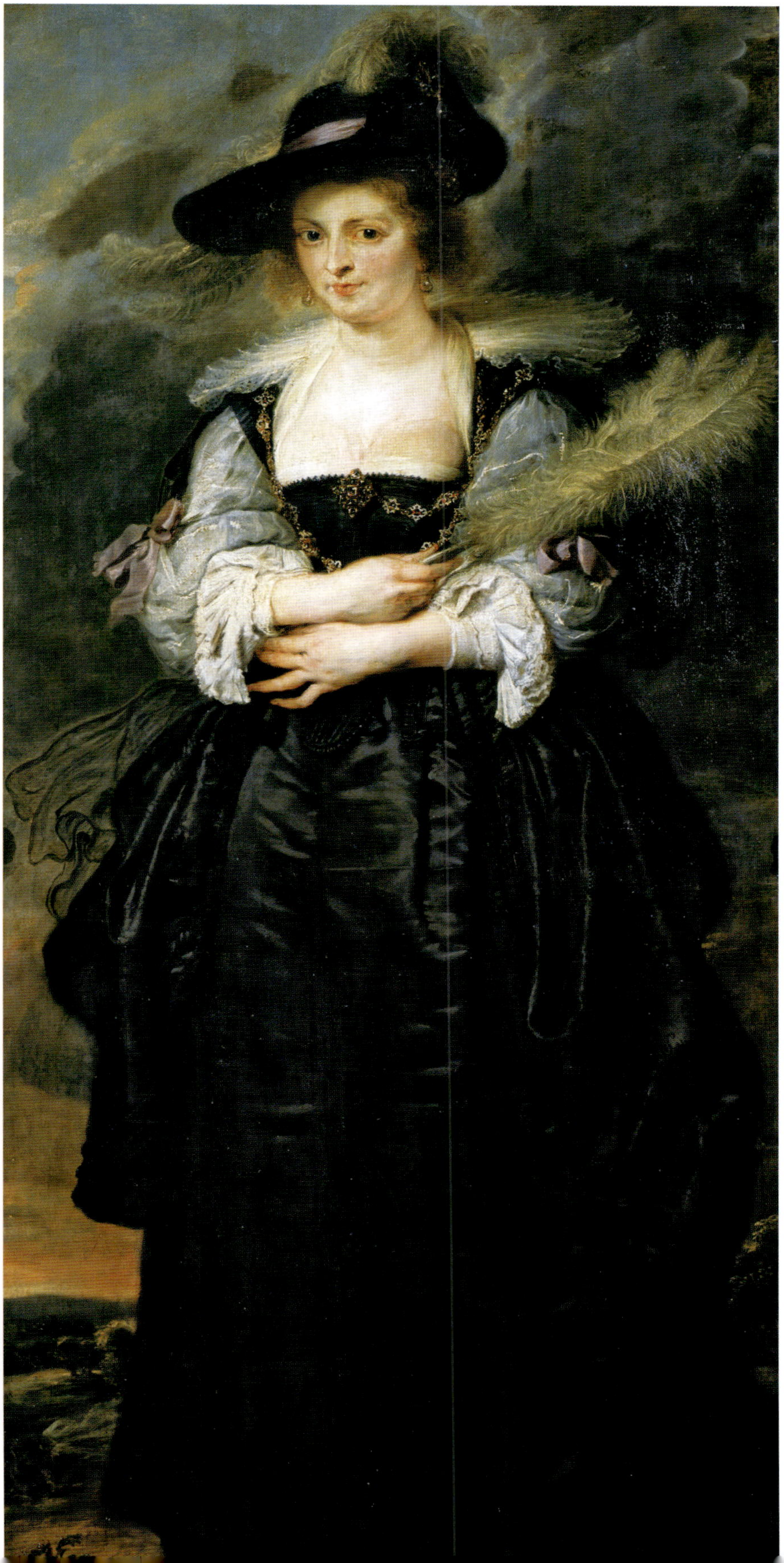

VOLUPTUOUS WOMEN

Unfortunately, the peace that Rubens had worked so hard for did not last, and for most of the next 20 years Europe continued to be embroiled in the Thirty Years' War. It was disheartening after all his efforts, but Rubens was now quite detached from it, living blissfully with his new young wife.

Hélène certainly gave Rubens a new impetus to paint beautiful and sensual women. She inspired him in nearly all his future paintings – whether he was representing her as a goddess or as a mortal, as herself or in another role; her soft, plump and rosy flesh became one of the most recognizable elements of Rubens's paintings. Her ample figure was considered to be the epitome of fashionable beauty and health, and a sign of prosperity and class. Variations of her appeared so often that they became his personal signature.

TACTILE BRUSHWORK

Although Rubens was in his 50s, his abundant energy, warm nature and robust powers of observation and comprehension were showing no signs of diminishing, and his glowing colours and sweeping brushwork were even more masterful than they had been earlier in his career. He began producing some of his most exuberant works, broadening his painterly style with looser, more tactile applications of paint, which was unusual among contemporary artists, who generally sought to paint tight, neat, realistic images with invisible brushmarks. By then, his influence across Europe was overwhelming, and many other artists began changing their styles, painting in a freer manner in emulation of his approach.

For Rubens, the female form represented mystery, seduction, fertility and comfort, but he was also attracted by many other qualities, including wealth, courtly grace, intellectual discussion, femininity, beauty, sumptuous fabrics and luxuriant textures – all of which emerge in his paintings. His zest for life can be seen in all of this, in his bountifully endowed figures and expressively rendered textures, and his love of humanity, of soft flesh and of the expression of emotion. All this is conveyed in his large and small works, but more specifically his intense feelings for Hélène emerge palpably in his paintings after 1630. Centuries later, some of his sensual imagery became uncomfortable to many viewers; the generous proportions of the women became outdated, but in the 17th century

Below left: The Alliance of Earth and Water, *Rubens, 1618. This union of two elements is represented by the goddess Cybele as Earth and Neptune as Water.*

Below: Drawing of a female head – a study for the head of Saint Apollonia, *Rubens, 1630. Hélène Fourment seems to have been the model for this drawing.*

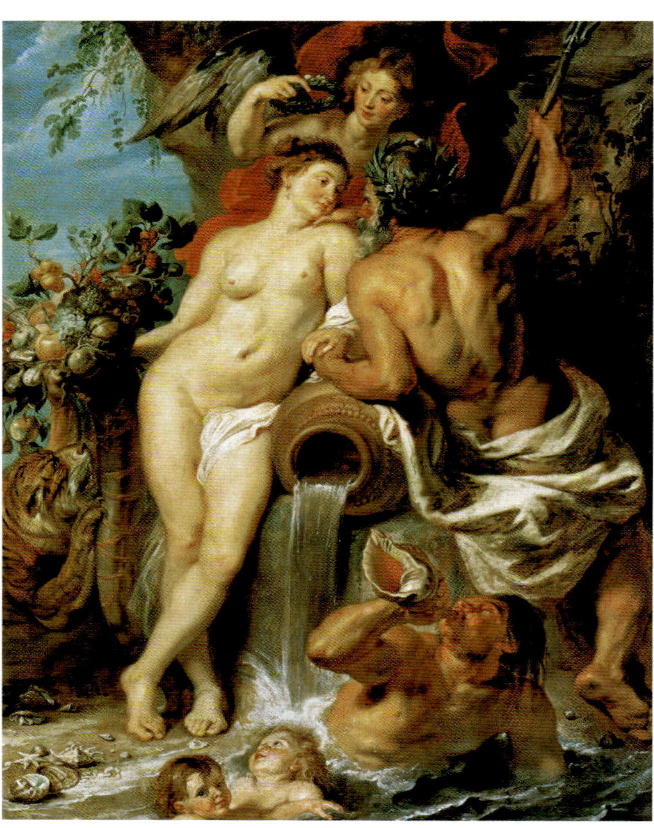

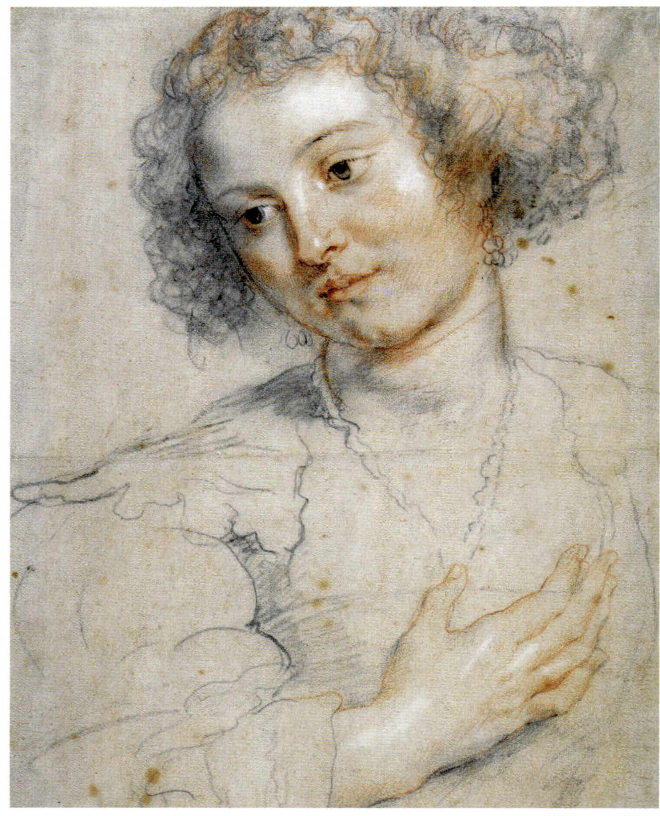

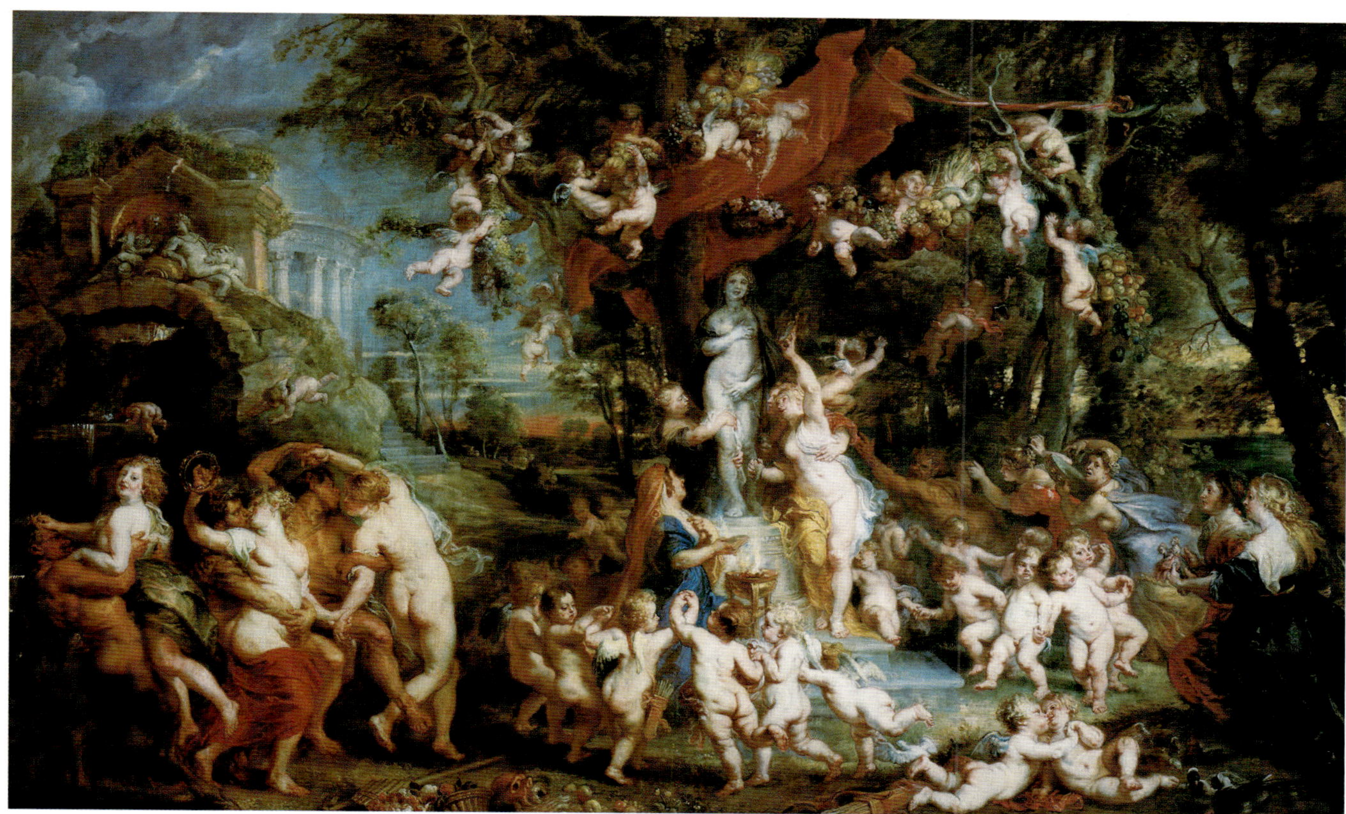

full, fleshy figures were fashionable, and Rubens's portrayals of lust and passion captured the spirit of the period.

INFORMAL PAINTINGS

Over their ten-year marriage, Rubens and Hélène had five children: Clara Johanna (1632–89), Frans (1633–78), Isabella Helena (1635–52), Peter Paul (1637–84), and Constantia Albertina (1641–1709/12), and his paintings of her with their children are among his most loving and gentle. He was at his happiest in the intimacy of his family circle, and his informal paintings of his children and Hélène are created with flowing, graceful brushwork, soft colours and natural gestures. Similarly, his portraits of Hélène are softer than any of the other portraits he painted.

Left: The Toilet of Venus, *c.1613. To Rubens, the combination of an ample frame, pale skin and delicate blonde hair was the epitome of womanhood.*

Far left: Deianira Tempted by Fame, *1638. In his depiction of the classical femme fatale, Rubens highlights the glowing white skin and voluptuous body.*

CELEBRATION OF LOVE

Fascinated by Greek and Roman mythology, Rubens depicted many stories, mostly for private commissions, relishing the opportunity to paint voluptuous women. The lyricism, eloquence and sensuality of his compositions became even more

Above: The Feast of Venus, *1636–37. Rubens's beauties were young and lively, full-figured and with pink-tinged skin.*

vigorous and earthy from 1620, and after his second marriage he took pleasure in painting mythological stories celebrating the power of love.

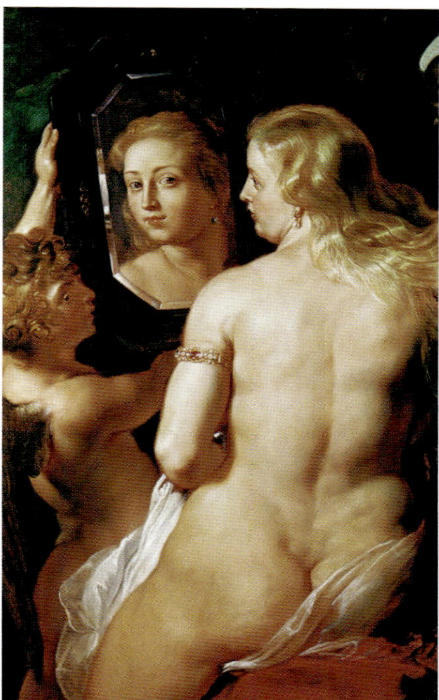

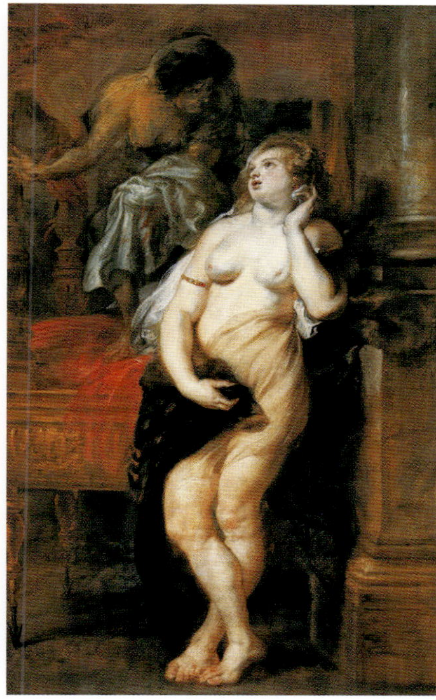

MONUMENTAL COMMISSIONS

Rubens became even more renowned after his diplomatic missions. He was famed for his prodigiousness, accomplished handling of paint, energetic compositions and dramatic, triumphal and sensual style. A shrewd businessman, he laboured fervently to meet the demand for his work.

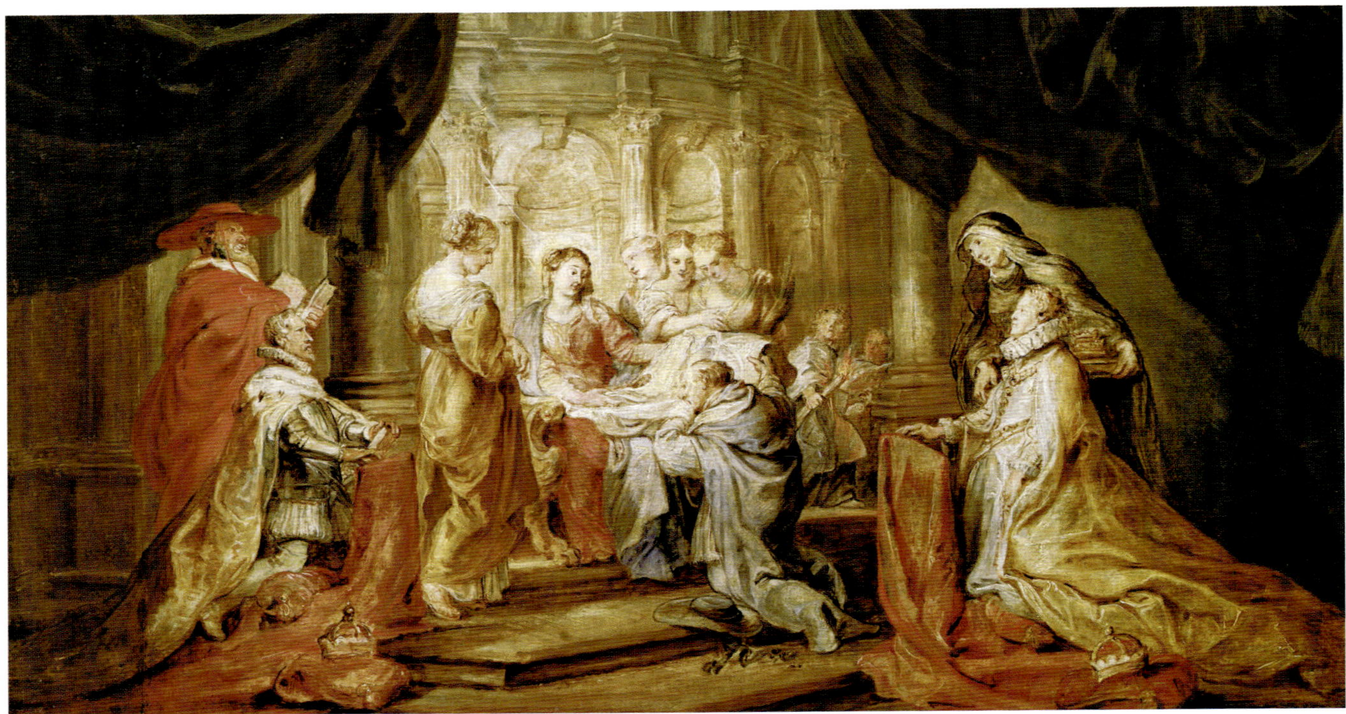

During the 1630s, Rubens produced some of his most significant monumental paintings. One was the Ildefonso altarpiece of 1630–32, commissioned by the Infanta Isabella for the altar of the Ildefonso Brotherhood in the church of St Jacopo op de Coudenberg in Brussels. The Brotherhood had been founded by the Archduke Albert, and the main panel of the triptych depicts a scene from Saint Ildefonso's life, while the wings show Albert and Isabella being presented to the Virgin Mary by their respective patron saints.

HUMANITY AND HEROISM

It has not been verified who commissioned Rubens to create his fourth and final tapestry cycle depicting the life of Achilles, a Greek hero who fought the Trojans. It may have been Philip IV or Charles I, or it might have been his father-in-law Daniel Fourment, who owned a set of the tapestries as well as eight preparatory sketches. The

expense of the tapestries make this last seem unlikely, as they were made of silk, wool and rare, costly silver thread, although Fourment may have been the agent for an unknown patron. It is also possible that Rubens created the designs as a gift for Fourment some time between 1620 and 1630. As usual, he did not portray a conventional view of the story. No single ancient literary source offers an entire biography of Achilles, yet Rubens depicted him in eight action-packed scenes from his life that convey both his humanity and his heroism. It is apparent from the paintings that Rubens studied all texts written on the subject, including Homer, Statius, Servius and Fulgentius.

As with his Achilles cycle, Rubens's expressiveness in the Whitehall ceiling was unconventional and unexpected. Briefed to celebrate the achievements of James I, he created complex allegorical stories to symbolize the benefits of national unity and peace, including

Above: A sketch by Rubens for the Ildefonso altarpiece commissioned by the Infanta Isabella, showing his mature, painterly and confident style.

Knowledge triumphing over Ignorance, Liberty overcoming Avarice, and Heroic Virtue defeating Envy. His fluidity and freedom of invention is apparent across the entire complex, a programme that he worked out in detailed stages for his students and assistants to follow.

JOYOUS ENTRY

After the Infanta Isabella's death, Philip IV appointed his younger brother Cardinal Infante Ferdinand (1609–41) as the new governor of the Netherlands. Ferdinand had been a cardinal since he was ten years old. He was also Infante of Spain, Infante of Portugal, Archduke of Austria, Archbishop of Toledo (1619–41) and a military commander during the Thirty Years' War. On April 17, 1635, he visited Antwerp, which became

Right: The Saint Ildefonso altarpiece: Mary Presenting a Liturgical Robe to Saint Ildefonso, *Rubens, c.1630–32.*

Far right: The Death of Achilles, Rubens, 1630–35. This is the final scene from Rubens's Achilles tapestry cycle. Here, Paris has just shot the fatal arrow through Achilles's vulnerable heel.

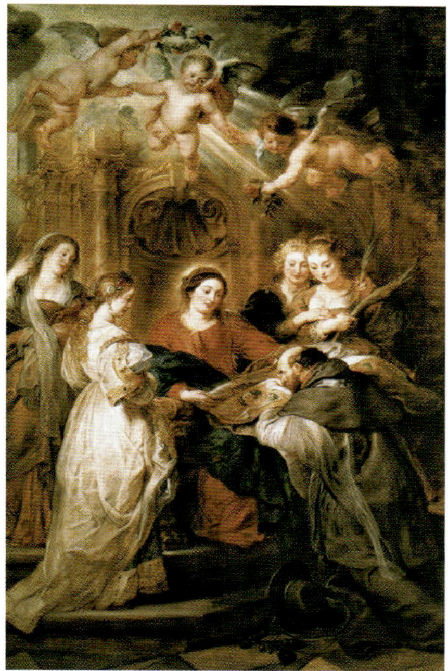

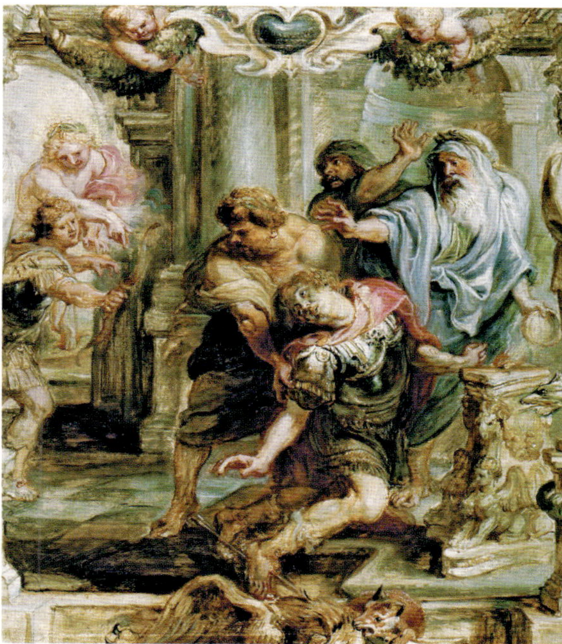

known as his 'Joyous Entry.' Rubens was commissioned to prepare temporary street decorations for the occasion, swiftly organizing teams of artists and craftsmen to produce his designs. State entries professed an agreement between ruler and people of renewed assistance and support in exchange for loyalty. In 1628, Rubens had described Antwerp as living on its savings, as along with the continued Dutch blockade of the Scheldt, Spain had deprived it of the right to trade with the Spanish Indies. The people of Antwerp were hopeful that Ferdinand would restore peace and prosperity to their city. The decorations represented both a loyal welcome and a desperate plea, and they surpassed all expectations by their magnificence. Consisting of nine huge scenic structures of wood and cloth, with cut-out figures, mouldings and banners, plus large canvases of portraits and allegories, the decorations were erected throughout the city, creating a route for Ferdinand to make his triumphal entry in a procession through a series of grand stages and arches. They celebrated Ferdinand's achievements, exalted the Habsburg dynasty and concluded with depictions of the plight of the Southern Netherlands and of Antwerp in particular. Ferdinand proclaimed his delight in the display publicly and to Rubens in person, although it failed in its ultimate mission of securing his aid.

Below: Whitehall Ceiling: The Peaceful Reign of James I. *Here, Rubens recalls the King Charles I's father signing a peace treaty with Spain in 1604.*

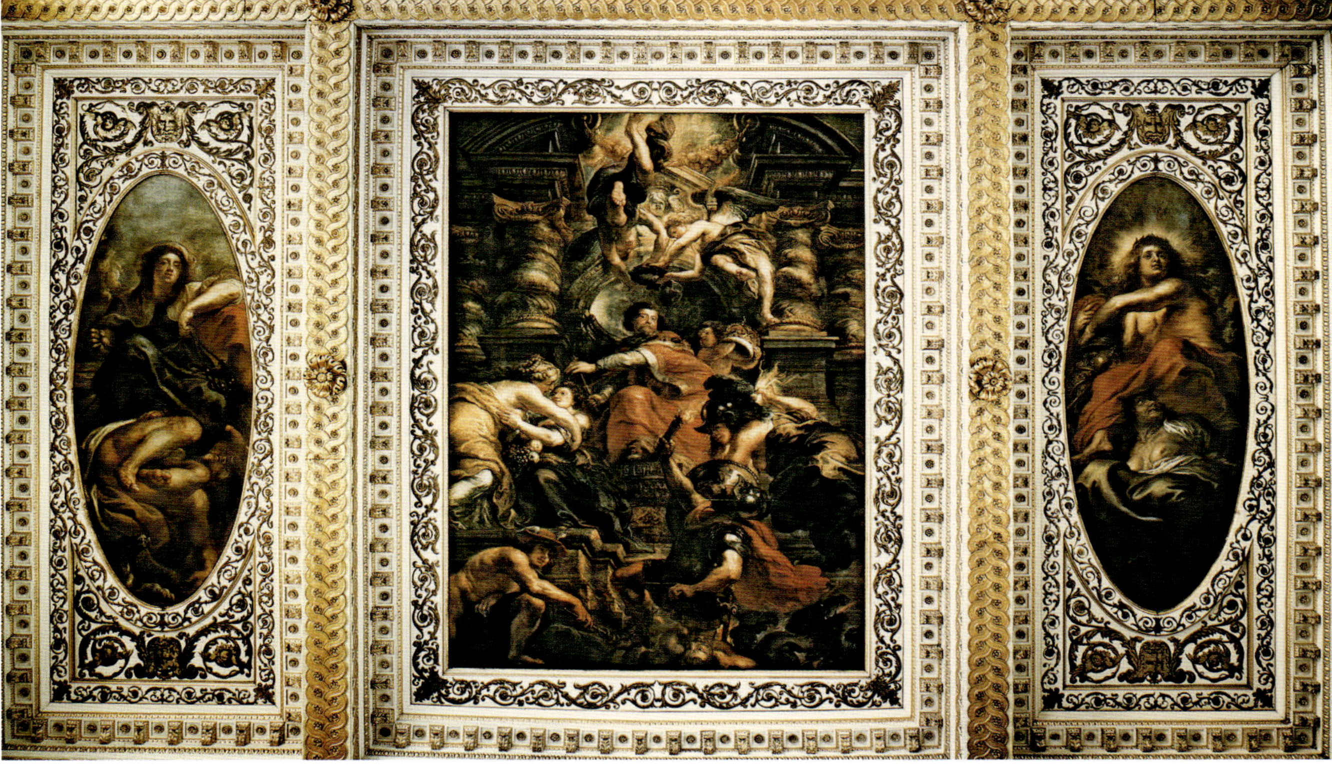

THE CASTLE OF STEEN

In 1635 Rubens bought a manor house, the Château de Steen, or *Het Steen* (which translates as 'Stone House'), near Malines, south of Antwerp. He began dividing his time between this idyllic rural retreat and his studio in town, enjoying the pleasures of being a member of the upper classes.

Het Steen means 'stone house'. The sales description of *The Stone House and the Hunting Lodge* stated: 'A manorial residence with a large stone house and other fine buildings in the form of a castle, with garden, orchard, fruit trees and a drawbridge, and a large hillock on the middle of which stands a high square tower, having also a lake and a farm . . . the whole surrounded by moats.' With the ownership came the title Lord of Steen, which amused Rubens immensely. In the year in which he bought Het Steen, he and Hélène had their third child, a daughter, Isabella Helena, and Jan Caspar Gevaerts (1593–1666) published a souvenir volume of prints of his Joyous Entry decorations, which further increased his renown. The following year, he was given his largest commission to date: the decoration of Philip IV's new royal hunting lodge, Torre de la Parada in Madrid. Ferdinand acted as his brother's agent, and kept in close contact with Rubens as he worked on the series, which was to be 100 paintings, completed in under a year. The works were to include arcadian subjects, animals, hunting scenes and portraits of

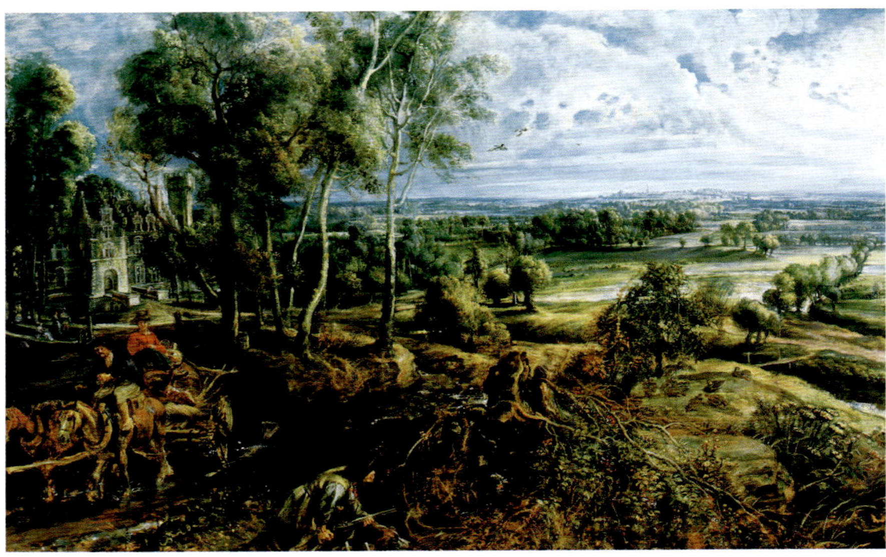

Above: An Autumn Landscape with a view of Het Steen in the Early Morning, *Rubens, c.1636. This is a view of Rubens's new manor house.*

the king. Although he planned many of the works, Rubens entrusted the execution of most final paintings to others, including Cornelis de Vos (1584–1651), Theodoor van Thulden (1606–69), Erasmus Quellinus the Younger (1607–78), and Jacob Jordaens.

VIEWS OF THE LAND

Concurrently, Rubens executed several new portraits of Ferdinand, including one commemorating his victory at Nördlingen, showing him on a horse with a goddess of Victory flying overhead and a battlefield in the background. Ferdinand also commissioned other works. Even though Rubens was engulfed with all these commissions, for his own pleasure he began painting images of his new manor, in informal landscapes filled with shimmering colour and atmospheric light effects, such as *Château de Steen with Hunter* (1636), *Landscape with a Rainbow* (1636), and *Landscape with Het Steen* (1636). Having spent his life painting commissioned works dominated by figures, these landscapes make nature the focus. Yet even in these tranquil pictures he rendered movement: in carts, cows, trees, birds, clouds and small figures at their daily tasks. He replaced the blues, pinks and golds of his regular palette with dark greens, lemons, cobalt

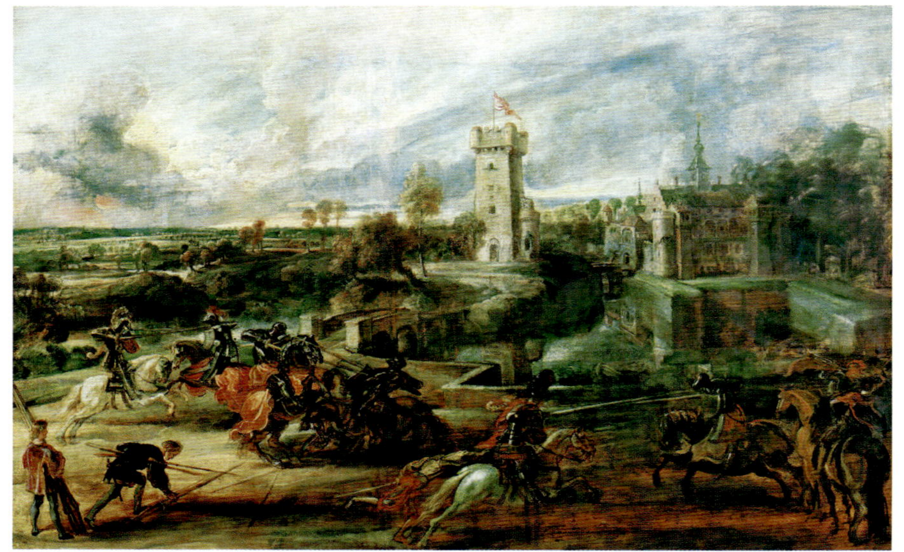

Left: Tournament by the Moat of Steen Castle, *Rubens, 1635–37. Rubens painted his largest and most luminous landscapes at Het Steen. This depicts an imaginary joust.*

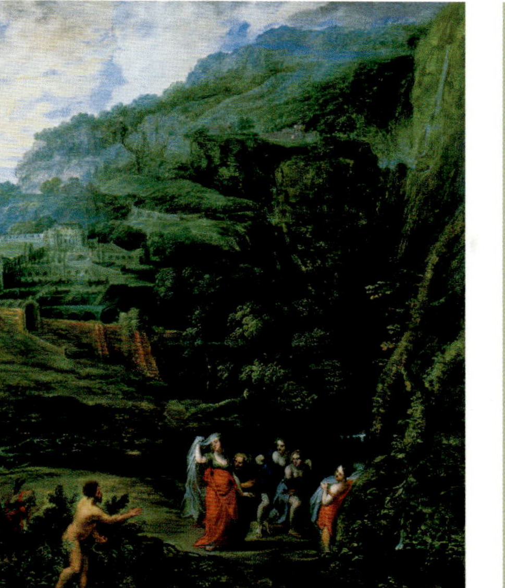

Above: Ulysses and Nausicaa, *1635. This scene from Homer's* Odyssey *also gave Rubens an opportunity to paint the scene.*

blue and pale orange. Colour changes of times of day and the seasons were all captured with his dynamic brushstrokes, and unlike his other works, his views of Het Steen and landscapes and have no allegorical, symbolic or spiritual meanings; they are simply recordings of what he saw, of the power of nature. In this, he was once again ahead of his time.

Right: Meeting of the Two Ferdinands, *1635. In this painting, Rubens commemorates the meeting of King Ferdinand III of Hungary and the Cardinal-Infante Ferdinand at Nördlingen.*

GOUT

Since 1626, when he was 49, Rubens had started to suffer with gout, a form of arthritis that causes pain in the joints. Attacks are sudden and acute, with the affected joints becoming hot, red and swollen. It was particularly distressing for Rubens as it prevented him from painting, and after his first feverish attack, his symptoms worsened and occurred more frequently. By 1636, the attacks were almost continuous, but Rubens had always been endowed with a rare *joie de vivre*, and this positive attitude kept him relatively buoyant.

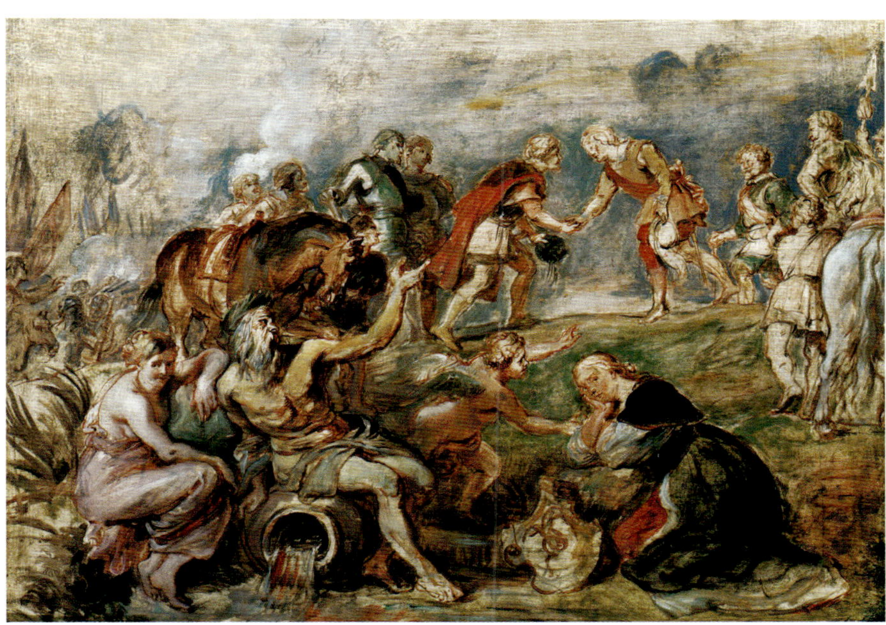

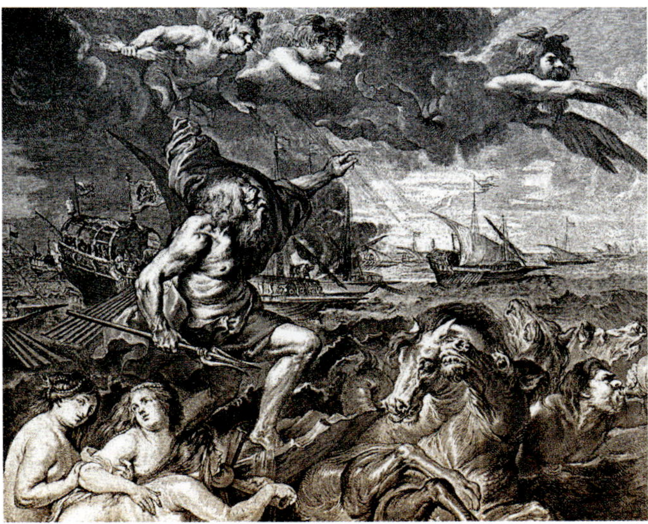

Left: The Voyage of Cardinal-Infante Ferdinand from Barcelona to Genoa, *etching after a painting by Rubens, 1635. This is an allegorical image of a journey by the Cardinal-Infante Ferdinand in a shell-chariot pulled by four sea horses. Nearby, Neptune grasps his trident.*

STAYING AT HOME

With his art, his gout, his new young family and Het Steen, Rubens preferred to stay close to home rather than to travel any more or enter into the intrigues of royal courts. So for most of his commissions from this period, even those from distant locations, he worked at home from precise measurements for each painting. In 1636, he wrote to Peiresc about his Whitehall paintings: 'I have a horror of courts. I sent my work to England in the hands of someone else. It has now been put in place, and my friends write that His Majesty is completely satisfied with it.'

LATE MYTHOLOGIES

Rubens kept abreast of all his commissions, but increasingly entrusted his apprentices and assistants to finish many of them. In later life, he chose which paintings he would complete, selecting subjects for their appeal to him personally rather than the prestige of the patron.

Religious and mythological themes intrigued Rubens, especially myths for the fantastic scope of their stories. Mythological themes gave him more freedom for individual expression than Bible stories, and he had an almost untiring enthusiasm for portraying these Greek and Roman stories, using his unique blend of lyricism, vigour and sensuality. He planned over 60 of Philip IV's Torre de la Parada mythological pictures, but was happy to give many of the final works to other artists to complete. Some were established artists and some were his assistants, including Frans Snyders, De Vos, Van Thulden, Quellinus, Jordaens, Borrekens (1611–65), Peeter Symons (fl.1629–36) and Jacob Peter Gowy (active c.1632–61). Unusually and for the first time, he encouraged these others to sign their own names on the paintings, which may

have been for altruistic reasons, or it may have been because he deemed the work inferior to his own and did not want to be associated with it.

By the time he undertook the Torre de la Parada paintings, he was as accomplished in mythological themes as he was in biblical subjects, and felt confident enough to change traditional mythological portrayals. His depictions are shown from various unexpected viewpoints, and often express Humanist schools of thought.

PERSONAL CHARACTER

As with all his figures, during the 1630s Rubens's goddesses took on a more intimate and personal character. *The Judgement of Paris*, which was one of the events that led up to the Trojan War and also to the foundation of Rome, was a theme that he portrayed

Below: Hercules Slays the Dragon in the Garden of Hesperides, *Rubens, 1635–40. This dramatic close-up shows Hercules wrestling with a vicious mythological beast.*

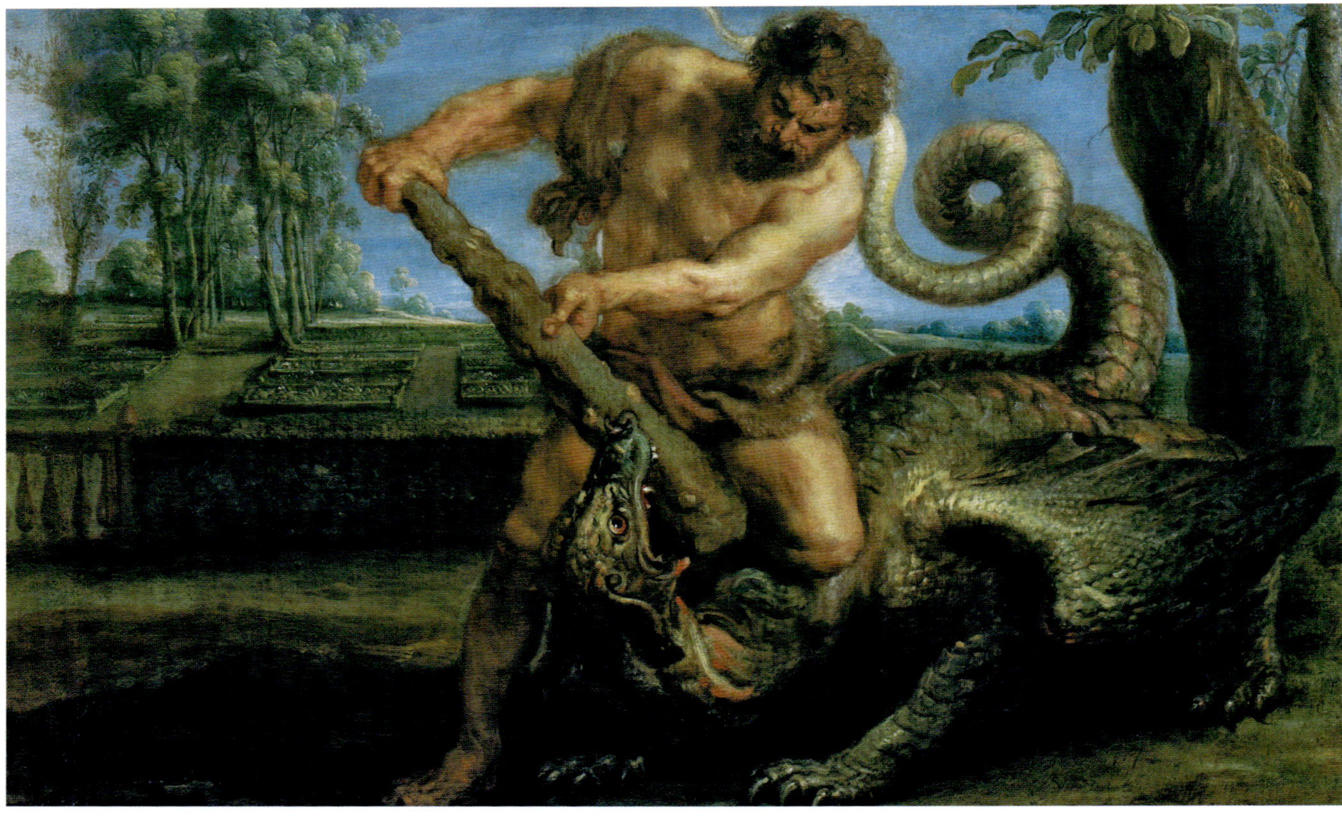

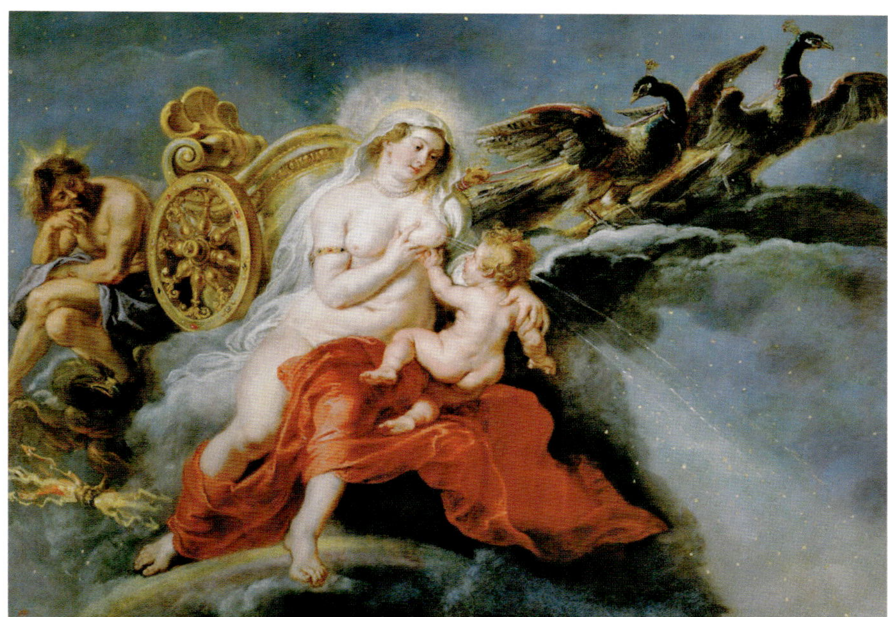

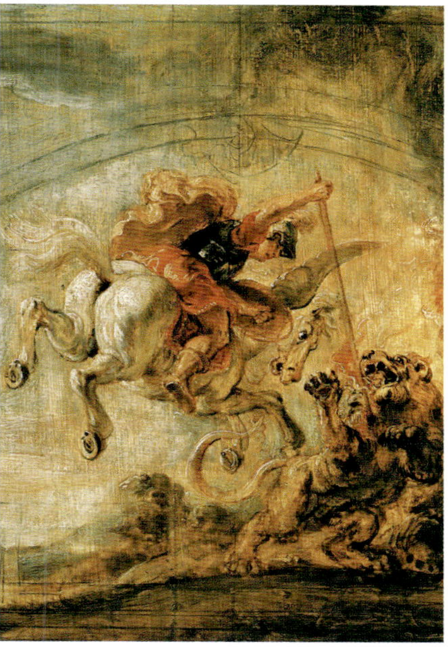

several times over his career, from his first in 1597–1600, to his last in 1638 for Philip IV. Despite Ferdinand reporting to his brother that Rubens had frequent incapacitating attacks of gout and was bed-ridden and incapable of painting for much of the time, Philip still insisted on Rubens painting the picture. He completed it for Philip, along with a sensual *Venus and Adonis*. In both of these paintings, Hélène was the model for Venus, the goddess of beauty. By then, he had become even freer with his compositions, and his plump young women were always inspired by Hélène. It amused the King of Spain to see, even in his Torre de la Parada paintings, that Rubens put his young wife in the title roles.

THE CONSEQUENCES OF WAR

During the previous year, Rubens had completed a commission for Ferdinand de' Medici, the Grand Duke of Tuscany (1610–70). In many ways, *The Consequences of War* is a complement to *The Allegory of Peace and War* of 1629–30. Italy had been less involved in the European wars that had dominated

Right: The Consequences of War, *Rubens, 1638–39. Commenting on the Thirty Years' War, this shows Mars, the Roman god of war, with his sword pointing to a deadly battle, while he looks at Venus, the goddess of love.*

Above: The Birth of the Milky Way, *1636–37. Rubens, as usual, has interpreted the classical myth in an original composition filled with human attributes.*

Rubens's life, and this painting expresses his personal view of the tragedy and hopelessness of the war. He wrote of it to Ferdinand de' Medici's court painter, Justus Sustermans (1597–1681): '. . . That grief-stricken woman clothed in black, with torn veil, robbed of all her jewels and other ornaments, is the unfortunate Europe who, for so many years now has suffered plunder, outrage,

Above: Bellerophon Riding Pegasus Fighting the Chimaera, *1635. No matter what Rubens was depicting, he always conveyed a sense of action.*

and misery.' In this work, Rubens once again articulates his originality: Mars, the god of war, marches from the Temple of Janus, encouraged by Alecto, the Fury of War, who is accompanied by two monsters symbolizing Plague and Famine, while Venus attempts to restrain him, but even her overwhelming beauty is ineffectual. A woman personifies the wretchedness of Europe.

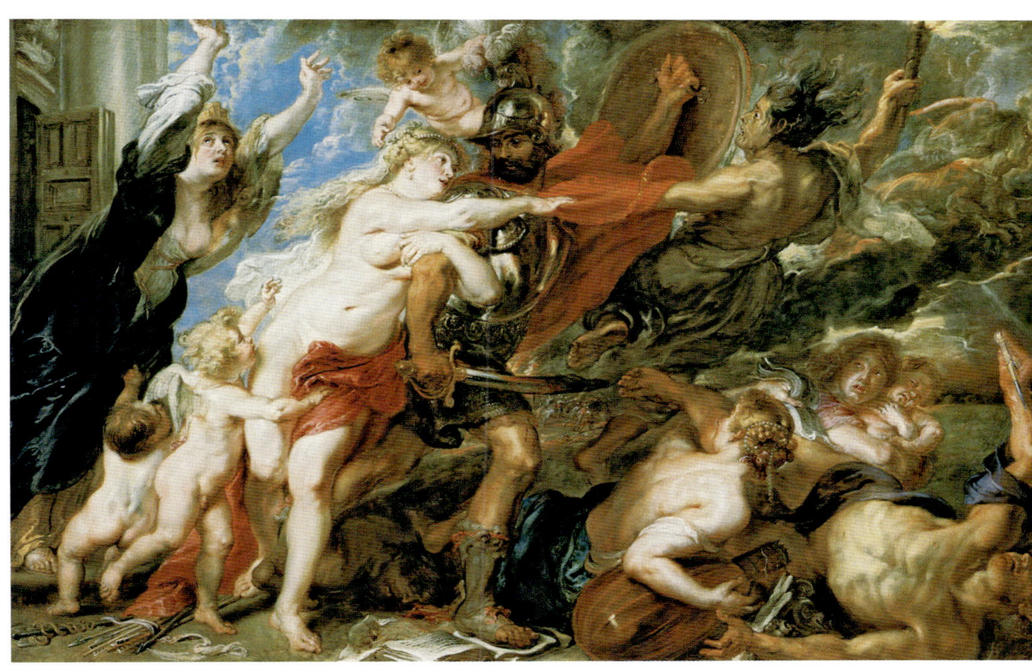

TROUBLING AILMENTS

Rubens's recurrent attacks of gout laid him up for weeks at a time. He wrote: 'The gout very often prevents my wielding either pen or brush, and taking up its usual residence so to speak, in my right hand, hinders me especially.' As if reflecting his suffering, his later allegories nearly all depict love overshadowed by pain.

Only in his landscapes did Rubens show calm, untroubled views of nature in all its beauty. The countryside was a respite for him from his hectic studio. In the country, he could forget the war, Antwerp's economic problems and his demanding diplomatic missions. He often preferred to stay at Steen, as is apparent in one of his letters to a pupil, Lucas Fayd'herbe (1617–97): 'I hope that this will find you still in Antwerp, for I have urgent need of a panel on which there are three heads in life-size, painted by my own hand, namely: one of a furious soldier with a black cap on

Right: Fortune, Rubens, 1636–37. This is the goddess Fortune who can bring happiness, but also misfortune – symbolized by the gathering storm.

Below: Deucalion and Pyrrha Repopulate the World by Throwing Stones Behind Them, c.1636. Here, Rubens depicts the first king and queen of Northern Greece.

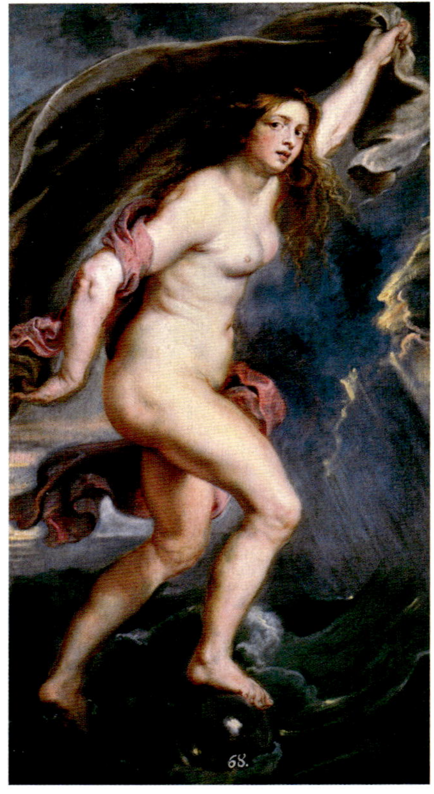

his head, one of a man crying and one laughing. You will do me a great favour by sending this panel to me at once or if you are ready to come yourself, by bringing it with you.'

SHIFTING THE FOCUS

Despite his debilitating pain, Rubens continued to work industriously. In c.1636–38 he painted Hélène, not as a goddess, nor in a conventional portrait, but naked, wrapping herself in fur. *Het Pelsken* is an intimate view of his cherished wife, while one of his final self-portraits also focuses on her and their young son Peter Paul. He presents himself in his early 60s, gazing at Hélène, while she looks at their child. All three are richly attired. Acknowledging his love for his family, no trace of his ill health is apparent, only pride, as he touches Hélène's hand to symbolize their union and his protectiveness of her. X-rays have shown that he altered the picture as he painted, shifting the focus

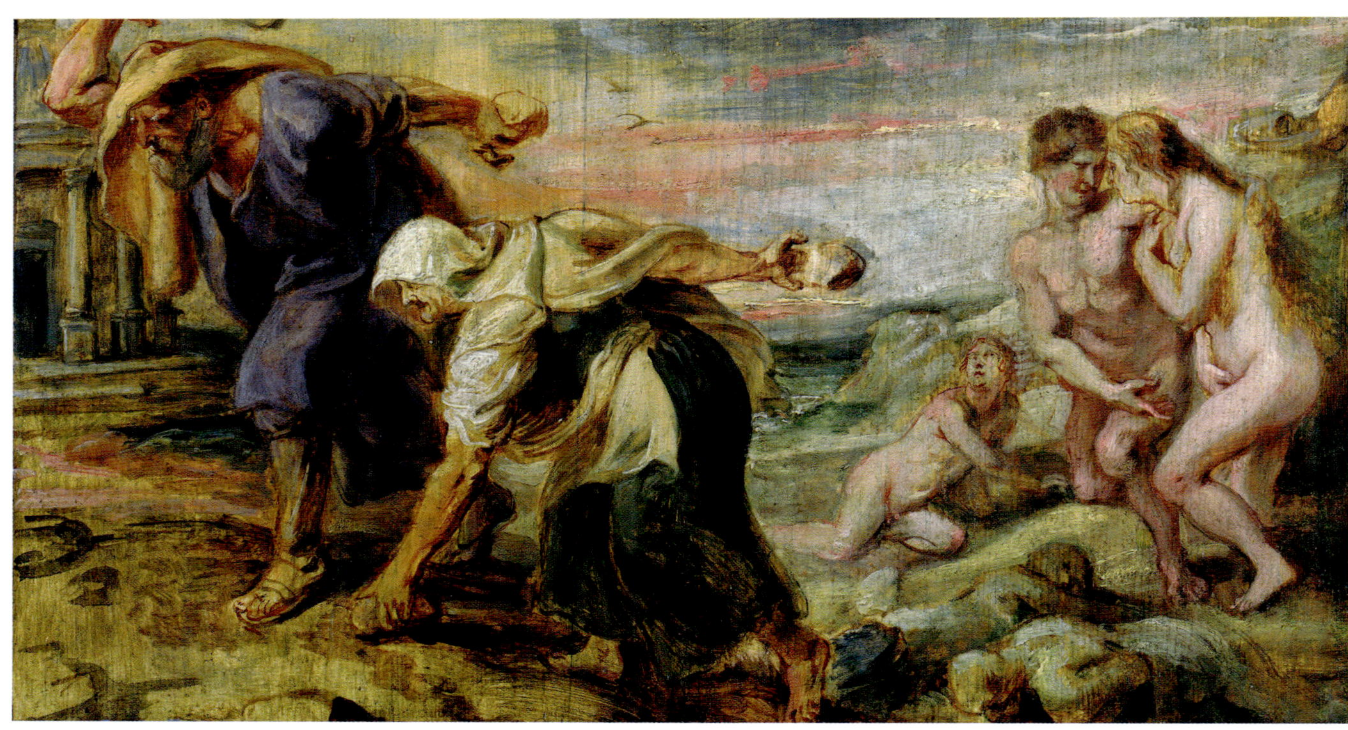

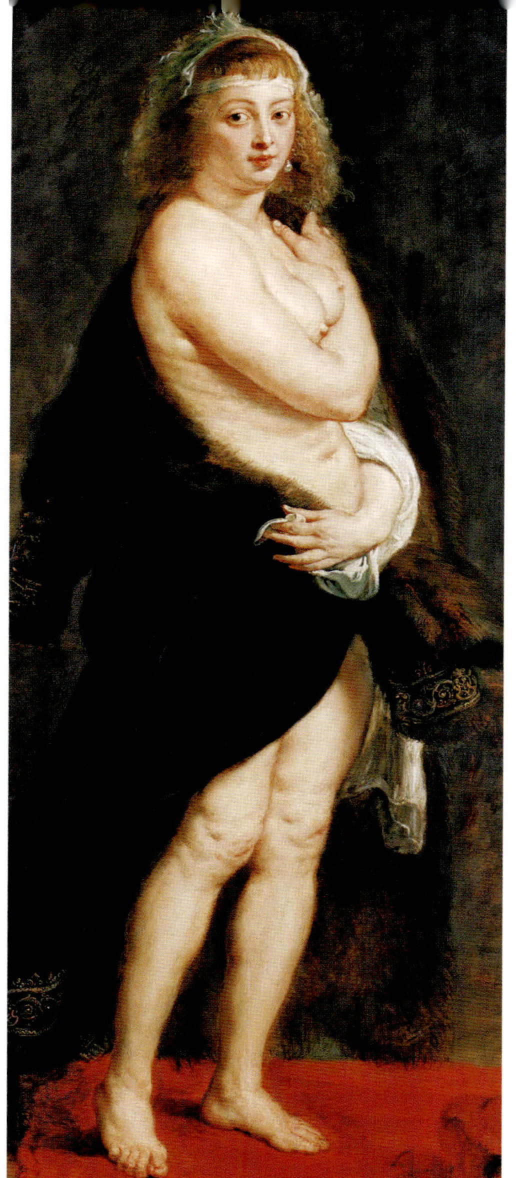

Above: Het Pelsken ('The Little Fur'), *Rubens, 1636–38. This is Rubens's favourite portrait of Hélène. He refused to part with this image of her, her naked body barely concealed by her fur wrap.*

from himself as head of the household to Hélène as the perfect wife and mother. The scene is filled with symbols of ideal motherhood: the parrot traditionally indicates the Virgin, and the fountain, caryatid and garden setting suggest fertility. It is an image of domestic bliss, love, elegance and prosperity.

In 1638, Rubens designed a triumphal carriage for the Cardinal Infante Ferdinand to celebrate the

Right: Saint Augustine, *1636, was an early Christian theologian and philosopher whose writings influenced the development of Western Christianity and philosophy.*

Spanish naval victory over Dutch forces at Calloo, or Kallo, that year. The battle was fought near the fort of Kallo, on the left bank of the River Scheldt. Ferdinand gained success when he led the Spanish army against the much larger Dutch forces by Ferdinand.

PICKING UP ON THE PAST

Having retained a few of the rarest jewels and his Egyptian mummy when he sold his collection to Buckingham, Rubens used them as the basis for a new collection. In 1637, he was commissioned by a wealthy German financier Everhard Jabach (1618–95) to paint an altarpiece focusing on the life of Saint Peter for Cologne's Church of Saint Peter. It meant a lot to Rubens, as it was the church of his boyhood, and where his father was buried. He wrote: 'I have great affection for the city of Cologne, because it was there that I was brought up until the tenth year of my life and I have often had the wish to see it again, after so long.' However, his health prevented him from travelling, so he took

the measurements and created a powerful image of Saint Peter's crucifixion from his Antwerp studies.

LAST DAYS

By early 1640, despite struggling to paint, Rubens was incapacitated by excruciating pain, and was receiving almost constant medical attention from Antwerp's specialist Dr Lazarus Marcquis (1605–47). On May 27, he wrote a new will. Four days later, his friend Gerbier wrote to Charles I from Brussels: 'Sir Peter Rubens is deadly sick.' The Cardinal Infante sent other physicians to him, but they were too late. Rubens had died on May 30, 1640 from heart failure, a result of his chronic gout. His youngest child was born eight months after his death.

Below: Andromeda, c.1640s. *Painted mainly by his workshop, this is one of Rubens's statuesque beauties as the mythological heroine tied to a rock.*

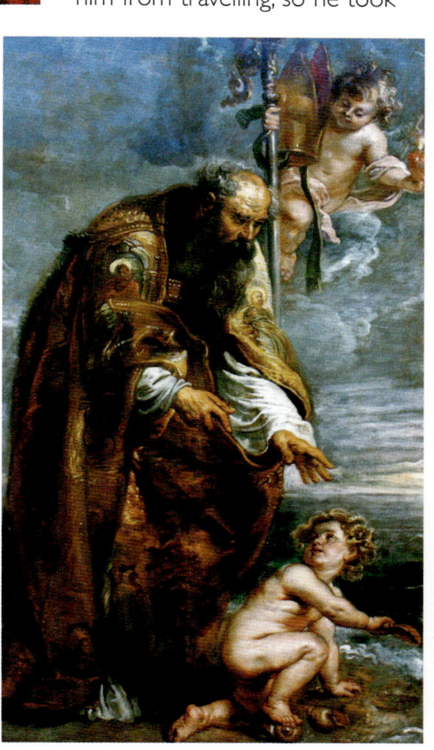

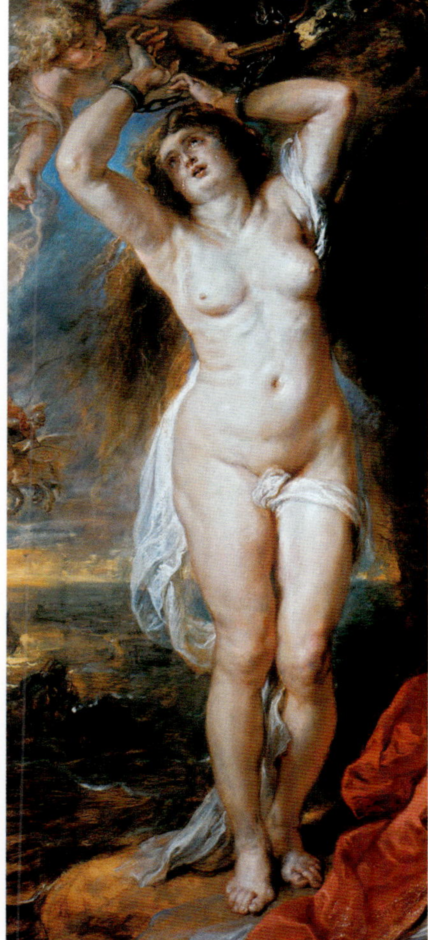

INFLUENCE AND LEGACY

For over six weeks following Rubens's death, hundreds of masses were said for him across Flanders and in other parts of Europe. His funeral cortège was befitting of one of Antwerp's most illustrious citizens and a knight of two realms, bedecked with 60 tapers, crosses of red satin and the music of the Church of Our Lady.

An international celebrity of his times, Rubens had become renowned for his artistic and diplomatic accomplishments. On the night he died, his body was interred in the Fourment family tomb in Saint Jacob's church in Antwerp. Three days later, the funeral mass took place; the chapel was adorned with candles and red satin crosses and a procession was led by the clergy, followed by prominent members of Antwerp society, his family and friends, and crowds of orphaned boys in acknowledgement of the financial assistance he had given them. In the year following his death, a funeral chapel was built especially for him, and one of his last paintings, *The Madonna and Child Surrounded by Saints*, was displayed above it. A white marble statue of the Virgin, made by Lucas Fayd'herbe, was placed above that, and his friend, the philosopher, poet and historian Gevaerts contributed the epitaph: 'Peter Paul Rubens, knight and Lord of Steen, who, among the other gifts by which he marvellously excelled in the knowledge of ancient history and all other useful and elegant arts, deserved also to be called the Apelles, not only of his own age, but of all time and made himself a pathway to the friendship of kings and princes.'

EXTRAORDINARY VERSATILITY

Rubens left his 26-year-old wife and seven children. In 1672, the Italian painter, antiquarian and writer Giovanni Pietro Bellori (1613–96) published *Lives of the Modern Painters, Sculptors and Architects*. In it, he wrote of Rubens: 'He was tall and well-formed with a pleasing complexion and temperament, a commanding presence too, and generous, elegant in his manners and of dignified mien.' In 1708, the critic and painter Roger de Piles (1635–1709) listed 56 painters in his *Cours de Peinture par Principes avec un Balance de Peintres*.

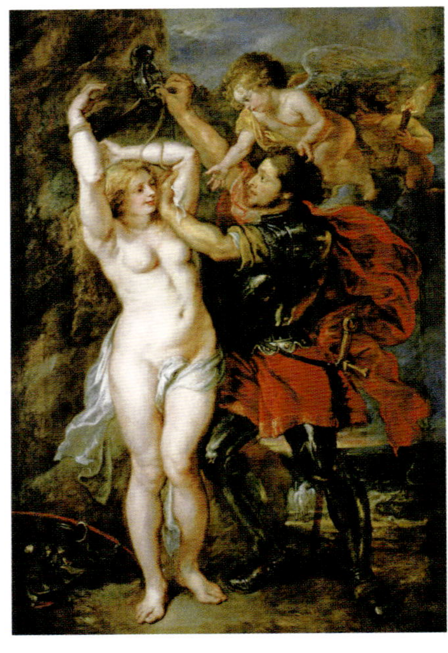

Above: Perseus Freeing Andromeda, *Rubens and Jordaens, 1639–41. This is one of Rubens's last paintings. After his death in 1640, it was finished by Jacob Jordaens.*

He awarded marks to each artist on the list for composition, drawing, colour and expression, and the highest marks went to Raphael and Rubens.

His work became sought after by collectors and princes, and emulated by both art students and established artists. He had an enormous influence on the development of the 18th-century Rococo style, and especially on Jean-Antoine Watteau (1684–1721) and François Boucher (1703–70). Watteau's *fête galantes* – paintings of figures frolicking in the countryside – were directly inspired by Rubens. During the Neoclassical era, his work became unfashionable, but the Romanticists embraced it wholeheartedly,

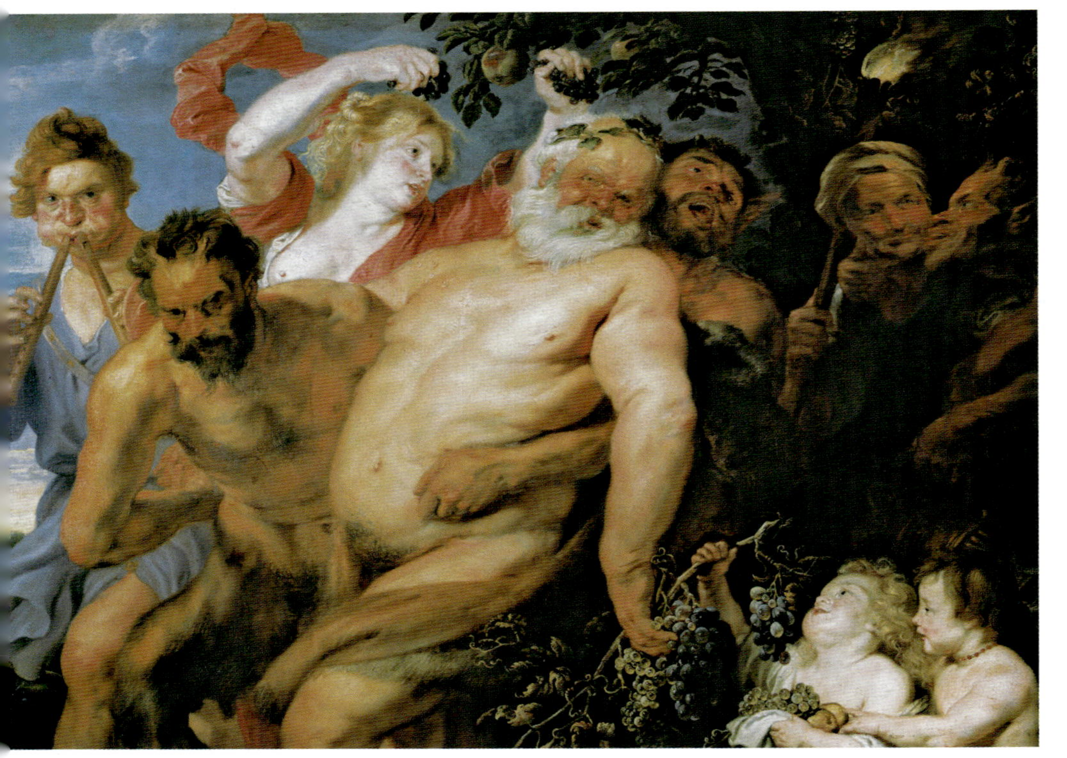

Left: Drunken Silenus Supported by Satyrs, *c.1620. This is believed to have been executed by Rubens's studio, including Jan Wildens, Frans Snyders and Van Dyck.*

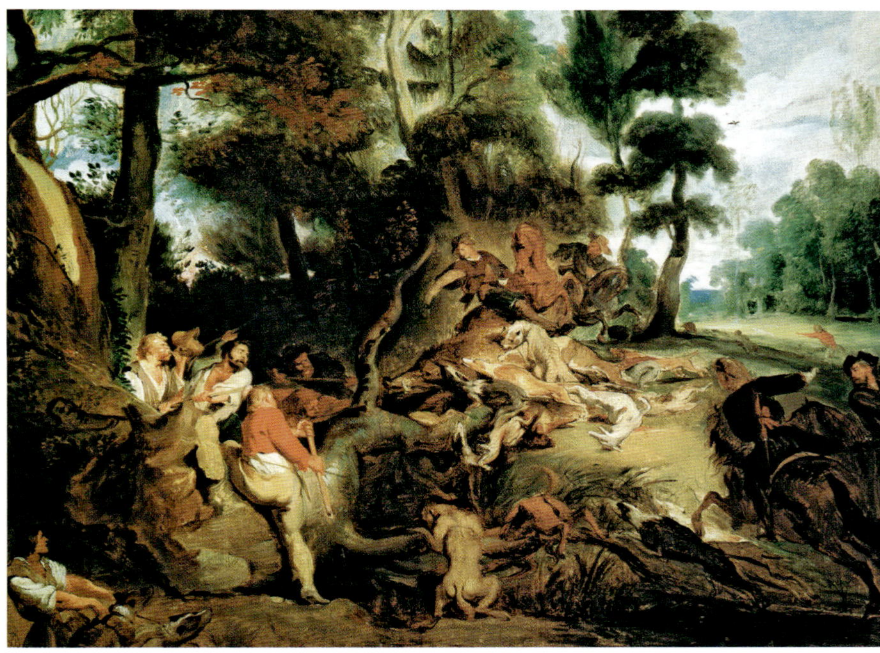

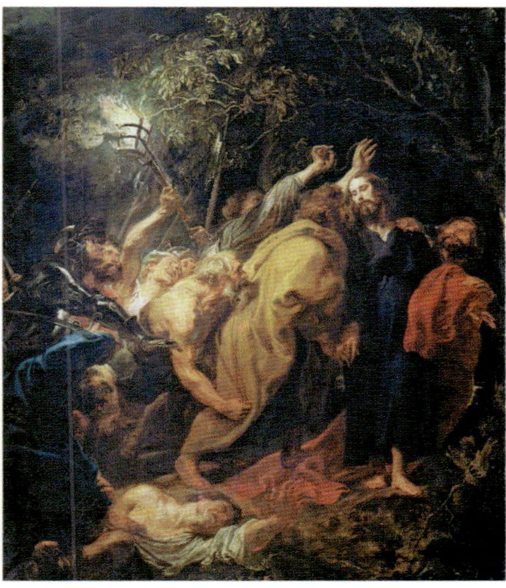

Above: The Arrest of Christ in the Gardens, *1618–20. From the brush of Rubens's greatest pupil, this is a copy of a Rubens painting by Van Dyck.*

Above: In a mark of the esteem with which he held Rubens, Delacroix copied his painting The Wild Boar Hunt *in c.1840–50.*

in particular Theodore Géricault (1791–1824) and Eugene Delacroix (1798–1863). Delacroix's journal is filled with references to Rubens, such as: 'He dominates, he overwhelms you with so much liberty and audacity.'

Several Impressionists and Post-Impressionists also became close followers, particularly Auguste Renoir (1841–1919) and Paul Cézanne (1839–1906), and Rubens's work continued to inspire artists in the 20th and 21st centuries, including Giorgio de Chirico (1888–1978), Lucian Freud (1922–2011), Jackson Pollock (1912–56), Sir Anthony Caro (1924–2013), and Jenny Saville (b.1970).

ENERGY AND INVENTIVENESS

Rubens's ability to assimilate, amalgamate and reinterpret other artists's styles and methods led him to produce profoundly innovative and versatile work. Characterized by bold colours, dynamic compositions and vigorous brushwork, his expressiveness shows his rare insights into how to use elements of others' work judiciously, to create his own unique style, and his abundant energy, inventiveness and vitality ensured that his legacy endured.

Below: Despite being classified as an Impressionist, Renoir always maintained that he admired the style of Rubens.

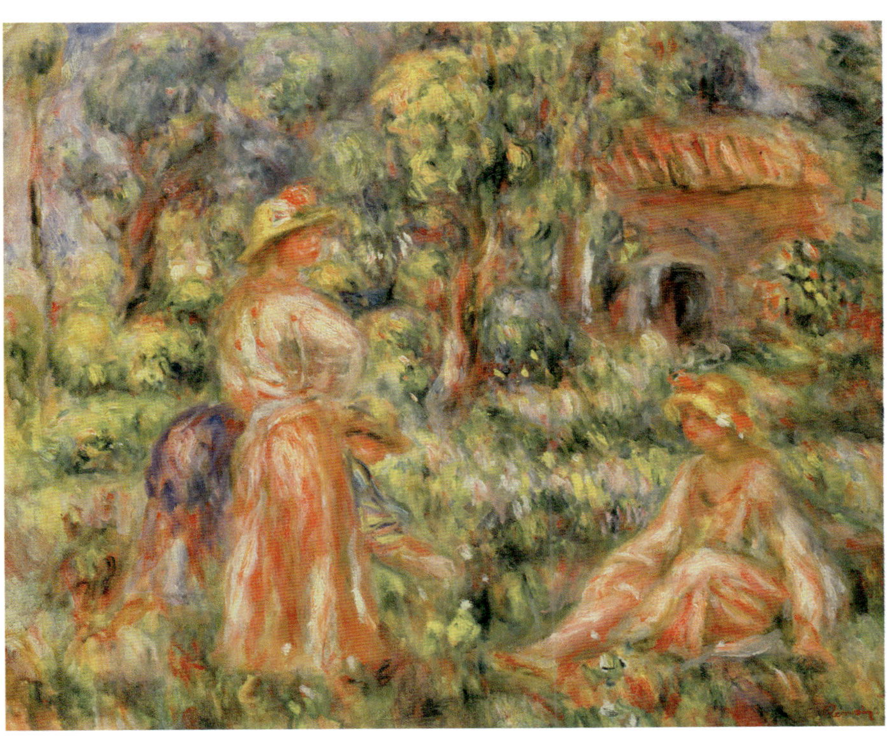

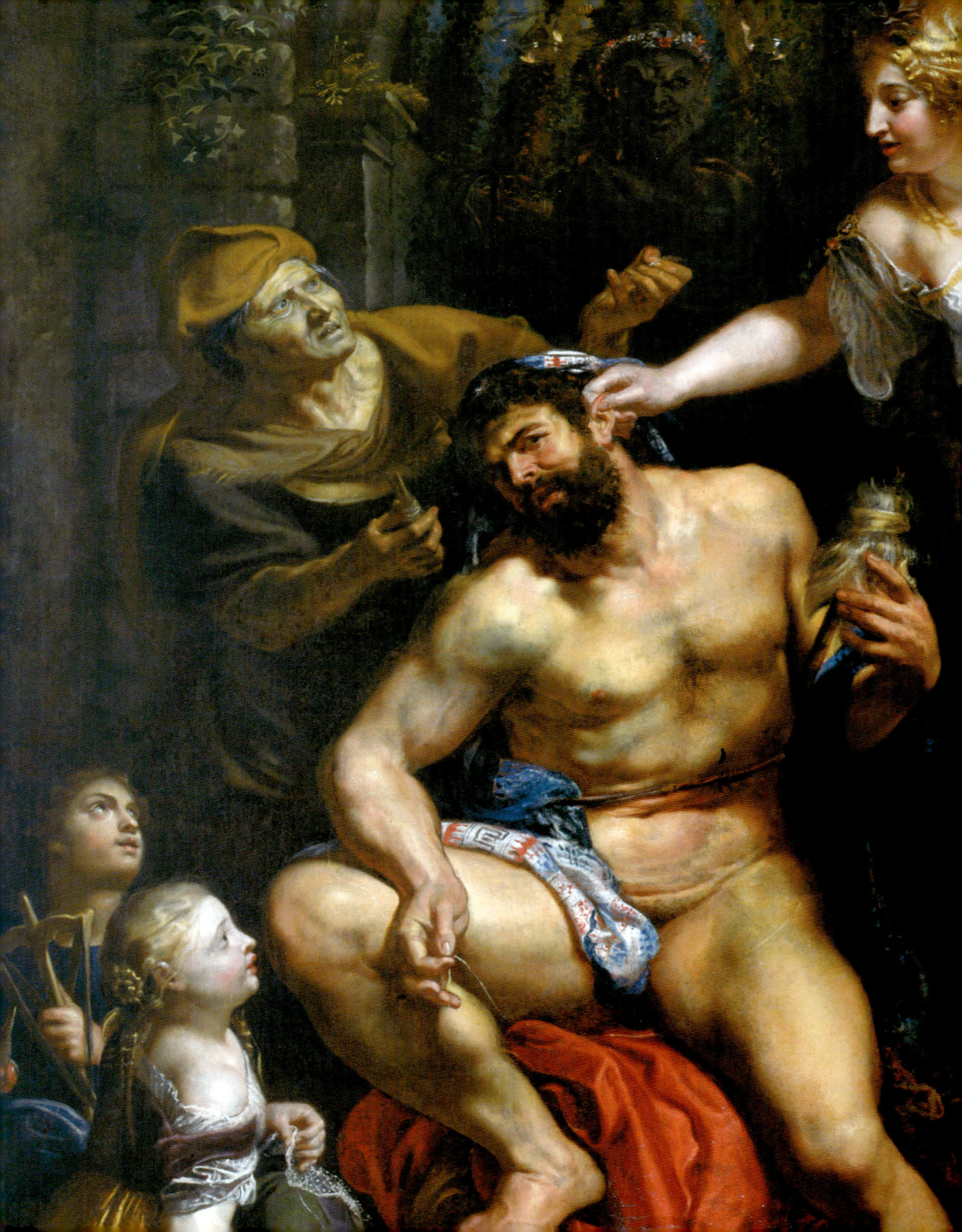

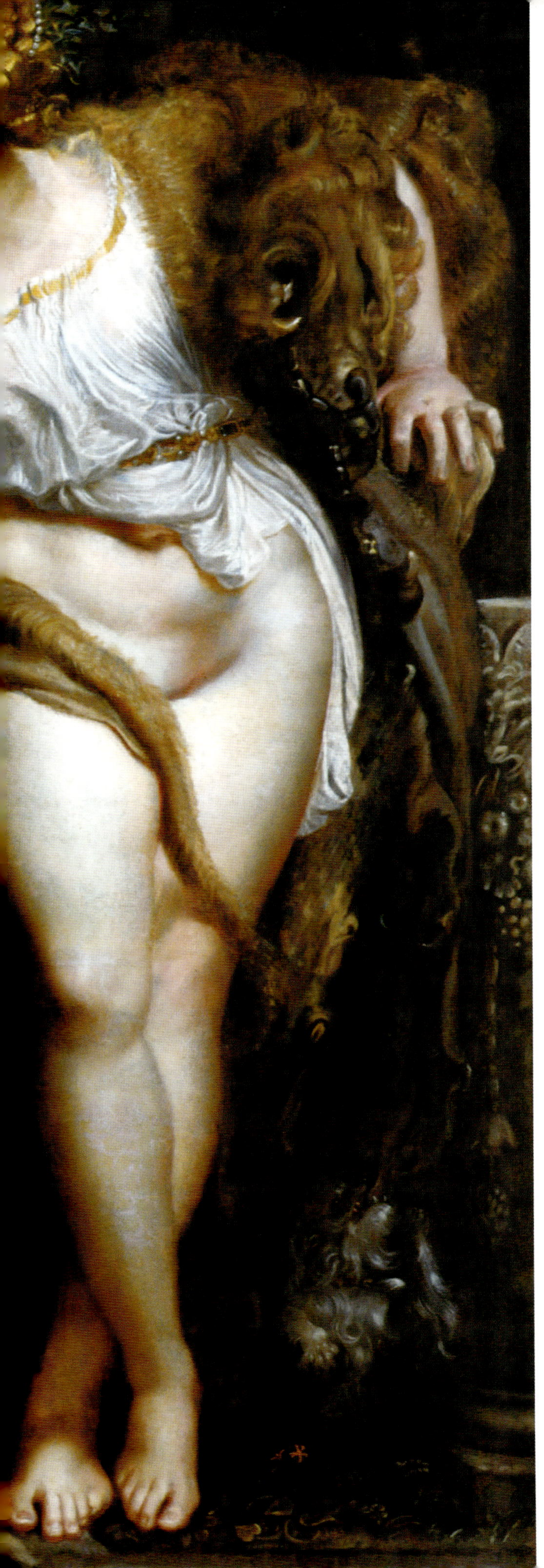

THE GALLERY

One of the most prolific and exciting painters of his time, Rubens used his acute powers of observation and exemplary artistic skills to cultivate and synthesize the diverse styles and methods of artists he admired, including Caravaggio, Michelangelo, Tintoretto and Veronese, and blended this with his own unique and vibrant approach. From the start of his career, he was noted for his intelligence, empathy and charm, which singled him out as eminently suited to become involved with the political intrigues and issues that dominated Europe. As a peacemaker and outstanding artist, he was welcomed at any European court he visited. From the time he had completed his artistic training, his career proceeded without setback. He travelled to Italy to study the great Renaissance and classical works that he knew from copies. With his creative proficiency, abundant energy and skills as a linguist and courtier, he found favour with the aristocracy, and he remained abroad for eight years, travelling, studying art and becoming a respected ambassador.

Left: Hercules and Omphale, *1602, oil on canvas. One of Rubens's early renditions of a mythological tale, this shows Hercules under the spell of Omphale, Queen of Lydia, who has made him spin wool. Despite being a Catholic and painting this work in Catholic Italy, Rubens's expression of sensuality, love, endeavour, strength and beauty had a universal appeal.*

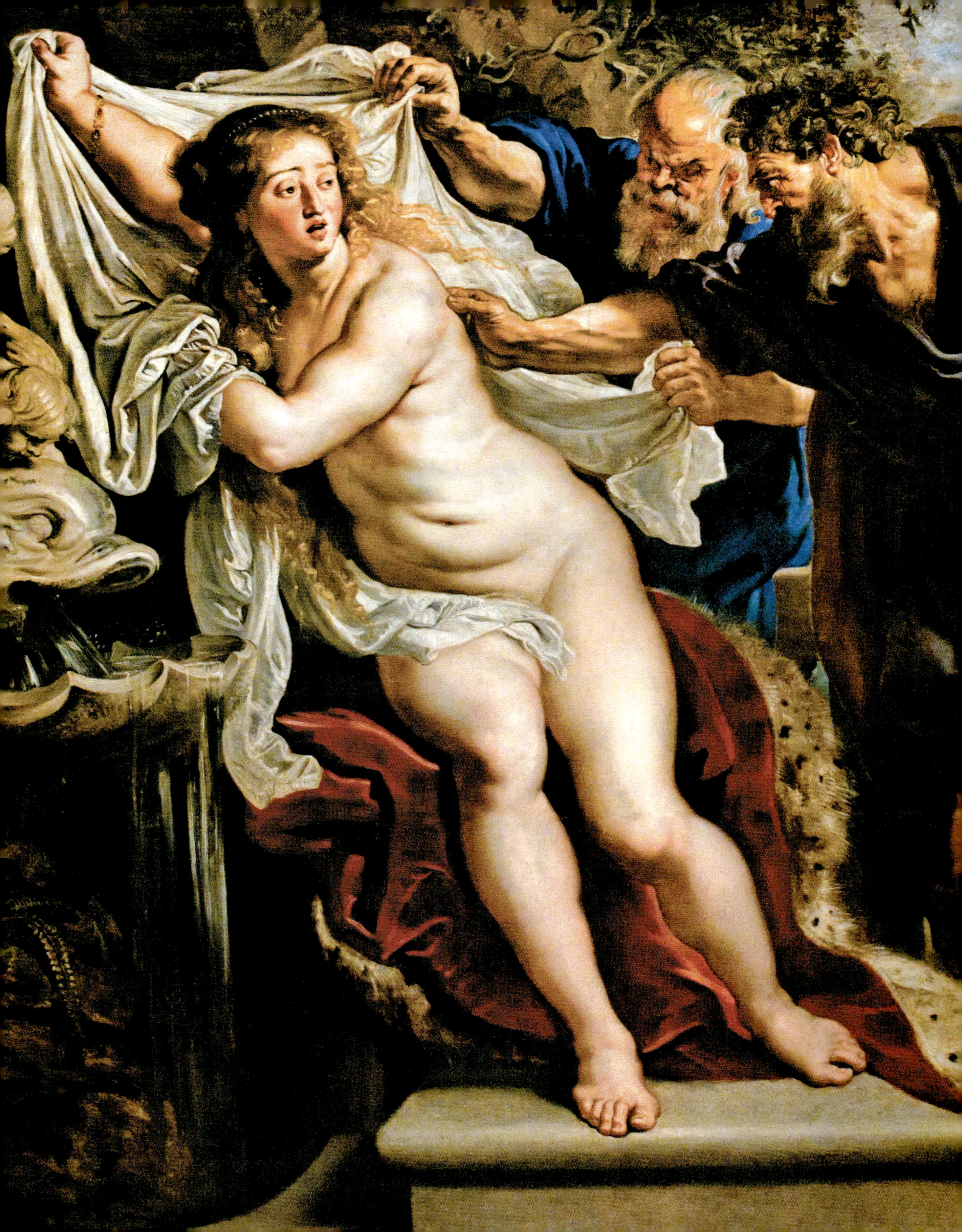

THE INFLUENCE OF ITALY

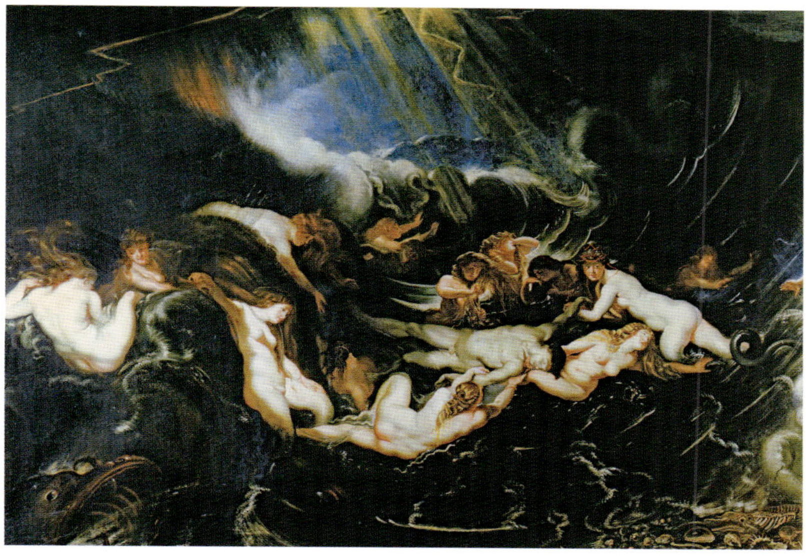

From the moment he qualified as a professional artist, Rubens showed an outstanding creative capacity. His early style shows the influence of his teachers, especially Otto van Veen, and from his time in Italy, he also assimilated ideas from ancient and more modern Italian artists. Yet his depictions were always personal, of the most passionate or dynamic moments in stories, and showing the closest details and personal gestures in portraits. Once he had studied in Italy, he could have returned to Antwerp, but he was asked to join the court of the Duke of Mantua and soon became much sought after in Italy for the beauty of his painting, his unconventional interpretations, and his fresh and passionate compositions.

Above: Hero and Leander, *1605–07, oil on canvas. This is a dramatic portrayal of two aspects of one story: Leander drowning on a dark, stormy night; and his love, Hero, throwing herself into the sea in despair. Here, Rubens focuses on the human body in extremes of movement, and imitates the dramatic lighting effects that he admired in the work of Tintoretto.*

Left: Susanna and the Elders, *1609–10, oil on panel. From a biblical story, this shows a beautiful young woman, Susanna, resisting two lecherous men – also highly respected judges – who secretly entered her garden while she was bathing.*

Portrait of a Man,
*c.*1597, oil on copper,
21.6 x 14.6cm (8½ x 5¾in),
The Metropolitan Museum
of Art, New York, USA

One of Rubens's earliest
known works, painted when
he was 26 before he left
Antwerp for Italy in May
1600. The unidentified, well-
groomed man could be an
architect, draughtsman or
geographer, suggested by the
square and dividers in his
hands, while the watch is
a reminder of mortality – a
vanitas symbol. Alternatively,
the square and dividers
could symbolize Temperance.
The precise contours and
lifelike details owe much
to the influence of
Otto van Veen.

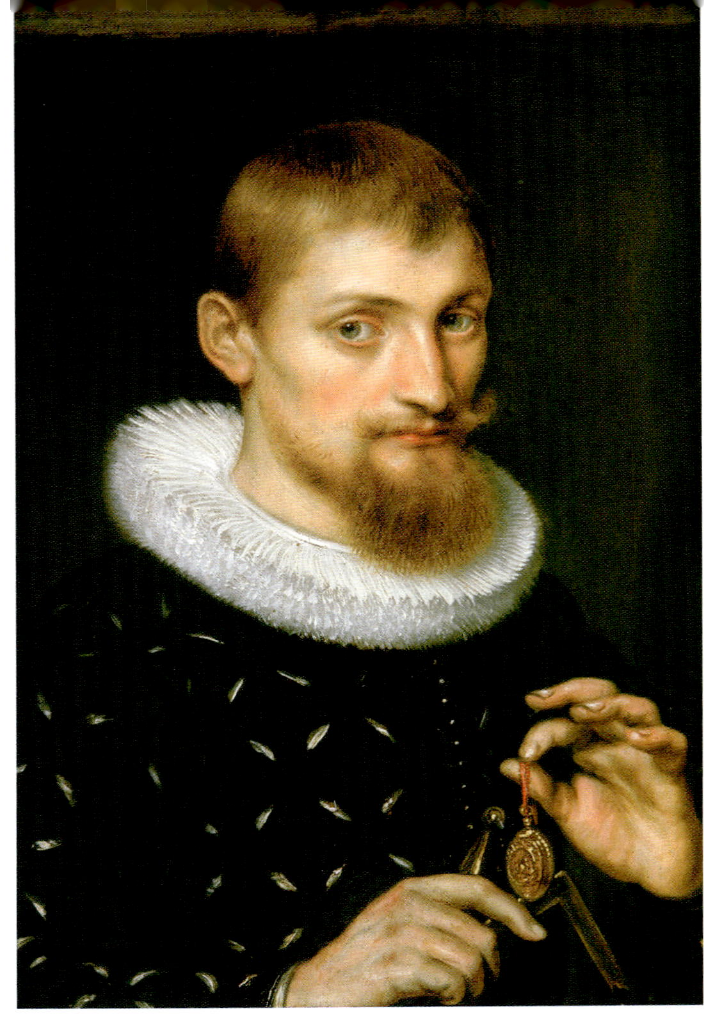

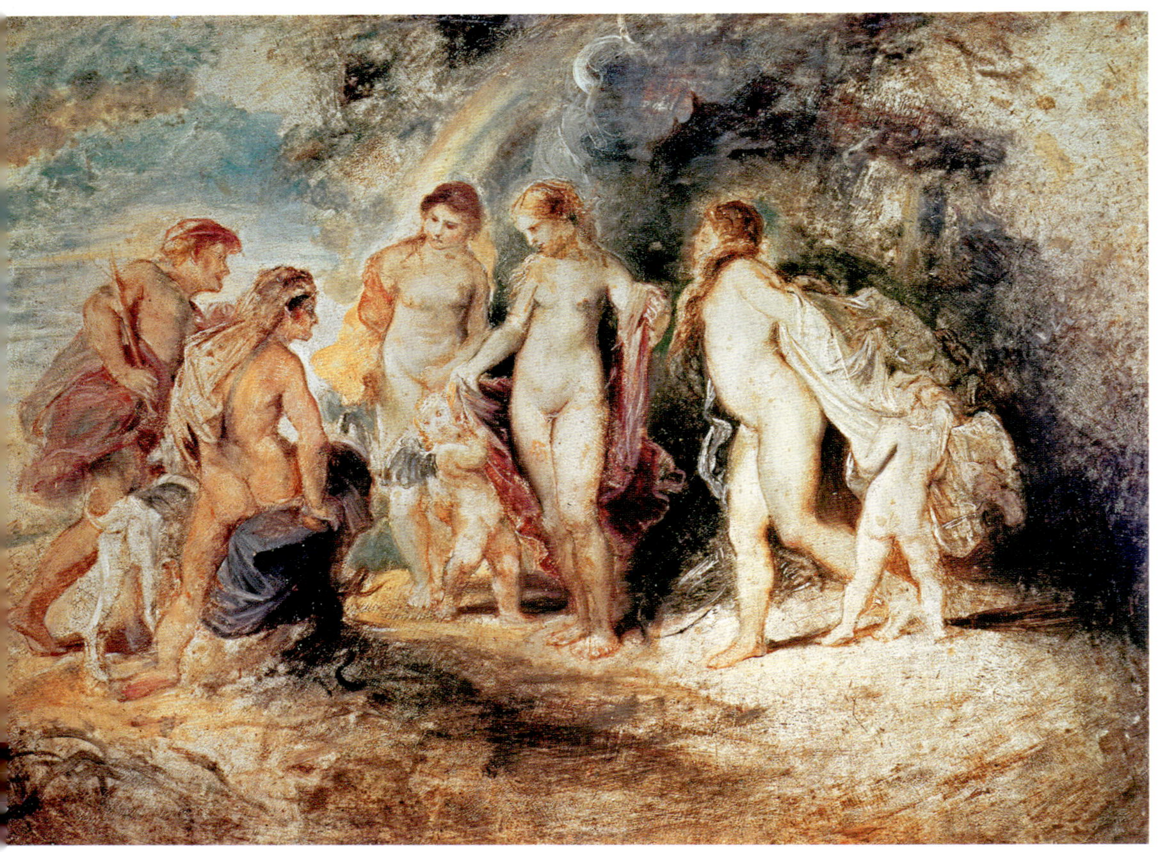

The Judgement of Paris,
*c.*1599–1601, oil on copper,
32.5 x 43.5cm (12¾ x 17in),
Akademie der Bildenden
Kunste, Vienna, Austria

One of his first attempts
at the subject, Rubens later
painted this story several
times. It is also one of his
few works on copper.
His patron for the work
has not been identified,
although it may have been
Cardinal Richelieu. Even
though Richelieu was not
in favour of Rubens for his
alignment with Spain, he
admired his art. Rubens
excelled at depicting the
three young goddesses in
different poses, as Paris
compares their beauty.

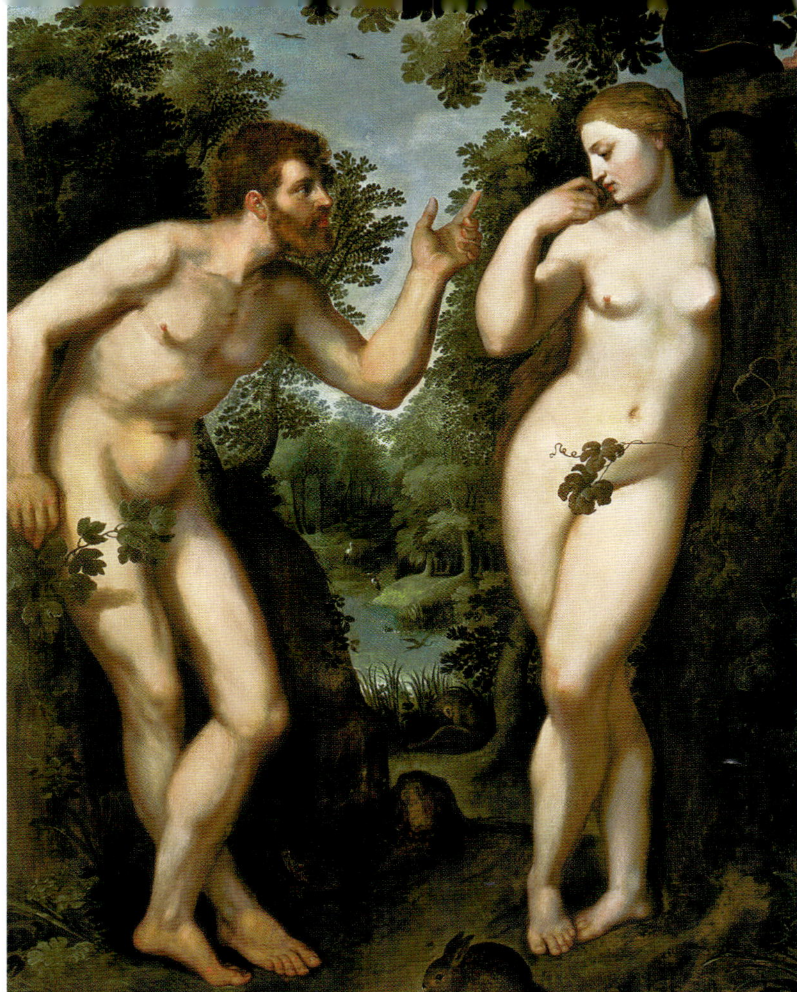

*Adam and Eve, c.*1599,
oil on panel, 180 x 158cm
(71 x 62in), Rubenshuis,
Antwerp, Belgium

Little is known about
Rubens's output from his
initial establishment as an
artist and his departure for
Italy in 1600. This is one
of the few extant paintings
from that period. The story
of Adam and Eve was often
painted by artists to blend
beauty with a moral
message. This derives directly
from a print by Marcantonio
Raimondi after Raphael,
although Rubens's Adam
is more muscular and
Eve more idealized.

Eleanor Gonzaga,
*c,*1600–01, oil on canvas,
76 x 49.5cm (30 x 19½in),
Kunsthistoriches Museum,
Vienna, Austria

Eleanor, Eleonore or
Eleonora Gonzaga
(1598–1655) was the
youngest daughter of Duke
Vincenzo I of Gonzaga and
Eleonora de' Medici. Rubens
painted her aged two, when
he was living at the Mantuan
court. She later became the
second wife of the Holy
Roman Emperor. Highly
educated, pious and
interested in art, she
founded several convents
and promoted cultural life at
the Viennese court. Rubens's
early portrait of her is a
little stiff and doll-like.

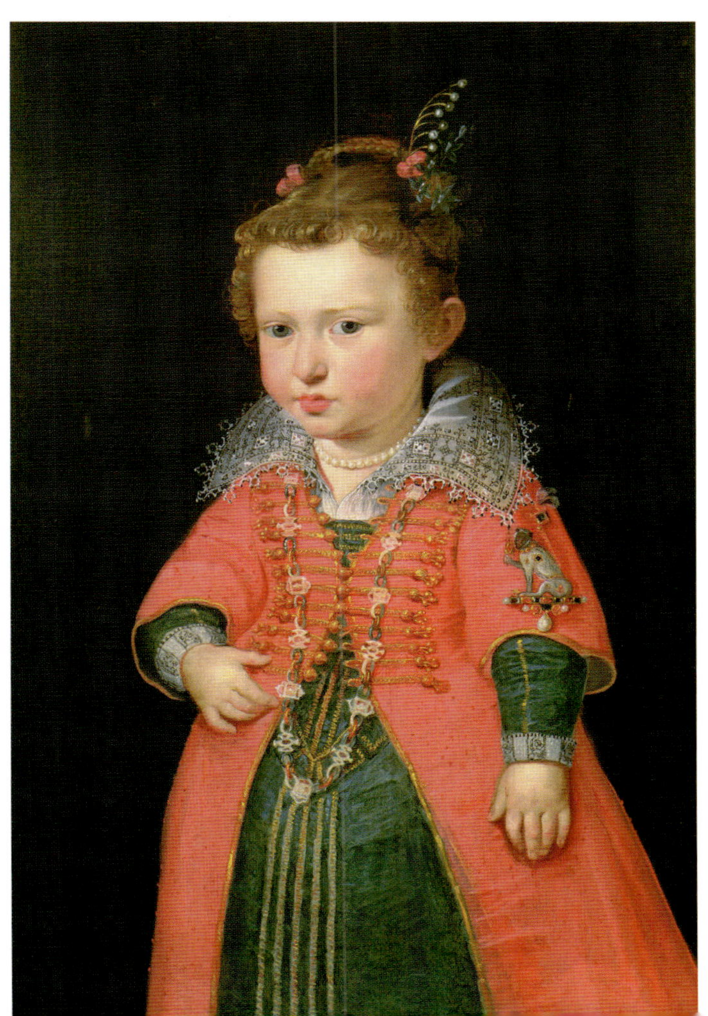

Battle between the Greeks and the Amazons, c.1602–04, pen and ink on paper, 25 x 42.8cm (10 x 16¾in), Private Collection

Four images of this subject by Rubens survive: two drawings and two paintings (see also page 176). This version began as a few marks in graphite, with firmer lines drawn with a fine pen. Rubens's fascination with the power and dynamism of horses in battle is apparent. The Amazons were a race of legendary female warriors from Asia Minor.

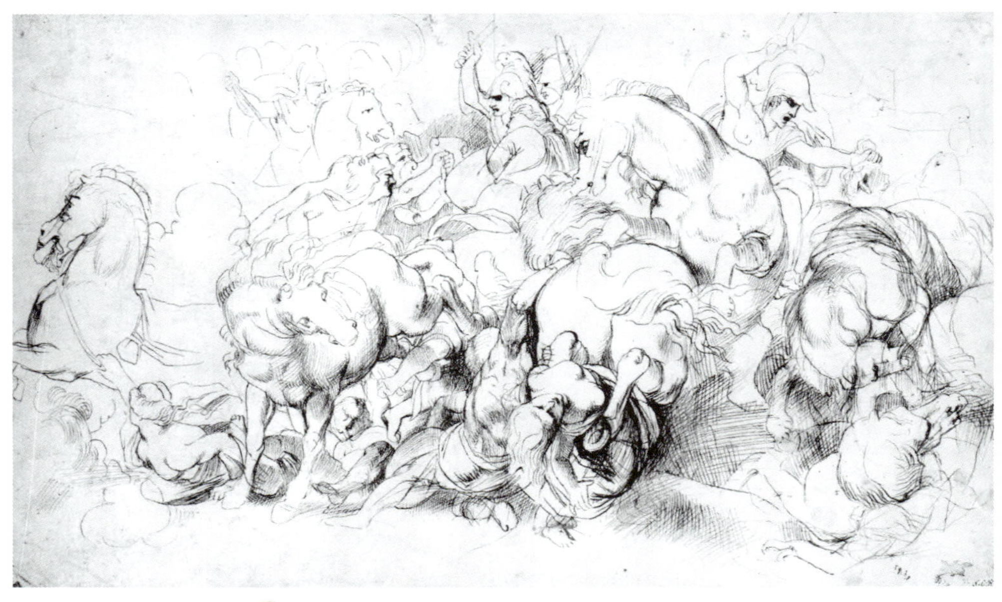

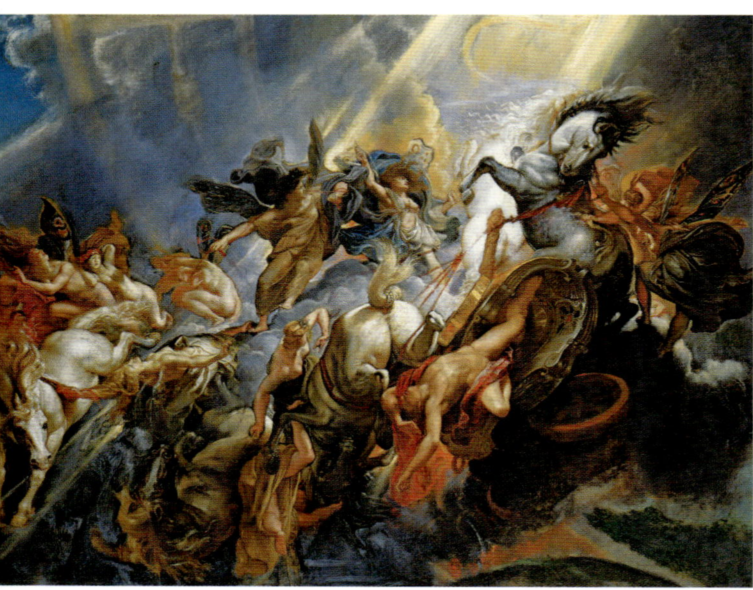

The Fall of Phaeton, 1604–05, oil on canvas, 98.4 x 131.2cm (38¾ x 51¾in), National Gallery of Art, Washington DC, USA

Here, Rubens depicted a moment of action in a Greek myth. Apollo allowed his son Phaeton to drive his Chariot of the Sun across the sky, but the boy could not control it. Horses, the chariot and Phaeton plunge into darkness, while Horae – female figures personifying the seasons – watch in horror as the Earth bursts into flames. Dramatic lighting, powerful dynamism and complex poses show Rubens's early genius.

Portrait of Emperor Charles (after Titian), 1603, oil on canvas, 76.3 x 56.6cm (30 x 22¼in), The Courtauld Gallery, London, UK

As the official painter to members of the Habsburg dynasty, Rubens took a particular interest in portraits of their great ancestor, the Holy Roman Emperor Charles V. This is a copy of the first of Titian's portraits of Charles, as a knight in armour. In painting such careful studies, Rubens learned the methods and approaches of the Italian masters he admired, while also providing his patrons with copies of works they coveted.

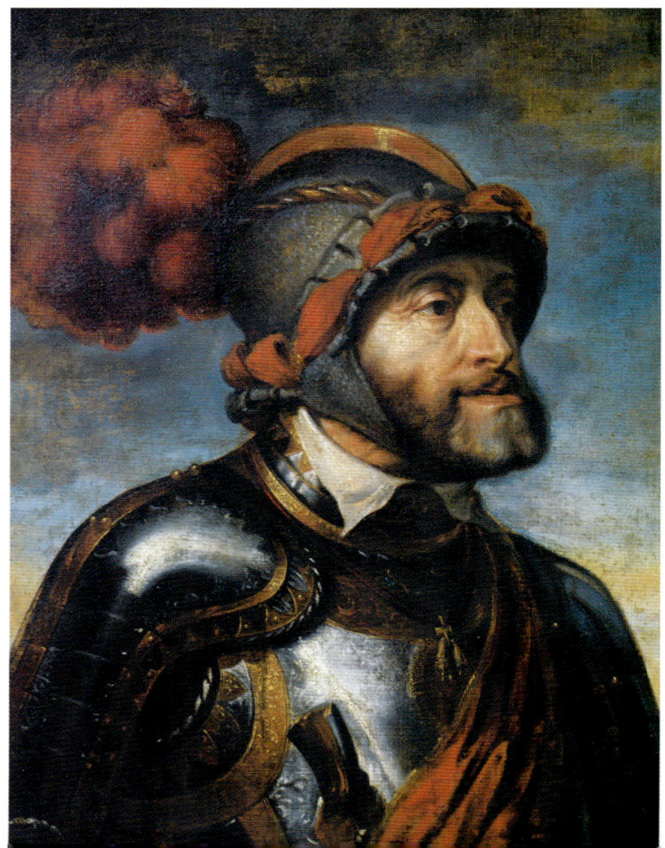

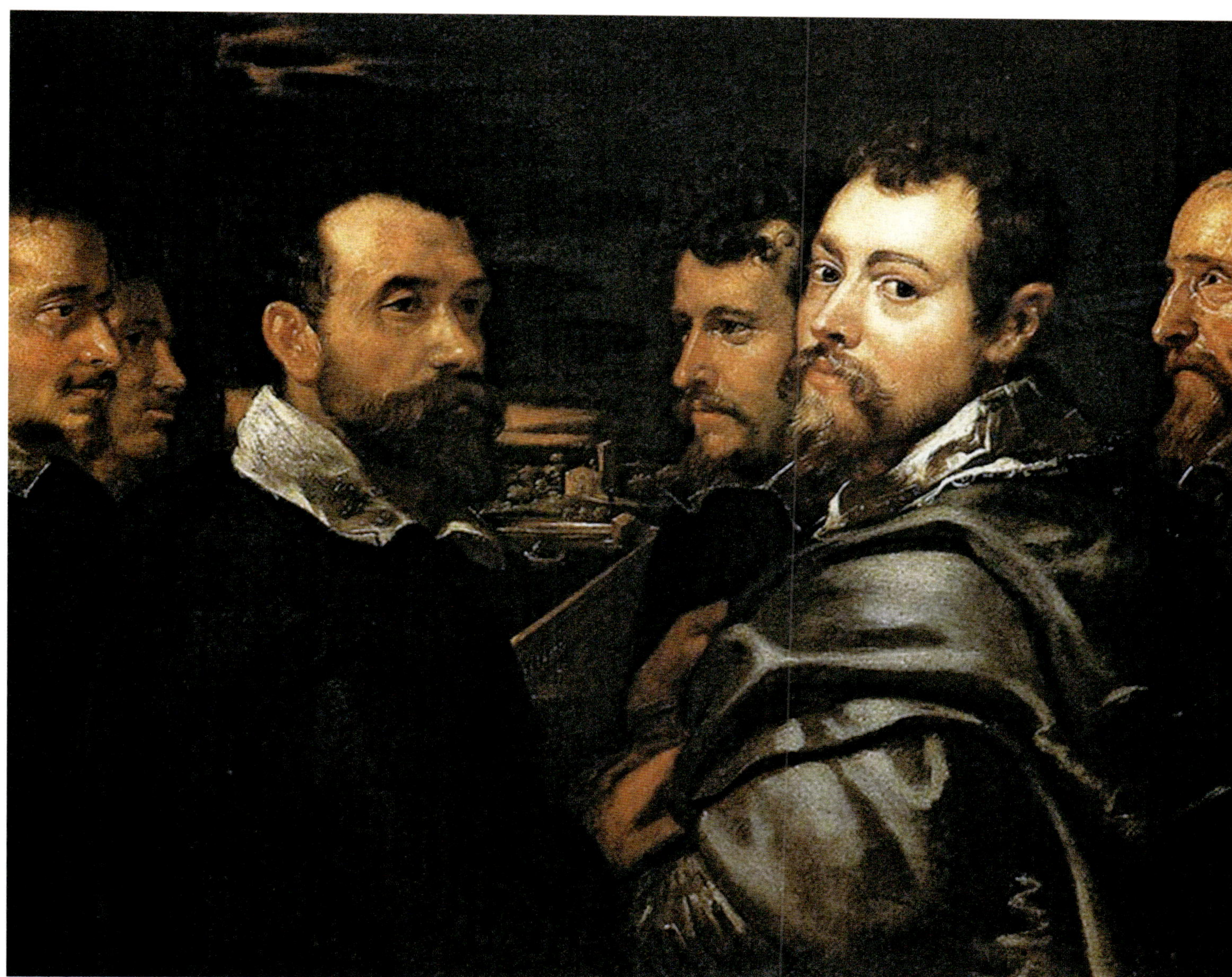

Self-portrait in a Circle of Friends from Mantua, c.1602–4, oil on canvas, 77.5 x 101cm (30½ x 39¾in), Wallraf-Richartz Museum, Cologne

This is Rubens's earliest known self-portrait. It includes prominent scholars of the day (from left to right): Frans Pourbus, Caspar Schoppe, William Richardot, Philip Rubens, Peter Paul Rubens and Justus Lipsius. Although most were probably painted from life, Lipsius was not. In comparison with the others, he appears rather stiff-looking, but Rubens included him as he was a leading philosopher of the time. Rubens is the only person looking directly out of the canvas at the viewer.

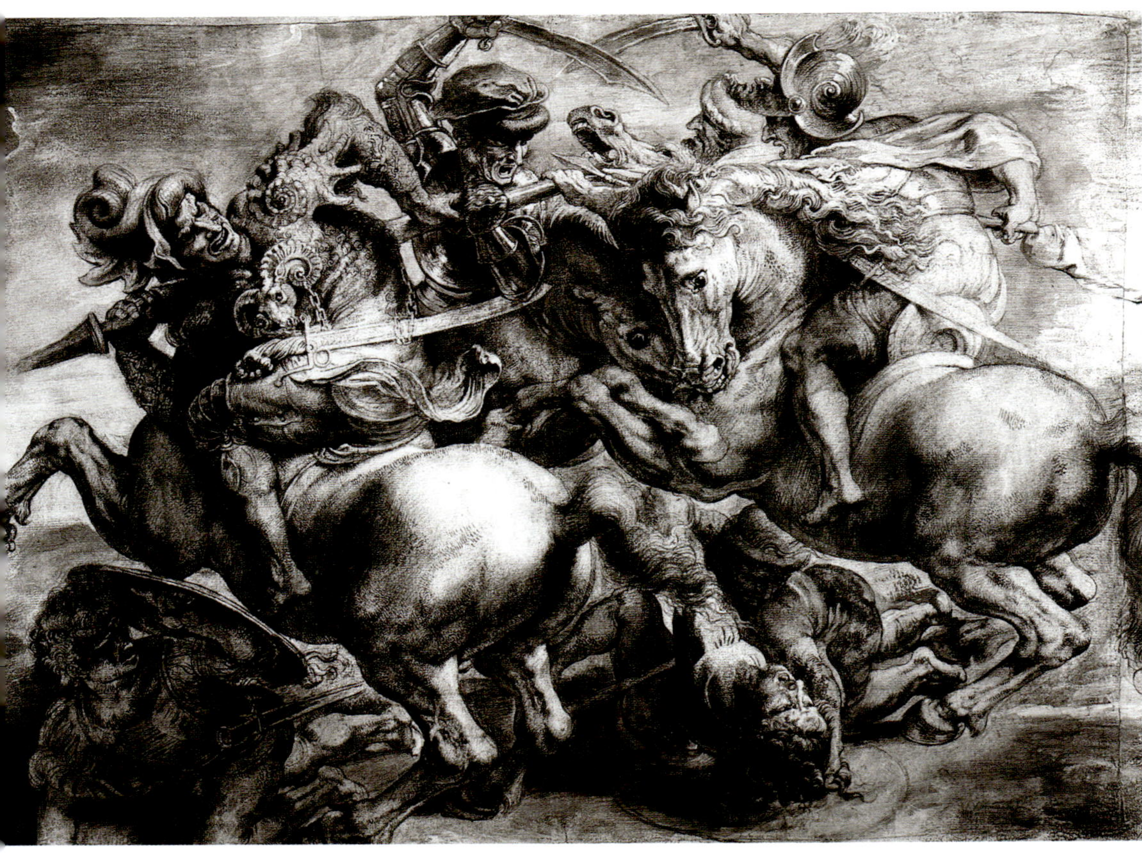

After the Battle of Anghiari by Leonardo da Vinci, 1604, black chalk, pen and ink, grey and white body colour on paper, 45.2 x 63.7cm (17¾ x 25in), Louvre, Paris, France

This is a copy of Leonardo's painting *The Battle of Anghiari*, now lost. As many of Leonardo's original sketches for the work still exist, it can be seen how closely Rubens's work captures the original drama and movement of the scene. The lessons Rubens learned in copying the lively horses and men, plus the intense emotions, movement and sense of power, informed much of his later work.

Portrait of Prince Vincenzo Gonzaga, 1604–05, oil on canvas, 67 x 51.5cm (26¼ x 20¼ in), Kunsthistorisches Museum, Vienna, Austria

The seventh Duke of Mantua and Monferrato from 1626–27, Vincenzo II Gonzaga (1594–1627) inherited the duchy at the death of his elder brother Ferdinand, and was the last direct Gonzaga to rule. As court painter, it was Rubens's duty to paint the family portraits, and this shows the prince aged 11, in the stiff, opulent fashions of the Mantuan court.

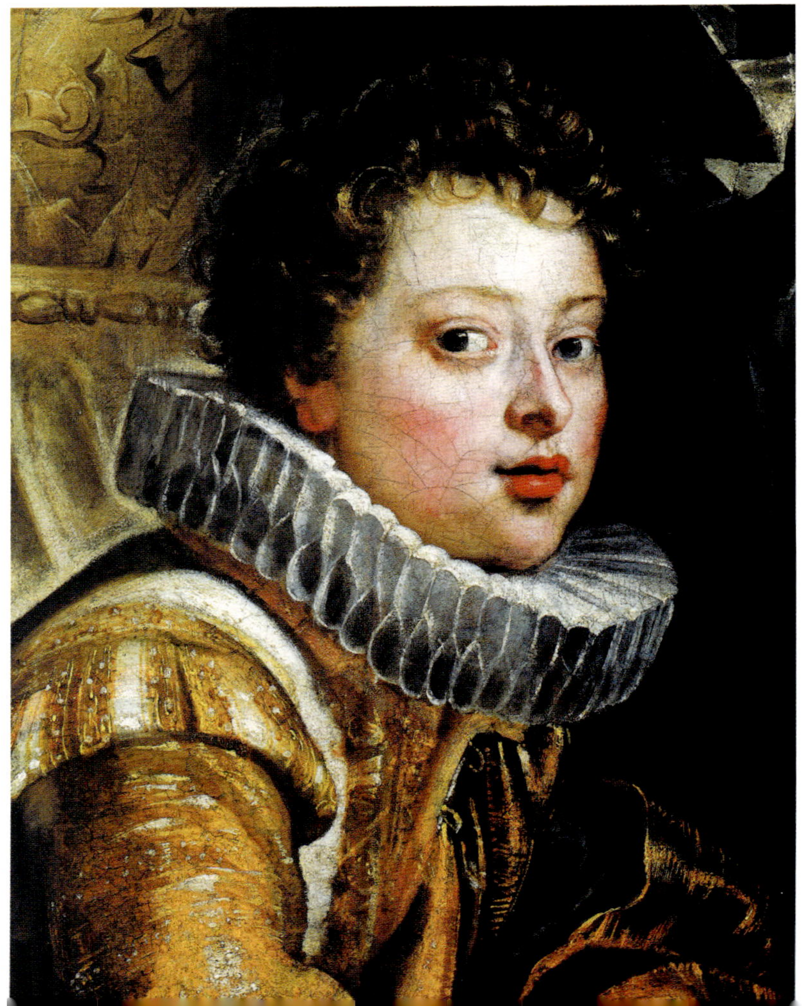

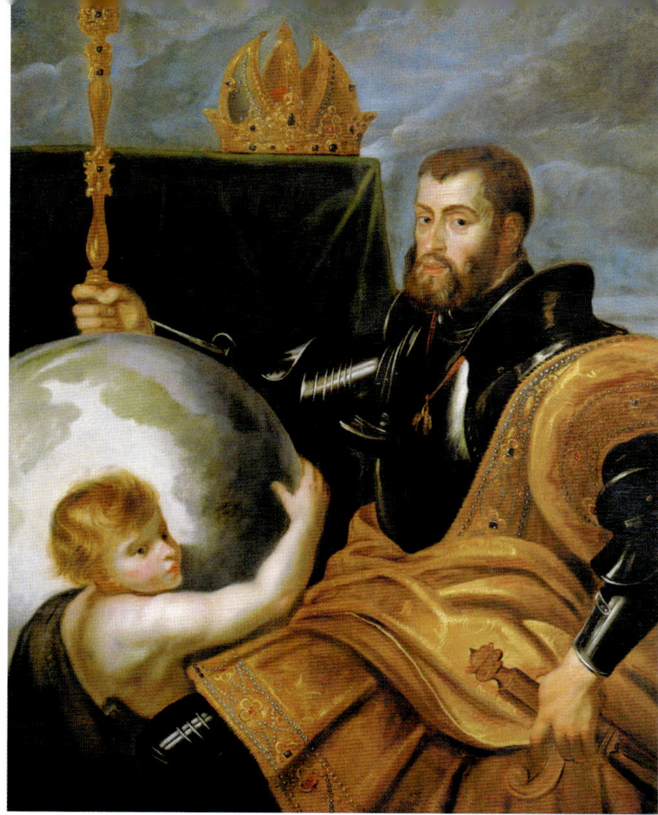

Allegory of Emperor Charles V as Master of the World, 1604, oil on canvas, 166.5 x 141cm (65½ x 55½in), Residenz Galerie, Salzburg, Austria

This was painted just after Rubens's first diplomatic mission to Spain in 1603–04. He perceived Charles V as the founder of the dynastic power of the imperial Habsburg family, which he held in high respect. Soon after his return to Italy, he executed this work, modelled on a painting by Parmigianino (1503–40) in the ducal collection. Painted 50 years after his death, Charles V is shown in ceremonial armour.

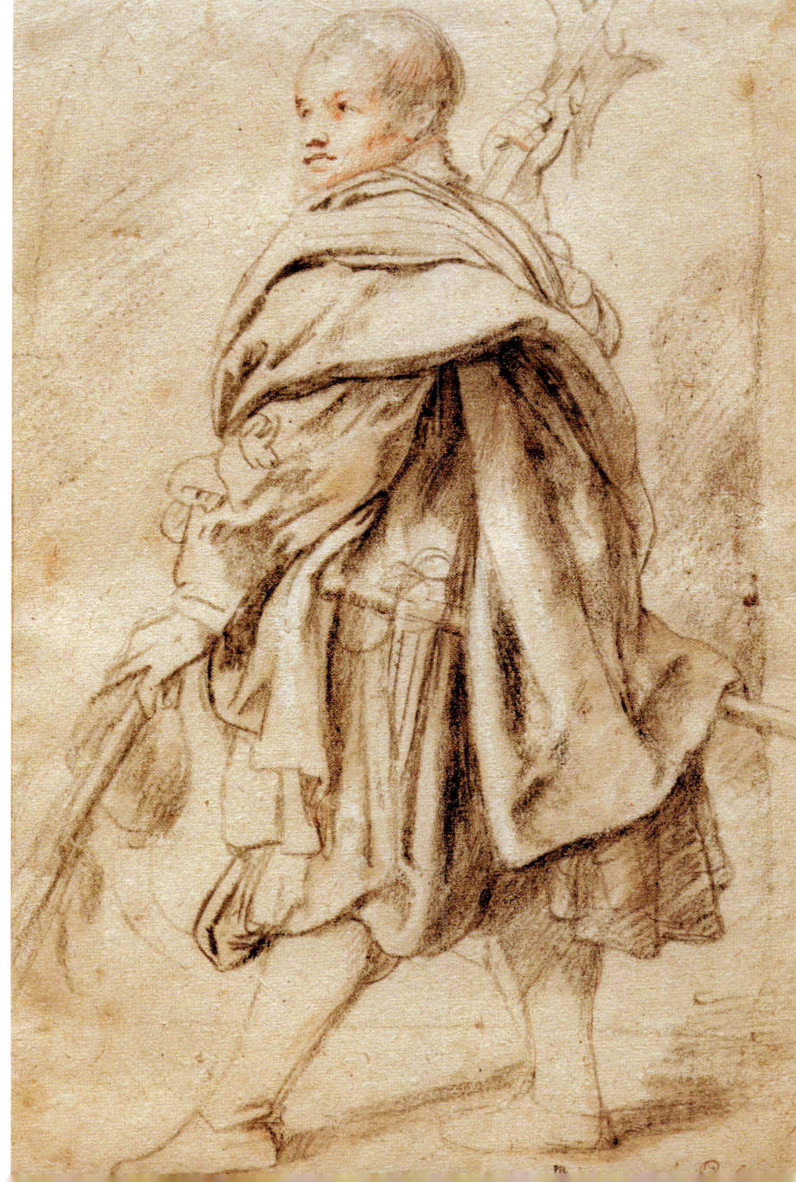

Study of a Halberdier, 1604, black and red chalk, pen and wash, white body colour on light grey paper, 40.7 x 26cm (16 x 10¼in), Bibliothèque Royale Albert Ier, Brussels, Belgium

This large study is a preliminary drawing for a guard who once stood at the lower right of the painting *Vincenzo Gonzaga and his Family Adoring the Holy Trinity*. It is one of Rubens's earliest studies of a single figure. The heavy contour lines and parallel hatched marks show few corrections or changes, and Rubens paid more attention to the clothing than to the head and limbs.

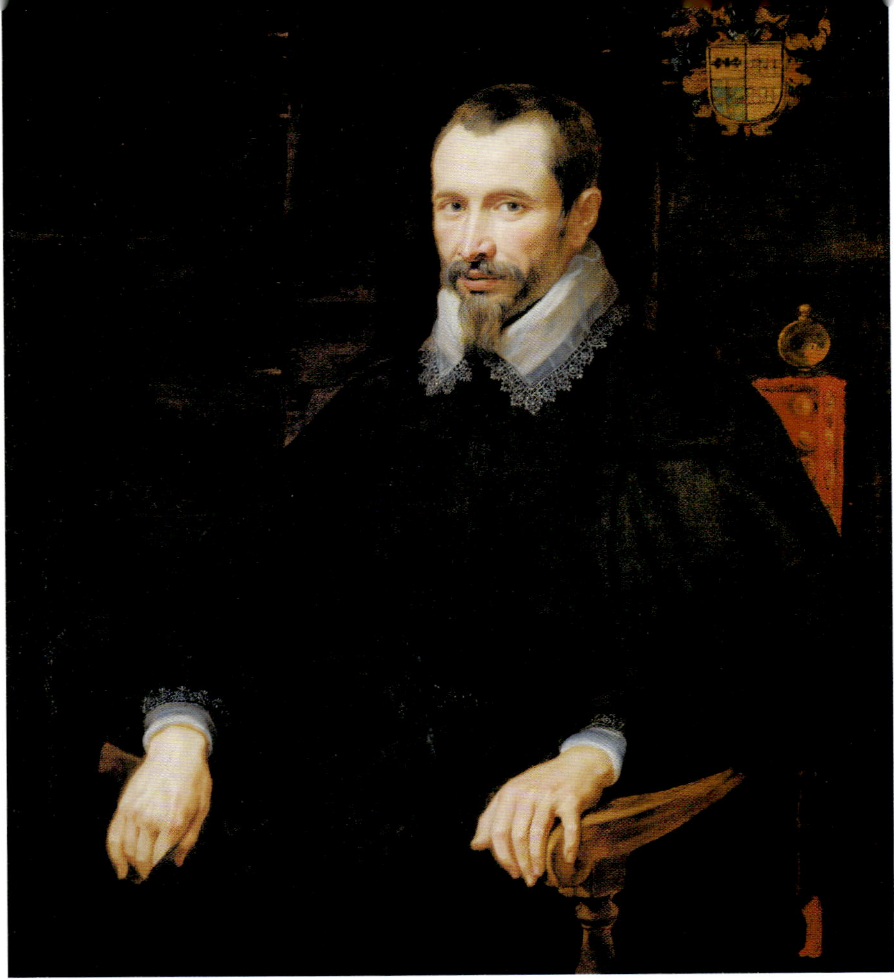

Portrait of Niccolò Pallavicino,
1604, oil on canvas,
105 x 92cm (41⅓ x 36¼ in),
Private Collection

Rubens's acquaintance with the powerful Genoan banker Niccolò Pallavicino or Pallavicini began with his return to Mantua early in 1604. Niccolò became godfather to Rubens's second son Nicolas, who was named after him, proving how easily Rubens slipped into close friendships with prominent figures of the upper classes. The Pallavicini family gave Rubens several significant commissions, including a number of coveted altarpieces and their portraits.

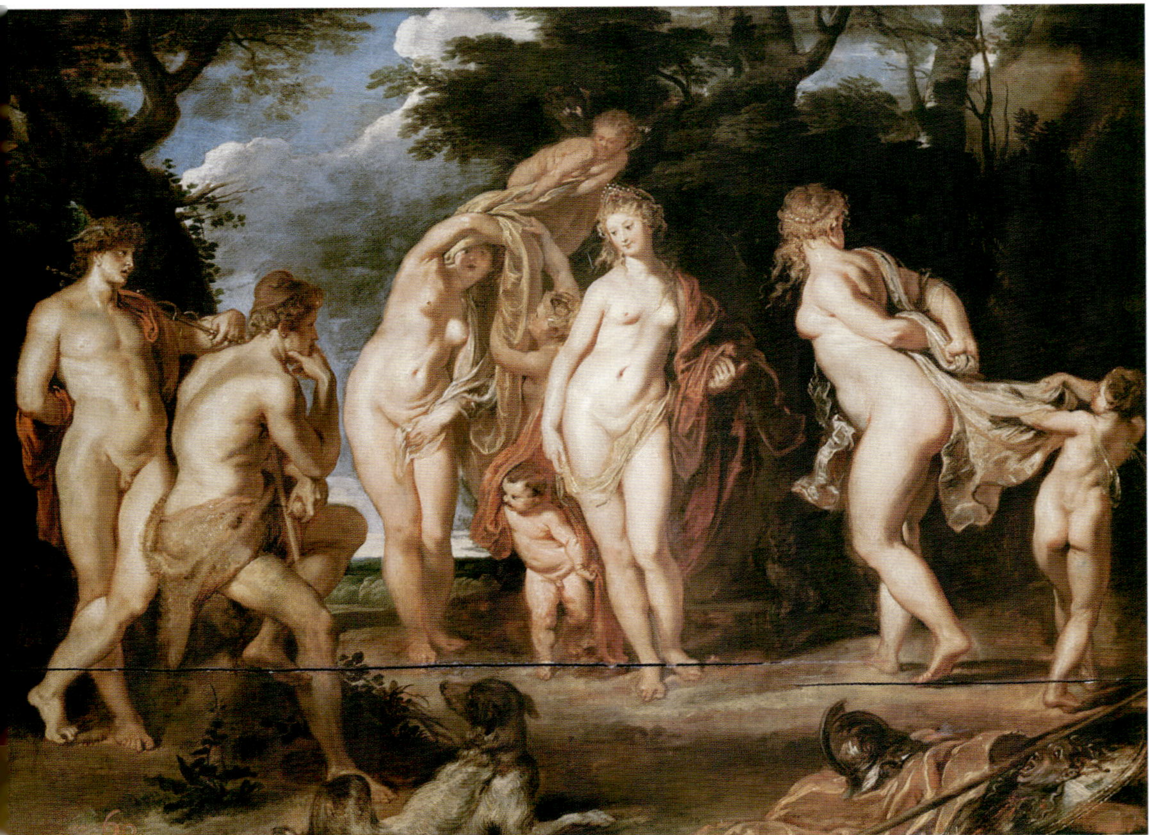

The Judgement of Paris,
c.1605, oil on panel,
89 x 114.5cm (35 x 45in),
Museo Nacional del Prado,
Madrid, Spain

According to Homer's *Iliad*, Paris, a shepherd, son of Priam, had to decide which of the three goddesses – Juno, Venus or Minerva – was the most beautiful, and give her the golden apple he had received from Mercury. Here, Paris still holds the apple, while his attention is on Venus. Minerva's weapons are in the foreground. The figures are based on classical sculptures and Mannerist ideas of twisting torsos.

The Gonzaga Family Adoring the Holy Family, 1604–05, oil on canvas, 381 x 477cm (150 x 188in), Ducal Palace, Mantua, Italy

Commissioned by Vincenzo I Gonzaga for the Jesuit church in Mantua, this is part of a huge triptych which was badly damaged during the French siege of Mantua in the early 19th century, when parts were cut off, including the heads of several family members. It portrays Vincenzo and his wife Eleonora, plus his parents Guglielmo Gonzaga and Eleonore of Austria, and several of their children with halberdiers, one of which is Rubens's self-portrait.

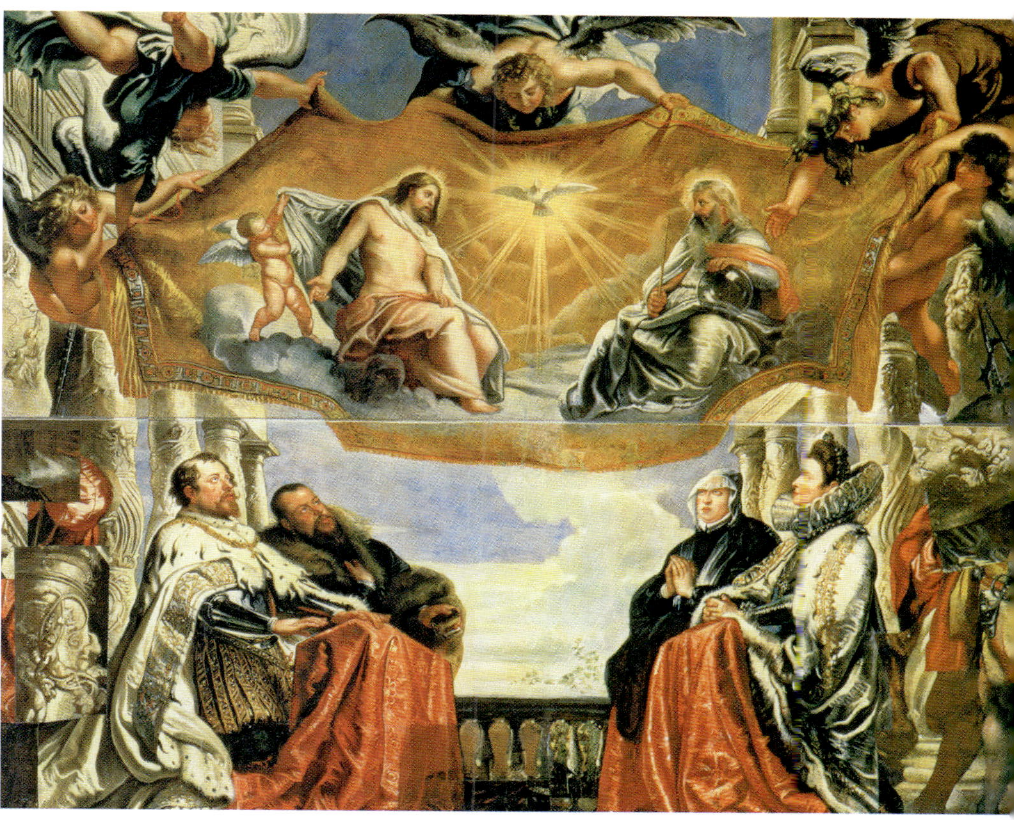

The Circumcision, 1605, oil on canvas, 400 x 225cm (160 x 89in), Chiesa del Gesù e dei Santi Ambrogio e Andrea, Genoa, Italy

Produced during Rubens's stay in Rome, commissioned by Marcello Pallavicino, brother of Niccolò, this is a theatrical rendition of Jesus as a baby at the centre of the Jewish ceremony of circumcision. Mainly influenced by paintings from the Mantuan court, the light and strongly foreshortened viewpoint heightens the drama of the moment and recalls paintings by Tintoretto, while the empathetic emotions portrayed are purely of Rubens's imagination.

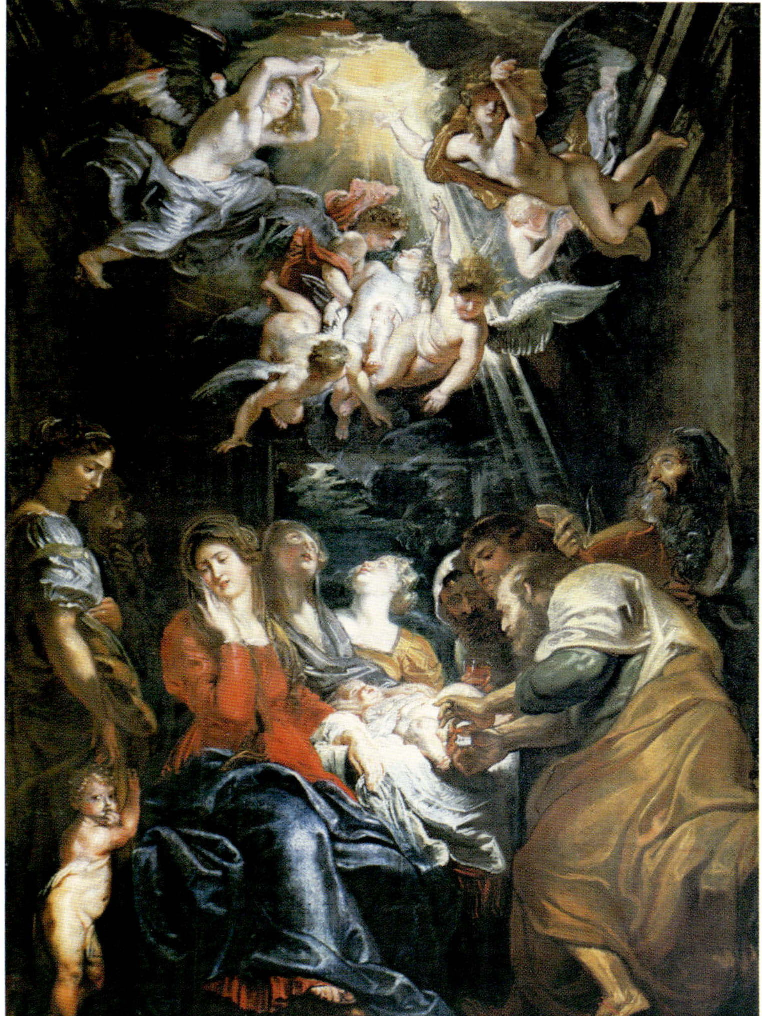

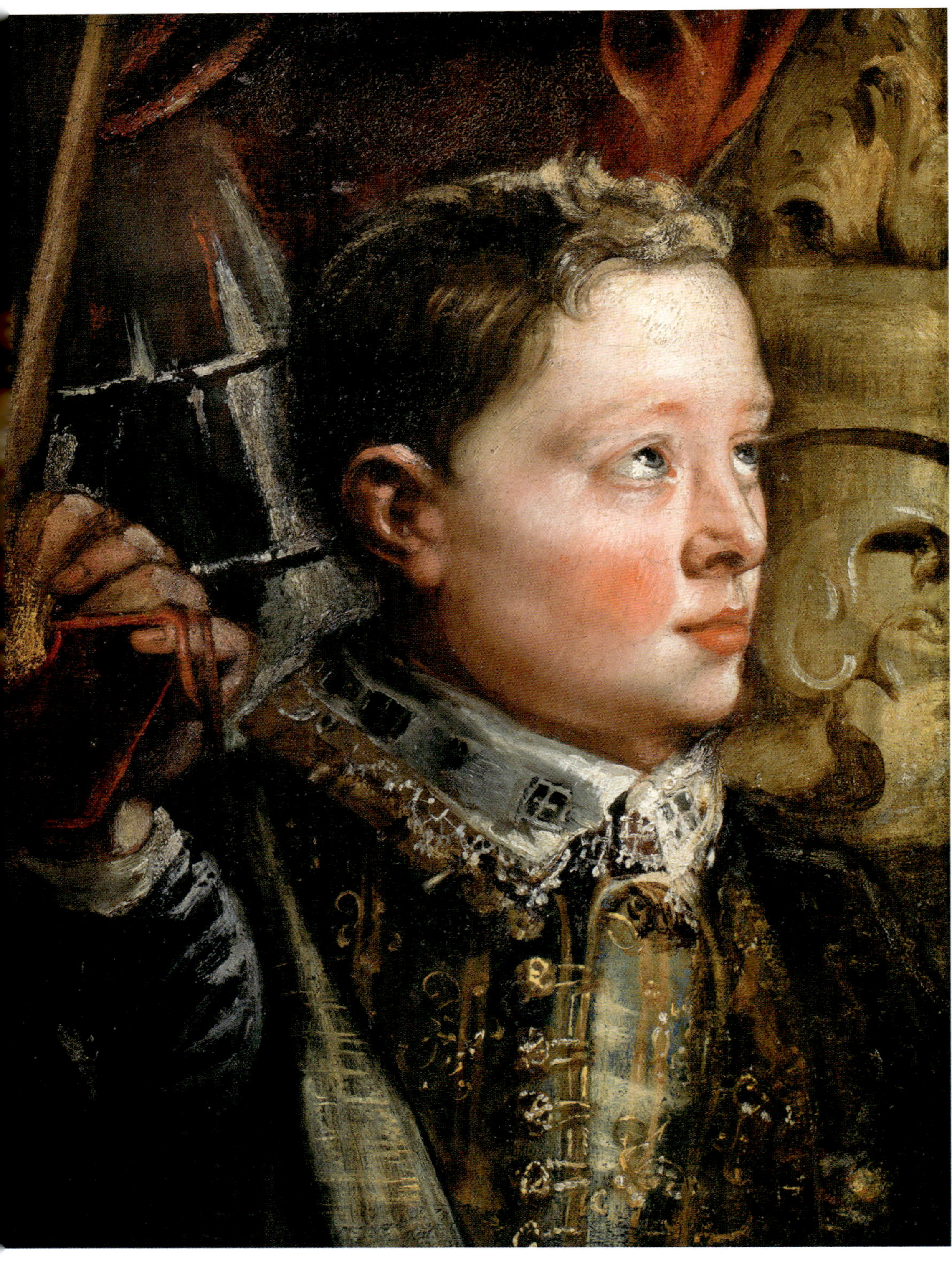

Portrait of Francesco IV Gonzaga, 1605, oil on canvas, 52 x 40cm (20½ x 15¾in), Romano Freddi Collection on loan to the Palazzo Ducale, Mantua, Italy

An early portrait by Rubens, this is the eldest son of Vincenzo Gonzaga, Duke of Mantua and Eleonora de' Medici. It shows the dexterity of the young artist and his understanding of what was wanted by his patrons; the young man looks noble and commanding, yet also sensitive, thoughtful and modest – the perfect qualities for a powerful future duke.

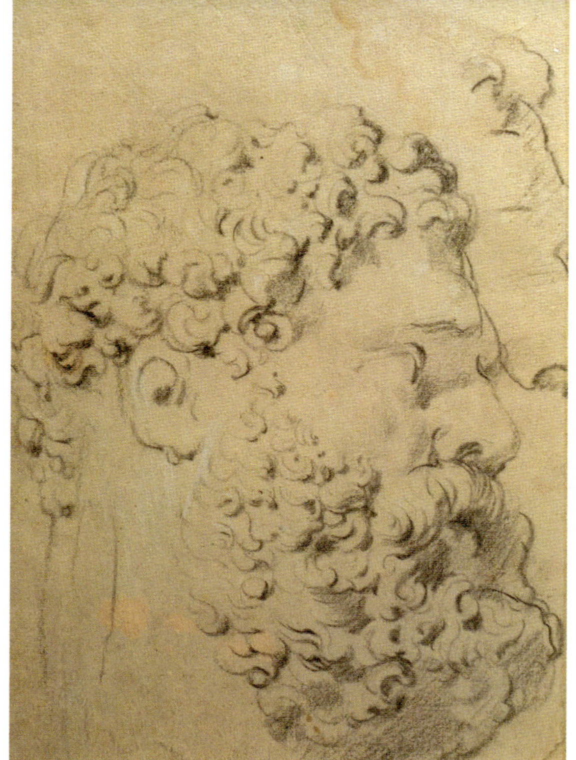

Study of the Head and Profile of the Farnese Hercules by Glycon, 1606–08, Rubens and Frans Snyders, black and white chalk on paper, 36.3 x 24.5cm (14¼ x 9¾in), The Courtauld Gallery, London, UK

An ancient statue of Hercules made in the early third century CE and signed by Glykon became a great inspiration to Rubens, who made many studies of it and wrote that 'The difference between men of our age and the ancients is the sloth and lack of exercise of those living; indeed one eats and drinks, exercising no care for the body...' As well as being Rubens's model for ideal manhood, the statue was an important element of his learning. Throughout his life, he maintained that the way to become a better artist was to study and imitate the great artists of the past.

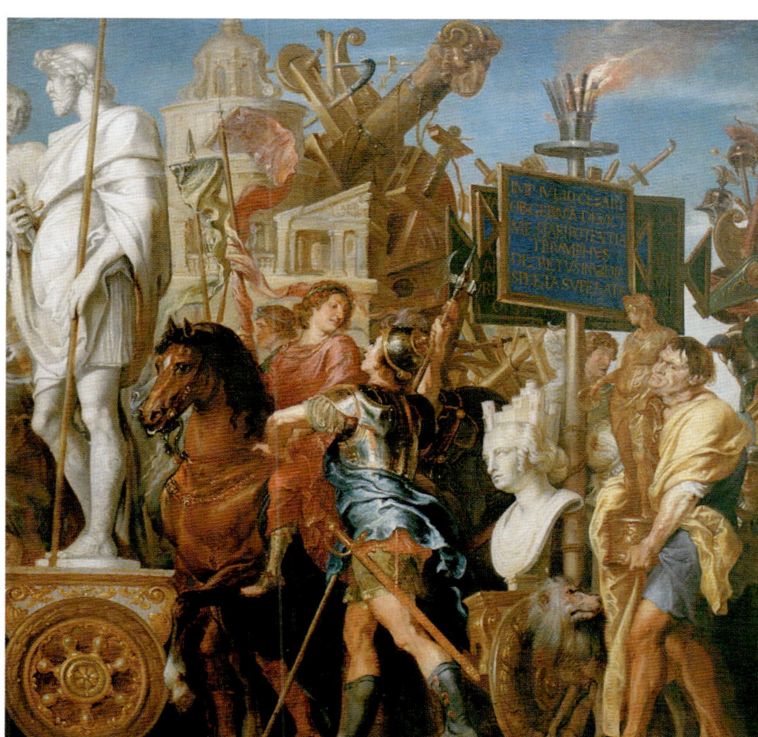

The Triumph of Caesar, 1607–08, oil on wood, 86.5 x 90.5cm (34 x 35½in), National Gallery, Prague, Czech Republic

Rubens made two skilful copies of Mantegna's series of paintings of 1486–1505. Rubens was attracted to Mantegna's work for his vivid, lifelike portrayals, especially in this lively triumphal parade with its fluid, dynamic figures and expressive colours. The liveliness of his own style arose from his speed of application, dexterity and ability to discern and convey moods and expressive gestures.

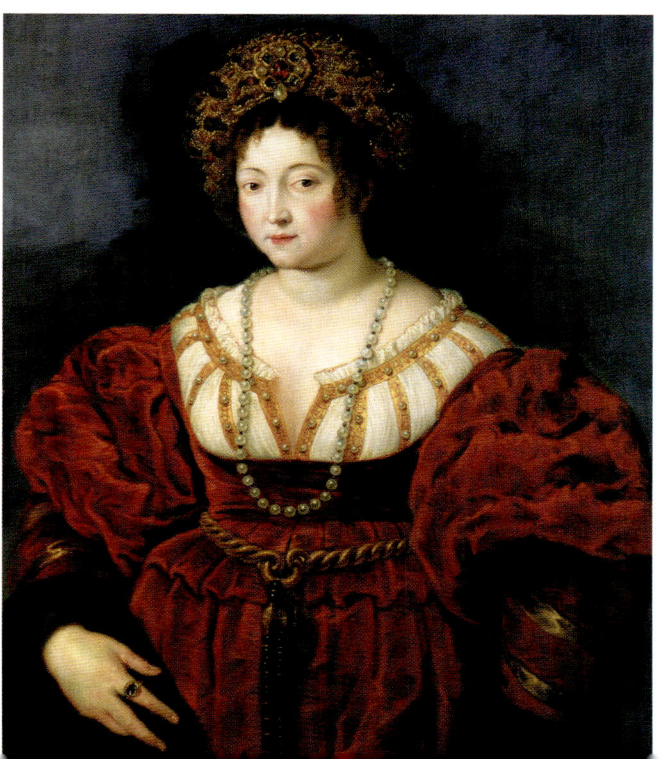

Isabella d'Este, 1605–08, oil on canvas, 101.8 x 81cm (40 x 32in), Kunsthistorisches Museum, Vienna, Austria

Isabella d'Este-Gonzaga was the Marquess of Mantua and wife of Francesco II Gonzaga. This is Rubens's copy of Titian's 1529 painting *Isabella in Red*. Isabella was 55 when the original work was painted, but as one of the most admired and sophisticated women of the Renaissance, she became unhappy with her ageing appearance and requested that Titian paint her as she was in her 20s.

Saint George and the Dragon,
c.1606–08, oil on canvas,
304 x 256cm (119¾ x
100¾in), Museo Nacional
del Prado, Madrid, Spain

In his 'Golden Legend,' the
archbishop of Genoa, Jacopo
de la Voragine (c.1230–98),
wrote that Saint George
killed a dragon that had been
terrorizing the people of
Silene, and saved a princess.
Here, George rides a white
stallion and brandishes his
sword against the dragon,
which attempts to extract
a lance stuck in its jaws.
Behind, the princess watches.
This is a clear example of
Rubens's use of directed light
and dynamic compositions.

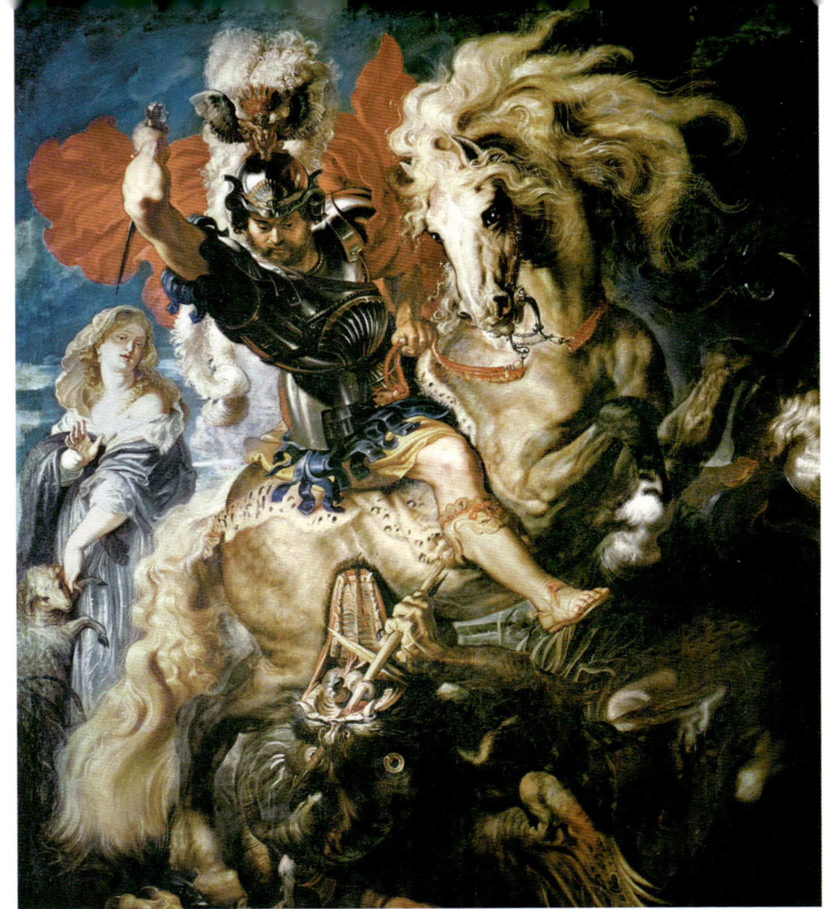

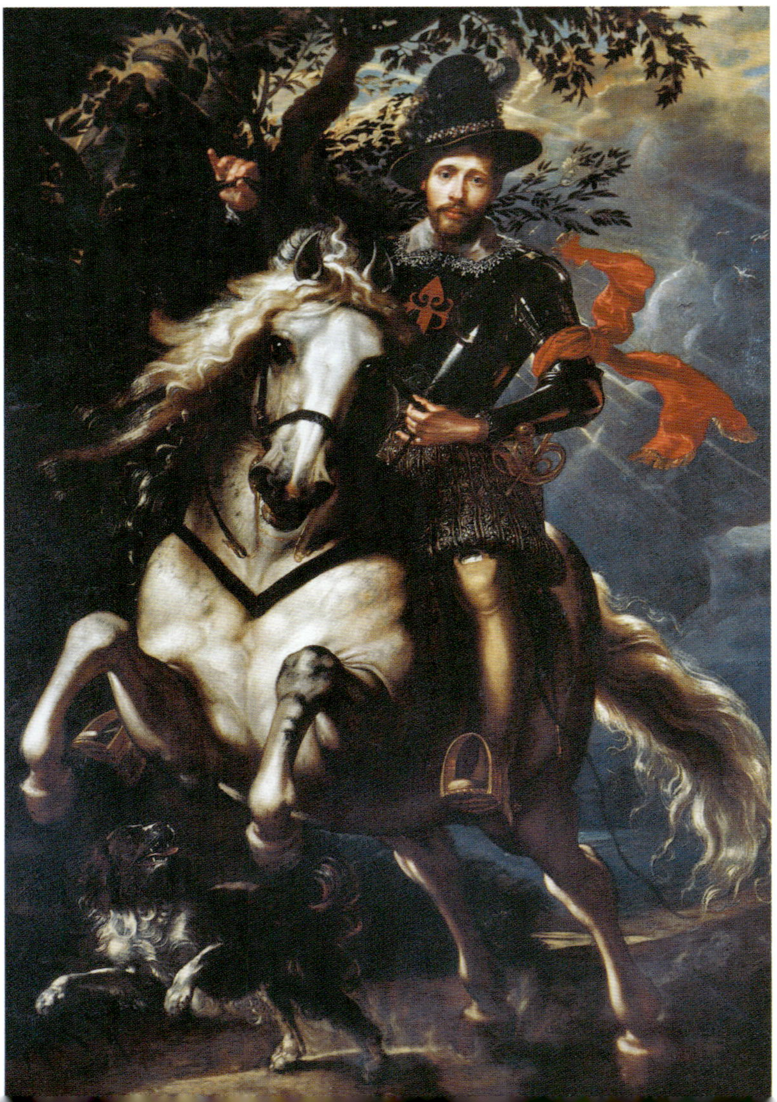

*Equestrian Portrait of
Giancarlo Doria,* 1606,
oil on canvas, 265 x 188cm
(104 x 74in), Galleria
Nazional della Liguria,
Genoa, Italy

One of two large equestrian
portraits that Rubens made
during his Italian period,
this powerful portrait
of Giancarlo Doria
(1577–1629) includes a
horse on its hind legs, a dog
echoing the horse's pose,
strong lighting, foreshortening,
and fluid, dashing contours.
Equestrian portraits were
not new, and Rubens once
again took his influence from
Tintoretto, but uniquely,
Rubens created a strong
sense of immediacy and
vitality in the painting.

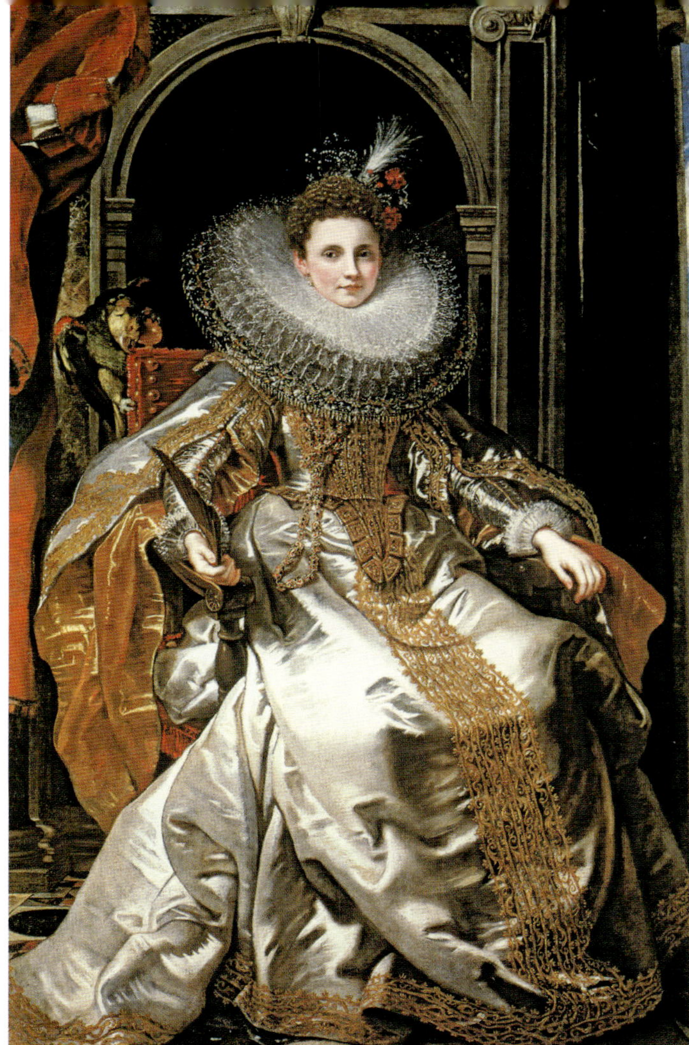

Portrait of Marchesa Maria Serra Pallavicino, 1606, oil on canvas, 233.7 x 144.8cm (92 x 57in), Kingston Lacy Estate, Dorset, UK

In a magnificent shimmering silk gown overlaid with gold embroidered lace, long golden over-sleeves, small ruff-cuffs at the wrist and a white and silver lace cartwheel neck ruff, Maria Serra Pallavicino (*c*.1575–*c*.1630) sits on a high-backed red chair with a parrot, her hair dressed with flowers, jewels and a white egret feather. All is grand, sumptuous and beautiful – as required by the aristocracy of Europe.

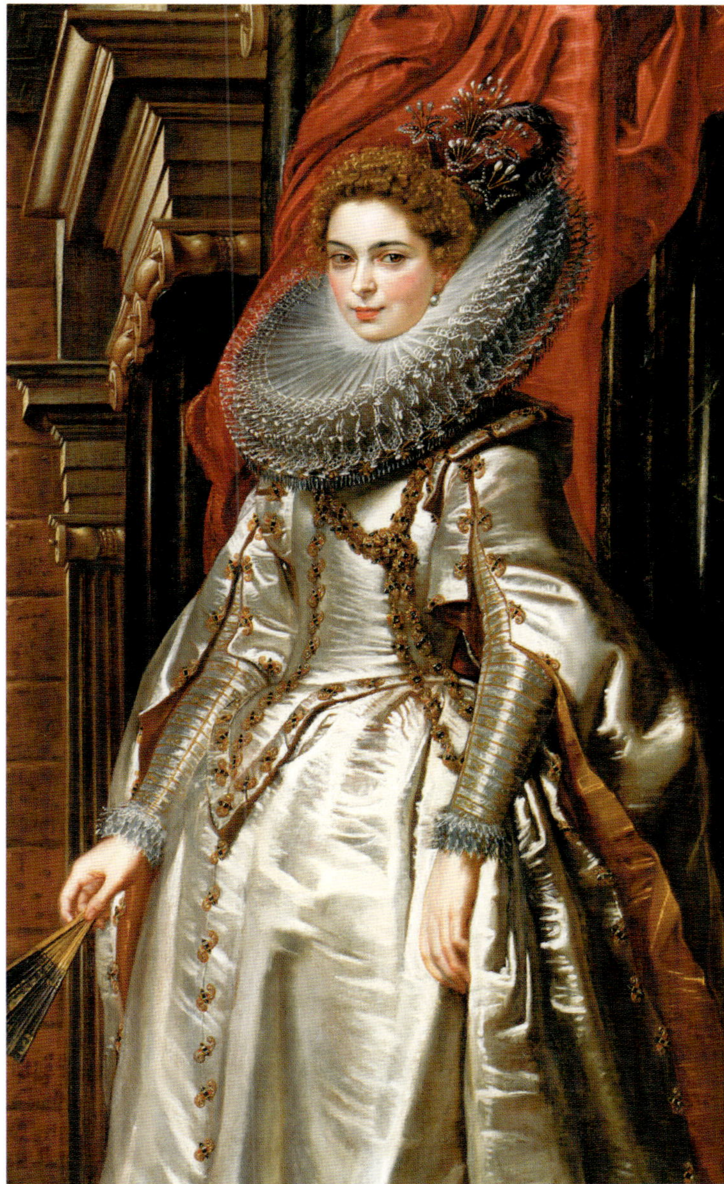

Marchesa Brigida Spinola Doria, 1606, oil on canvas, 152.5 x 99cm (60 x 39in), National Gallery of Art, Washington DC, USA

Rubens worked in Genoa at least four times during his stay in Italy. This is one of several female portraits he made there. Brigida was 22 years old at the time, in the year of her marriage. Rubens uses dry paint to convey the stiffness of her lace collar, cuffs and glittering hair adornments. The light, diagonal lines and bravura brushwork builds up her silvery satin dress in layers of translucent glazes, highlighted with thick, freely painted strokes.

Madonna Adored by Angels,
1608, 44.9 x 34.6cm
(17⅔ x 13⅔in), red chalk and
graphite on paper, Pushkin
Museum of Fine Arts,
Moscow, Russia

While Rubens was in Rome,
the Priests of the Oratory,
or the Oratorians,
commissioned him to paint
the high altar of their main
church, Santa Maria in
Vallicella. This was his sketch,
incorporating their fresco of
the Virgin Mary, that the
Oratorians specified had to
be in his altarpiece. With
several putti holding the
image aloft, the image is
inspired by Barocci, Carracci
and Correggio, and met
the requirements of
the fraternity.

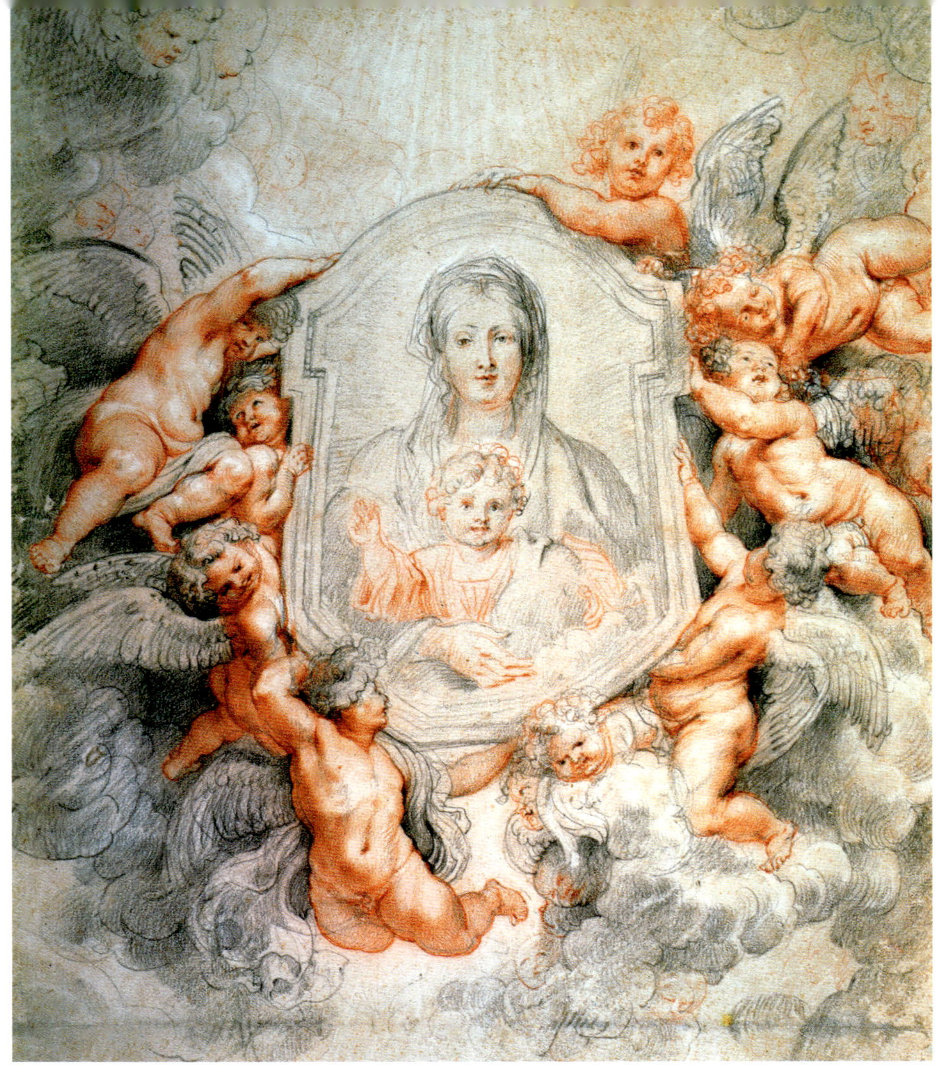

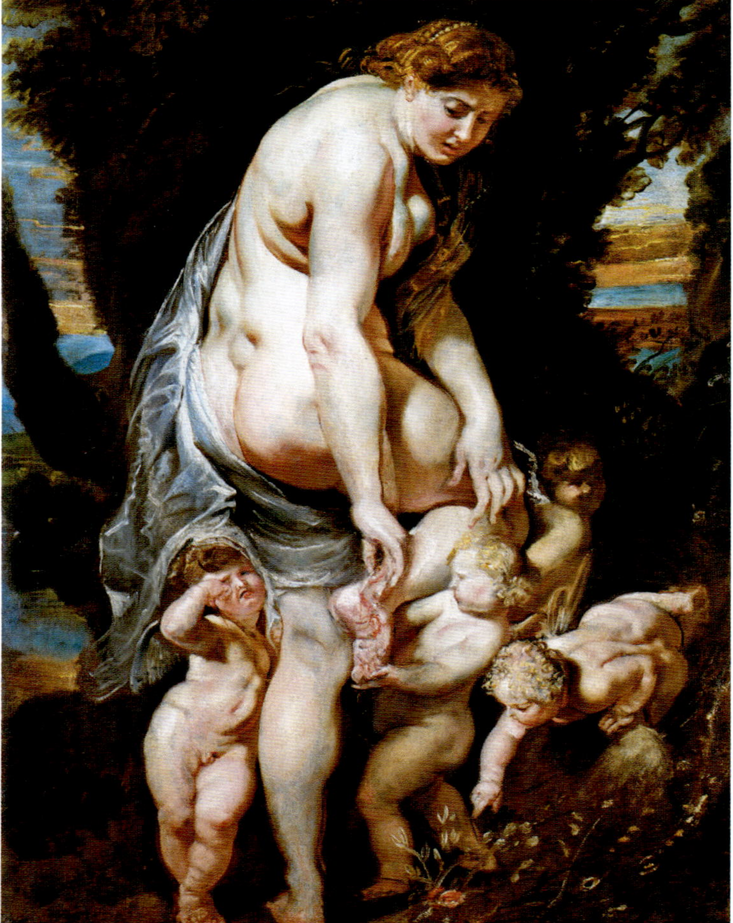

Venus Wounded by a Thorn,
c. 1608–10, oil on canvas,
55.8 x 81.2cm (22 x 32in),
USC Fisher Museum of Art,
Los Angeles, USA

According to an ancient
poem by Bion of Smyrna
(c.100 BCE), this follows
the moment when Venus
stepped naked from a
fountain and ran through a
forest to try to help Adonis
escape from Mars. A thorn
pierces her foot, and as she
pulls it out, her blood stains
the petals of a rose bush.
According to the legend,
roses were always white, but
after being touched by her
blood, many turned red.

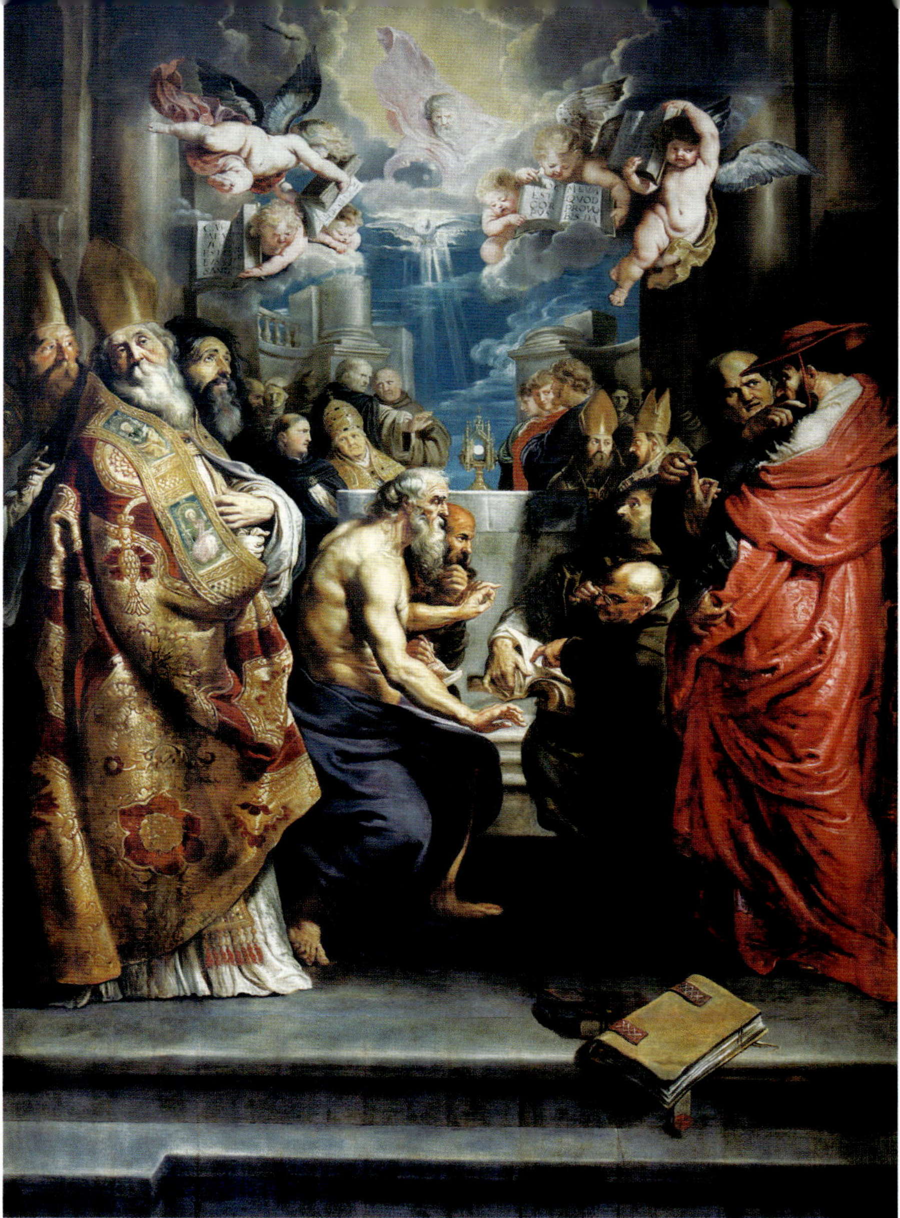

Disputation of the Holy Sacrament, 1608–09, oil on panel, 377 x 146cm (148¼ x 96½in), St Paul's Church, Antwerp, Belgium

The main area of the Catholic faith that instigated the Protestant Reformation was the Disputation. While Catholics believe that in the Eucharist the bread and wine actually becomes Christ's body and blood, Protestants believe that it is merely symbolic and there is no actual transubstantiation. This painting represents the Fathers of the Church discussing the issue.

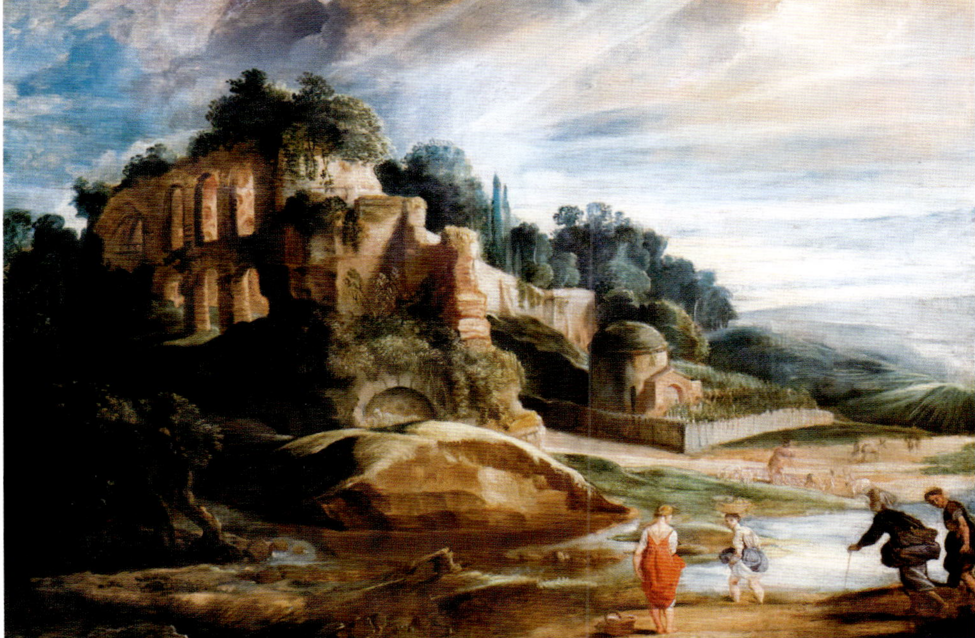

Landscape with the Ruins of Mount Palatine in Rome, c.1608, oil on panel, 76 x 106.8cm (30 x 42in), Musée du Louvre, Paris, France

Largely a pastoral scene depicted in dramatic chiaroscuro, this was painted while Rubens was in Rome, before he returned to Antwerp. It is a view of the Palatine Hill, and picks up the classical style of Annibale Carracci, whom Rubens particularly admired. Palatine Hill is the most central of the Seven Hills of Rome, and one of the most ancient parts of the city.

*Cain Slaying Abel, c.*1608–09, oil on panel, 131.2 x 94.2cm (51⅔ x 37in), The Courtauld Gallery, London, UK

This is the Old Testament story in which Adam's eldest son Cain kills his younger brother Abel in a fit of jealousy, and was painted soon after Rubens returned to Antwerp. In his combination of Italian and Belgian skills and styles, Rubens uses close details, expressive brush marks and subtle colours to portray the violent scene. It made an immediate impact on all who saw it, influencing many contemporary artists.

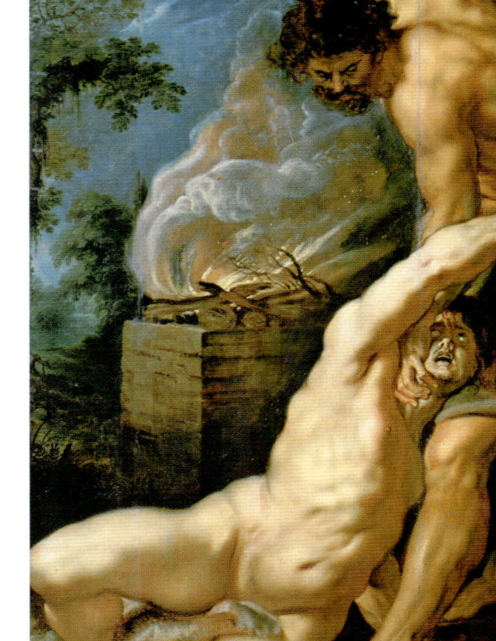

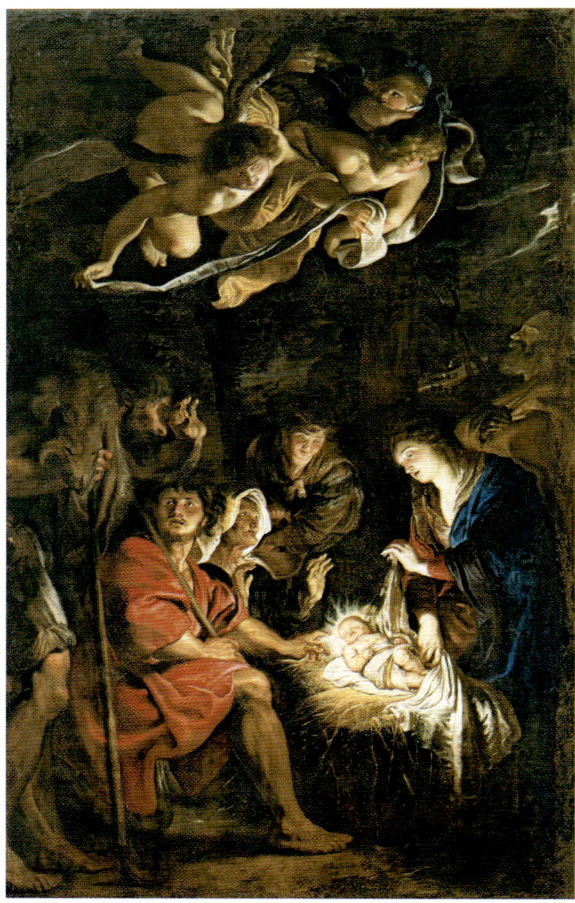

Adoration of the Shepherds, 1608, oil on panel, 300 x 192cm (120 x 76in), Municipal Art Gallery, Fermo, Italy

This painting was rediscovered in the early 20th century. Rubens spent approximately three months painting it for the church of Saint Philip Neri in Fermo, Italy. Following the chiaroscuro of Caravaggio, it portrays the shepherds at the Nativity stable, paying homage to the baby Jesus. Four angels hover above them, holding a scroll announcing Jesus's birth. Light radiates around Mary and the baby.

*The Holy Family with Saint Elizabeth, Saint John, and a Dove, c.*1608–09, oil on wood, 66 x 51.4cm (26 x 20¼ in), The Metropolitan Museum of Art, New York, USA

This work, created shortly after Rubens came back to Antwerp from Rome, shows his amalgamation of the cool skin tones and smooth contours of his Flemish training with the lively, twisting figures he admired in Italian painting. Although it was early in his career, he was already established as one of the leading artists of the Baroque movement. Following the ideas of the Council of Trent, his image of the Holy Family inspires affinity.

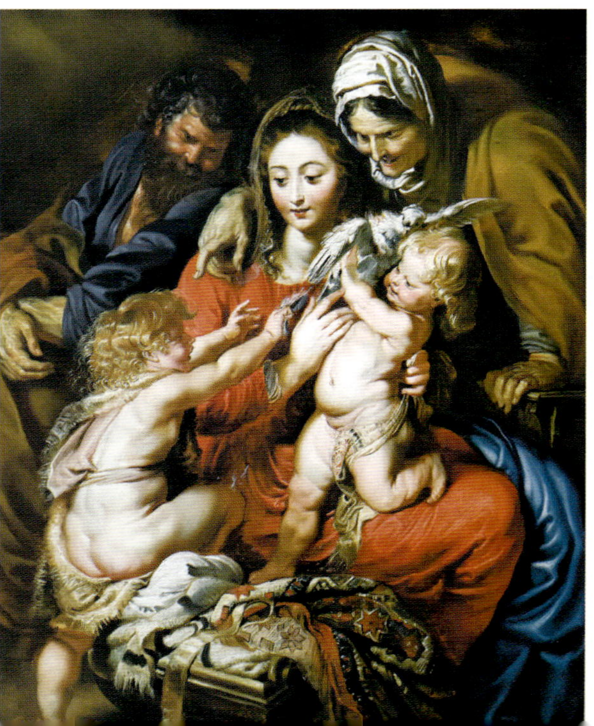

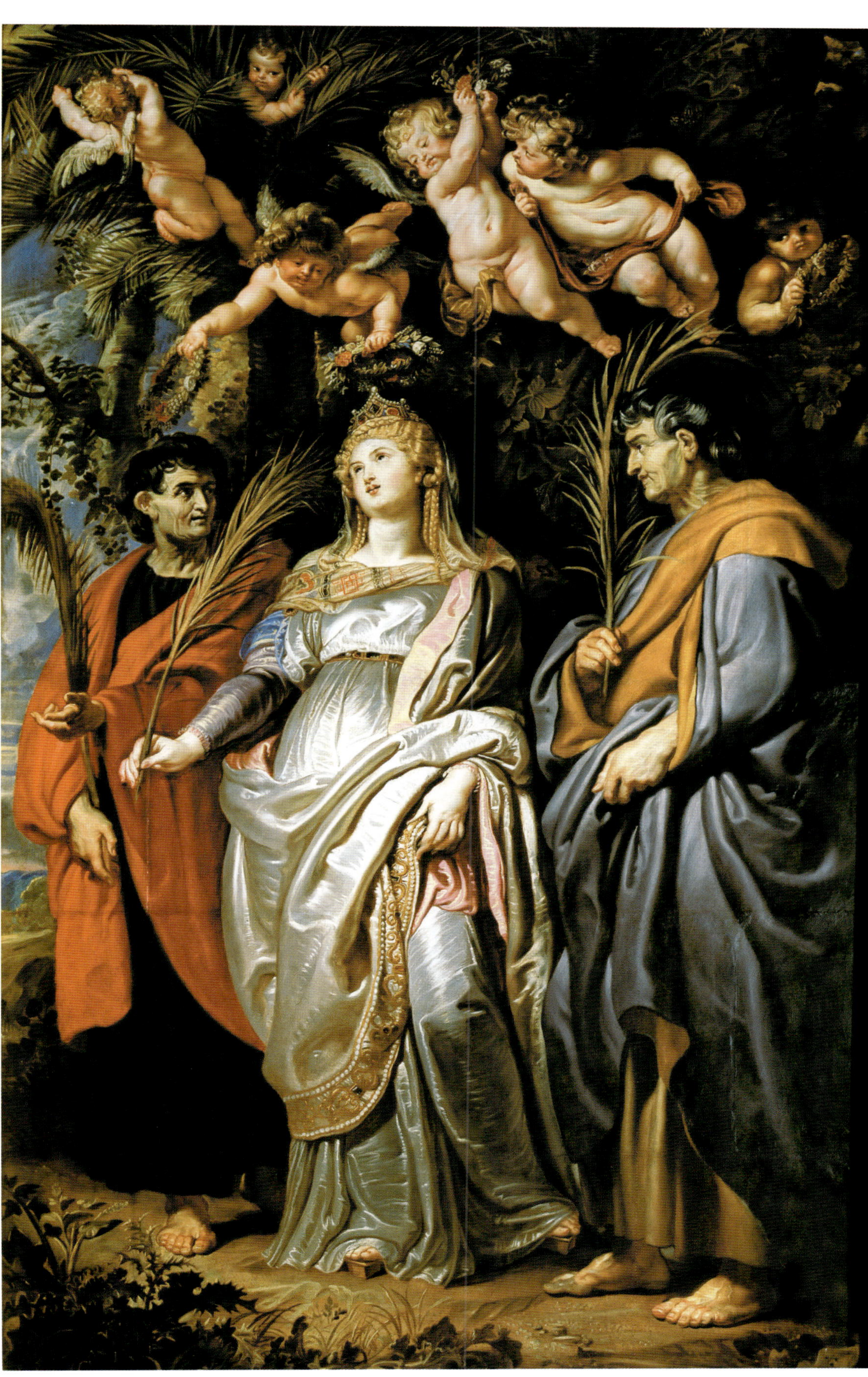

Saint Domitilla, Flanked by the Saints Nereus and Achilleus, 1608, oil on canvas, 425 × 280cm (167⅓ × 110⅛in), Santa Maria in Vallicella, Rome, Italy

Nereus and Achilleus are two Roman Christian martyrs who, according to legend, were eunuchs and chamberlains of Flavia Domitilla, a niece of the Roman Emperor Domitian. All three died as martyrs and were popular saints in Rome, where they were born. So this attracted particular interest in its position in the church of Santa Maria in Vallicella in Rome.

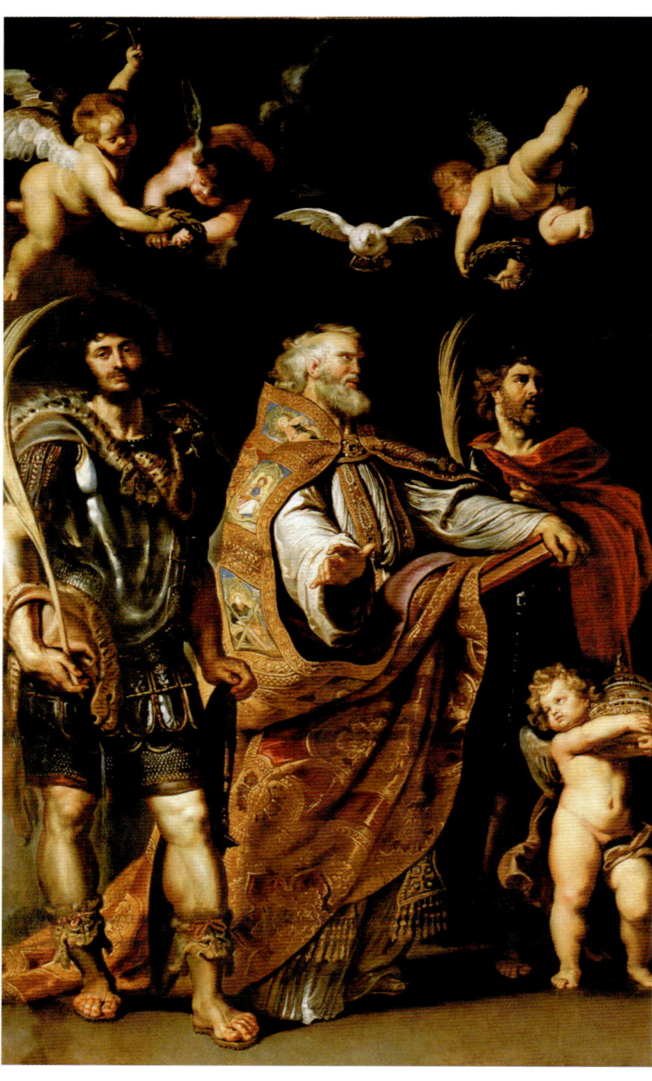

Saints Gregory the Great, Papia and Mauro, 1608, oil on canvas, 425 x 280cm (167⅓ x 110⅓in), Santa Maria in Vallicella, Rome, Italy

In this altarpiece, Rubens expressed his great respect for the work of Carracci, Correggio and Barocci, who were all influential on the emergence of the Baroque style. Here, Saint Gregory (the Pope) is in the centre, to his right is Saint Papia in a red cloak, and to the left is Saint Mauro in armour. In venerating the saints, Rubens blatantly celebrates the success of the Counter-Reformation.

Saints Catherine and Eligius, c.1610, oil on canvas, 66 x 25cm (26 x 10in), Dulwich Picture Gallery, London, UK

An oil sketch for the altarpiece of the Church of St Walburga (or Walpurgis) representing the *Raising of the Cross,* this is of Saints Eligius and Catherine, which went on the back side of the wings. Saint Eligius was a blacksmith and bishop and the patron saint of Antwerp's blacksmiths. Saint Catherine of Alexandria stands in front of him, holding her martyr's sword and palm branch, while a putto or cherub flies above them.

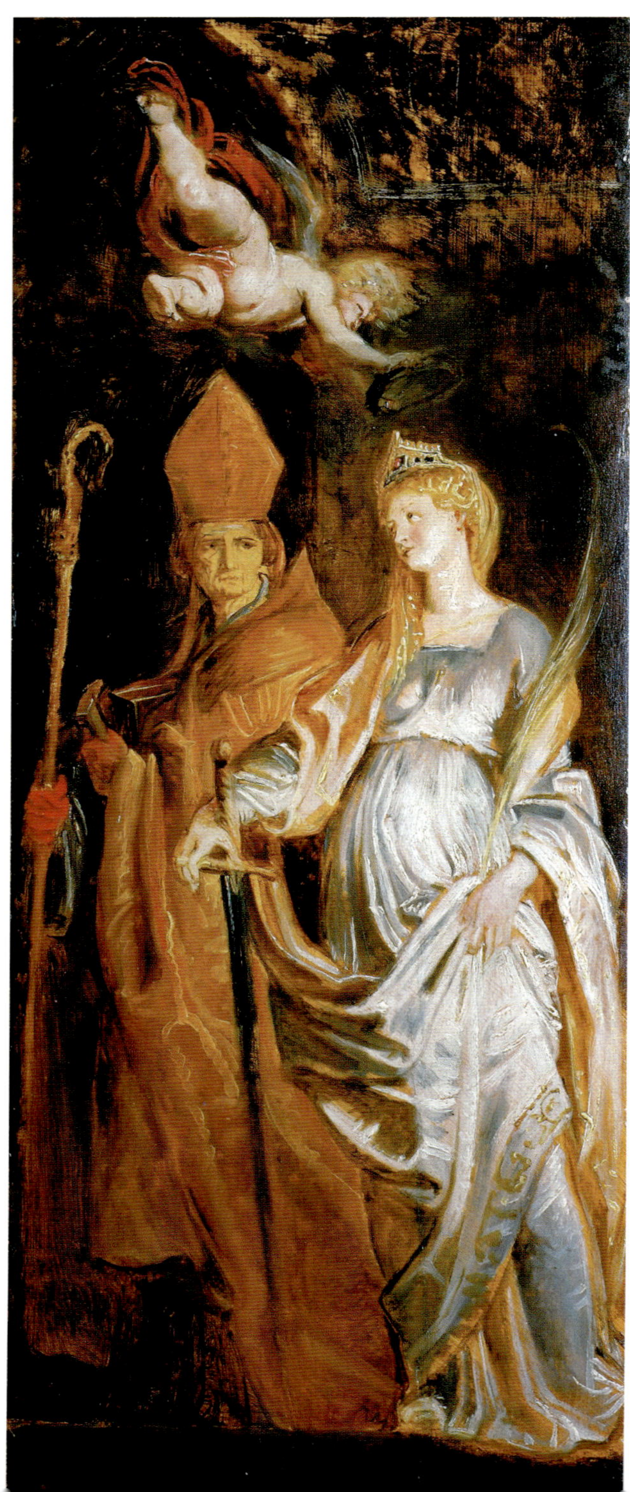

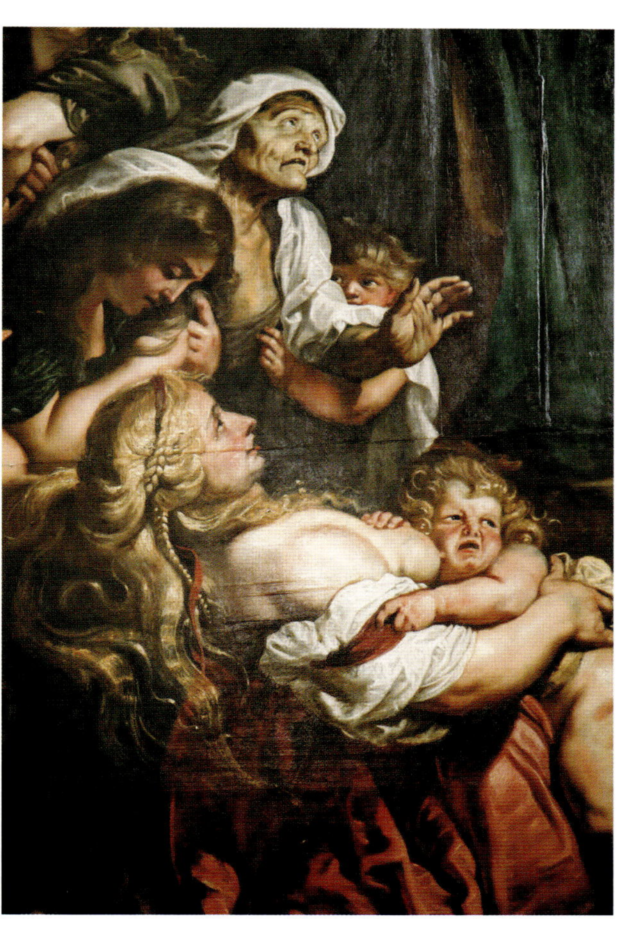

Side panel from
The Raising of the Cross,
1610, oil on panel, 460 x
150cm (181 x 59in),
Cathedral of Our Lady,
Antwerp, Belgium

Rubens's dynamic, ground-breaking triptych (see pages 50–51) extends to the outer panels where here on the left-hand side, Saint John, the Virgin Mary and a group of weeping women and children witness the dramatic action. Mary is suffering internally – a sign of her strength, courage and acceptance of God's will. A nursing mother, horrified at what she is witnessing, forms a diagonal connection with Christ's eyes in the central panel.

Moses and the Brazen Serpent, 1609–10, oil on panel, 161.2 x 146.1cm (63½ x 57½ in), The Courtauld Gallery, London, UK

This colourful painting portrays an episode from the Old Testament in which the Israelites are punished with a plague of poisonous snakes. Moses points to a brass serpent arranged on a cross in the centre of the composition. Those that gaze on it are miraculously restored to health. The influence of Michelangelo is evident in the depictions of the human body.

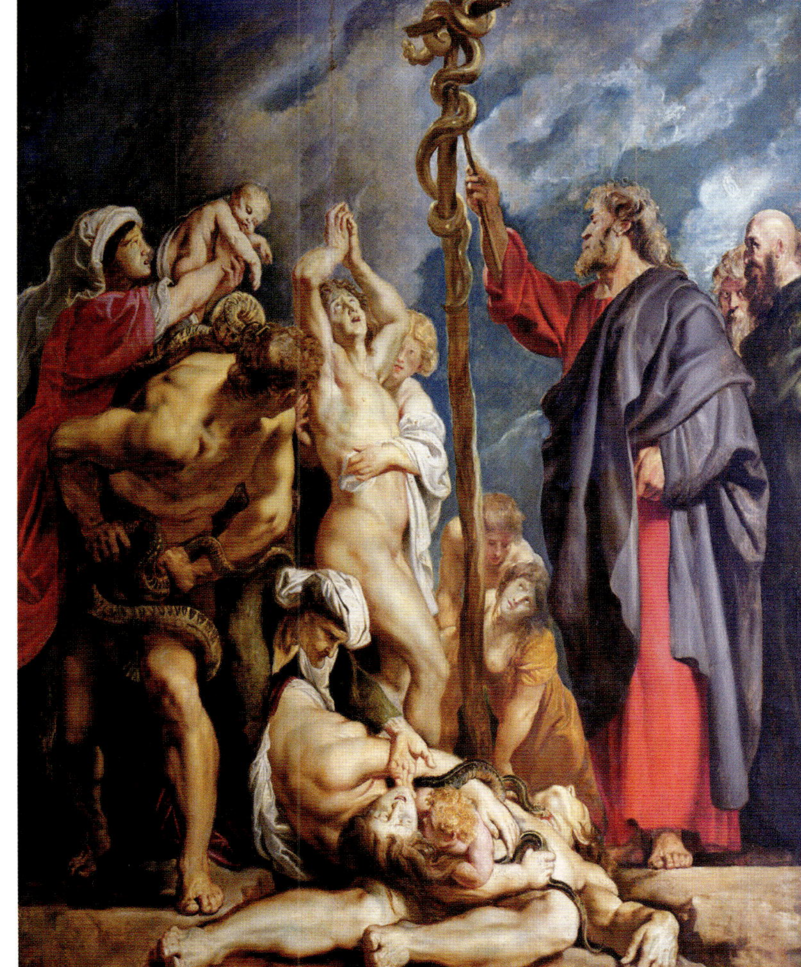

*Mulay Ahmad, c.*1609, oil on panel, 99.7 x 71.5cm (39¼ x 28⅛in), Museum of Fine Arts, Boston, USA

This is a copy of a lost portrait by Jan Cornelisz Vermeyen (1500–59) that was

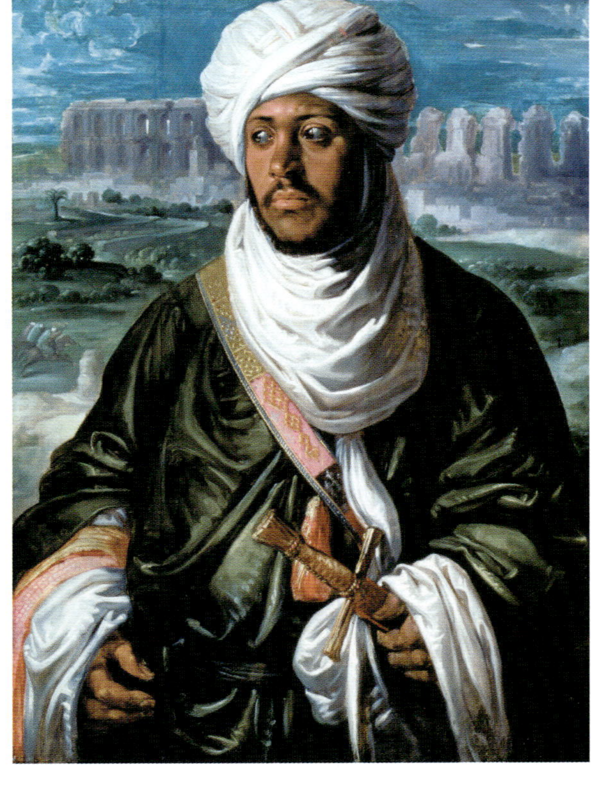

probably in Rubens's own collection. Mulay Ahmad had been the King of Tunis and was in fact a brutal leader, but Rubens idealized him and used his exotic image later in his paintings of *Adoration of the Magi*. Rubens kept this painting throughout his life.

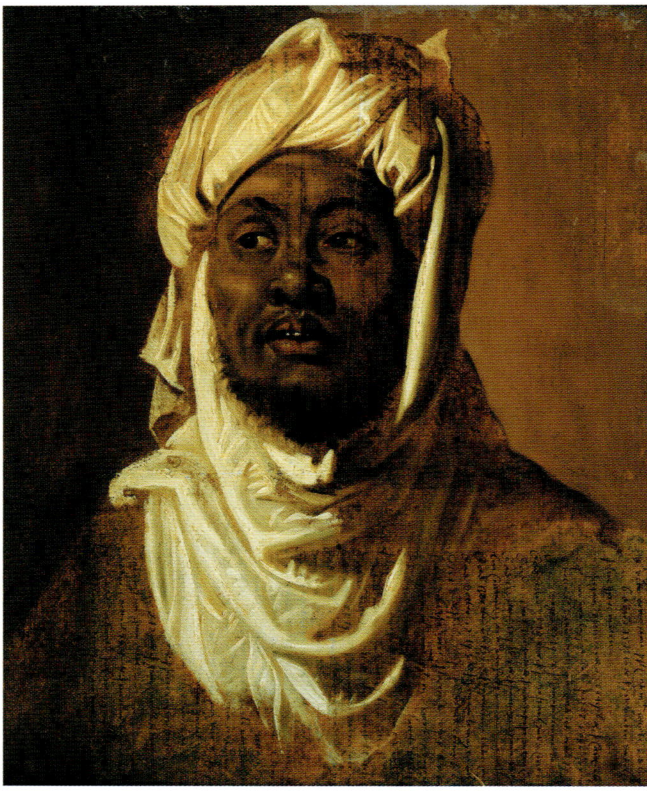

*Study for Balthazar in Adoration of the Magi, c.*1608–09, oil on paper laid on panel, 54 x 47.2cm (21¼ x 18½in), Private Collection

Names of the Magi are not given in the New Testament, but in the Western Christian church they are: Melchior, a Persian scholar, Gaspar, an

Indian scholar; and Balthazar, an Arabian scholar. The names are derived from an ancient Greek manuscript, and as well as scholars, Balthazar is often described as a king of Arabia, Melchior a king of Persia, and Gaspar a king of India. Rubens directly translated this sensitive study into a finished painting.

*Study of Two Heads, c.*1609, oil on wood, 69.9 x 52.1cm (27½ x 20½in), The Metropolitan Museum of Art, New York, USA

Rubens made studies of heads from live models and other works of art, creating various characters that he used later

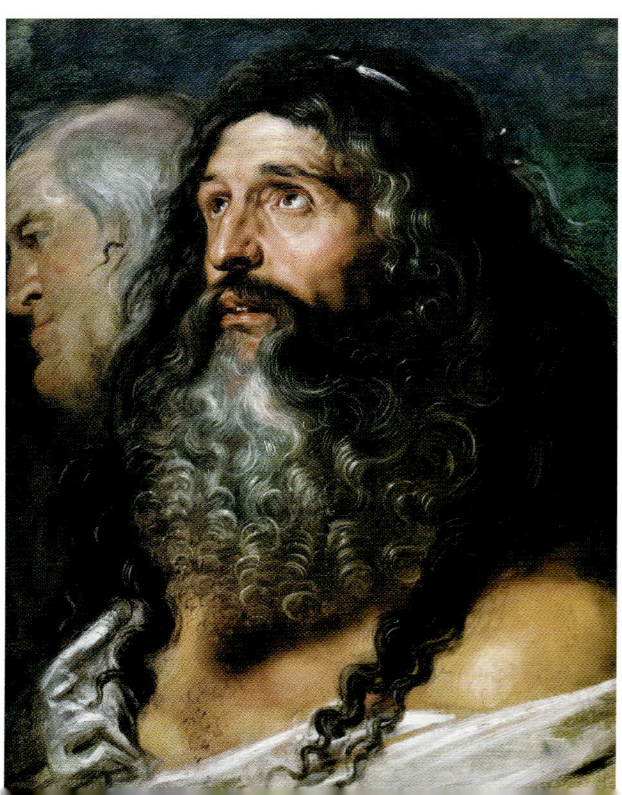

in religious and mythological works. The main head here became a saint in an altarpiece of 1609, a priest in 1612, a river god, and then Plato. The other head was derived from a work by Mantegna. Rubens's disciples Jacob Jordaens and Van Dyck followed this practice.

Portrait of Philip Rubens,
1610–11, oil on oak,
68.5 x 53.5cm (27 x 21⅛in),
Detroit Institute of Arts,
Michigan, USA

With bravura paint application and a predominantly monochrome palette, Rubens created a sensitive portrait of his beloved elder brother. Despite not always living in the same country, the siblings remained close throughout their lives, sharing their great intelligence and numerous friends. This was painted fairly quickly, with thin paint and rapid brush marks, resulting in a sketchy, relaxed and dynamic appearance.

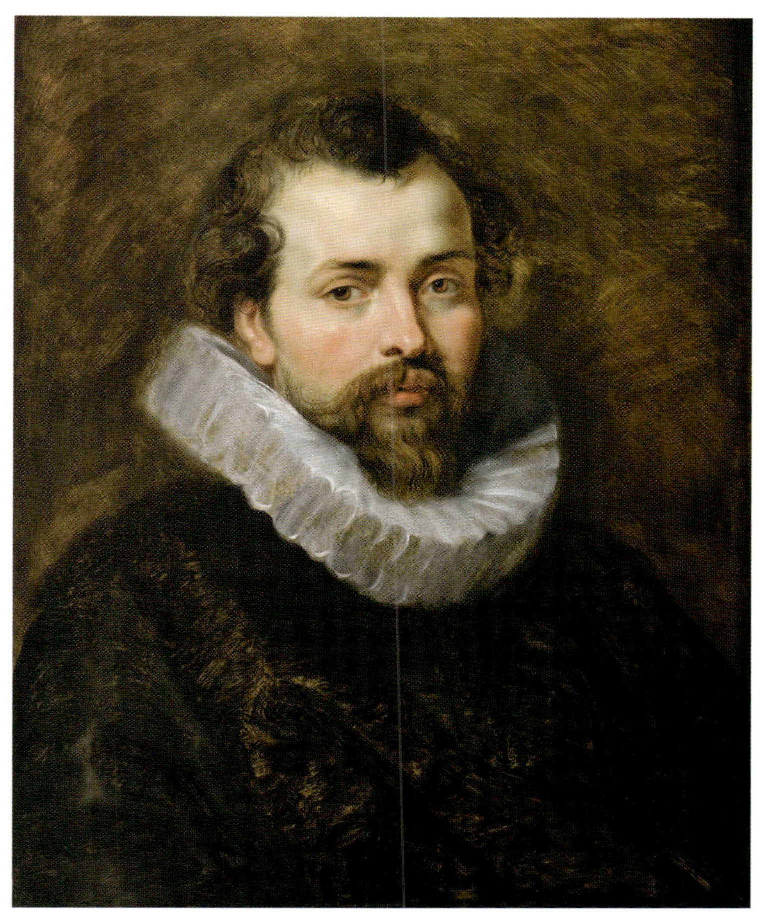

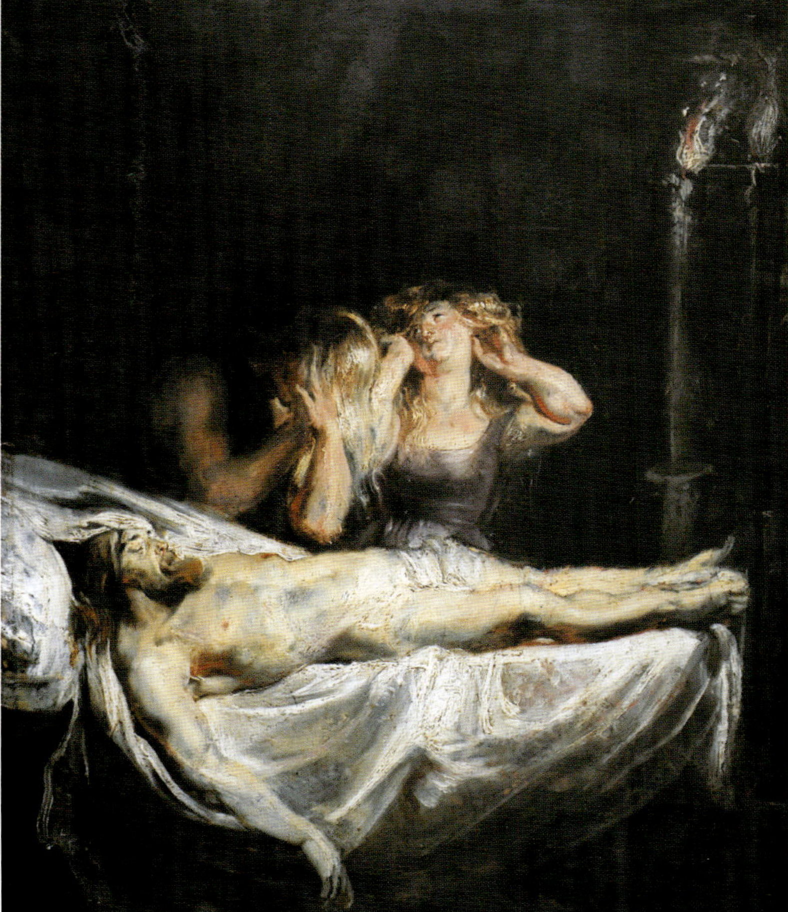

*Lamentation, c.*1609,
oil on panel, 34 x 27cm
(13⅓ x 10⅔in), Staatliche
Museen, Berlin, Germany

The naked body of Christ stretches across this composition, while a grief-stricken Virgin Mary and Mary Magdalene sob next to him. Unlike many of his works, here Rubens has imbued the Virgin with unbridled emotions. Two large torches in the background cast a glow, focusing attention on the figures and the shroud. This sketch was one of his first versions of this theme, but it was never followed into a final work.

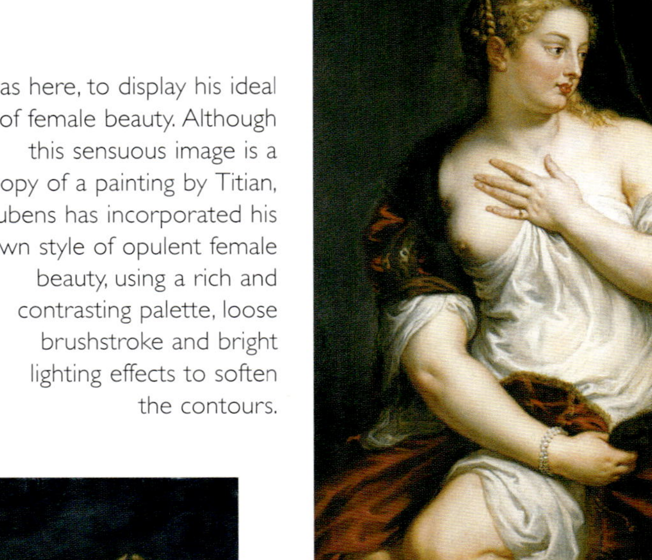

The Toilet of Venus, c.1608, oil on canvas, 137 x 111cm (54 x 43¾in), Museo Thyssen-Bornemisza, Madrid, Spain

Rubens was always drawn to mythological stories, as they gave him the opportunity to express passion, violence and movement – and also as here, to display his ideal of female beauty. Although this sensuous image is a copy of a painting by Titian, Rubens has incorporated his own style of opulent female beauty, using a rich and contrasting palette, loose brushstroke and bright lighting effects to soften the contours.

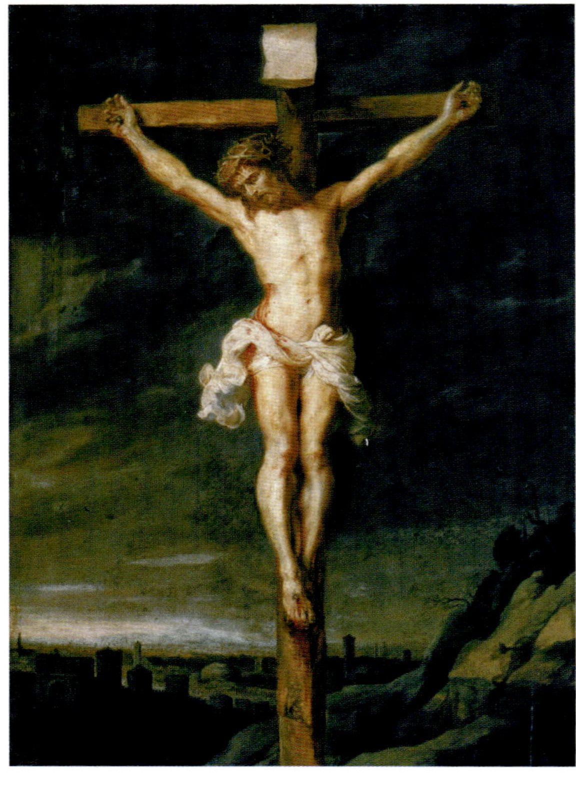

Crucifixion, c.1610, oil on wood, 107 x 76cm (42⅛ x 30in), Ciurlionis State Art Museum, Kaunas, Lithuania

One of many versions of this subject painted by Rubens, this work portrays Jesus as a muscular young man put to death in his prime, once again evoking an immediate sense of reality and compassion in viewers. Set against a dark background with an eerie light on the horizon, Christ on the cross is a lone figure, his skin glowing. It is clear that he is no ordinary man.

Study of Horsemen in Three Positions, c.1610–15, oil on panel, 36 x 65.7cm (14¼ x 26in), The Royal Collection, London, UK

This is believed to have been executed by Rubens and one of his pupils as a training exercise. Horses and riders often appear in Rubens's work, yet this is not as fluid as many of his other sketches. Training a student to follow his lead like this was a common part of art teaching.

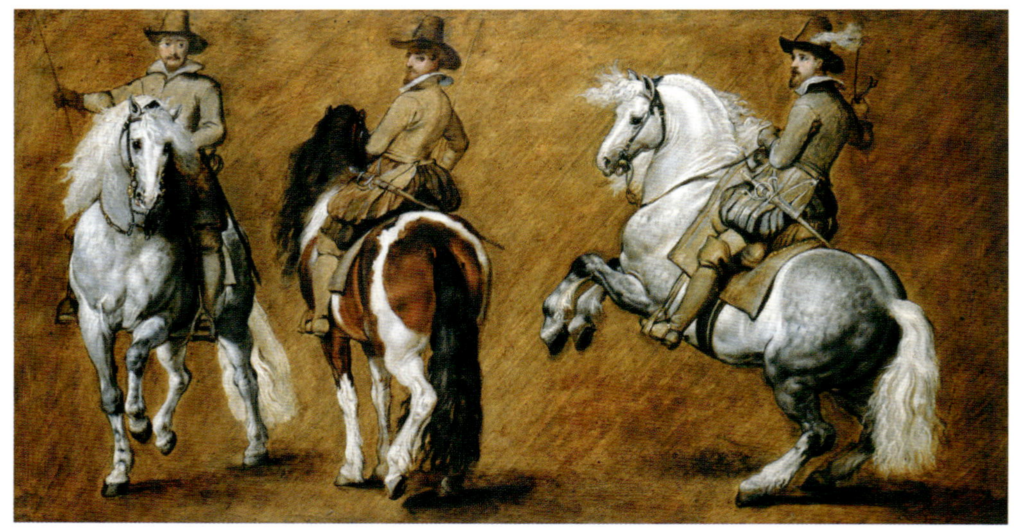

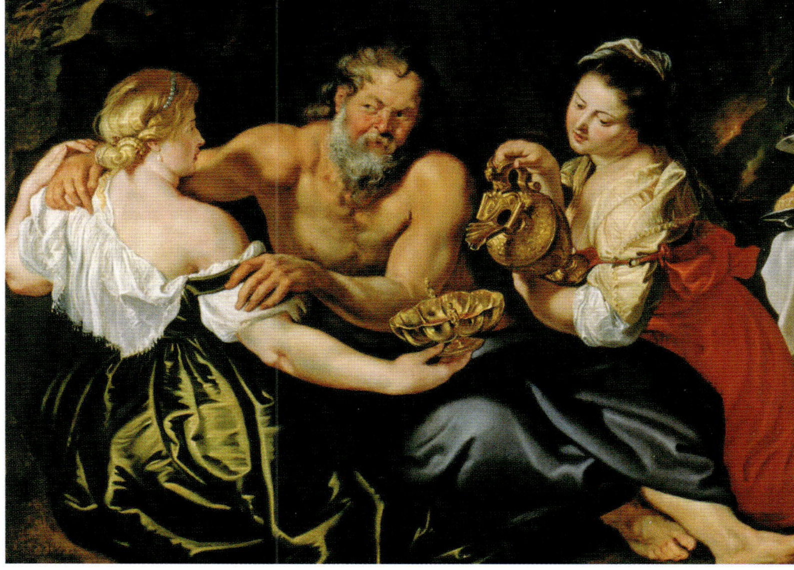

Lot and his Daughters, c.1610–11, oil on canvas, 108 x 146cm (42½ x 57½in), Staatliches Museum, Schwerin, Germany

Sumptuous fabrics, shimmering light, gleaming vessels, glowing skin – all expressing a biblical story from the Book of Genesis that could be difficult to portray. Fearing that they are the only survivors of Sodom, Lot's daughters seduce their father to ensure that he will have descendants. Rubens conveys the story in a luxurious manner, focusing on feminine beauty, clear light, rich colour and contrasting textures.

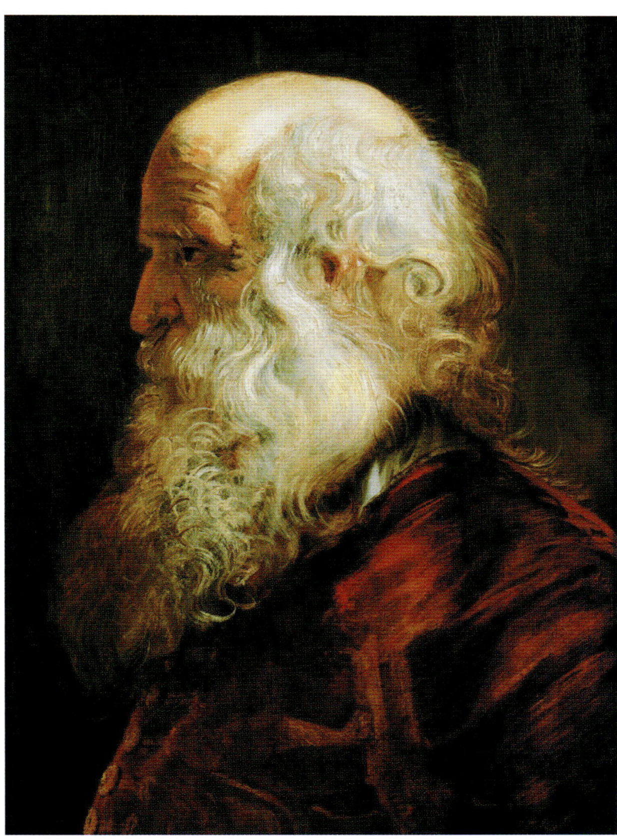

Study for the Head of an Old Man, 1610–15, oil on oak, 67 x 56.5cm (26⅔ x 22¼in), Kunsthistoriches Museum, Vienna, Austria

Using a characteristic light touch, layers of directional strokes and a rich palette, Rubens built up a bank of many different, lifelike characters, using them later in paintings to represent elders of the church, saints, biblical characters and pagan gods. These portraits were taken from life, and the same figures frequently appear in several different works over the years to come.

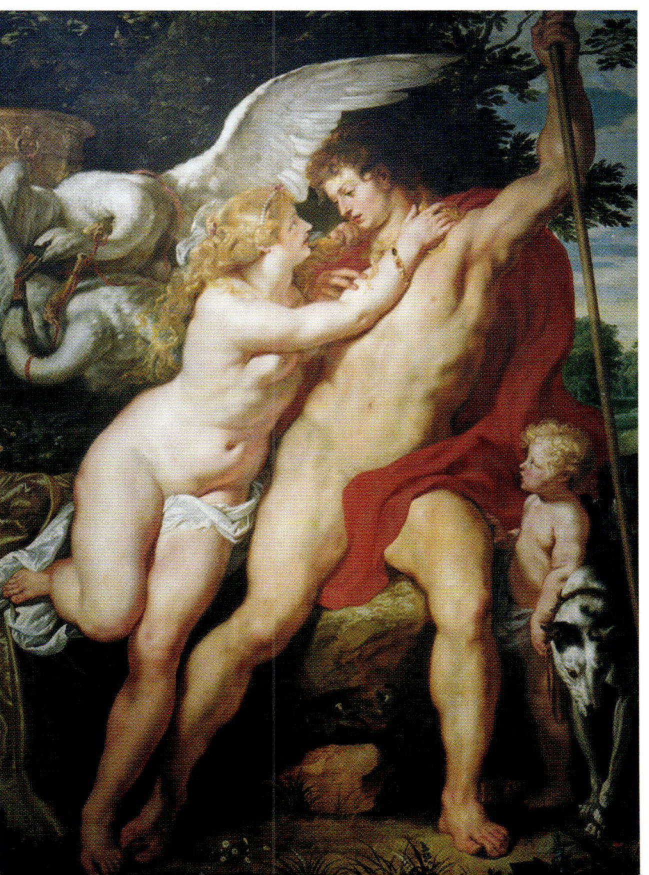

*Venus and Adonis, c.*1610, oil on panel, 276 x 183cm (108¾ x 72in), Museum Kunst Palast, Düsseldorf, Germany

The goddess Venus had a helpless passion for the young hunter, Adonis. When she left him at dawn one morning, she begged him not to hunt that day. But he broke his promise and was killed by a wild boar. This painting depicts Venus pleading with her lover not to hunt. Femininity for Rubens included soft, plump, pale flesh and long blonde hair, while virility was epitomized with powerful muscles and golden skin.

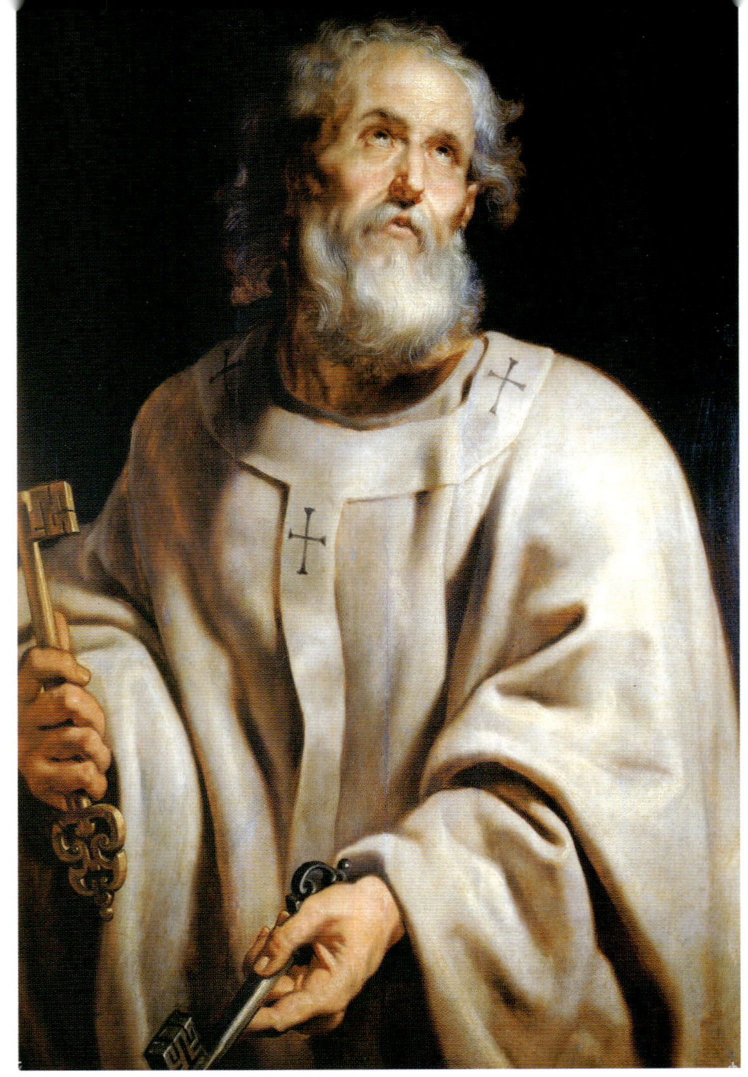

Saint Peter, c.1610–12,
oil on panel, 107.5 x 83cm
(42¼ x 32⅔in), Museo
Nacional del Prado,
Madrid, Spain

From the Twelve Apostles
series commissioned by
the Duke of Lerma, this
represents Saint Peter, life-
sized for full impact, holding
the keys to the Kingdom of
Heaven, the symbol by which
he is usually identified.
Rubens created each of his
apostles in this series as a
strong man, usually mature,
filling the space, reminiscent
of Michelangelo's style and
monumental approach.

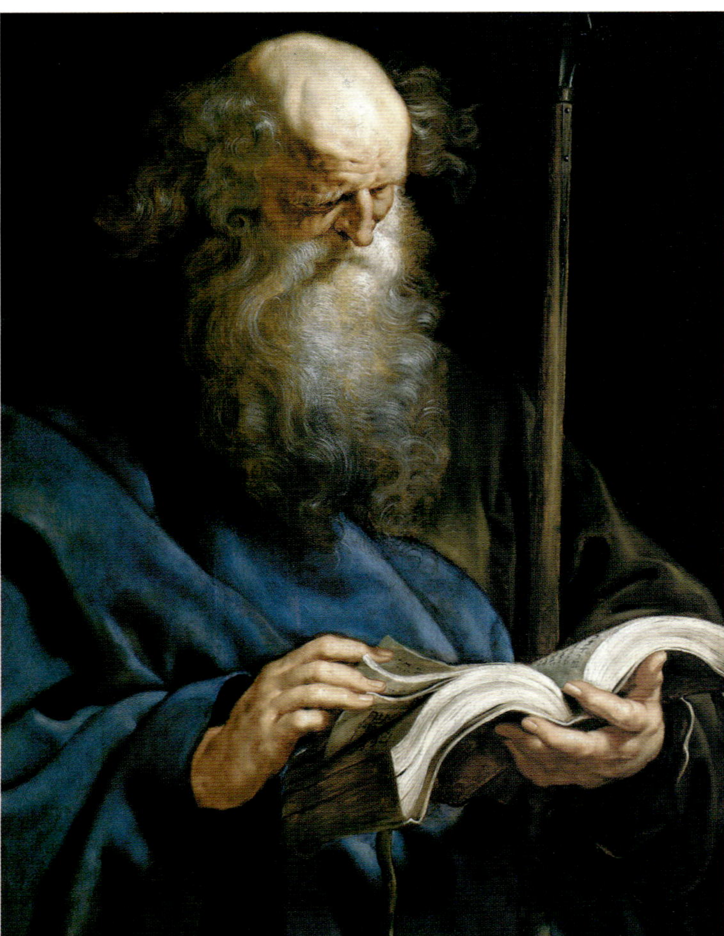

Saint Thomas, c.1610–12,
oil on panel, 107.5 x 83cm
(42¼ x 32⅔in), Museo
Nacional del Prado,
Madrid, Spain

Another apostle from the
series of 12 commissioned
by the Duke of Lerma, this
impressive-looking elderly
man shows his wisdom by
reading a heavy tome, so
can be identified as Saint
Thomas. Working as an
evangelist in Persia and India,
Saint Thomas built a church
with his own hands before
being shot with arrows,
stoned and left to die.

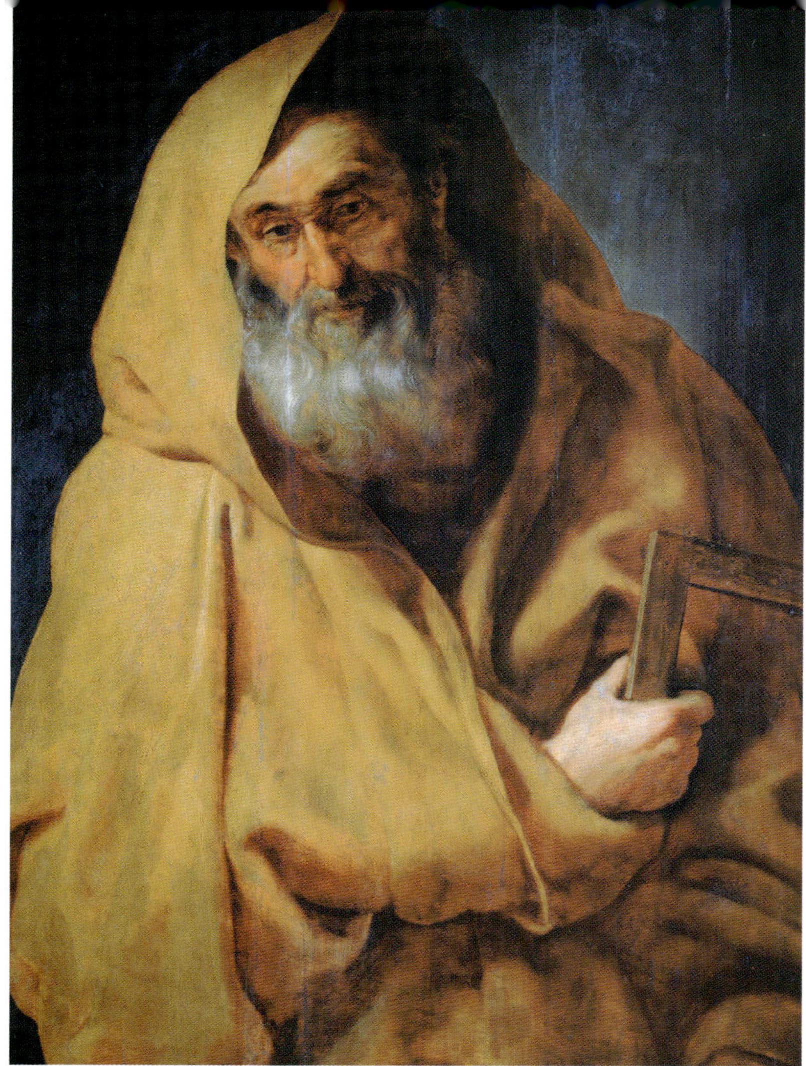

James the Younger,
c.1610–12, oil on panel,
107.5 x 83cm (42¼ x
32⅔in), Museo Nacional
del Prado, Madrid, Spain

Also known as James the
Lesser, or the Minor, this
forceful-looking man
swathed in a voluminous
cloak is identified by the
fuller's tool he holds, with
which he was killed. He was
probably the first bishop in
Jerusalem. As with all the
saints in this series, Rubens
illuminates him from a single
light source and sets him
against a dark background,
so in essence he emerges
from the shadows, creating
a mystical presence.

Saint Bartholomew,
c.1610–12, oil on panel,
107.5 x 83cm (42¼ x
32⅔in), Museo Nacional
del Prado, Madrid, Spain

Saint Bartholomew probably
preached Christianity near
the border of India and in
Armenia. According to the
Bible, he was introduced to
Jesus by Philip, and also died
a martyr's death; he was
flayed alive, crucified and
then beheaded. Rubens
depicts him here with a
knife, referring to his horrific
death. Matching the rest of
the series, this is life-sized,
and the lighting highlights
the figure as if in a spotlight,
creating an instant impact.

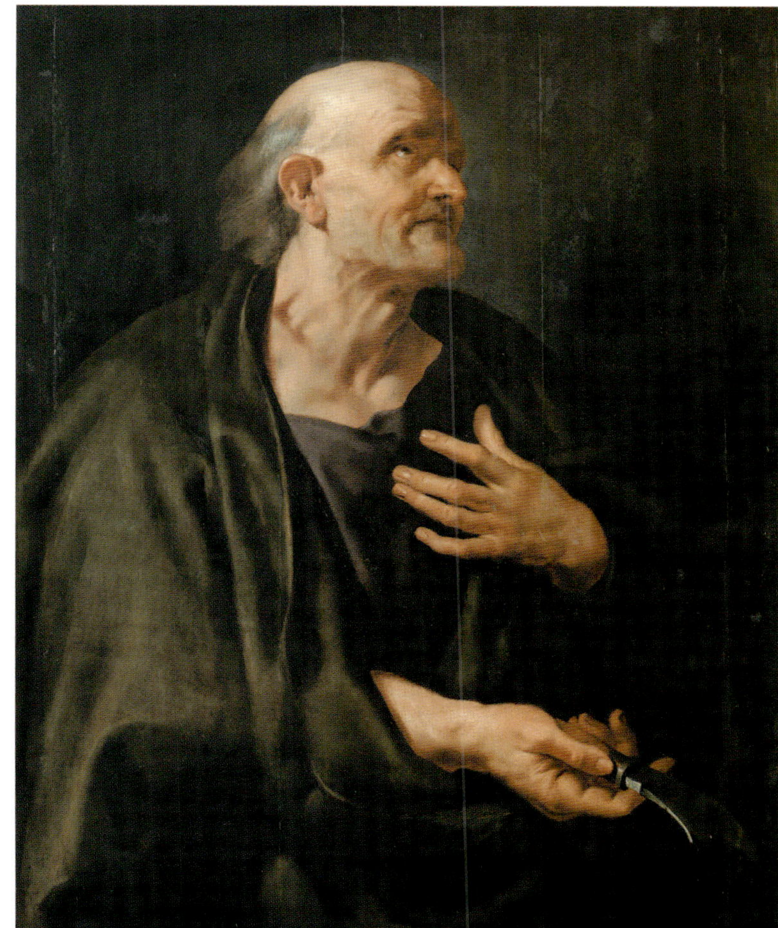

Saint Matthew, c.1610–12,
oil on panel, 107.5 x 83cm
(42¼ x 32⅔in), Museo
Nacional del Prado,
Madrid, Spain

Rubens's Matthew is younger
than most of his other
apostles. Originally a tax
collector, Matthew travelled
to Ethiopia after preaching to
the Jews in Palestine. Leaning
slightly back at an animated
angle, as if conversing with
someone beyond the
painting, Matthew holds a
weapon that refers to his
suffering and martyrdom,
although the means of his
death is often disputed.

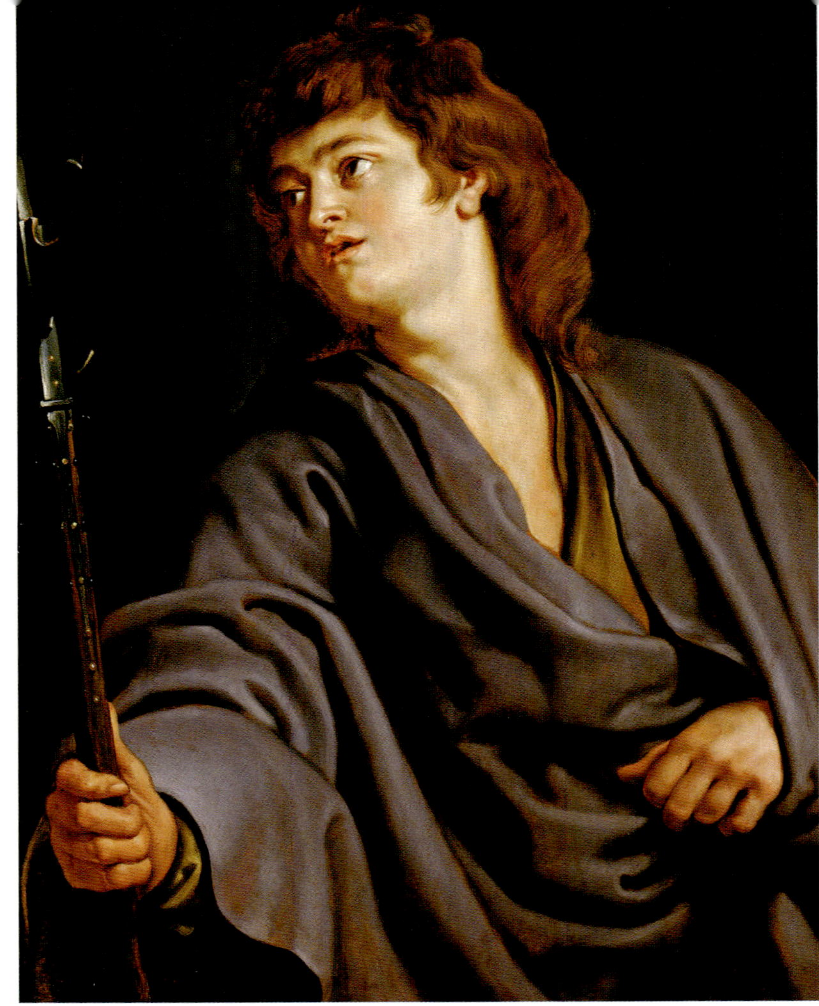

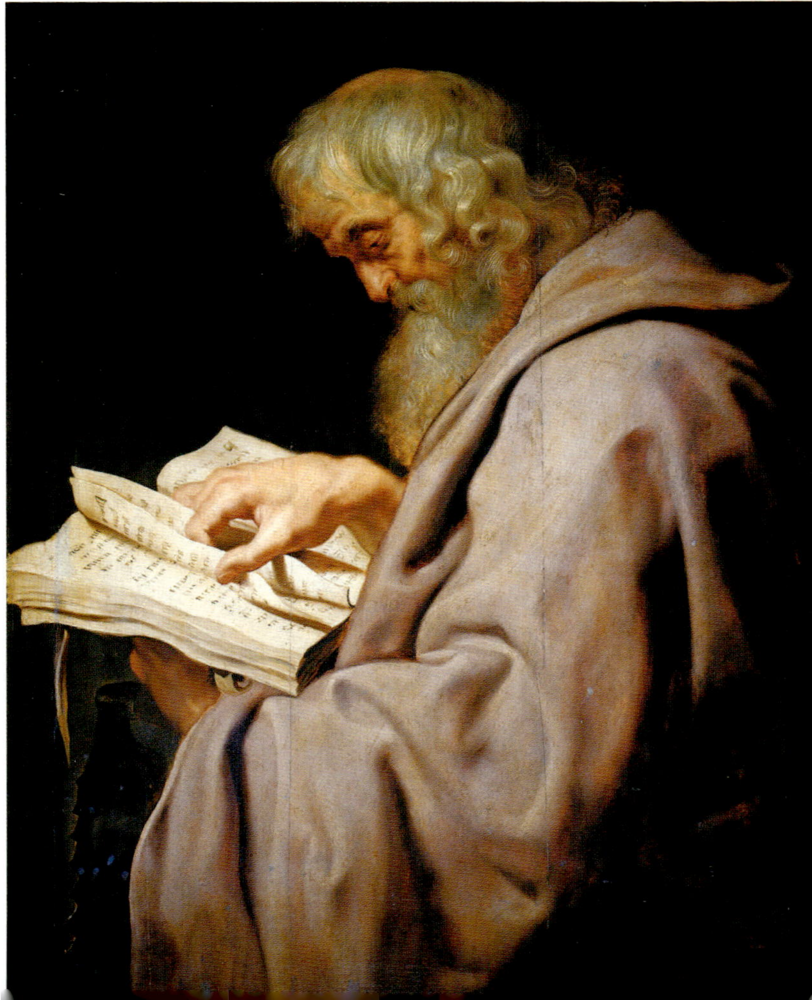

Saint Simon, c.1610–12,
oil on panel, 107.5 x 83cm
(42¼ x 32⅔in), Museo
Nacional del Prado,
Madrid, Spain

Also known as Simon
the Zealot, this apostle
is variously said to have
worked near Palestine, or to
have accompanied Jude on
his travels. In his left hand
he holds a saw, as according
to a tradition, he was
put to death with one. He
also gained a reputation as
a 'fisher of men' through his
preaching of the gospel. This
image clearly follows several
of Michelangelo's figures on
the Sistine Chapel ceiling.

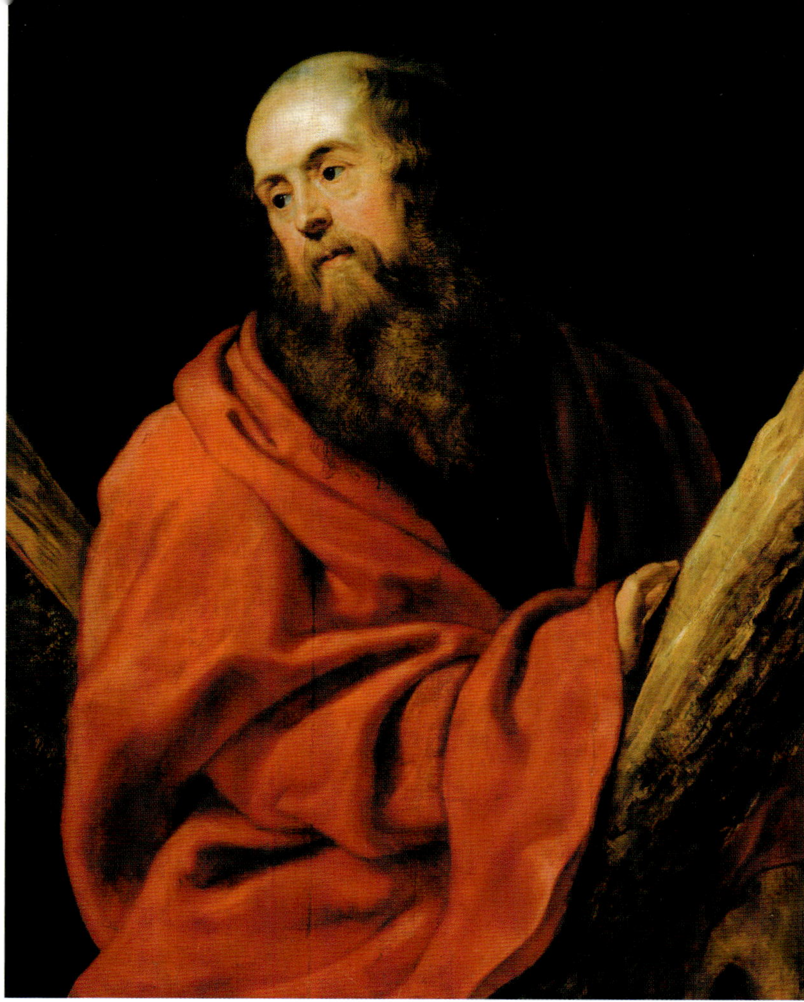

Saint Andrew, c.1610–12, oil on panel, 107.5 x 83cm (42¼ x 32⅔in), Museo Nacional del Prado, Madrid, Spain

The brother of Peter, Andrew is said to have founded the Russian church, and is the patron saint of both Russia and Scotland. Tradition holds that he was crucified in Greece on a cross saltire, and here he is carrying that cross he may have died on. The credibility of Rubens's characters helped to authenticate stories from the Bible for viewers.

Saint James the Elder, c.1610–12, oil on panel, 107.5 x 83cm (42¼ x 32⅔in), Museo Nacional del Prado, Madrid, Spain

With his arresting gaze, James can be identified by his pilgrim's attributes, that is, a hat and staff, which follows accepted medieval traditions of iconography about his life. After working in Jerusalem, James allegedly preached across Spain, and he is the only apostle whose death is recorded in the scriptures: he was beheaded by Herod Agrippa, the same King Herod mentioned in the Bible's Acts of the Apostles.

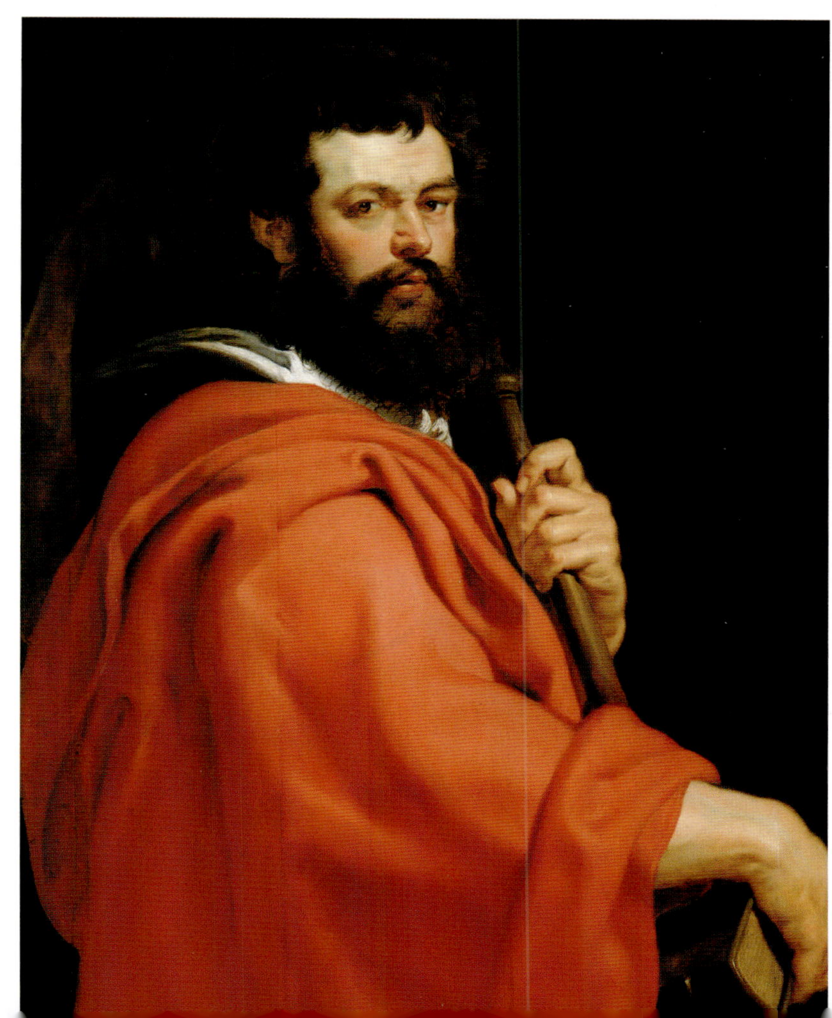

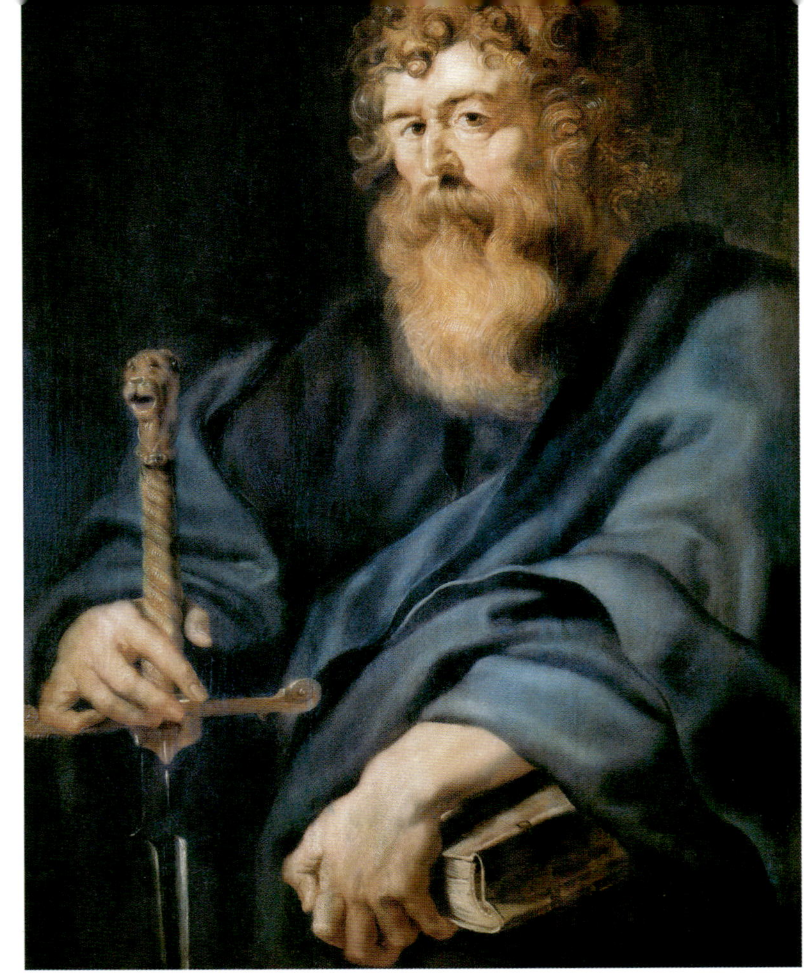

Saint Paul, 1610–12, oil on panel, 107.5 x 83cm (42¼ x 32⅔in), Museo Nacional del Prado, Madrid, Spain

One of a series of 12 panels, each showing one of Christ's apostles, this portrayal of Saint Paul shows him to be a powerful figure, set against a dark background. Light falls directly on to his face and clothing, recalling both Michelangelo and Caravaggio. Each saint is depicted with his Christian emblem, so here Paul carries the sword and Holy Scriptures, symbolizing his battle for the Faith and his work in spreading the Gospel.

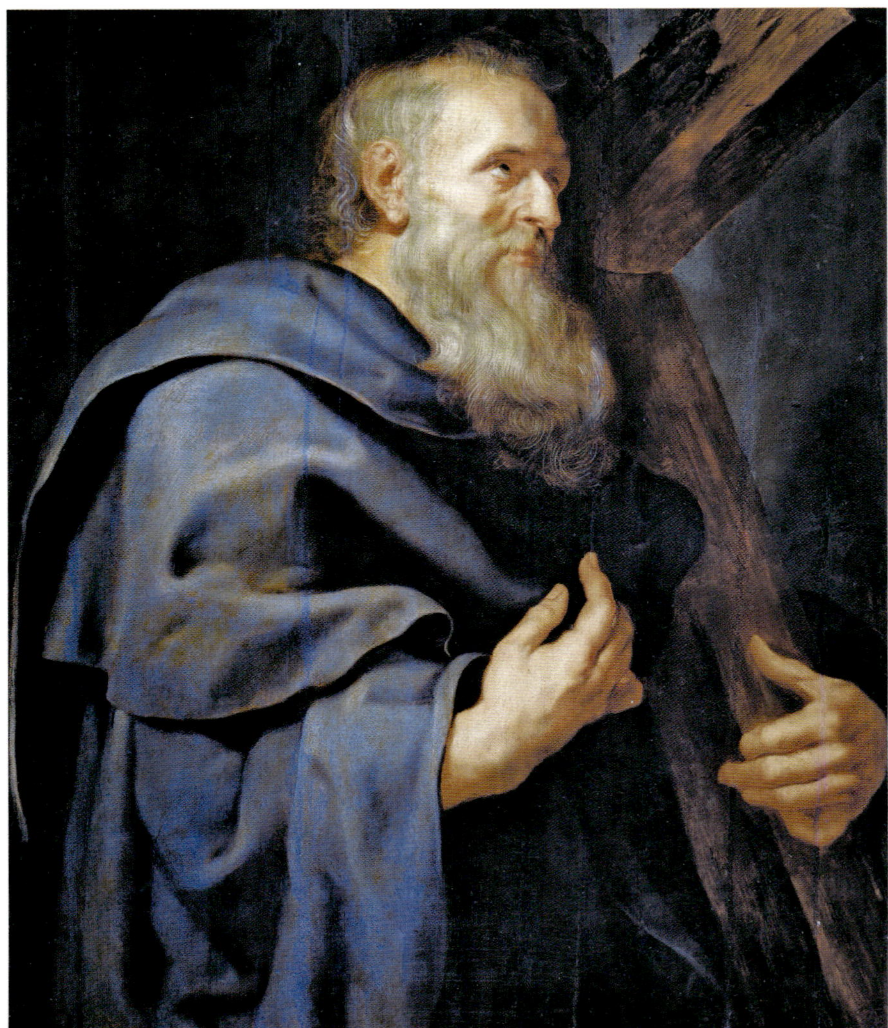

Saint Philip, 1610–12, oil on panel, 107 x 82.5cm (42⅛ x 32⅓in), Museo del Prado, Madrid, Spain

Part of the series of the 12 apostles, Saint Philip emerges from the dark background in strong tenebrism. The influence of Michelangelo's powerful figures and his method of intensely directed light arise from Rubens's recent trip to Italy. Saint Philip carries a cross because he was martyred in a crucifixion. According to the Bible, he was among those surrounding John the Baptist when he described Jesus as the Lamb of God, and he was also one of the attendees at the wedding at Cana. Additionally, he is often perceived as a link to the Greek community.

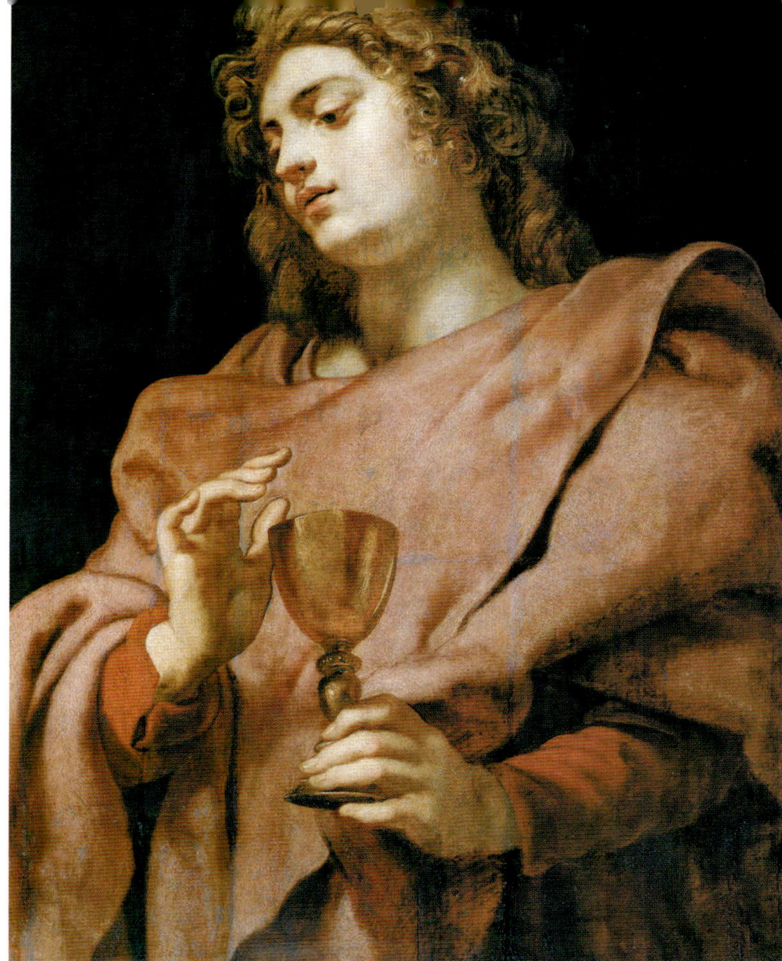

Saint John the Evangelist, c.1610–12, oil on panel, 107.5 x 83cm (42¼ x 32⅔in), Museo Nacional del Prado, Madrid, Spain

A rather beautiful young man holds his emblem of a goblet with which he was intended to be poisoned. He is Rubens's version of Saint John the Evangelist. Legend says that someone tried to kill him by serving him poisoned wine, but the attempt to kill him failed, and he later died naturally. A fisherman and the brother of James, Saint John is often mentioned as the one whom Jesus most loved.

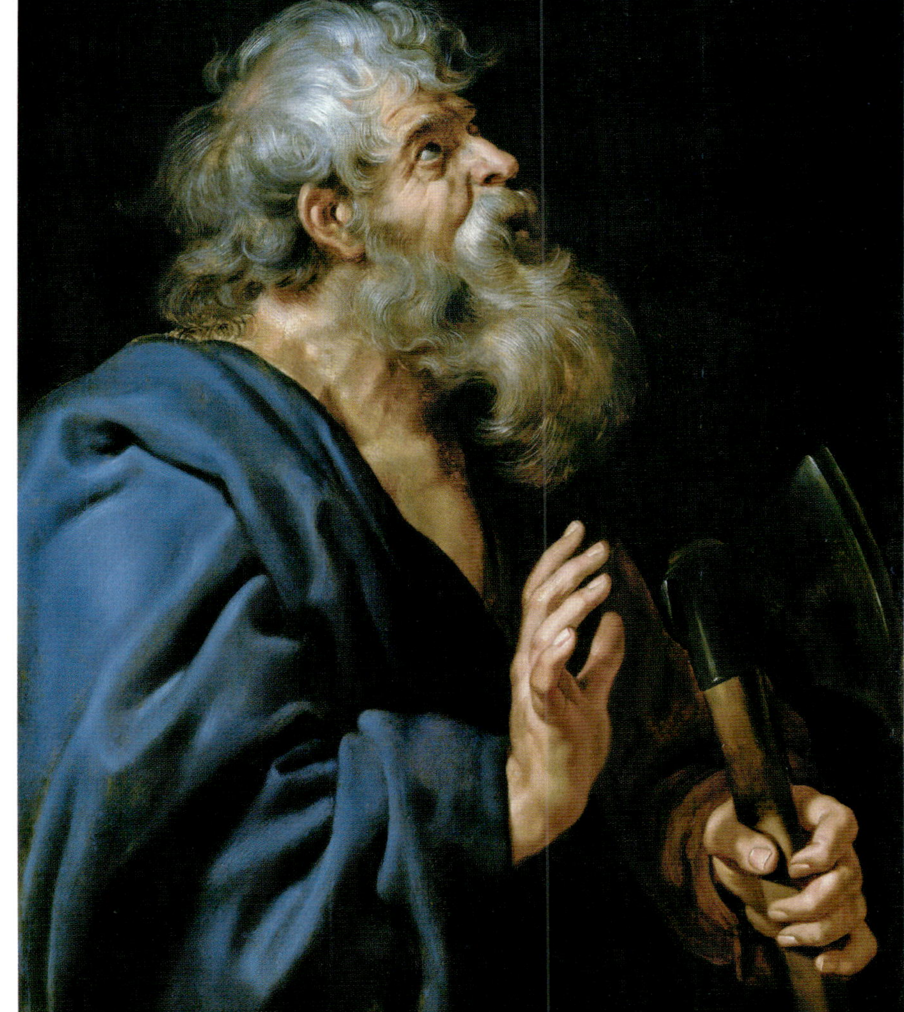

Saint Matthias, 1610–12, oil on panel, 107 x 82.5cm (42⅛ x 32⅓in), Museo del Prado, Madrid, Spain

According to the Acts of the Apostles, after Judas had betrayed Jesus, the remaining apostles chose Matthias to join them. The Acts of the Apostles also explains that Matthias was a follower of Jesus from the time he was baptized by John to his ascension into heaven, 43 days after the crucifixion. As with each painting in this series, Rubens has painted Matthias in strong chiaroscuro, holding his Christian emblem. This is an axe that refers to the unconfirmed story that says he was stoned and then beheaded in Jerusalem.

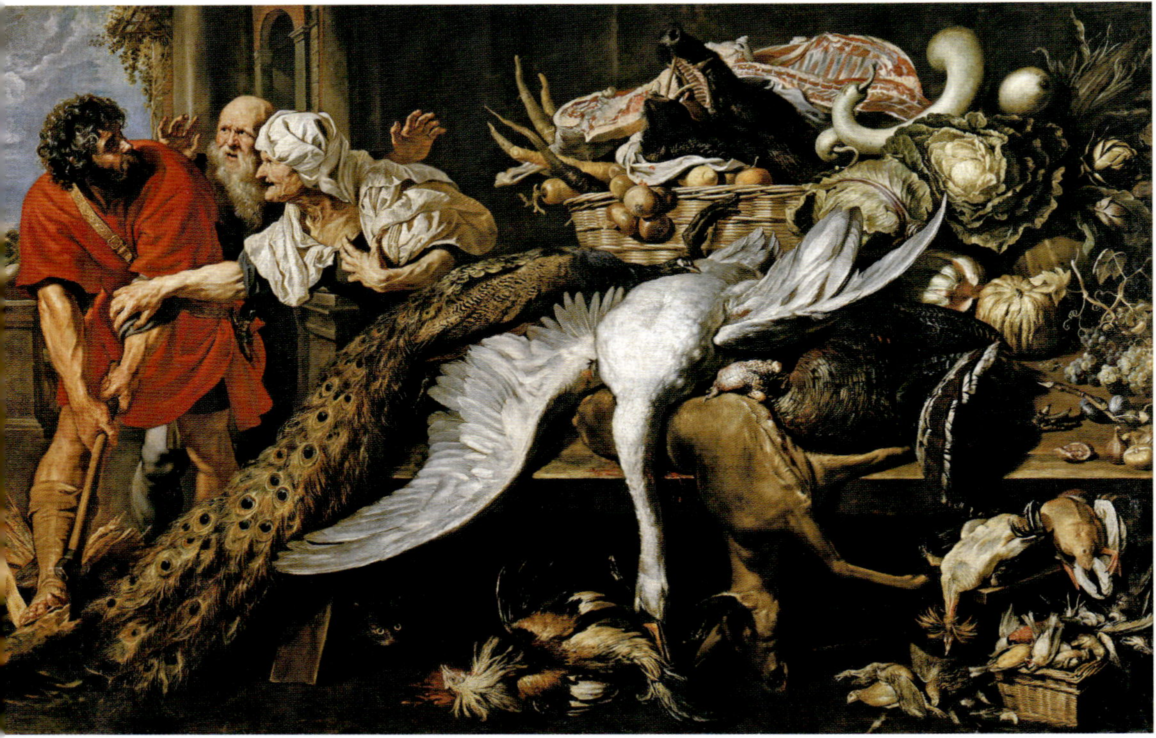

The Recognition of Philopoemen, Rubens and Snyders, c.1609, oil on canvas, 201 x 313.5cm (79 x 123⅓in), Museo Nacional del Prado, Madrid, Spain

In collaboration with Snyders, Rubens painted this scene of Philopoemen, a Greek general and statesman renowned for his courage. According to Plutarch, Philopoemen visited a grand house, and through his modest appearance the lady of the house confused him with a servant and put him to work. This depicts the moment when two elderly servants recognize him. Rubens painted the figures, and Snyders painted the large still life in the foreground.

Juno and Argus, c.1610, oil on canvas, 249 x 296cm (98 x 116½in), Wallraf-Richartz-Museum, Cologne, Germany

From Ovid's *Metamorphoses*, Jupiter, the supreme Roman god, had a lover, Io, a priestess. His wife Juno sent Argus to capture Io and turn her into a cow. In retaliation, Jupiter sent Mercury to kill Argus. In a scene filled with colour and light, Rubens's image depicts the gory result: Argus decapitated, with Juno removing his hundred glowing eyes to decorate the plumage of a peacock.

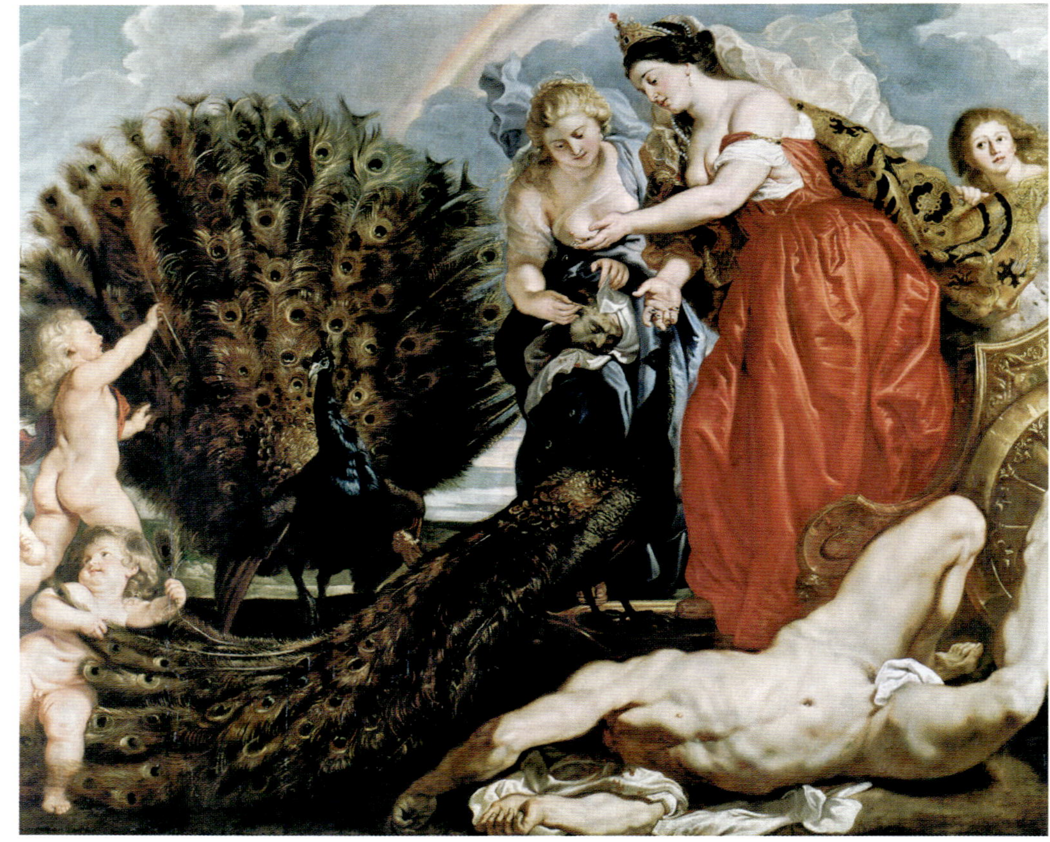

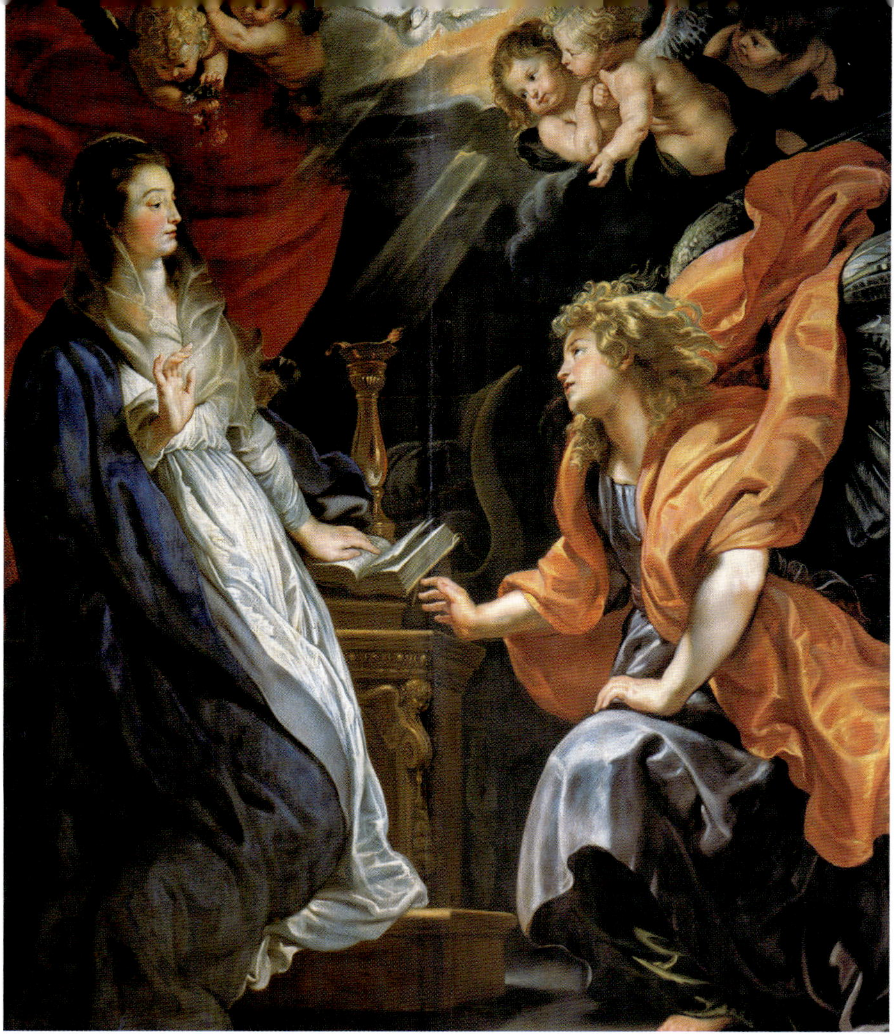

The Annunciation, c.1610, oil on canvas, 224 x 200cm (88 x 78¾in), Kunsthistorisches Museum, Vienna, Austria

A common subject for Counter-Reformation artists, this subject was portrayed in its most dramatic format by Rubens soon after his return from Italy for the Antwerp Jesuit College. Depicting the moment the Angel Gabriel visits Mary, he chose to portray it as a striking night scene, focusing on fluid brushwork, contrasting colours of warm and cool, expressive gestures and expressions, and an impressive play of light and shadows.

Annunciation of the Virgin's Death, 1609–12, oil on panel, 92 x 73.1cm (32¼ x 28¾in), The Courtauld Gallery, London, UK

In Catholic orthodoxy, the Archangel Michael carries the souls of the dead to Heaven. Not often portrayed in art is the story of the Archangel visiting the Virgin Mary three days before her death, to warn her to prepare. Rubens portrays the event as a moment of action, giving Mary a serene expression of acceptance as she watches the angel descend.

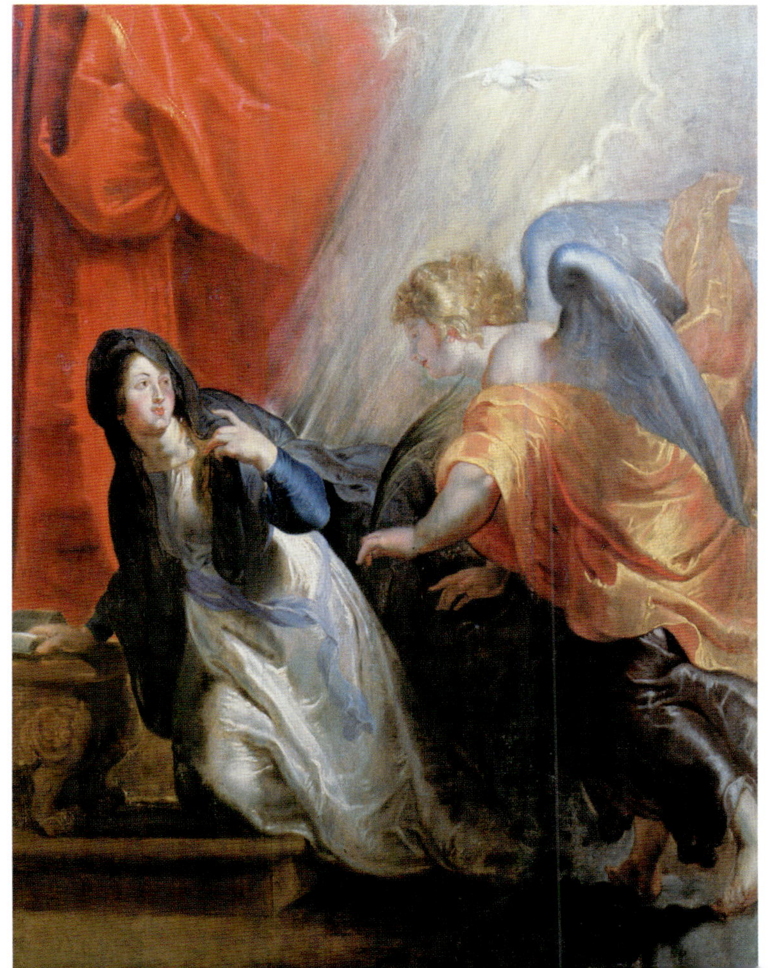

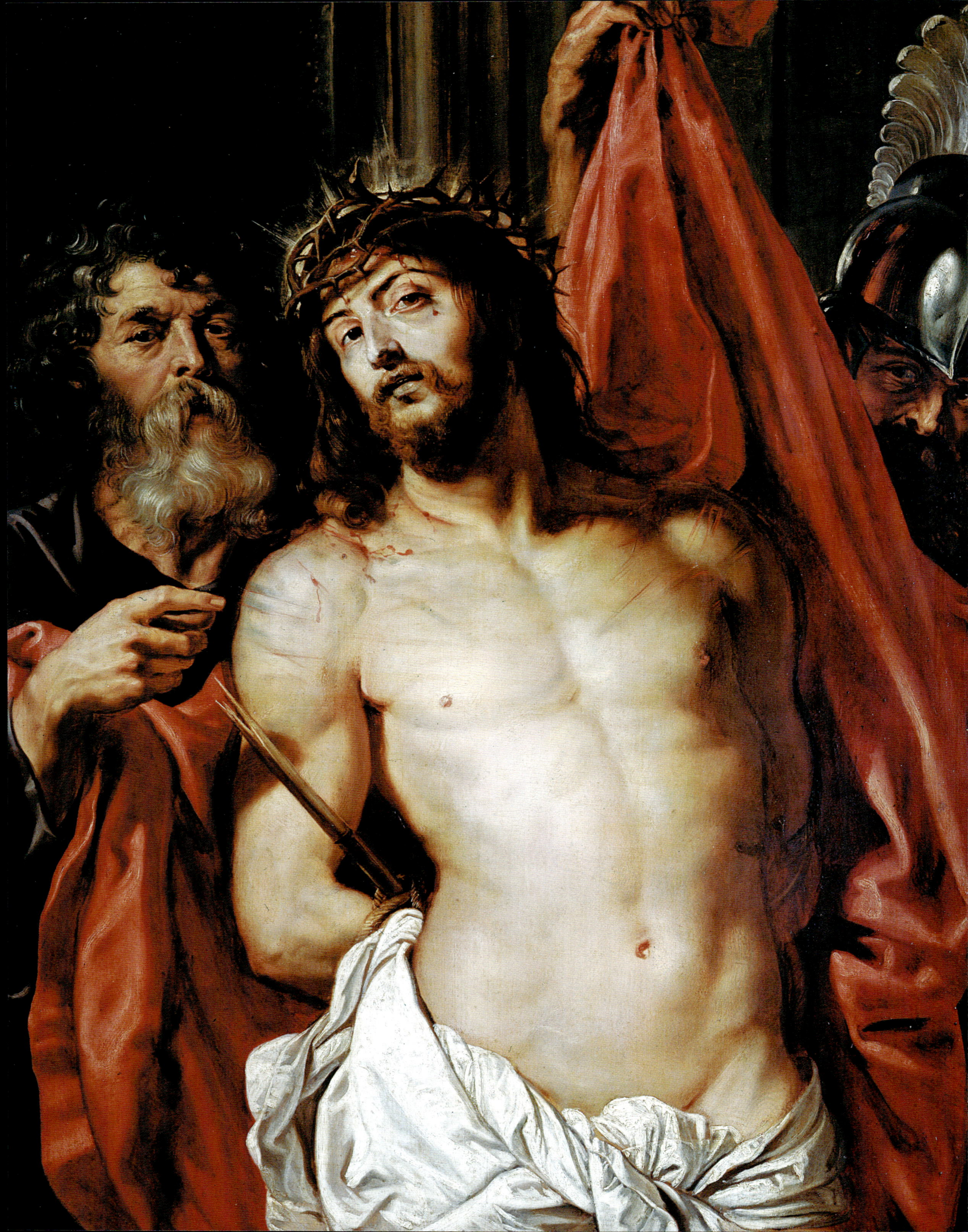

EMINENCE IN EUROPE

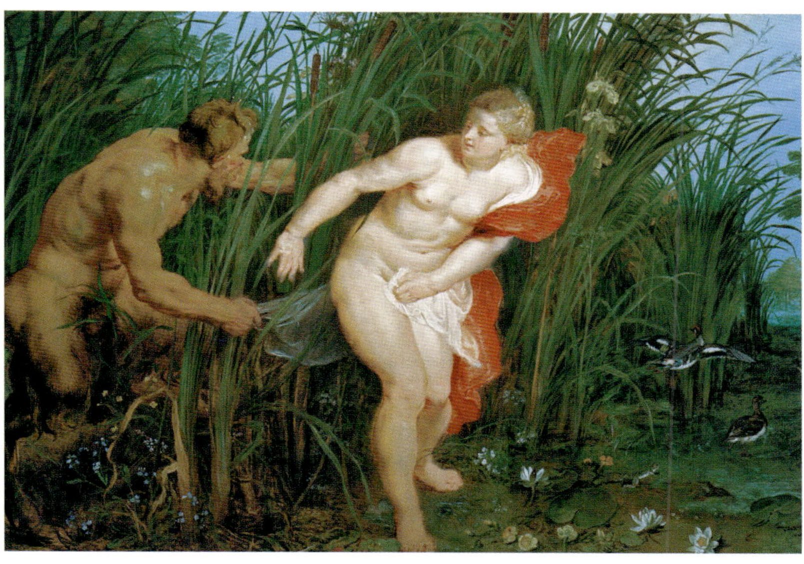

By 1611, Rubens was the most acclaimed artist in Europe. Outstandingly accomplished in every genre, his work held no secrets or undercurrents, he suffered no angst or self-doubt, and he had no enemies. By that time, he had bought and renovated his house, and incorporated a large studio to keep up with his burgeoning workload. Business acumen was not a common attribute of artists, but Rubens began extending his fame by selling prints of his works across Europe.

Above: Pan and Syrinx, *1617–18, oil on oak. According to Ovid's* Metamorphoses, Syrinx *is a nymph who flees from the lecherous satyr Pan. To help her escape his clutches, the gods turn her into a reed. Here, Rubens paints her as a voluptuous nude. Predominantly in green, rose and flesh tones, the painting is abundant with nature, including reeds, flowers, ducks, herons and kingfishers.*

Left: Christ with the Crown of Thorns, *c.1612, oil on wood. Viewers are confronted by Jesus, semi-naked, pushed forward on the picture plane, his pale skin in stark contrast with the red cloth behind him. The Roman governor Pontius Pilate points at him as he presents the prisoner, humiliated in his crown of thorns, to viewers, inviting them to participate in the biblical story.*

Visitation, left panel from *Descent from the Cross* triptych, 1611–14, oil on panel, 420 x 150cm (165⅓ x 59in), Onze Lieve Vrouwekerk, Antwerp, Belgium

This is the left-hand panel from *Descent from the Cross* depicting the New Testament story of The Visitation, showing Mary visiting her cousin Elizabeth, who is pregnant with John the Baptist. Behind the two women are their husbands, Joseph and Zacharias. The figures are typical middle-class women of the period, and Rubens's rich, painterly Baroque technique exploited the intense colour of Venetian painting along with the chiaroscuro of Caravaggio, blended with his own unique approach.

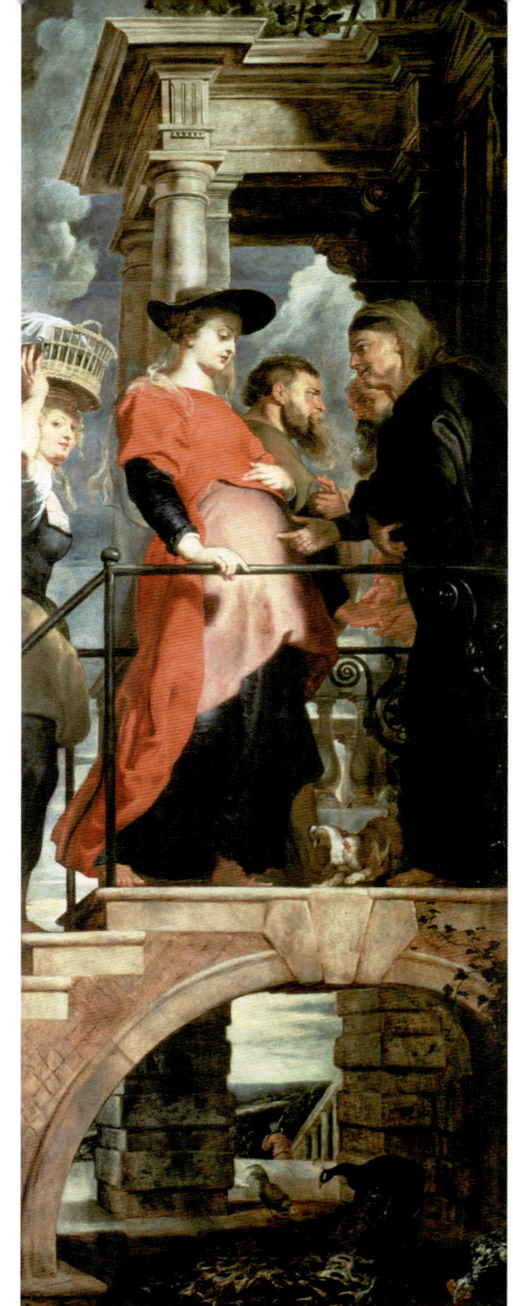

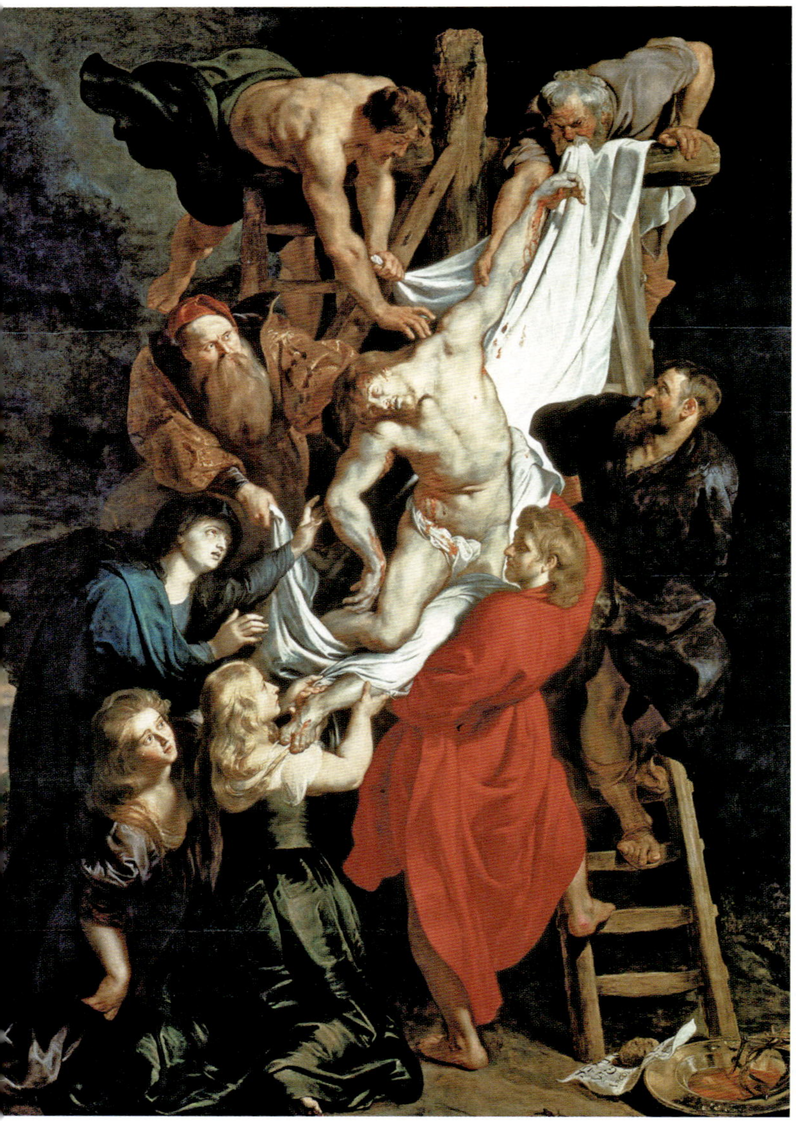

Descent from the Cross, centre panel, 1611–14, oil on panel, 421 x 311cm (165¾ x 122⅓in), Onze Lieve Vrouwekerk, Antwerp, Belgium

Churches in Antwerp were decorated with unusual splendour for northern Europe. Commissioned by the Arquebusiers' Guild through the instigation of Rubens's friend Nicolaas Rockox, this is the second of his great altarpieces for Antwerp Cathedral. Paid 2400 florins for it, the result propelled Rubens to fame. The dramatically diagonal composition attracts attention with its chiaroscuro and rich colours, while the power of human emotion is almost palpable. Never before had the Deposition been painted with such forceful dynamism and passion. Eight figures surround the corpse of Jesus, which is being tenderly lowered from the Cross by workmen on ladders. A blonde Mary Magdalene takes the weight of his foot.

Saint Christopher Carrying the Christ Child, c.1612, oil on panel, 420 x 310cm (165⅓ x 122in), Onze Lieve Vrouwkerk, Antwerp Cathedral, Belgium

These images form the exterior or back wings of the *Descent from the Cross* triptych. According to medieval legend, Saint Christopher carried the Christ Child across a river on his shoulders. These paintings are devoted to Saint Christopher, as he was the Arquebusiers' patron saint. When the triptych was closed, these two scenes were on show. The hermit saint lights Christ's way with a lantern. These panels were not completed until after Rubens finished the front. The entire triptych is about carrying Christ in some way, from *Visitation,* where he is being carried in his mother's womb, to the right-hand panel, where he is being held by Simeon, and here on these outer panels.

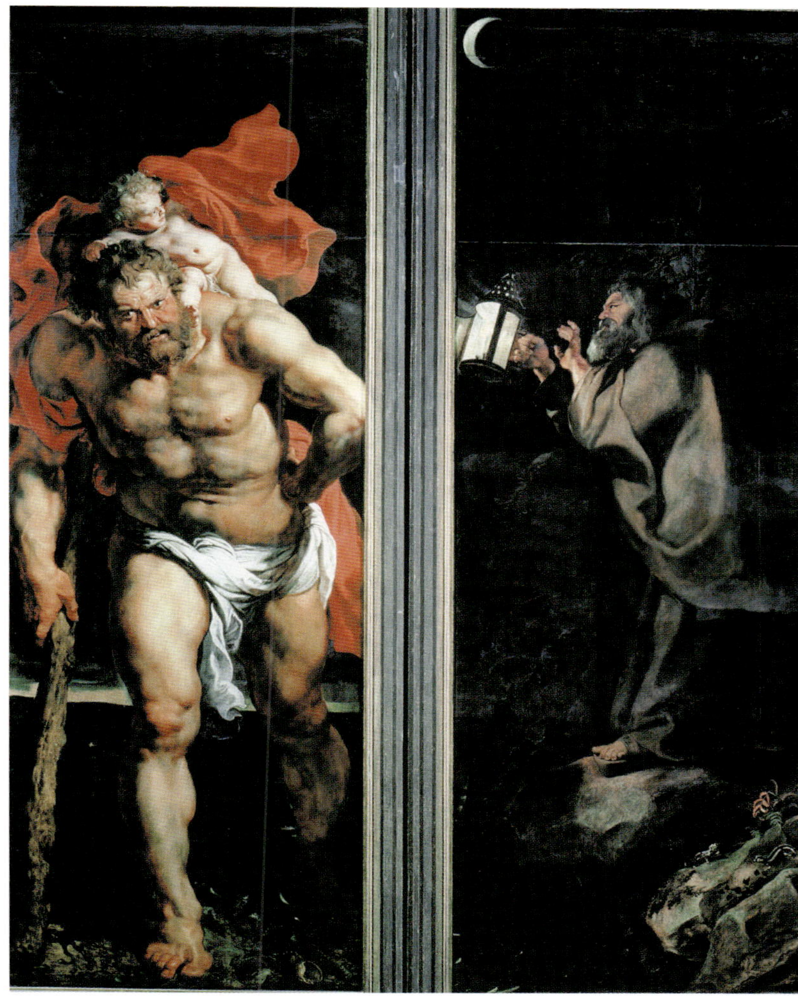

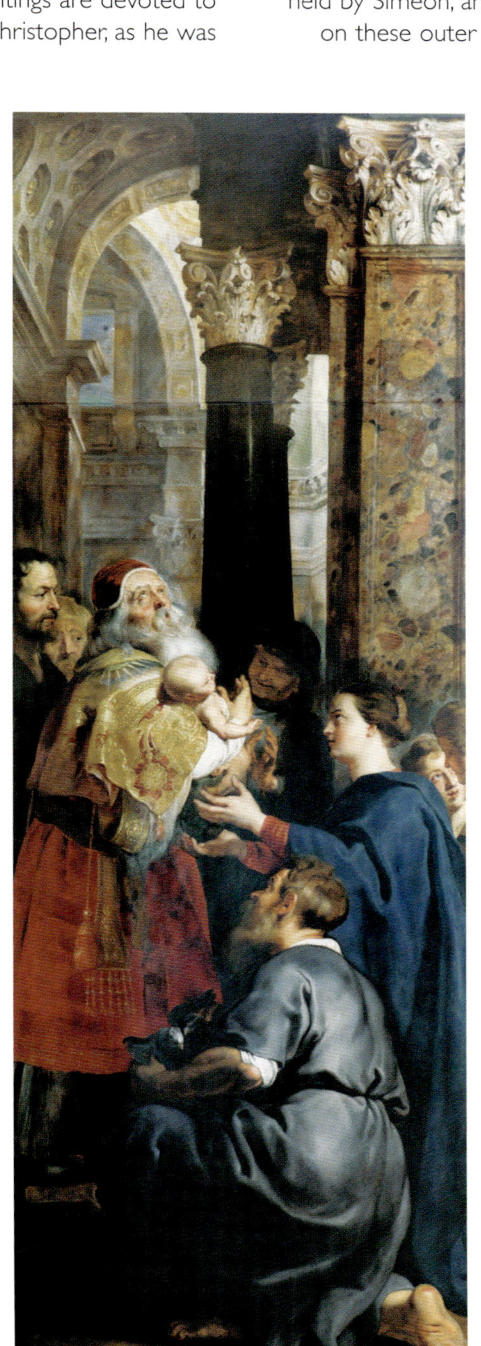

Presentation in the Temple, right panel from *Descent from the Cross* triptych, 1611–14, oil on panel, 420 x 150cm (165⅓ x 59in), Onze Lieve Vrouwkerk, Antwerp Cathedral, Belgium

The first great altarpiece painted by Rubens after his return from Italy was *Descent from the Cross* for the chapel of the Arquebusiers' Guild in Antwerp Cathedral. The triptych was dedicated to Saint Christopher, the guild's patron saint. This is the right-hand panel; Simeon carries the infant Jesus, Mary supports her son, and Joseph kneels. The spectator behind Simeon is Nicolaas Rockox, Rubens's friend, mayor of Antwerp and president of the Arquebusiers' Guild.

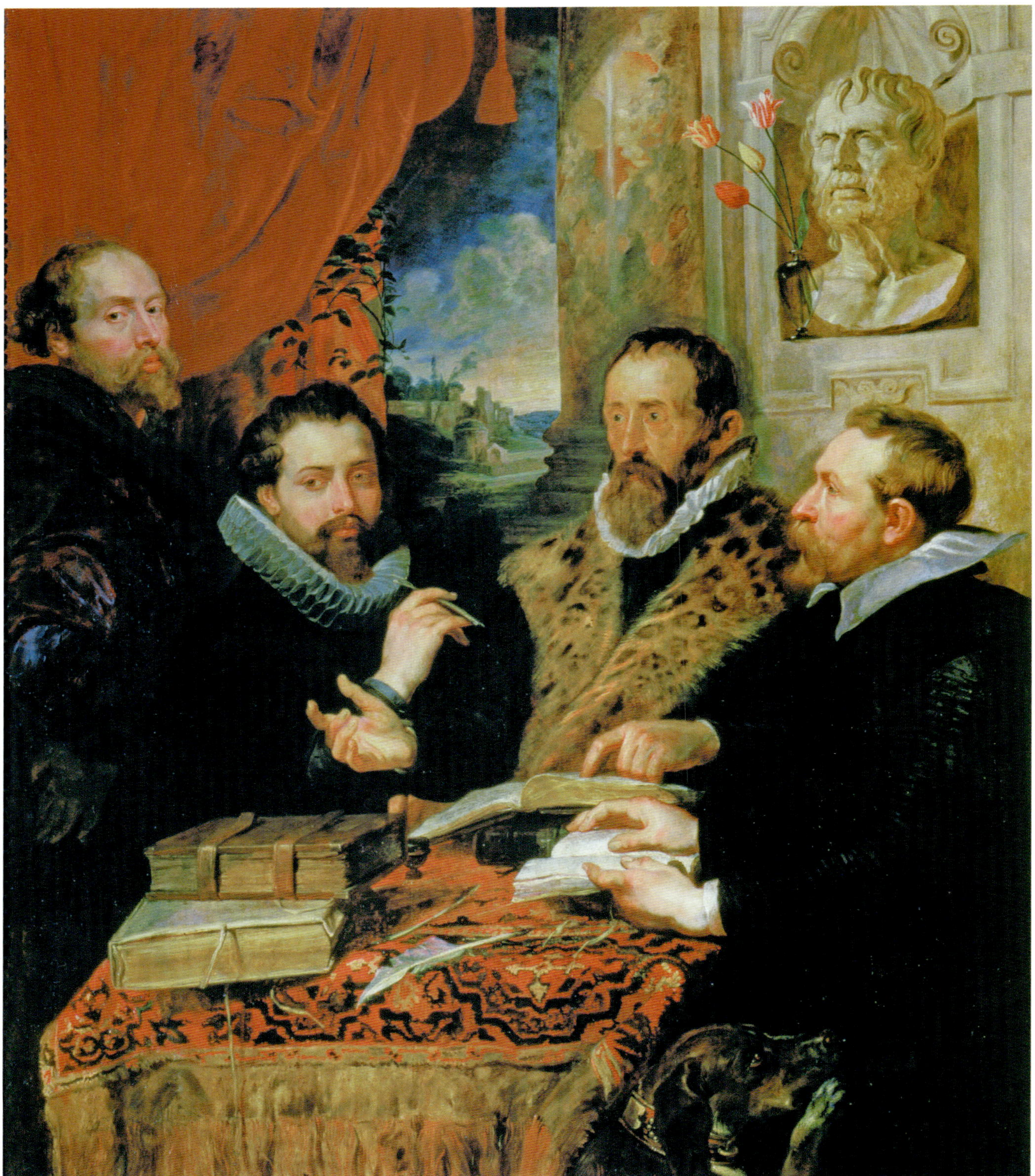

The Four Philosophers,
1611–12, oil on canvas,
164 x 139cm (64½ x
54¾ in), Pitti Palace, Galleria
Palatina, Florence, Italy

Embodying intellectual
significance, this group
portrait shows Rubens with
three Humanists: his brother
Philip; the philosopher Justus
Lipsius; and Jan Woverius.

Rubens produced this in
memory of his beloved
brother just after Philip had
died. Symbols throughout
express the underlying
principles of Stoic philosophy,

including a bust of Seneca
(see opposite) and books,
while the four tulips show
that two of the men are
alive (the two tulips in
bloom) and two are dead.

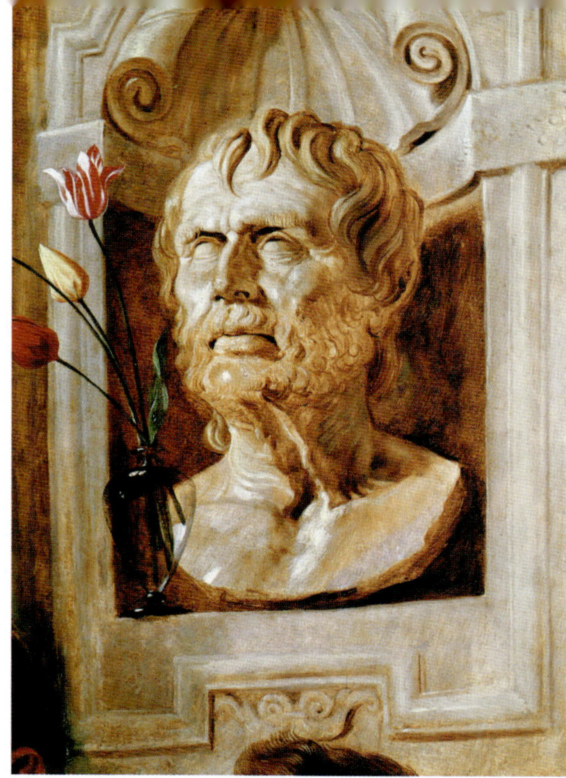

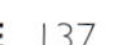

Detail from The Four Philosophers, 1611–12, oil on canvas, 164 x 139cm (64½ x 54¾ in), Pitti Palace, Galleria Palatina, Florence, Italy

In the group portrait on the page opposite, a bust of the ancient Roman philosopher Seneca is placed directly above Lipsius.

This represents the group's admiration for him and signifies their shared belief in Stoicism, a school of thought that stood for the control of human behaviour by reason rather than emotion. As well as a memorial of Rubens's brother, the painting was meant to provoke a discussion of humanistic thinking.

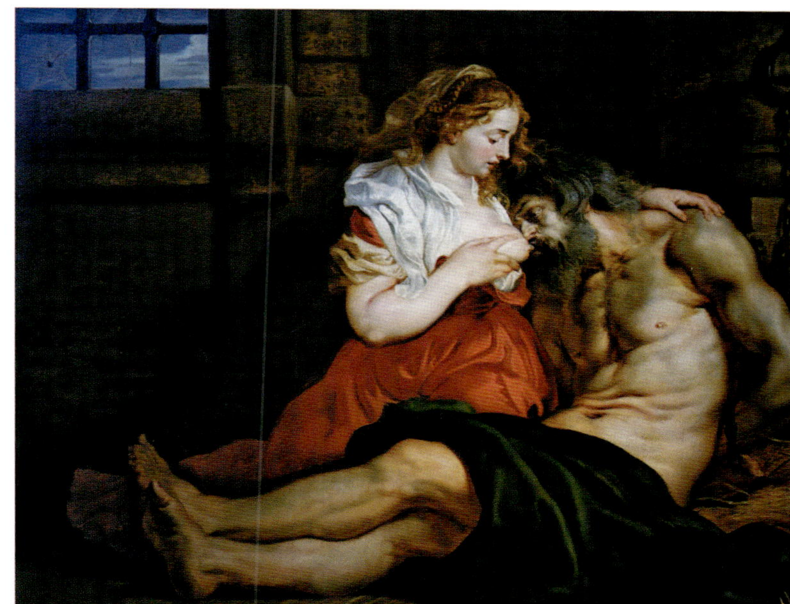

Roman Charity, 1611–13, oil on canvas, 140.5 x 180.3cm (55⅓ x 71in), The State Hermitage Museum, St Petersburg, Russia

This depicts the story of Cimon, who has been incarcerated and sentenced to death by starvation. His daughter secretly breastfeeds him to keep him alive, but she is discovered by a jailer. Despite this, her act of selflessness impresses officials and wins her father's release. In the 17th and 18th centuries, many European artists depicted the scene, and Rubens painted several versions, but the incestuous connotations became distasteful to later generations.

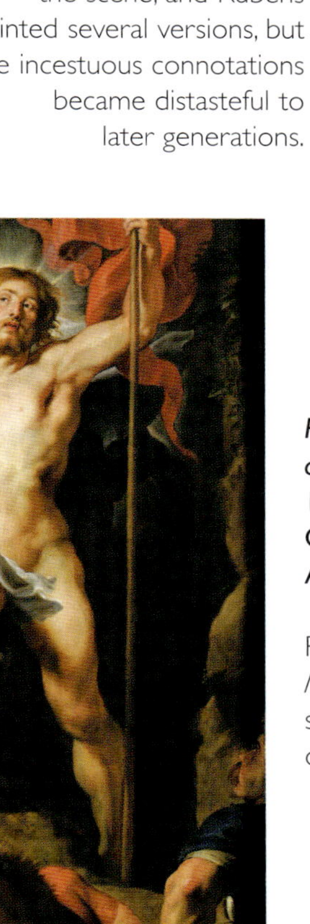

Resurrection of Christ, c.1611–12, oil on panel, 138 x 98cm (54⅓ x 38½in), Onze Lieve Vrouwekerk, Antwerp, Belgium

Rubens painted this, the *Moretus* triptych, at around the same time as the centre panel of *Descent from the Cross* (see page 134). Jan Moretus's widow Martina Plantin placed the commission. Christ strides powerfully from his open, rocky tomb, radiating a supernatural glow, as astonished guards look on. Both Martina and Jan's patron saints are present on the outer panels, that is, John the Baptist and Saint Martina.

Assumption, 1611–14,
oil on panel, 458 × 297cm
(180⅓ × 117in),
Kunsthistorisches
Museum, Vienna, Austria

A subject frequently
depicted by Rubens, the
Assumption of the Virgin
comes from *The Golden
Legend,* written by
Archbishop Jacobus de
Voragine (*c.*1230–98) in
1260, also in the biblical
apocrypha. They state that
the apostles gathered at
Mary's empty tomb and saw
her Assumption to Heaven.
Symbolizing her purity,
the Virgin is in white, but she
is surrounded by heavenly
blue. Every figure in the
painting is depicted in
different poses, gestures
and emotions.

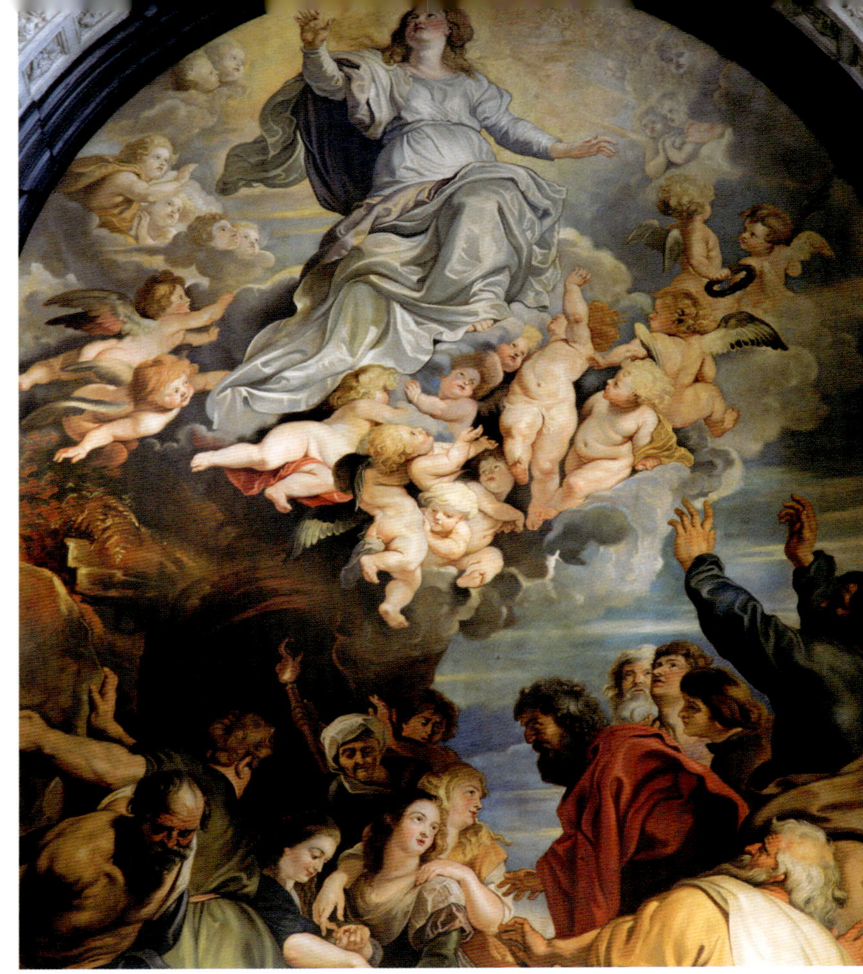

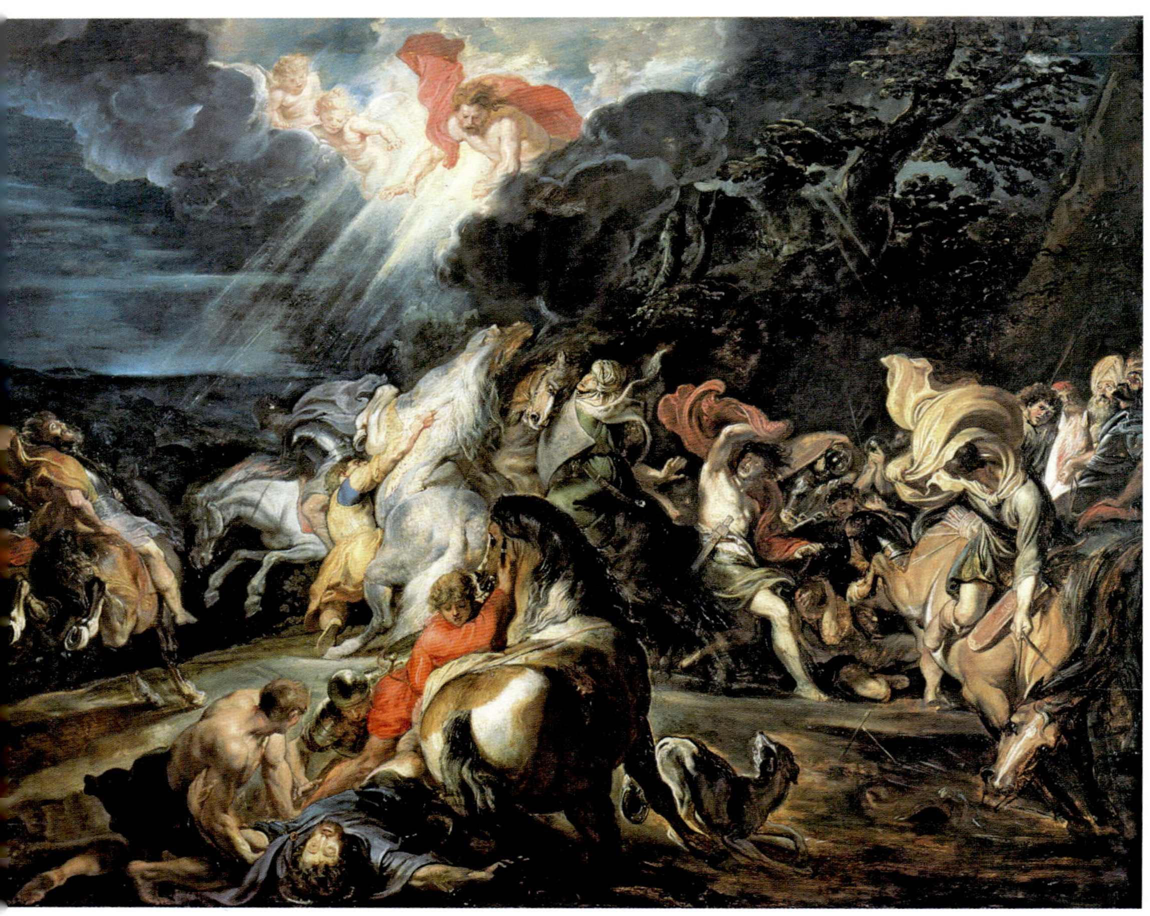

*Conversion of St Paul, c.*1611,
oil on panel, 95.2 × 120.7cm
(37½ × 47½in), The
Courtauld Gallery,
London, UK

Rubens painted this subject
several times. This is an oil
sketch, and is noticeably
different from the finished
painting he later produced.
Characteristically, he has
captured a moment of the
most dramatic potential.
The scene is full of swirling
activity, when Paul, stunned
by the supernatural light and
sudden appearance of Christ
in the sky, falls from his horse
to the ground, while his
frightened companions
struggle to restrain their
alarmed horses.

Modello for the Ghent altarpiece, 1611–12, oil on oak, 106.7 x 82.1cm (42 x 32⅓in), National Gallery, London, UK

This is an oil sketch for Rubens's altarpiece for St Bavo in Ghent. Saint Bavo was a knight before his conversion to Christianity, and this shows him being received as a monk into the church by Saints Floribert and Amandus. On the right, the kings Clothar and Dagobert argue with a herald about a decree that forbade knights to become monks, while on the left are Bavo's sisters – Saints Gertrude and Begga.

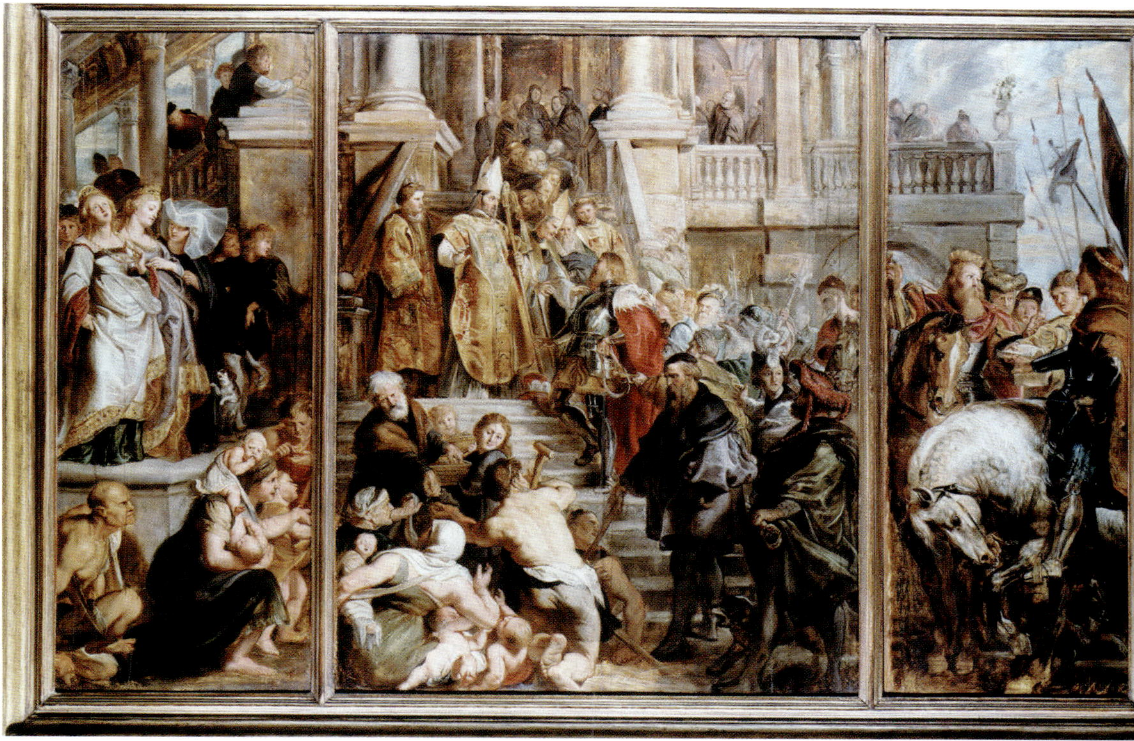

Ansegisus and Bega, 1612–15, oil on oak, 94 x 76cm (37 x 30in), Kunsthistorisches Museum, Vienna, Austria

This painting was commissioned by Duke Albert and the Infanta Isabella. Ansegisus was the son of the bishop Arnulf of Metz, and married to Bega, a princess and the daughter of the Carolingian prince Pepin the Elder. After her husband's death in 661, Bega founded and became Abbess of the convent of Ardenne. Rubens has represented them in close-up as a portrait of a wealthy, contemporary Flemish couple.

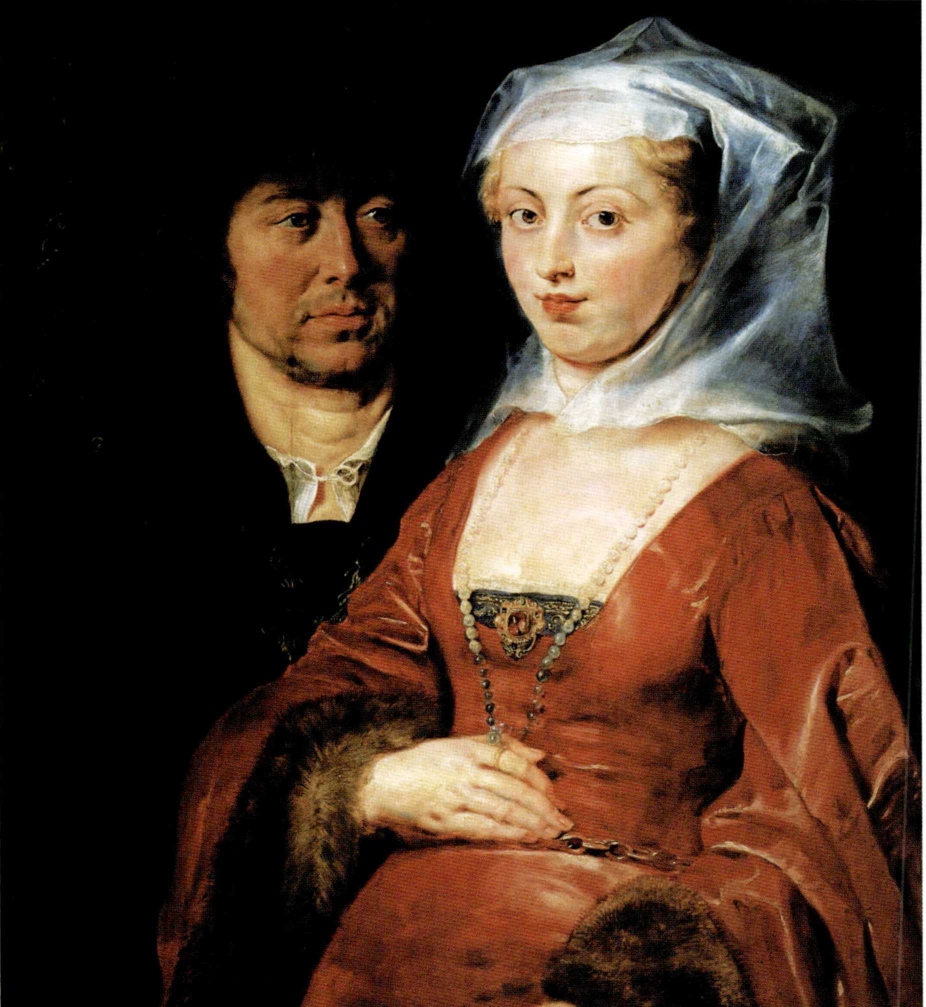

Romulus and Remus,
1615–16, oil on canvas,
210 x 212cm (82⅔ x
83½in), Palazzo dei
Conservatori Pinacoteca
Capitolina, Rome, Italy

Twins Romulus and Remus
were the legendary founders
of Rome. Their mother, a
Vestal Virgin, explained her
pregnancy by claiming she
had been violated by Mars,
the god of war, but she
was imprisoned and her
sons were ordered to be
drowned in the River Tiber.
Instead, they were found and
reared by a she-wolf and a
woodpecker. The wolf and
infants can be seen, while
Faustulus, the herdsman
who discovered them, is
approaching. On the left are
Tiberius, the god of the River
Tiber, and Fortuna, the
goddess of good fortune.

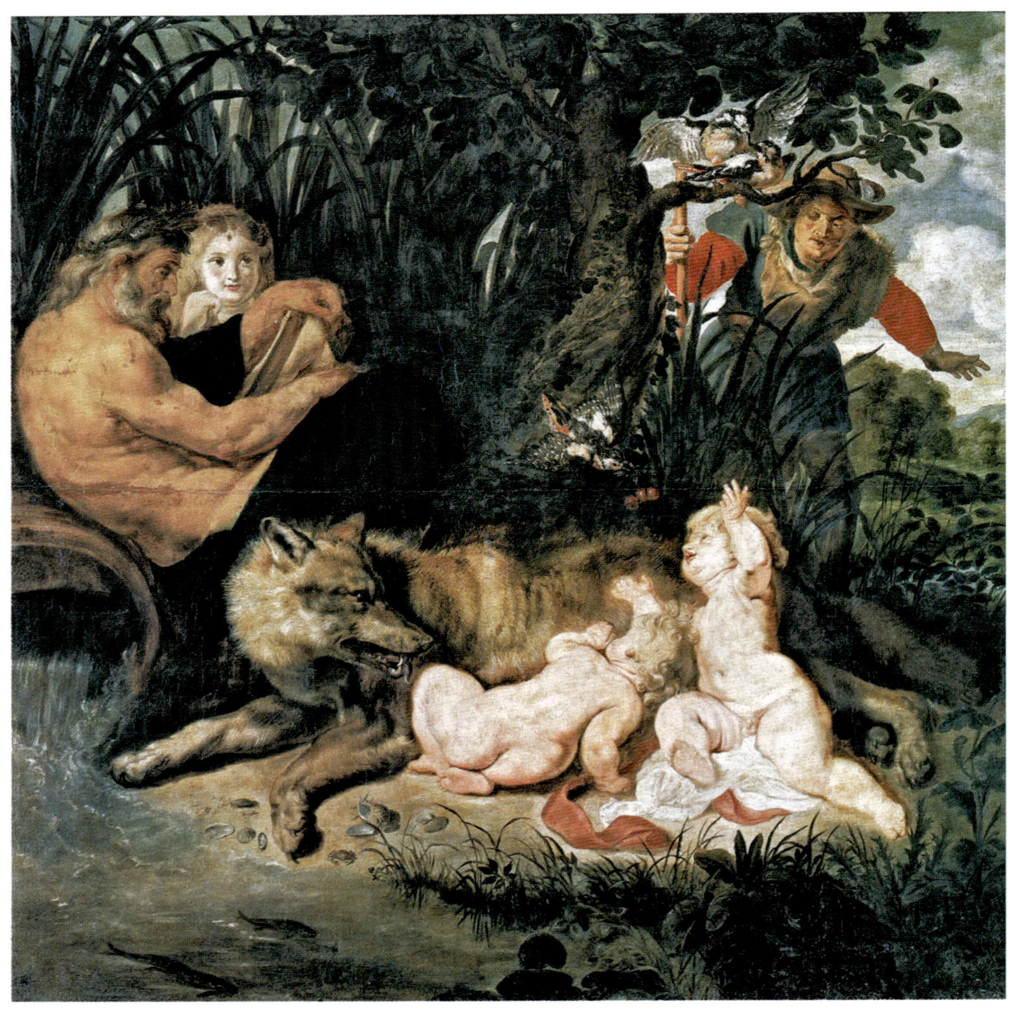

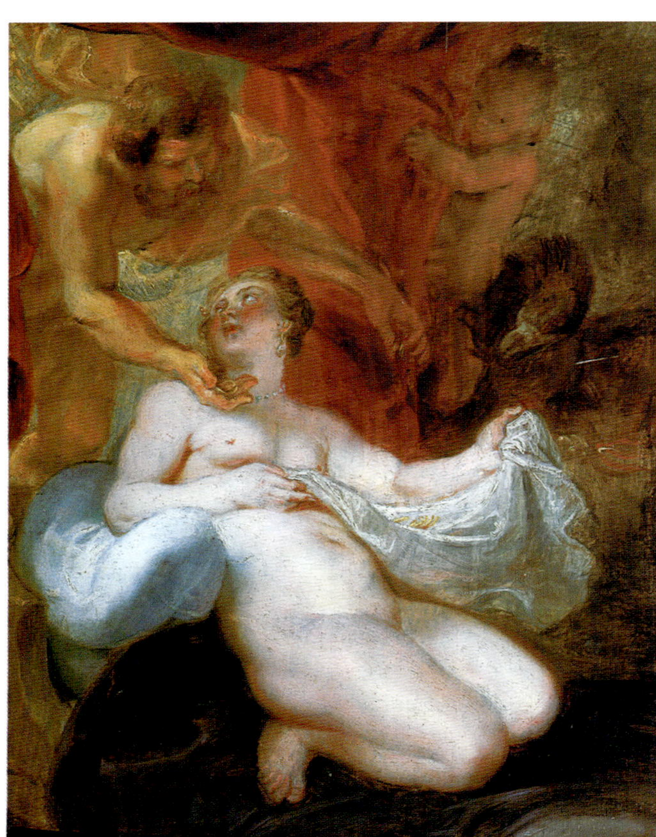

Jupiter and Danaë,
date unknown, oil on
wood, 27.8 x 21cm
(11 x 8¼in), Private
Collection

Expressing the Greco-
Roman myth of the beautiful
princess Danaë who is
seduced by the king of the
gods, Jupiter, Rubens paints
swathes of fabric to enhance
the softness of the figures'
naked, voluptuous flesh.
As always, Rubens's female
has paler skin than her
male counterpart, and this
alabaster-coloured skin is
tinged with the rosy-pink
hues that he loved.

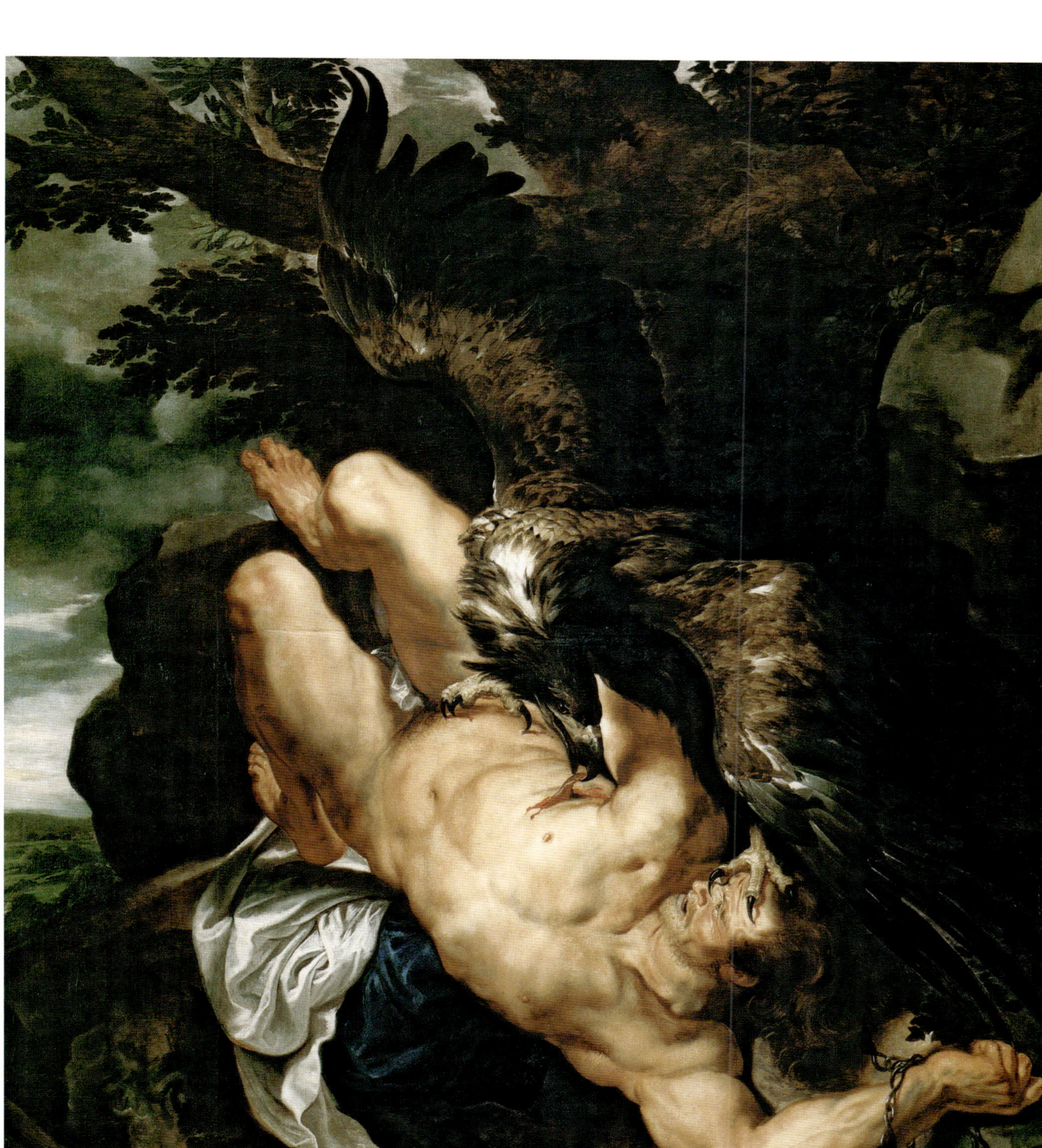

Prometheus Bound, started c.1611–12, completed by 1618, oil on canvas, 242.6 x 209.5cm (95½ x 82½in), Philadelphia Museum of Art, Pennsylvania, USA

Rubens kept this painting in his personal collection and listed it as 'A Prometheus bound on Mount Caucasus with an eagle which pecks his liver. Original by my hand, the eagle done by Snyders.' The broad, muscular figure of Prometheus follows Michelangelo, while the asymmetrical composition was inspired by a 1548–49 painting by Titian of the giant Tityus. The myth of Prometheus inspired many moral, religious and philosophical interpretations. Punished for stealing fire from heaven by Zeus, he was fastened to Mount Caucasus where an eagle pecked at his liver until Hercules set him free.

The Death of Hippolytus,
c.1611–13, oil on copper,
49.5 x 70.2cm (19½ x
27⅔in), Fitzwilliam Museum,
Cambridge, UK

The sea monster that
Hippolytus, the son of the
Greek hero Theseus, has
been sent to destroy rises
up out of the waves, toppling
his chariot and terrifying
the horses. The fearsome
monster makes the horses
rear, their flowing manes
reflected in the crashing
waves, and creates a
frenzied and horrific scene.
The copper surface gives
clarity to small details,
enhancing the colours.

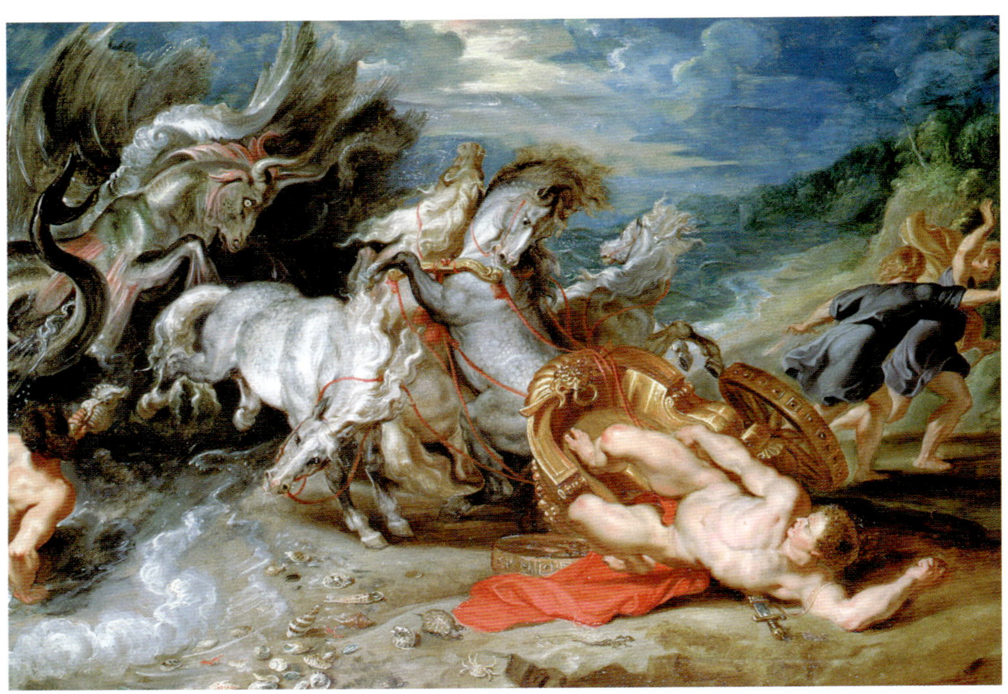

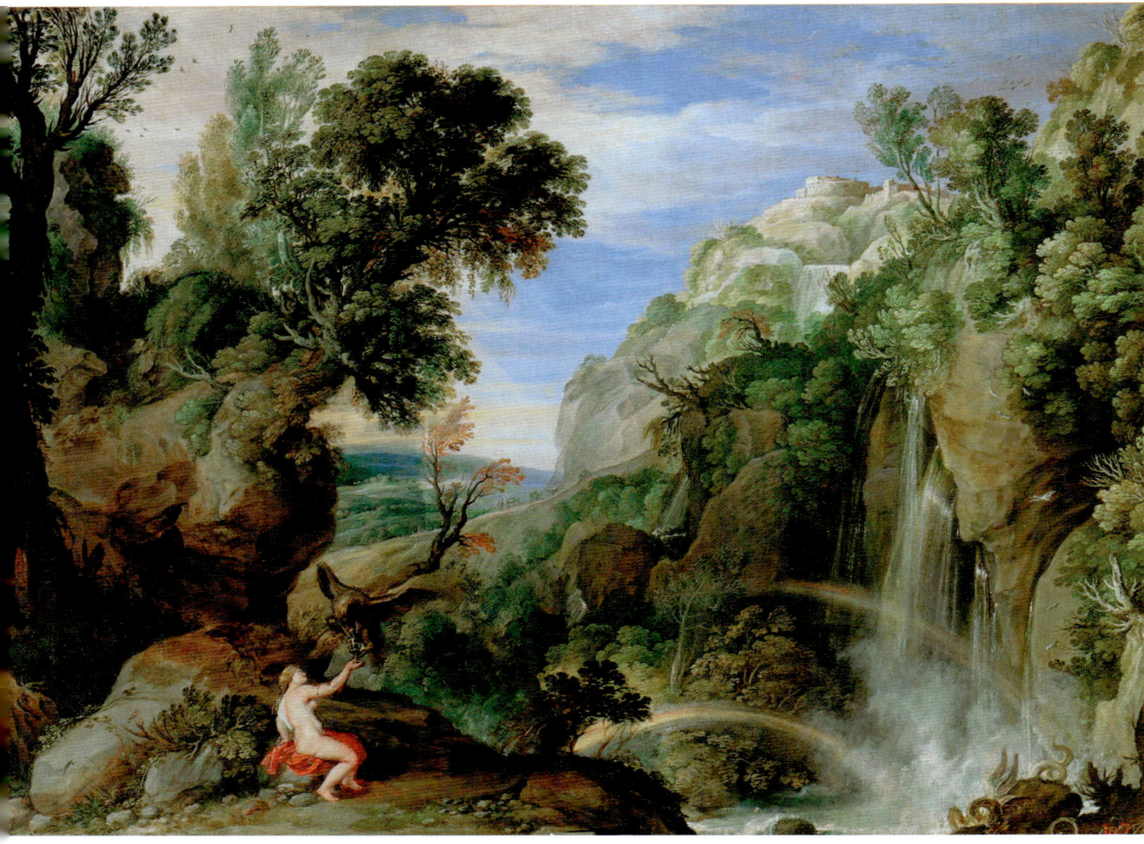

*Landscape with Psyche and
Jupiter,* 1611, oil on canvas,
95 x 129cm (37⅓ x 50¾in),
Museo Nacional del Prado,
Madrid, Spain

Through jealousy of the
mortal Psyche's beauty that
was admired by too many,
Venus, the goddess of love
and beauty, has set her
impossible tasks. Jupiter helps
Psyche by transforming
himself into an eagle and
collecting water from
the River Styx. Painted in
collaboration with Paul Bril
(1554–1626), Rubens added
the expressive figures to
Bril's luminous landscape
setting. Although Flemish,
Bril spent most of his career
painting landscapes in Rome.

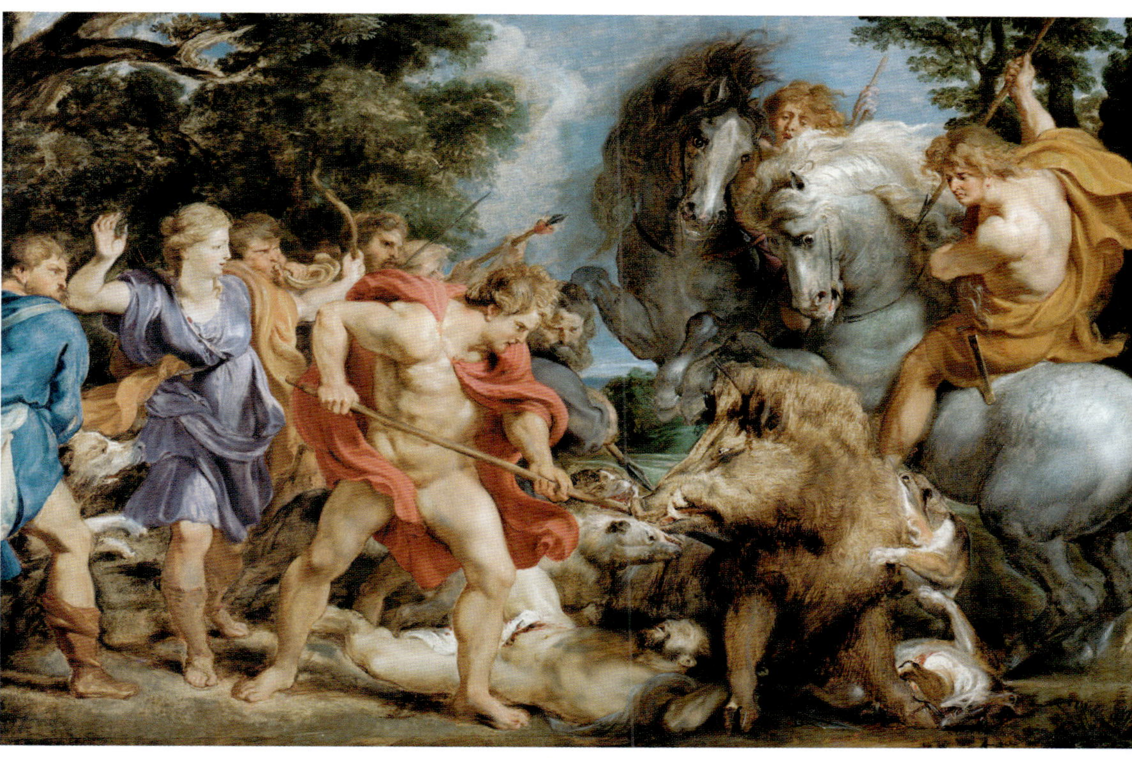

Calydonian Boar Hunt,
1611–12, oil on panel,
59.2 x 89.7cm
(23¼ x 35¼ in),
J. Paul Getty Museum,
Los Angeles, USA

The story of the Calydonian
boar hunt was told in Ovid's
Metamorphoses. When King
Oeneus of Calydon failed to
honour the goddess Diana,
she released a terrifying
boar on his land. The king's
son Meleager took a
group of huntsmen to kill
the beast, and after several
were killed or maimed,
Meleager defeated it and
presented its head as
a trophy to his beloved,
the huntress Atalanta.

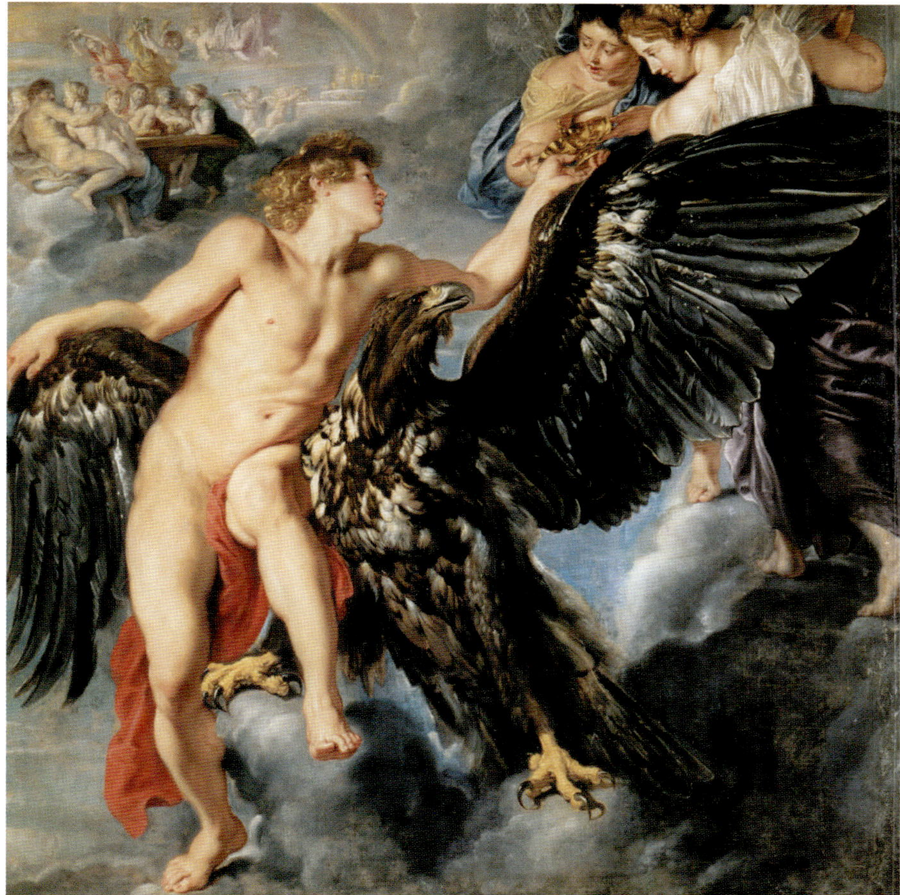

Abduction of Ganymede,
1611, oil on canvas,
203 x 203cm (80 x 80in),
Schwarzenberg Palace,
Vienna, Austria

Ganymede was an
outstandingly beautiful son of
a legendary king of Troy, and
Jupiter fell in love with him.
According to Ovid, Jupiter
transformed himself into an
eagle, and carried Ganymede
to Olympus where he made
him his cup-bearer. Using
powerful chiaroscuro and
a predominantly primary-
coloured palette, Rubens
creates an emotive image
of a beautiful young man
being carried on the eagle's
wing, with gods feasting
on a cloud behind him.

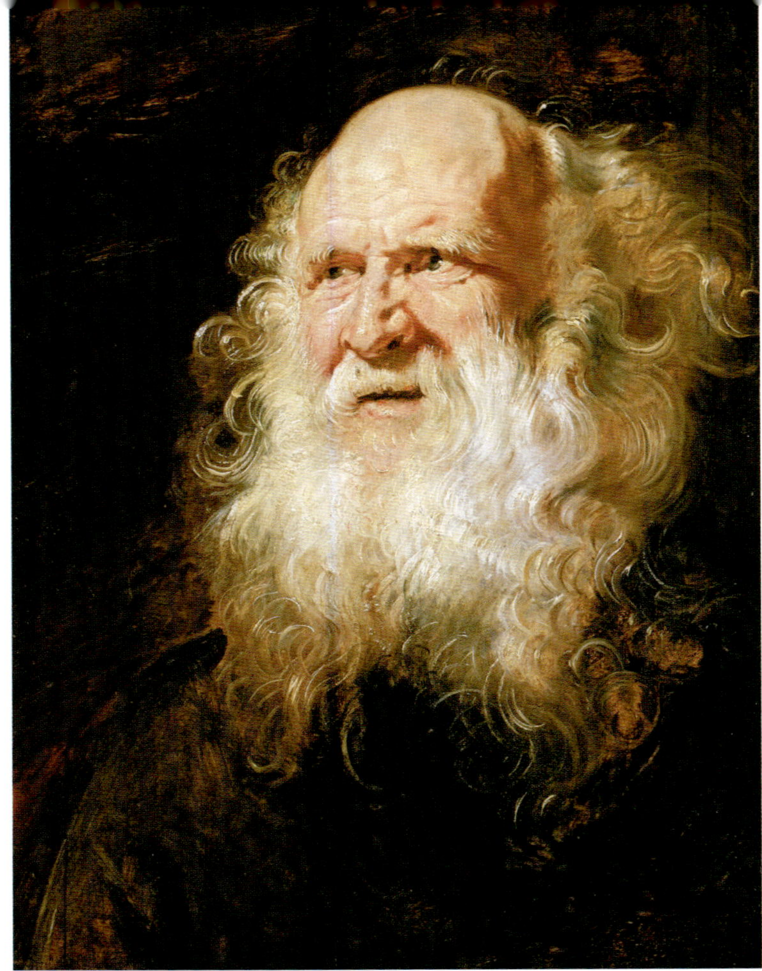

Study of the Head of an Old Man, c.1612, oil on oak, 67.3 x 50.2cm (26½ x 19¾in), The Dayton Art Institute, Ohio, USA

With confident handling of paint, Rubens evokes the craggy look and feel of the old man's furrowed face. Through sensitive use of light and dark, and soft and hard gradations, he creates depth in the eyes, while fine, loose strands of hair are delineated with the tip of a brush. This attention to detail and accuracy was essential when he transferred this face to large, finished paintings.

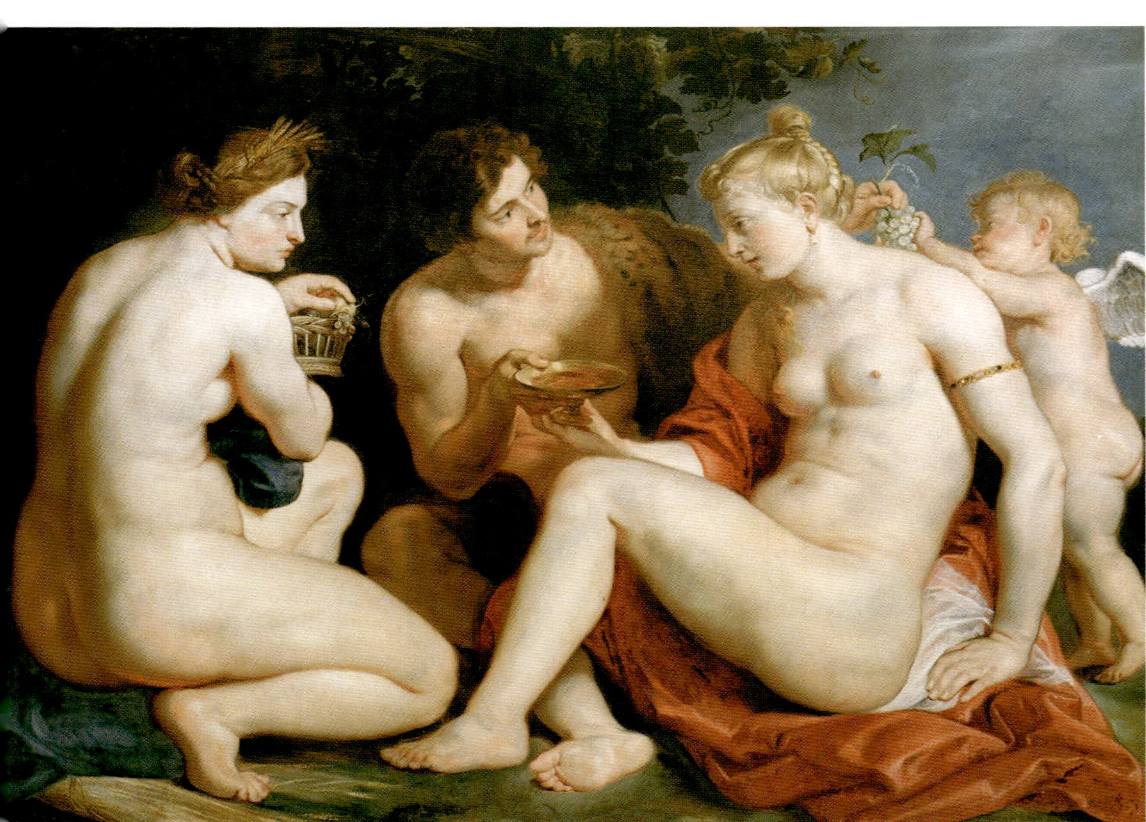

Venus, Cupid, Bacchus and Ceres, 1613, oil on canvas, 141 x 200cm (55½ x 78¾in), Staatliche Museen, Kassel, Germany

Venus and her son Cupid are being offered food and wine by Ceres, the goddess of the fruits of the field, and Bacchus, the god of wine. This suggests that love is impossible without food and drink. This is a cool, calm scene, often perceived as implying moderation in pleasure – which is unusual in Rubens's depictions. The poses of the figures are taken directly from ancient statuary, which for him signified perfection.

The Entombment, c.1612,
oil on canvas, 131.1 ×
130.2cm (51½ × 51¼ in),
J. Paul Getty Museum,
Los Angeles, USA

This emotive work
deliberately shocked, with
Christ's corpse draped
diagonally across the
composition. Christ's body
is being placed into his
tomb, assisted by John
the Evangelist in red.
Mary Magdalene is in the
background; Mary, the mother
of James the Younger and
Joseph, is bowing her head in
sorrow, and his mother is
looking to Heaven for
support. Blatantly shocking,
Christ's blue-white skin and
livid wounds announce his
sacrifice and suffering.

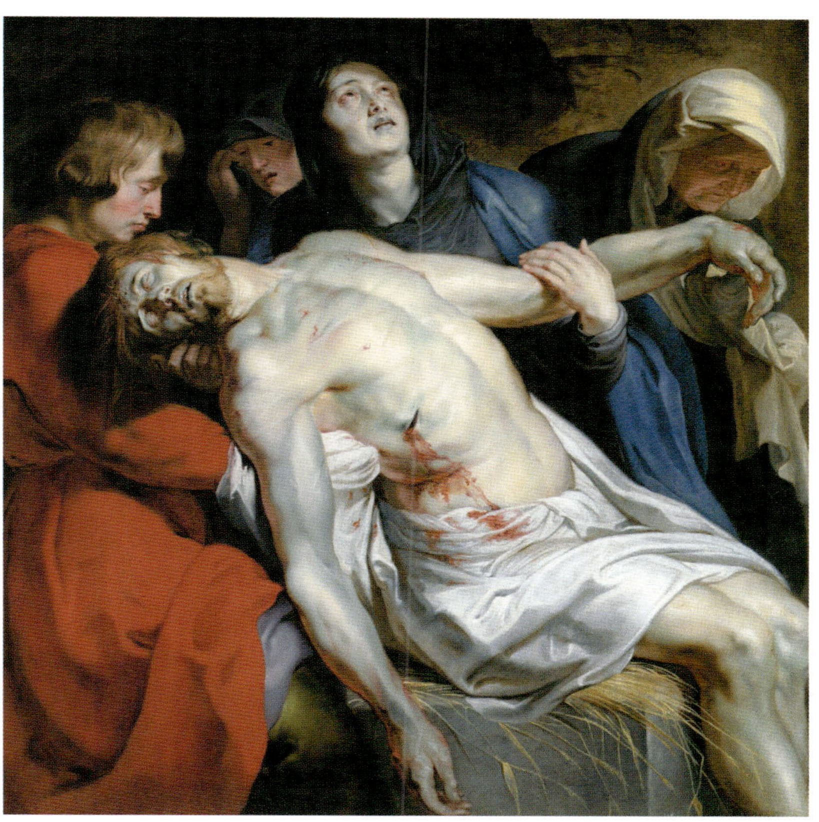

*The Family of Jan Brueghel
the Elder, c.1612–13,* oil on
panel, 125 × 95.2cm (49¼ ×
37½ in), The Courtauld
Gallery, London, UK

Here, Rubens depicts his
good friend Brueghel with
his second wife Catharina
van Mariënburg and their
eldest surviving children,
Elisabeth and Pieter. The
picture is one of intimacy
and informality, shown by
intertwined hands and
relaxed, affectionate
expressions and gestures,
while their rich clothing and
jewellery suggest elegance,
wealth and respectability.
It is probable that this
work was a gift from
Rubens to Brueghel.

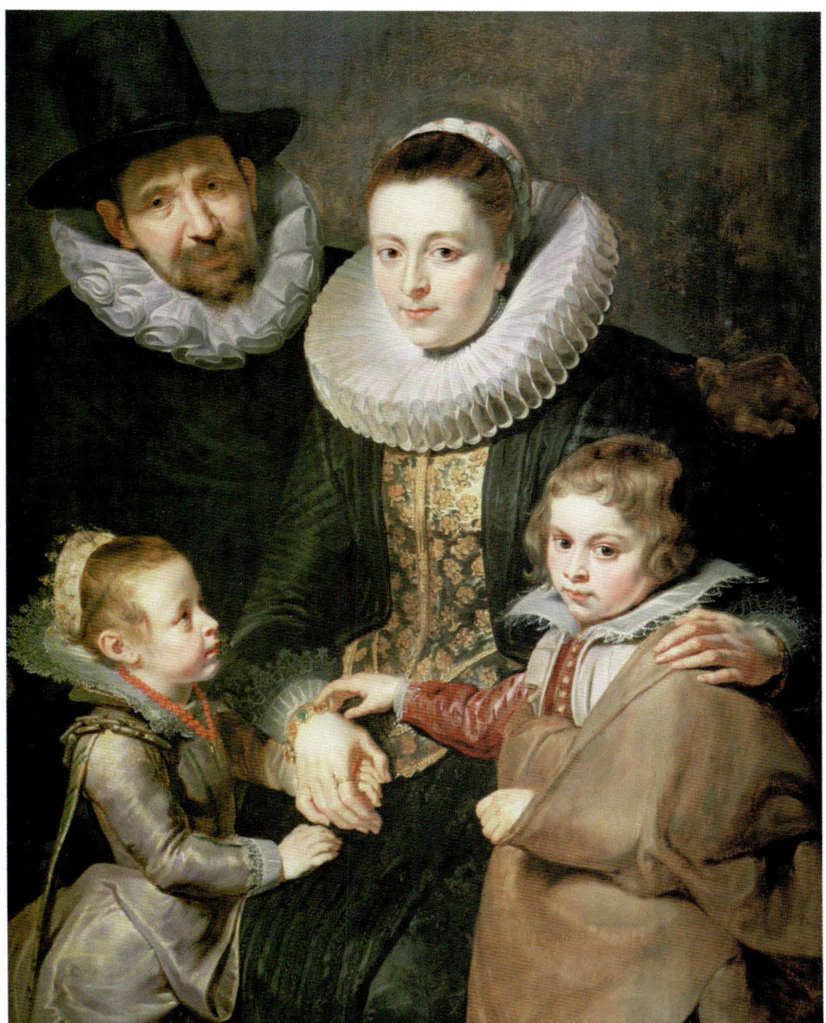

Jupiter and Callisto, 1613,
oil on canvas, 202 x 305cm
(79½ x 120in), Staatliche
Museen, Kassel, Germany

Taken from Ovid's
Metamorphoses, Diana's nymphs
were expected to be as chaste as
the goddess herself, but one of
them, Callisto, was seduced by
Jupiter. In order to reach Callisto,
Jupiter disguised himself as Diana.
Callisto's subsequent pregnancy
was eventually noticed by Diana,
who punished her by changing
her into a a bear and setting dogs
on her. Once again, Jupiter came
to her, and snatched her up to
heaven before she was hurt.

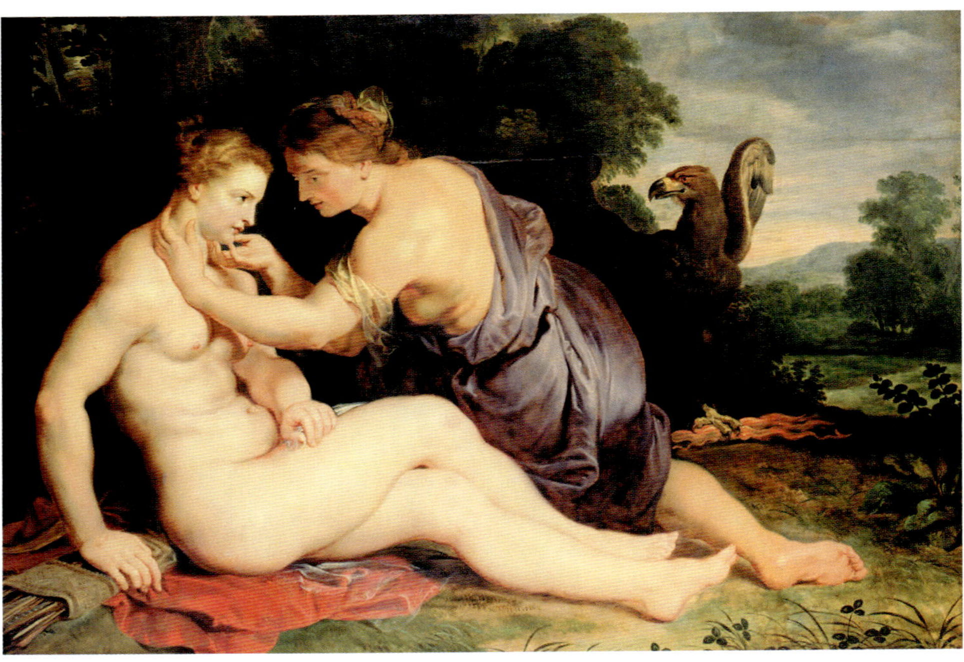

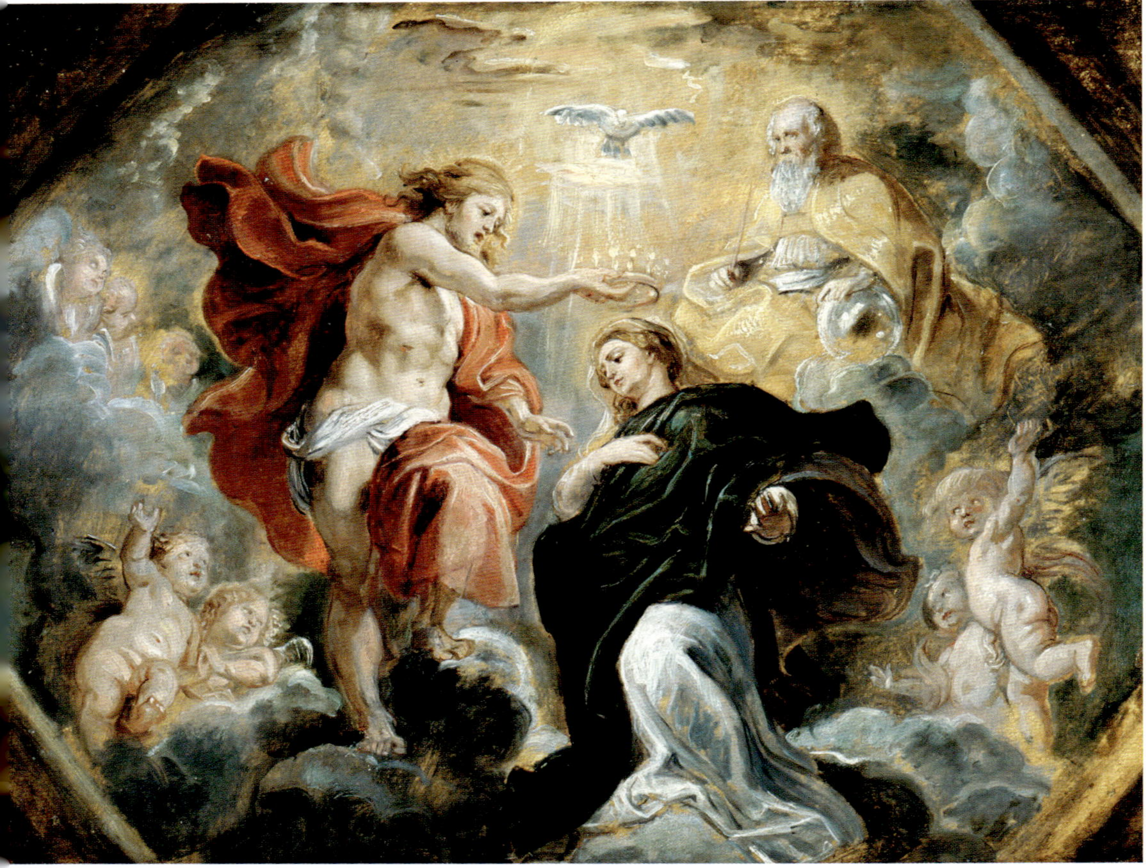

*The Coronation of the
Virgin, c.*1613, oil on panel,
46.2 x 61.7cm (18 x 24¼ in),
The Courtauld Gallery,
London, UK

The Virgin Mary has arrived
in Heaven and is being
crowned as Queen of
Heaven by the Holy Trinity.
Predominantly painted in the
three primary colours of red,
blue and yellow, this is also
strongly foreshortened,
as it was a modello for a
ceiling painting in Antwerp
Cathedral. When Rubens
won the commission, it
caused a rift between him
and his former teacher
Van Veen, who was initially
commissioned for the work.

Death of Adonis, c.1614, oil on panel, 212 x 325cm (83½ x 128in), The Israel Museum, Jerusalem, Israel

The goddess Venus bends over the lifeless body of her human lover Adonis, who has been fatally wounded by a boar while out hunting. Based on a famous antique statue, this work began as a commission, possibly ordered by a relative of Rubens's first wife. Creating a fluid and sensual composition, this expresses Rubens's perception of ideal beauty, love and sorrow.

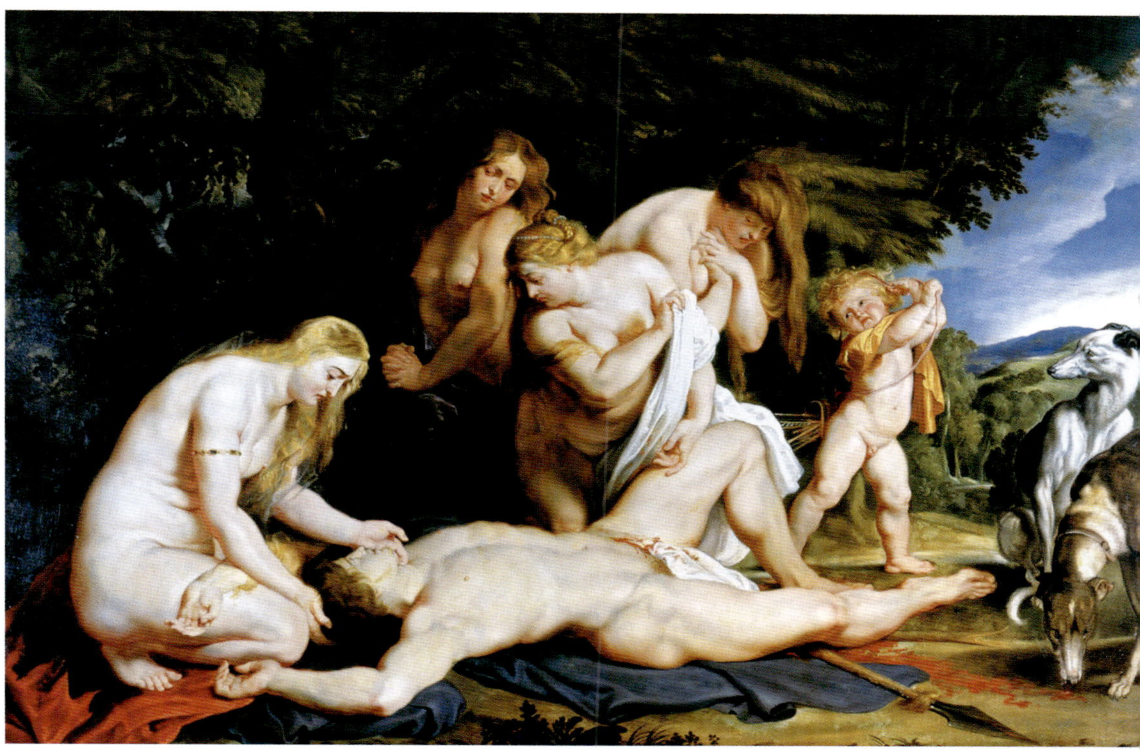

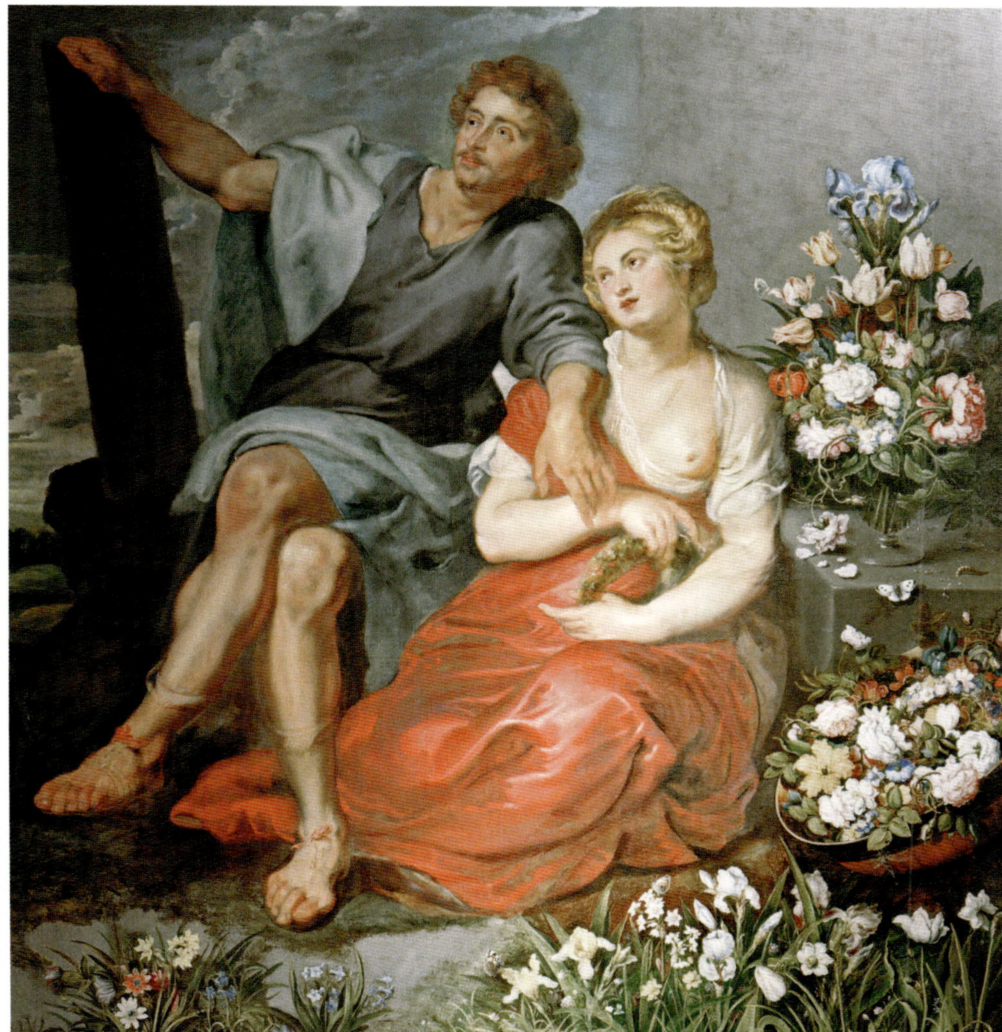

Pausias and Glycera, 1612–15, Rubens and Osias Beert the Elder (*c.*1580–1624), oil on canvas, 203.2 x 194.3cm (80 x 76½in), The John and Mabel Ringling Museum of Art, Florida, USA

A nearly life-sized young couple sit before a deep blue, cloud-dappled sky, surrounded by tulips, irises, narcissi, violets, roses and cyclamen. Rubens executed the figures in broad, fluent, confident strokes, while Osias Beert the Elder (*c.*1580–1624) painted the flowers in exacting botanical detail. Pausias and Glycera is an ancient Roman love story. Glycera made floral garlands and Pausias, a master of an illusionistic painting technique, painted them with precision.

Commander Being Dressed for Battle, 1612–14, oil on panel, 122.6 × 98.2cm (48¼ × 38⅜in), Private Collection

This was painted at the time Rubens was enjoying great success after the unveiling of his great triptychs, *The Raising of the Cross* (see page 51) and *Descent from the Cross* (see pages 53 and 134–5). Although unnamed, the curly-haired, bearded man can be identified as a commander in battle by his long baton and powerful demeanour. As a blonde-haired page secures his armour, the commander looks out of the canvas with a strong, bold, yet somewhat melancholy expression.

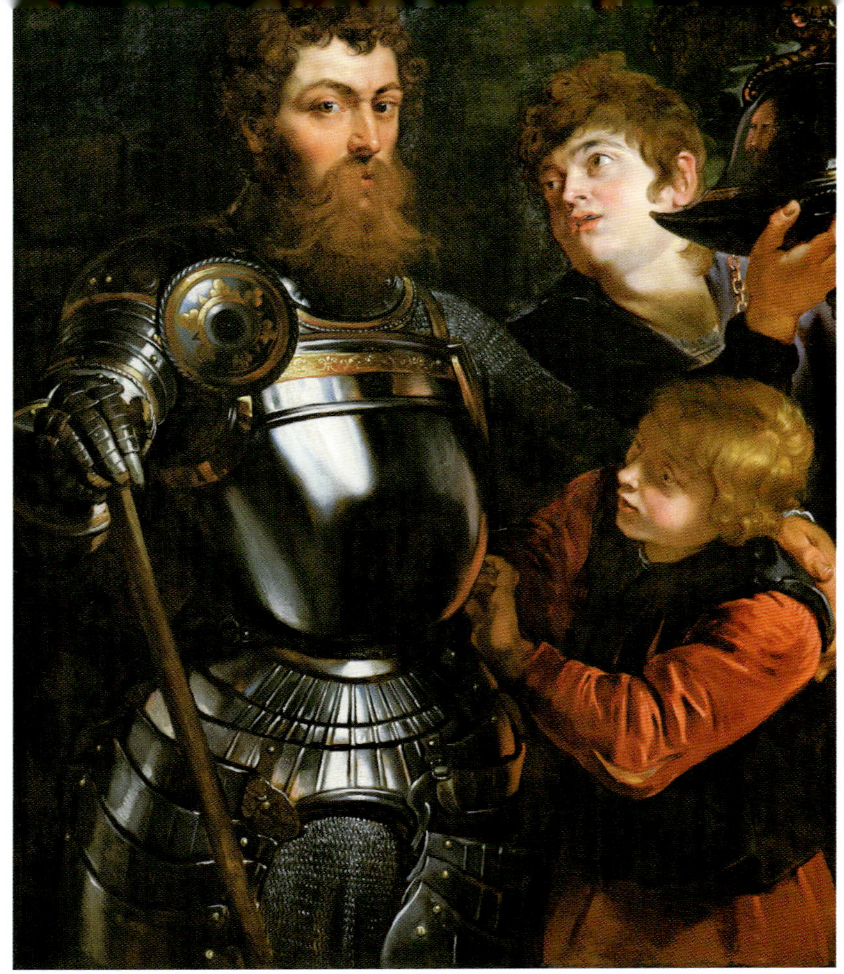

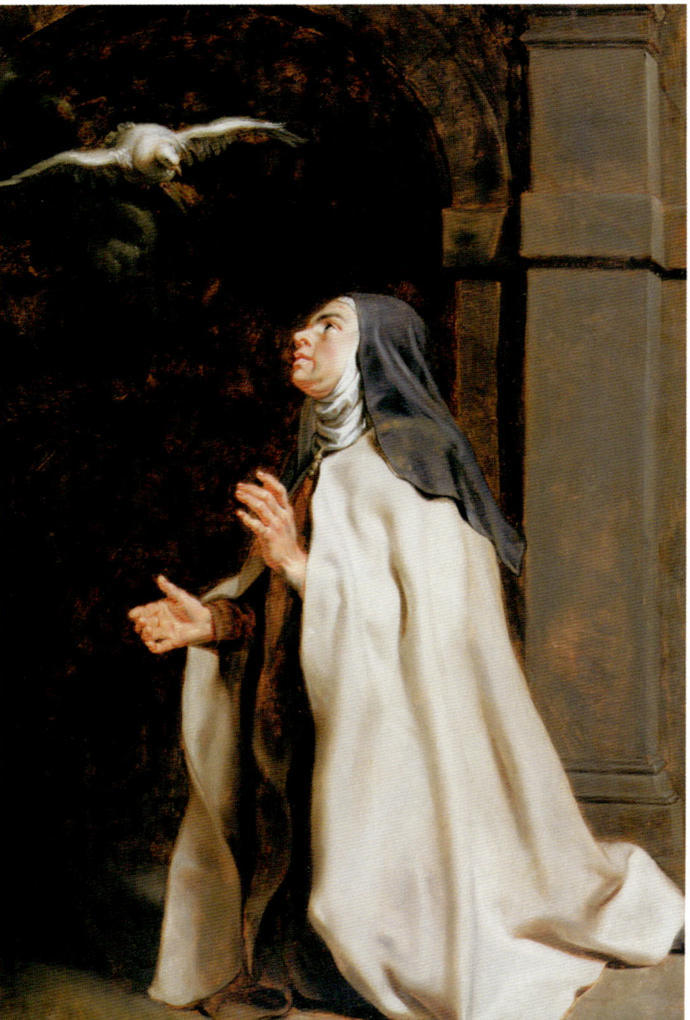

Teresa of Avila's Vision of a Dove, c.1614, oil on panel, 97 × 63cm (38¼ × 24⅞in), The Fitzwilliam Museum, Cambridge, UK

Beatified in the year this work was painted, Saint Teresa of Avila was a prominent Spanish mystic and Carmelite nun, extremely popular in her native country. She captured the imagination of several Counter-Reformation artists, mainly for her achievements for the Church and her vivid mystical visions. Rubens also painted a larger version of this for the chapel of Saint Teresa in the church of the Barefoot Carmelite nuns in Antwerp.

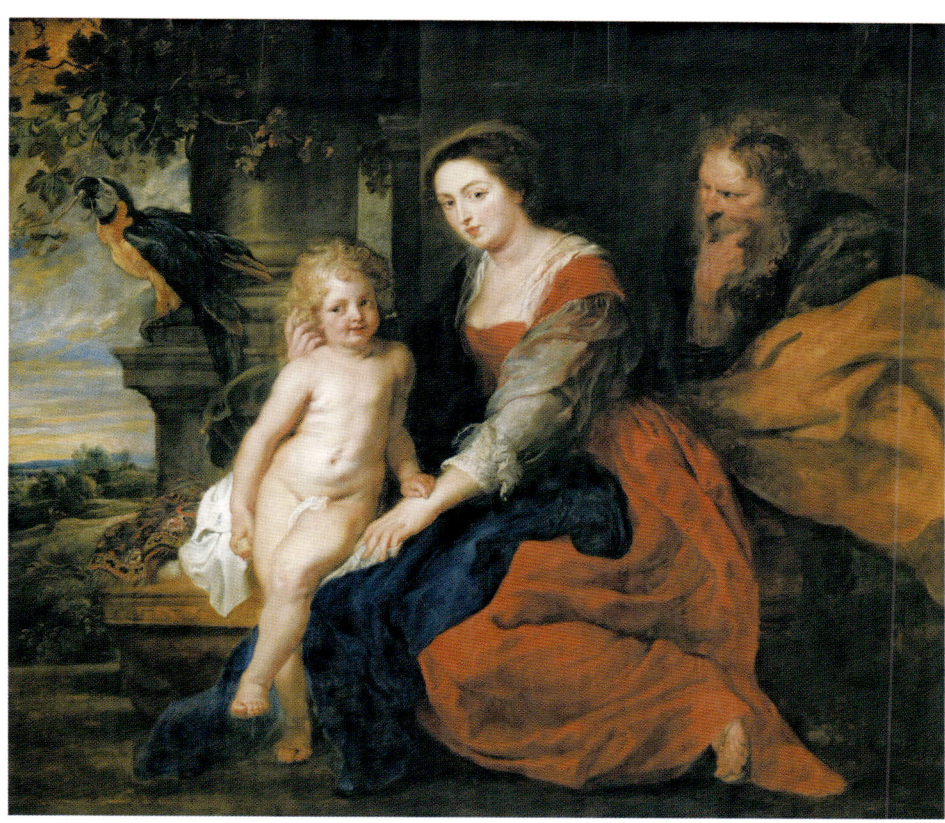

Holy Family with a Parrot,
1614, oil on panel,
167.7 x 191.4cm (66 x
75⅓in), Royal Museum of
Fine Arts, Antwerp, Belgium

In 1633, Rubens was
appointed dean of the Guild
of St Luke in Antwerp, and
he donated this work in
thanks. Joseph is a protective
presence, while Mary
and Jesus are the focal
characters. Mary wears
fashionable clothes, and she
and her son are in front of
a building where a colourful
parrot perches on a pillar.
Parrots frequently appear in
pictures of the Madonna and
Child, as they traditionally
symbolize the prophecy
of Mary's redemptive role.

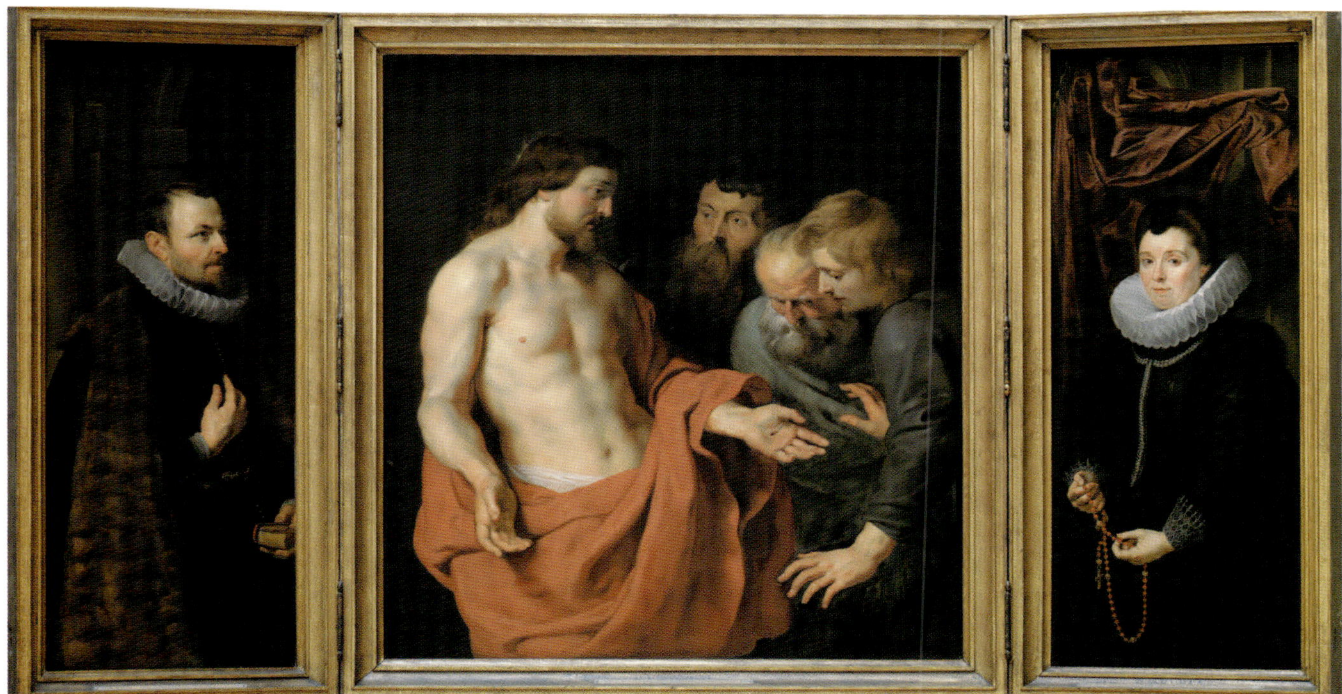

*Epitaph of Rockox and
his Wife Adriana Perez,*
1613–15, oil on panel,
146 x 233cm (57½ x
91¾in), Royal Museum of
Fine Arts, Antwerp, Belgium

This triptych was
commissioned by Nicolaas
Rockox. The centre panel
portrays Doubting Thomas,
the biblical story of the
apostle who, after the

Crucifixion, did not believe
that he was seeing the
resurrected Christ. Rockox
and his wife are depicted on
the outer panels, and their
coat of arms is on the back.

The work was painted for
the Rockox family memorial
chapel – the Chapel of the
Immaculate Conception in
the Minorite Church (now
destroyed) in Antwerp.

The Flight into Egypt, 1614,
oil on oak, 40.5 x 53cm
(16 x 21in), Gemäldegalerie Alte
Meister, Kassel, Germany

With dramatic use of
chiaroscuro, this image of Mary
and Joseph, fleeing with the infant
Jesus by moonlight and guided
by angels, both humanized and
romanticized the theme known
to most contemporary viewers
of the biblical story in which
the Holy Family learn that
King Herod intends to kill
all infants in their area.

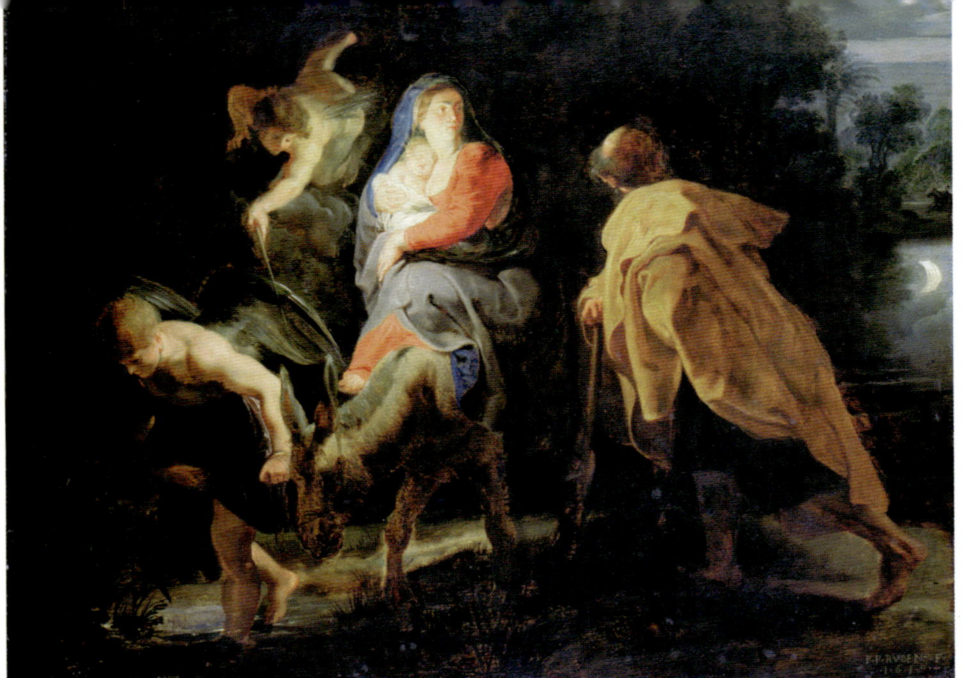

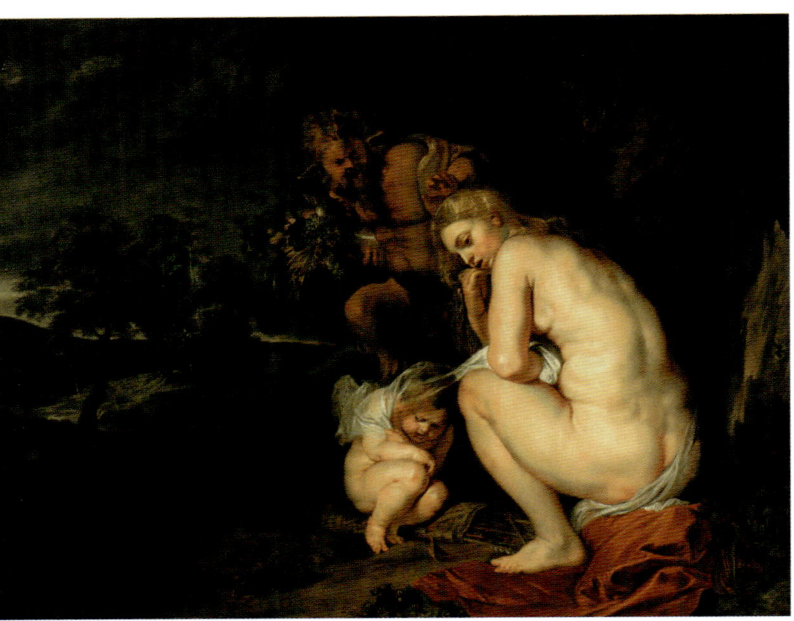

Venus Frigida, 1614, oil on
panel, 142 x 184cm (56 x
72½in), Royal Museum of
Fine Arts, Antwerp, Belgium

Venus is a Mediterranean
goddess, but Rubens has
depicted her in northern
Europe, shivering with cold.
The painting illustrates a
classical proverb that says:

'Without Bacchus and
Ceres, Venus freezes.'
In other words, 'There
is no love without bread
and wine.' Venus crouches
in the foreground, while
Cupid also tries desperately
to keep warm. This work
is one of the few paintings
that Rubens actually
signed and dated.

Descent from the Cross,
1614, oil on canvas, 338 x
194cm (133 x 76⅓in),
Musée des Beaux-Arts,
Valenciennes, France

One of several versions
of this subject painted by
Rubens, this work is a skilful
use of the space. Christ's

body is propped up by
those closest to him in life,
as they ease him down
from the cross. The
predominant palette of
red, white, green, blue,
flesh and brown combine
with the dynamic poses
to draw viewers' eyes
around the image.

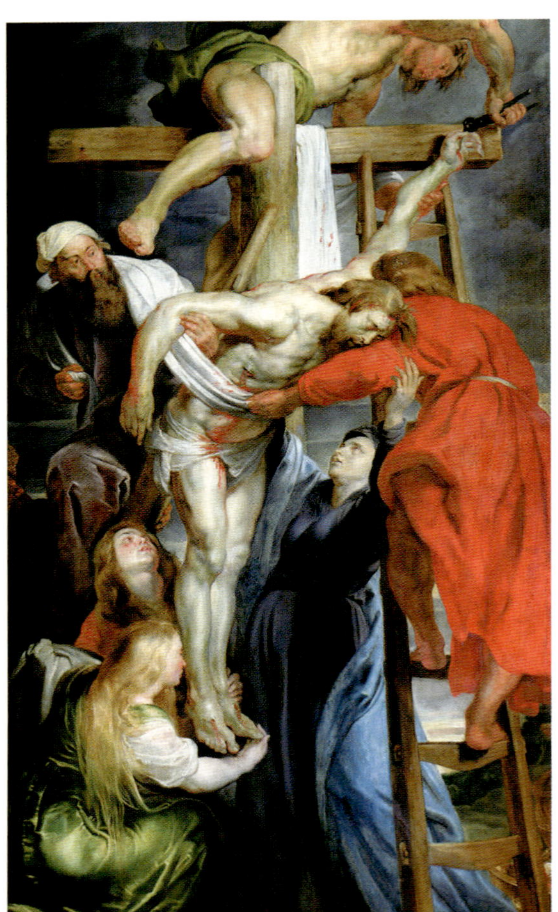

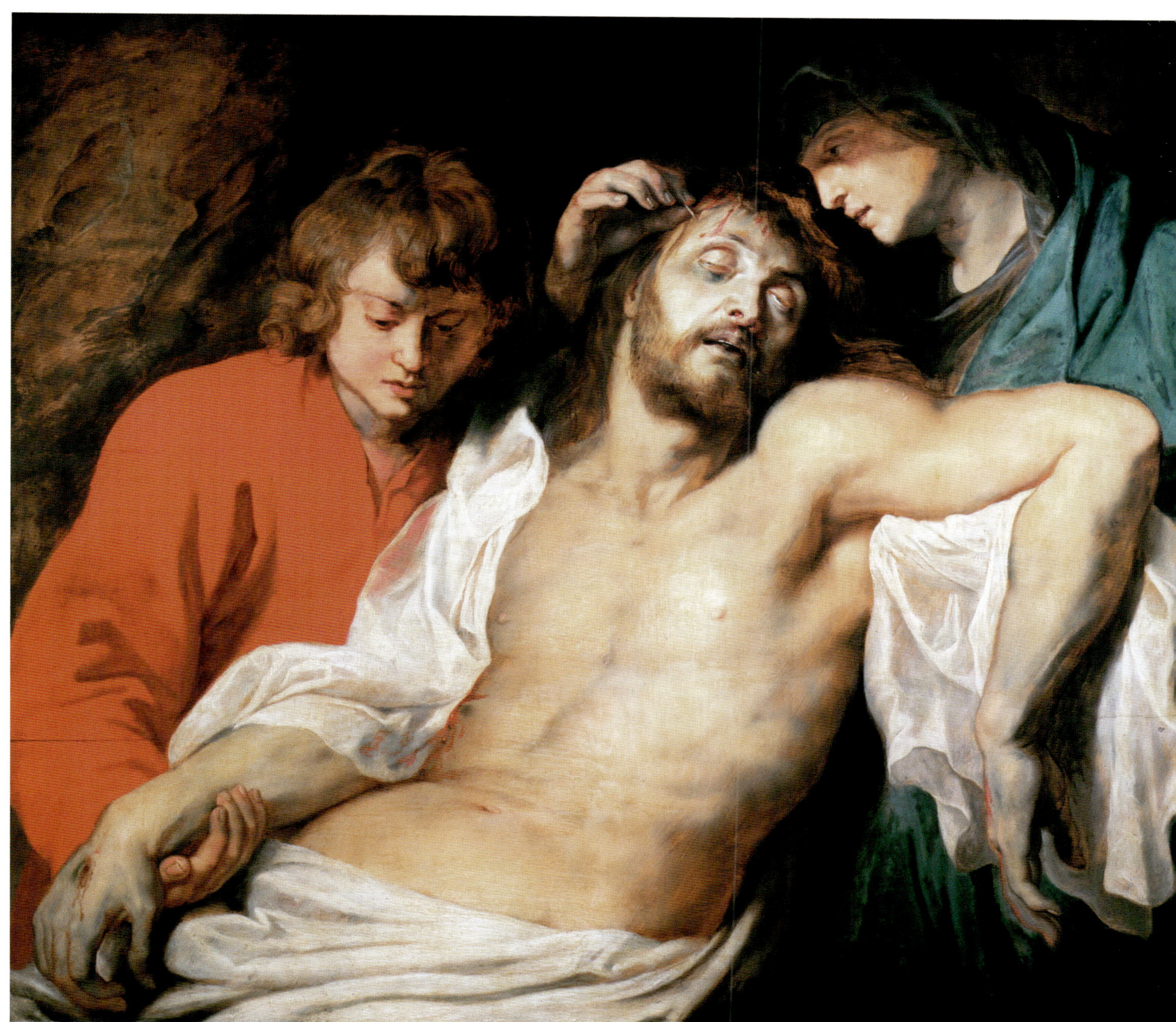

Lament of Christ by the Virgin and Saint John, 1614–15, oil on panel, 107.5 x 115cm (42⅓ x 45¼ in), Kunsthistorisches Museum, Vienna, Austria

The Lamentation had been a popular subject for Roman Catholic artists since the Renaissance, and consequently it was often depicted during the Counter-Reformation. As usual, Rubens has created an unexpected composition, bringing Christ's corpse into strong, immediate close-up, dramatically projecting from the picture plane, leaning against his mother. Looking down in sorrow, Saint John holds Christ's arm, while the Virgin tenderly cradles her dead son's head.

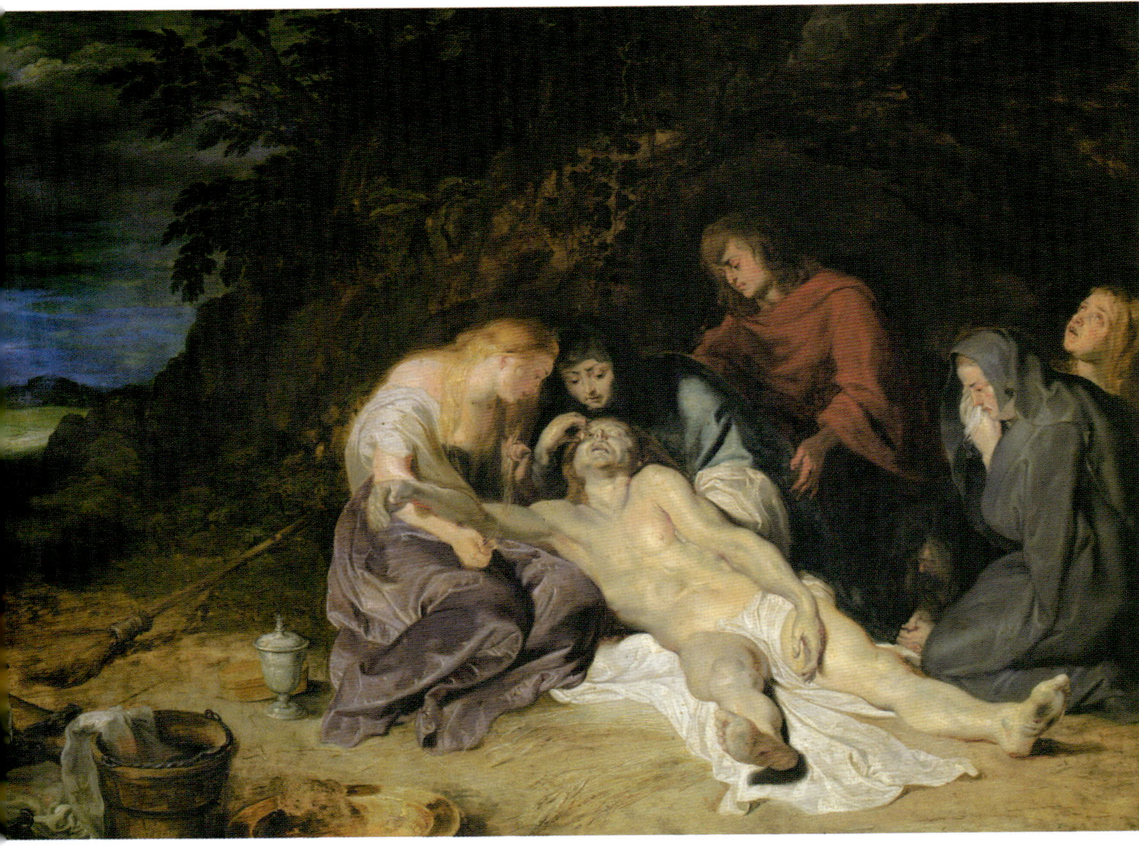

Lamentation over the Dead Christ with Saint John and the Holy Women, 1614, oil on panel, 55 x 73cm (21⅔ x 28⅞in), Royal Museum of Fine Arts, Antwerp, Belgium

In a scene of horror and desolation, Christ's body has been taken down from the cross and put on the ground by his close friends and his mother. The anguish of their bereavement is palpable; each person is so preoccupied with his or her own pain that no one comforts the Virgin Mary as she weeps silently before her son. The group is vividly illuminated against the dark background.

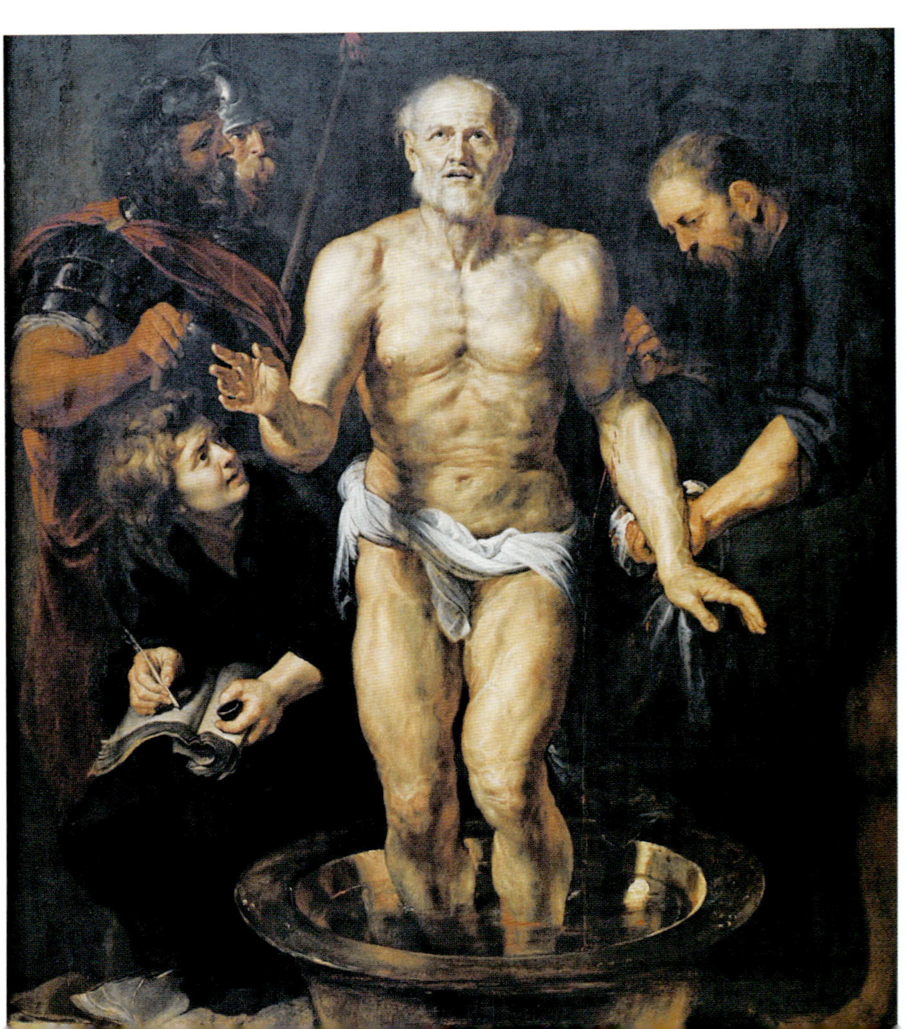

The Death of Seneca, 1614, oil on panel, 185 x 154.7cm (72¾ x 61in), Alte Pinakothek, Munich, Germany

The ancient philosopher Seneca (3BCE–65CE), having been accused of treason by his own student, the Emperor Nero, was forced to commit suicide. A doctor and friend have cut open Seneca's veins in warm water to speed the flow of blood. A scribe attempts to record the last words of the philosopher: 'Vir[tus]' (virtue), which implies Seneca's composure as he died.

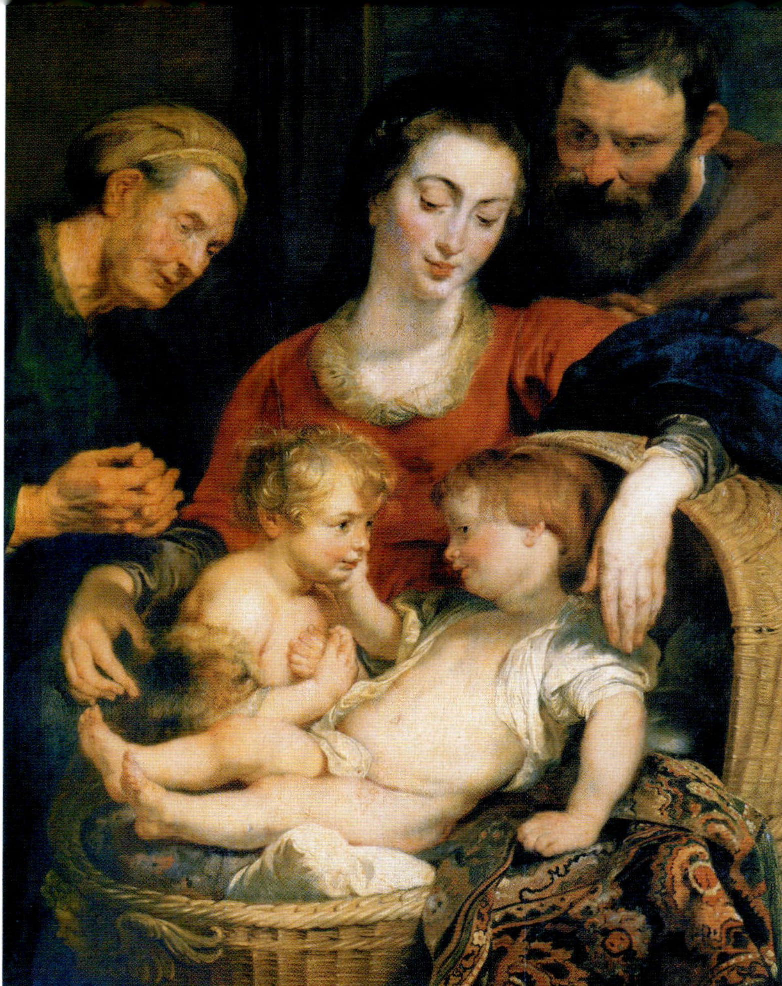

The Holy Family with Saints Elizabeth and John the Baptist, 1614–15, oil on panel, 114 x 80cm (45 x 31½in), Pitti Palace, Galleria Palatina, Florence, Italy

Rubens always treated images of the Holy Family as intimate domestic scenes, thus enabling viewers to identify with them. Unlike his idealistic mythological paintings, Rubens made these as real and provincial as he could under the guidelines of the Counter-Reformation. This warm and natural image portrays a mother showing her baby to his cousin, watched by doting adult relatives.

Two Sleeping Children, c.1612–13, oil on panel, 50.5 x 65.5cm (20 x 25¾in), The National Museum of Western Art, Tokyo, Japan

The two innocent sleeping children shown here are thought to be Clara and Philip, the children of Rubens's brother Philip. On his death, he left two children, born in 1610 and 1611. Rubens later used the faces of these two children in large-scale paintings in oils, respectively *Madonna with a Garland of Flowers* (see page 177) and *Madonna Adored by Angels* (see page 114). This fresh handling comes from Rubens sketching the subject from direct observation.

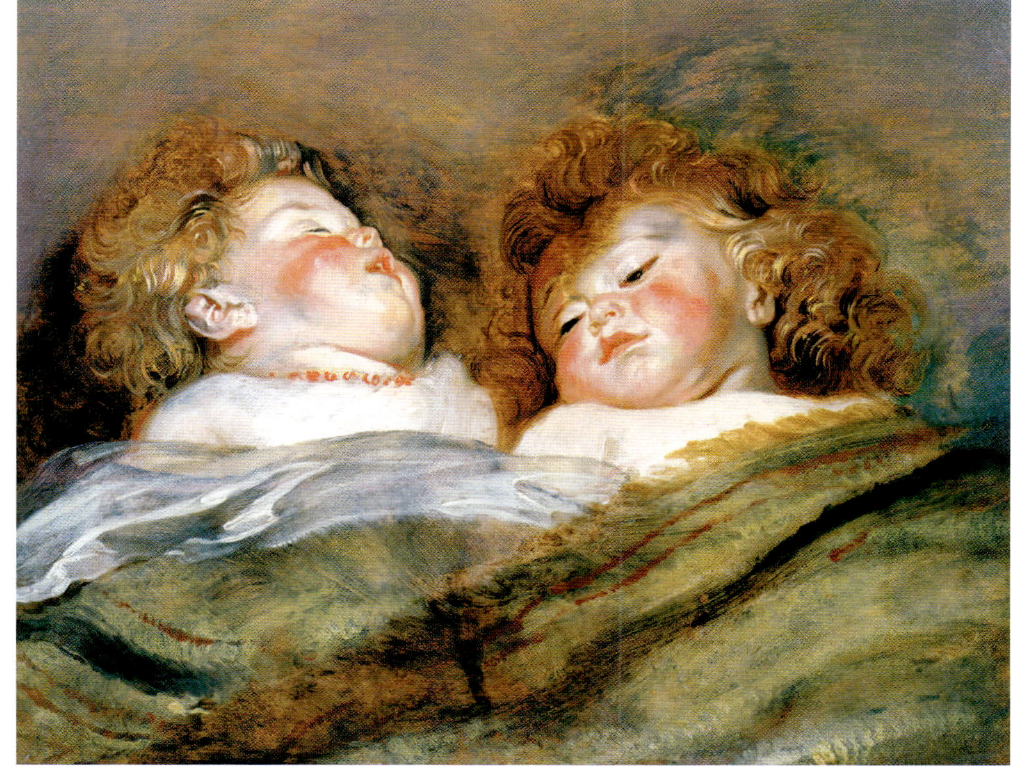

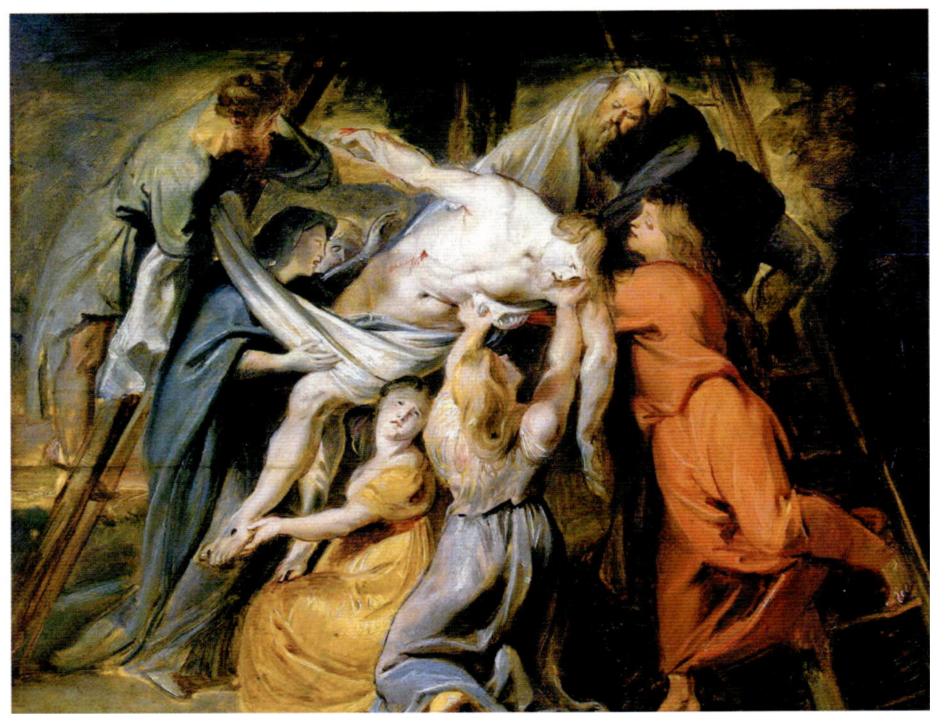

Descent from the Cross,
1612–14, oil on panel,
48.7 x 52cm (19 x 20½in),
Shuvalov House Museum,
Leningrad, Russia

Using vivid colours and
lively poses that suggest
continual movement,
Rubens demonstrates his
ability to portray several
people crowding into a
composition, all in different
dynamic positions, and all
occupied with their own
upsetting tasks. Their
bodies and limbs form
a network as they ease
Christ's body down from
the cross. Christ's limp
body echoes the cross he
has just been taken from.

*The Holy Family with Saints
Elizabeth and John the
Baptist,* 1614–15, oil on
oak, 136 x 100cm (53½ x
39⅓in), The Wallace
Collection, London, UK

Commissioned by the
Archduke Albert and hung
in his private oratory at the
Ducal Palace in Brussels, this
work earned Rubens 300
guilders in 1615. The subject
is taken from a 13th-century
text, *Meditations on the Life
of Christ.* Christ is with his
mother, Joseph, Mary's cousin
Elizabeth and her son, Saint
John the Baptist. Christ
wears a coral necklace,
which symbolizes the
blood he will later shed.

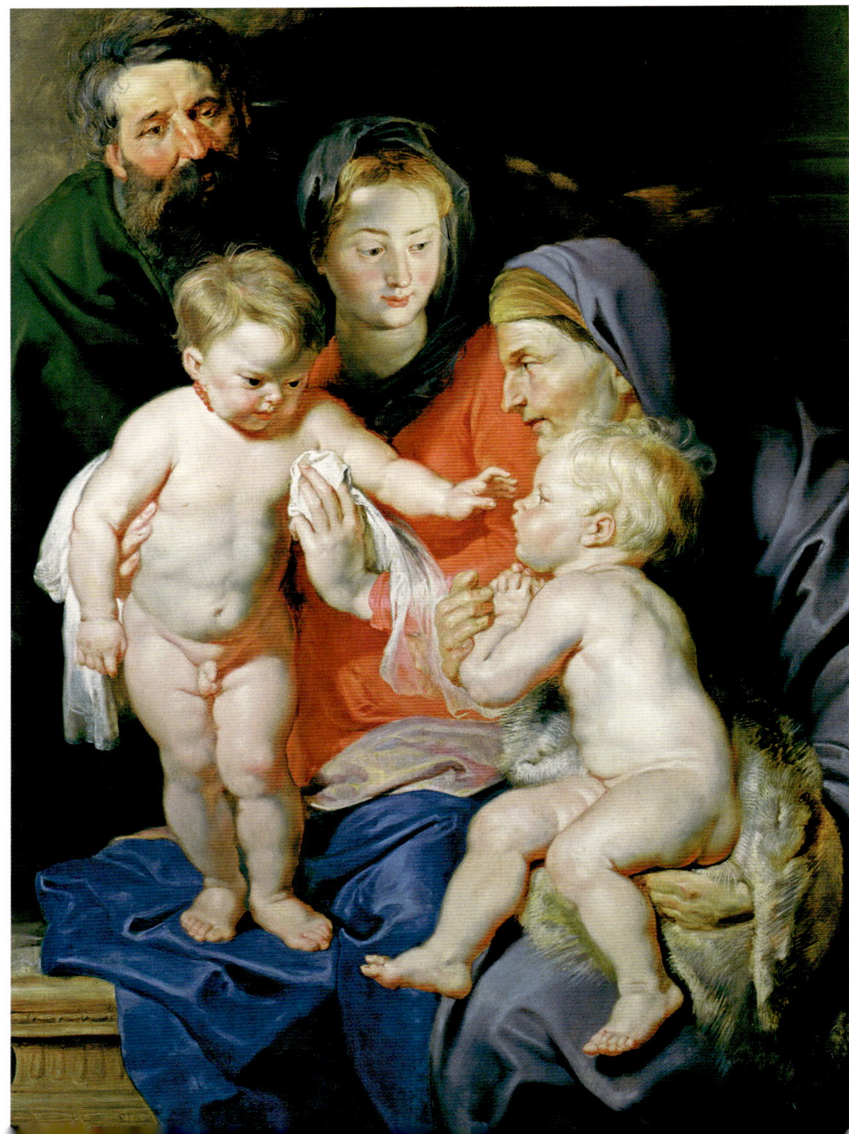

The Infant Christ with John the Baptist and Two Angels, 1615, Rubens and Snyders, oil on panel, 76.5 x 122.3cm (30 x 48in), Kunsthistorisches Museum, Vienna, Austria

Proving that his empathy with children was as astute as his understanding of adults, Rubens painted this group of babies and toddlers deliberately to evoke empathy and tenderness in viewers. They represent Jesus as an infant, his slightly older cousin John the Baptist, and two angels with fruit and a lamb. The expressions and gestures display the natural impudence of children of this young, carefree age.

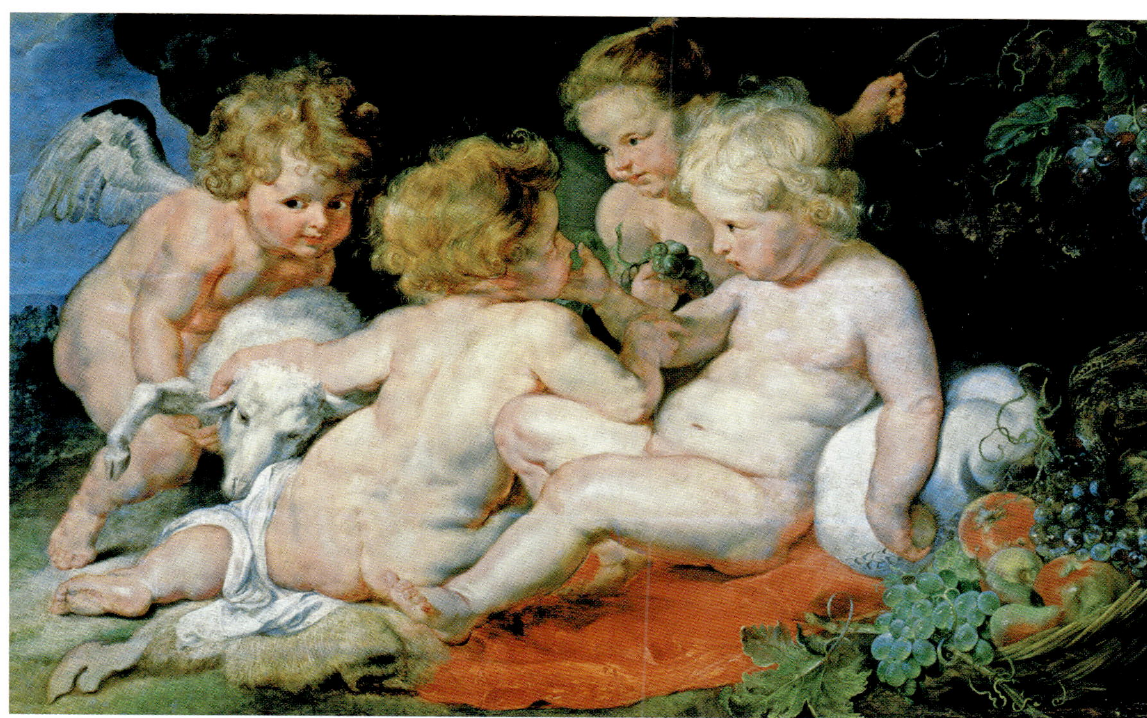

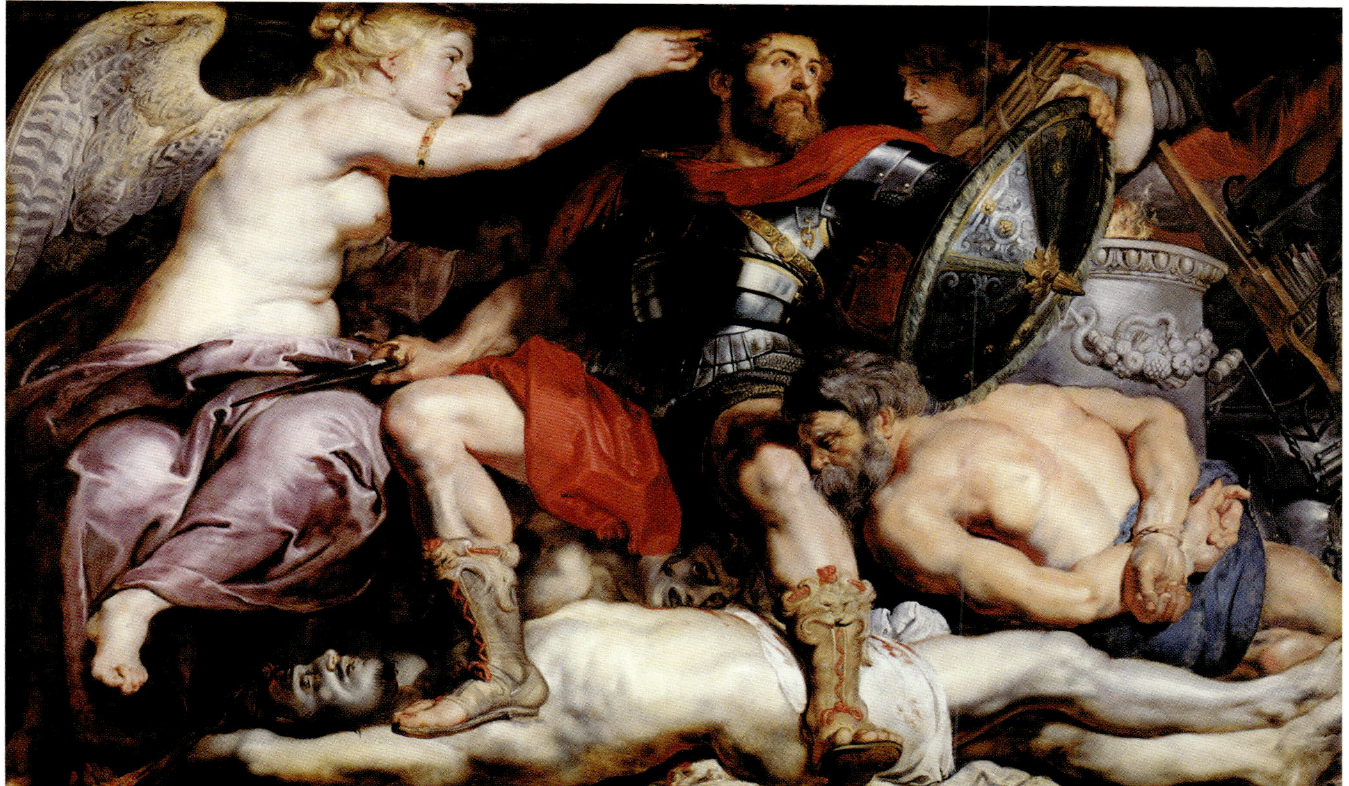

The Triumph of Victory, c.1614, oil on oak, 161 x 236cm (63⅓ x 93in), Staatliche Museen, Kassel, Germany

Rubens painted this moral and political allegory for the Guild of St George, the Antwerp archers' company, while the Eighty Years' War continued to rage. Here, Victory is a hero in antique armour, a bloody sword in his hand. He sits on the defeated figure of Rebellion, while the goddess of victory crowns him with a wreath of oak leaves. On the right, Barbarism lies with his hands tied, and above him, a guardian spirit carries a bundle of crossbow bolts, a symbol of harmony.

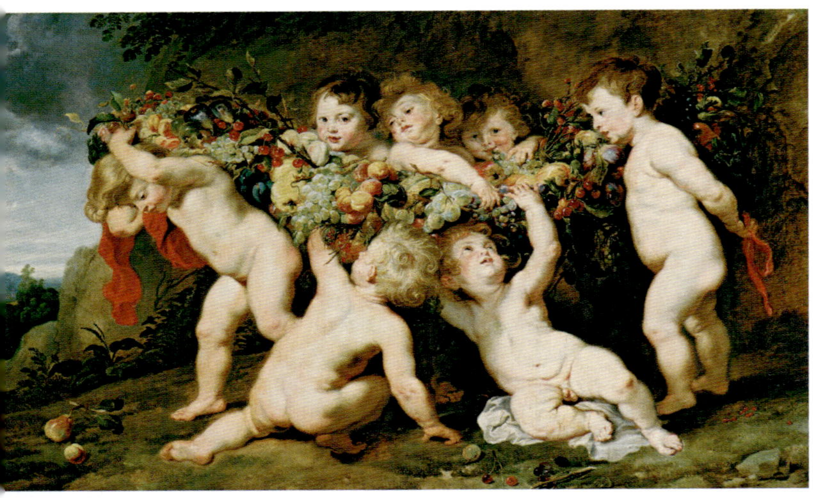

Garland of Fruit, c.1615–17, Rubens and Snyders, oil on canvas, 120 × 203.8cm (47¼ × 80¼ in), Alte Pinakothek, Munich, Germany

Against Snyders's landscape, Rubens captures a scene of six charming putti playing with a garland of fruit. Putti are chubby male infants that were used by artists to represent angels or mythological creatures. Often depicted to embody spirits of sacred love during the Baroque period in particular, putti were also used to infer God's presence. Like Raphael, Rubens was an expert at rendering engaging putti in many situations.

The Four Continents, 1615, oil on canvas, 208 × 283cm (81¾ × 111½ in), Kunsthistorisches Museum, Vienna, Austria

This represents the four continents of Asia, America, Europe and Africa. (Australia was only discovered nine years before this painting was executed and was as yet uncharted territory.) In the foreground, the river Nile has his arm around Africa. Behind them is Europe with the river god of the Danube. On the right is Asia, and at the back is America with the god of the Rio de la Plata.

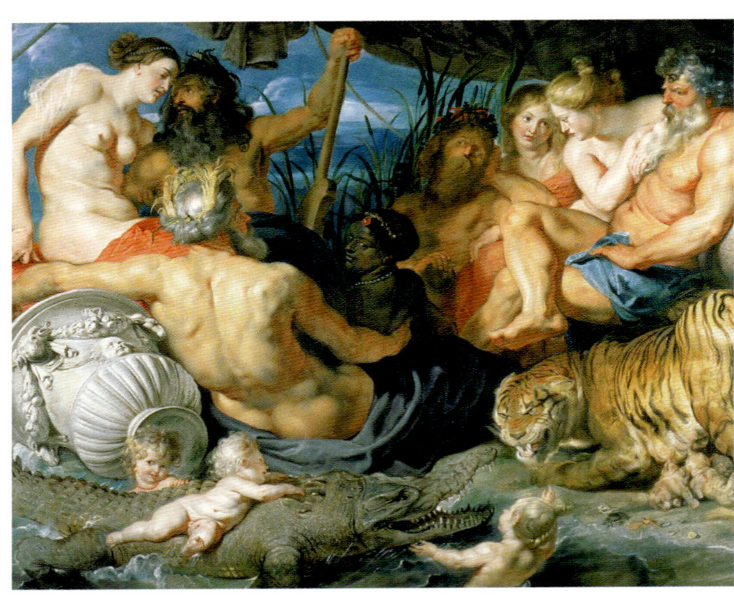

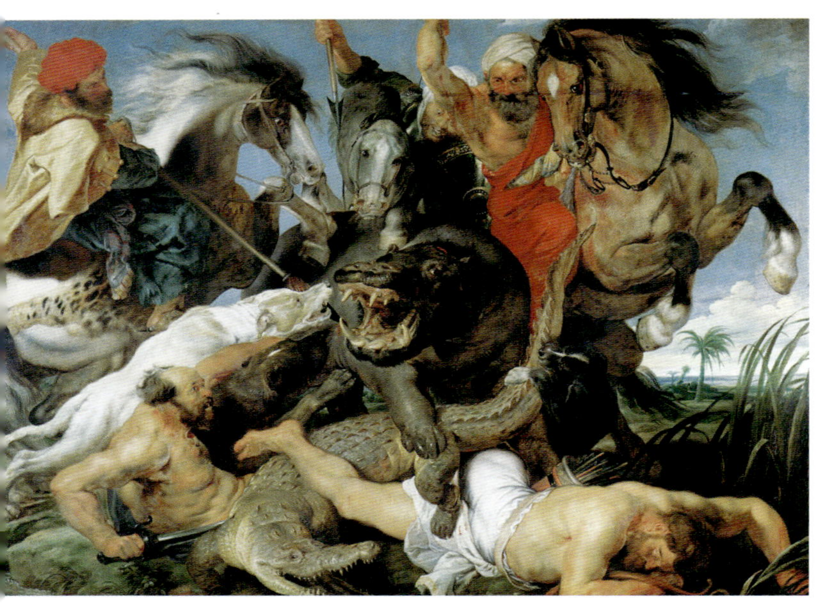

Hippopotamus and Crocodile Hunt, 1615–16, oil on canvas, 248 × 321cm (98 × 126in), Alte Pinakothek, Munich, Germany

One of four hunting paintings commissioned by Maximilian I, Elector of Bavaria, to decorate the old Schleissheim Palace, this is a wild hippopotamus and crocodile with three Moorish riders and hunting dogs. An allegory about humanity's struggle in the world, it is also a painting of opposites between smooth and scaly, dark and light, high and low, beauty and barbarism. Vivid colours portray a dramatic, violent and emotional scene.

Wolf and Fox Hunt, c.1616, oil on canvas, 245.4 x 376.2cm (95⅝ x 148⅛in), The Metropolitan Museum, New York, USA

This is another of Rubens's first large paintings of a hunt made between 1616–21. This canvas, which was originally more symmetrical, was made to fit a domestic interior. As with many of his works at this time, Rubens painted with the help of assistants. Although it is not clear exactly what he painted, he did declare that the wolves were his own work, and the landscape was painted after all the figures were completed.

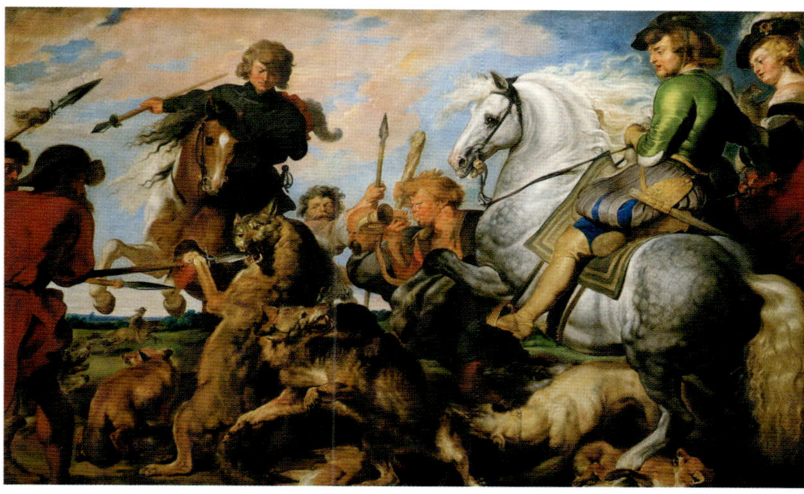

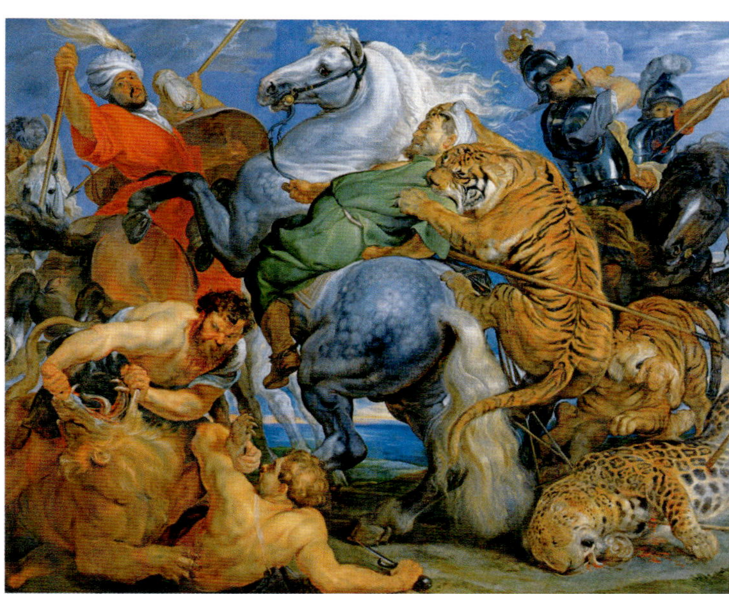

Tiger Hunt, 1615–16, oil on canvas, 256 x 324cm (34¼ x 52½in), Musée des Beaux Arts, Rennes, France

Another of the hunting paintings commissioned by Maximilian I, Elector of Bavaria, this violent, fierce fight is a tumult of colour and aggressive action. A frenzy of spears, jaws, teeth and claws depict a ferocious scene. A dead leopard lies on the ground, while a tiger has jumped on the back of a huntsman and is pulling him off his horse. It is an allegory of the civilized and the savage.

Boar Hunt, 1615–18, oil on canvas, 250 x 320cm (98½ x 126in), Musée des Beaux-Arts, Marseille, France

This is another of four hunting scenes painted by Rubens for the Elector Maximilian of Bavaria. A boar is threatened by men with spears. For a period, Rubens painted these rather graphic displays of aggression, fuelled in part by the passions of the Counter-Reformation, but mainly by vexation of the constant wars that were fought throughout his life.

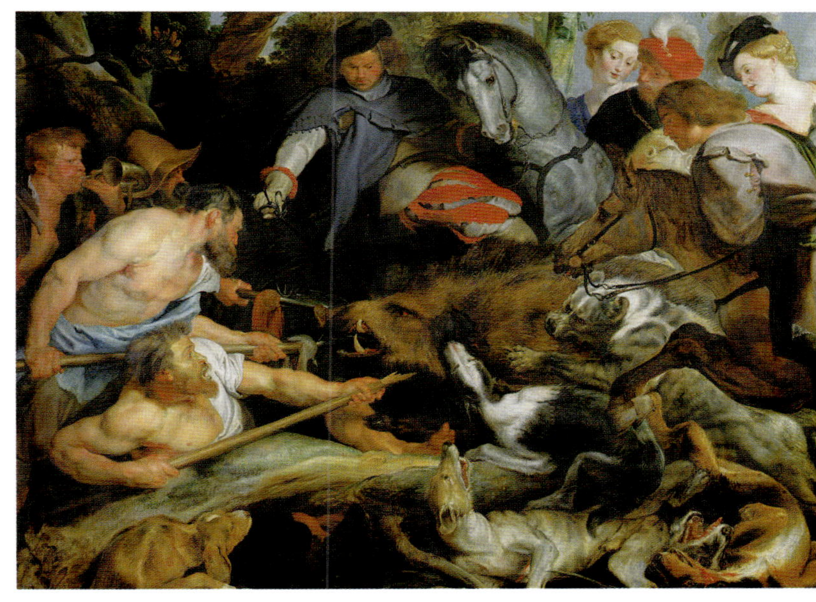

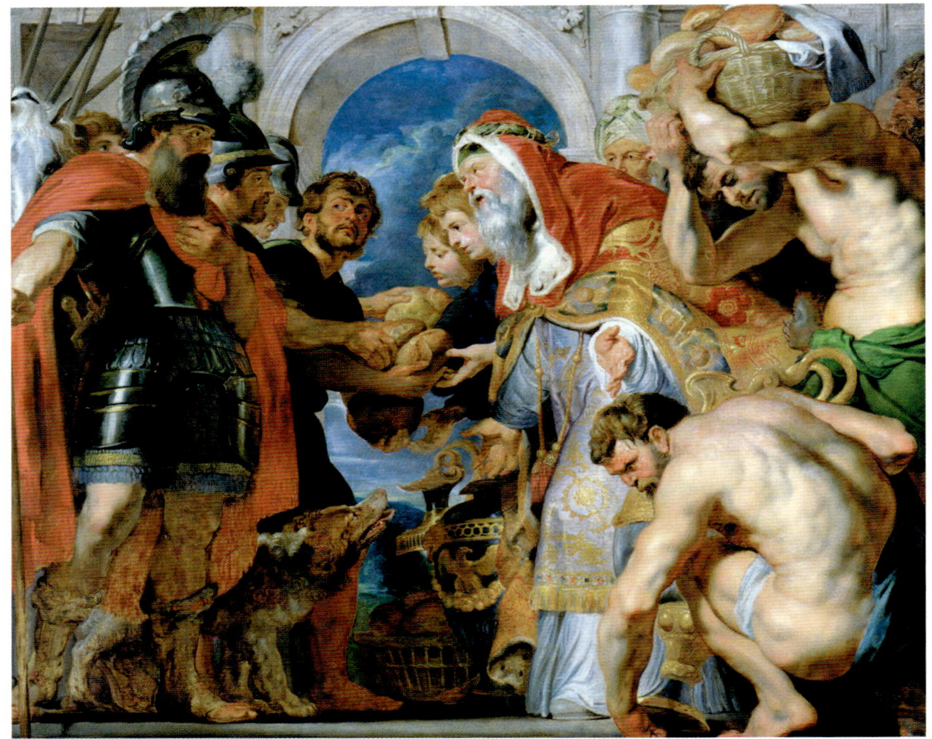

The Meeting of Abraham and Melchizedek, 1616–17, oil on canvas, 204 x 250cm (80 x 98in), Musée des Beaux-Arts, Caen, France

From the Old Testament book of Genesis, this depicts Abraham meeting the Priest-King of Salem (Jerusalem), Melchizedek. It portrays the gifts of bread and wine that Abraham was given after returning from a battle. Set before a grand arch, Abraham stands in armour with his soldiers, receiving loaves of bread from Melchizidek, who is with his servants. The light shines on Melchizedek while Abraham is in shadow, and brilliant colours are juxtaposed across the work, including red, blue, white, gold, purple and green.

Hygeia, Goddess of Health, c.1615, oil on oak, 106.2 x 74.3cm (41¾ x 29¼in), Detroit Institute of Arts, Michigan, USA

In both Greek and Roman mythology, Hygeia was the daughter and attendant of the god of medicine Asclepius, and a companion of the goddess Aphrodite. She personified health, cleanliness and hygiene, or the goddess of good health. Her sisters included Panakeia (All-Cure) and Iaso (Remedy). In classical sculpture, she was represented as a woman holding a large serpent in her arms. Rubens's version portrays her as a wealthy woman of his times.

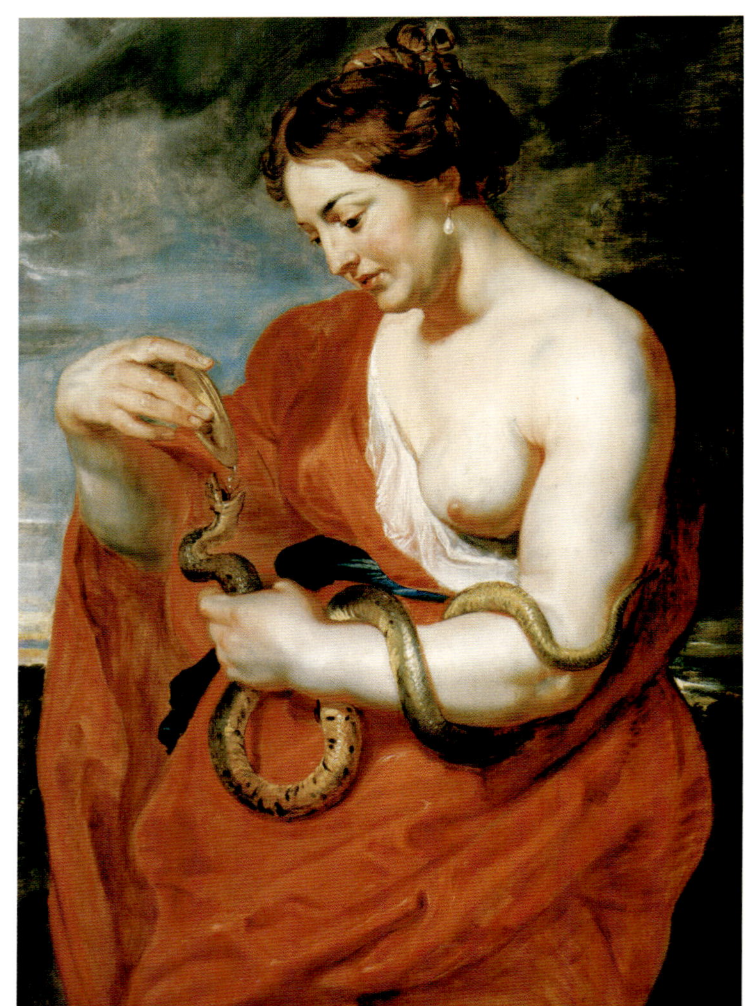

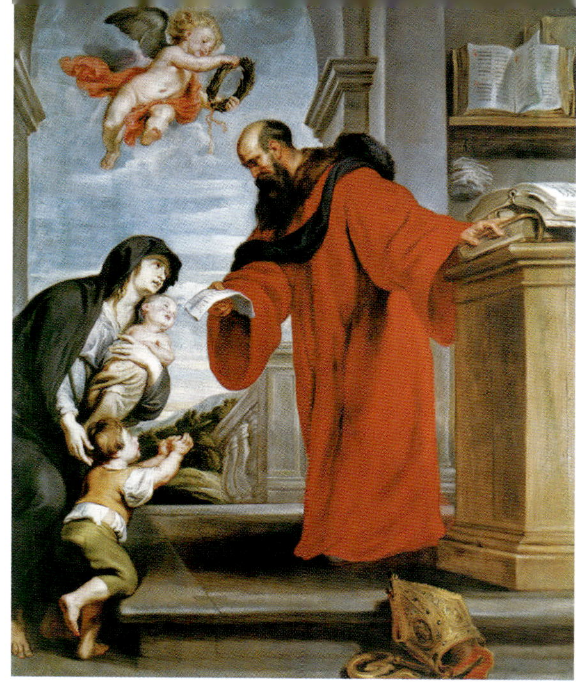

Saint Ives of Tréguier, 1615–20, oil on canvas, 287 x 221cm (113 x 87in), Detroit Institute of Arts, Michigan, USA

Saint Ives, the patron saint of lawyers and defender of widows and orphans, was a French lawyer of the 13th century. Born in 1253 in Brittany, France, he graduated in civil law, was appointed ecclesiastical judge of the Bishop of Tréguier, and championed the poor. His popularity rose in France during the 16th century, and then spread to the Netherlands. Rubens has painted him defending a widow and an orphan.

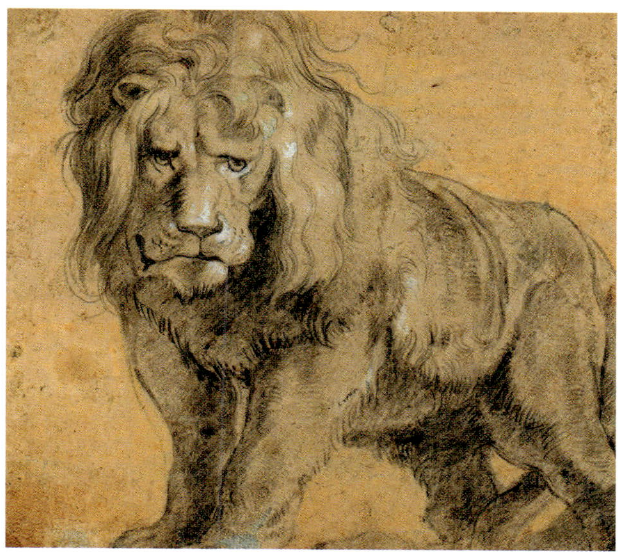

*Lion, c.*1612–13, black, white and yellow chalk on paper, 25.2 x 28.3cm (9⅞ x 11⅛in), National Gallery of Art, Washington DC, USA

Fascinated by lions, Rubens often visited the Royal Menagerie in Brussels to sketch and paint them from direct observation. This is a confident study of a lion for his painting of the Old Testament story, *Daniel in the Lions' Den*, which he completed a couple of years later. The story of persecution was a strong subject for the Counter-Reformation, and in his painting, Rubens gave his lions individual expressions.

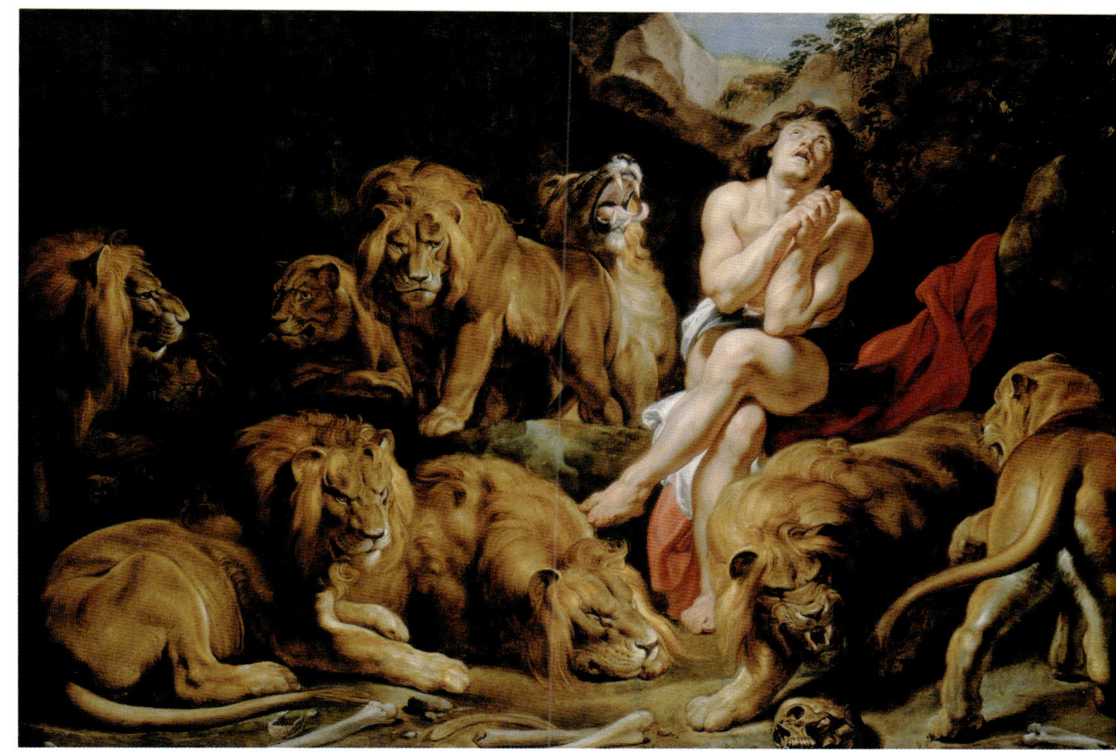

*Daniel and the Lions' Den, c.*1614/16, oil on canvas, 224.2 x 330.5cm (88¼ x 130⅛in), National Gallery of Art, Washington DC, USA

'Daniel among many lions, taken from life. Original, entirely by my hand,' wrote Rubens of this painting. It represents the biblical prophet Daniel, chief counsellor to the Persian king Darius, who aroused jealousy among other royal ministers. They forced Darius to imprison Daniel in a lions' den. The next morning, Darius anxiously had the stone removed that sealed the entrance, and discovered Daniel still alive. Here, the lions squint and yawn at the morning light streaming into their lair.

Saint Jerome, c.1615, oil on canvas, 236 × 163cm (93 × 64in), Gemäldegalerie, Dresden, Germany

One of several paintings of Saint Jerome executed by Rubens, this shows the most learned of the Fathers of the Catholic Church. Jerome was the son of Eusebius, best known for his translation of most of the Bible into Latin and his commentaries on the Gospels. Jerome is often depicted with a lion, as one story relates that he tamed a lion in the wilderness by healing its paw.

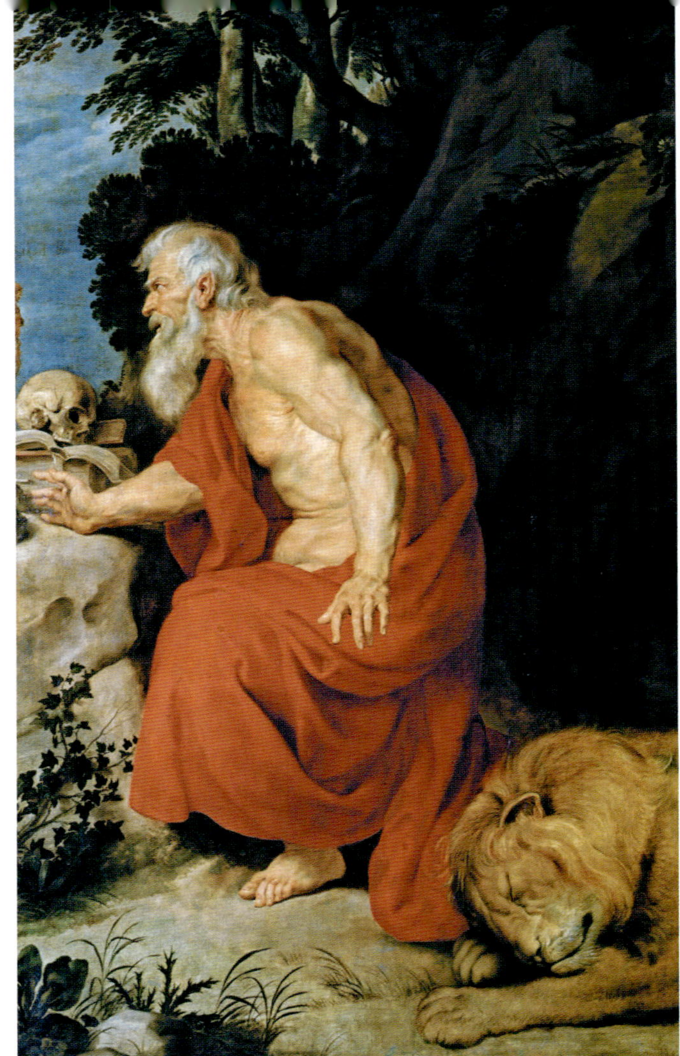

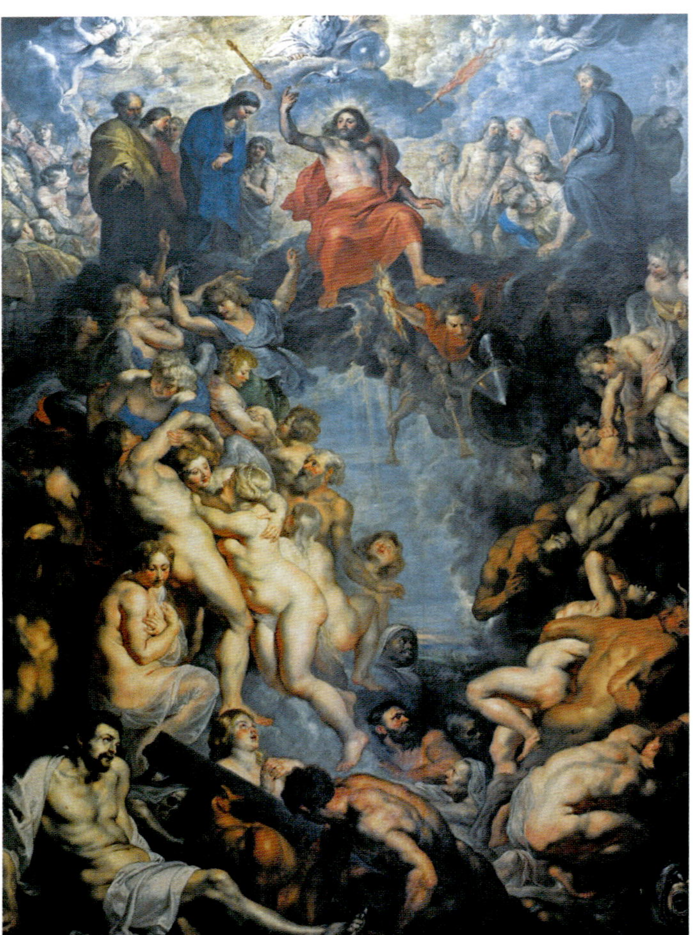

The Great Last Judgement, 1617, oil on canvas, 608.5 × 463.5cm (239½ × 182½in), Alte Pinakothek, Munich, Germany

Here, Christ is judging humankind. Tombs are open, and the dead have risen and await the decision about who is blessed and who is damned. This painting was commissioned by Duke Wolfgang Wilhelm of Pfalz-Neuburg for the high altar of the Jesuit church in Neuburg an der Donau, but the nudity within it shocked many worshippers, so it was covered up for much of the time.

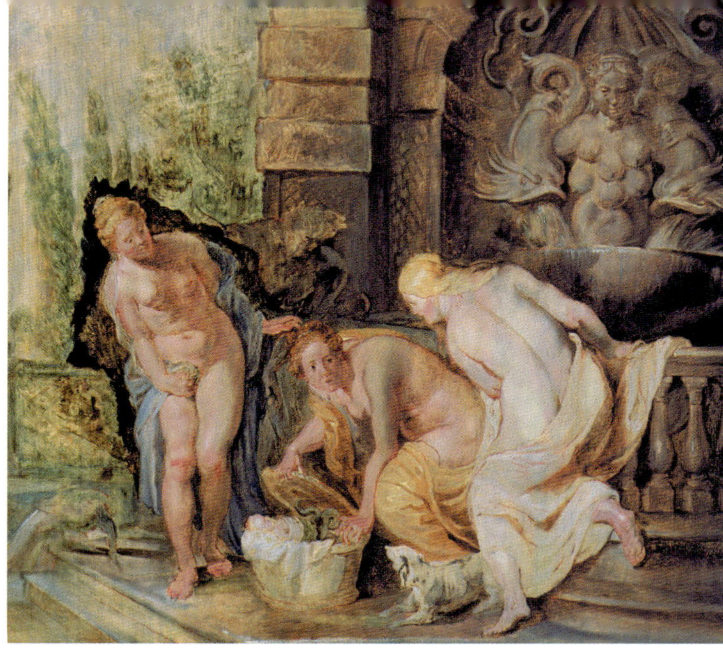

The Daughters of Cecrops discovering Erichthonius, c.1615, oil on panel, 41 x 50cm (16 x 19⅔in), The Courtauld Gallery, London, UK

King Erichthonius was a mythical early ruler of ancient Athens, raised by the goddess Athena. This is a study for a much larger painting of Erichthonius as a baby.

The daughters of King Cecrops have just discovered the baby in a basket. This shows Rubens's bold bravura brushwork, his confident placement of marks, robust figures and his lightness and spontaneity of touch. This study was for a painting of about 1616. Sixteen years later, Rubens painted another work of the same subject.

Entombment, c.1616, pen and brush in brown ink on paper, 22.2 x 15.3cm (8¾ x 6in), Rijksmuseum, Amsterdam, The Netherlands

This is an image of Christ's body being lowered into his tomb. It was a strong image for Counter-Reformation artists. In this preparatory work, Rubens shows his concern with the effects of light, exploring the range of tonal gradations, from the white of the paper to the darkest brown of the ink. Despite his overwhelming workload, Rubens always created several preparatory works before completing his final paintings.

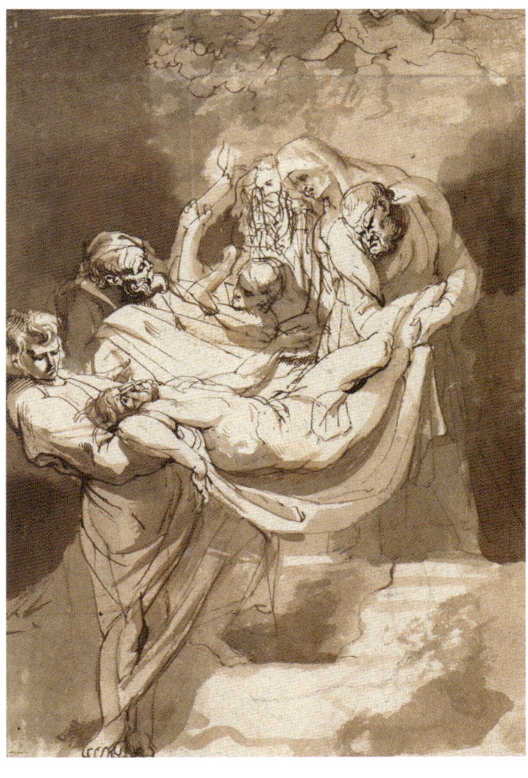

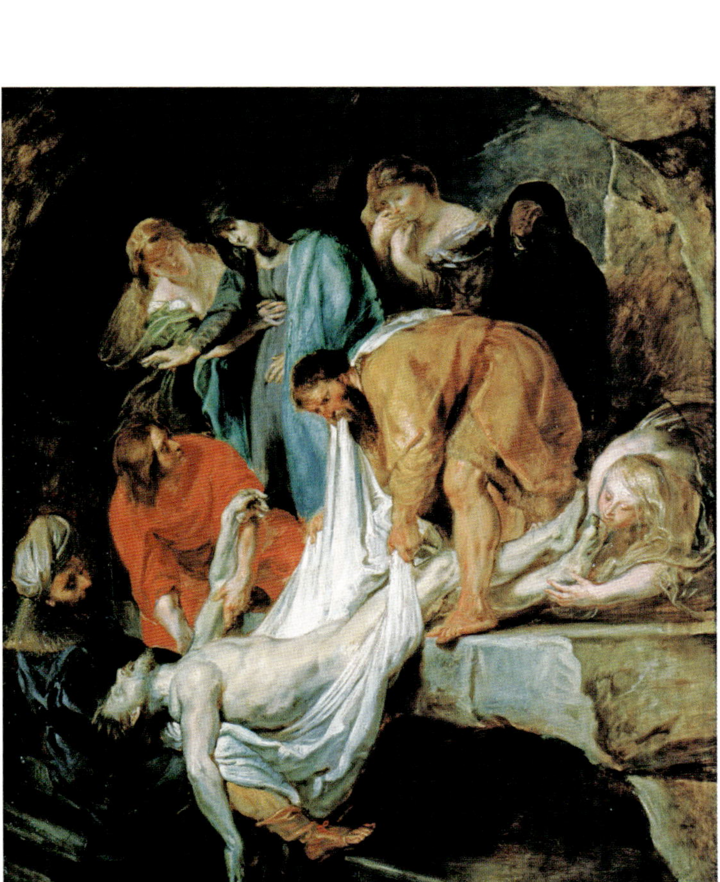

Entombment, 1615–16, oil on panel, 83.1 x 65.1cm (32¾ x 25⅔in), The Courtauld Gallery, London UK

This oil sketch shows the moment after the Crucifixion when Christ's body is lowered into a tomb by his friends. His pale, limp body dominates the painting, focusing viewers' attention on the horror of the scene; it was intended to make the viewer's religious experience personal. Human elements, such as John the Baptist gripping a corner of the sheet in his teeth, shows viewers the physical and emotional stress of the event.

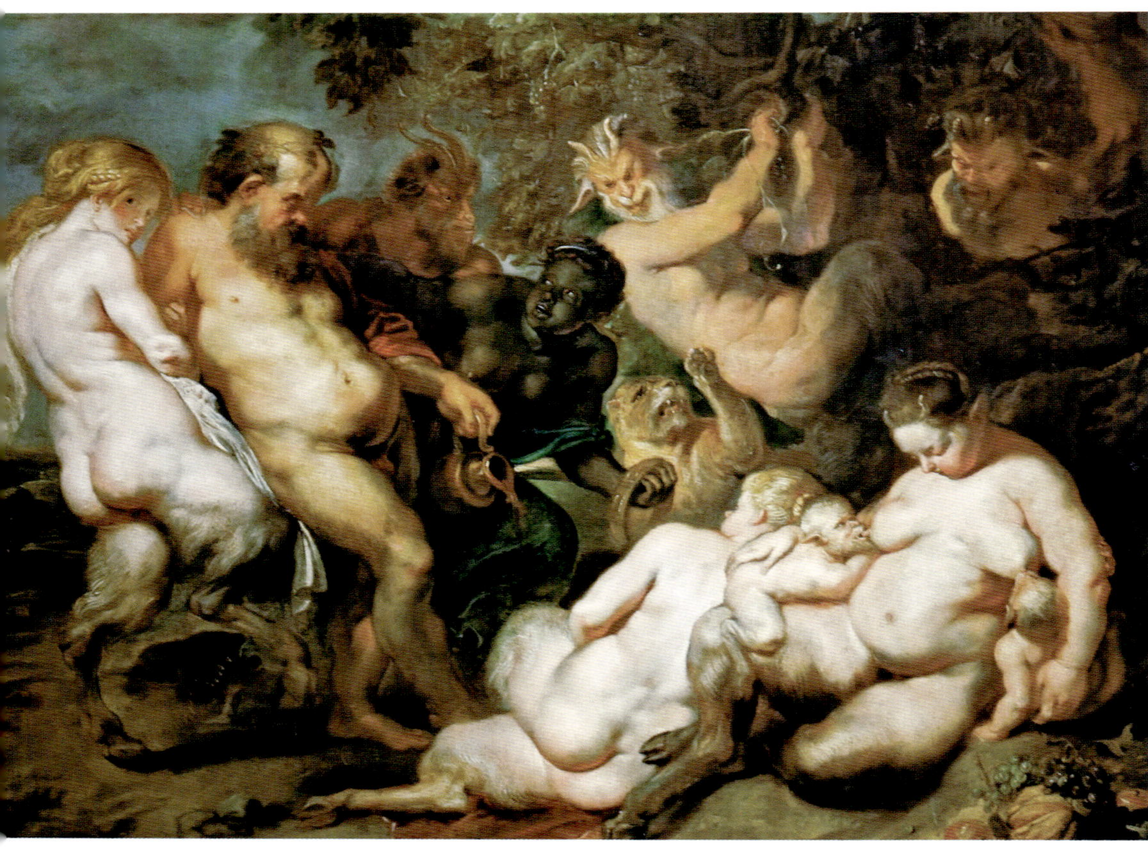

*Bacchanalia, c.*1615, oil on canvas, 91 x 107cm (35¾ x 42in), Pushkin State Museum of Fine Arts, Moscow, Russia

This is one of the paintings that Rubens kept until the end of his life. It depicts the ancient Roman festival celebrating Bacchus. As Bacchus represented the power of intoxication, the festivals were often excuses for bawdy drunkenness and wanton behaviour. This painting was extremely popular among Rubens's friends and other visitors, for its fat, frolicking figures and the painting style of loose, almost sketchy brushwork and sense of vivacity.

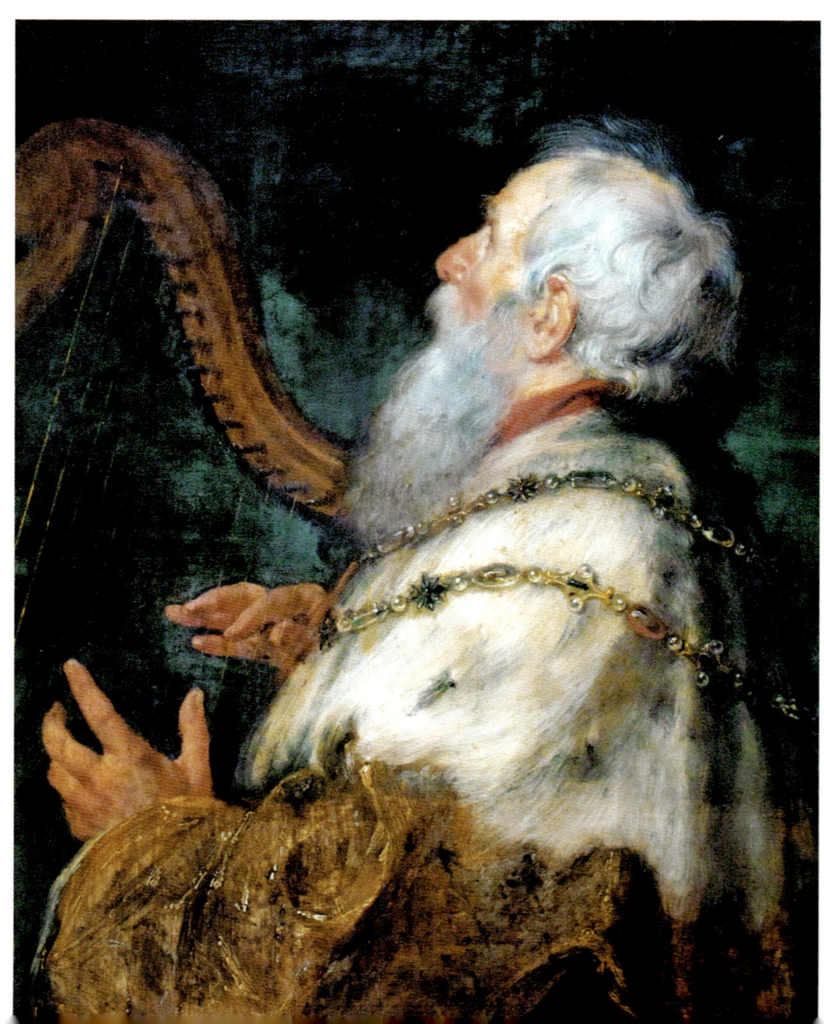

King David Playing the Harp, Rubens and Boeckhorst, 1616, oil on panel, 84.5 x 69.2cm (33¼ x 27¼ in), Städel Museum, Frankfurt, Germany

Only partially painted by Rubens, this work was simply a study of a head when completed by him, but after his death, his former employee Jan Boeckhorst (*c.*1604–68) enlarged the work, adding two further panels and creating more of a complete image. It was probably originally a 'tronie', which was a portrait made by an artist to practise capturing a particular character, and later used in a finished work.

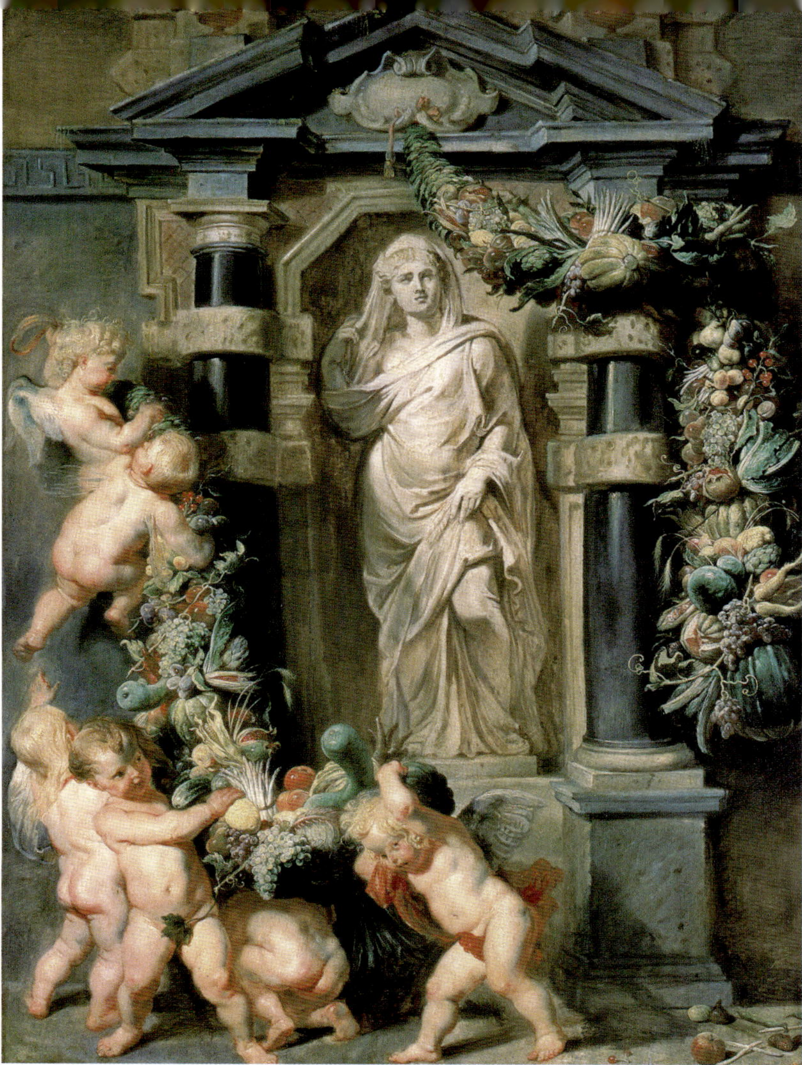

Statue of Ceres, Rubens and Frans Snyders, 1615, oil on panel, 90.5 x 65.5cm (35⅔ x 25¾in), The State Hermitage Museum, St Petersburg, Russia

This small painting is very still and calm in comparison with most of Rubens's more dynamic, large works. In clear and radiant colours, he depicts a Hellenistic statue of Ceres, the goddess of vegetation and earthly fertility. Rubens saw this statue in Rome, but he altered it to imbue it with fresh energy. Rubens painted the statue and Snyders added the garland of plucked fruits that decorates the niche containing the figure.

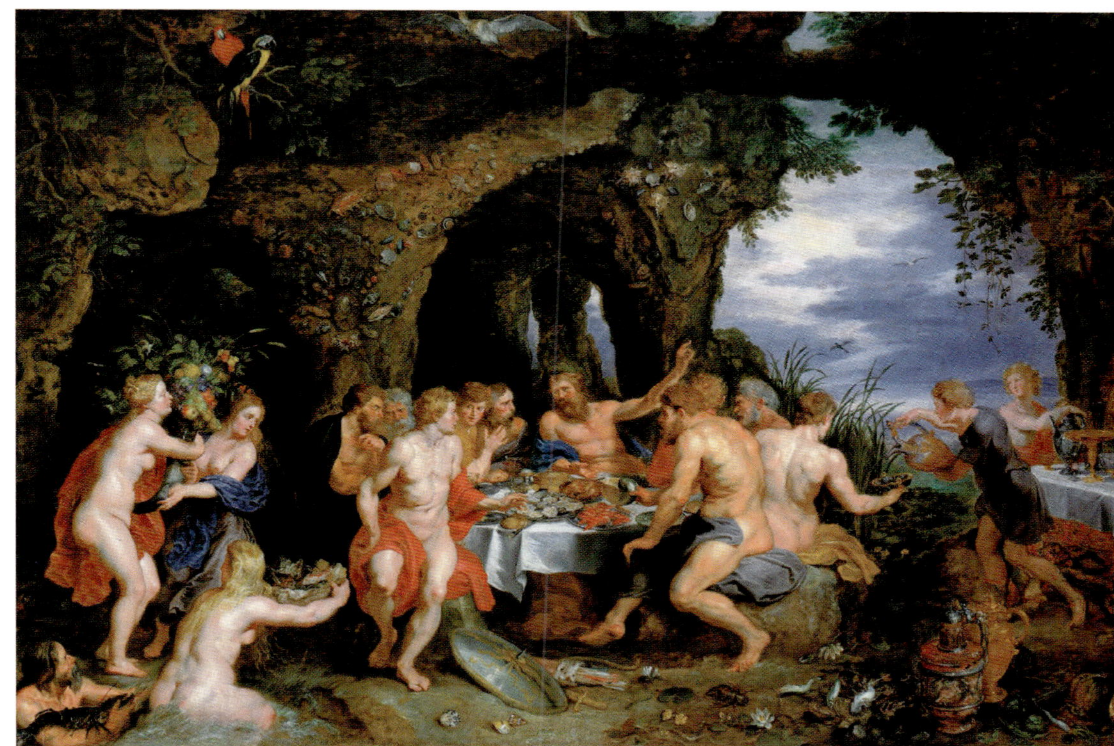

The Feast of Acheloüs, Rubens and Brueghel the Elder, c.1615, oil on wood, 108 x 163.8cm (42½ x 64½in), The Metropolitan Museum of Art, New York, USA

One of the most admired collaborations between Rubens and his friend Jan Brueghel, this mythological painting was planned completely by Rubens, who also painted the figure group, while Brueghel painted the landscape. It represents a tale from Ovid's *Metamorphoses*. The river god Acheloüs explains to the Greek hero Theseus that a distant island is his former lover Perimele, transformed by Neptune so that she could remain forever within the river's embrace.

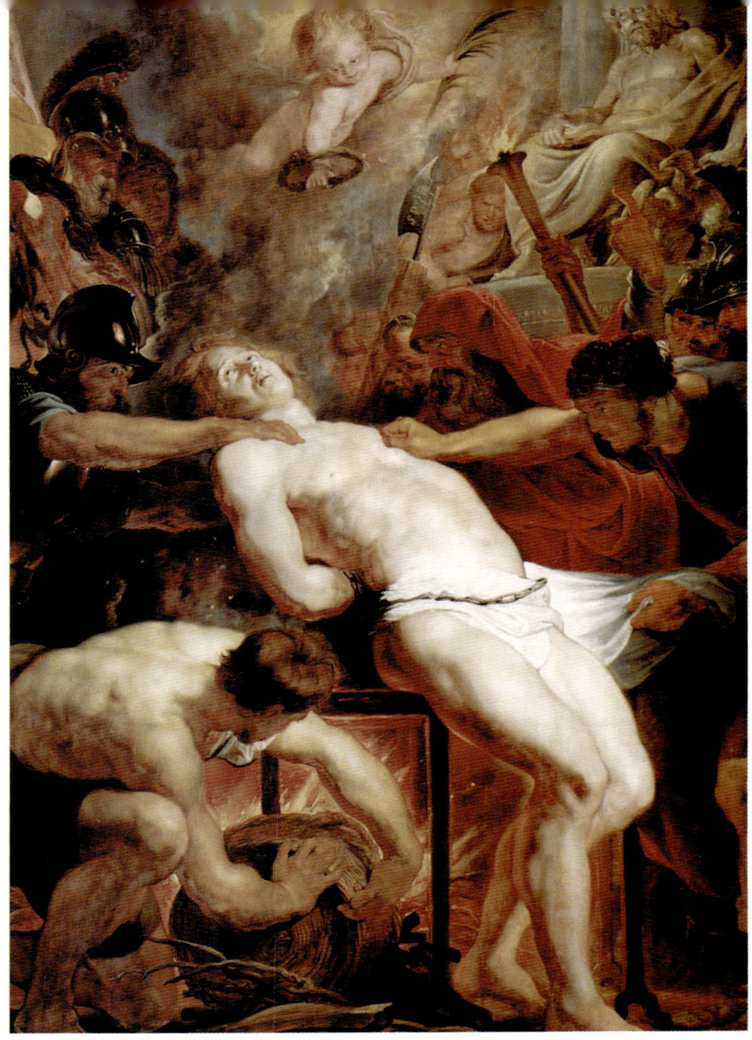

The Martyrdom of Saint Lawrence, c.1613–15, oil on panel, 250 × 178.5cm (98⅓ × 70¼ in), Alte Pinakothek, Munich, Germany

Saint Lawrence (or Laurence), a deacon under Pope Sixtus II, suffered martyrdom in Rome in 258. According to legend, he was tortured and then put to death by being roasted on a gridiron. Rubens was particularly adept at illustrating the vividly human side of biblical stories to create an immediate sense of reality among viewers. This shows the ghastly reality of his death.

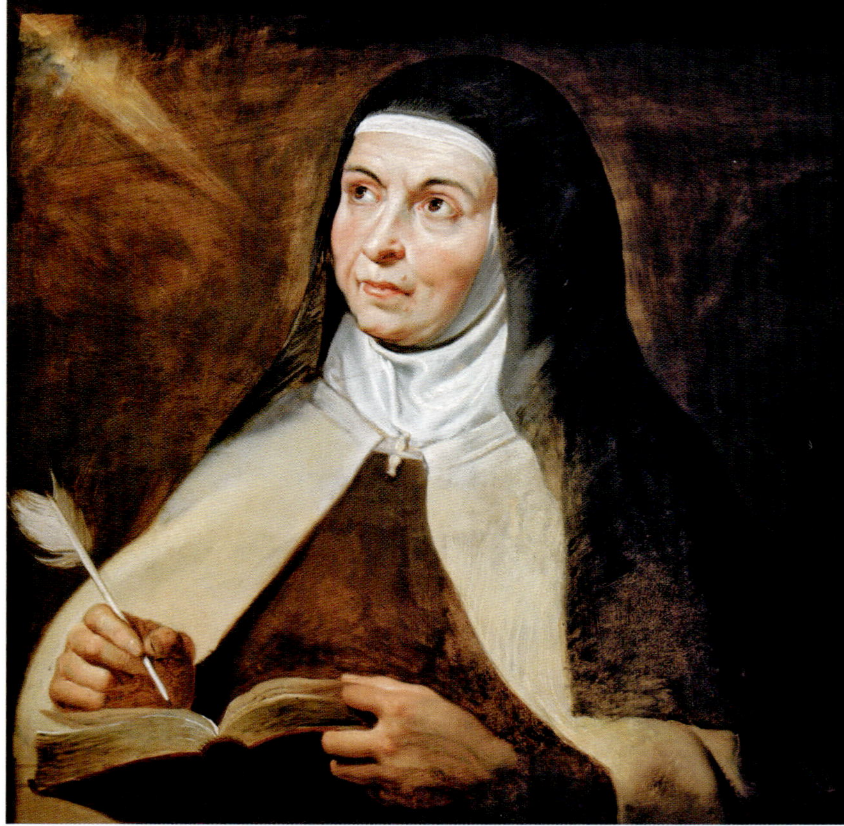

Saint Teresa of Ávila, c.1615, oil on oak, 67 × 69cm (26⅓ × 27¼ in), Kunsthistorisches Museum, Vienna, Austria

Teresa of Ávila, also called Saint Teresa of Jesus, was a prominent Spanish mystic, Carmelite nun, author and theologian. After her death, her cult increased in Spain during the 1620s, and for a time she was considered as a candidate to become a national patron saint. In Rubens's representation, she holds a book and quill, referring to her authorship of several important books about her experiences as a mystic.

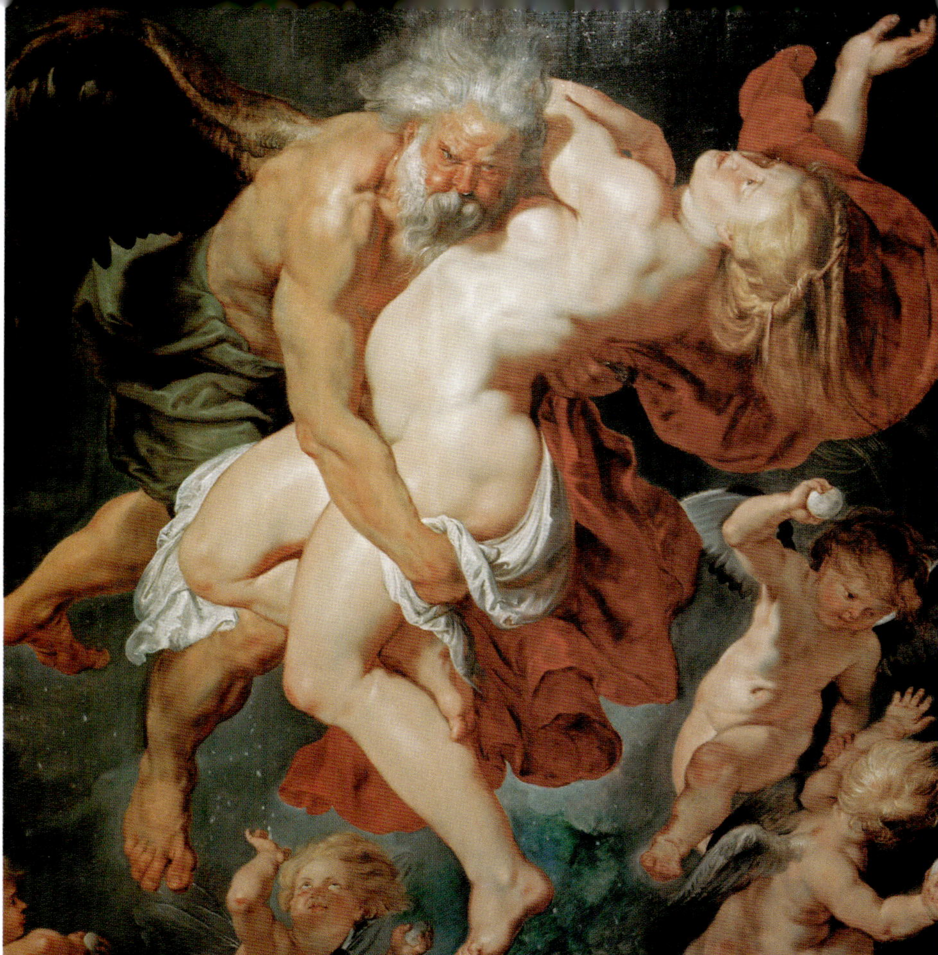

Boreas abducts Oreithyia,
*c.*1615, oil on wood,
146 x 140cm (57½ x 55in),
Akademie der Bildenden
Künste, Vienna, Austria

In this episode from
Ovid's *Metamorphoses*,
Rubens creates a powerful
image of Boreas, the ruler
of the north wind. He is old
with flowing grey locks and
wings. He loved Oreithyia,
the daughter of the
legendary King Erechtheus
of Athens and, against her
will, carried her off to be his
bride. Here, he flies away
with the naked girl. Putti
play with snowballs, while
Boreas and Oreithyia fill
the rest of the composition.

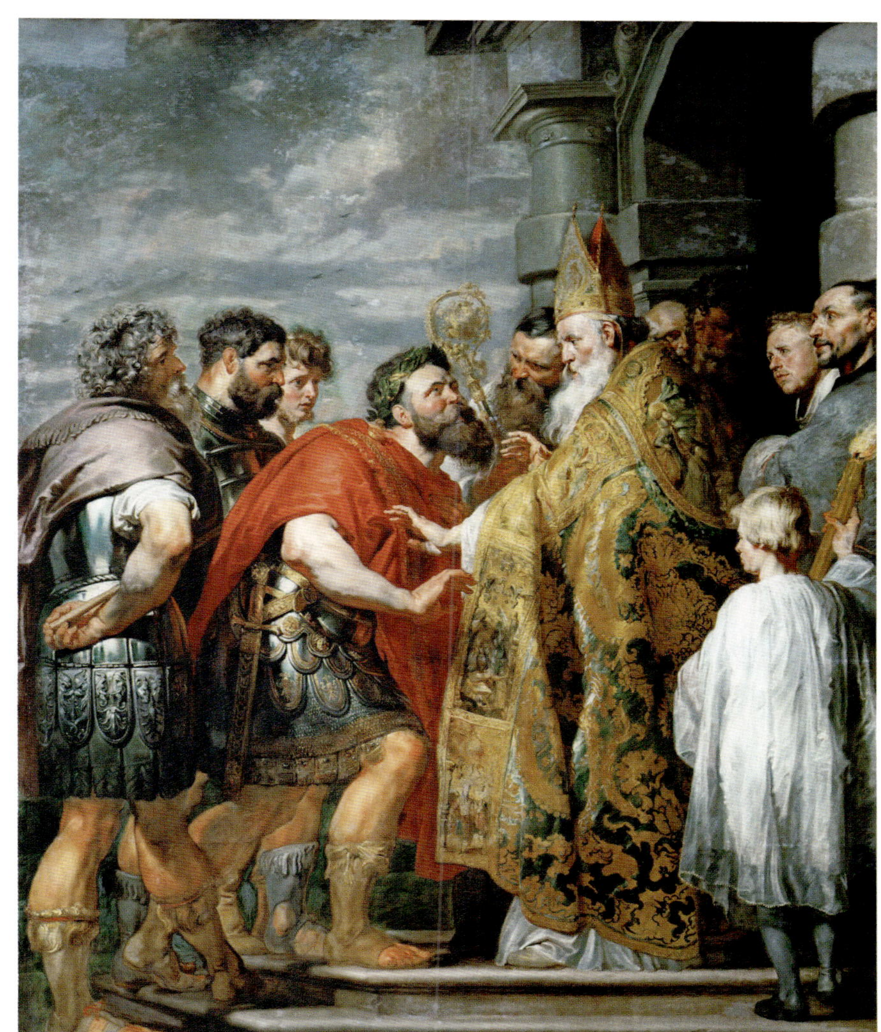

Saint Ambrose and Emperor
*Theodosius, c.*1615, oil on
canvas, 362 x 246cm (142½
x 96¾in), Kunsthistorisches
Museum, Vienna, Austria

Executed by Rubens with
assistance from his main
pupil Van Dyck, this shows
the Roman emperor
Theodosius I and his
entourage being barred from
Milan Cathedral by its
archbishop Saint Ambrose,
in punishment for their
Massacre of Thessalonica.
Van Dyck later painted his
own similar version of the
story, which can be seen
to have been inspired
particularly strongly by
his master's approach.

Head of a Franciscan Friar,
*c.*1615, oil on canvas,
52 x 44cm (20½ x 17⅓in),
The State Hermitage
Museum, St Petersburg,
Russia

Strong chiaroscuro has
the effect of commanding
attention on this monk's face.
As if under a spotlight, his skin
is highlighted against his brown
cassock and black background.
The focus is deliberately
centred on the man's facial
features, bringing to the fore
the honesty and intensity of
his gaze. In contrast with many
of his brightly coloured works,
for this painting Rubens
employed an extremely
restricted palette.

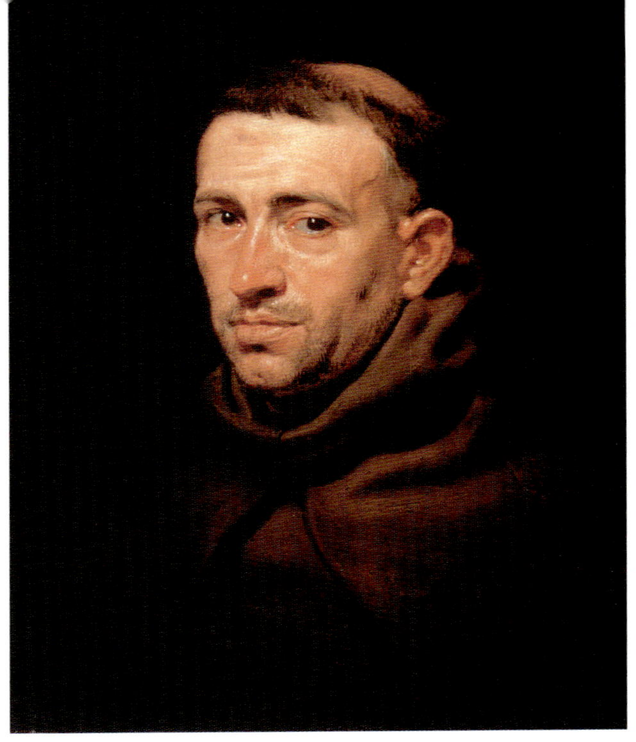

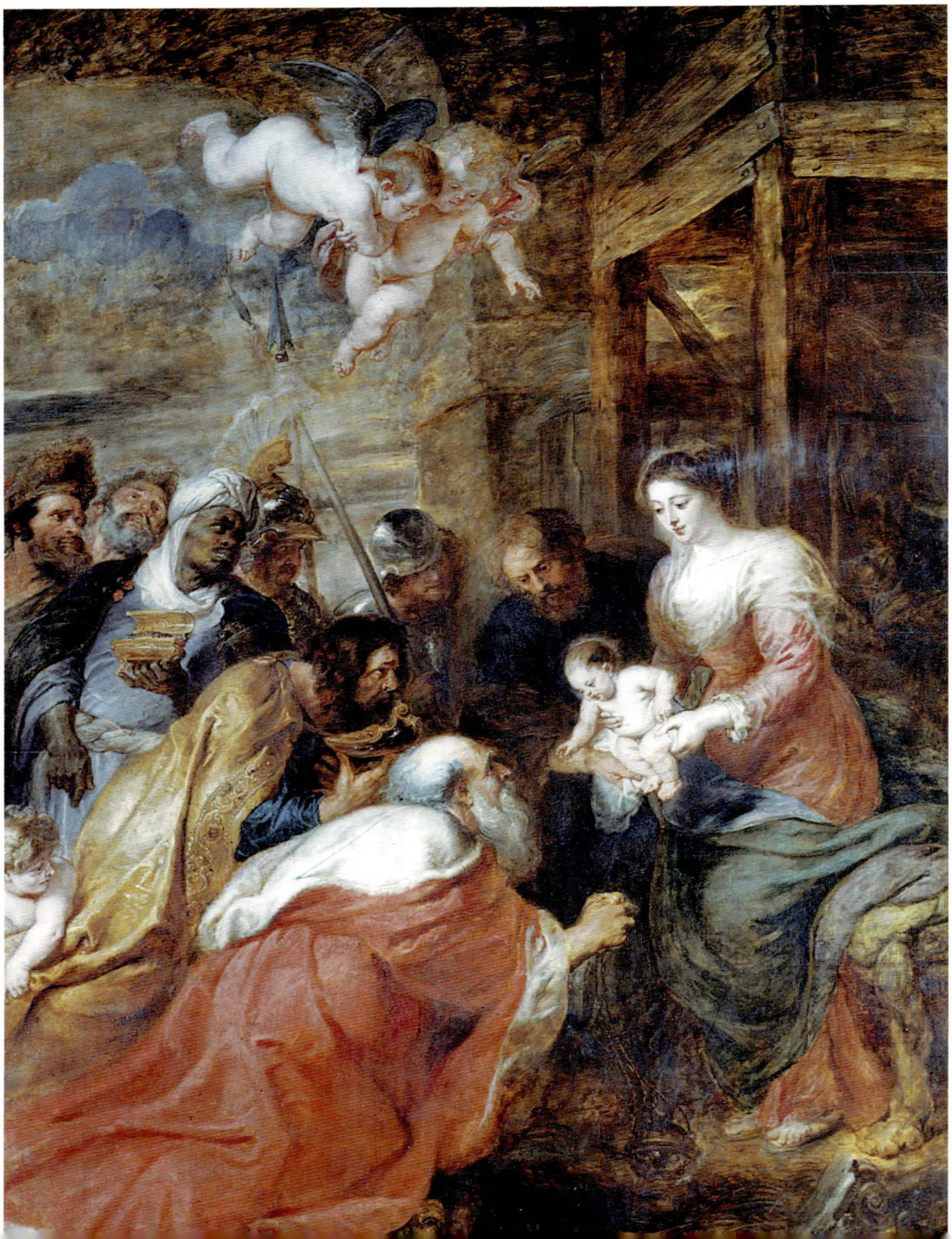

Adoration of the Magi,
*c.*1616–17, oil on canvas,
338 x 251cm (133 x 99in),
King's College Chapel,
Cambridge, UK

While this was a popular subject
during the Renaissance, Rubens
produced more personalized,
unique and widely varied
interpretations of the theme.
This features the interior of a
17th-century Flemish farm. The
Magi have arrived at the stable
where the Holy Family is
temporarily residing. They are
dressed in magnificent clothes
and jewels, so Rubens has
combined sumptuous colours
with powerful chiaroscuro to
create a magnificent scene,
which is also nonetheless
intimate. The brightest light falls
on the Virgin and Child. Even
though she was a poor Jewish
girl, Mary is dressed richly in a
shimmering 17th-century silk
gown, which contrasts from
traditional depictions of her
in simple blue and white.

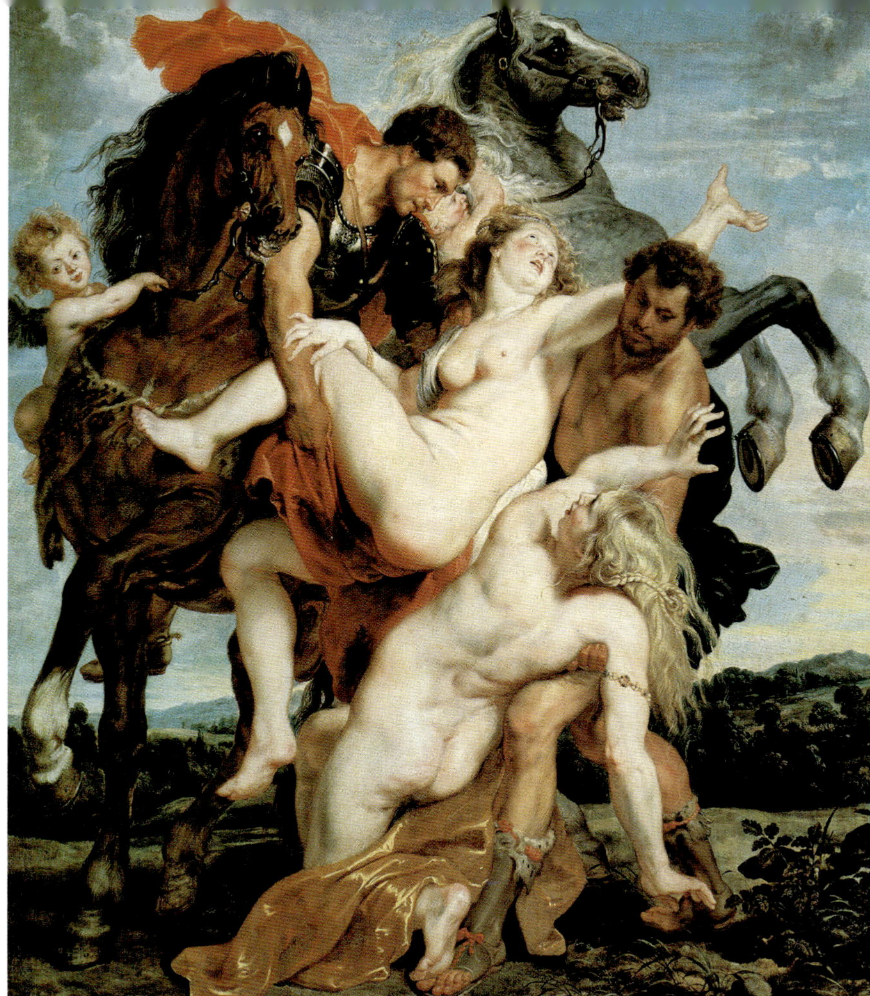

Rape of the Daughters of Leucippus, c.1617, oil on canvas, 224 x 211cm (88¼ x 83in), Alte Pinakothek, Munich, Germany

The mythological ancient Greek philosopher Leucippus had two daughters, Phoebe and Hilaeira. This depicts the mortal Castor and the immortal Pollux abducting them. Castor is a horse-tamer, recognizable from his armour, whilst Pollux, a boxer, is stripped to the waist. Castor's horse is well behaved and supported by a putto, while Pollux's is rearing. With flaying limbs, the two young women fight helplessly against their abductors.

The Union of Earth and Water, c.1618, oil on canvas, 223 x 181cm (87¾ x 71¼in), The State Hermitage Museum, St Petersburg, Russia

In the 16th and 17th centuries, the four elements, Earth, Air, Fire and Water, were often represented as classical gods and goddesses. As a woman, Earth is represented by Cybele, the Mother of the Gods, who holds a horn of plenty in her right hand. Neptune represents Water, with an overturned urn. Their union is blessed by the goddess of Victory who has descended from Mount Olympus.

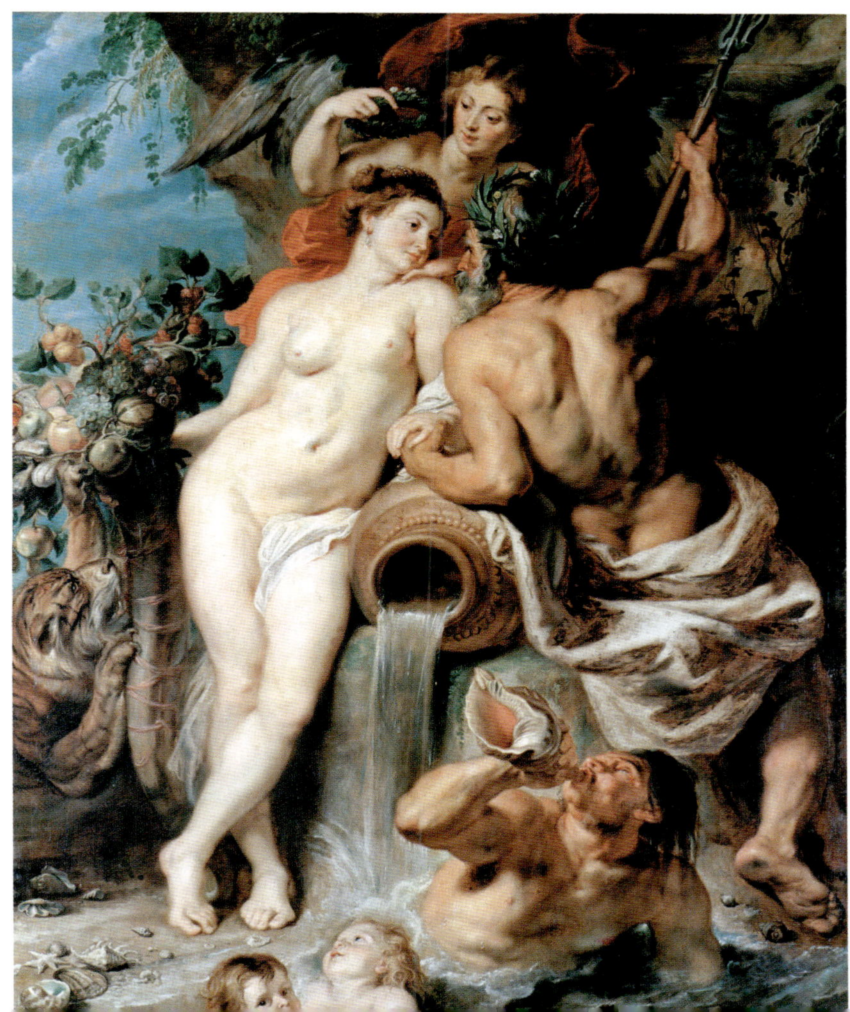

Young Man with a Black Hat, 1615–18, oil on oak, 44.1 x 35.3cm (17⅓ x 14in), Alte Pinakothek, Munich, Germany

An unidentified young man is depicted close to the picture plane, his long, artistic fingers suggesting a sensitive, artistic nature. Rubens often used strong chiaroscuro for his male portraits, also employing an extremely restricted palette. He has used rich, dark tones and broadly massed shadows, but the facial features are detailed and the eyes, in particular, show depth.

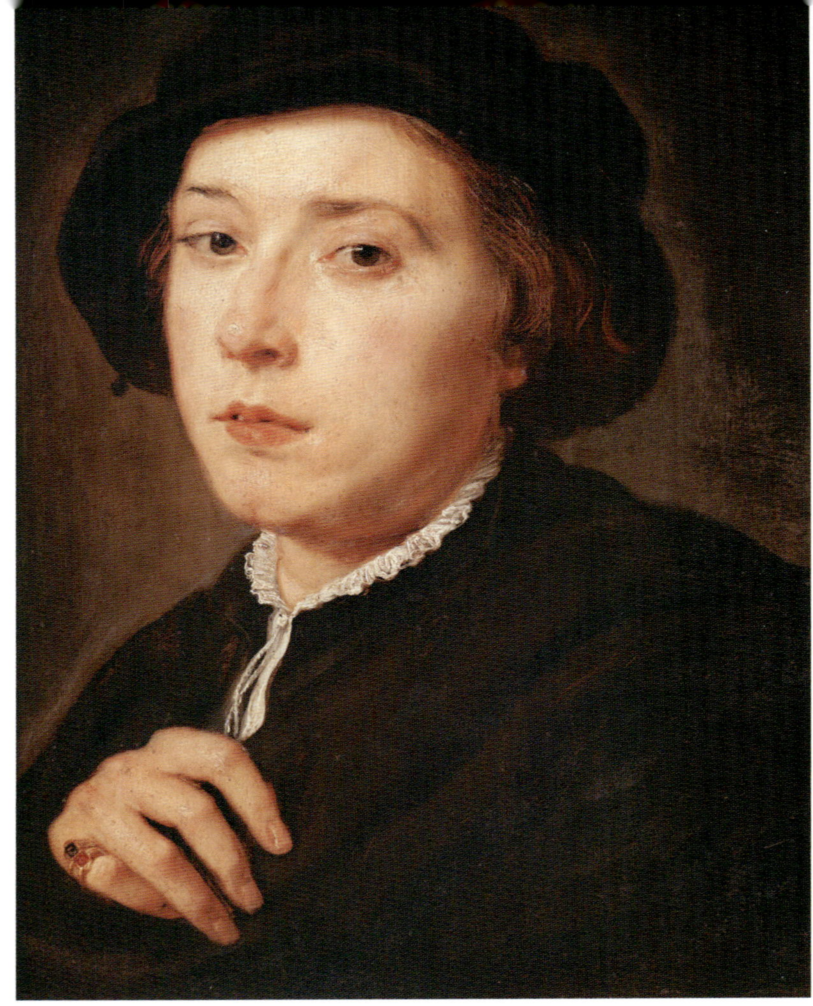

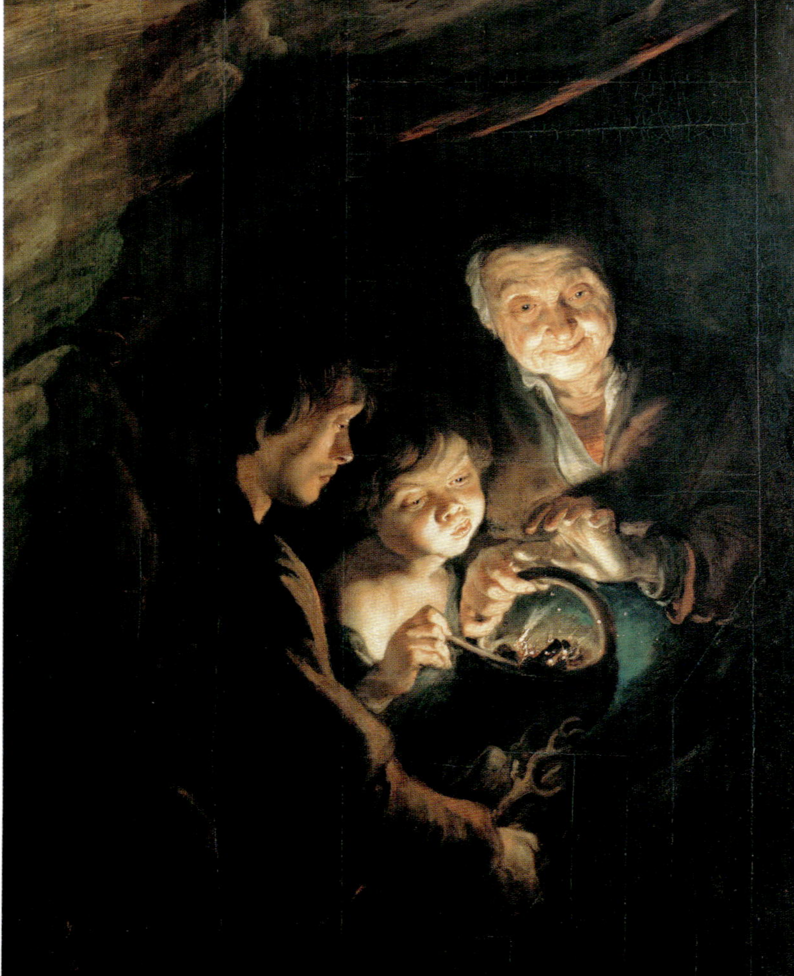

Old Woman with a Basket of Coal, 1618–20, oil on panel, 115 x 92cm (45⅓ x 36¼ in) Gemäldegalerie, Dresden, Germany

Using the dramatic tenebrism made popular by Caravaggio, this painting depicts three people in a cave, gathered around a coal basin. A smiling elderly woman warms her outstretched hands, a boy blows on the embers to coax the flames to provide them with more warmth, and a youth looks into the fire with a pensive expression.

A Shepherd with his Flock in a Woody Landscape, 1615–22, oil on oak, 64.3 x 94.3cm (25⅓ x 37in), The National Gallery, London, UK

Rubens initially worked on the central part of this painting and then enlarged it. Although landscapes were not fashionable as works of art at that time, he enjoyed painting them because they offered him a complete contrast with his normally complex compositions of so many figures. This painting naturally leads the eye through the scene, with the stream leading from the tall, dark trees to the glowing light in the distance.

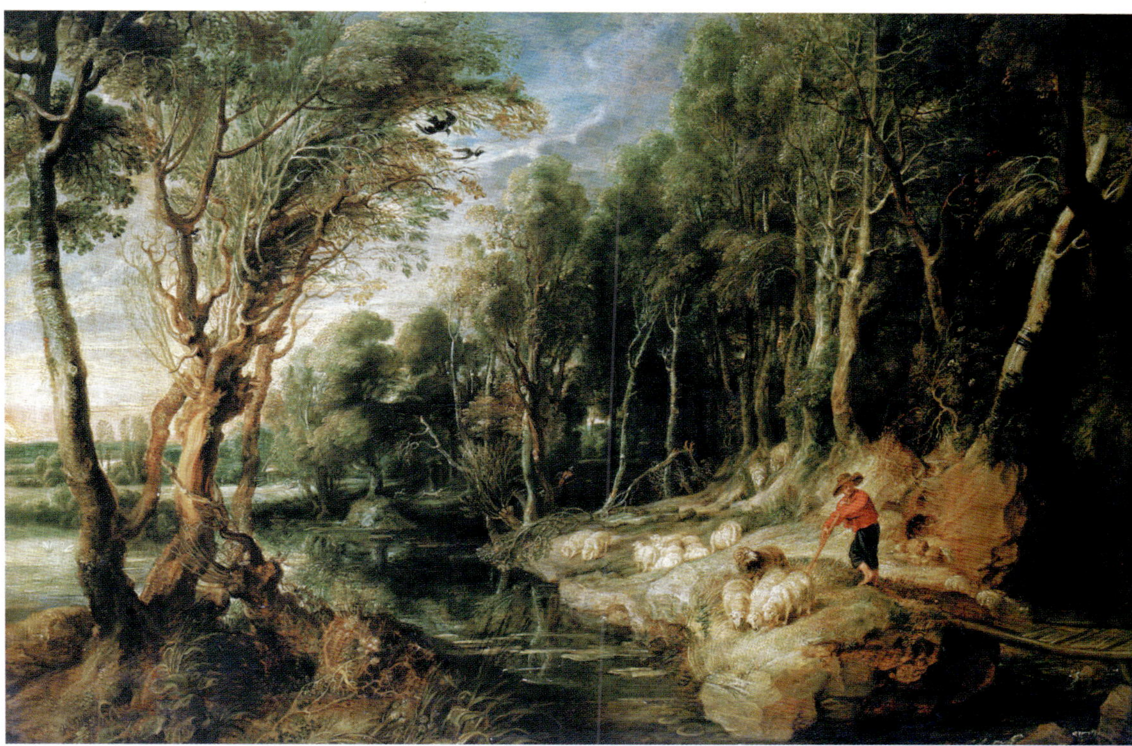

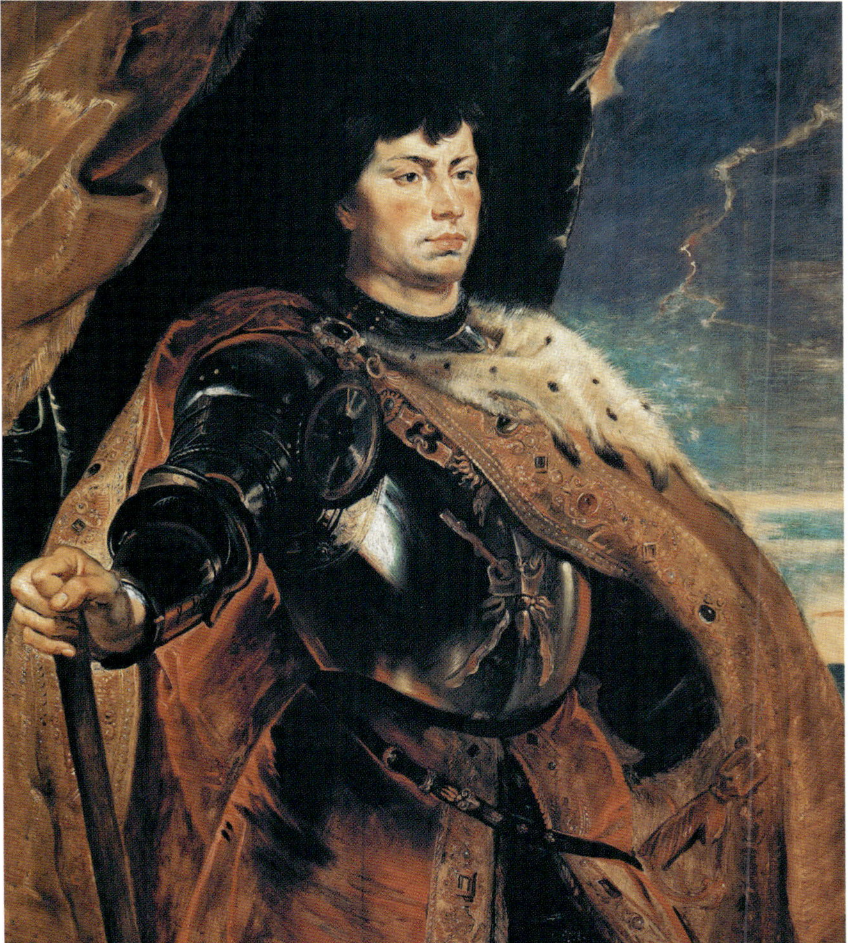

Charles the Bold, Duke of Burgundy, c.1618, oil on canvas, 118.5 x 102cm (46¾ x 40⅛in), Kunsthistorisches Museum, Vienna, Austria

Full of contradictions, Charles, Duke of Burgundy (1433–77), was known to be cruel and clever, and a lover of splendour, fashion and art. Yet his conceit and audacity caused him to fail in various conflicts. Dying at just 44, he left sumptuous treasures and became somewhat of a legend. Rubens painted this portrait of him nearly two centuries after his death.

Seven Studies of Heads, c.1616, pen and ink with chalk on paper, 17.4 x 22.4cm (7 x 8¾in), Collection of the Duke of Devonshire, Chatsworth, UK

These pen and ink studies of the head of an elderly bearded man, two further men's heads and two women, one wearing a cap, are similar to many of Rubens's studies that he made from life. They were not for any particular painting, but Rubens usually incorporated them into later works. Some of the characters shown here appear in his *Adoration of the Magi* (below).

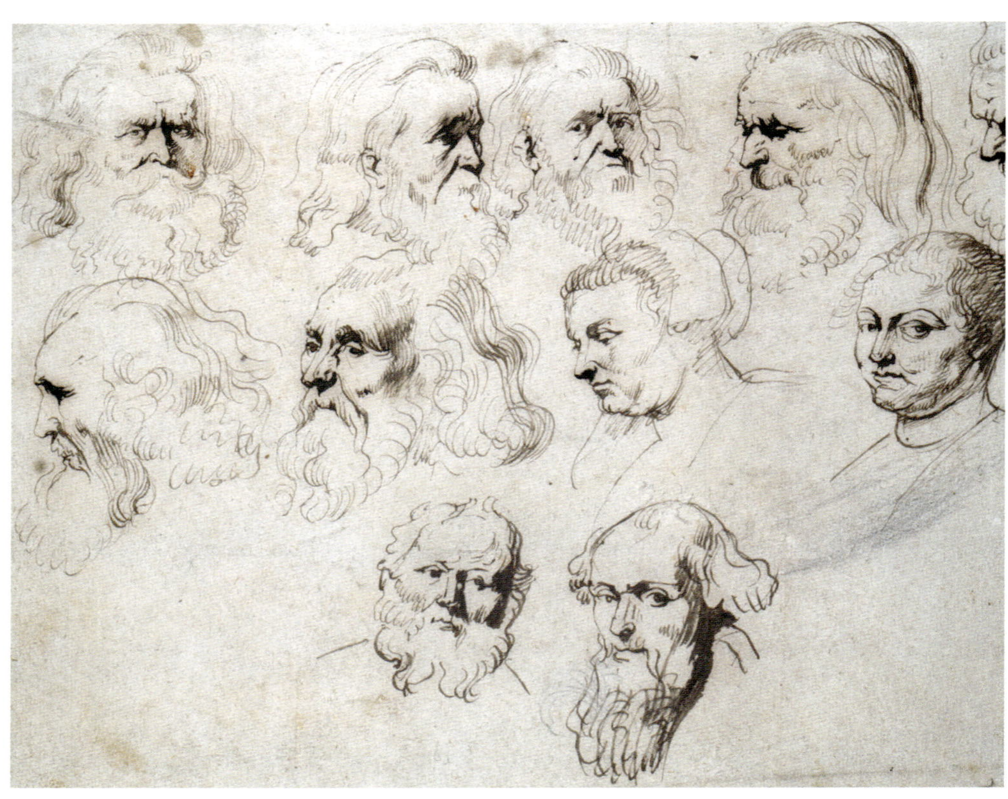

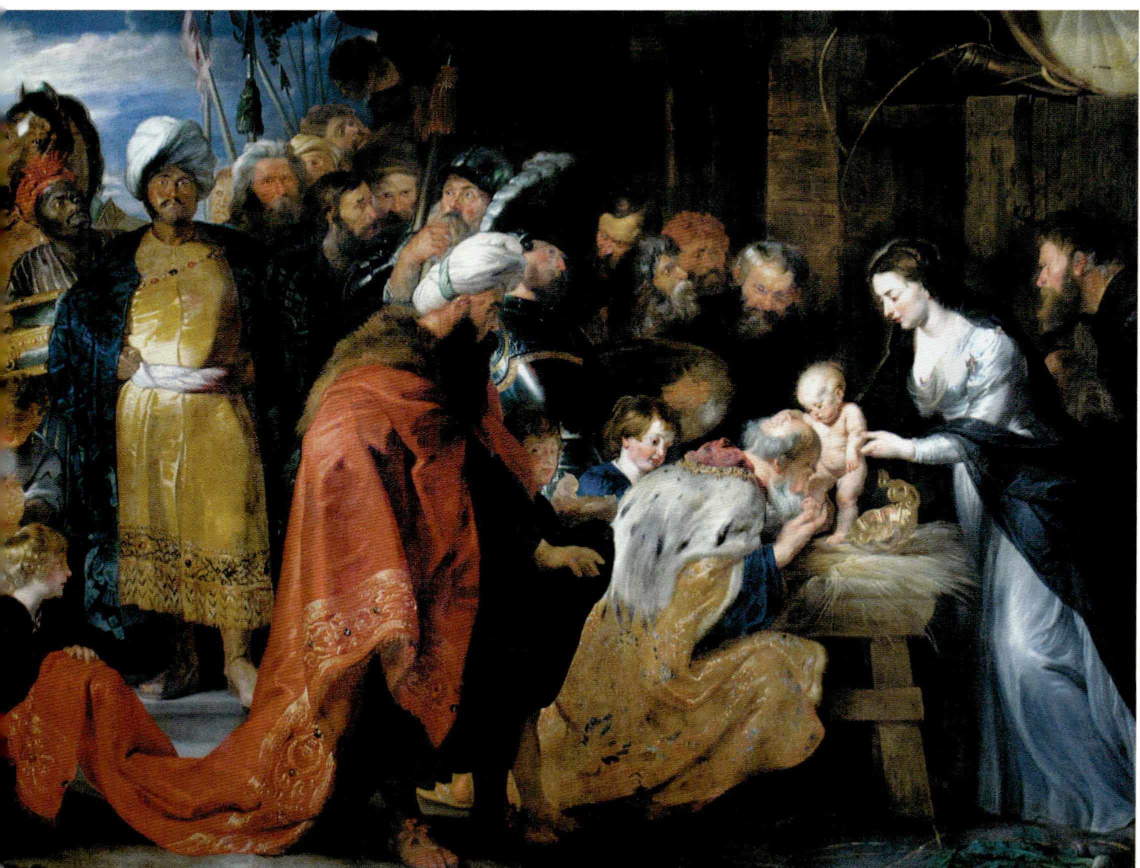

Study for Adoration of the Magi, c.1617–18, oil on panel, 48.2 x 64.8cm (19 x 25½in), Private Collection

Rubens painted this subject more often than any other episode from the life of Christ. The horizontal composition allowed Rubens to make the most of the magnificently attired kings and the Holy Family. The rich colours, contrasting textures and different emotions suited his empathy with the whole of mankind. A tiny foot is held and kissed by the Assyrian king Caspar, who kneels in gold and blue drapery and an ermine stole.

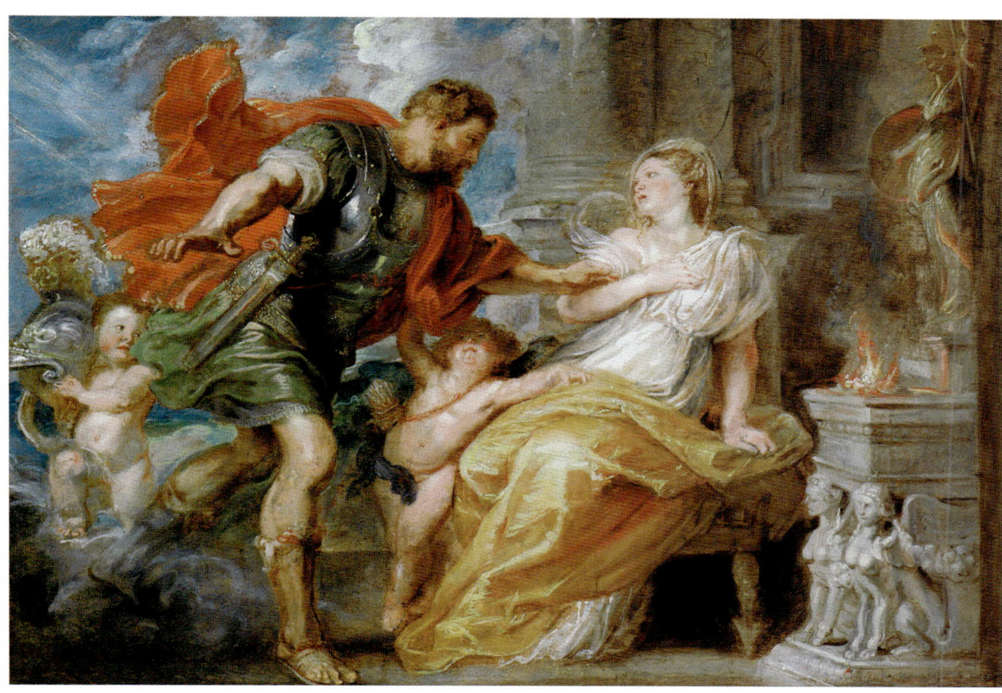

Mars and Rhea Silvia,
c.1616–17, oil on canvas,
208 x 272cm (82 x 107in),
Liechtenstein Museum,
Vienna, Austria

This painting depicts Ovid's
myth of Mars raping Rhea
Silvia, which resulted in the
birth of Romulus and Remus,
the founders of Rome.
According to the story,
Cupid, the god of love,
leads Mars to Rhea Silvia,
a priestess of Vesta, the
goddess of the hearth,
protector of the family,
hospitality and community
life. Mars overpowered the
Vestal Virgin while she slept.

Clara Serena, c.1616, oil on
canvas mounted on panel,
37 x 27cm (14½ x 10⅔in),
Liechtenstein Museum,
Vienna, Austria

This is Rubens's 5-year-old
daughter from his marriage
to Isabella Brant, showing
her clear resemblance to her
mother. The naturalness of
the image and the closeness
of her face to the picture
plane is not typical of
contemporary portrait
painting, but demonstrates
the closeness between
Rubens and his first-born
child. Her rosy cheeks and
the highlights on her nose
and forehead give an
impression of vivacity.

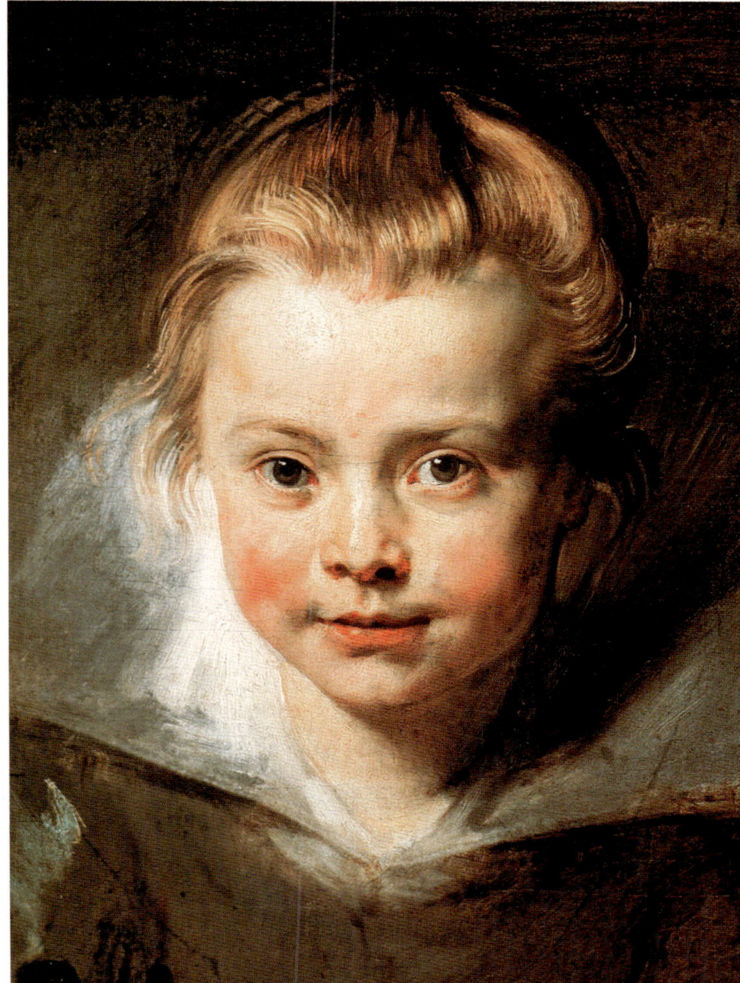

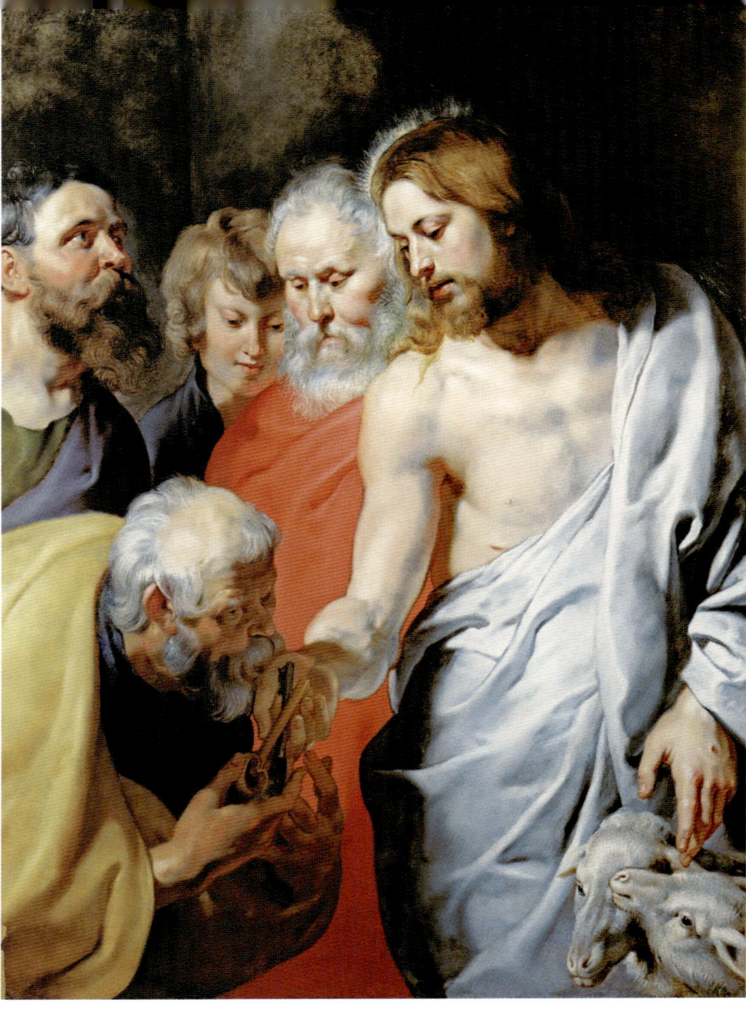

Christy's Charge to Peter,
1616, oil on oak,
139.2 x 114.8cm (55 x
45¼ in), The Wallace
Collection, London, UK

In the Gospel of Saint
Matthew, Christ charges
Saint Peter with the keys of
the Kingdom of Heaven. In
the Gospel of Saint John,
Christ appears to the
Apostles after his death and
tells Peter to 'feed his sheep'.
As he often did, Rubens
combined two moments:
Christ giving the keys to
Peter, while simultaneously
pointing at two sheep.
Rubens painted this
for Nicholas Damant
(c.1531–1616), an advisor
to the Archdukes
Albert and Isabella.

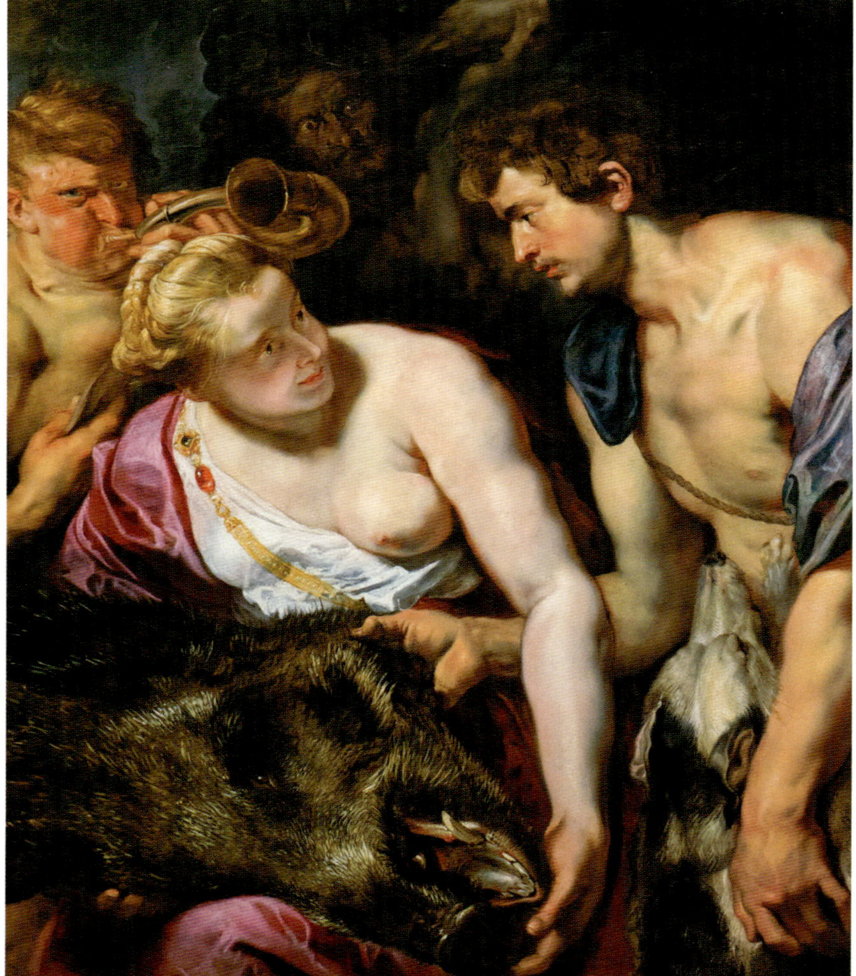

Atalanta and Meleager,
c.1616, oil on wood, 133.4 x
106.7cm (52½ x 42in),
The Metropolitan Museum
of Art, New York, USA

From Ovid's *Metamorphoses*,
a king's son, Meleager, killed a
wild boar that ravaged the
countryside, and presented its
head to the huntress Atalanta,
whom he loved. Atalanta
turns to thank Meleager, who
has one hand on the boar's
head and another on his dog,
as he gazes adoringly into her
eyes. This part of the story
is presented by Rubens in
compelling close-up.

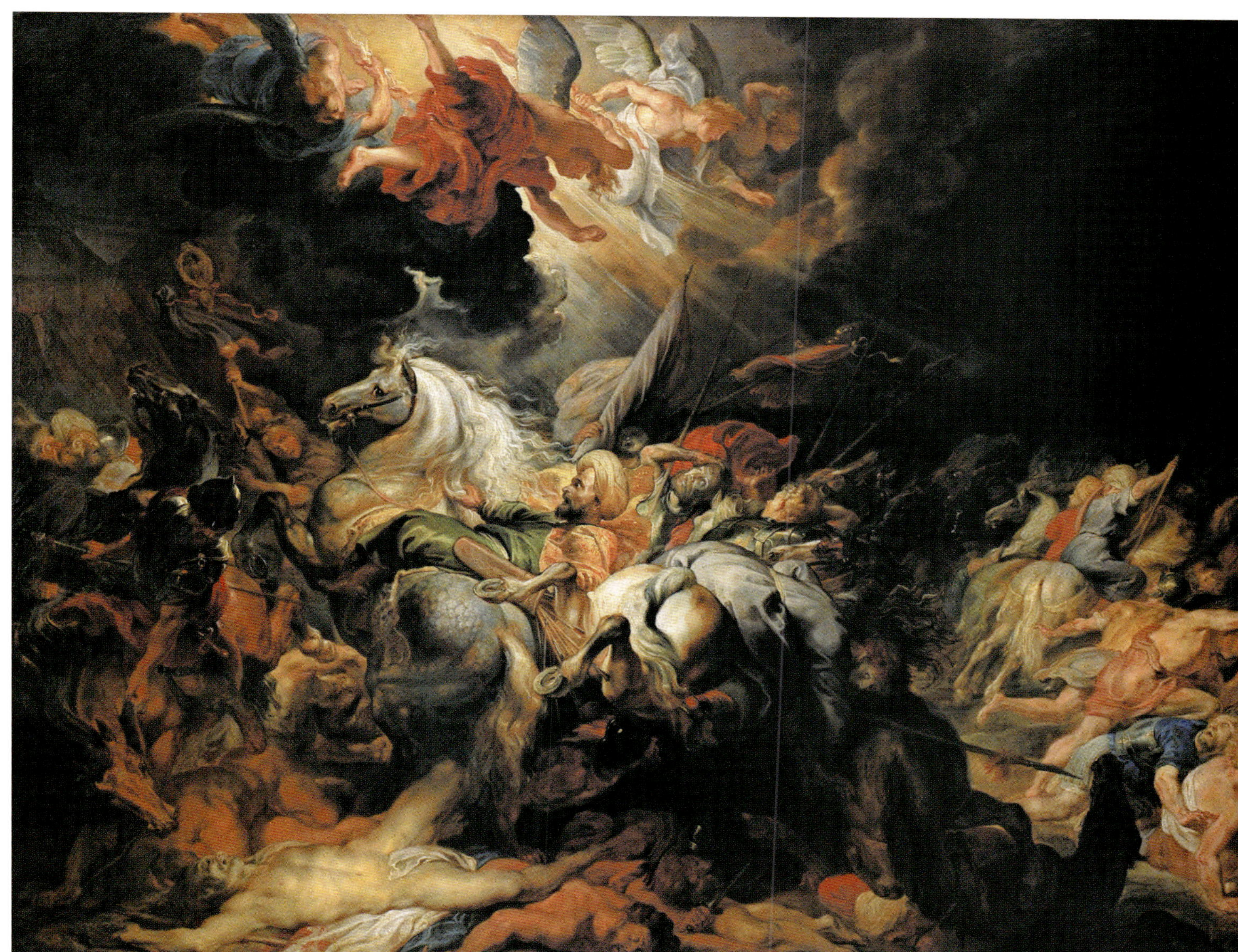

Defeat of Sennacherib, 1612–14, oil on panel, 98 x 123cm (38⅖ x 48⅓in), Alte Pinakothek, Munich, Germany

This tells the story of King Sennacherib, whose Assyrian warriors conquered all the cities of Judah and then attacked the holy city of Jerusalem, but that city was assisted by the angel of the Lord. The painting shows the Assyrian king riding across the country with the leaders of his army, when suddenly a ray of light flashes from the darkness, and four angels with thunder bolts appear in the sky. Under the fear of the angels, the Assyrian army takes flight, Sennacherib's horse rears, and the other horses scatter in terror. On the ground, the dead and wounded are trampled in the panic-stricken chaos. The dramatic effects of light add to the powerful impression of confusion and disarray. Rubens painted this violent image as a pendant to the equally unnerving *Conversion of Saint Paul.*

The Last Judgement, 1615,
oil on panel, 81 × 54cm
(32 × 21¼in), Musée des
Beaux-Arts, Pau, France

In this disturbing religious
scene, Rubens worked in an
unusually coloured grisaille –
brown rather than grey. It is
a powerful Christian image
of the final and eternal
judgement by God of all
humanity. Painted at the
same time as his violent
hunting scenes, the painting
is filled with writhing,
contorted, naked bodies,
male and female, tangled
and intertwined.

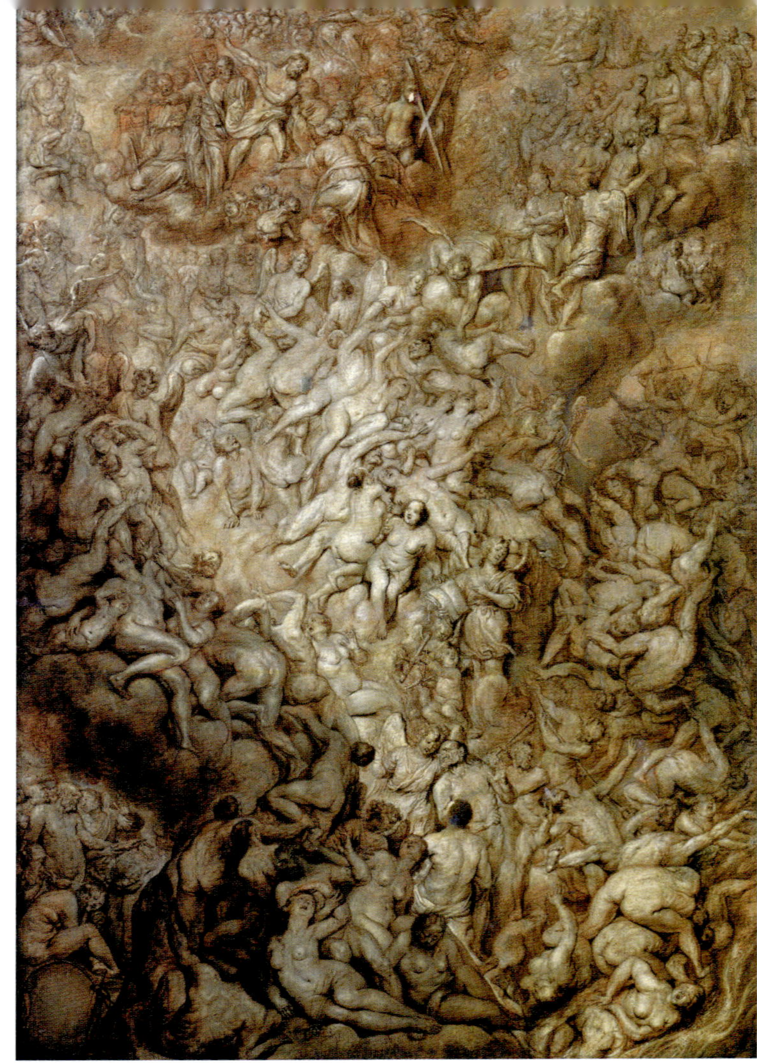

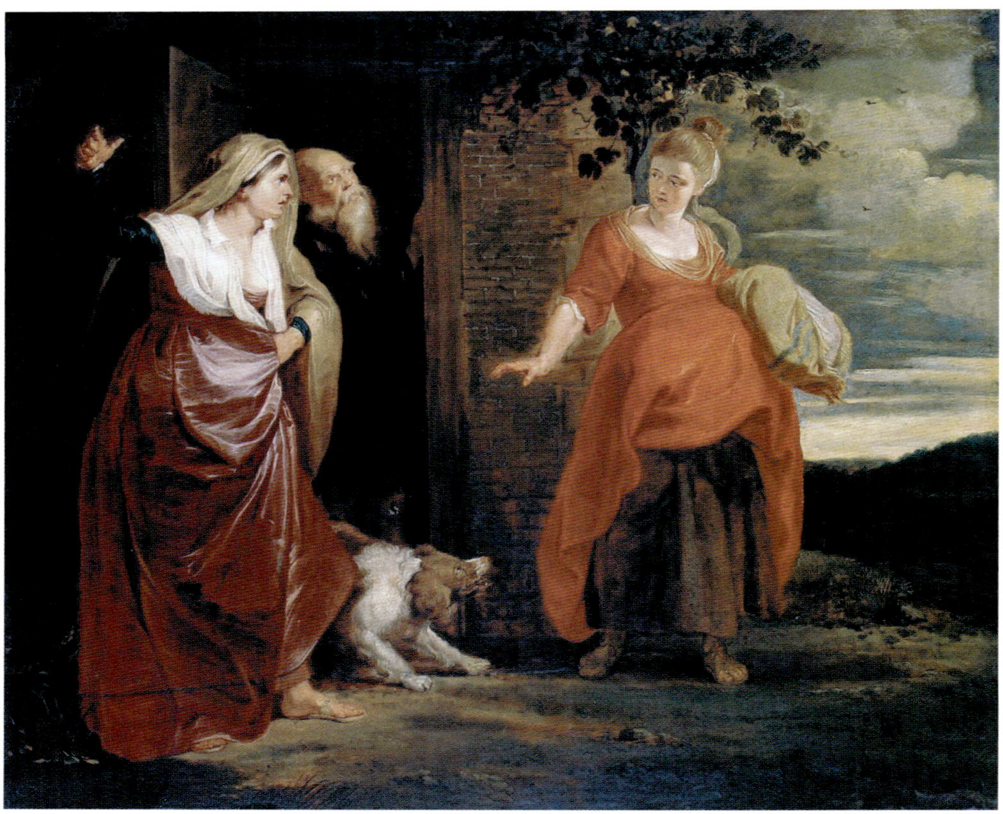

*Hagar Leaves the House
of Abraham*, 1615–17,
oil on panel, 62.8 × 76cm
(24¾ × 30in), The State
Hermitage Museum,
St Petersburg, Russia

In the biblical story, Abraham
and Sarah could not have
children of their own,
so Sarah suggested that
Abraham tried for a child
with Hagar, their Egyptian
maid. Once Hagar became
pregnant, however, Sarah
thought the maid looked
contemptuously at her
mistress. So she and
Abraham dismissed the
maid and sent her away.
Rubens shows Hagar
looking proud as she leaves,
Sarah watching angrily, and
Abraham also looking on.

Resurrection, c.1615–16, oil on canvas, 183 x 155cm (72 x 61in), Palatina Gallery, Pitti Palace, Florence, Italy

Here, Rubens celebrates Christ's victory over death. Rising from the tomb, Christ discards his shroud. It is taken by the angel in red just behind him, while on the left-hand side two angels, or putti, carry away his crown of thorns. The tomb itself is covered with sheaves of wheat that symbolize the bread of the Eucharist. Looking directly at viewers, Christ's eyes suggest that his Resurrection enables their redemption.

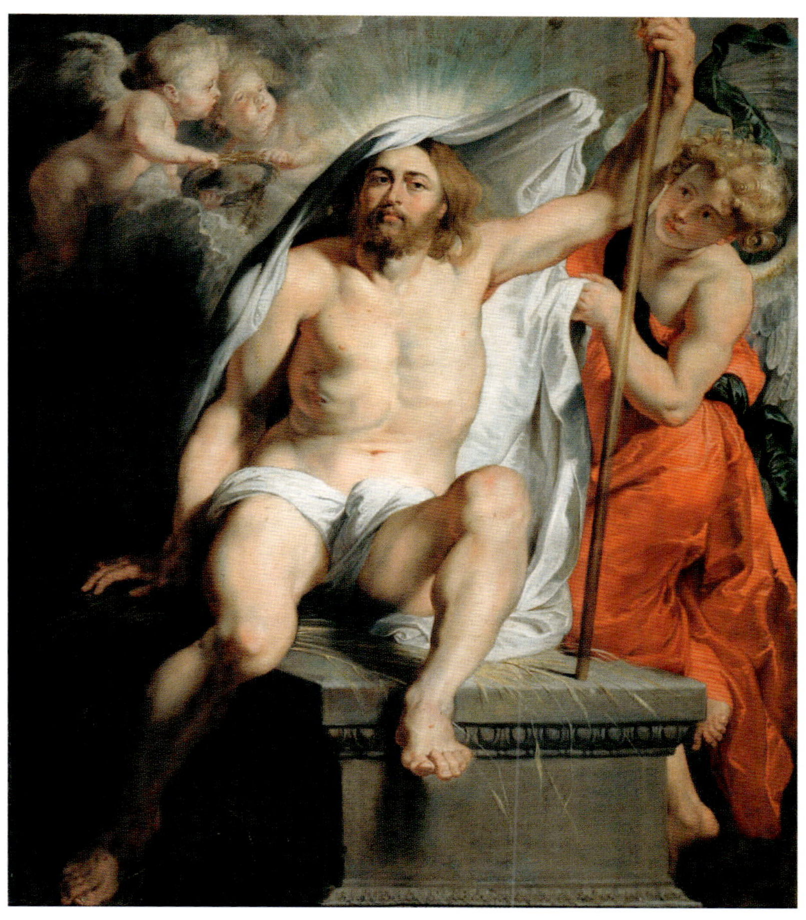

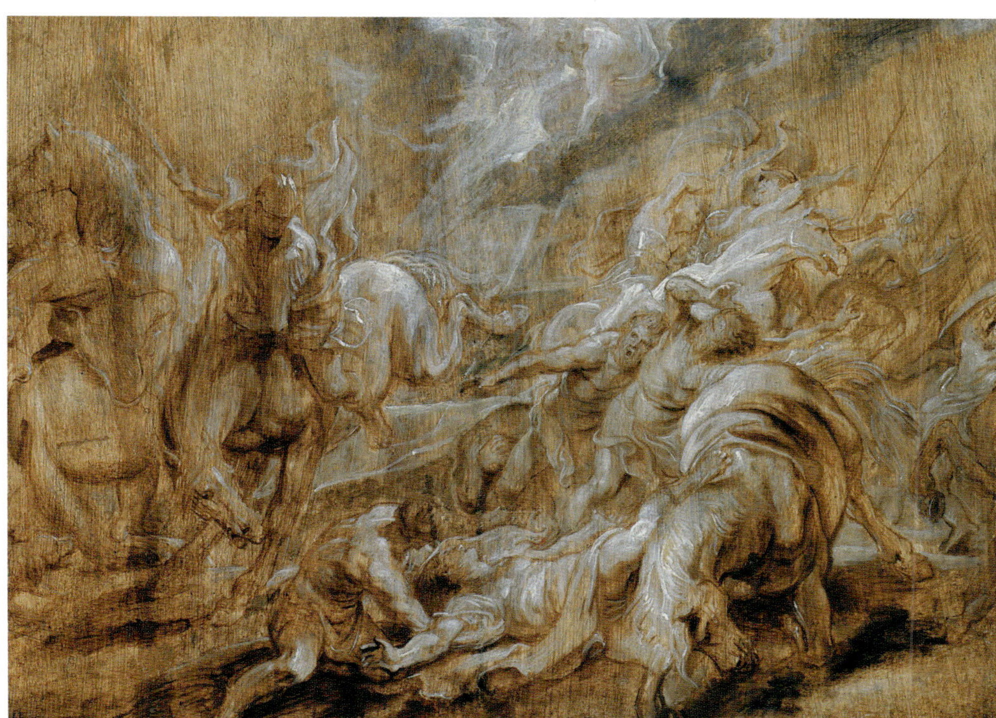

The Conversion of Saint Paul, 1616–20, oil on panel, 72 x 103cm (28⅓ x 40½in), Ashmolean Museum, University of Oxford, UK

In the Bible, Saul was a Roman Jew, and a fervent persecutor of Christians. Travelling to Damascus, he was blinded by a Heavenly light, and God's voice asked him why he was persecuting Christians. Subsequently, he converted to Christianity, and with Peter became seen as one of the founders of the Christian Church. This study for a large canvas formerly in Berlin (destroyed in 1945) is in brown monochrome, with touches of white and colour.

Madonna and Standing Child,
c.1616/18, oil on wood,
62.5 x 49cm (24⅔ x
19¼ in), Lower Saxony
State Museum,
Hanover, Germany

In Roman Catholic art,
depictions of the Virgin
Mary were common, and
this work is devotional
rather than narrative,

intended to help the faithful
concentrate on prayer.
Rubens was particularly
adept at capturing the
Christ Child as both a
mischievous little boy and
a deity. This image, with
the obvious tenderness
between mother and child,
and the little boy standing
on her lap, derives from
similar paintings by Raphael.

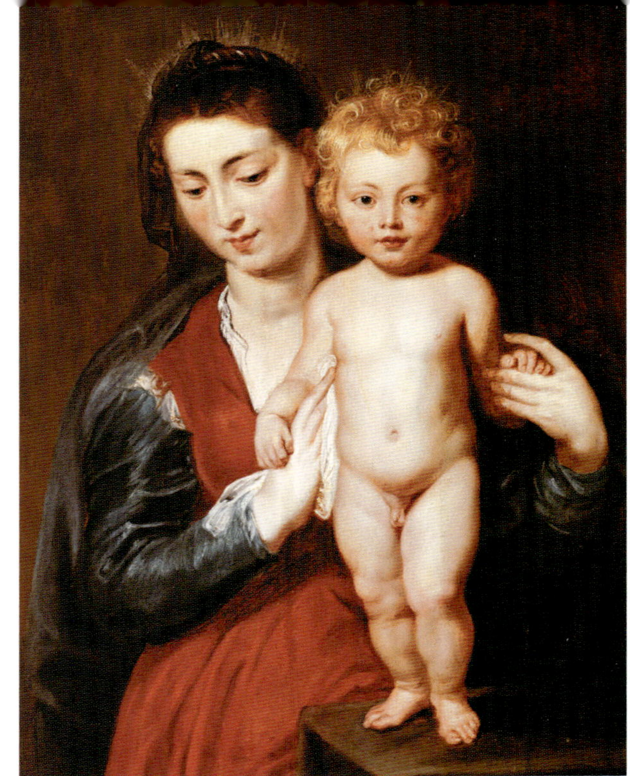

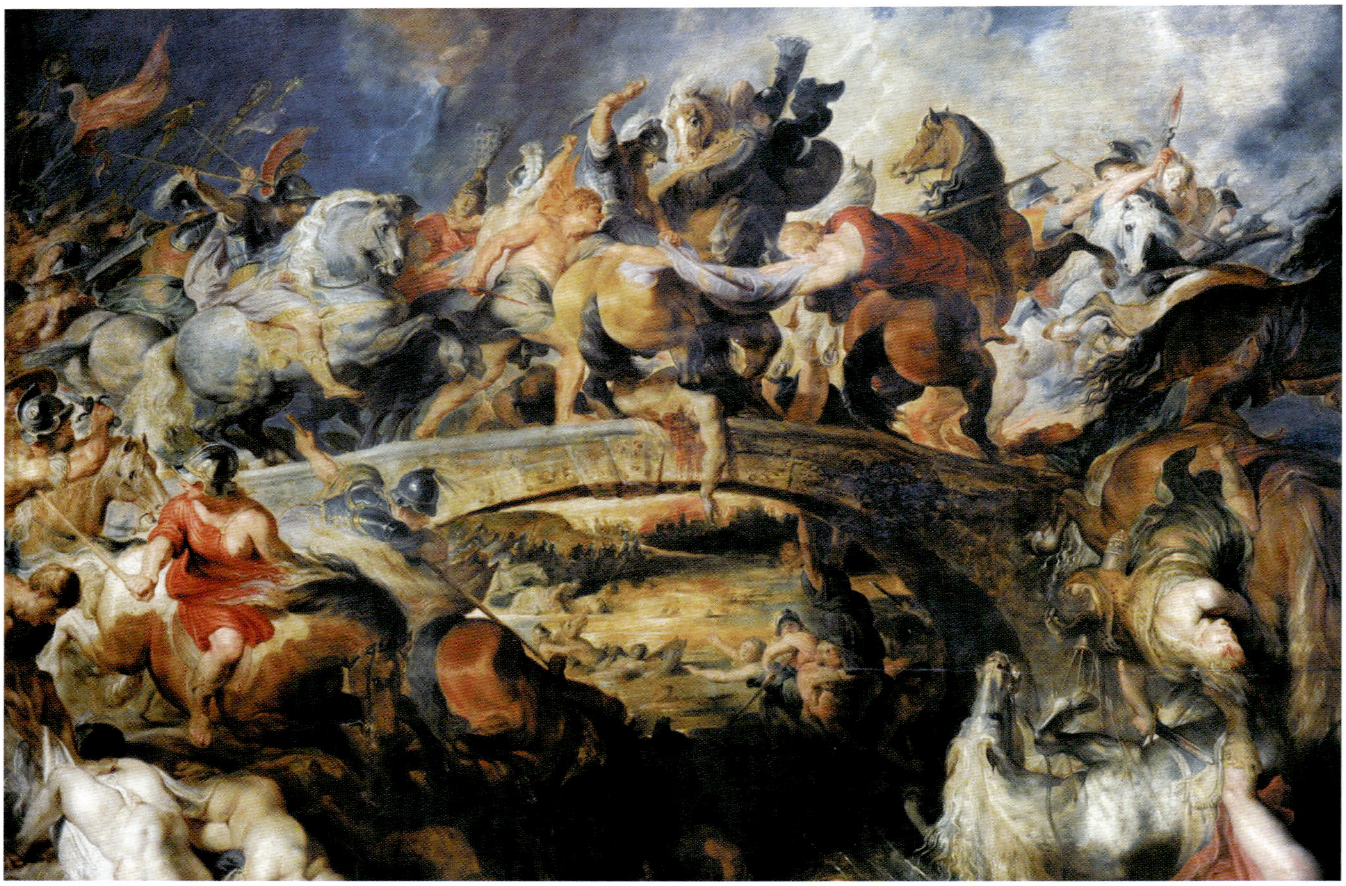

Battle of the Amazons,
1615, oil on wood,
121 x 165.5cm (48 x
65¼ in), Alte Pinakothek,
Munich, Germany

In Greek mythology,
Amazonomachy was a
mythical battle between
the ancient Greeks and the
Amazons, a mythical race
of warrior women in Asia

Minor. The Amazons were
portrayed as a savage and
barbaric race, while the
Greeks were depicted as
civilized. Crowded with
figures, action and incidents,

this work has elements
taken from Leonardo da
Vinci's *Battle of Anghiari*
of 1505, now lost. This
work is full of both furious
energy and exacting detail.

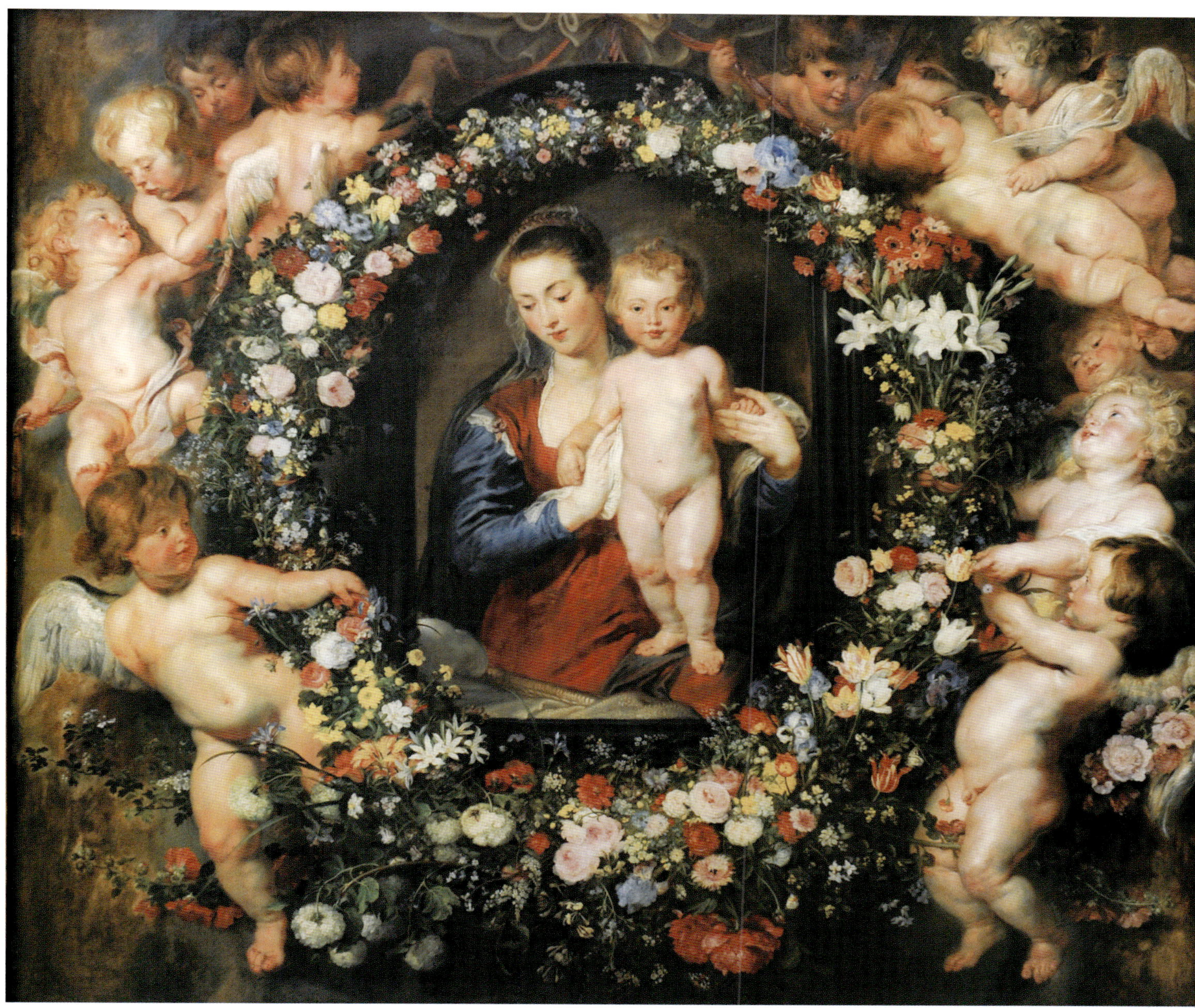

Madonna with a Garland of Flowers, Rubens and Brueghel, 1616–17, oil on oak, 185 x 209.8cm (72¾ x 82½in), Alte Pinakothek, Munich, Germany

One of Rubens's many collaborations with his friend Brueghel (who was nicknamed 'Velvet Brueghel' because of his softly depicted flowers), this painting is also known as *Virgin and Child in a Flower Garden with Angels*.

It was a common type of devotional image during the Counter-Reformation, as it encouraged private contemplation, and it blends decoration with religious symbolism. Veneration of the Virgin Mary was a central element of the Catholic Church. Possibly painted for George Villiers, the Duke of Buckingham, the Virgin, Child and winged cherubs were painted by Rubens, while Brueghel painted the flower garland.

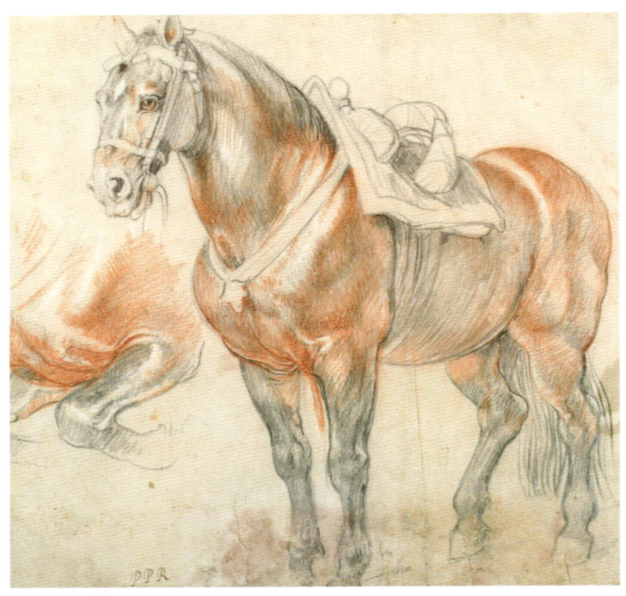

Saddled Horse, c.1615–18, black and red chalk heightened with white chalk, 41.3 x 42.8cm (16¼ x 17in), Albertina, Vienna, Austria

Rubens drew avidly and for many purposes. His first planning for a commission usually began with a rapid sketch, often in pen and brown ink and wash. These were his first thoughts or *primi pensieri*. His next stage was to prepare a coloured and detailed modello or oil sketch to be shown to the customer. Finally, he would work out close details by making detailed individual drawings, often with chalk, and using models. This image of a horse is one of the last – subtle, delicate and strong.

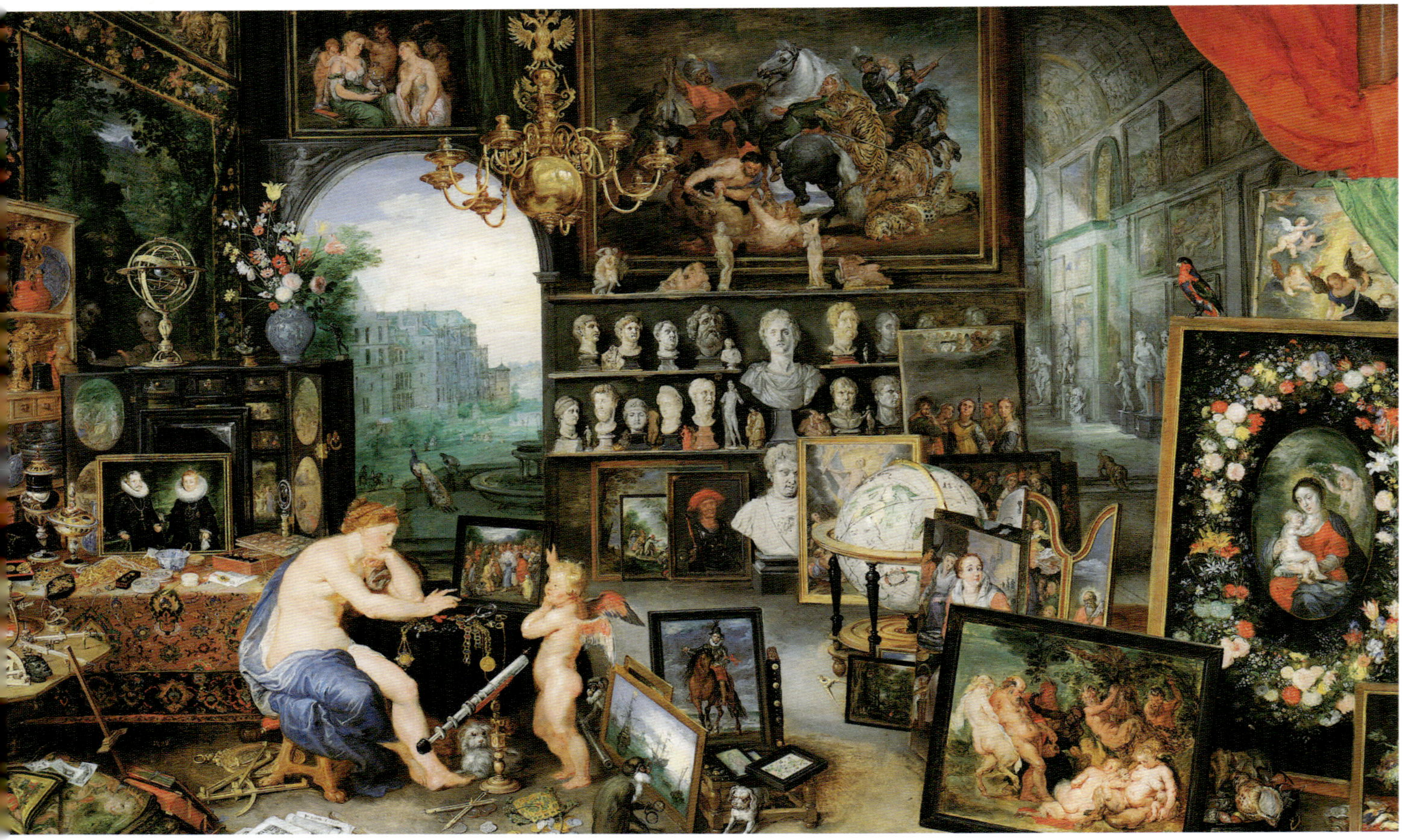

The Sense of Sight, Rubens and Brueghel, 1617, oil on panel, 65 x 109cm (25½ x 43in), Museo Nacional del Prado, Madrid, Spain

The Five Senses is a set of allegorical paintings by Rubens and Brueghel the Elder. The representation of the five senses as female figures started in the previous century. Here, the female figure contemplates a painting of Christ restoring the sight of a blind man. Saint Cecilia, the patron of eyesight, is present. This was probably commissioned by Albert and Isabella, as several details allude to them.

Taste, Rubens and Brueghel, 1618, oil on panel, 64 x 110cm (25½ x 43⅓in), Museo Nacional del Prado, Madrid, Spain
This is one of five allegorical paintings of the five senses: Sight, Hearing, Smell, Taste and Touch, and it was one of the most successful collaborations of Rubens and Brueghel the Elder. Rubens's figures appear in Brueghel's courtly scenes. A satyr pours nectar of the gods into a goblet held by a nymph leaning on a table of food. The garland and the three paintings in the background have Christian connotations.

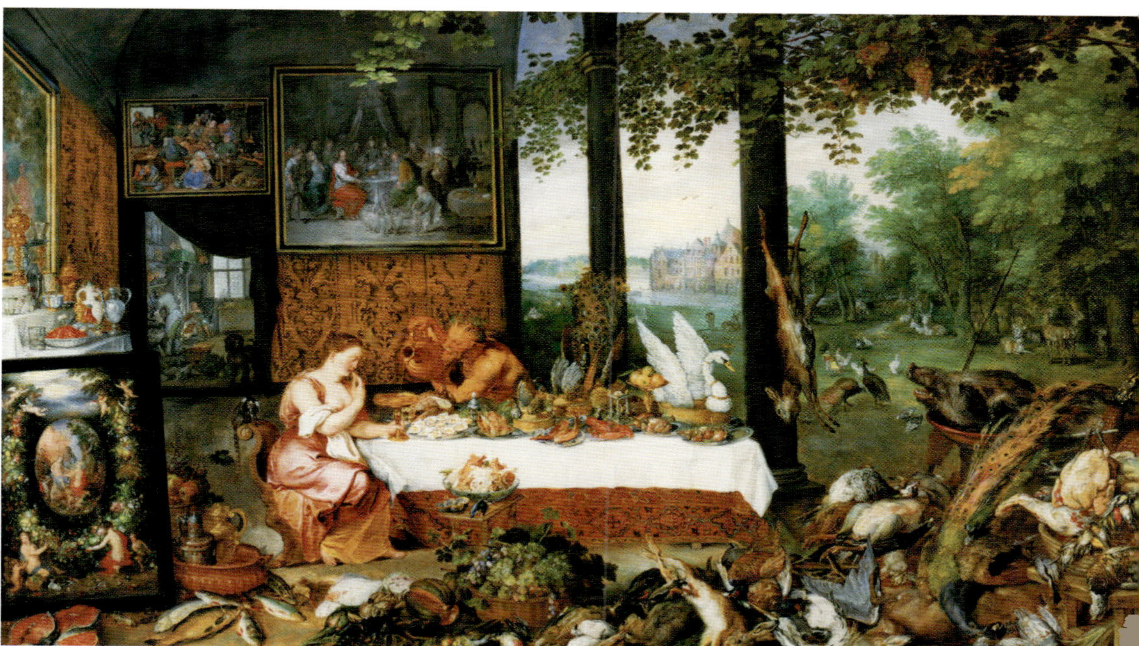

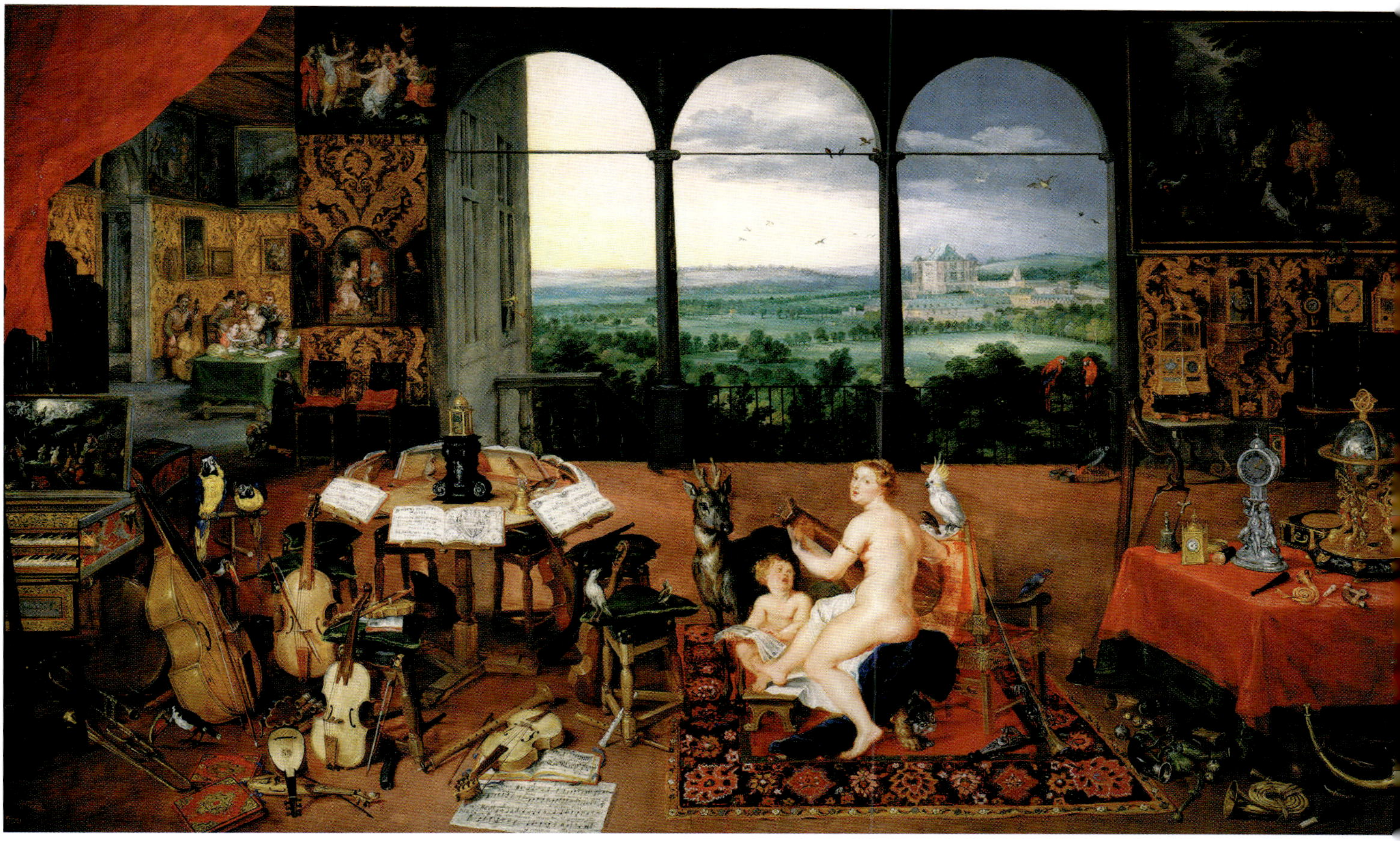

Hearing, Rubens and Brueghel, 1617–18, oil on panel, 65 x 107cm (25½ x 42in), Museo Nacional del Prado, Madrid, Spain

In this allegory of hearing, music is referred to in a madrigal dedicated to Albert and Isabella. The work belongs to a set of five paintings depicting allegories of the senses. Amid many references to hearing, Venus plays the lyre and sings, accompanied by Cupid.

Musical instruments fill the composition, including clavichord, drum, trumpet, trombone, pipe, bell, cornetto, flutes and violas.

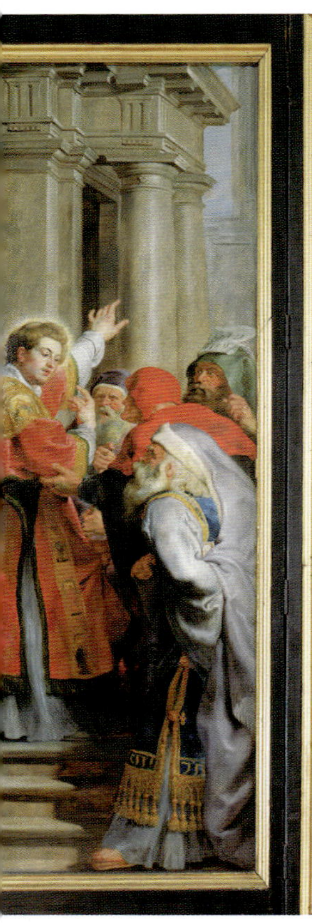
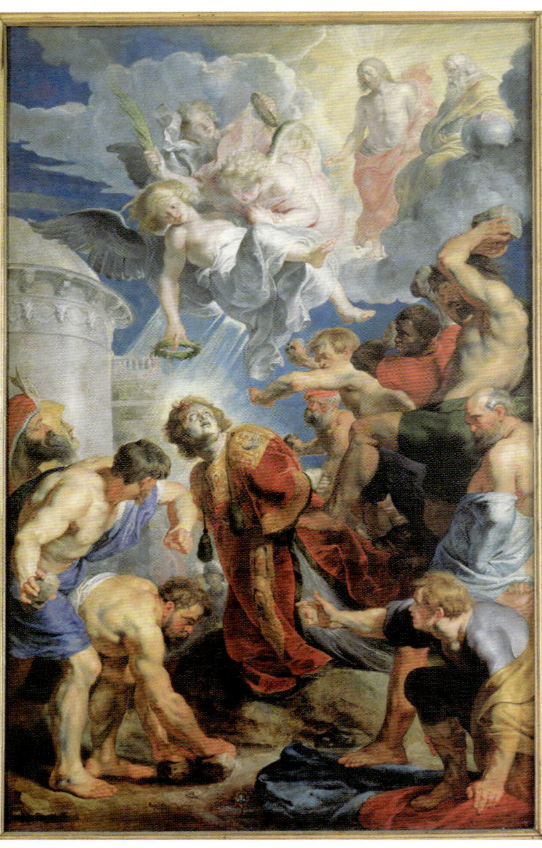
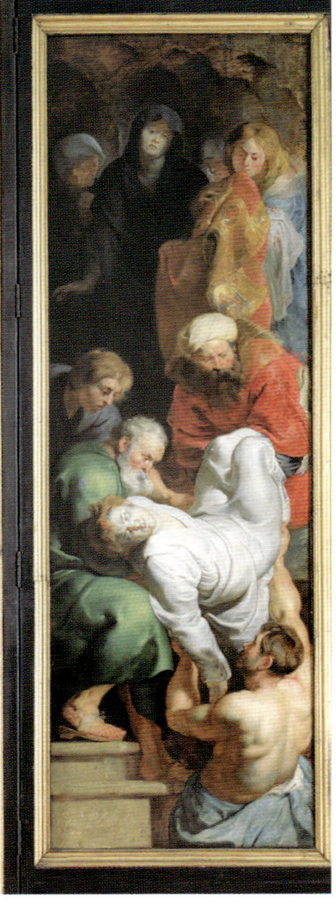

*The Martyrdom of Saint Stephen, c.*1617, oil on canvas (centre), oil on panel (sides), centre: 437 × 278cm (172 × 109⅛in), side panels: 228.6 × 71cm (90 × 28in), Musée des Beaux-Arts, Valenciennes, France

This triptych was commissioned by the rich Benedictine Abbey Saint-Amand, near Valenciennes. The open panels show powerful depictions of the martyrdom of Saint Stephen, as well as scenes from his life, including angels bringing him a martyr's crown and palm branch as he is stoned to death. When the triptych is closed, an Annunciation can be seen on the back and side panels (see below).

*The Annunciation, c.*1617, oil on panel, 228.6 × 71cm (90 × 28in), Musée des Beaux-Arts, Valenciennes, France

From the reverse of the triptych of *The Martyrdom of Saint Stephen* (above), this Annunciation scene is on view when the triptych is closed. It represents the Virgin Mary as a demure, lavishly dressed contemporary young woman, with the Angel Gabriel descending on her with zest and grace. She is surrounded by putti, who are witnesses to the momentous news the angel is giving her.

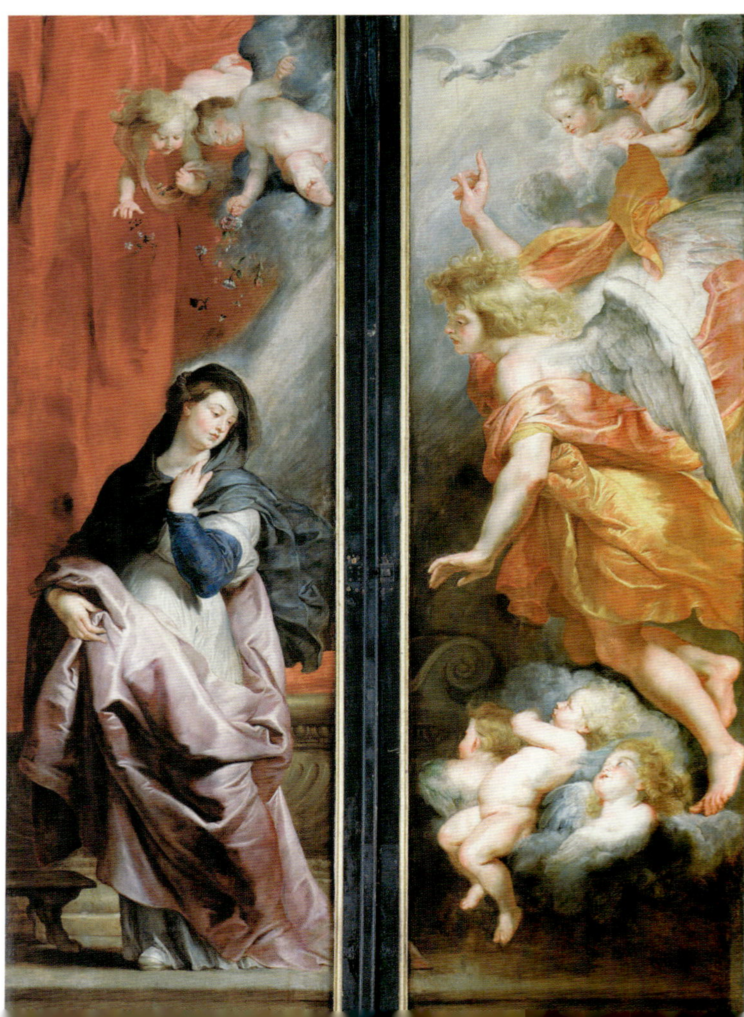

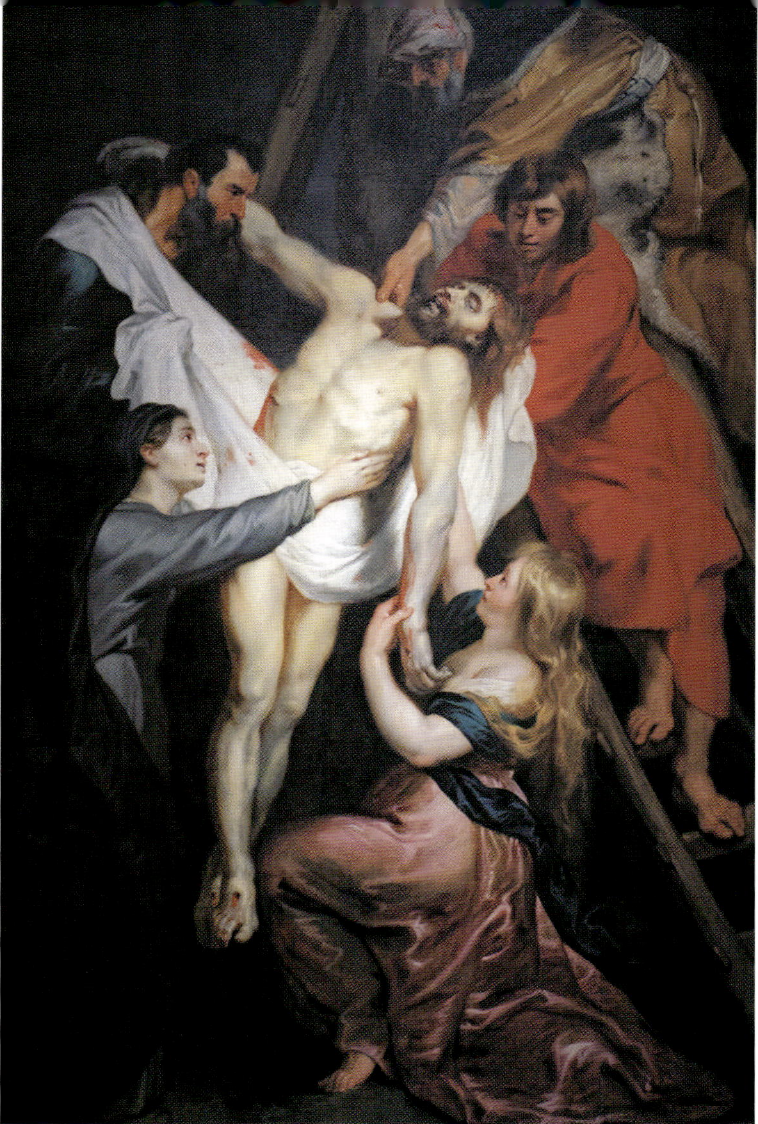

Descent from the Cross, 1617–18, oil on canvas, 297 x 200cm (117 x 78¾ in), The State Hermitage Museum, St Petersburg, Russia

After Rubens's success with his *Descent from the Cross* for Antwerp Cathedral in 1612, he was commissioned to produce several more by different churches. This was for the Capuchin church in Lierre, France. In comparison with his earlier, more famous *Descent*, this has fewer figures, while Christ is larger. His friends and family all wear richly coloured garments, drawing viewers' eyes and accentuating Christ's deathly pallor.

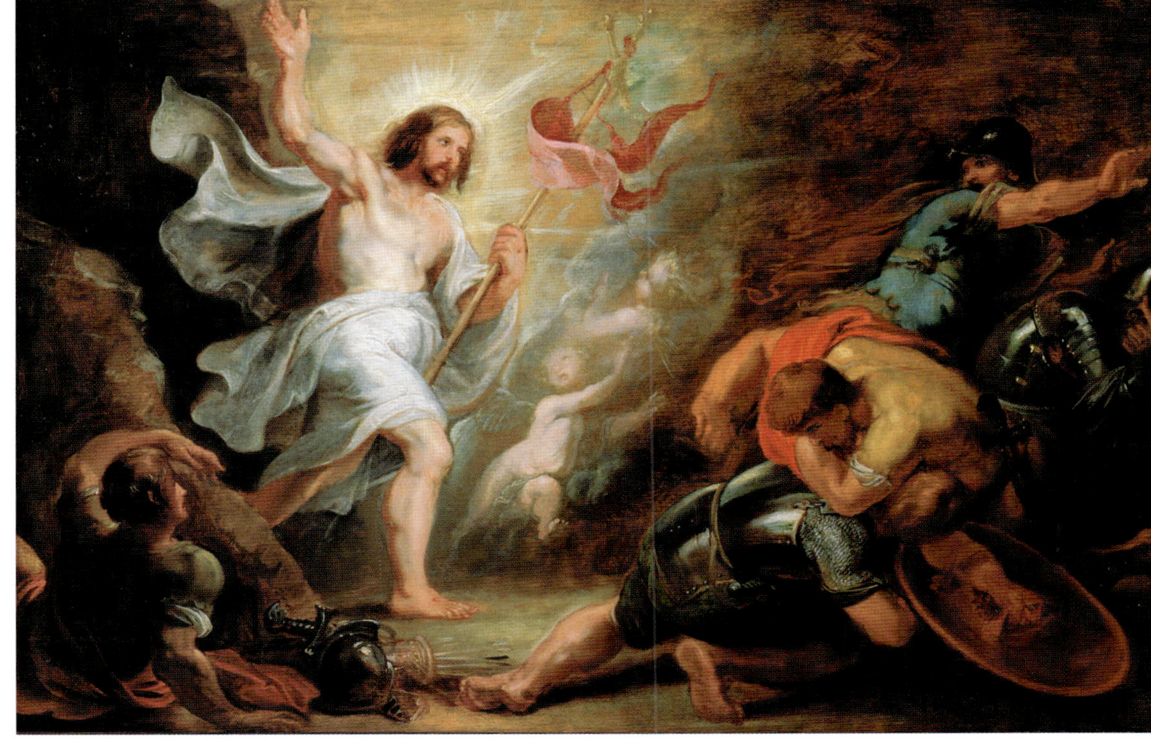

The Resurrection of Christ, c.1617–19, oil on panel, 102 x 67cm (40¼ x 26 in), Musée des Beaux-Arts, Marseille, France

This panel was made for an altarpiece in the Janskerk, or St John's Church, a 15th-century Gothic church in Mechelen, near Antwerp. It represents Christ bursting forth from his tomb, where his body had been laid less than two days before. The guards scramble in terror as Jesus emerges, no longer a corpse, emitting a dazzling holy light and carrying a banner that traditionally represented triumph over death.

The Flagellation of Christ,
1617, oil on panel,
37.4 x 35.1cm (14¾
x 13¾in), Museum
voor Schone Kunsten,
Ghent, Belgium

Rubens made this
modello for a large work
in the Antwerp church
of St Paul, formerly
the church of the
Dominicans. It displays a
strong contrast between
the pale, suffering body
of Christ and his brutal
torturers. The final work
was one of 15 works by
11 artists, including Van
Dyck and Jordaens. The
series is devoted to
the 'Mysteries of the
Rosary' which in the
Catholic religion include
sorrowful, joyful, glorious
and luminous.

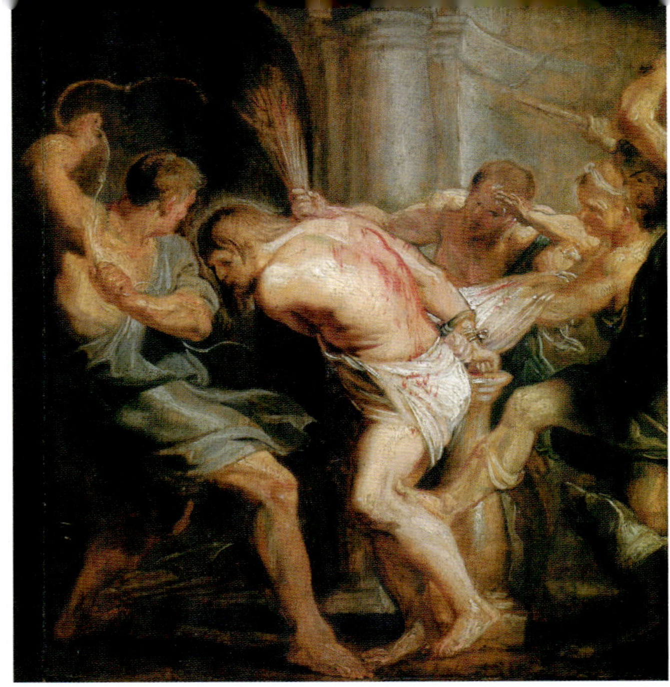

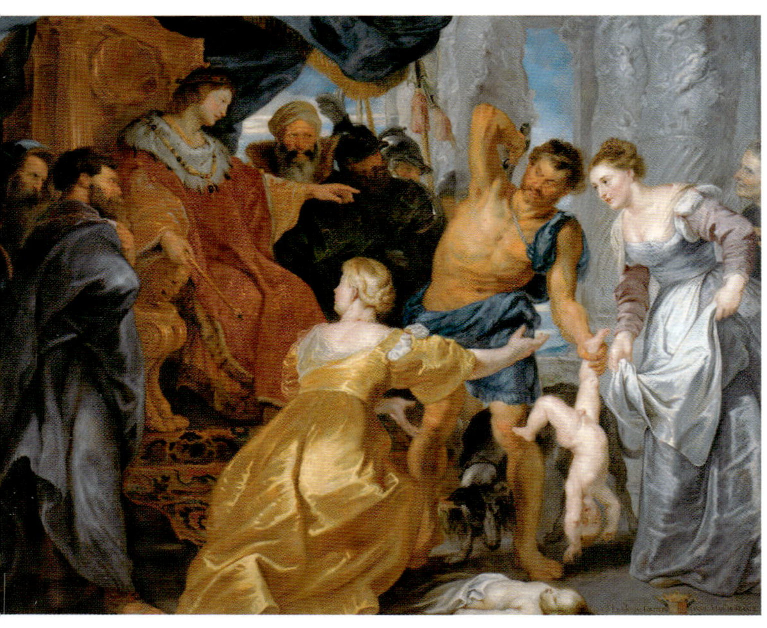

The Judgement of Solomon,
c.1617, oil on canvas, 234 x
303cm (92 x 119¼in),
Statens Museum for Kunst,
Copenhagen, Denmark

In a biblical story of King
Solomon, two women both
claimed that a baby was
their child. So Solomon
ordered it to be cut in
two for the women to share.
Immediately, the true mother
gave up her half to save its life.
The painting is also divided in
two; warm colours include
the true mother's clothes,
Solomon's cloak and throne,
while cold colours include
the executioner's sash, the
false mother's dress, and
columns behind her.

*Saint Francis Holding the Jesus
Child,* 1617, oil on canvas, 234 x
184cm (92 x 72½in), Musée des
Beaux-Arts, Lille, France

As he usually did, Rubens
has depicted the Virgin in
a brilliant vermilion dress. Here
it contrasts with a fairly muted
palette in the rest of the
composition. Traditionally, Mary was
depicted in blue, as ultramarine
pigment was the most expensive
after gold. In Rubens's time,
vermilion had replaced ultramarine
as the most costly pigment.

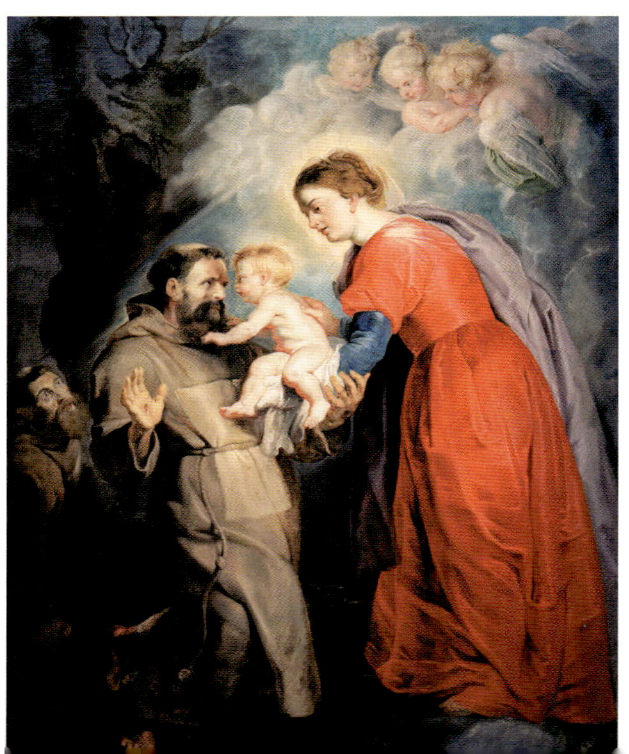

Cimon and Iphigenia, Rubens and Wildens, 1617, oil on canvas, 208 x 282cm (82 x 111in), Kunsthistorisches Museum, Vienna, Austria

As in most of his collaborations, here Rubens planned the composition for this work and painted the figures, while the other artist, Wildens in this case, painted the surrounding landscape. This Greek myth depicts Cimon, the son of a Cypriot lord, who discovered the sleeping Iphigenia when out walking, and instantly fell in love with her. Wildens became related to Rubens through marriage some years later.

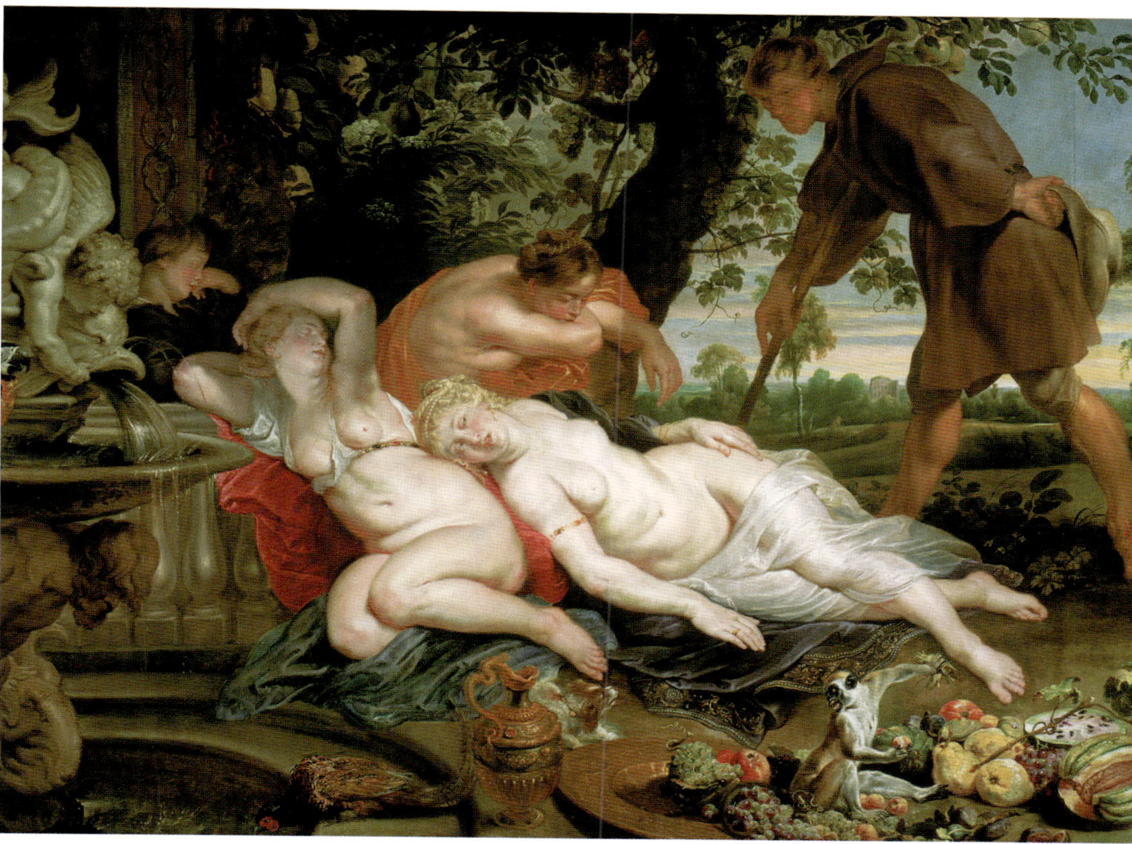

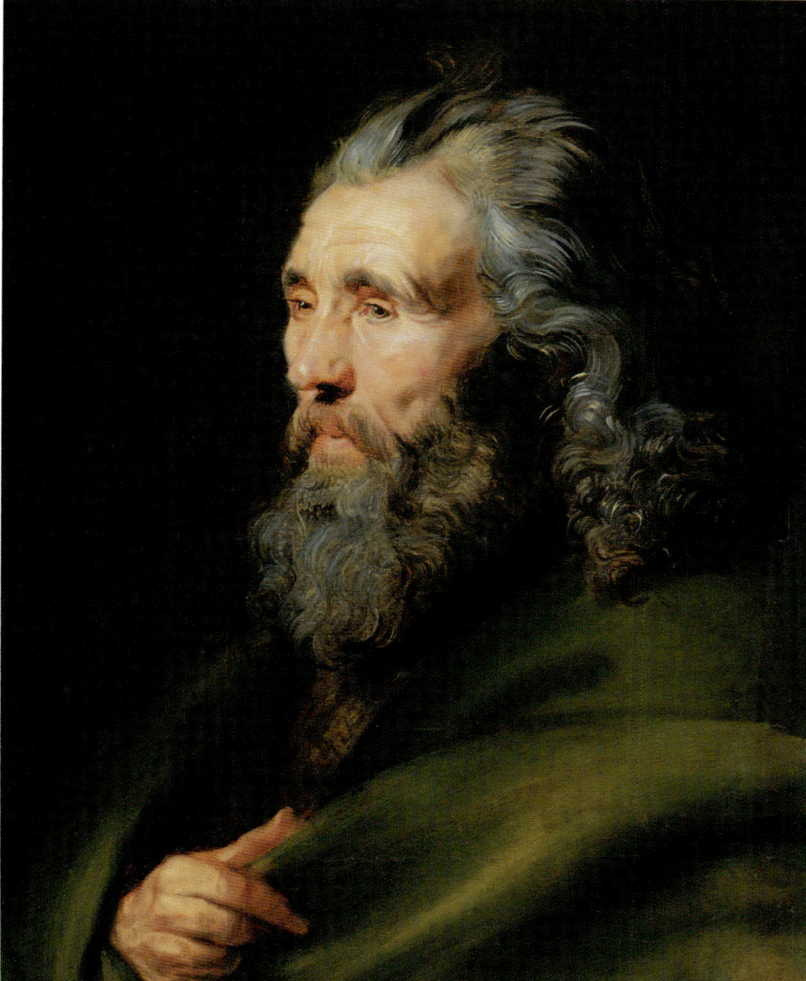

Head Study of a Bearded Man, c.1617, oil on oak, 68.6 x 53.3cm (27 x 21in), Fitzwilliam Museum, University of Cambridge, UK

This is a study for the head of one of Rubens's depictions of the Magi that he made for the Janskerk, or St John's Church, in Mechelen, near Antwerp. It is of Caspar, the oldest Magi, and one of the three 'kings' who visited Mary and Joseph to pay homage to Jesus soon after he was born. Rubens often made detailed yet spontaneous-looking studies from models in his studio.

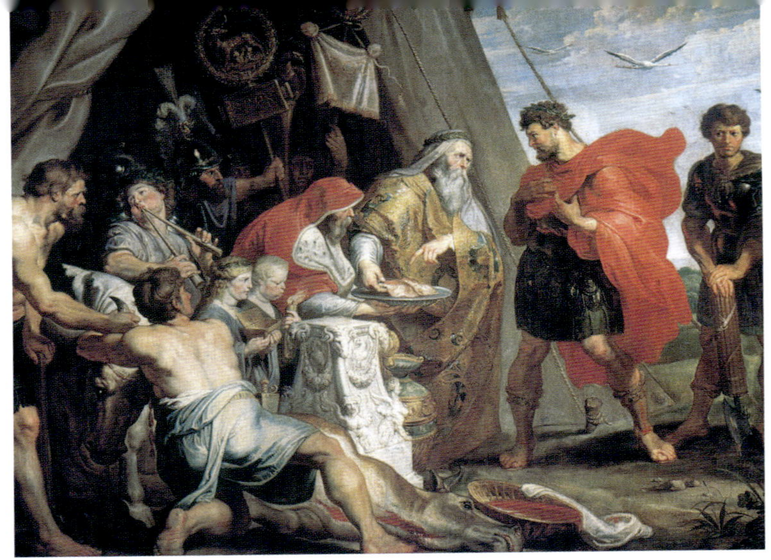

Decius Mus Consulting the Auspices, 1617, oil on panel, 74.6 x 104.1cm (29⅓ x 41in), Oskar Reinhart Art Collection, Winterthur, Switzerland

In one of Rubens's series of eight paintings featuring stories of Decius Mus, here a priest examines the entrails of a sacrificial bull and finds that Decius Mus will have to sacrifice his life to save Rome. The bold colours and painterly brushwork create a lively scene showing the courage of the Roman consul.

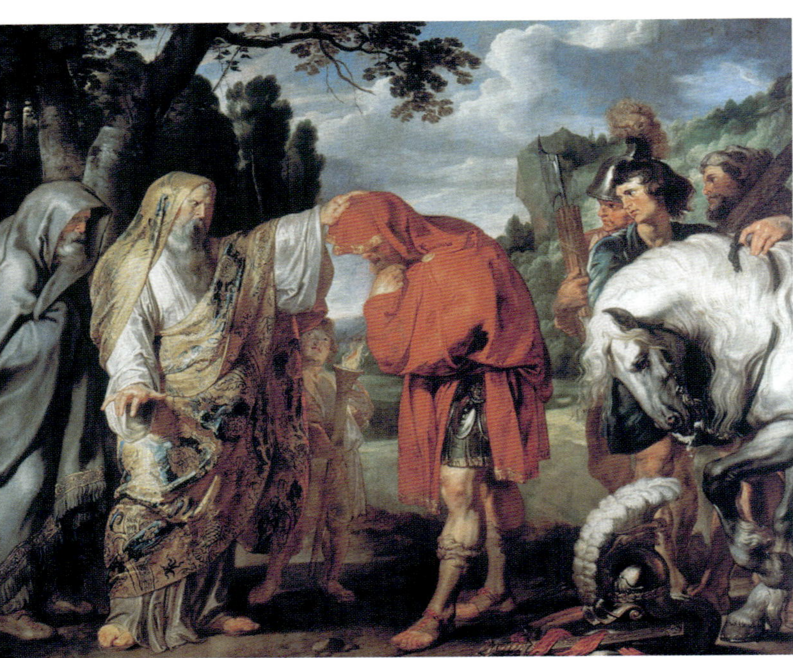

The Consecration of Decius Mus, 1616/17, oil on panel, 284 x 334cm (111⅞ x 131½in), Liechtenstein Museum, Vienna, Austria

Of the four tapestry cycles he designed, Rubens's *Decius Mus* series is the only one for which he completed the monumental cartoons. These were created exactly to scale and colour for the weavers to follow. The first two sets were woven by the Brussels workshop of Jan Raes the Elder, but the series was extremely popular and numerous further sets were produced from Rubens's designs by other manufactories.

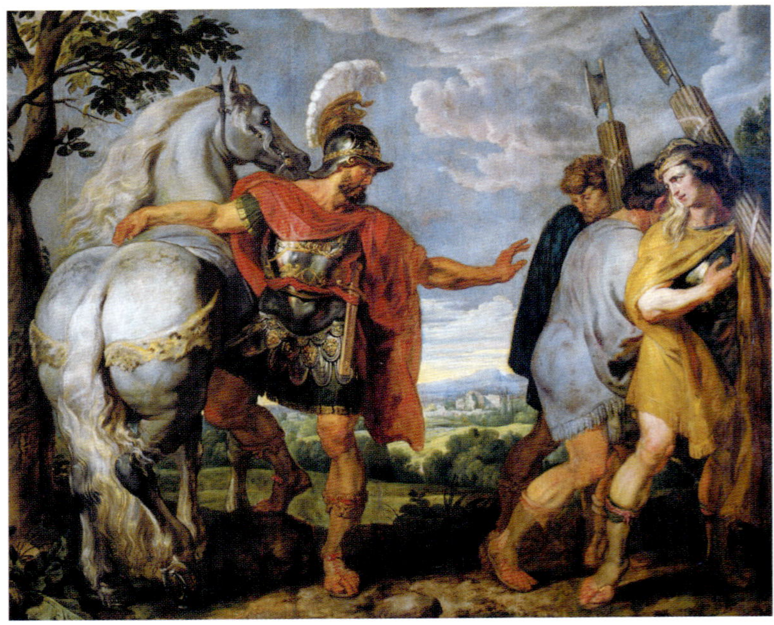

*Decius Mus Dismissal of the Lictors, c.*1617, oil on panel, 284 x 342cm (112 x 134¾in), Liechtenstein Museum, Vienna, Austria

The *Decius Mus* cycle was Rubens's first foray into tapestry design, and one of his earliest ancient Roman history paintings. As a member of a circle of humanists, Rubens was well acquainted with antique thought, literature and art. This is the fourth in a series of eight tapestry designs on the theme of Decius Mus. The work was enlarged by his assistants into the cartoon and sent to weavers in Brussels.

Death of Decius Mus,
1617, oil on panel, 88 x
138cm (34⅔ x 54⅓in),
Liechtenstein Museum,
Vienna, Austria

This is the moment
where Decius Mus is
run through by a lance
in battle, so securing
victory for his country.
His white stallion rears
as he slips off its back in
a graceful movement,
showing the greatness
of the consul as he
falls in sacrificial death.
Rubens here fuses
Christianity and
antiquity in the image as
a divine light shines on
the hero, as it did upon
Saul in the Bible. This
was entirely acceptable
to the Catholic Church
at that time.

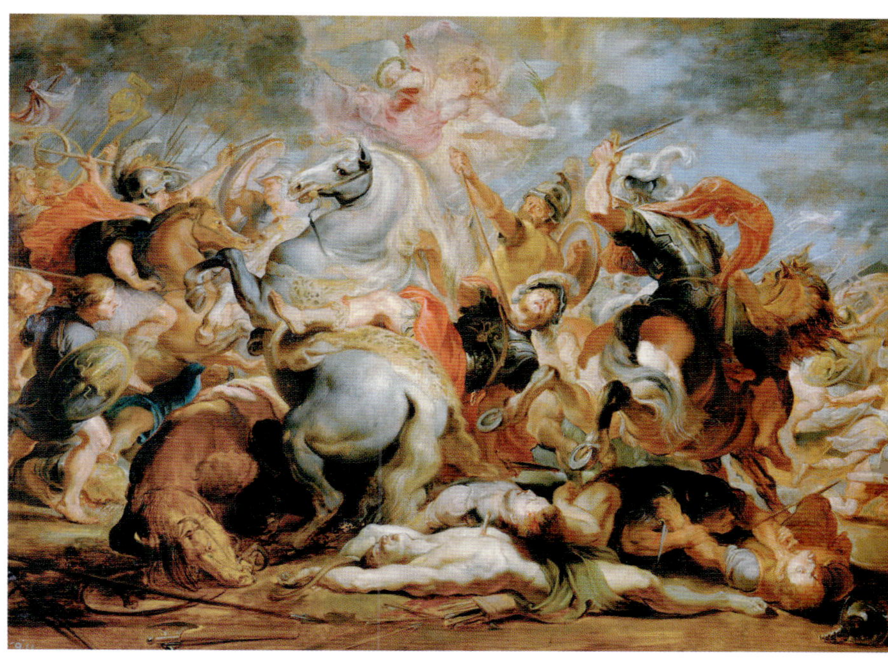

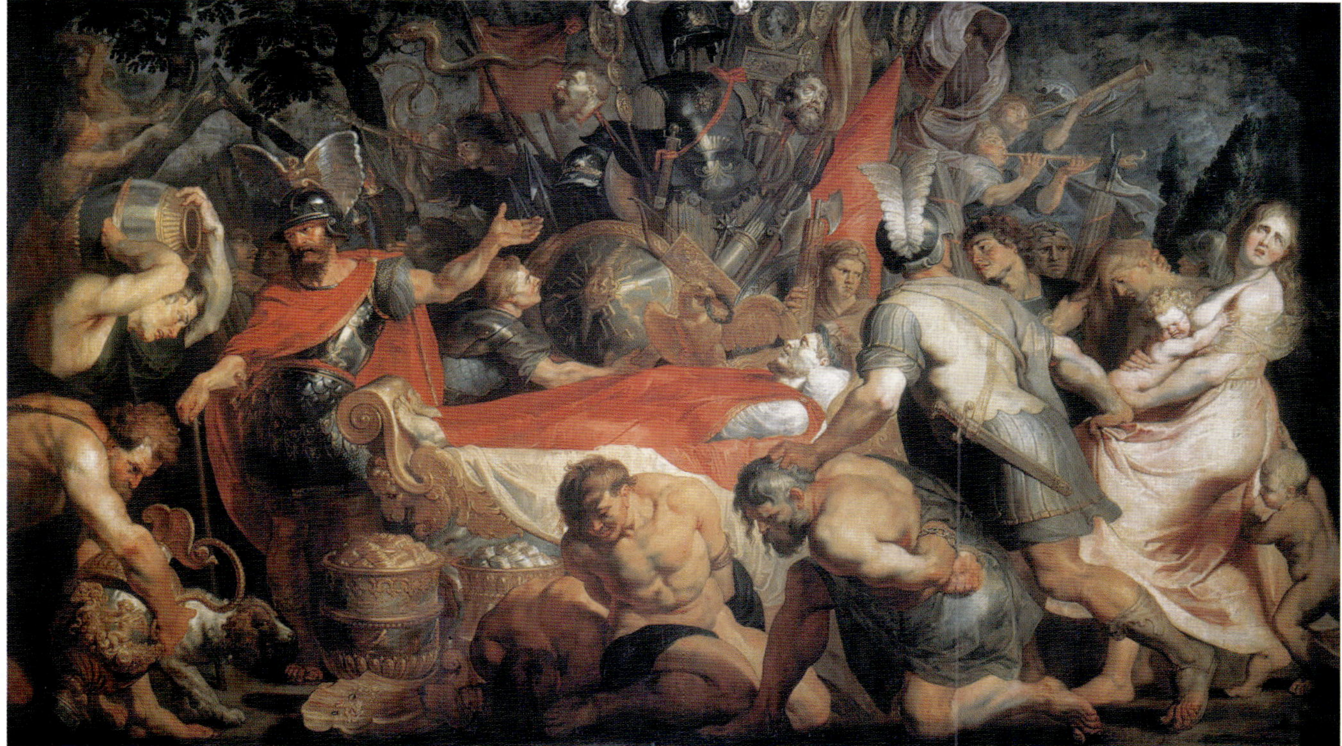

The Funeral of Decius Mus,
1616–17, oil on panel,
288 x 519cm (113⅓ x
204⅓in), Liechtenstein
Museum, Vienna, Austria

In a red toga, the body
of Decius Mus lies in the
centre of an ornately carved
and gilded couch. The
figures' poses derive from
an ancient Greek relief.
Rubens deliberately created
an emotionally charged
scene, with activity
surrounding the motionless
corpse of Decius Mus. This
was one of his cartoons,
and broke new ground in
tapestry design by its vigour
and complex design.

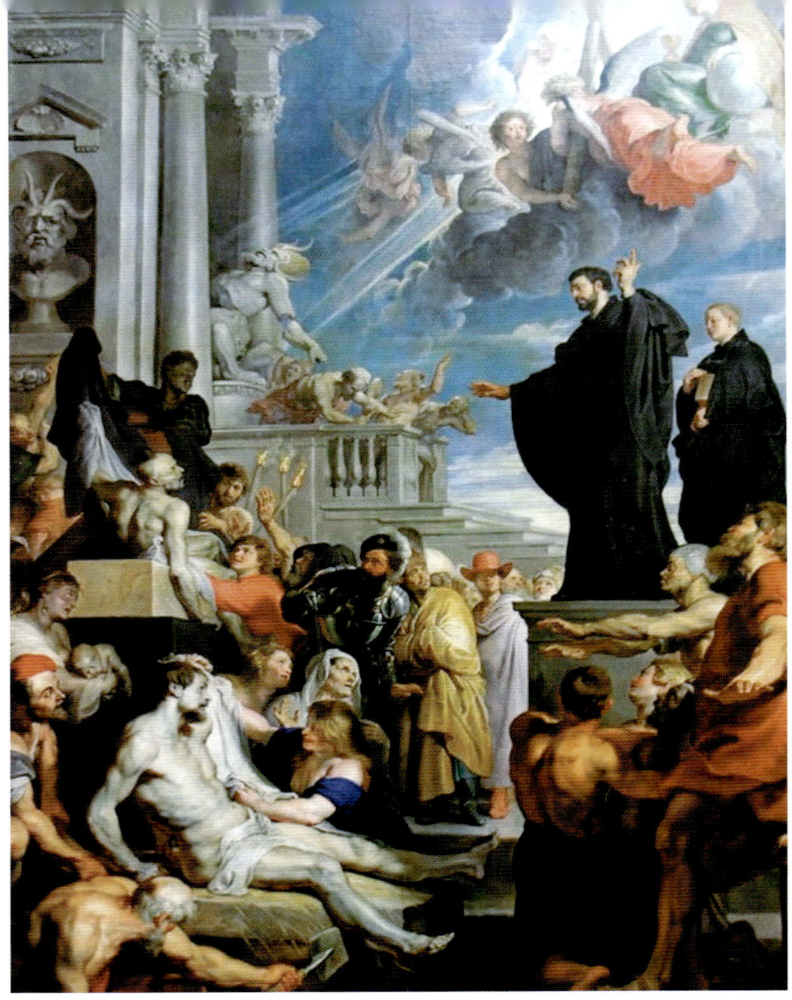

The Miracles of Saint Francis Xavier, 1617–18, oil on canvas, 535 x 395cm (210⅔ x 155½in), Kunsthistorisches Museum, Vienna, Austria

Painted for the Jesuit church in Antwerp, Rubens depicts a Hindu idol that is being destroyed by rays of light emanating from an allegory of the Catholic faith. The idol plays an important role in the full decorative scheme of the Jesuit church designed by Rubens, and it includes several other images of the destruction of idols by early Christian saints, such as Saint Eugenia and Saint John Chrysostom.

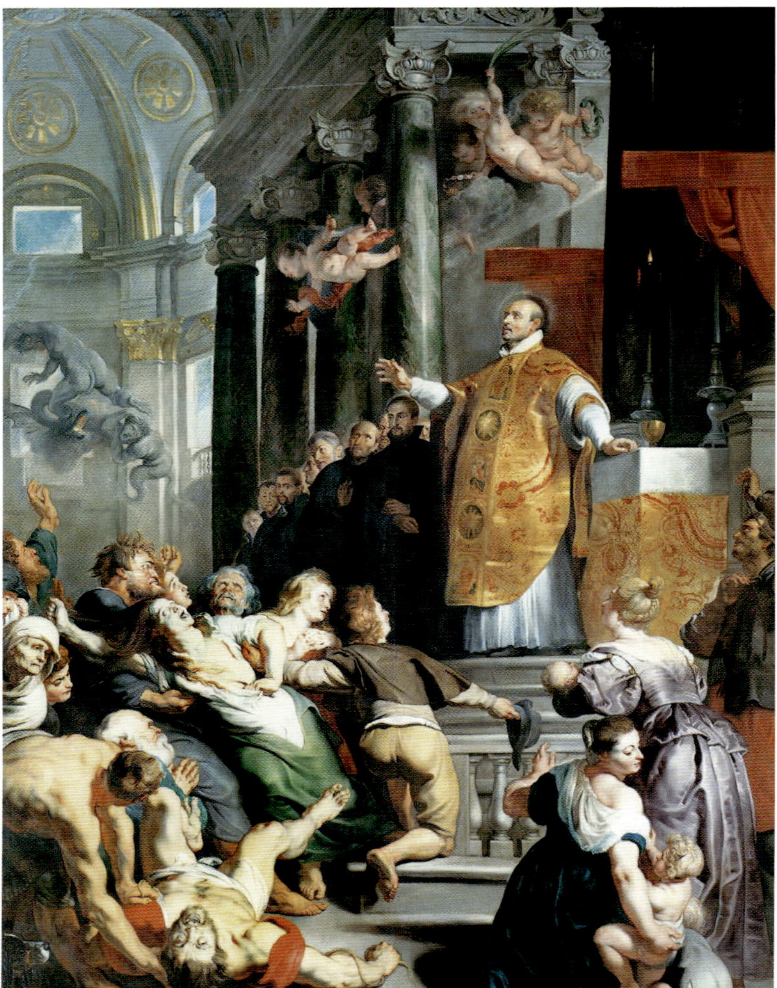

The Miracles of Saint Ignatius of Loyola, c.1617/18, oil on oak, 535 x 395cm (210⅔ x 155½in), Kunsthistorisches Museum, Vienna, Austria

This altarpiece alternated with *The Miracles of Saint Francis Xavier* (above) in the Jesuit church at Antwerp. Rubens was in charge of the whole decorative scheme of the church, and here combined different scenes from the life of the founder of the Society of Jesus. Saint Francis and Saint Ignatius were connected with the Jesuit order, but at that time they had not yet been canonized, and Rubens's paintings of them served as propaganda.

Return of the Prodigal Son,
*c.*1618, oil on canvas,
107 x 155cm (42⅛ x 61in),
Royal Museum of Fine
Arts, Antwerp, Belgium

This painting was found in
Rubens's own collection after
his death. He painted the
rural scene for his own living
room, so it must have given
him a great deal of pleasure.
The biblical subject in just a
small part of the canvas
serves merely as a vehicle
for the painting of one of
his earliest landscapes, and a
close observation of farming,
which fascinated him.

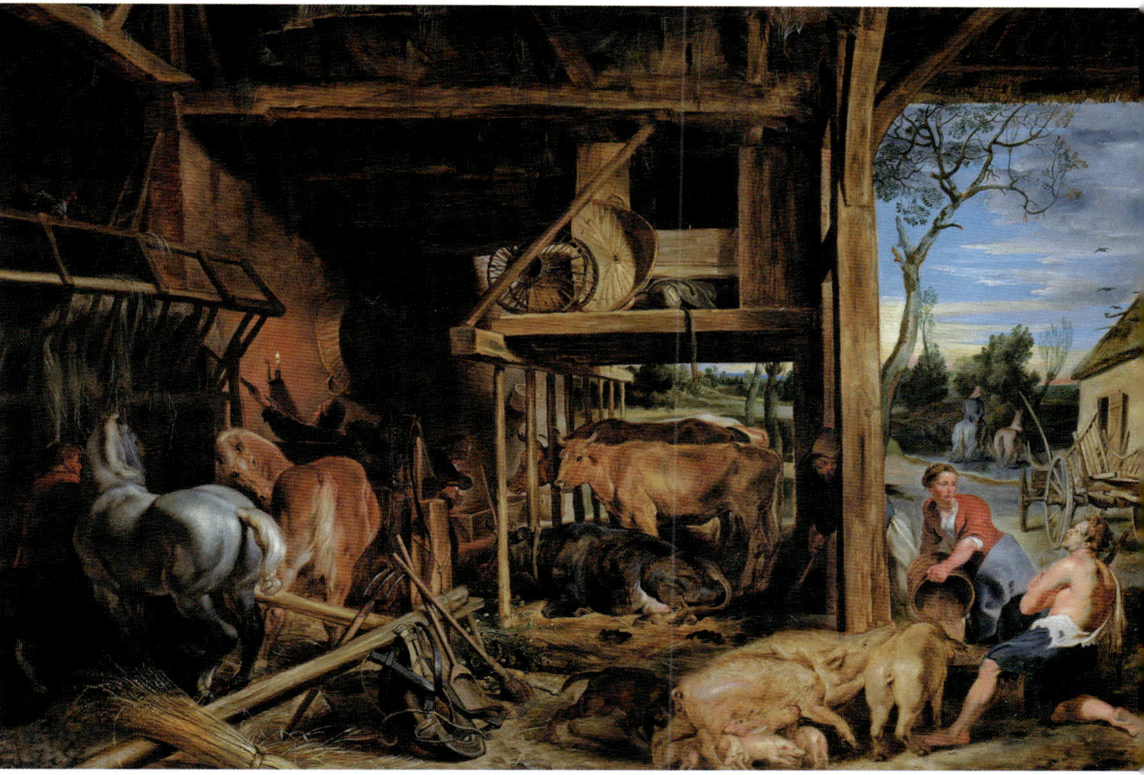

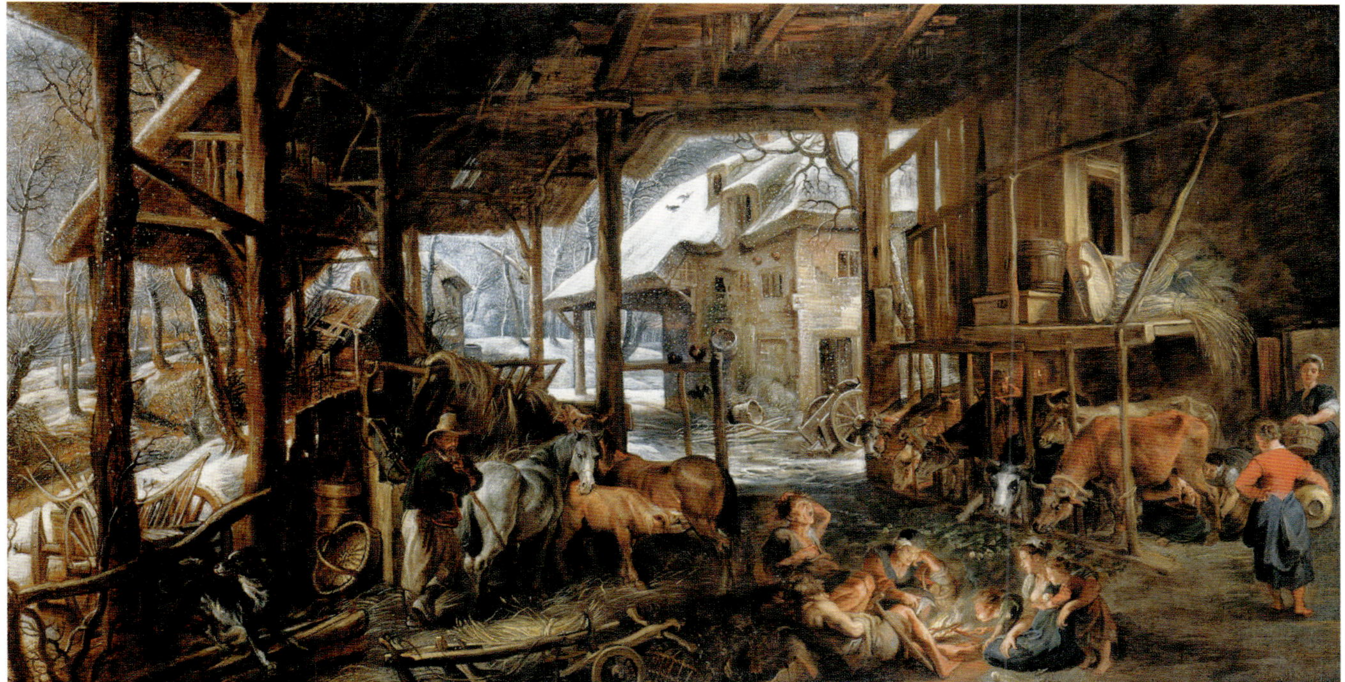

Winter, Interior of a Barn,
1618–19, oil on canvas,
121.4 x 223.1cm
(47¾ x 87¾in), The Royal
Collection, London, UK

This landscape and another
entitled *Summer* were a pair
in the Duke of Buckingham's
collection, but Rubens
painted them for himself
because he enjoyed painting
landscapes, was interested in
farming, and also seems to
have been exploring ideas
for religious works. This has
great resemblances to *Return
of the Prodigal Son* (above).
For a man who worked all
his life, pleasing others, to
paint a natural view was a
way in which he could relax,
but he was also gathering
information for a nativity or
adoration scene. The personal
details, glowing light and sense
of depth are compelling.

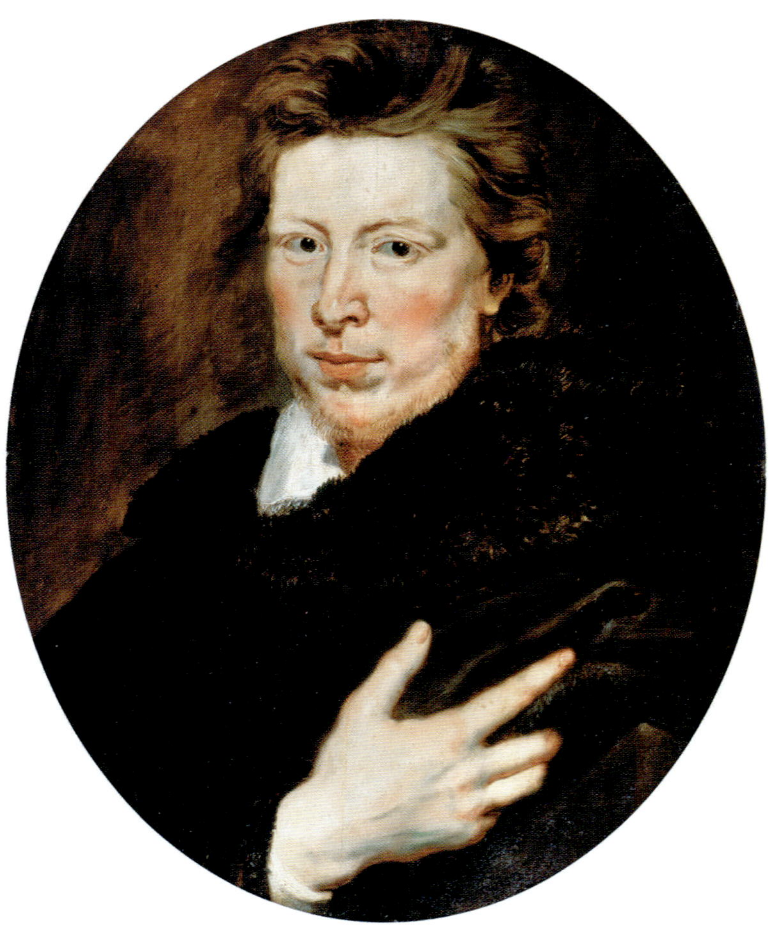

George Gaidge, c.1616–17, oil on panel, 60 x 49.4cm (23⅔ x 19½in), The State Hermitage Museum, St Petersburg, Russia

George Gaidge, or Gage, (1592–1638) was an English diplomat and a Roman Catholic. It is likely that he received priest's orders in Rome in 1614. In Antwerp in 1616–17, he negotiated the purchase of some pictures from Rubens for King James I, and Rubens painted this portrait of him. He was later involved in the ill-fated negotiations for the marriage of the English Prince Charles with the Spanish infanta.

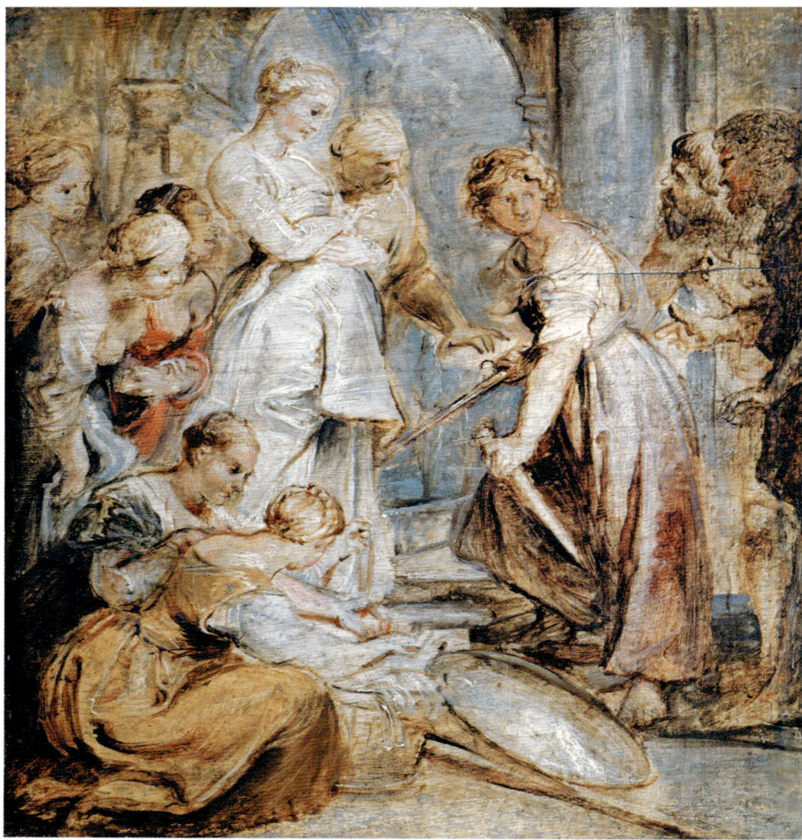

The Discovery of Achilles Among the Daughters of Lycomedes, c.1618, oil on panel, 28.5 x 26cm (11¼ x 10¼in), Fitzwilliam Museum, University of Cambridge, UK

According to prophecy, Achilles was to die in the Trojan War. To avoid this, his mother hid him in the court of King Lycomedes disguised as a woman. However, Ulysses and Diomedes knew that he was hiding, but wanted him to help them fight the war. Disguised as merchants, they showed jewels to the ladies of the court. As they guessed, Achilles gave himself away by showing more interest in their weapons.

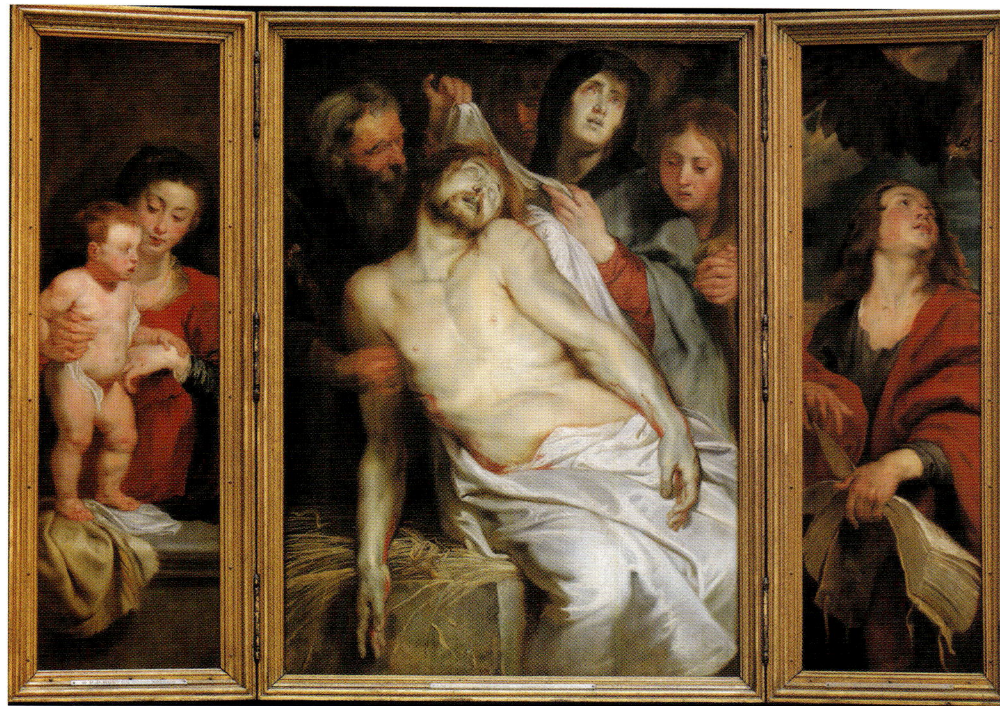

Epitaph of Jan Michielsen and his Wife Maria Maes, 1618, oil on panel, 138 x 178cm (54⅓ x 70in), Royal Museum of Fine Arts, Antwerp, Belgium

This triptych commemorates the merchant Jan Michielsen and his wife Maria Maes, who are interred in the Cathedral of Our Lady in Antwerp. The central panel shows Joseph of Arimathea laying the body of Christ on straw. Beside him, his mother holds a cloth to cover his face, while Saint John and Mary Magdalene watch. The work includes the patron saints of the couple: Mary with Child, and John the Evangelist.

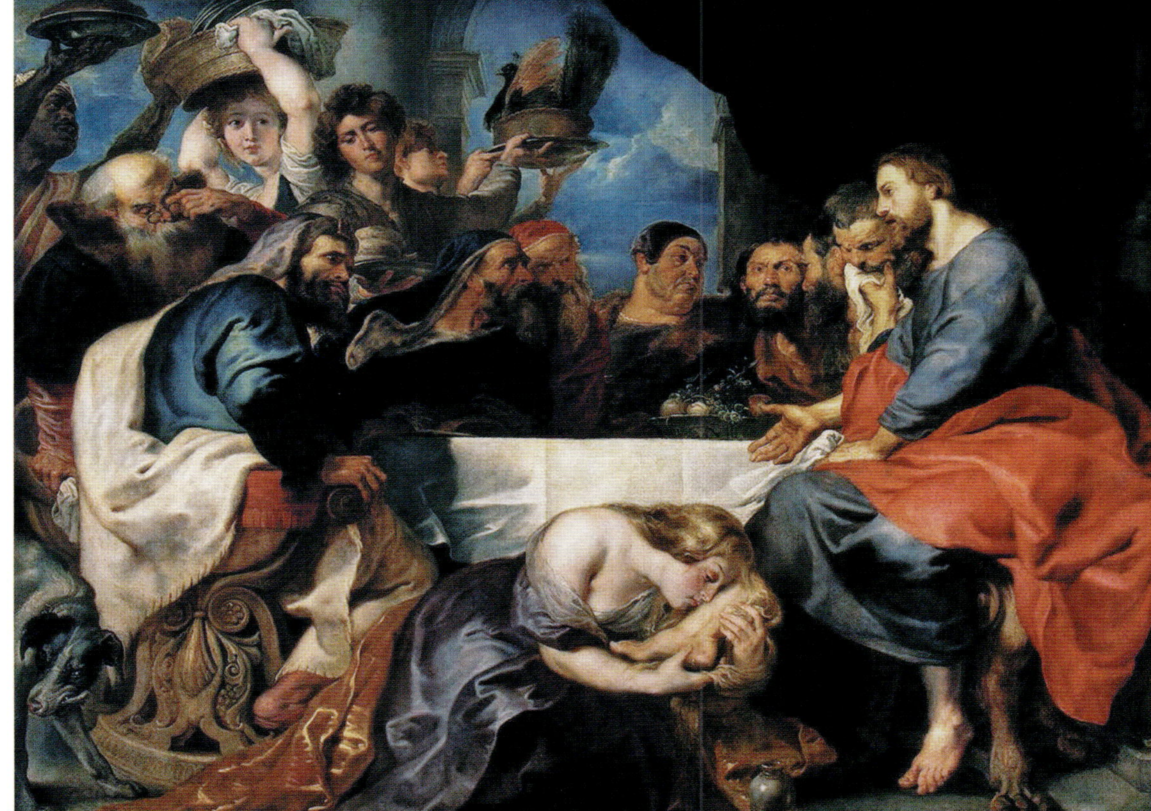

Feast in the House of Simon the Pharisee, 1618–20, oil on canvas transferred from wood, 189 x 285cm (74⅓ x 112¼ in), The State Hermitage Museum, St Petersburg, Russia

Also known as *Christ in the Home of Simon the Pharisee,* this depicts an incident from the Bible where Jesus visits Simon the Pharisee. A sinful woman goes to the house and anoints Christ's feet. Simon says he should not have allowed her to touch him. Jesus says to her: 'Thy sins are forgiven. Thy faith hath saved thee.' To Simon he says: 'Her sins, which are many, are forgiven; for she loved much.'

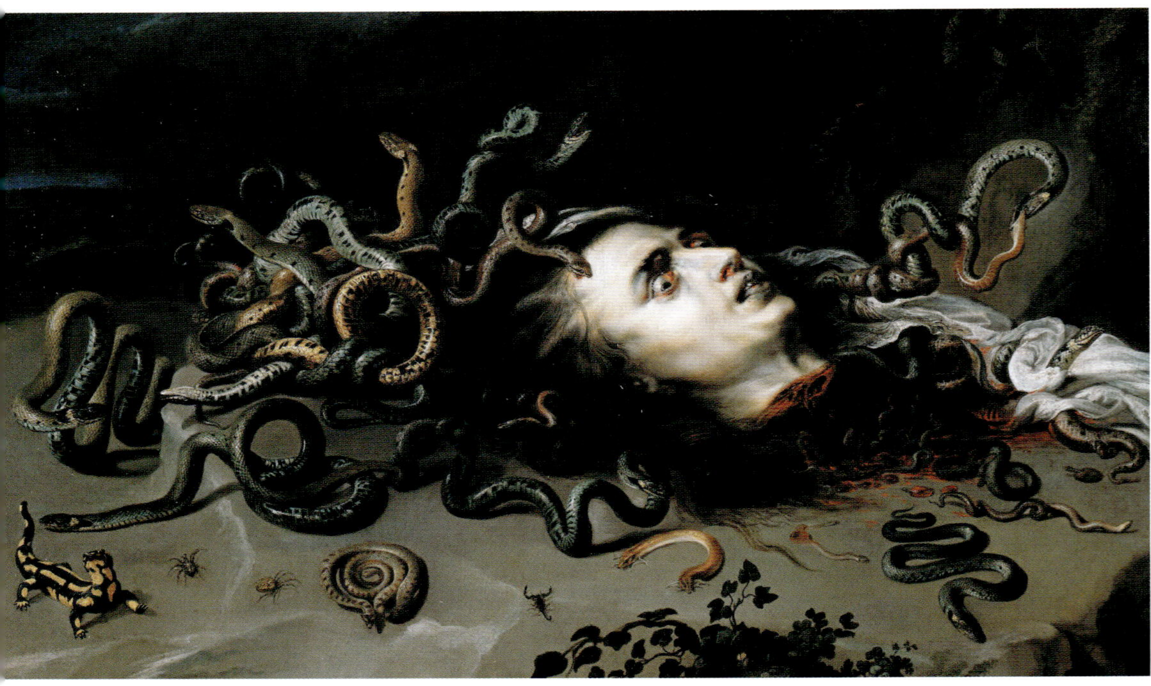

Head of Medusa, c.1617–18, oil on canvas, 68.5 x 118cm (27 x 46½in), Kunsthistorisches Museum, Vienna, Austria

Medusa's head has been depicted on soldiers' shields and building entrances traditionally to ward off danger. Rubens's version is a dead Medusa lying on a stony ledge. Her deathly pale face has a frozen gaze with glassy eyes and a half-open mouth, and although she is dead, the snakes of her 'hair' continue to live, while the drops of blood that have fallen from her metamorphose into new snakes.

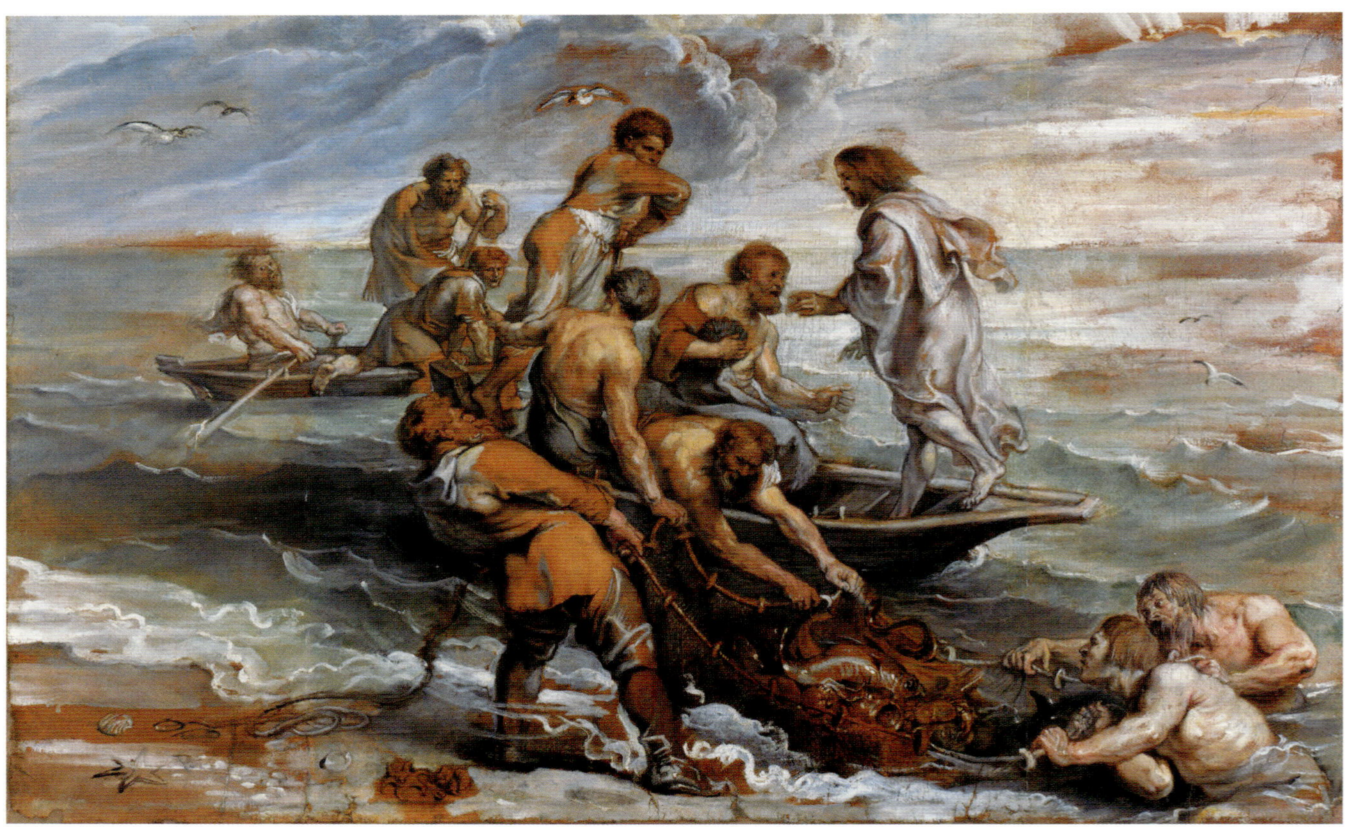

The Miraculous Draught of Fishes, 1618–19, black chalk, pen and oil on paper, stuck on canvas, 55 x 85cm (21⅔ x 33⅓in), The National Gallery, London, UK

In the New Testament, Jesus used Simon Peter's boat to preach to fishermen. When he finished, they could not catch any fish, so were about to go home when Jesus urged them to try one more cast of the net. They were rewarded with a miraculous catch of fish. Jesus then called for them to be 'fishers of men' and encourage others to follow him. Here, Rubens creates a dynamic composition evoking a sense of movement. Every figure is captured with solidity and credibility.

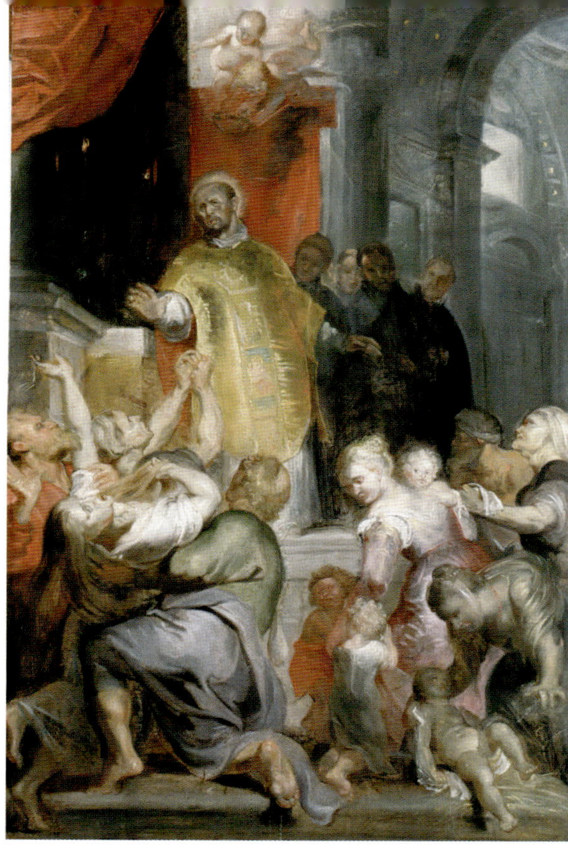

Saint Ignatius Loyola Exorcising, c.1619, oil on panel, 73.7 x 50.2cm (29 x 19¾in), The Dulwich Picture Gallery, London, UK

The founder of the Jesuit Order, Saint Ignatius of Loyola, was canonized three years after the believed date of this modello, which was preparation for part of an altarpiece depicting the Miracles of Saint Ignatius for the chapel in the Jesuit church of Sant'Ambrogio in Genoa. It refers to the curing of a possessed woman, a woman whose withered arm was healed when she washed Ignatius's linen, and also his intercessionary role in difficult births.

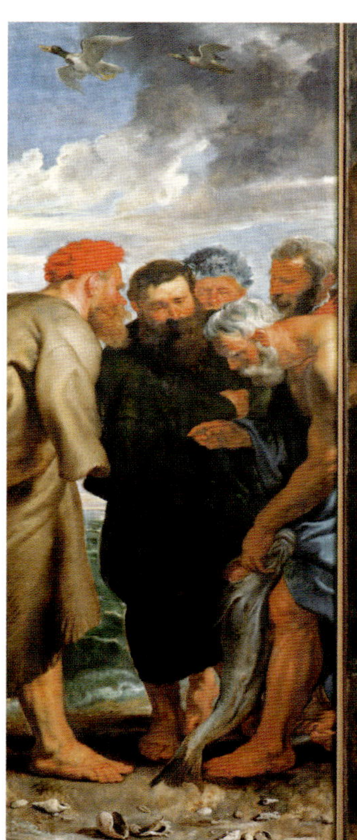
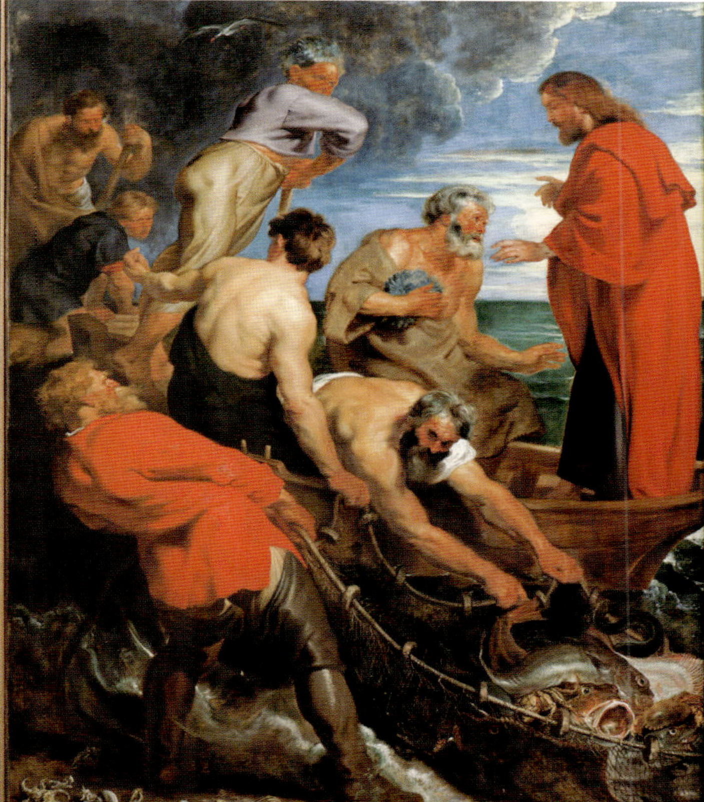
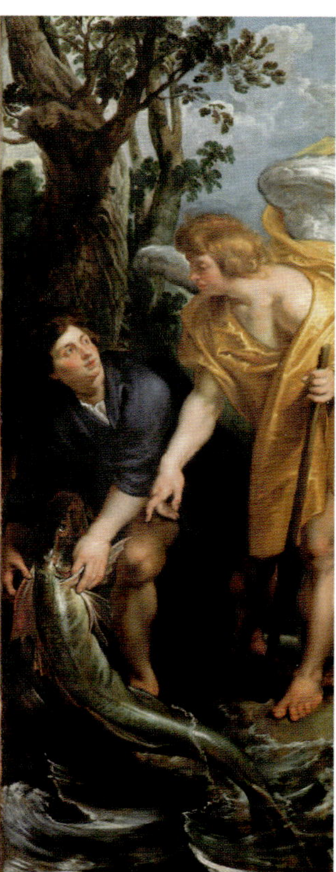

The Miraculous Draught of Fishes, 1618, oil on panel, dimensions unknown, Our Lady on the Dijle Church, Mechelen, Belgium

In a vibrantly coloured interpretation of the Bible story of Jesus encouraging the fishermen to preach his word after he performs a miracle, Rubens painted this triptych originally as the altarpiece of a local church, commissioned by the Fishmongers' Guild. The central part of the triptych follows the painting opposite, with the men in the same dynamic poses, but Rubens used brighter, bolder colours to capture the eyes of worshippers. He was paid 1600 guilders for this work.

Saint Sebastian, c.1614,
oil on canvas, 200 x 128cm
(78¾ x 50⅓in), Staatliche
Museen, Berlin, Germany

An early Christian saint,
Sebastian was killed during
the Roman emperor
Diocletian's persecution of
Christians. According to
legend, he was tied to a
tree or post and shot with
arrows, but was rescued and
healed by Irene of Rome.
Later, he was clubbed to
death. Rubens depicts him
bound to a tree, his eyes
turned heavenward. The
details of the work derive
from Caravaggio's example.

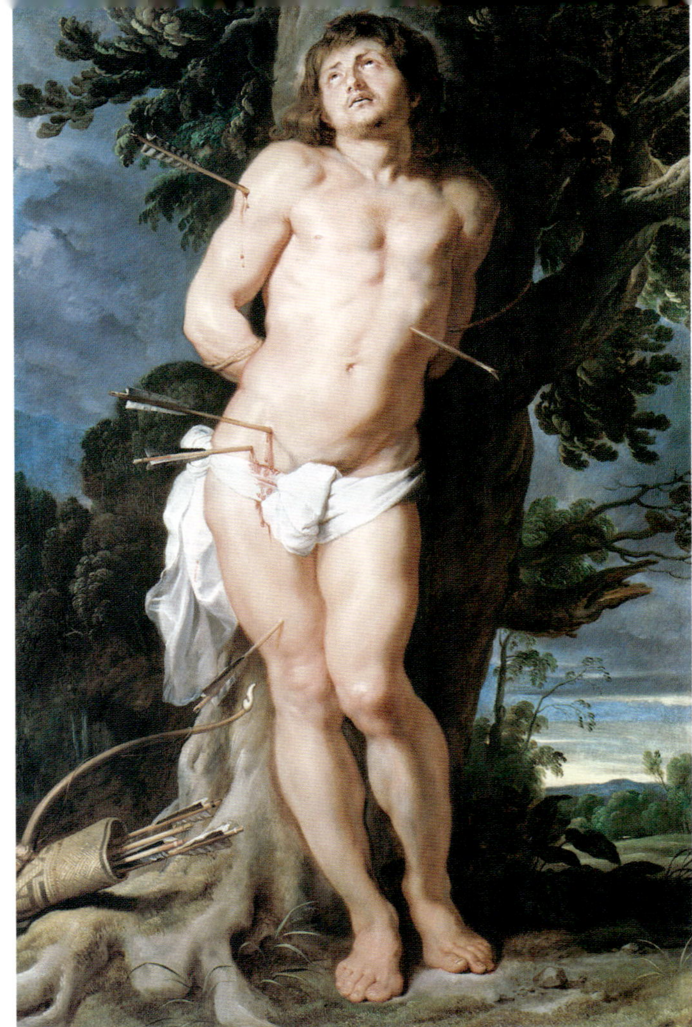

Head of a Magi, c.1618,
oil on panel transferred
to canvas, 66.8 x 51.5cm
(26⅓ x 20¼ in), The
National Gallery of Art,
Washington DC, USA

This is Melchior, the Assyrian
king and one of the three
Magi. Rubens painted it for
his friend Balthasar Moretus
the Elder, owner of the
prestigious Plantin Press in
Antwerp. The profile of a
bearded, middle-aged man
in a scarlet robe, opening
his gilded vessel to reveal his
gift for the baby Jesus of
frankincense is full of
character. In biblical times,
frankincense symbolized
sacrifice, prayer and
Christ's divine majesty.

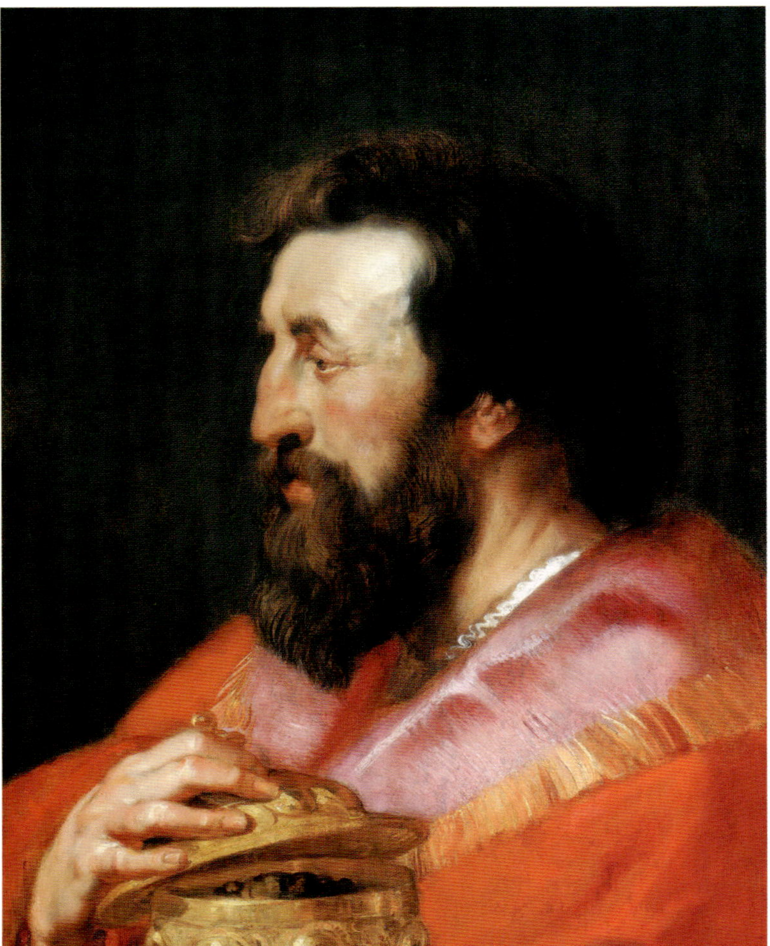

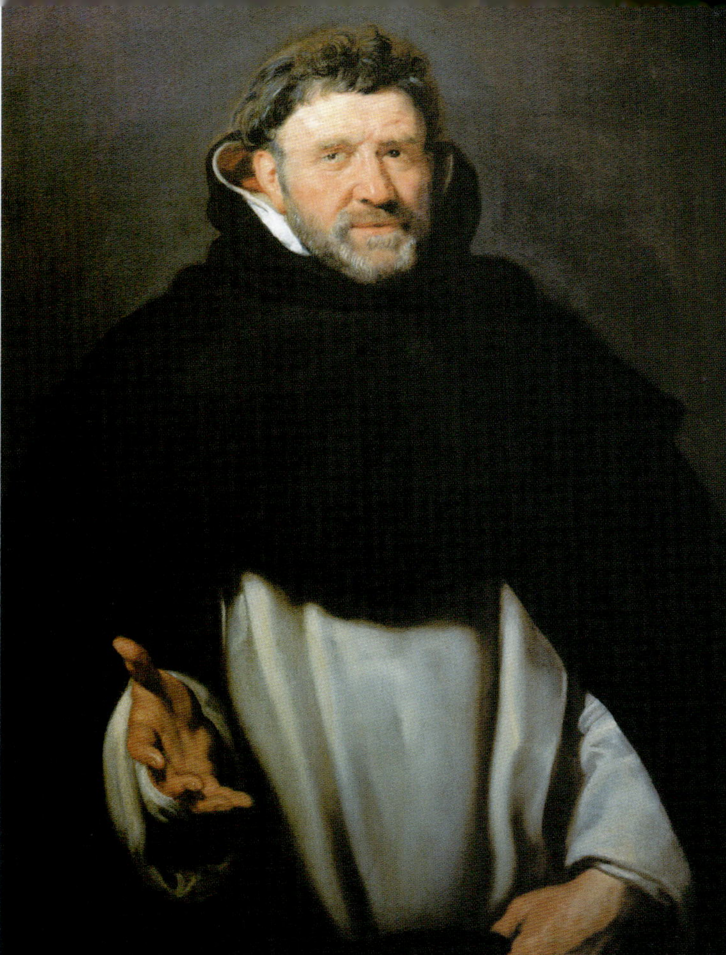

Michael Ophovius, c.1615–17,
oil on canvas, 111.5 x
82.5cm (43⅞ x 32½in),
Royal Picture Gallery
Mauritshuis, The Hague

One of Rubens's good
friends, Michiel Ophovius
(1570–1637) was Prior of
the Dominican monastery
of Saint Paul in Antwerp.
This portrait shows him
in the habit of his order: a
white woollen tunic and long
black cloak with a red-lined
hood. His mouth is slightly
open and with his right hand
he makes a gesture. This
refers to his eloquent skills
as a speaker – he was also
a lecturer at the Dominican
study house in Louvain.

*The Virgin Presents the Infant
Jesus to Saint Francis,* 1618,
oil on wood, 179 x 155cm
(70½ x 61in), Musée des
Beaux-Arts, Dijon, France

Differing from most other
artists, Rubens rarely painted
the Virgin Mary in blue and
white, but usually in striking
scarlet. Here, he presents her
as a beautiful young woman
of the times, with an
individual personality. She
holds out her baby for Saint
Francis to venerate, and
naturally, her chubby boy
looks back to his mother
for reassurance.

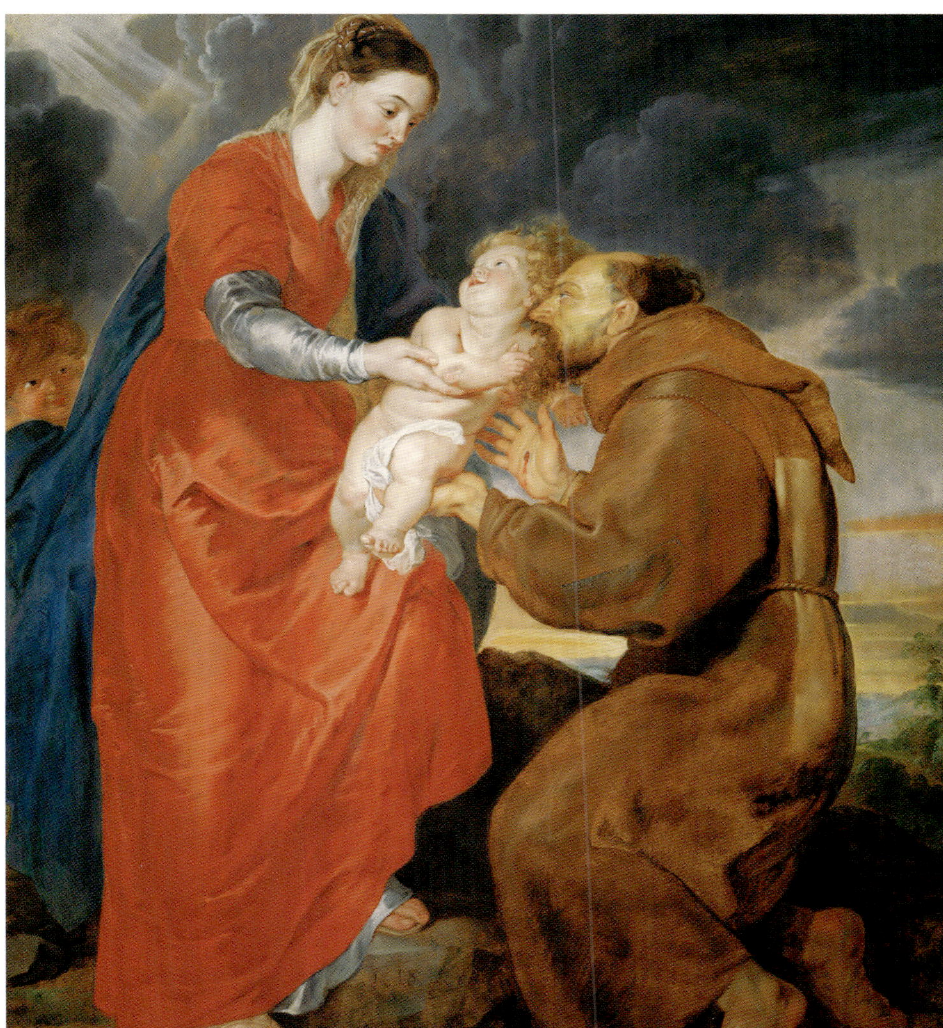

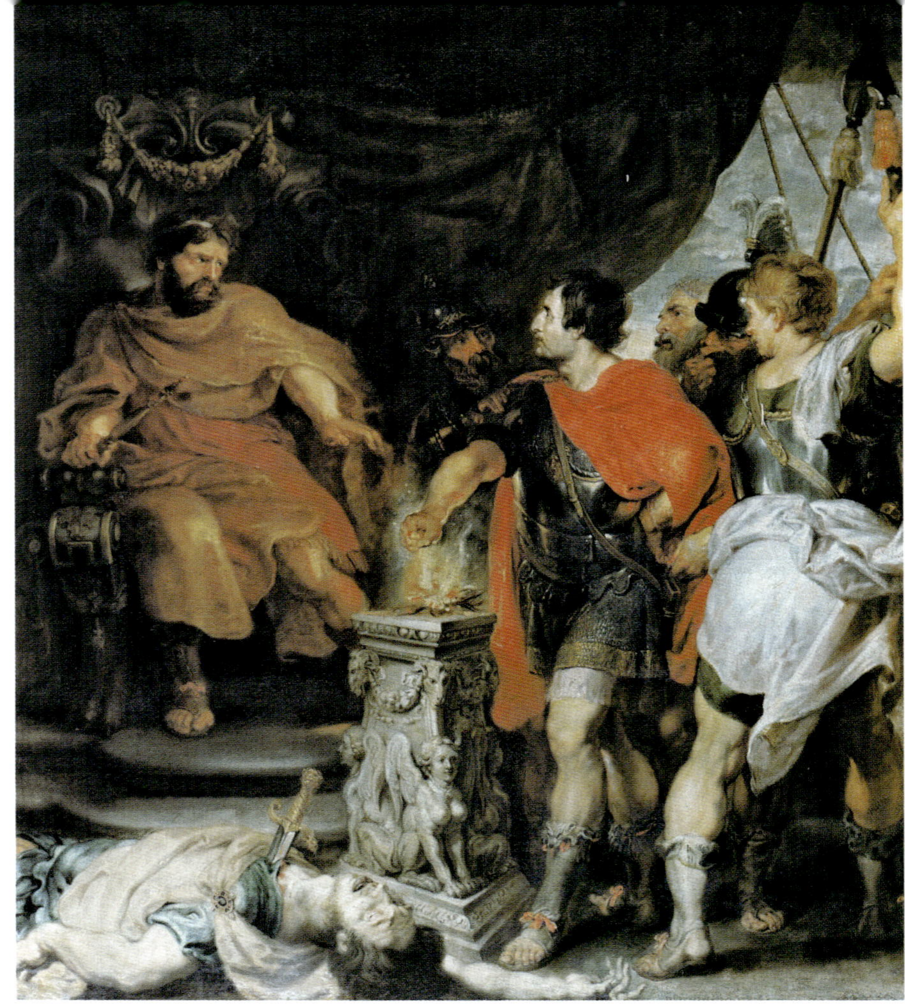

Mucius Scaevola before Lars Porsena, c.1618–20, oil on canvas, 187 x 156cm (73⅔ x 61⅓in), Museum of Fine Arts, Budapest, Hungary

The story of Mucius Scaevola, found in Livy, Plutarch and Valerius Maximus, describes how, during the siege of Rome by the Etruscans, a young Roman soldier attempted to kill the Etruscan king, Lars Porsena, but Musius Scaevola killed the wrong man in error. When captured and threatened with torture, he demonstrated his courage by holding his right hand in the fire of an altar.

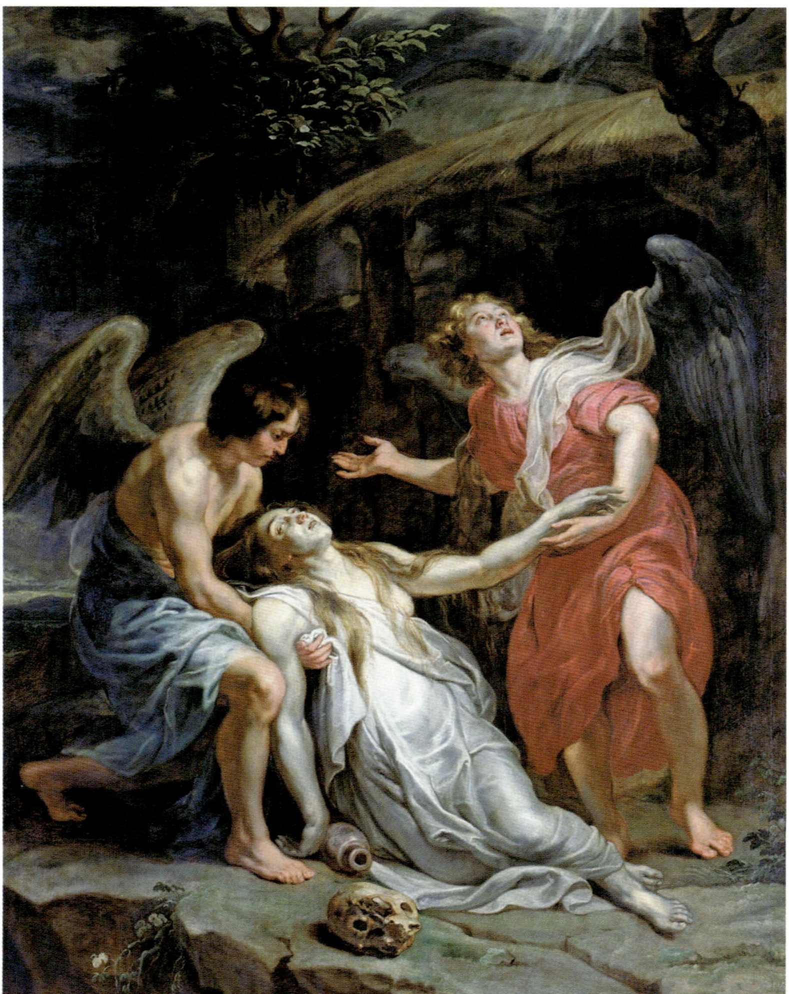

The Ecstasy of Mary Magdalene, c.1619–20, oil on canvas, 295 x 220cm (116 x 86⅔in), Musée des Beaux-Arts, Lille, France

The inspiration for this painting came from *The Golden Legend* by Jacques de Voragine, c.1260. On a rocky ledge at the mouth of a cave, Mary Magdalene appears to be in a trance-like state; her skin is white and the folds of her white robe cling to her body. Two angels support her – one looks down on her in concern, and the other looks up at a divine shaft of light.

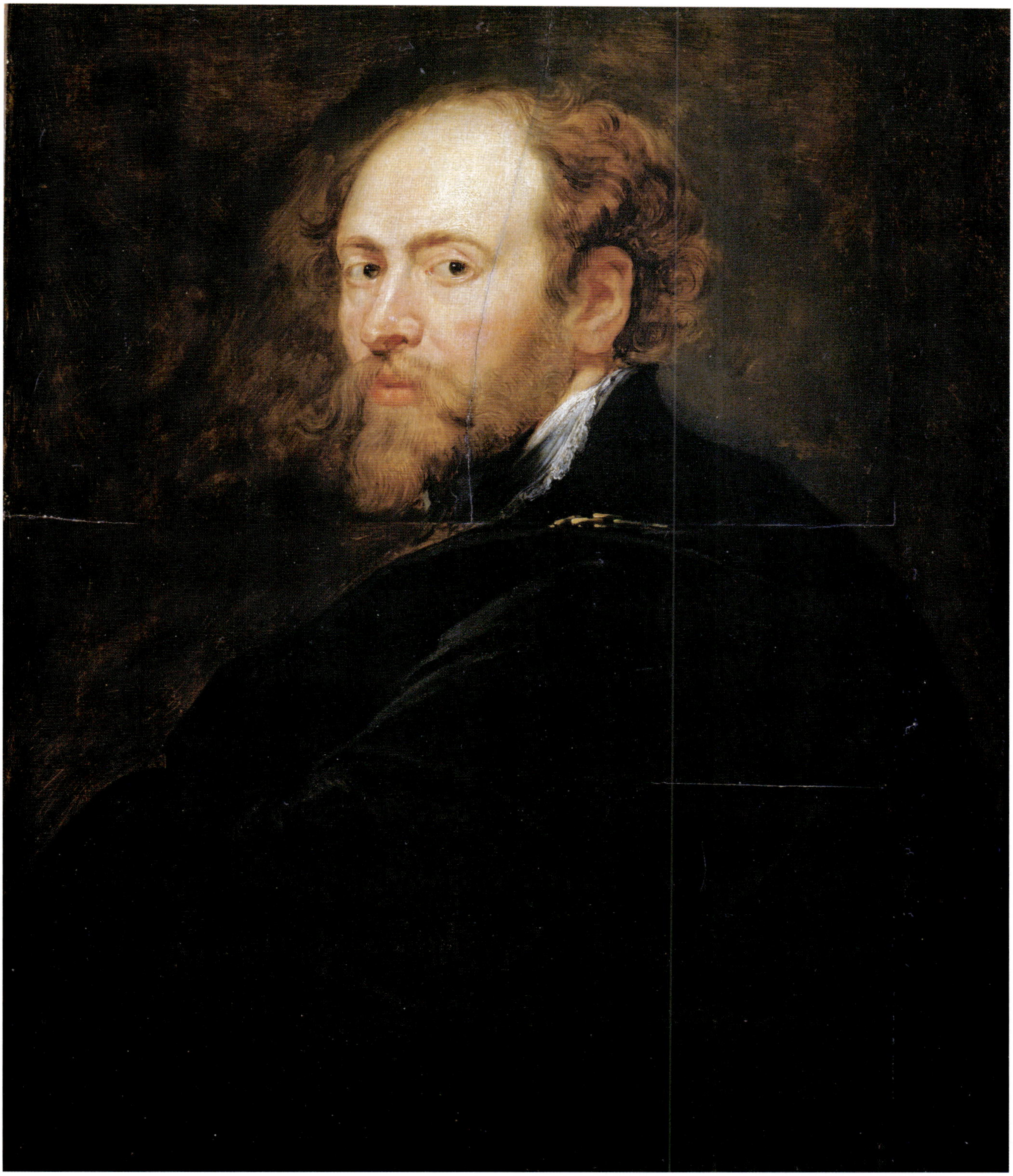

Self-portrait, *c.*1615–34, oil on oak, 78 x 61cm (30¾ x 24in), Galleria degli Uffizi, Florence, Italy

It is not clear when Rubens painted this self-portrait; suggestions vary between 1615 and 1634. It appears to be later than other self-portraits that show him as somewhat dandified, such as *Self-portrait in a Hat* (see page 211). Here, he is clearly a wealthy and dignified member of society, perhaps even a little melancholy. He is also slightly portlier than in other images of himself. The receding hairline is another aspect of his features that he had not previously portrayed.

Christ on the Cross Between the Two Thieves, 1619–20, oil on panel, 429 x 311cm (169 x 122⅓in), Royal Museum of Fine Arts, Antwerp, Belgium

Also called *Pierced with a Lance*, this painting was created as an altarpiece for the Recollects Church in Antwerp. As with most of his altarpieces, Rubens designed it to inspire strong emotions in viewers. Christ is on the cross. Longinus, a soldier on a horse thrusts a lance into his side to speed up the process. Mary Magdalene leans forward, imploring Longinus, while the sun is eclipsed in the sky.

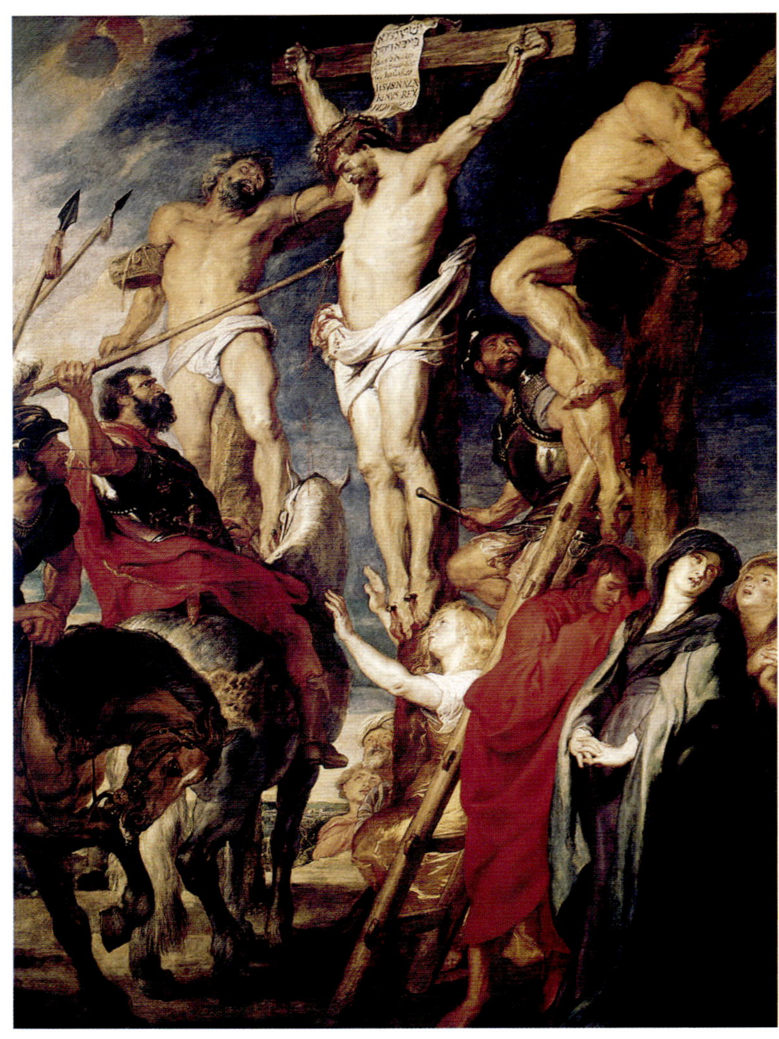

Nicolaas Rubens Wearing a Coral Necklace, 1619, white chalk, black chalk and sanguine on paper, 25.2 x 20.2cm (10 x 8in), The Albertina, Vienna, Austria

A charming drawing of his young son Nicolaas, Rubens captured this chubby-cheeked image of the toddler wearing a coral necklace, which was traditionally worn for the beauty of its colour and because it was believed to protect the wearer as it symbolizes the blood of Christ. Nicolaas was the second son of Rubens and Isabella Brant. A placid child, Rubens depicted him at least three times.

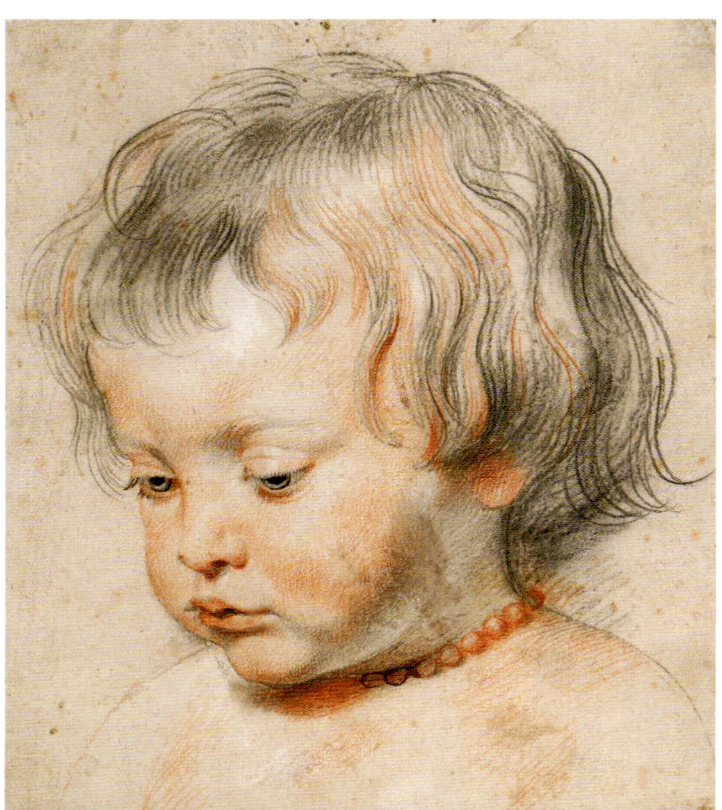

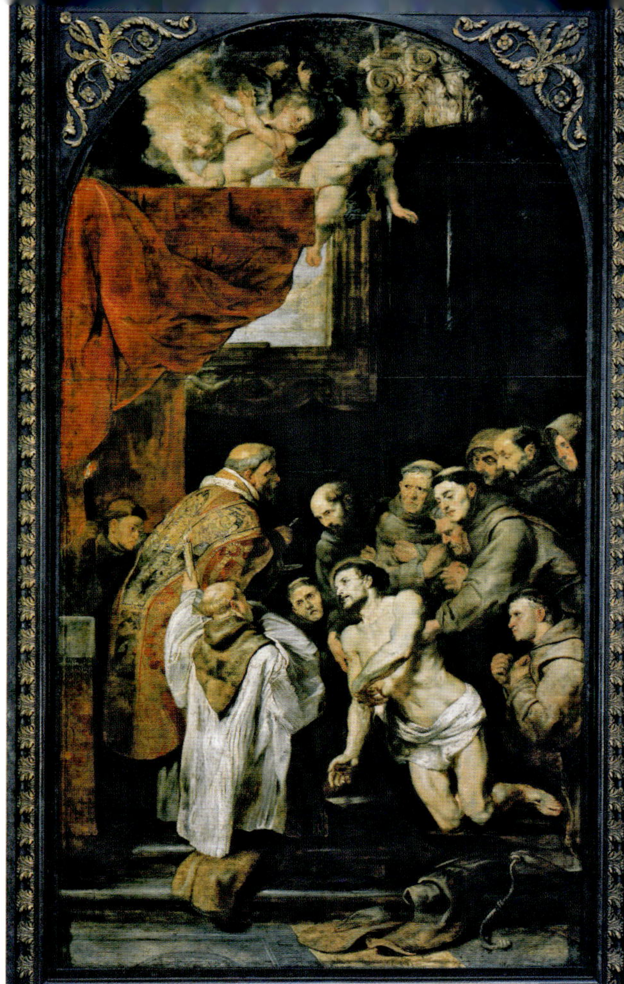

The Last Communion of Saint Francis, 1619, oil on panel, 422 x 226cm (166 x 89in), Royal Museum of Fine Arts, Antwerp, Belgium

While arguments still raged across the Christian world about transubstantiation – or whether or not the Eucharist was actually the body and blood of Christ – Counter-Reformation artists such as Rubens painted images of revered saints taking Communion, and so visually verifying the argument for transubstantiation. This represents Saint Francis taking his last Communion before he died.

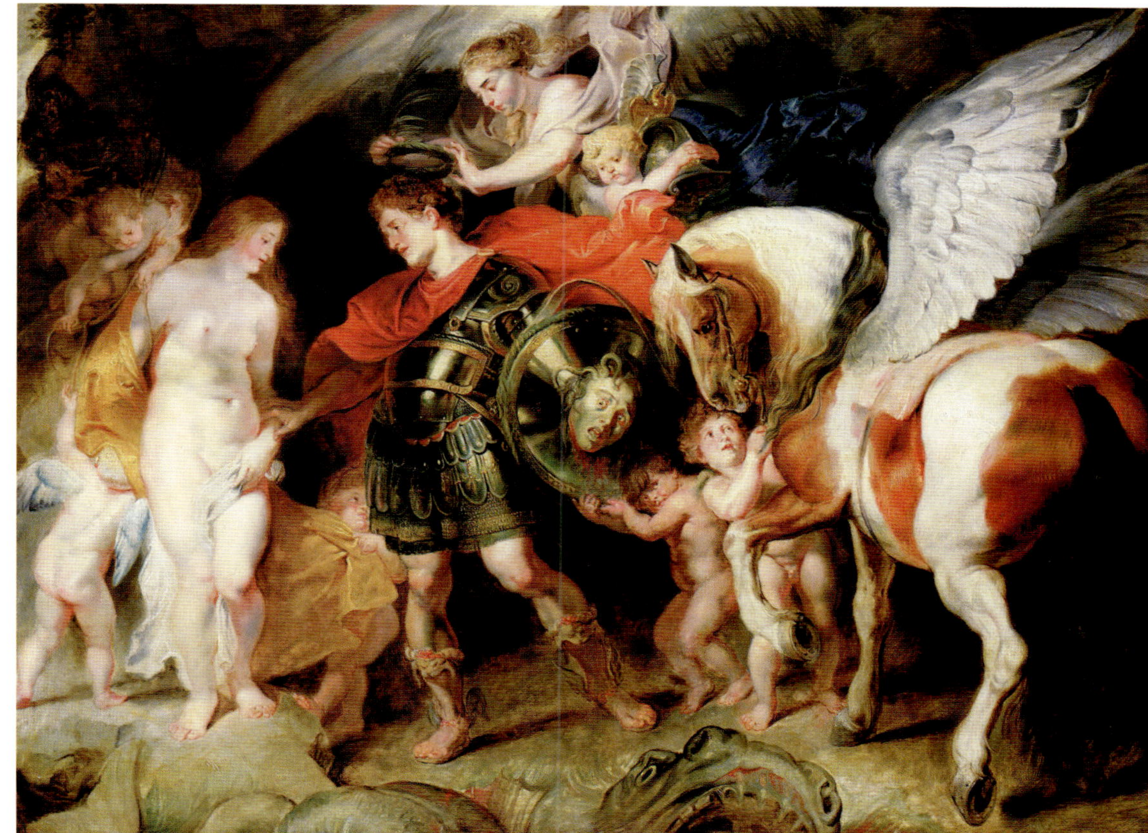

Perseus Freeing Andromeda, c.1622, oil on oak, 100 x 139cm (39⅓ x 54¾in), Staatliche Museen, Berlin, Germany

Chained to a rock, Andromeda, the daughter of the King of Ethiopia, was to be sacrificed to a sea monster. On his return from vanquishing Medusa, Perseus, on his winged horse Pegasus, catches sight of the chained Andromeda and saves her. Overcome by her beauty, he declares his love. Rubens depicts Perseus in gleaming armour and a red cloak as he loosens Andromeda's chains, assisted by putti, with Pegasus nearby.

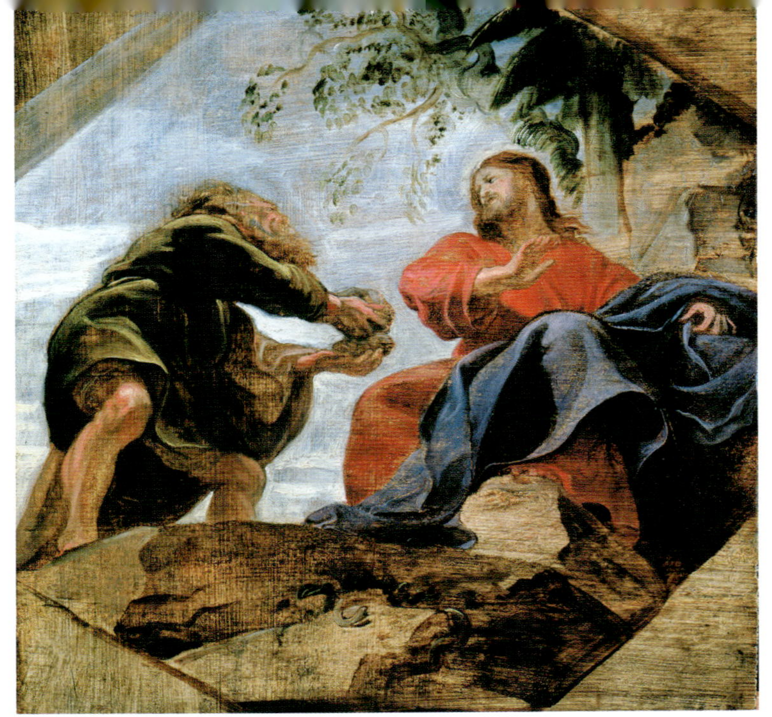

The Temptation of Christ, 1620, oil on panel, 32.9 x 31.6cm (13 x 12½in), The Courtauld Gallery, London, UK

This is one of several oil sketches for Rubens's decoration of the Jesuit church at Antwerp. He was commissioned to provide 39 paintings for the church, but all were unfortunately destroyed by fire in 1718. His contract required him to paint the sketches while his assistants completed the finished paintings. Here, Christ is being tempted by the Devil to turn stones into bread while he is fasting for 40 days and nights in the wilderness.

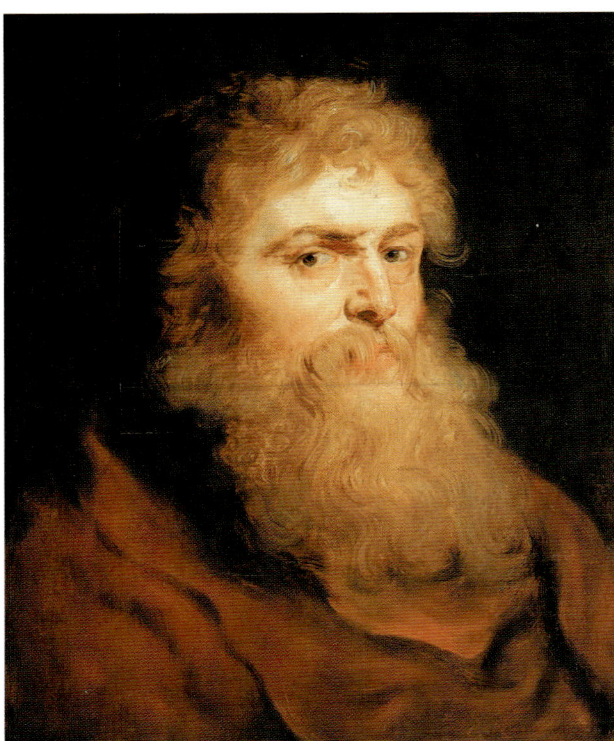

Head of a Bearded Man, c.1617–18, oil on panel, 69.7 x 53.4cm (27½ x 21in), Museo Soumaya, Mexico City, Mexico

With rapid brushstrokes, a restricted palette of colours and a confident approach, this portrait of an unidentified man shows Rubens's assured handling of any subject matter. Textures are conveyed masterfully with long and short brush marks and powerful tenebrism. The character of the man is powerfully depicted, largely through the expressive yet sensitive eyes. Judging by the relaxed expression of the sitter, this was probably one of Rubens's friends.

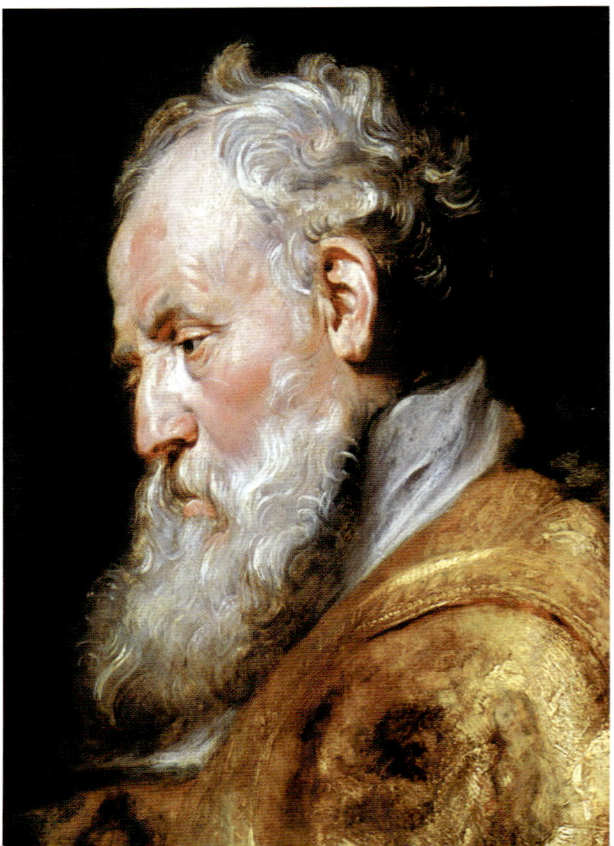

A Study of a Head (Saint Ambrose), c.1618, oil on panel, 49.6 x 38.1cm (19½ x 15in), The Scottish National Gallery, National Galleries of Scotland, Edinburgh, UK

This is a preparatory study for the head of Saint Ambrose in the large altarpiece of *Saint Ambrose Refusing the Emperor Theodosius Admission to the Church of Milan* (Kunsthistorisches Museum, Vienna). Ambrose was a Bishop of Milan in the 4th century, who stood against the powerful Theodosius over his horror of the emperor's Thessalonian massacre.

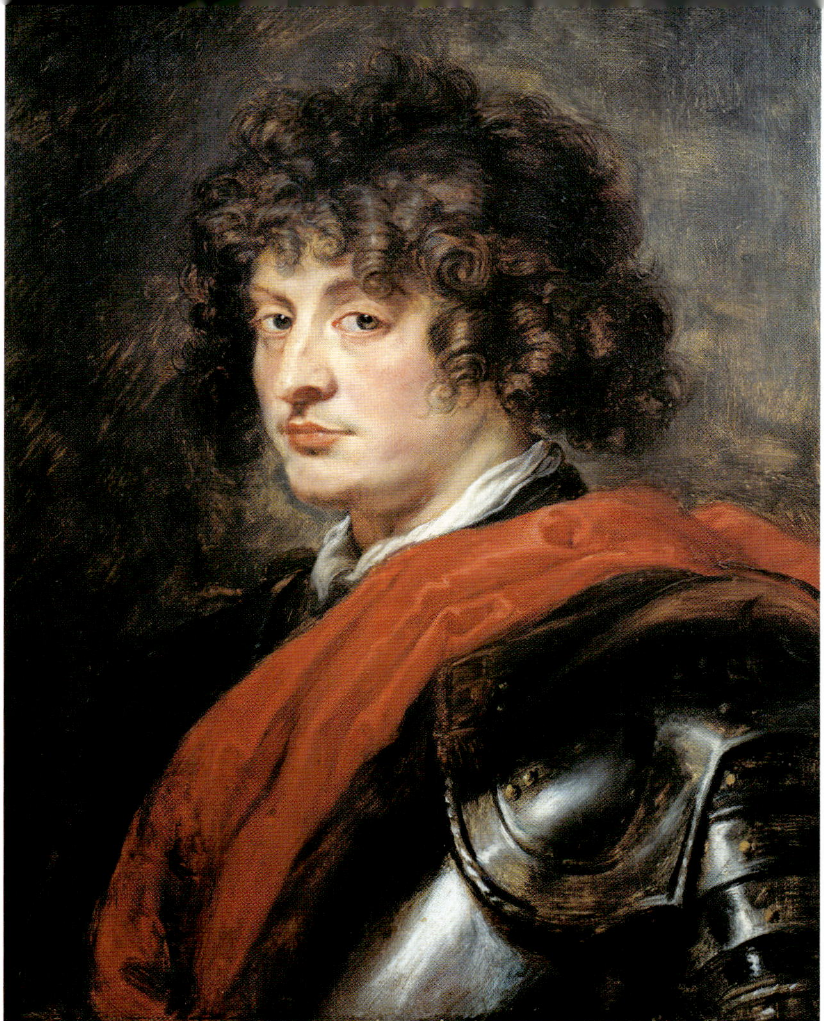

Portrait of a Young Man in Armour, c.1620, oil on canvas, 64.8 x 50.8cm (25½ x 20in), Timken Museum of Art, San Diego, USA

By the 1620s, Rubens was renowned across Europe. This bust-length portrait of a young man has traditionally been identified as a young captain, but is now believed to be a tronie, used for reference by Rubens or his assistants in the painting of other works. The curly-haired unknown sitter wears armour with a rather dashing red sash over one shoulder.

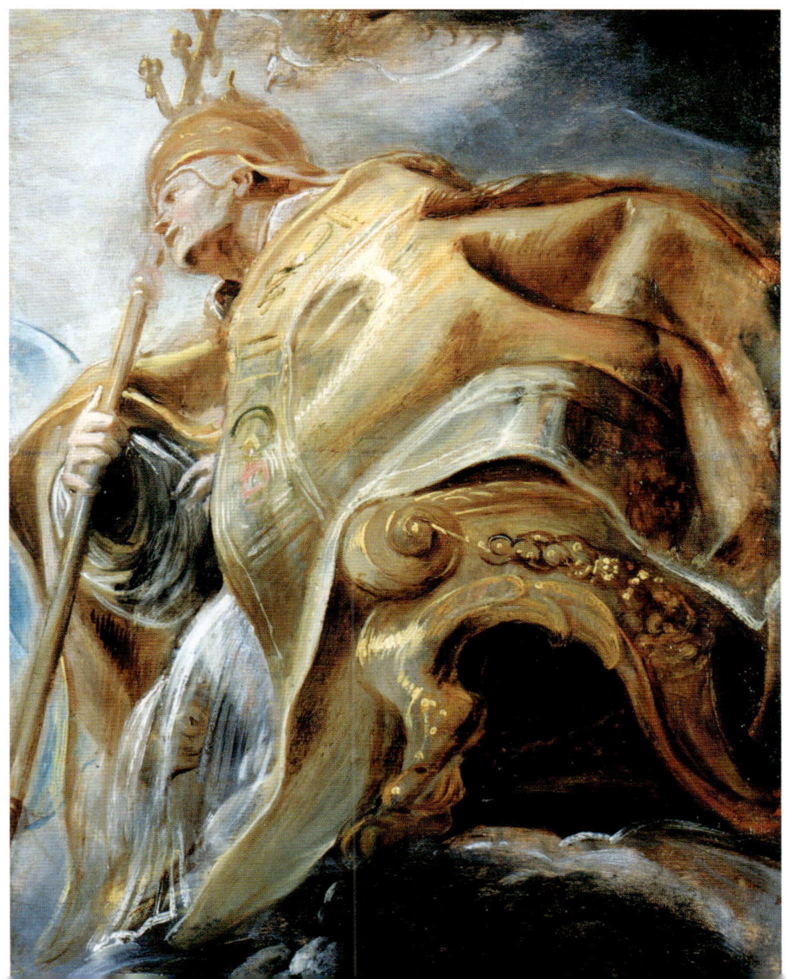

Saint Gregory the Great, 1620, oil on panel, 46.2 x 34.6cm (18¼ x 13⅗in), The Courtauld Gallery, London, UK

This is one of Rubens's oil sketches for his decoration of the Jesuit Church in Antwerp. Pope Gregory I (c.540–604) was commonly known as Saint Gregory the Great and was also called 'the Father of Christian Worship' because of his writings and efforts to revise Roman Catholic worship. In both the Catholic and Eastern Orthodox Churches, he is also the patron saint of musicians, singers, students and teachers.

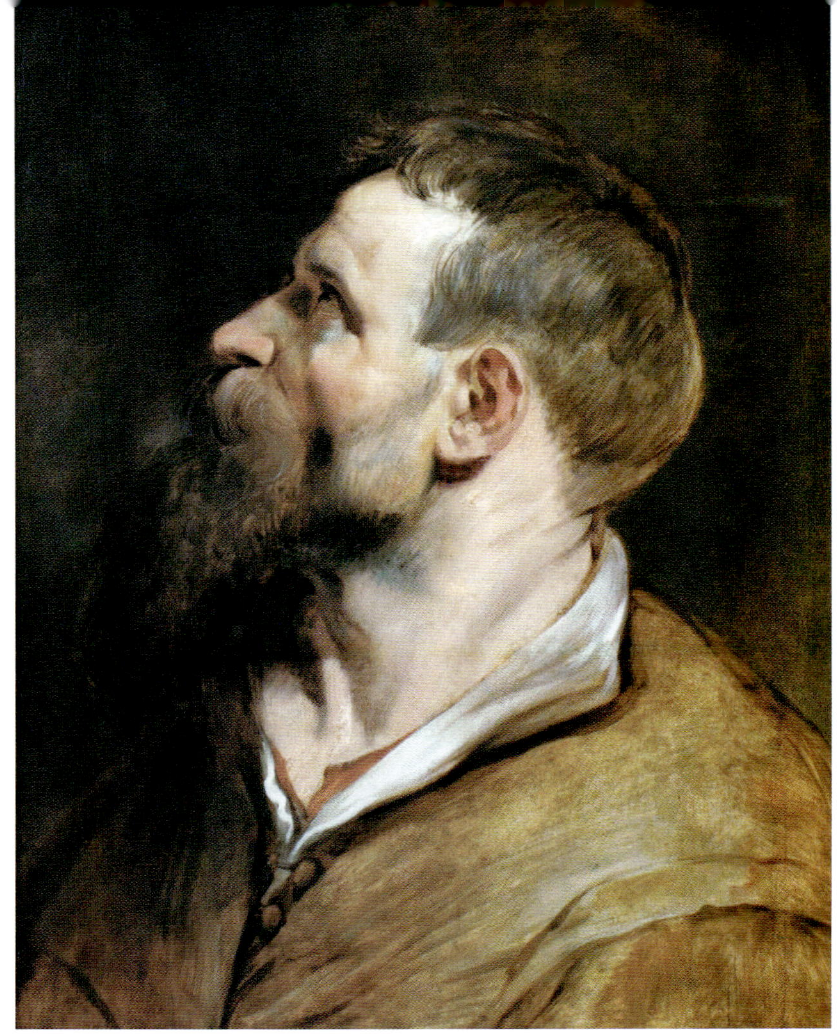

Head of a Bearded Man,
1620–21, oil on panel,
69 x 51cm (27¼ x 20in),
Národní Galerie, Prague,
Czech Republic

Rubens did not study anatomy, and unlike many artists he admired, he did not draw cadavers – this was not part of his style. Instead, he drew people who were alive and full of energy, with obvious personalities. This study epitomizes his quest for creating animated life on flat, static surfaces. These studies were used later in his finished narrative works, where they continue to exude life and zest.

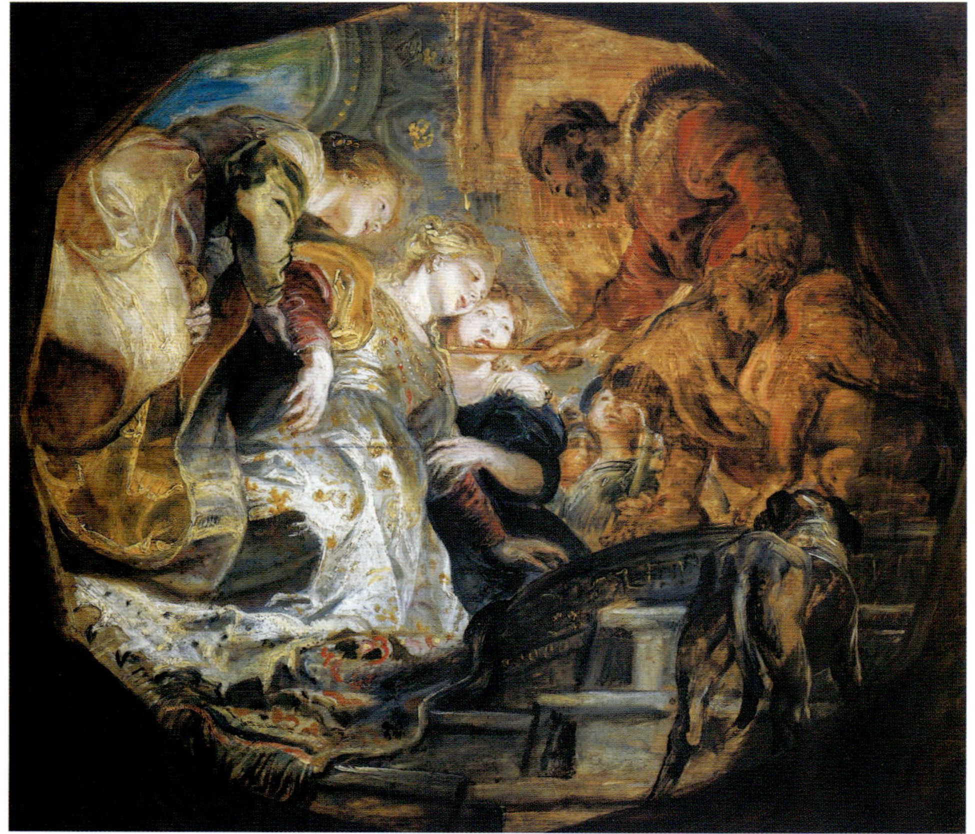

Esther before Ahasuerus,
1620, oil on wood,
33 x 32cm (13 x 12½in),
Academy of Fine Arts,
Vienna, Austria

This sketch was one of the first in a series of Rubens's 39 preparatory studies for the ceiling paintings in the Jesuit church in Antwerp. He copied elements of Veronese's ceiling painting in San Sebastiano, Venice. Although most of the finished work was executed by his pupils and assistants, Rubens retouched many of the paintings once they were in place.

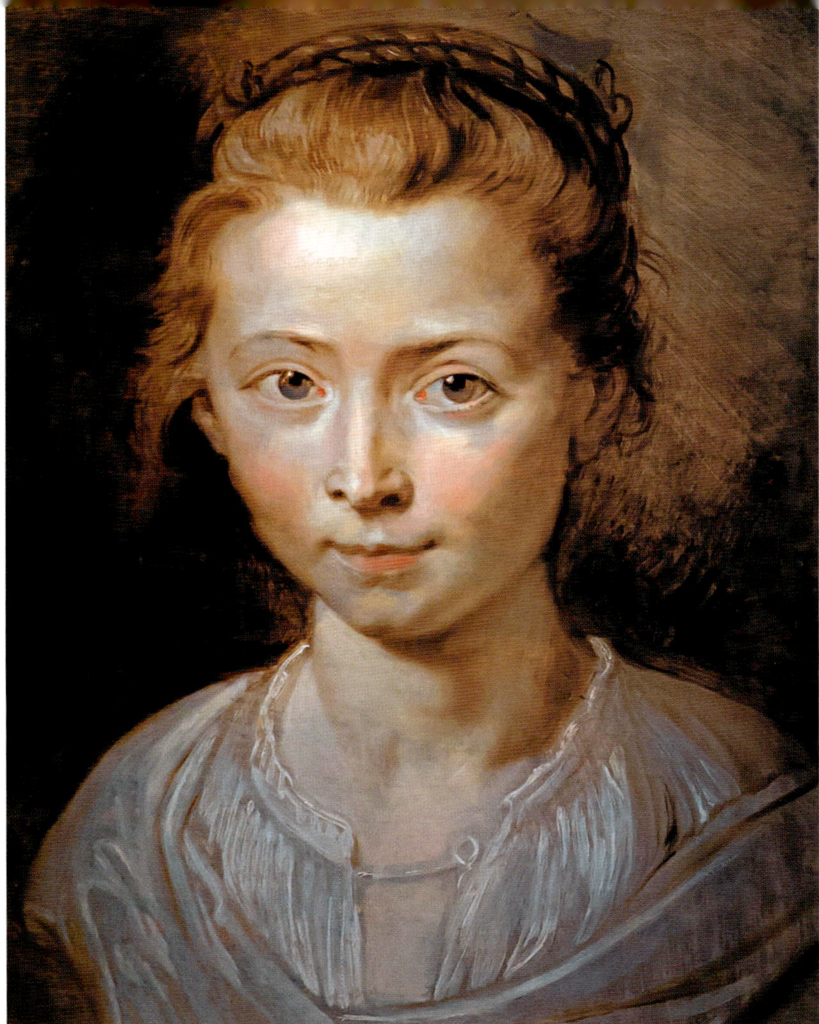

Portrait of a Young Girl, possibly Clara Serena Rubens, 1620–23, oil on panel, 35.6 x 26cm (14 x 10¼ in), Rubenshuis, Antwerp, Belgium

Although it has never been verified, this is almost certainly a portrait of Clara Serena by Rubens. It resembles the drawing of her on page 212, and another portrait of her that Rubens produced at around the same time. The resemblance to her mother Isabella Brant is also apparent. The painting has only recently been verified as being by Rubens, probably completed when Clara was about 12, just before she died. It demonstrates the close relationship between them, both by the child's expression as she looks at her beloved father, and by the way in which he has lovingly painted his daughter.

Whitehall Ceiling: The Apotheosis of James I, 1630–34, oil on canvas, 64 x 49cm (25 x 19¼ in), Banqueting House, Whitehall, London, UK

Preferring to paint grand, monumental works, Rubens planned and painted these ceiling paintings carefully by himself before undertaking the final works with the help of assistants. In the central oval canvas, he depicts the Apotheosis of the late King James, who is being carried by Jove's eagle and assisted by the figure of Justice, with Minerva (Wisdom) overhead. On either side, the four smaller works feature personifications of the king's royal qualities, including Liberality triumphing over Avarice, Discipline over Wantonness, Knowledge (Minerva again) over Ignorance, and Heroic Virtue (Hercules) over Envy. Across the top and bottom are cherubs, animals and garlands of produce that symbolize the advantages of the national unity, harmony and peace that James created in Britain during his reign.

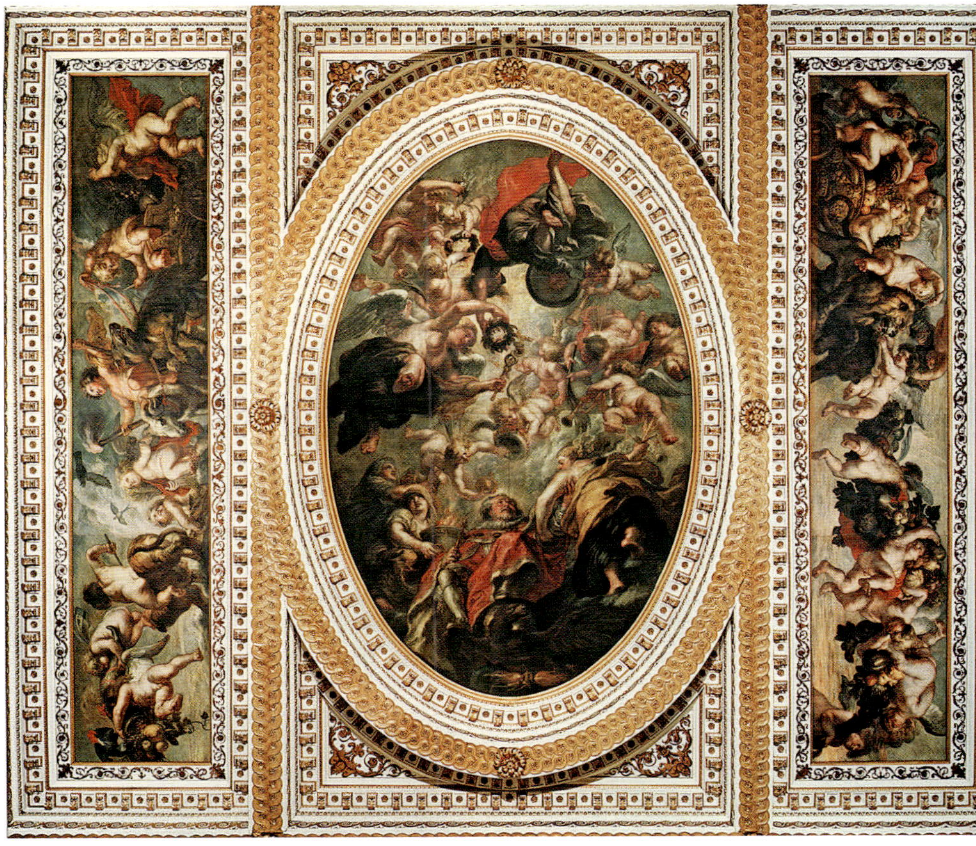

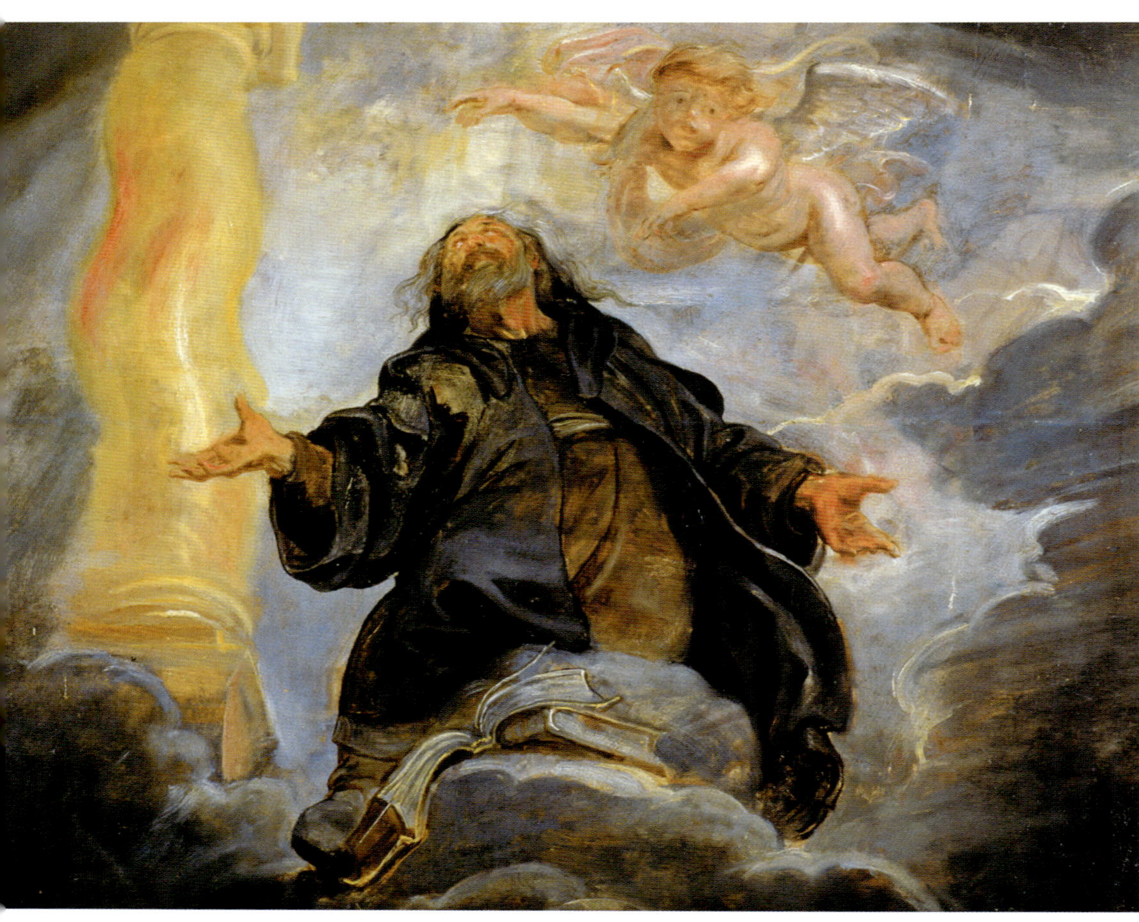

Saint Basil, 1620, oil on board, 50 x 64.8cm (19⅔ x 25½in), Schlossmuseum, Schloss Friedenstein, Gotha, Germany

Saint Basil the Great was Greek, the Bishop of Caesarea in Cappadocia, highly intellectual, influential and powerful during his lifetime, *c.*329–379, and one of the most distinguished and respected Doctors of the Church. He is often classed with his friend Gregory of Nazianzus and his brother Gregory of Nyssa as 'The Three Cappadocians' or the 'Cappadocian Fathers'.

Isabella Brant, 1621, red and black chalk with brown wash on paper, 38.1 x 29.4cm (15 x 11½in), British Museum, London, UK

Before her untimely death in 1626 at the age of 35, Isabella Brant sat for her husband on several occasions. The couple had a close and affectionate relationship and shared several interests, including Rubens's art and artefact collection. This sensitive work, drawn with a light touch, was used as the basis for three oil paintings, one of which was painted by Van Dyck as a gift to Rubens.

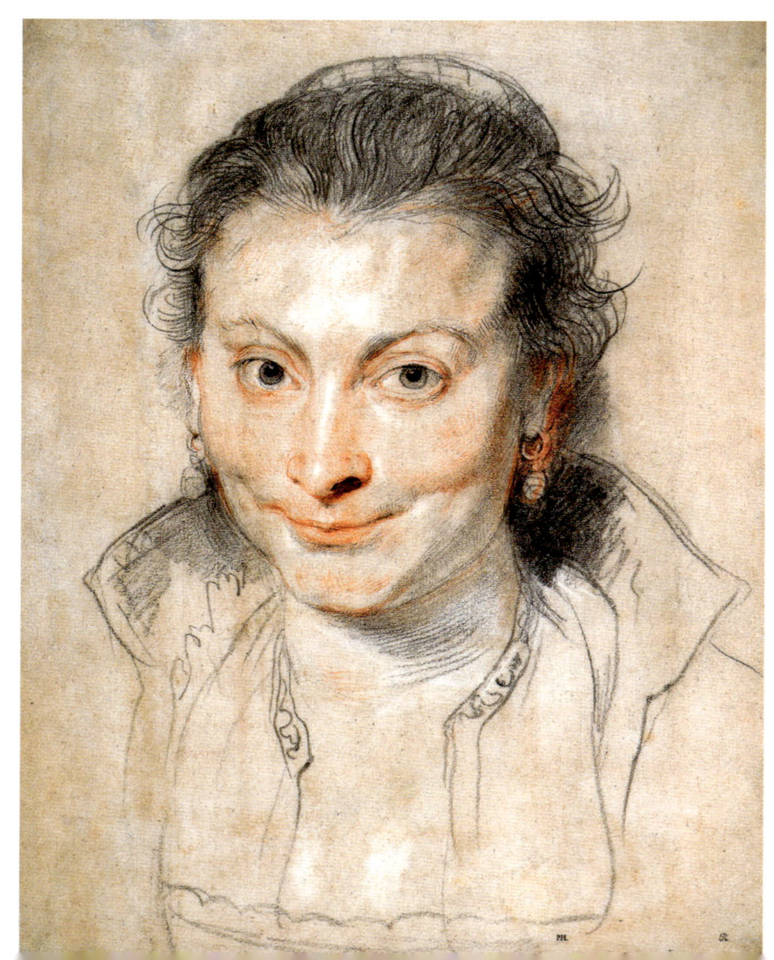

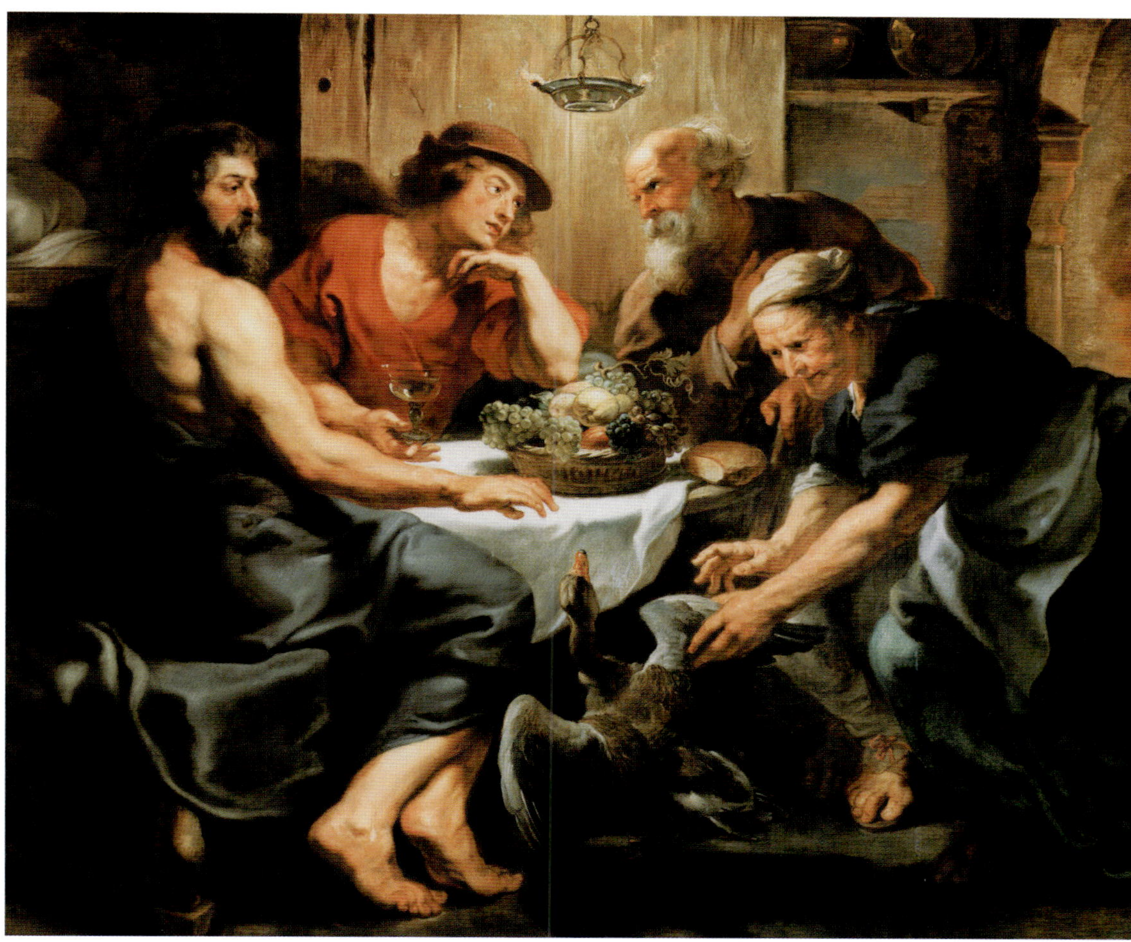

Jupiter and Mercury Visiting Philemon and Baucis, c.1620–25, oil on canvas, 153.5 x 187cm (60¼ x 73½in), Kunsthistorisches Museum, Vienna, Austria

Painted predominantly by Rubens's workshop but planned by him, this work portrays a story from Ovid's *Metamorphosis*. The gods Jupiter and Mercury travel to Earth disguised as weary travellers to test the honour and generosity of mortals. They seek help in a village, where they are refused at every door, until they knock at the house of an old married couple, Philemon and Baucis, who offer them rest, wine and food. The gods punish the other villagers, but save the kindly couple.

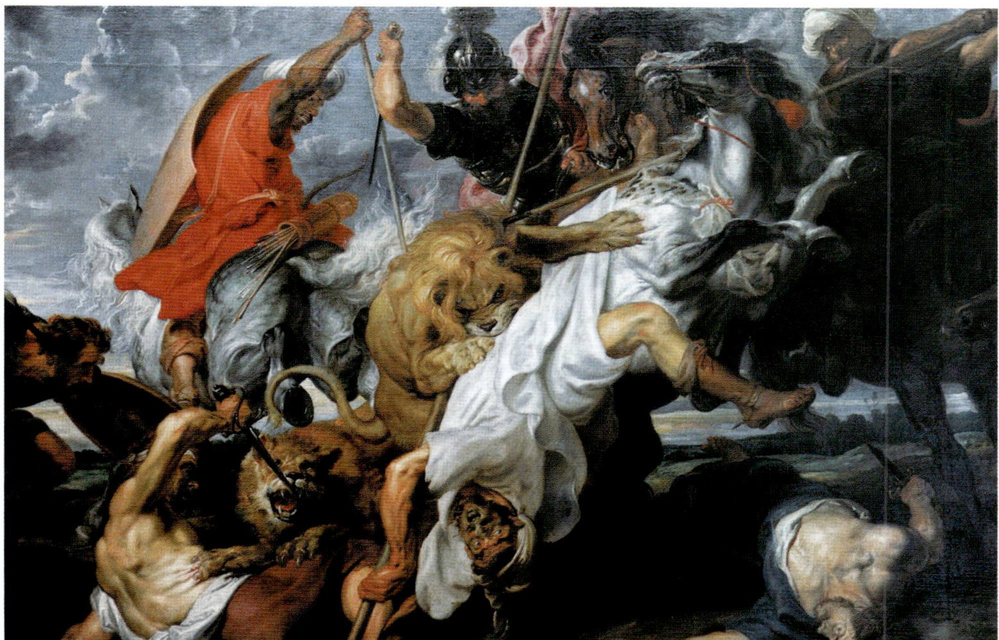

Lion Hunt, 1621, oil on canvas, 249 x 377cm (98 x 148⅛in), Alte Pinakothek, Munich, Germany

Battle scenes were a life-long preoccupation for Rubens. Gaining insights from Leonardo's *Battle of Anghiari*, this ferocious and violent image portrays two lions being attacked by hunters, both riding and on foot. With the lions also attacking the hunters, this was not intended to be a straightforward painting of a hunt, but an allegorical image in the midst of the Eighty Years' War.

The Medici Cycle: Education of the Princess, 1622–25, oil on canvas, 394 x 295cm (155 x 116in), Musée du Louvre, Paris, France

A maturing Marie de' Medici is studying. Her education is given a divine grace by the presence of three gods: Apollo, Athena and Hermes. The implication is that the gods offer her a combination of spiritual and earthly relationships. Also present are Rubens's three ideal beauties, representing the three Graces: Euphrosyne, Aglaea and Thalia, who give her beauty. Along with guidance, the gods bestow gifts on the Princess, including wisdom, knowledge of the arts and eloquence. The caduceus represents Marie's peaceful reign.

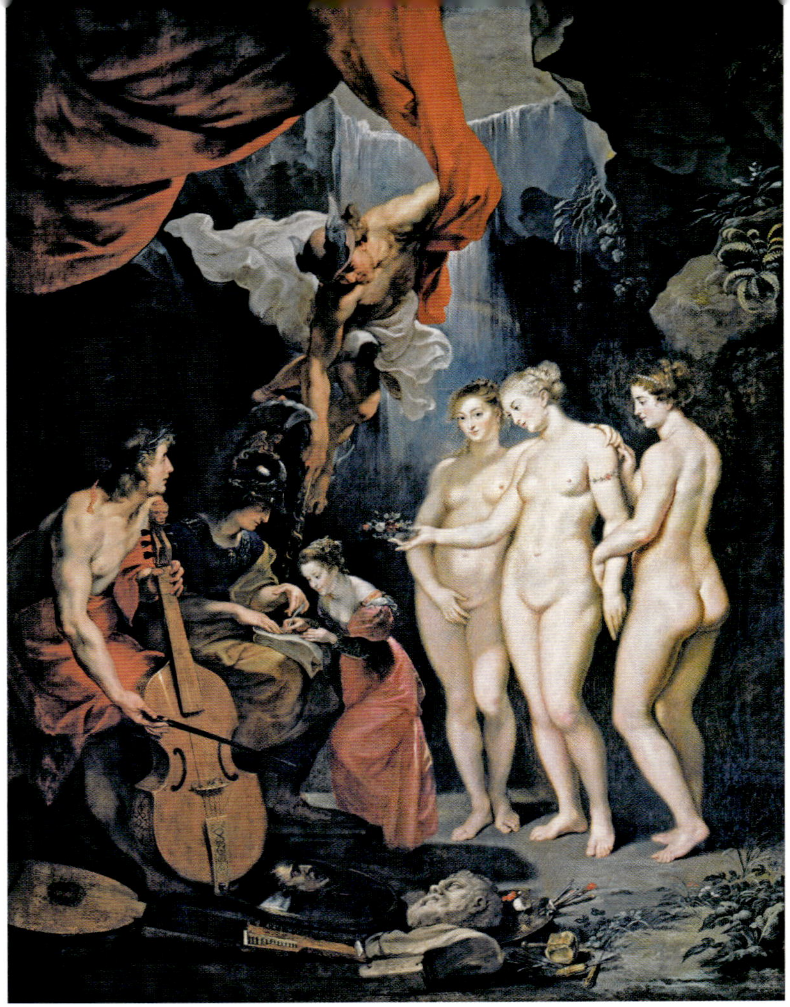

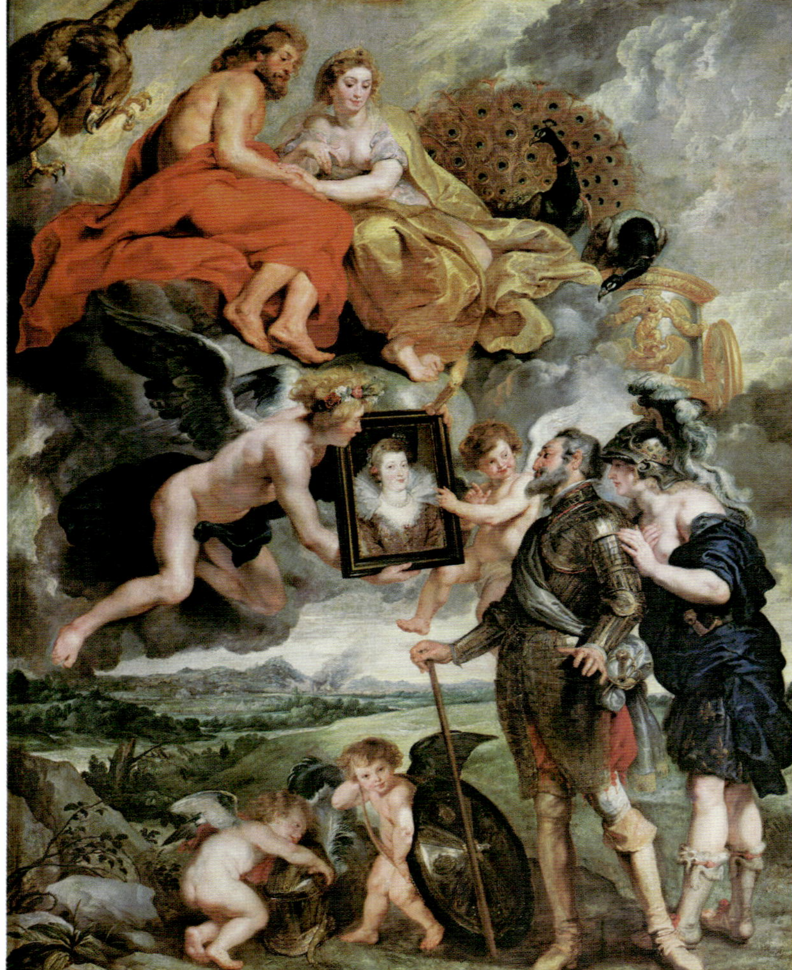

Henri IV Receiving the Portrait of Marie de' Medici, c.1622–25, oil on canvas, 394 x 295cm (155 x 116in), Musée du Louvre, Paris, France

In negotiating the marriage between Marie de' Medici and Henri IV, several portraits were exchanged. Here, Henri IV of France falls in love with a portrait of Marie. Cupid and Hymen, the gods of love and marriage, are showing him the portrait while Jupiter and Juno are sitting on clouds looking down on Henri. As they are happily married, this suggests their approval of the marriage. A personification of France is behind Henri, showing a closeness between the king and his country.

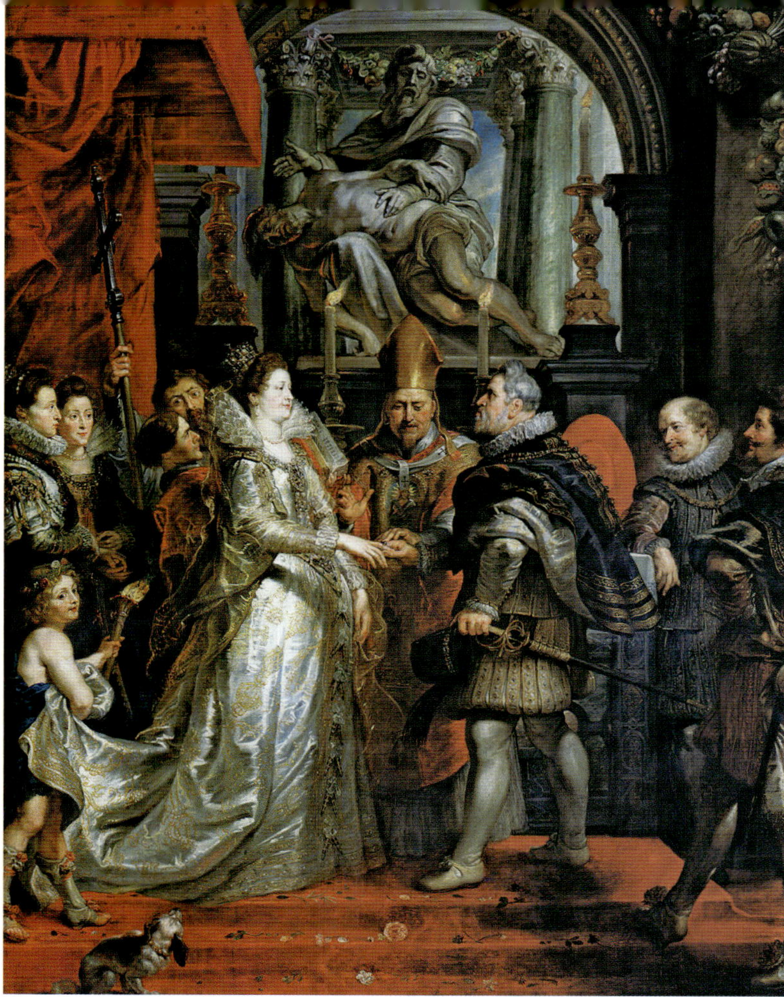

The Wedding by Proxy of Marie de' Medici to King Henri IV, c.1622–25, oil on canvas, 394 × 295cm (155 × 116in), Musée du Louvre, Paris, France

The proxy marriage ceremony of Marie and Henri took place in October 1600 in Florence cathedral, with Rubens in attendance as a member of the Gonzaga household. Here, Cardinal Pietro Aldobrandini presides over the ritual, and the bride's uncle, the Grand Duke Ferdinand of Tuscany, stands in the king's place and puts a ring on his niece's finger. The surrounding figures are identifiable as notable people of the time, including Rubens himself.

The Disembarkation at Marseilles, c.1622–25, oil on canvas, 394 x 295cm (155 x 116in), Musée du Louvre, Paris, France

This shows Marie arriving in Marseilles after her proxy marriage to Henri in Florence. Rubens depicts her leaving the ship, accompanied by the Grand Duchess of Tuscany and her sister, the Duchess of Mantua, into the welcoming, allegorical, open arms of a personification of France, who wears a helmet and royal blue mantle with golden fleur-de-lys. Sea gods rise from the water to watch, having escorted Marie safely to her destination.

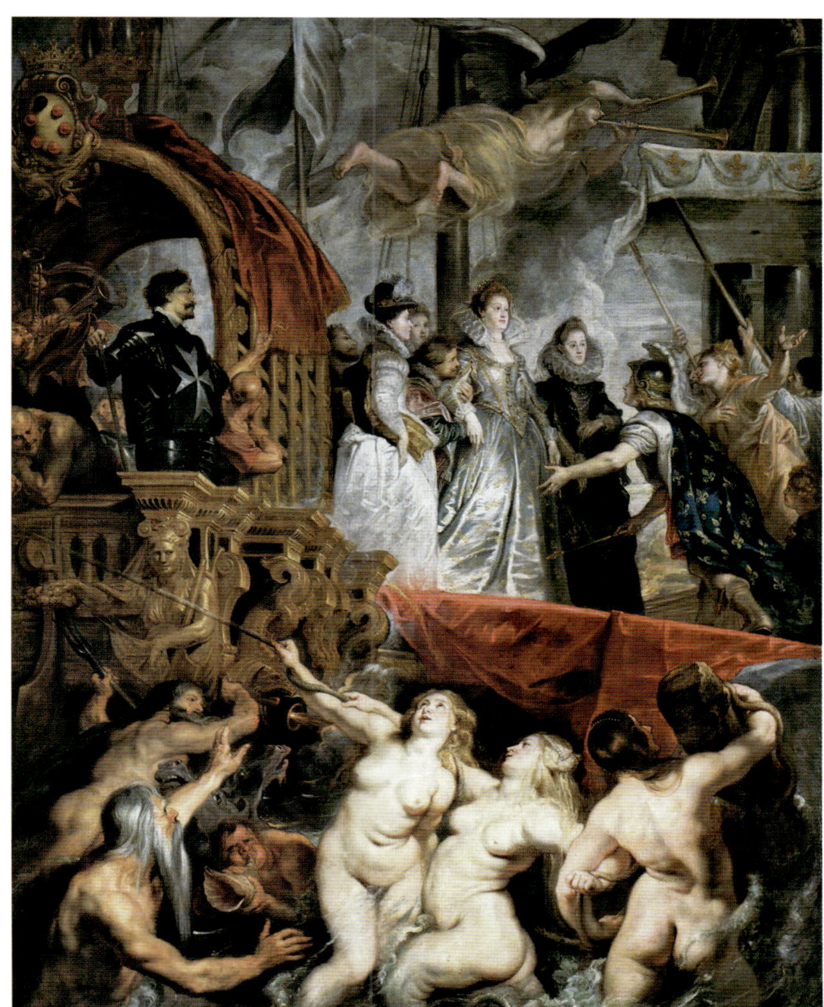

The Meeting of Henri IV and Marie de' Medici at Lyons, c.1622–25, oil on canvas, 394 x 295cm (155 x 116in), Musée du Louvre, Paris, France

This depicts the first meeting of Marie and her future husband, Henri. At the top of the painting, Marie and Henri are represented as the mythological Roman gods Juno and Jupiter. The joining of their right hands symbolizes the marriage union. Above them stands Hymen, the god of marriage, who unites them. A rainbow promises peace and harmony, while below, lions pull a chariot, conveying the allegorical figure of the city of Lyons.

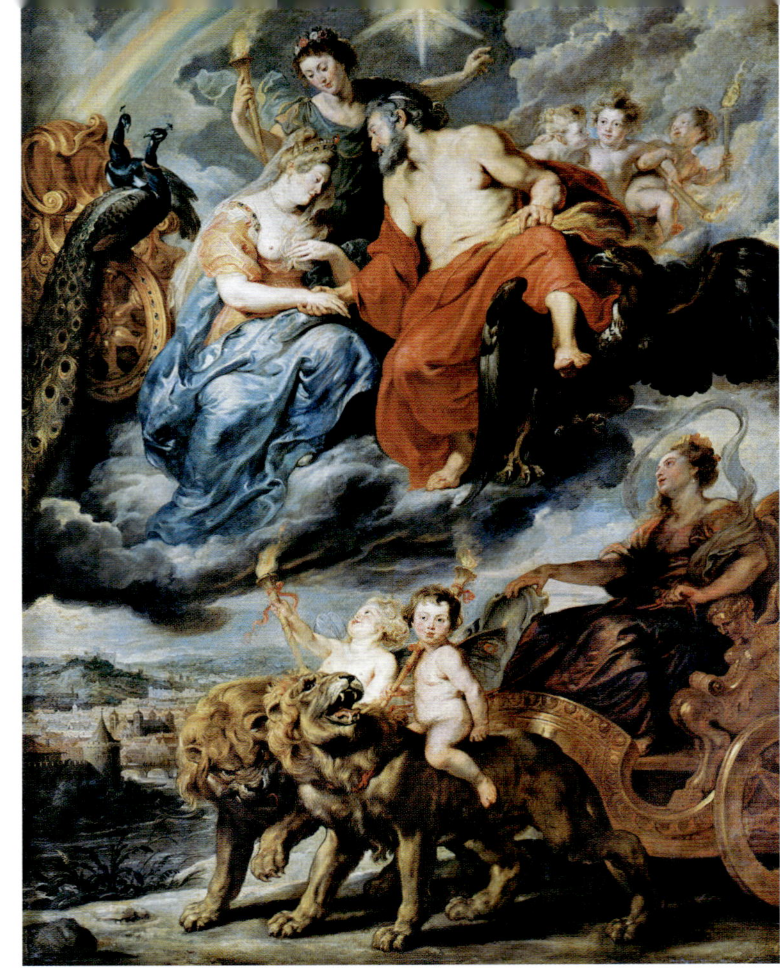

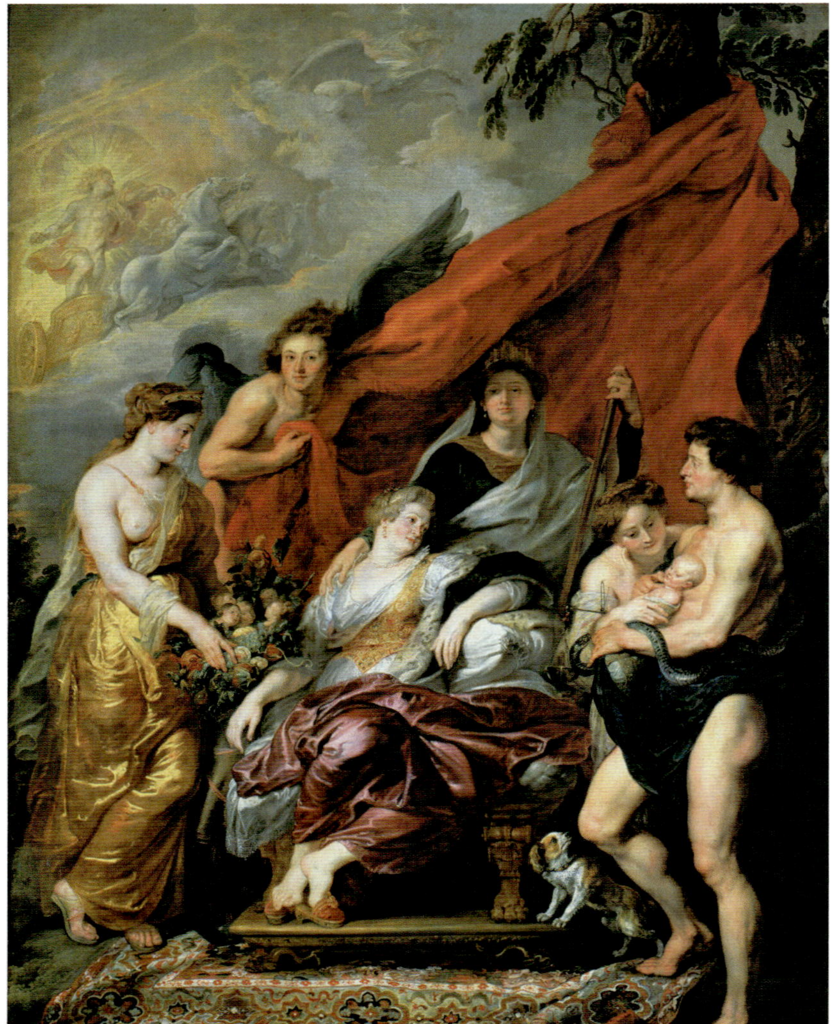

Birth of the Dauphin at Fontainebleau, c.1622–25, oil on canvas, 394 x 295cm (155 x 116in), Musée du Louvre, Paris, France

This represents the birth of Marie de' Medici's first son, who will become Louis XIII. Overall, the scene depicts political peace, as the birth of the first male heir brings security to the royal family. By representing Marie as Juno, the image implies that Henri is Jupiter, suggesting that his promiscuous ways will now be over. Louis is nursed by Themis, the goddess of divine order, implying that the gods have ordained that he will eventually become king.

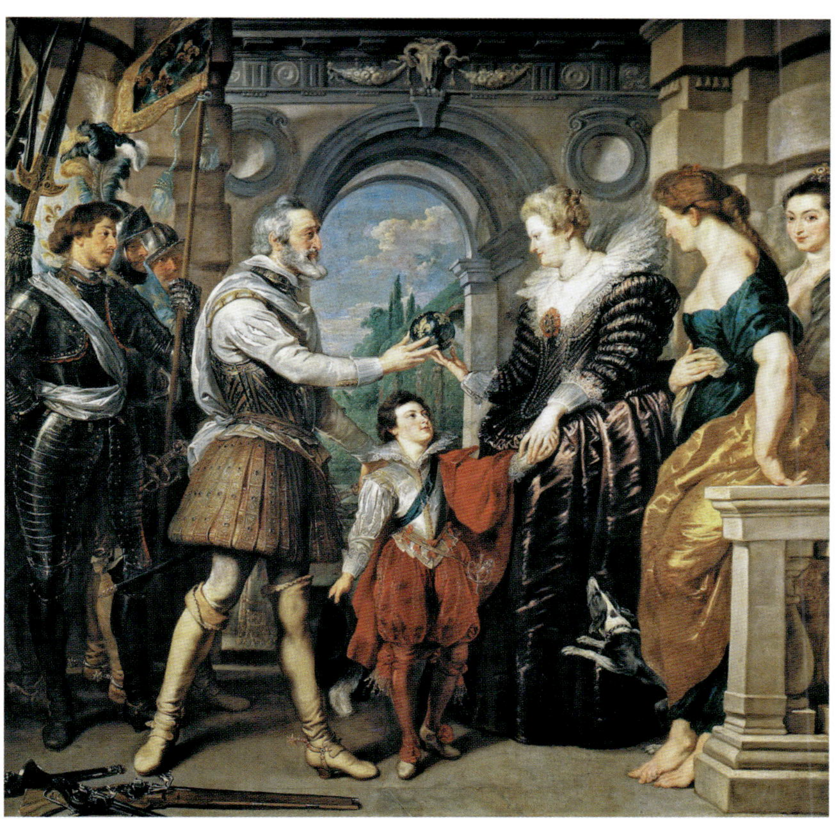

The Consignment of the Regency, c.1622–25, oil on canvas, 394 x 295cm (155 x 116in), Musée du Louvre, Paris, France

Here, Henri entrusts his wife with the Regency of France. Rubens had to create these images tactfully, so as not to put either Marie or Henri in a negative light. Because of the king's infidelities, it was rumoured that Marie had some involvement in his assassination. The orb alludes to the Roman *orbis terrarum* (sphere of earth), suggesting domain and power.

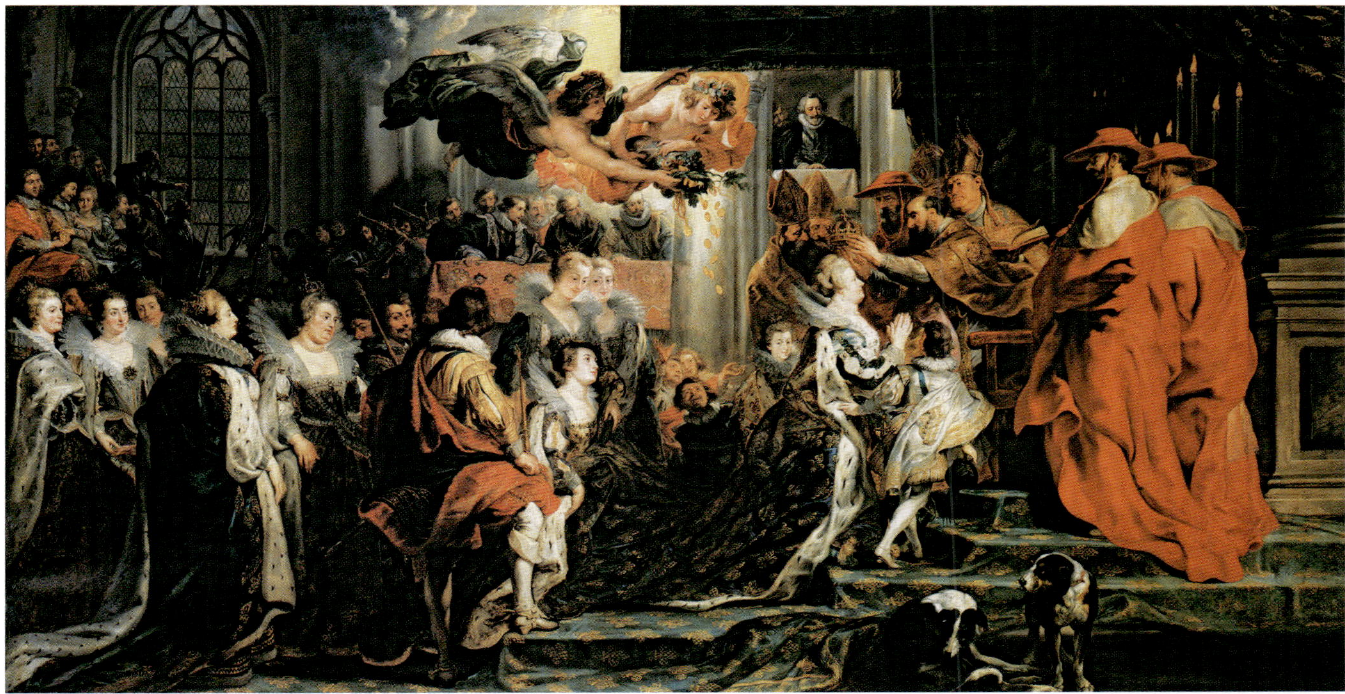

Coronation in Saint-Denis, c.1622–25, oil on canvas, 394 x 727cm (155 x 286¼in), Musée du Louvre, Paris, France

This shows Marie's coronation in Paris. She is conducted to the altar by the Cardinals Gondi and de Sourdis, and the ceremony is officiated by Cardinal Joyeuse. The Princess of Conti and the Duchess of Montpensier (the mother of Marie's future daughter-in-law) carry her train. Above, the classical personifications of Abundantia and a winged Victoria are showering blessings of peace and prosperity on Marie's head by pouring out the golden coins of Jupiter.

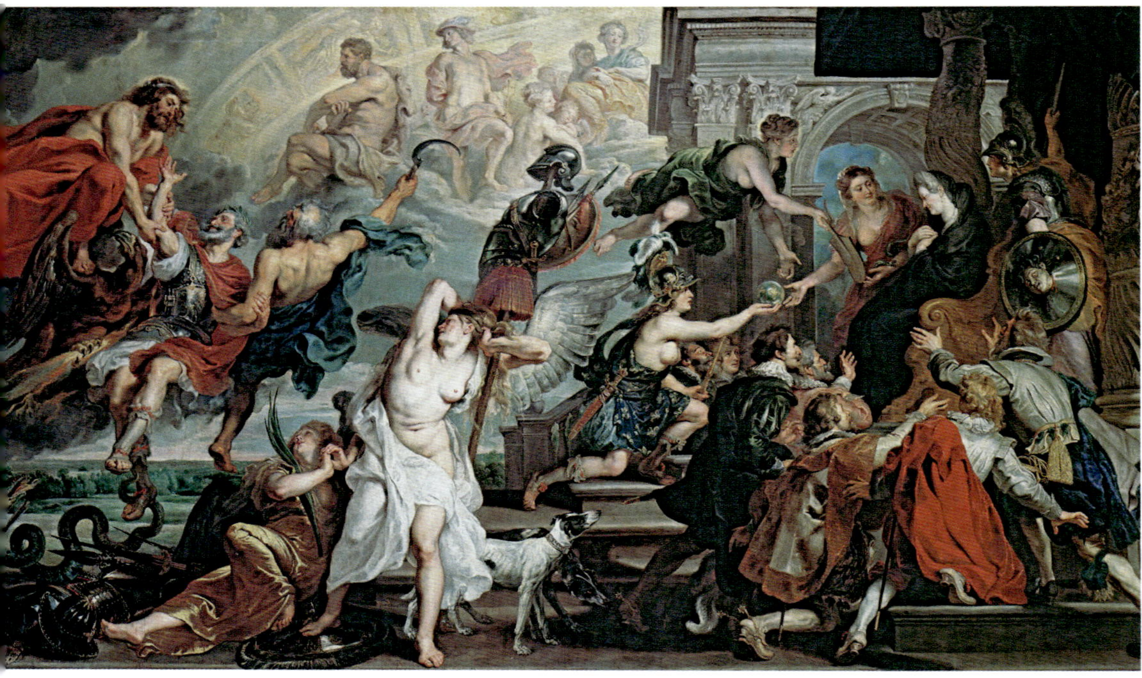

Apotheosis of Henri IV and the Proclamation of the Regency, c.1622–25, oil on canvas, 394 x 727cm (155 x 286¼in), Musée du Louvre, Paris, France

Two scenes feature here: the assumption of Henri IV to the heavens, and the assumption of Marie to the crown. Jupiter and Saturn welcome the assassinated King of France as he ascends to Olympus as a Roman emperor. The Queen accepts an orb, a symbol of government from personified France, suggesting that the Regency was offered to her, although she actually claimed it for herself on the day of her husband's murder.

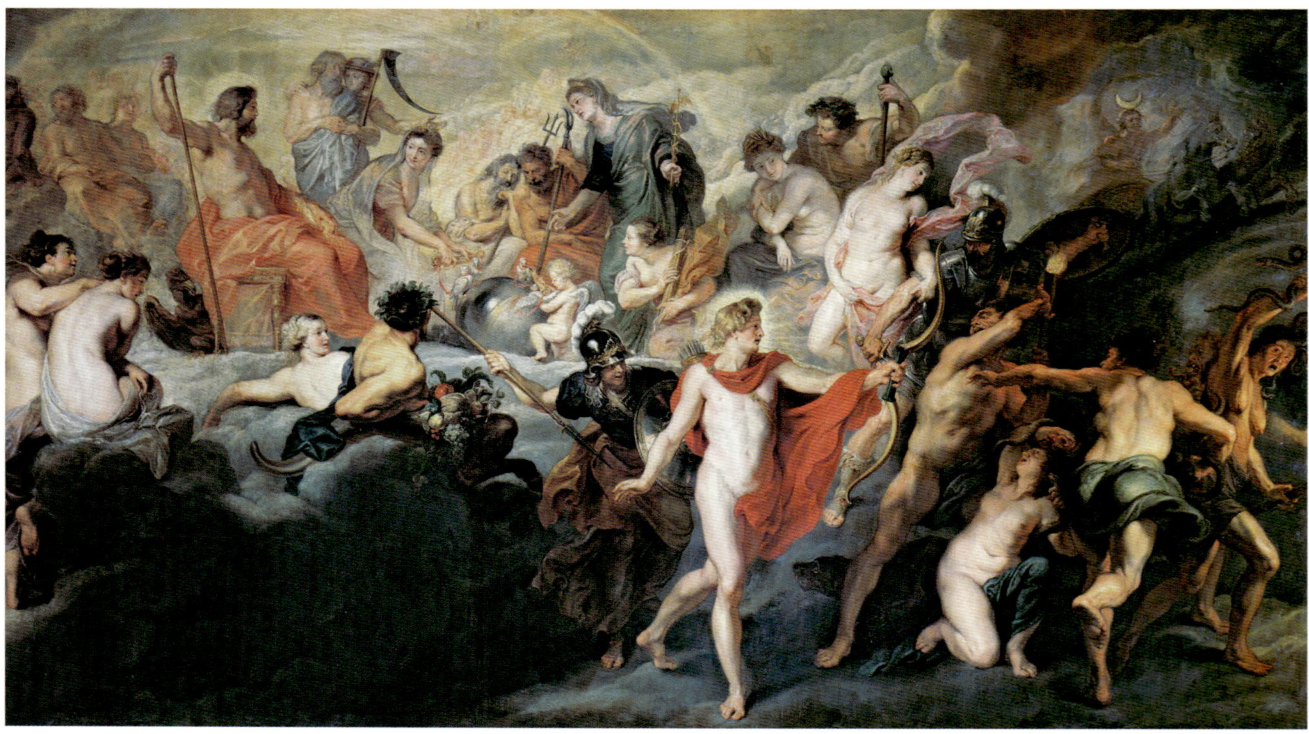

The Council of the Gods, c.1622–25, oil on canvas, 394 x 727cm (155 x 286¼in), Musée du Louvre, Paris, France

This painting commemorates Marie taking over the government as Regent. Marie wanted her son Louis to marry the Spanish Infanta, and for her daughter Elizabeth to marry the future king of Spain, Philip IV, so allying France and Spain, since peace in Europe was her primary goal. Overall, the painting represents her care of the kingdom while she was Regent. It also suggests that she perpetuated the policies of her late husband during his life and after his death.

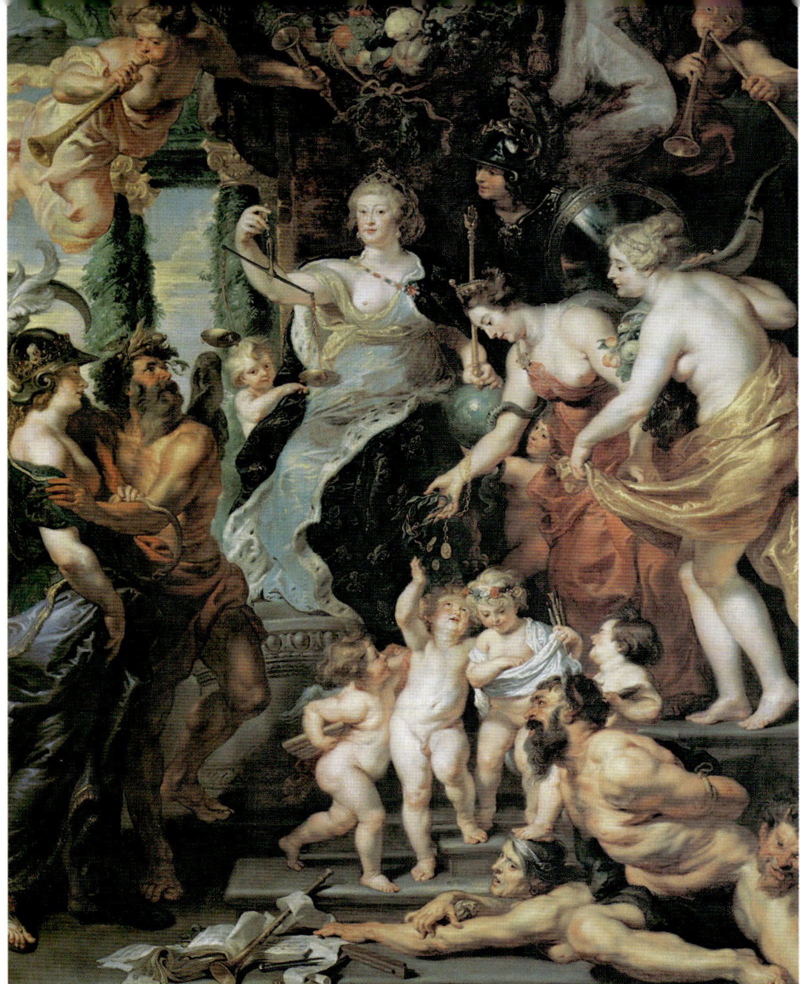

The Felicity of the Regency of Marie de' Medici, c.1622–25, oil on canvas, 394 x 295cm (155 x 116in), Musée du Louvre, Paris, France

This was painted entirely by Rubens on the spot, rather than by him and his studio assistants, to replace another more controversial depiction of Marie's expulsion from Paris by her son Louis in 1617. It is the final painting in Rubens's cycle. Surrounded by Cupid, Juno, Prudence, Abundance, Saturn and Pheme, Marie is shown as the personification of Justice. Representations of envy, ignorance and vice are also present, implying that she was unjustly judged.

Louis XIII Comes of Age, c.1622–25, oil on canvas, 394 x 295cm (155 x 116in), Musée du Louvre, Paris, France

Here, power is transferred from Marie to her son Louis on his coming of age. As Marie hands her son his kingdom, her control of France is represented by a ship. Louis now steers the vessel; the rowers can be identified by their emblematic shields. Louis looks up to his mother for guidance on steering the ship. The figure adjusting the sail is probably Prudence or Temperance. In actuality, Louis had rejected his mother's regency.

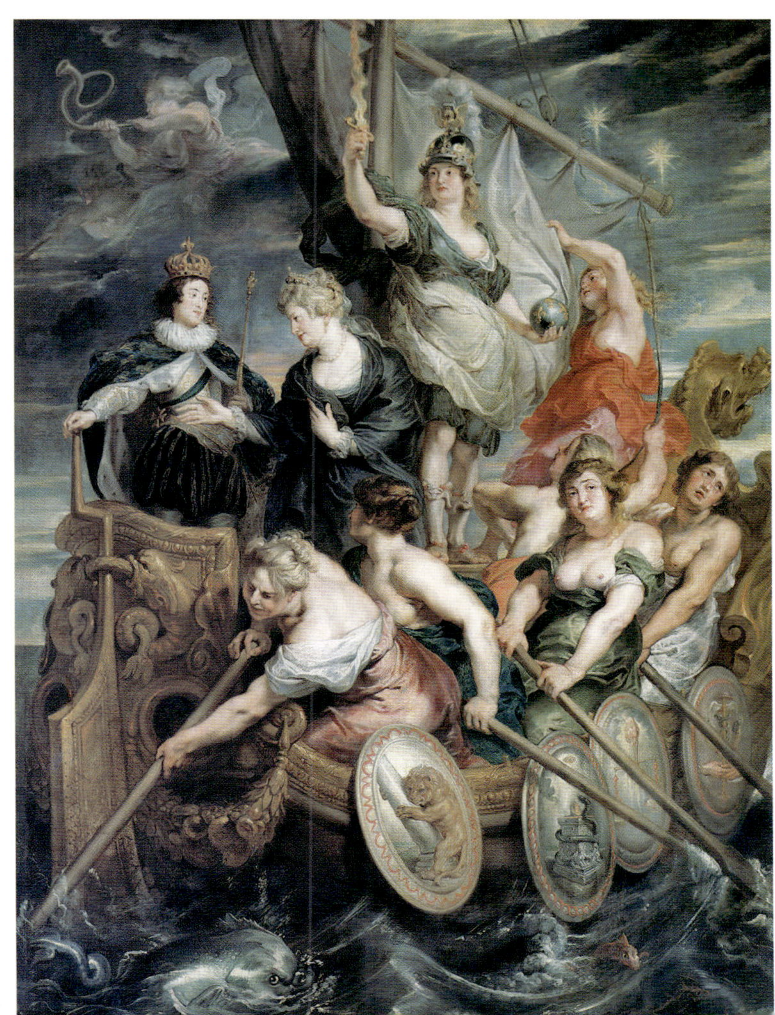

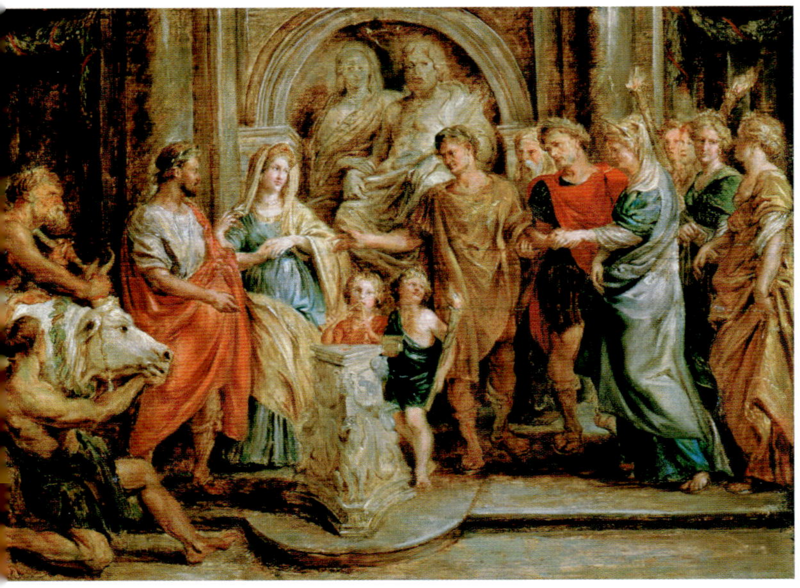

The Marriage of Constantine and Fausta and Constantia and Licinius, 1622, oil on panel, 47.3 x 64.4cm (18⅛ x 25⅜in), Private Collection

Rubens intended to evoke parallels here with the double marriage of Louis XIII of France with the Archduchess Anne of Austria and his sister Isabella (or Elisabeth) with Anne's brother Philip XIV of Spain in November 1615. The couples are ancient Roman siblings who married in a similar way: Constantine and Fausta, and Licinius and Constantia.

*Louis XIII, c.*1622, oil on paper on wood panel, 42.8 x 32.5cm (16¾ x 12¾in), National Gallery of Victoria, Melbourne, Australia

This is a small, somewhat pensive portrait of Louis, who, after being so dominated by his mother and certain ministers, turned out to be a weak and ineffectual king. Despite being aligned with the young king's controversial mother, Rubens befriended Louis and put him at ease while painting this informal portrait. This was quite an achievement at such an autocratic court.

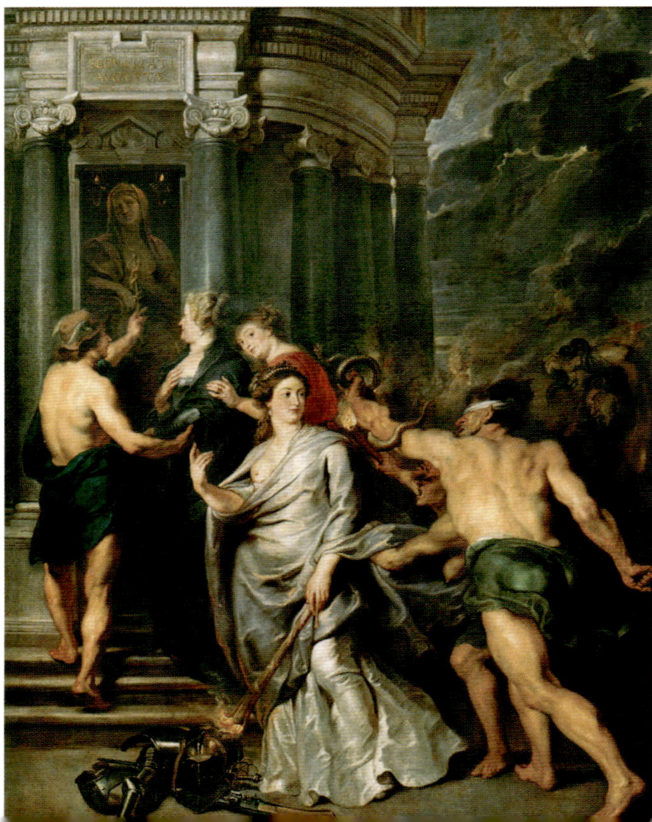

*The Peace Treaty of Angers, c.*1623–25, oil on canvas, 394 x 295cm (155 x 166in), Musée du Louvre, Paris, France

Also known as *The Queen Opts for Security,* this is one of Rubens's paintings of Marie de' Medici that belongs to the third group of works representing her widowhood and regency. It depicts an event when she was compelled to sign a truce in Angers after her armies had been defeated. The representation of the Temple of Security (which is rounded to represent the world) directly suggests Marie's wish for safety. Her attire and the light falling on her face imply that she is a goddess, further emphasized by Mercury next to her brandishing a caduceus swirled with writhing snakes.

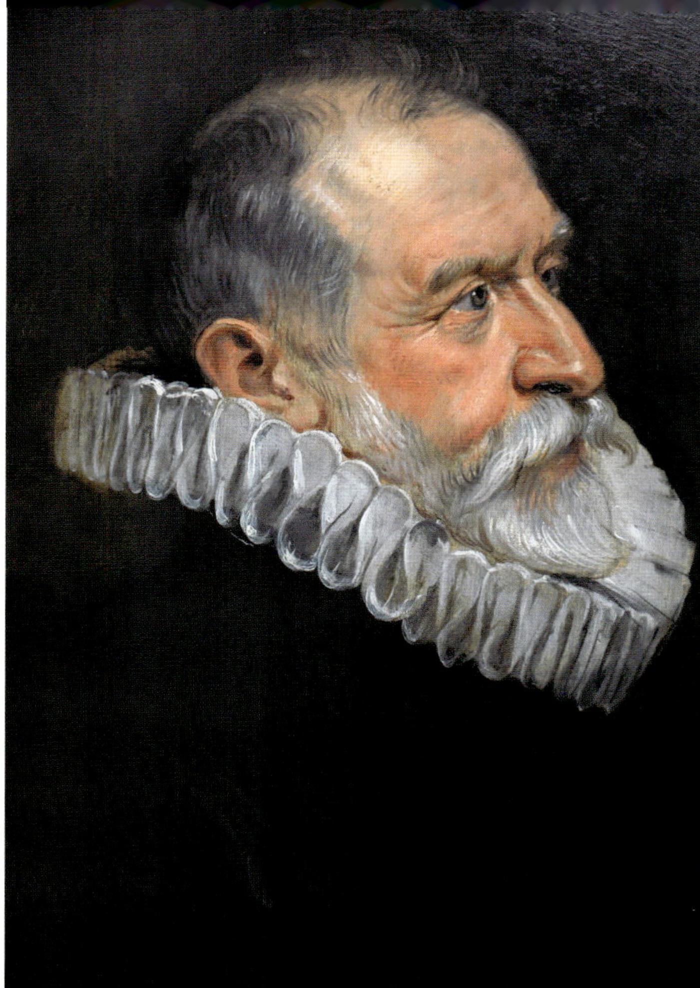

Portrait of an Old Man, 1622–25, oil on panel, *c.*1622–25, 64.7 x 49.5cm (25½ x 19½in), Gemäldegalerie, Staatliche Museen zu Berlin, Berlin, Germany

While working on the vast project for Marie de' Medici, Rubens continued his diplomatic duties and also painted several portraits. This is believed to be of Jan van Ghindertalen, a lawyer, magistrate and alderman of Brussels, closely involved in the city's government and known to Rubens through Albert and Isabella. In great detail, the face and ruff are strikingly highlighted against a black background.

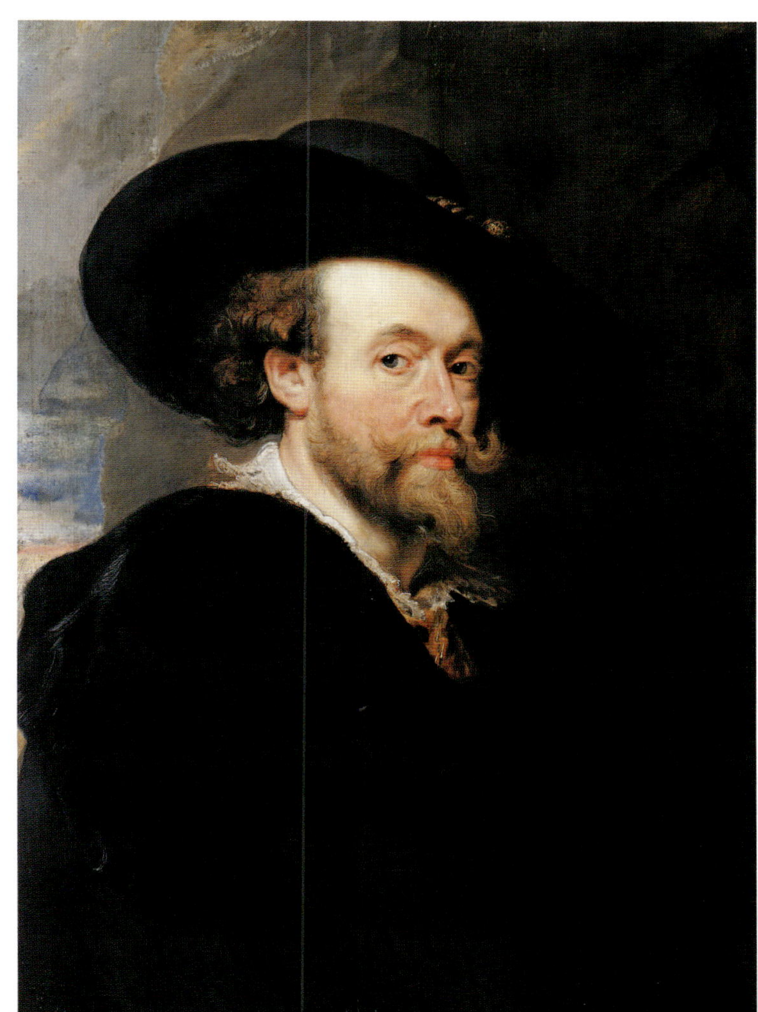

Self-portrait in a Hat, 1623, oil on panel, 85.7 x 62.2cm (33¾ x 24½in), Royal Collection, London, UK

Commissioned by Henri Danvers, Earl of Danby (1573–1643) as a present for King Charles I when he was Prince of Wales, this self-portrait caused Rubens some consternation. He said he was concerned at the arrogance of sending the future king a self-portrait. Lord Danvers asked for this, as he had wanted to ensure that the work was executed by Rubens alone and not his assistants. The painting expresses Rubens's skills in portraiture, including tonal contrast, luminous skin and light brush marks.

*Clara Serena, c.*1623, black, red and white chalk on paper, 35.3 x 28.3cm (14 x 11¼in), Albertina Museum, Vienna, Austria

It is not confirmed that this is Rubens's daughter Clara Serena, but the features show a close resemblance to her mother Isabella Brant, and also of the younger child portrait painted by her father a few years earlier, also believed to be her. It is probable that the drawing was a preparatory sketch for a portrait (now lost) in oil. The noble dress suggests that the Infanta Isabella accepted the girl as a lady-in-waiting.

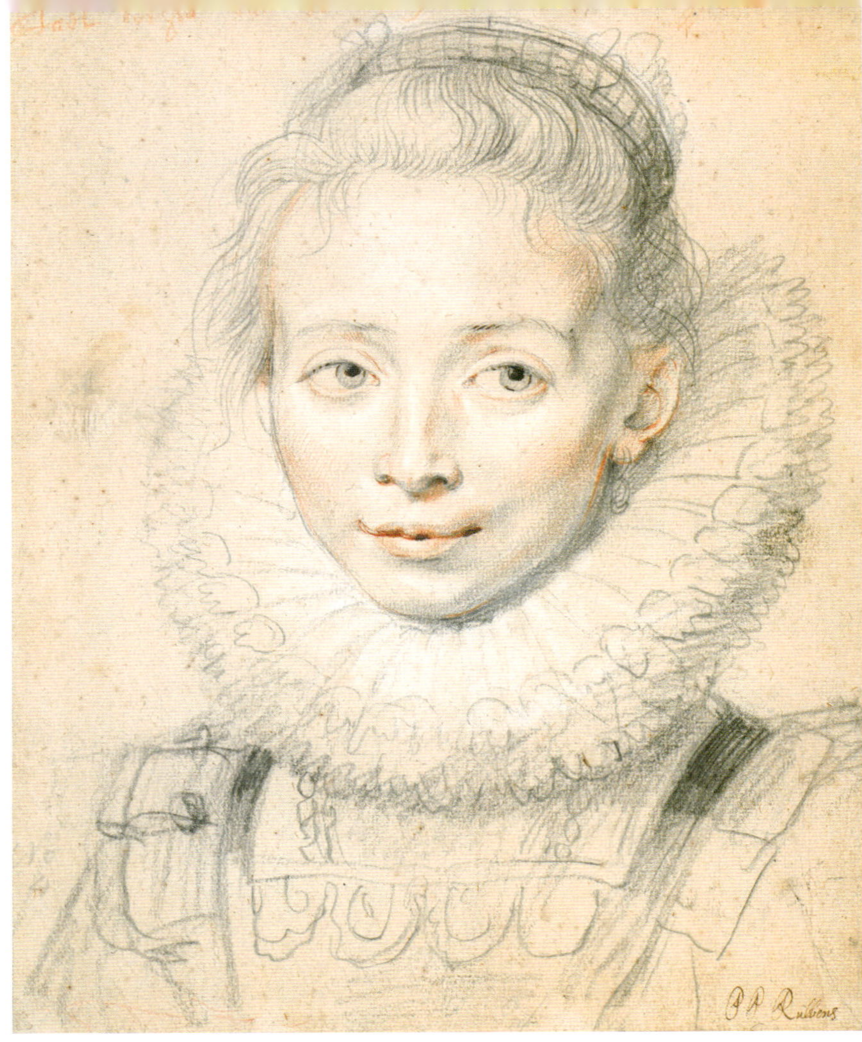

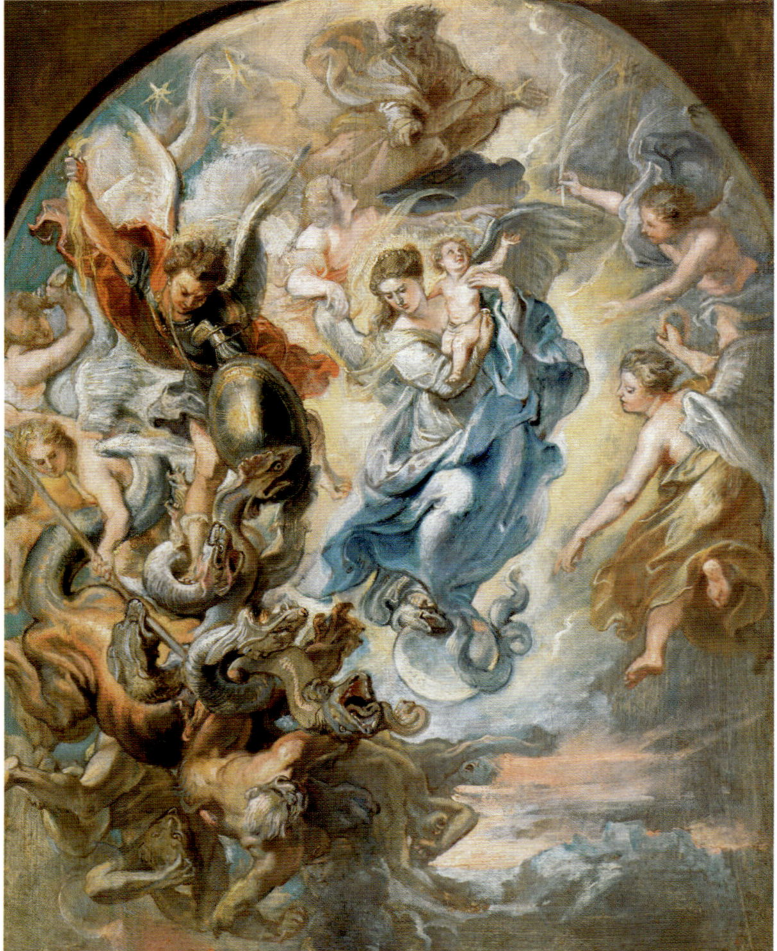

*The Virgin as the Woman of the Apocalypse, c.*1623–24, oil on panel, 63.5 x 49.2cm (25 x 19¼in), J. Paul Getty Museum, Los Angeles, USA

This modello was commissioned by Prince-Bishop Adam Friedrich Graf von Seinsheim (1708–79) for the main altarpiece of Freising Cathedral in southern Germany. The Virgin Mary holds the Christ Child while stamping on the serpent of sin, who curls around the moon at her feet. The Archangel Michael and angels banish Satan and other demons, while God instructs an angel to give the Virgin angel's wings.

*The Triumph of Rome,
Youthful Emperor Constantine
Honouring Rome, c.1622–23,
oil on panel, 54 x 69cm
(21¼ x 27in), Mauritshuis,
Den Haag, The Netherlands*

This was Rubens's thirteenth
sketch for his History
of Constantine series of
tapestry designs. Crowded
with allegorical figures, it
includes liberated Rome,
two winged Victories, and
Romulus and Remus, but was
rejected as part of the cycle
as it focused too much on
myth and not enough
on authentic events in
Constantine's life. It was
replaced by *The Death
of Constantine.*

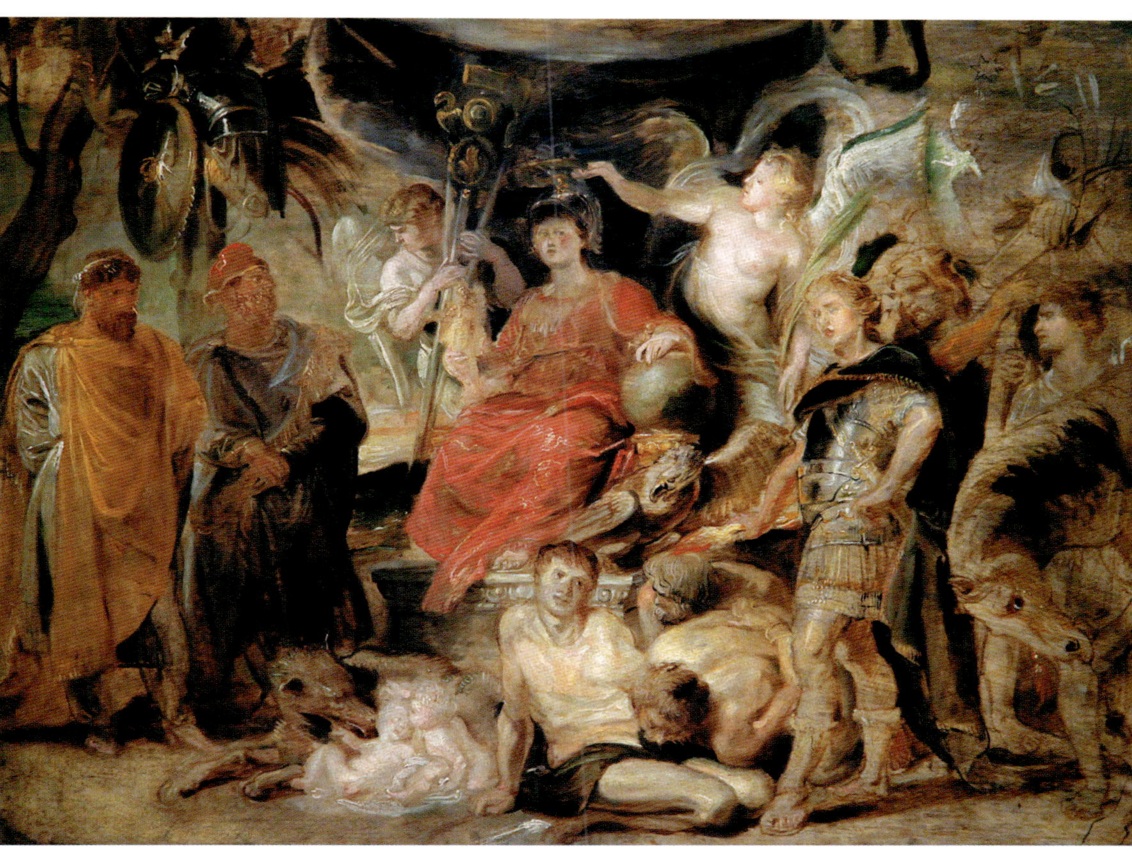

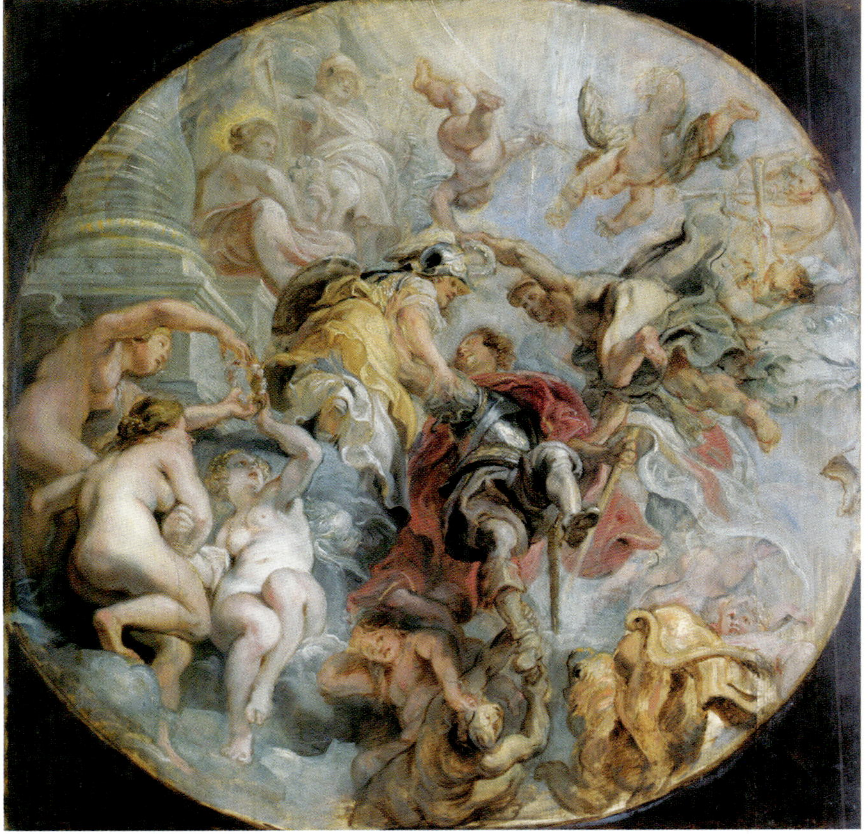

*Apotheosis of the Duke
of Buckinghamshire,
before 1625, oil on oak,
64 x 63.7cm (25 x 25in),
The National Gallery,
London, UK*

In a preparatory sketch
for a ceiling painting for
the Duke's London home,
George Villiers, the Duke
of Buckingham, is carried
upwards by Minerva and
Mercury to a marble temple.
The three Graces present
him with a crown of flowers,
while Envy tries to pull him
down and a lion challenges
him. Buckingham was the
favourite of both James I
and Charles I, and this is
an allegory of his political
aims and the forces that
hindered him.

Anne of Austria, 1622–25, oil on canvas, 120 x 96.8cm (47¼ x 38in), Norton Simon Museum, Colorado, USA

Painted during one of Rubens's visits to Paris when he was directing the decoration of the Luxembourg Gallery, Anne of Austria (1601–67) was the wife of Louis XIII of France, daughter-in-law of Marie de' Medici. As Queen of France, she is dressed with a 'Medici'-style pleated lace ruffle around her neck, jewelled crown, a satin dress embroidered with repeated fleur-de-lys, and an ermine-lined mantle.

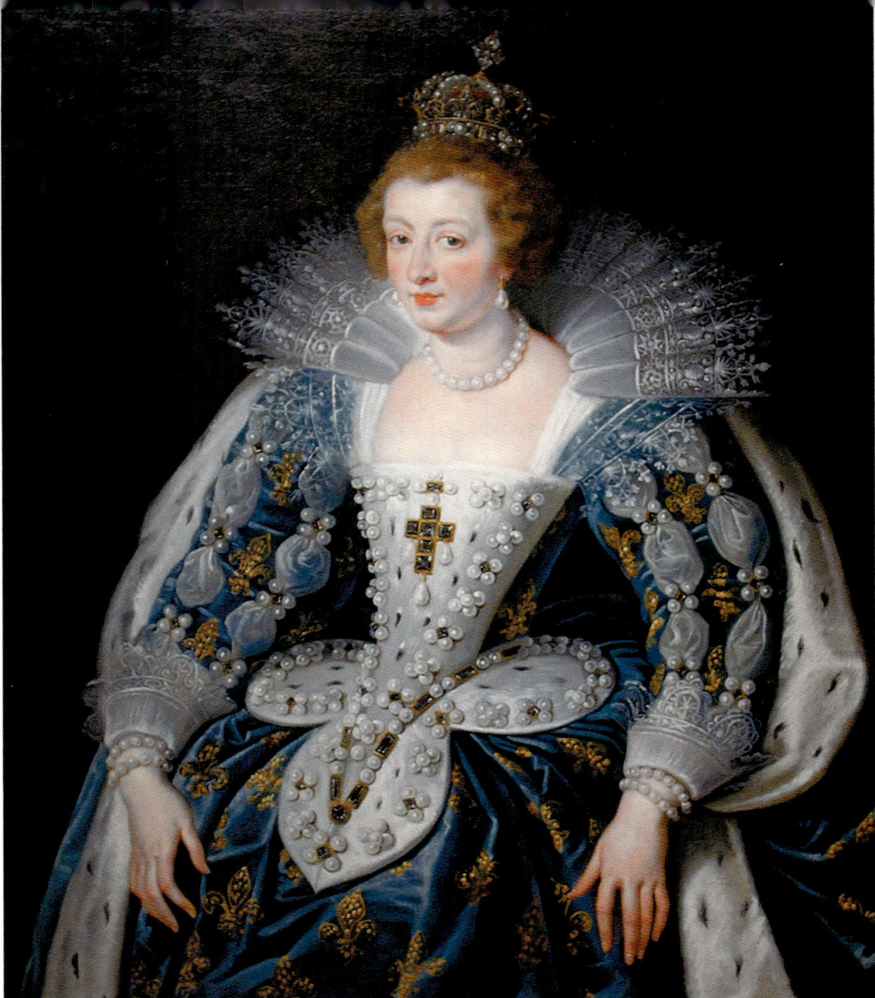

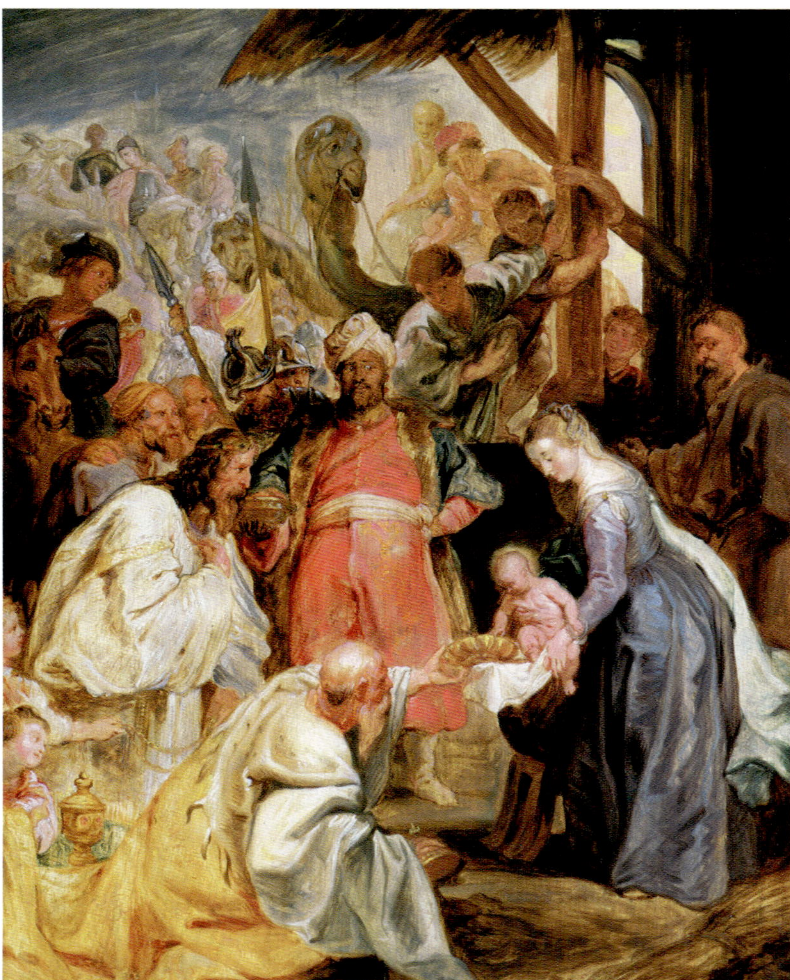

Adoration of the Magi, c.1624, oil on oak, 63.6 x 48.2cm (25 x 19in), Wallace Collection, London, UK

During the substantial programme of church building and restoration undertaken during the Twelve Year Truce in the war between Spain and the Netherlands, from 1609–21, Rubens painted this version of the Bible story. This painting is the modello for his altarpiece for the convent of the Dames Blanches in Louvain, commissioned by the prioress, Anna van Zevendonk, and paid for in 1634.

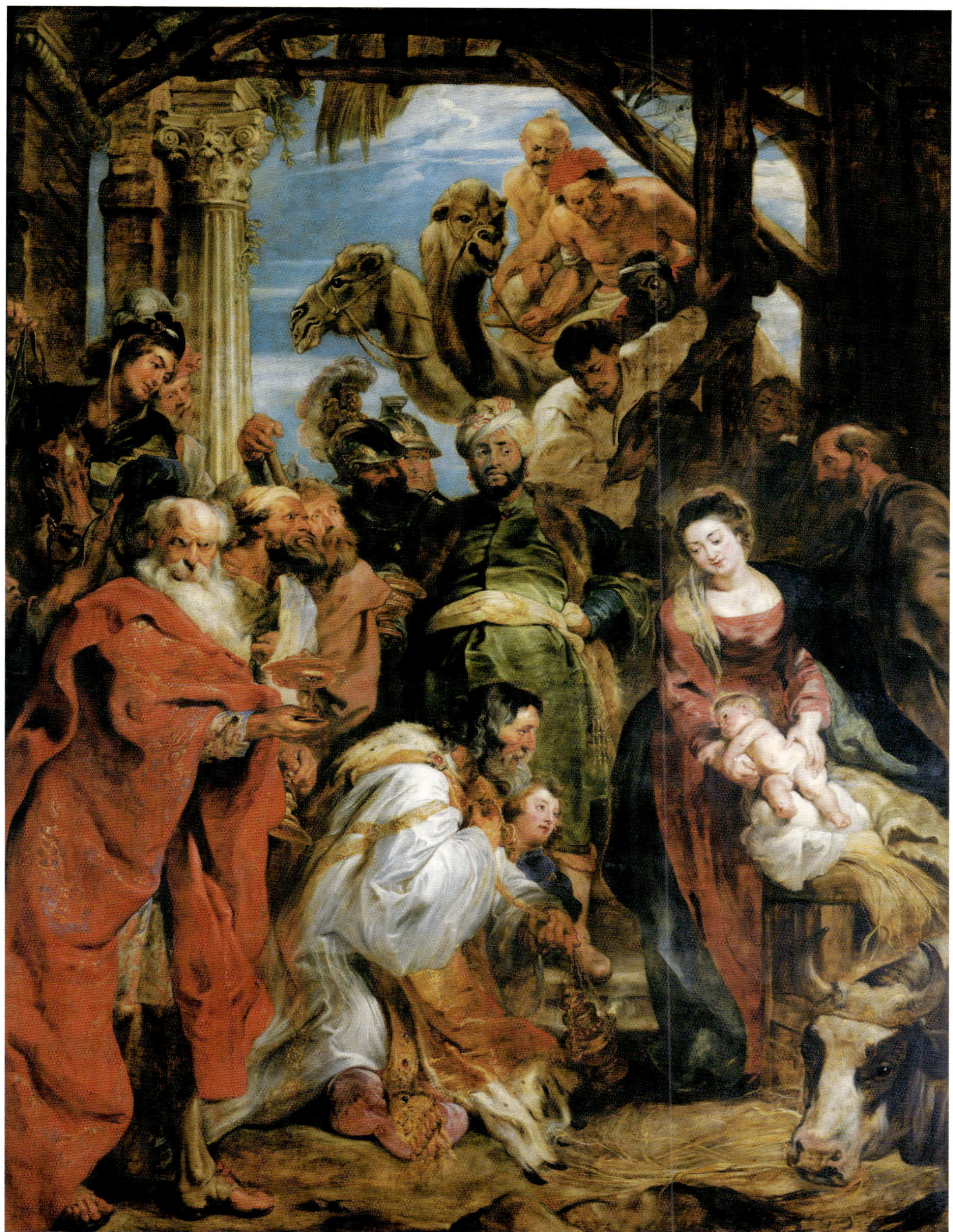

Adoration of the Magi, 1624, oil on panel, 447 x 336cm (176 x 132¼ in), Koninklijk Museum voor Schone Kunsten, Antwerp, Belgium

Made for the church of Saint Michael's Abbey in Antwerp, the Virgin Mary here is believed to be modelled by Isabella Brant. The central Magi is dressed as a priest, and seems to be celebrating mass. Behind him, looking rather disturbed, is the second wise man, while the third wears a turban. Each can be identified by the gifts they are bringing for the Christ Child, as well as their characterful faces.

Ceres with Two Nymphs, Rubens and Snyders, c.1620, oil on canvas, 224.5 x 166cm (88⅓ x 65⅓in), Museo Nacional del Prado, Madrid, Spain

Ceres, the goddess of grains and the harvest, holds some corn cobs in one hand and a horn of plenty in her other. Two nymphs fill this bountifulness with fruits, symbolizing the Earth's generosity. Inspired by Ovid's *Metamorphoses*, this was a collaboration between Rubens and Snyders. Rubens painted the figures of the goddess and her companions, while Snyders, who specialized in still lifes and animals, painted the fruit, the monkey and the birds.

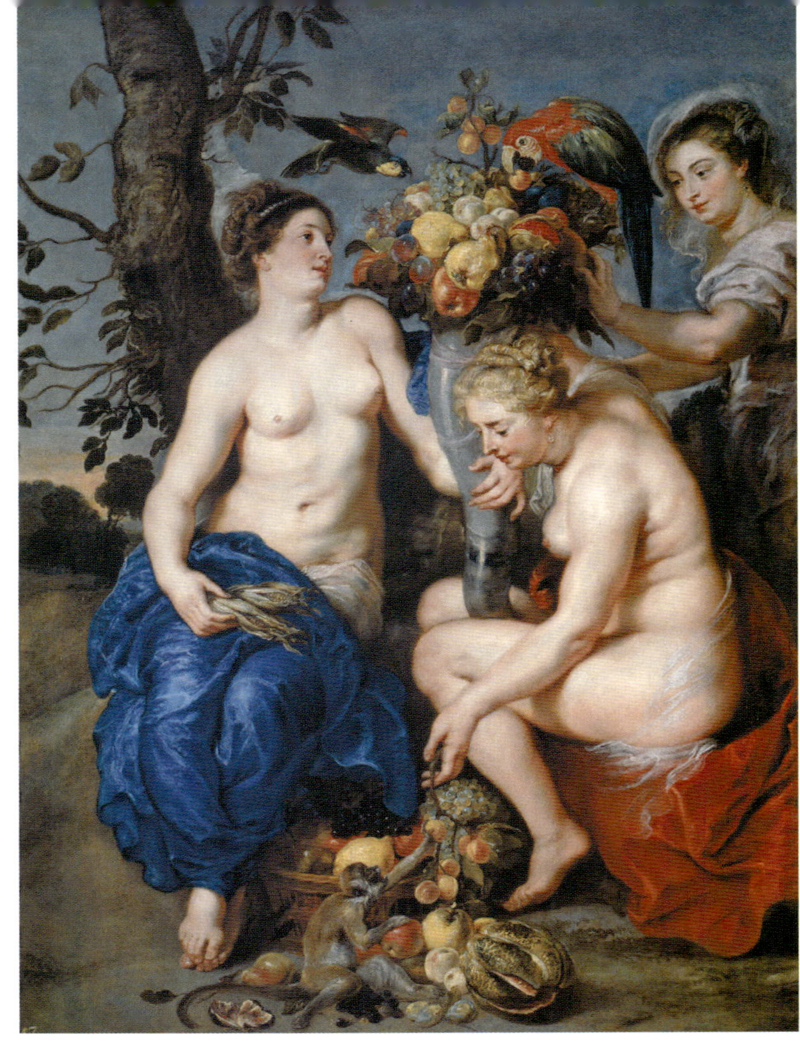

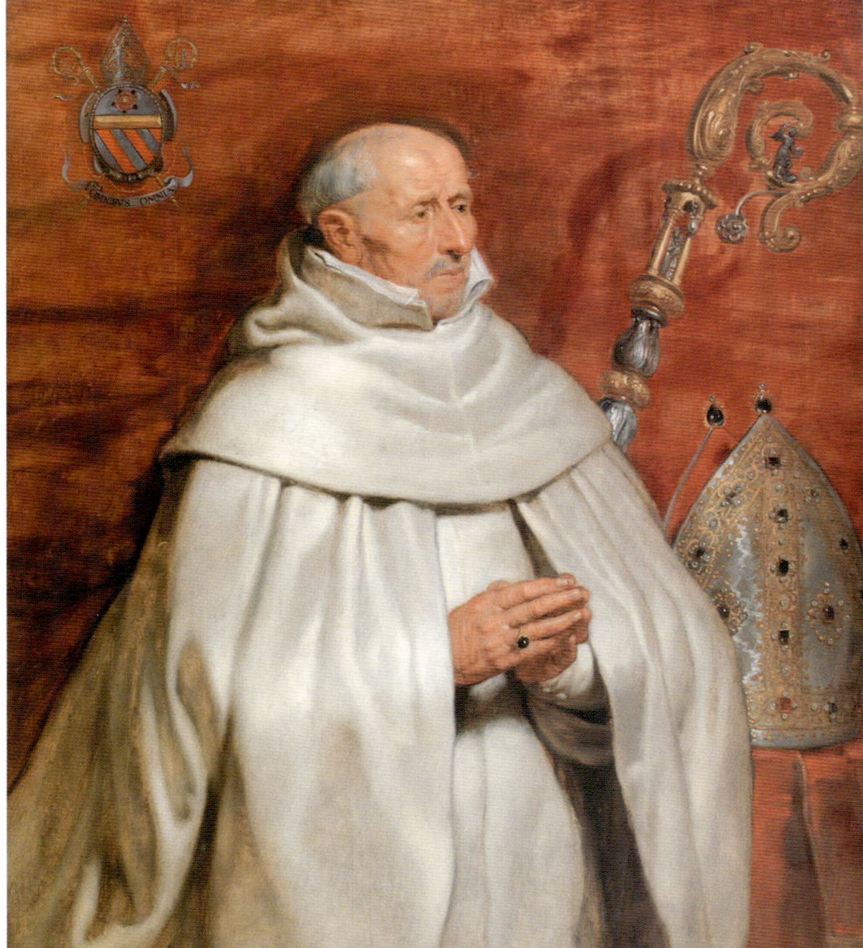

Matthaeus Yrsselius, c.1624, oil on oak panel, 120 x 102.5cm (47¼ x 40⅓in), Statens Museum for Kunst, Copenhagen, Denmark

The Abbot of Saint Michael's Abbey in Antwerp, Matthaeus Yrsselius (1541–1629), had commissioned *Adoration of the Magi* (see page 214) for his church, and Rubens painted this to be placed nearby, so that the abbot would be looking towards the high altar with his hands folded in prayer. The softly pious portrait was later placed on the abbot's grave, also in the abbey.

Lot and His Family Leaving Sodom, 1625, oil on panel, 74 x 118cm (29 x 46½in), Musée du Louvre, Paris, France

The story of Lot and his family leaving Sodom is told in the Old Testament Book of Genesis. Rubens illustrates the figures fleeing the sinful city of Sodom after being warned of its destruction by God. God had been willing to save Lot and his family because Lot had been kind and protective of two angels who had been sent to Sodom as messengers. The angels told Lot to take his family into the mountains and not to look back at Sodom, otherwise they would also be consumed by God's wrath.

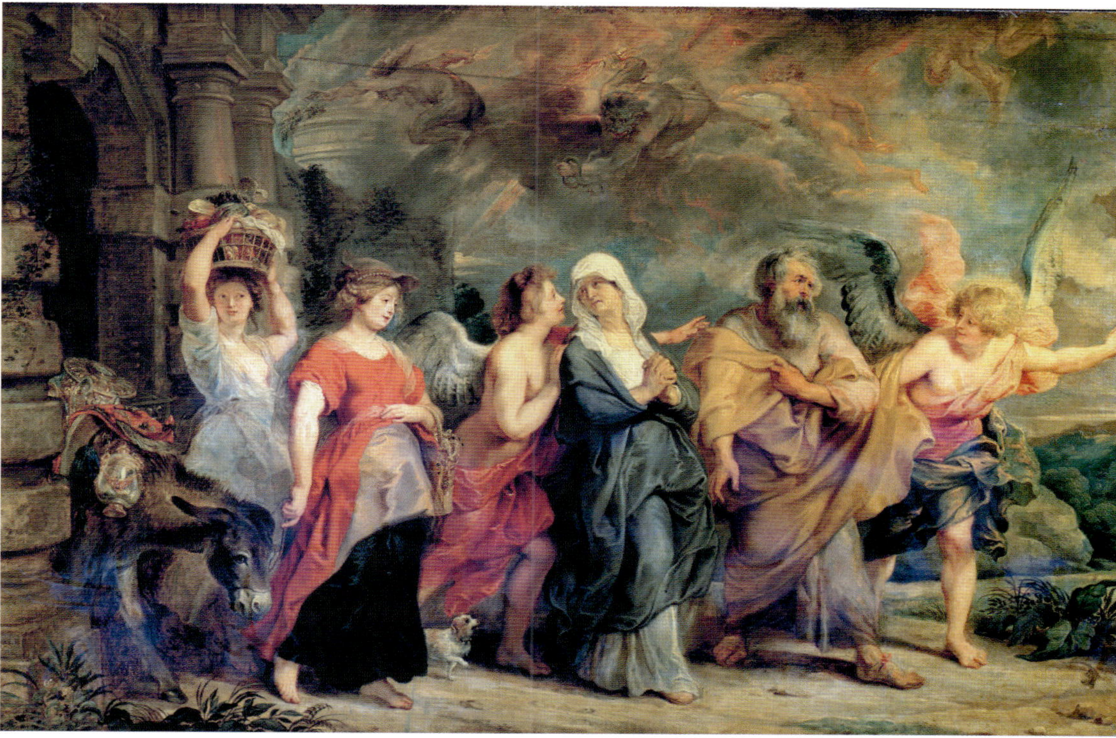

Portrait of Isabella Brant, c.1625 oil on panel, 86 x 62cm (34 x 24½in), Galleria degli Uffizi, Florence, Italy

Painted in the year before her untimely death, this closely observed and intimate portrait shows Rubens's first wife looking elegant and contented with her husband's companionship – he was also now famous. While Rubens did not paint Isabella as frequently as he painted his second wife, the love between the couple is almost palpable here.

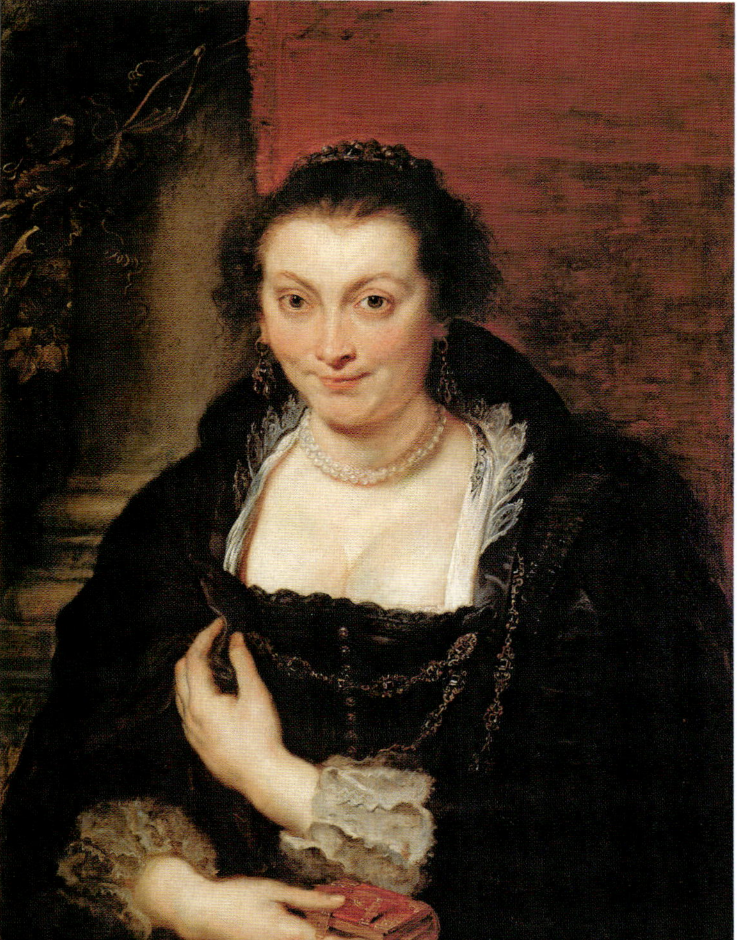

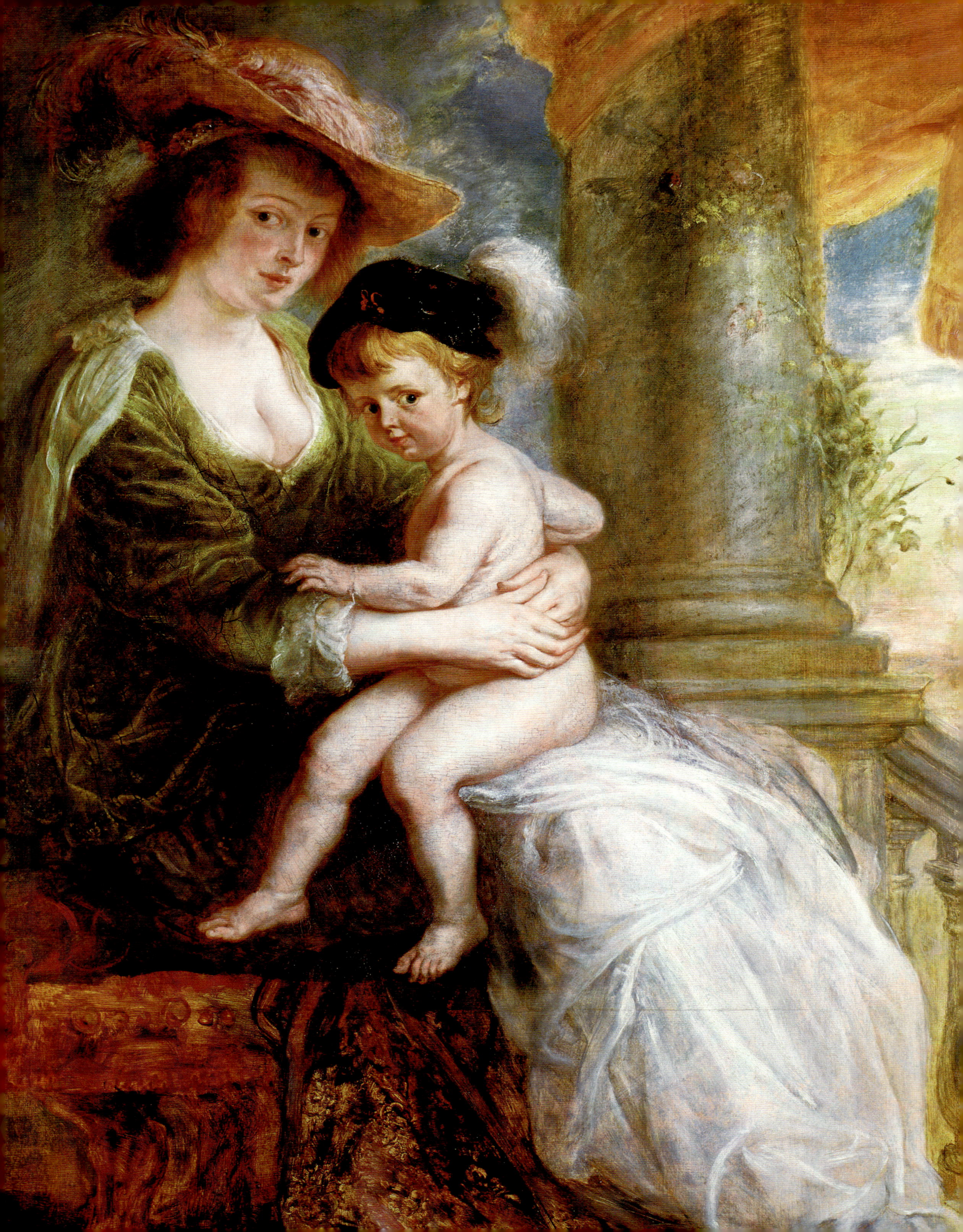

EVERLASTING VITALITY

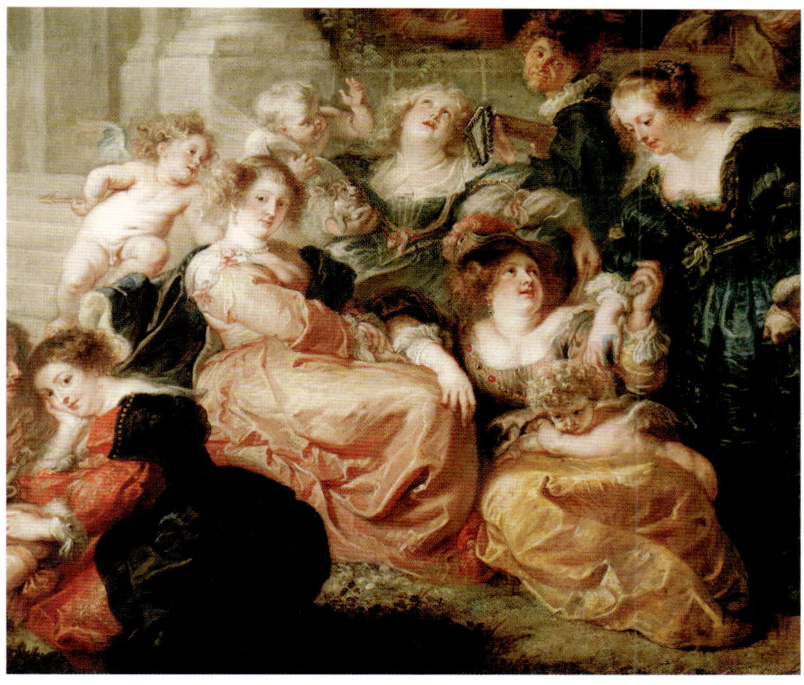

On Isabella's death in July 1626, Rubens's happiness came to an abrupt halt. By then he had experienced several deaths of close family and friends, and although he was professionally successful and had many friends, he was lonely. Art was his salvation, and he continued working frenetically despite his eyesight weakening. Four years later, he married his second wife Hélène, and his dynamic style evolved even more, his approach becoming looser and more painterly. He painted an even broader range of subjects, including the voluptuous nudes for which he has become known, as well as portraying personalities in religious and mythological works, portraits and country scenes, all with his new, more tactile brushwork.

Above: The Garden of Love, *1633–34. This is a detail of the painting on page 235 that depicts richly attired individuals flirting in a garden while chubby-cheeked Cupids fly overhead. Painted soon after Rubens's second marriage, most of the women were modelled by his new wife Hélène Fourment.*

Left: Hélène Fourment and her Son Frans, *c.1635, oil on panel. An intimate, personal scene, not a commission, this softly painted work conveys Rubens's love for his new wife and for his children.*

Portrait of a Woman, c.1625–30, oil on panel, 84.8 x 59.3cm (33⅓ x 23⅓in), The Royal Collection, London, UK

In 1622 Arnold Lunden married Susanna Fourment, and in 1630 Rubens married Susanna's younger sister Hélène. In 1660 Arnold's nephew Jean-Baptiste Lunden married Rubens's granddaughter Hélène-Françoise Rubens, which made the family particularly closely connected by marriage. This portrait is believed to be another Fourment sister, probably Elizabeth (1606–date of death unknown). The work remained in the family collection until after Rubens's death. On the back of the portrait is an oil sketch by Rubens for an allegorical painting.

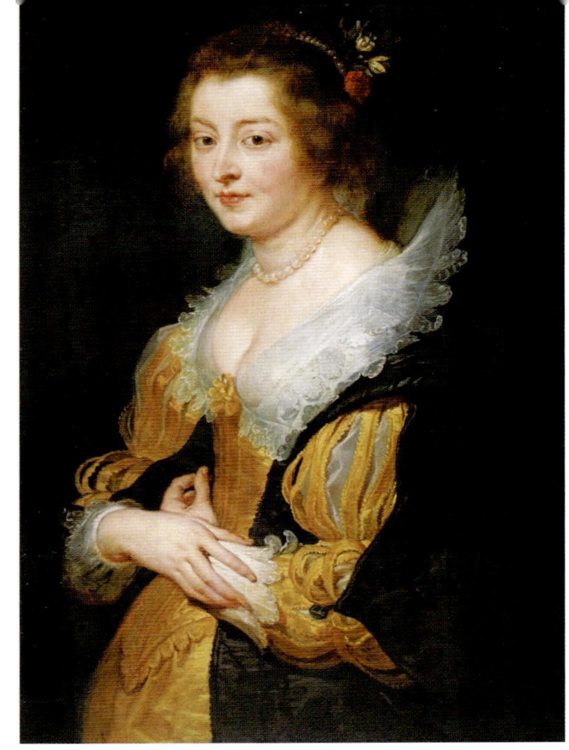

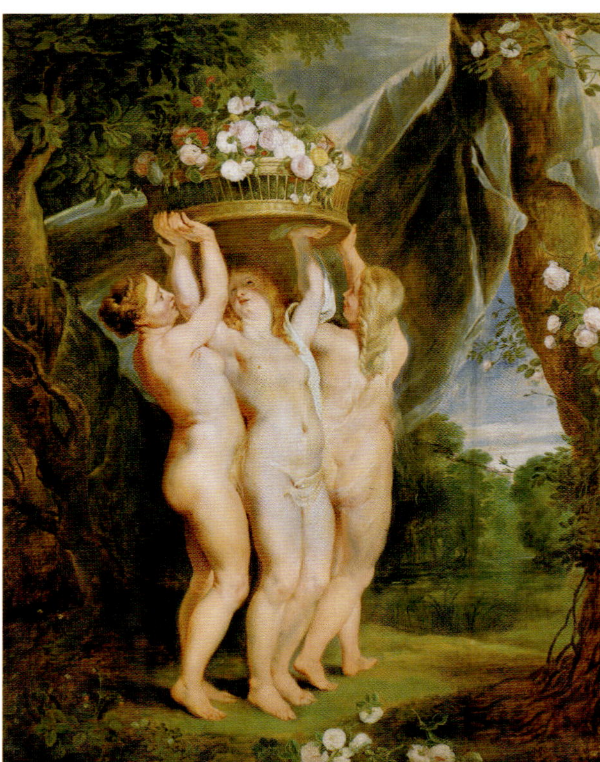

The Three Graces, Rubens and Brueghel, c.1625, oil on oak, 119 x 99cm (47 x 39in), Academy of Fine Arts, Vienna, Austria

A celebration of the abundance of Nature, the scenery here is intentionally idyllic. The focus is the three beautiful goddesses with pink-tinged alabaster skin who hold up a huge circular wreath of flowers – painted by Brueghel – representing the glory of Nature. The blonde, pale-skinned goddesses – painted by Rubens – are framed and offset by tree branches and a grey cloth. The entire composition was planned predominantly by Rubens.

Portrait of a Woman, (Susanna Lunden), 1625–27, oil on wood, 76.8 x 60cm (30¼ x 23 in), The Metropolitan Museum of Art, New York, USA

Believed to be one of the Antwerp silk merchant Daniel Fourment's seven daughters and soon to be Rubens's sister-in-law, this is Susanna Lunden (née Fourment), who remained a close friend throughout her life. Two other female portraits by Rubens appear to bear a familial resemblance, although not verified as being of Susanna. However, this lady appears to be the same as in the painting on page 78, here richly dressed as a wealthy Flemish lady.

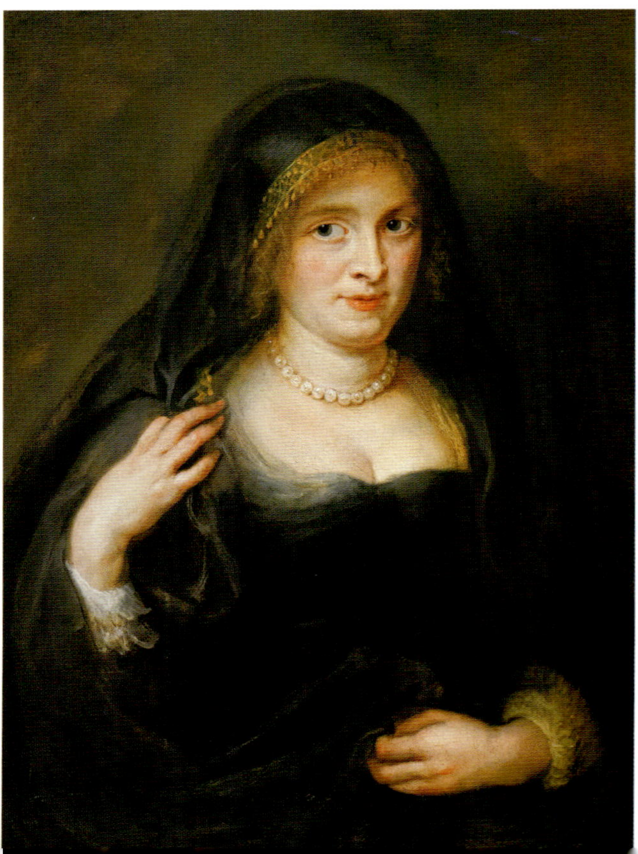

Landscape with Philemon and Baucis, c.1625, oil on panel, 146 x 208.5cm (57½ x 82in), Kunsthistorisches Museum, Vienna, Austria

Originally just a stormy landscape, Rubens added a mythological element – mere landscapes were not common subjects for paintings in Flanders, but moralizing images were. On a forest path, four figures walk: two elderly assisted by sticks, and two gods. From Ovid's *Metamorphoses*, the picture shows the forces of nature destroying others behind the four figures who did not show generosity. The gods are saving Philemon and Baucis for their kindness.

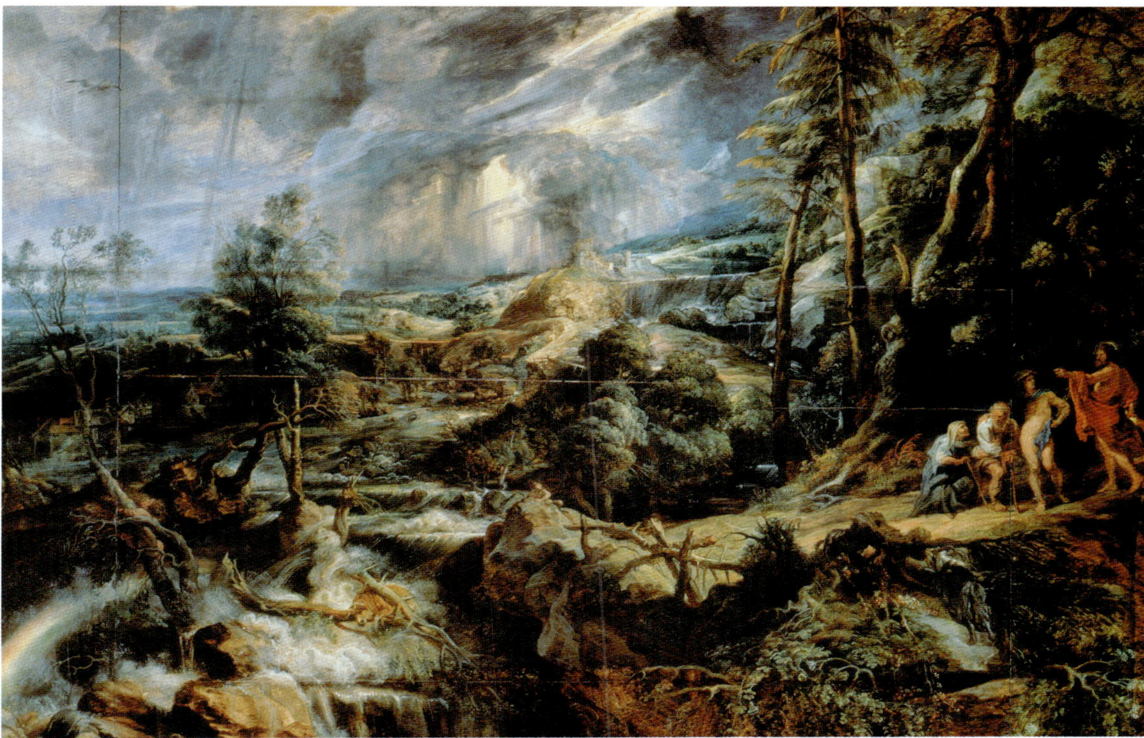

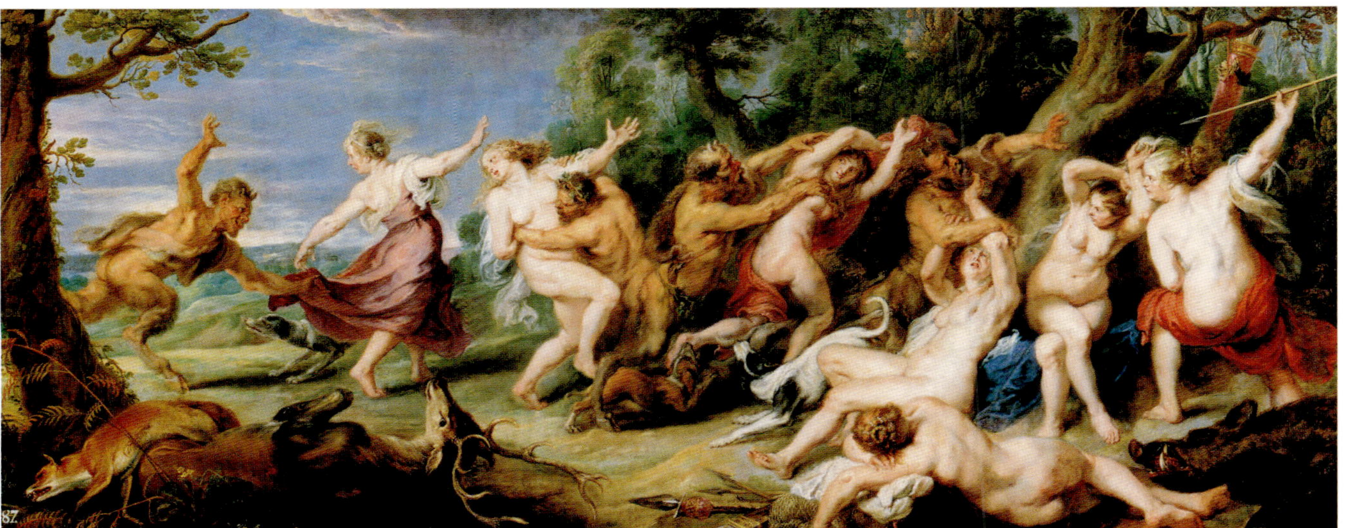

Diana and her Nymphs, 1639–40, oil on canvas, 129.5 x 315.2cm (51 x 124in), Museo Nacional del Prado, Madrid, Spain

Diana the huntress was resting with her court of nymphs in a clearing in the woods when she was attacked by a group of Satyrs. This scene is one of composed chaos, as the nymphs try to escape from the satyrs, including dead animals – trophies of their hunt – and the violent, attacking satyrs themselves, all filling the elongated canvas, which resembles a running frieze.

Portrait of George Villiers, 1625, oil on canvas, 63 x 48cm (24⅞ x 18⅞in), Pitti Palace, Florence, Italy

The 1st Duke of Buckingham virtually ruled England during the last years of the reign of James I and the first years of Charles I's monarchy. He was extremely unpopular. The failure of his aggressive and erratic foreign policy inflamed tensions in Britain and eventually erupted in the Civil War between the Royalists and the Parliamentarians. Villiers was also a connoisseur of art and admired Rubens (when they met in Paris in 1626) above all artists.

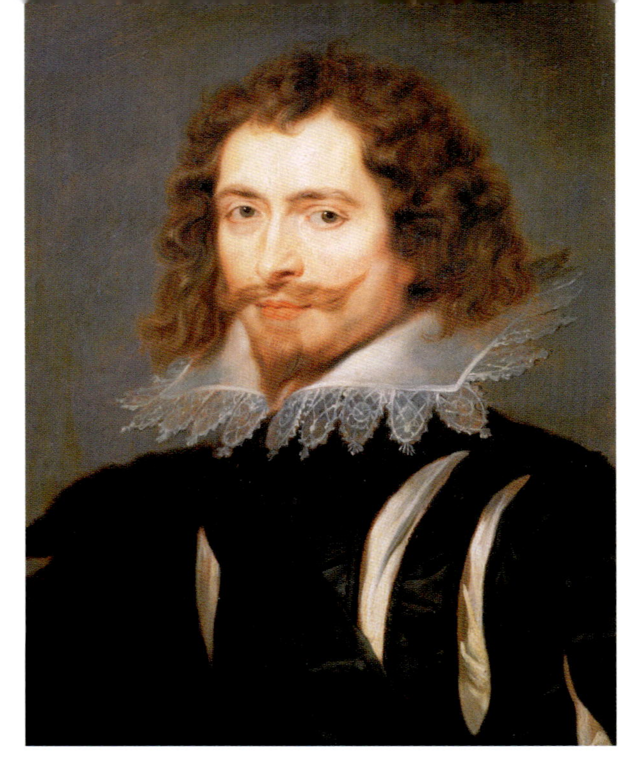

The Sacrifice of the Old Covenant, c.1626, oil on panel, 70.5 x 87.6cm (27¾ x 34½in), Museum of Fine Arts, Massachusetts, USA

This is a design for Rubens's *Triumph of the Eucharist* cycle of tapestries. The Old Testament sacrifice of a lamb is shown as a prophecy of the sacrifice of Christ in the New Testament, commemorated by Christians in the sacrament of the Eucharist, or Holy Communion. Rubens's scene is deliberately portrayed as if on a tapestry suspended from the surrounding architecture.

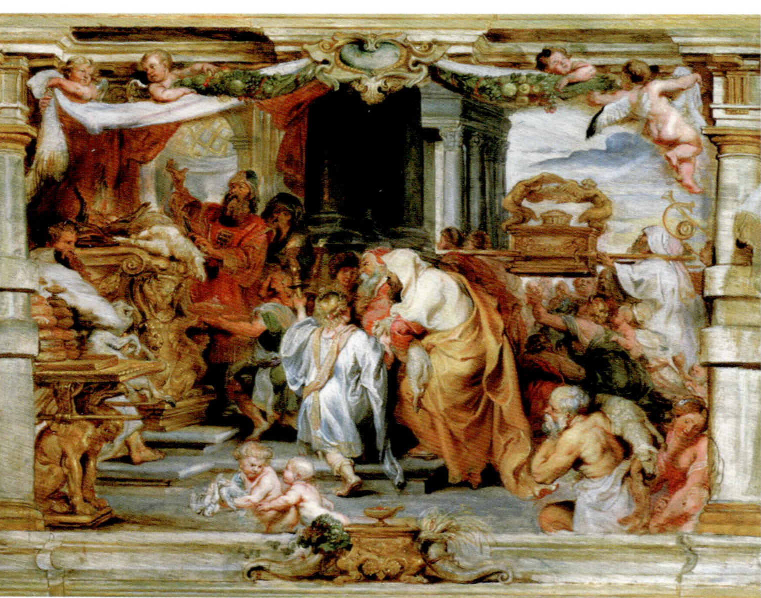

Ludovicus Nonnius, c.1627, oil on wood, 124.4 x 92.2cm (49 x 36¼in), The National Gallery, London, UK

Considered the founder of medical dietetics, Ludovicus Nonnius (1553–1645) was a Belgian doctor of Portuguese descent and also a humanist and friend of Rubens. The book he holds and the objects surrounding him refer to his accomplishments and writings – one of which was the first book that considered how dietary habits affect health. The presence of the bust of Hippocrates (the Greek founder of medicine) identifies his profession.

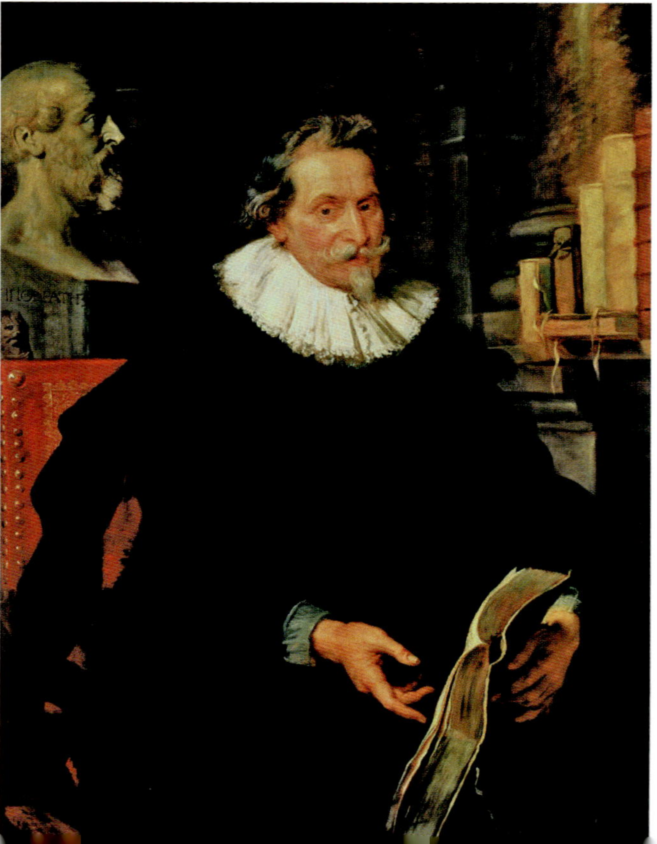

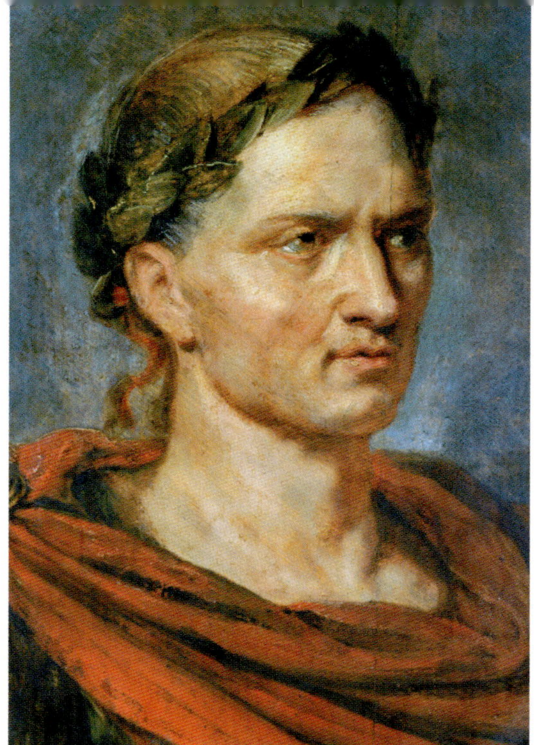

Julius Caesar, c.1625, oil on oak panel, 33 × 26.6cm (13 × 10½in), Private Collection

One of a group of portraits of ancient Roman emperors by Rubens, this was probably intended to be one in a series of the first 12 Roman emperors, which had been a fairly common theme of artists since antiquity. Here, Rubens portrays Caesar in his armour and laurel wreath, with a red cloak swathing his neck, held in place by a gold ornament. His stern expression conveys a formidable ruler. It is not clear exactly who commissioned these emperor portraits, or even if Rubens painted them as a gift for a friend, but either way, it is an individual and unique image.

The Miracles of Saint Francis of Paola, c.1627–28, oil on panel, 97.5 × 77.2cm (38½ × 30½in), J. Paul Getty Museum, Los Angeles, USA

Surrounded by divine light, Saint Francis of Paola levitates while his expression conveys his communion with God. Famed for his miraculous healing powers, Saint Francis was invited to France by the sickly King Louis XI, who is depicted with his royal court. In the foreground, a man and woman in convulsions of insanity are restrained while awaiting their cure, and a dead man comes to life – a sheet is symbolically lifted from his face.

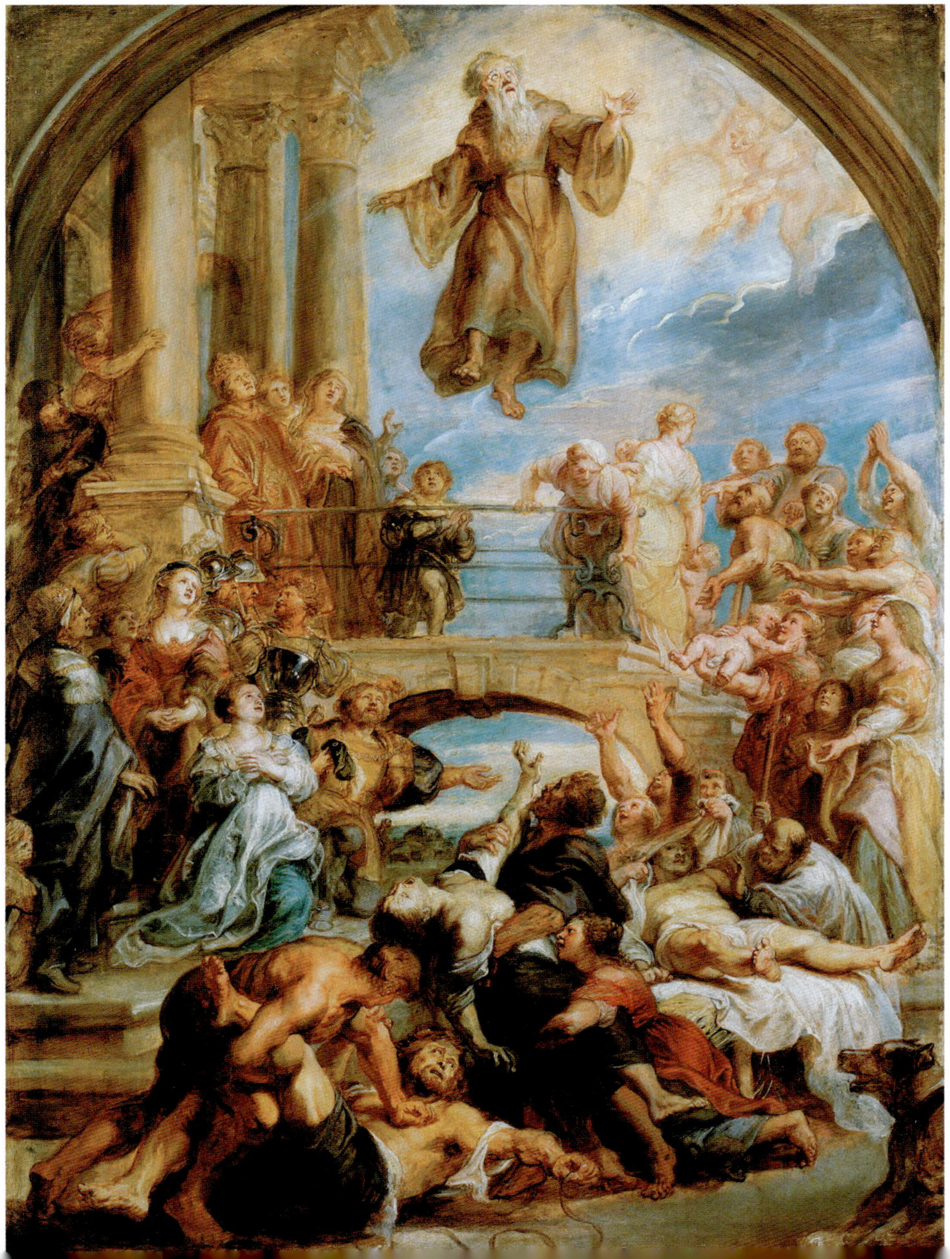

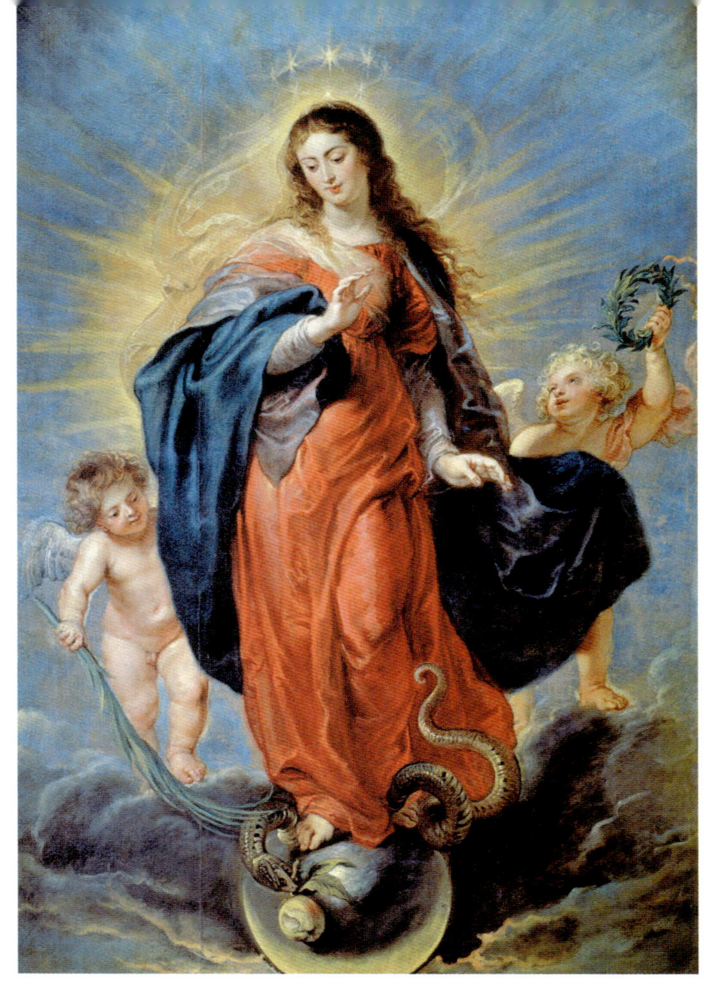

Immaculate Conception, 1628–29, oil on canvas, 198 x 135cm (78 x 53in), Museo Nacional del Prado, Madrid, Spain

Wearing a red tunic, blue robes and a crown of stars, the Virgin Mary crushes a serpent with her foot that carries the apple of Sin. Two angels holding a palm leaf and a laurel-leaf crown are classical symbols often associated with the Virgin. In another reference to Antiquity, Rubens based her figure on a classical sculpture. Painted by Rubens for the Marquis of Leganés, who gave the work to Philip IV, this shows elements of Rubens's mature style, combining Baroque dynamism with ideal beauty.

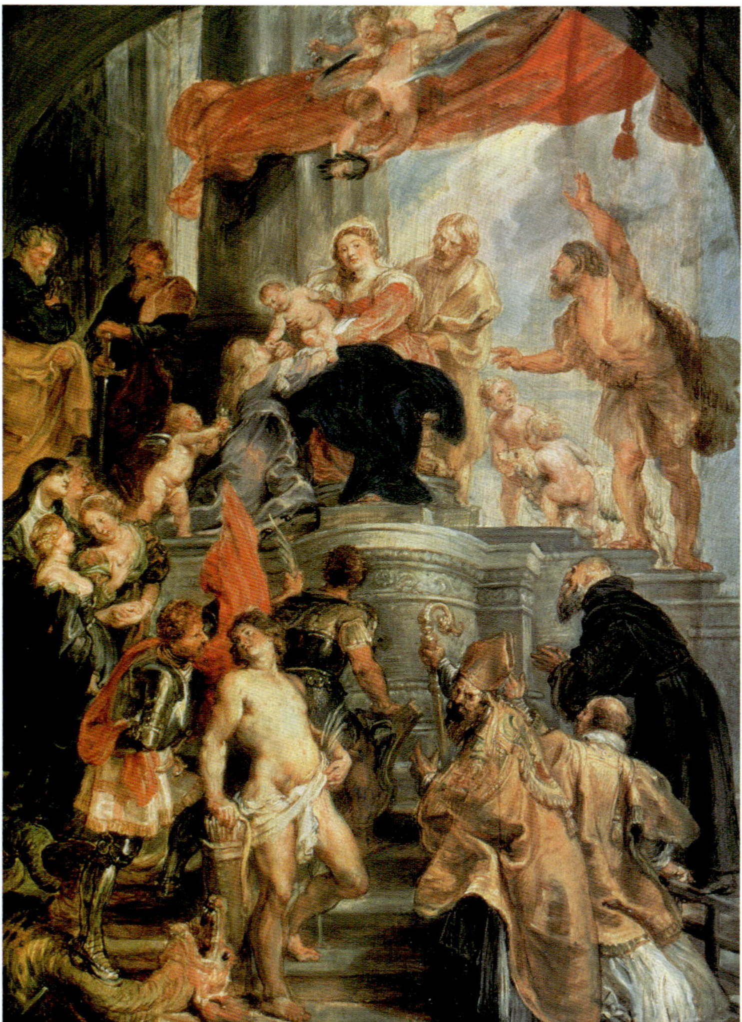

Madonna and Child Enthroned with Saints, c.1627–28, oil on canvas, 564 x 401cm (222 x 157¾in), Staatliche Gemaldegalerie, Berlin, Germany

Painted as an altarpiece for the high altar in Saint Augustine's church in Antwerp, this dynamic oil sketch reveals Rubens at his most powerful. The Virgin is on a high pedestal, and Jesus plays with the little surrounding putti, while various saints fill the foreground, including Saint Sebastian, Saint Gregory and Saint Francis. Contemporary viewers would understand this *Sacra Conversazione* – an Italian Renaissance invention.

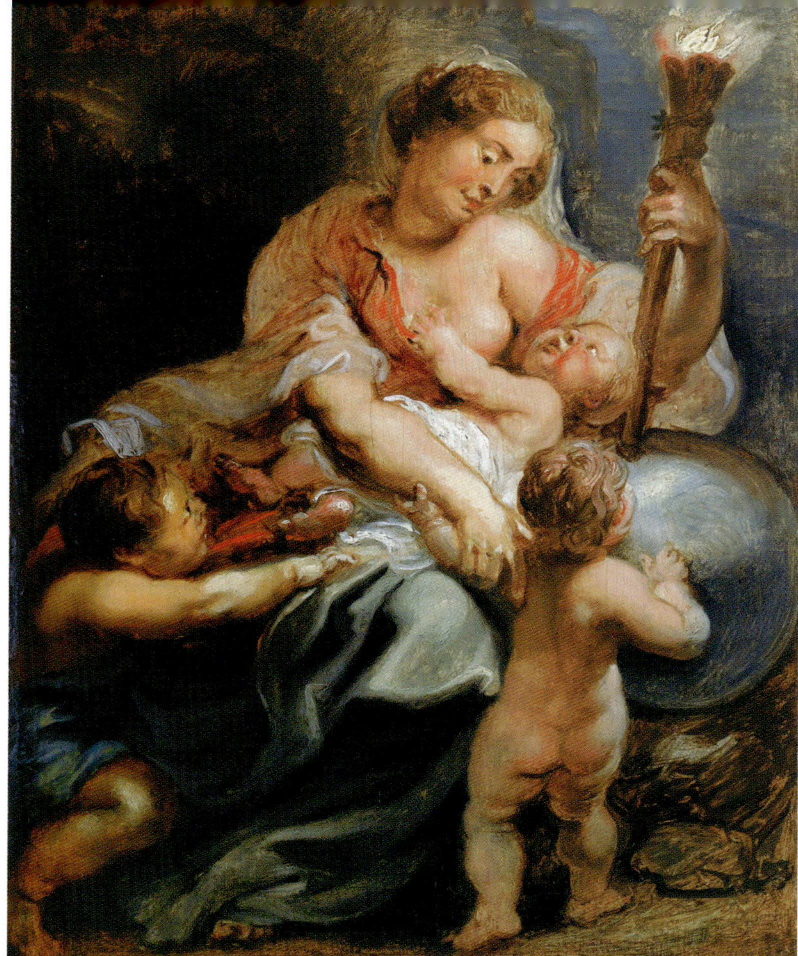

Charity Enlightening the World, c.1627–28, oil on panel, 36.8 x 29.2cm (14½ x 11½in), Mead Art Museum, Massachusetts, USA

Charity sits with three small children. This work is a modello for a tapestry in the *Triumph of the Eucharist* series, and one of three studies for smaller tapestries, all dealing with allegorical subjects that complement the theme of the Eucharist. Since the 13th century, Charity had been depicted as a maternal figure with children, usually three – a significant number in the Christian Church.

The Negotiations at Angoulême, 1622–25, oil on canvas, 394 x 295cm (155 x 116in), Musée du Louvre, Paris, France

The Treaty of Angoulême was signed on August 10, 1619 between Marie de' Medici and her son, King Louis XIII of France. It officially ended the civil war in France between the supporters of Marie and those of Louis, and it also established the reconciliation between mother and son. In the painting, Marie takes an olive branch from Mercury, the messenger god, in the presence of her priests.

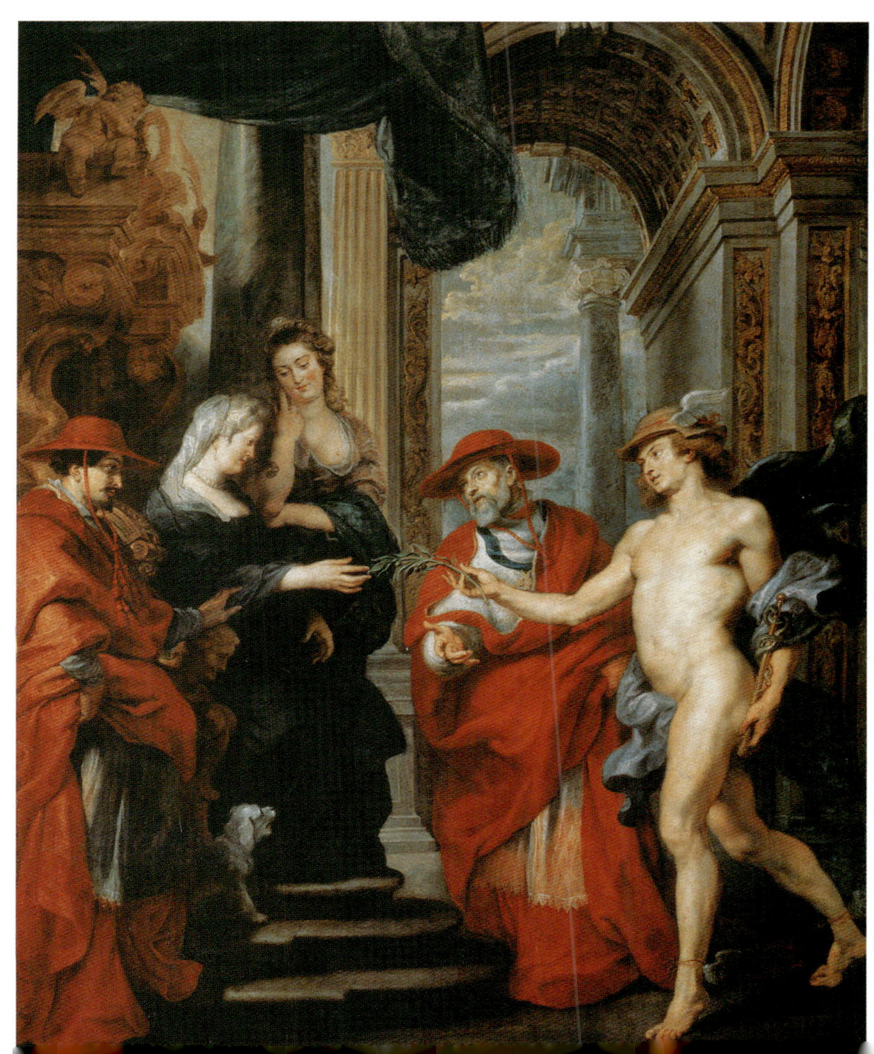

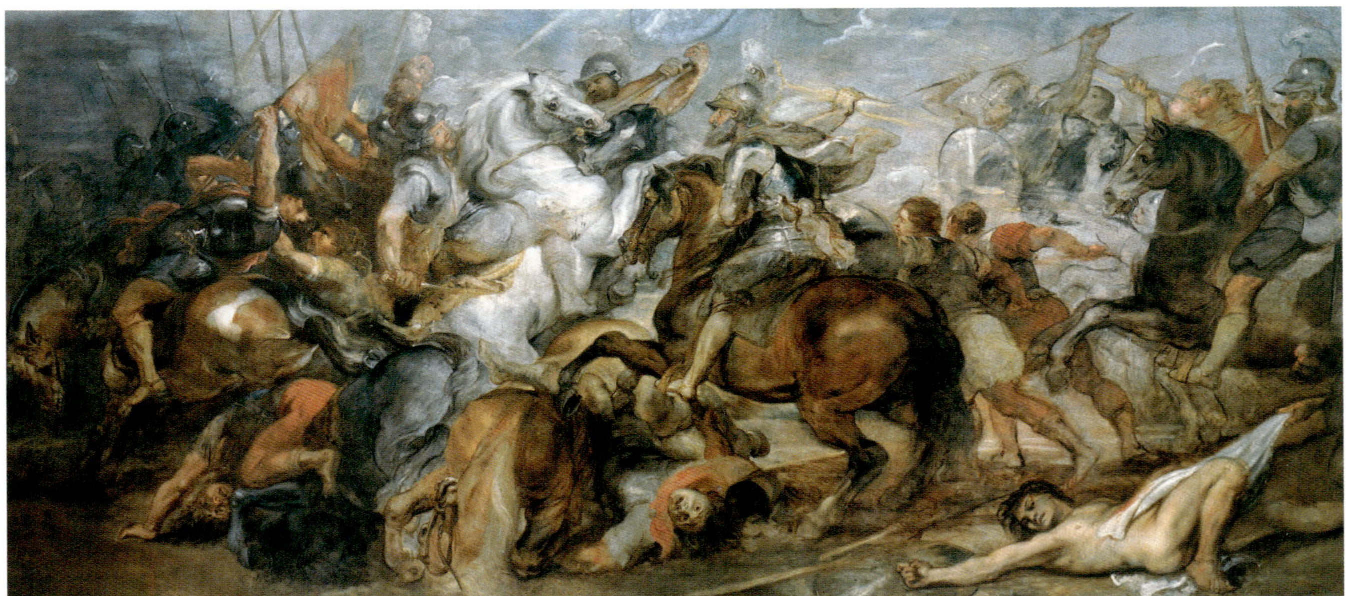

Henri IV at the Battle of Ivry, c.1627, oil on canvas, 380 x 692cm (149½ x 272in), Galleria degli Uffizi, Florence, Italy

The Battle of Ivry was fought at Ivry in Normandy on March 14, 1590 during the French Wars of Religion. It was a decisive victory for Henry, who then became claimant to the throne of France. He was, however, subsequently defeated in a siege of Paris, but finally took the French throne in 1594, after converting to Roman Catholicism. This battle of four years previously was won by Henry and his troops as Protestants against the Catholic League led by the Duc de Mayenne. By 1594, when he realized that the only way the French people would accept him was if he was Catholic, he famously declared Paris was 'worth a Mass' and converted.

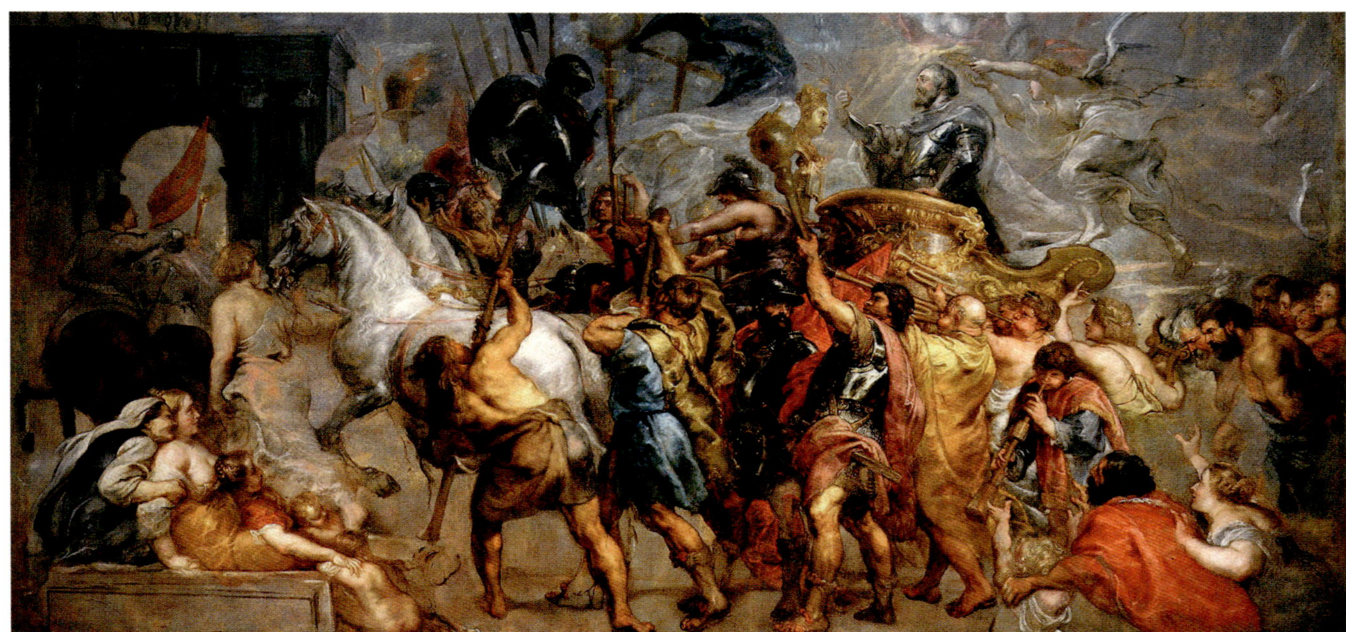

Triumphal Entry of Henri IV into Paris, 1627, oil on canvas, 380 x 692cm (149½ x 272in), Galleria degli Uffizi, Florence, Italy

Forming a pair with the *Henri IV at the Battle of Ivry* (above), this is part of the unfinished cycle that Rubens planned, dedicated to Henri IV. It shows the king, converted to Catholicism and victorious, entering Paris on March 22, 1594 after a long struggle. With no reference to time or place, Rubens has portrayed a complex allegorical image, comparing Henri to a triumphant Roman emperor. The triumphal arch derives from the ancient Roman arch of Titus.

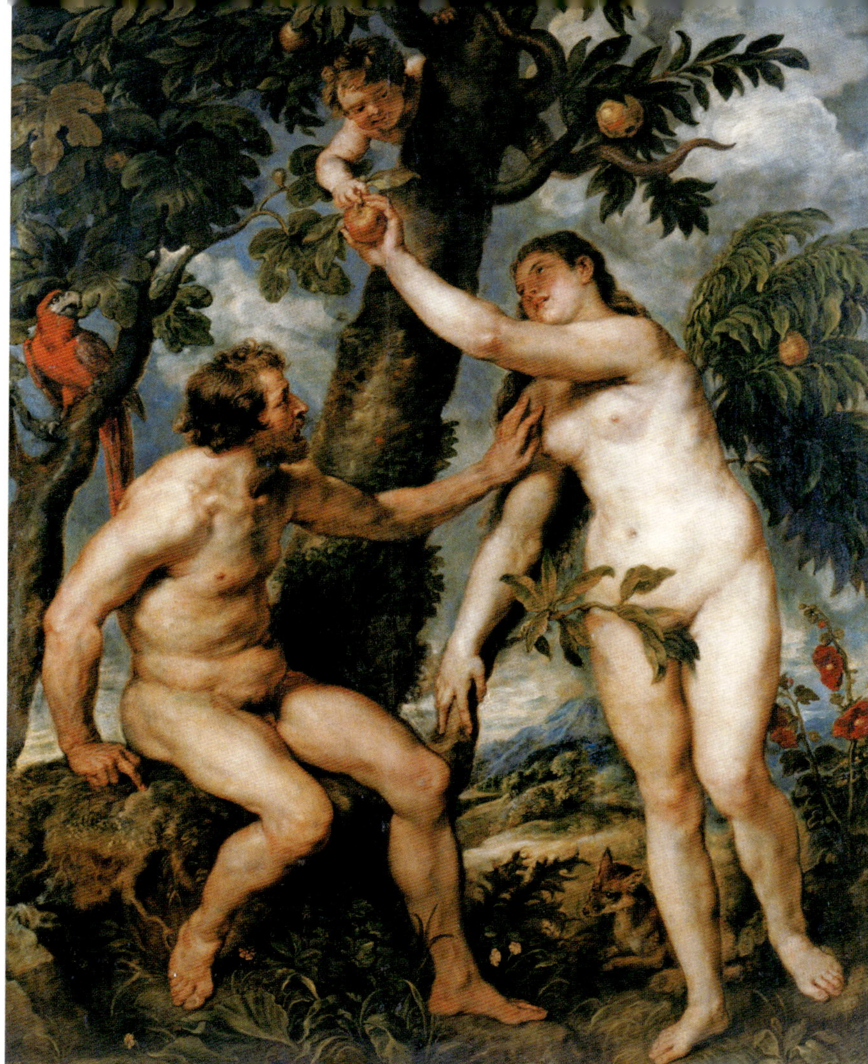

Adam and Eve, 1628–29, oil on canvas, 237 x 184cm (93¼ x 72½in), Museo Nacional del Prado, Madrid, Spain

This is a copy by Rubens of a painting by Titian during his 1628–29 trip to Madrid. Adam attempts to stop Eve from taking the forbidden apple from the serpent. Titian's work shows an influence of Raphael, while Rubens's version shows the influence of both Titian and Brueghel. Rubens added a parrot and changed Adam's posture, musculature, age and expression.

Ana Dorotea, Daughter of Rudolph II, 1628, oil on canvas, 73 x 65.4cm (28¾ x 25¾in), Apsley House, The Wellington Museum, London, UK

Having just taken her vows as a Carmelite nun – the habit was also worn by members of the Spanish royal family – this painting is of 17-year-old Ana Dorotea, the daughter of Emperor Rudolf II by his mistress Catherine de Strada. It is generally believed to belong to a series of portraits of members of the Spanish royal family painted by Rubens during his visit to Madrid in 1628.

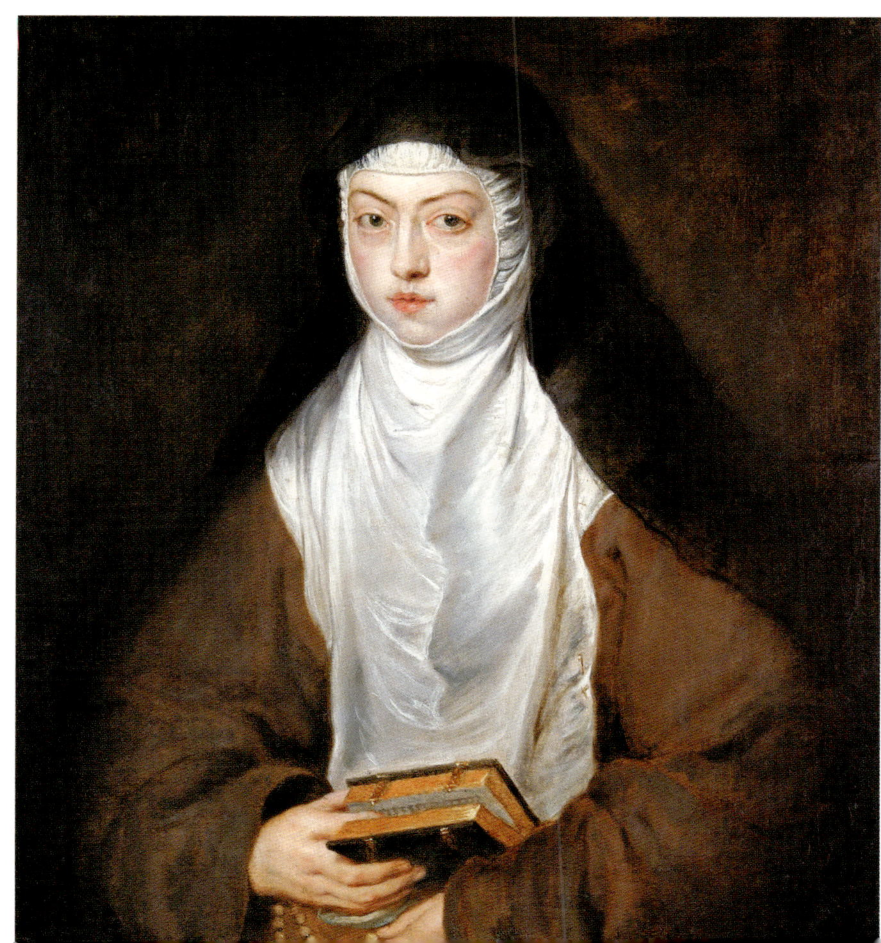

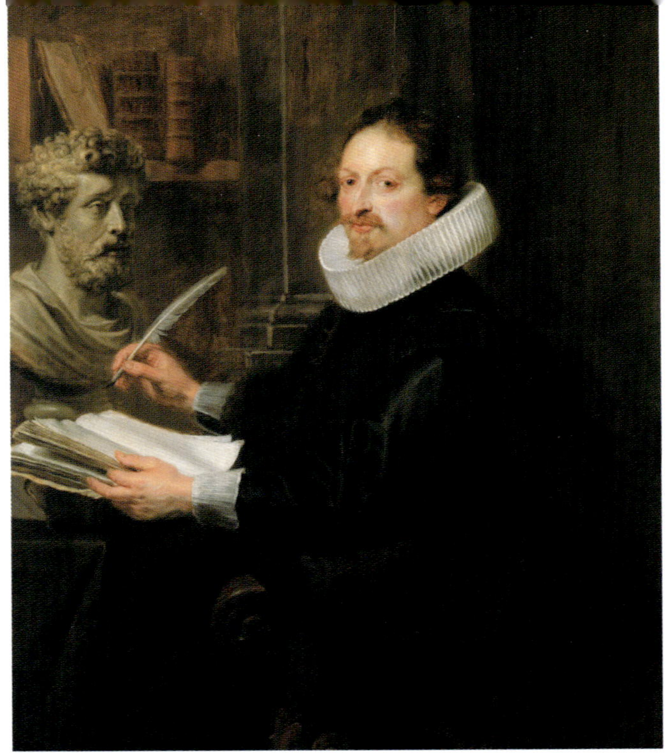

Gaspard Gevartius, 1628, oil on panel, 119 x 98cm (46¾ x 38½in), Koninklijk Museum voor Schone Kunsten, Antwerp, Belgium

Antwerp city secretary Jan Gaspar Gevartius, or Gevaert (1593–1666) was a friend of Rubens. He sits at his writing desk, making notes with a quill. On the table is a bust of Marcus Aurelius, as a reference to an unpublished work that Gevartius wrote on the Roman emperor and philosopher. The books in the background refer to his respected position in the city.

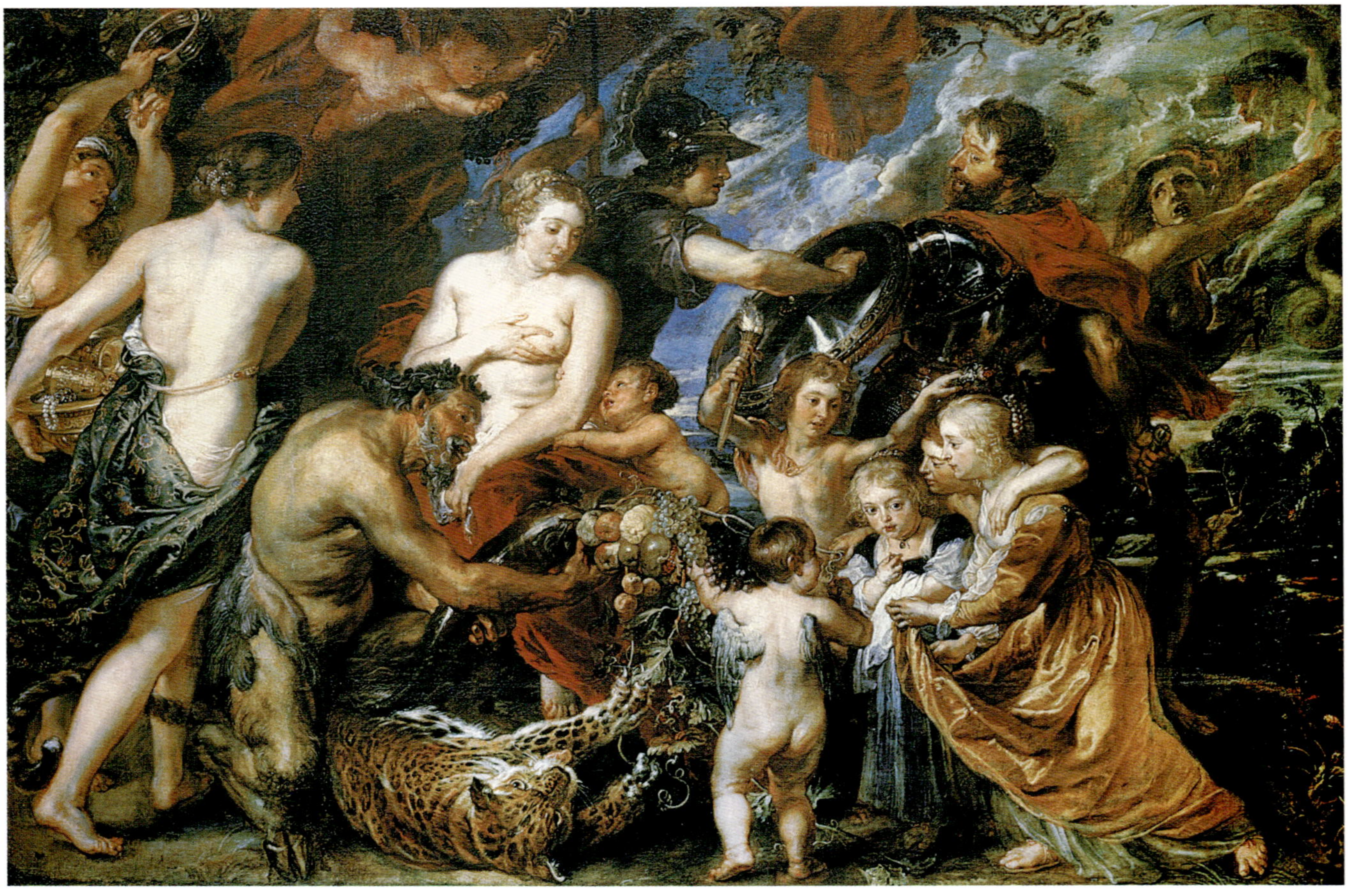

Allegory of Peace and War, or Minerva Protects Pax from Mars, 1629–30, oil on canvas, 203.5 x 298cm (80 x 117⅓in), The National Gallery, London, UK

Executed while he was in England, this illustrates Rubens's hopes for the peace he was trying to negotiate between England and Spain in his role as envoy to Philip IV of Spain.

He gave the painting to Charles I as a gift. The central figure represents Pax (Peace) in the person of Ceres, goddess of the earth, sharing her bounty with the figures in the foreground.

To her right is Minerva, the goddess of wisdom, who drives away Mars, the god of war, and Alecto, the fury of war. A putto holds an olive wreath, a further symbol of peace.

The Family of Sir Balthasar Gerbier, c.1629–40, oil on canvas, 217.2 x 310cm (85½ x 122in), The Royal Collection, London, UK

The children of Sir Gerbier seen here were also models in *Allegory of Peace and War* (opposite below). Balthasar Gerbier became close to Rubens during his stay in England – Rubens lodged with him in London. This was probably painted during that stay, as a glimpse of the river landscape in the background is the view from the Gerbiers' home, York House. As Rubens added and took away elements, the canvas became a composite, resulting in this final composition with full-length figures.

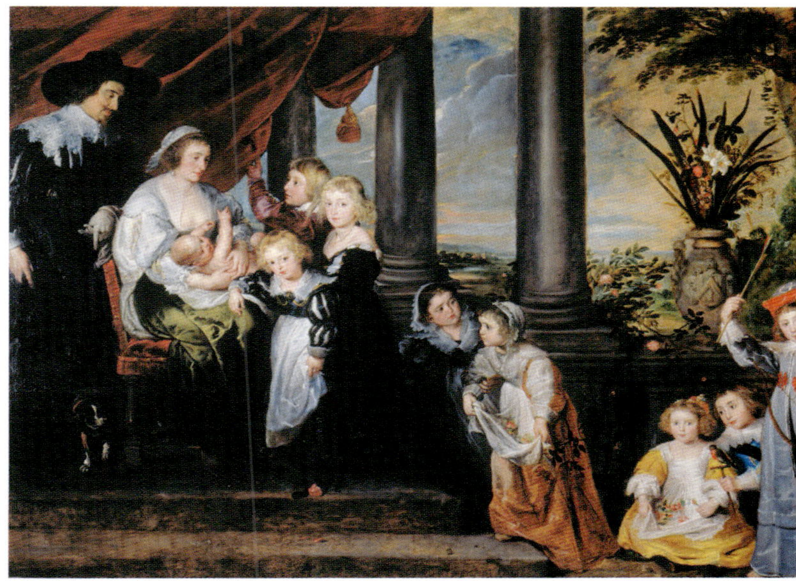

Venus, Mars and Cupid, c.1635, oil on canvas, 195.2 x 133cm (76¾ x 52⅓in), Dulwich Picture Gallery, London, UK

As usual, Rubens's Venus is soft, fleshy and sensual, echoing the version of Venus in his painting *Allegory of Peace and War* (opposite). Greek and Roman gods embody certain virtues, and what initially seems to be a mythological family is in fact an allegory of the triumph of Peace over War, and Love over Hate. Mars, the god of war, is disarmed by Love, and Venus nourishes her baby, Cupid.

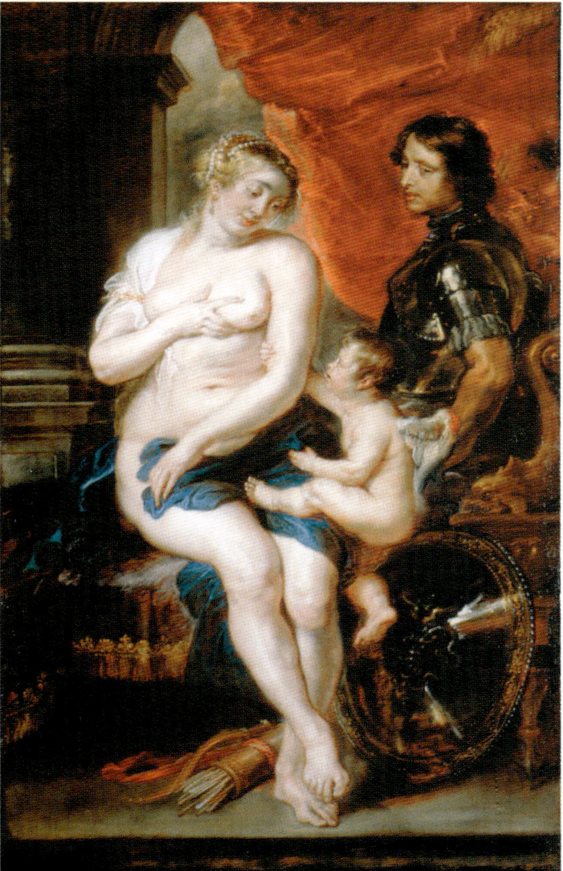

Portrait of Elisabeth of France, c.1628, oil on panel, 48.5 x 40.5cm (19 x 16in), Kunsthistorisches Museum, Vienna, Austria

Elisabeth, or Isabella, of France (1602–44) was the eldest daughter of King Henri IV of France and his second spouse Marie de' Medici. She became Queen consort of Spain from 1621 to 1644, and of Portugal from 1621 to 1640, as the first wife of King Philip IV of Spain. As Philip had recently been to France and spent a great deal of time with her mother and brother, Elisabeth welcomed Rubens to the Spanish court.

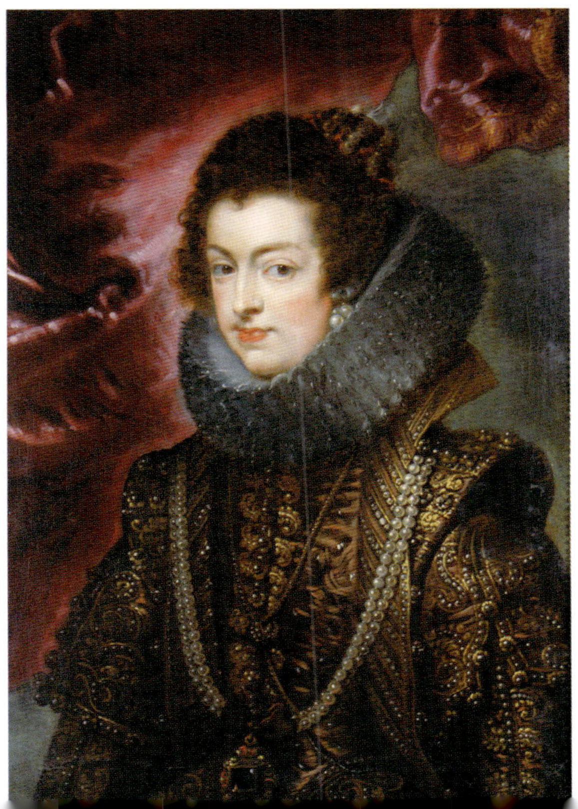

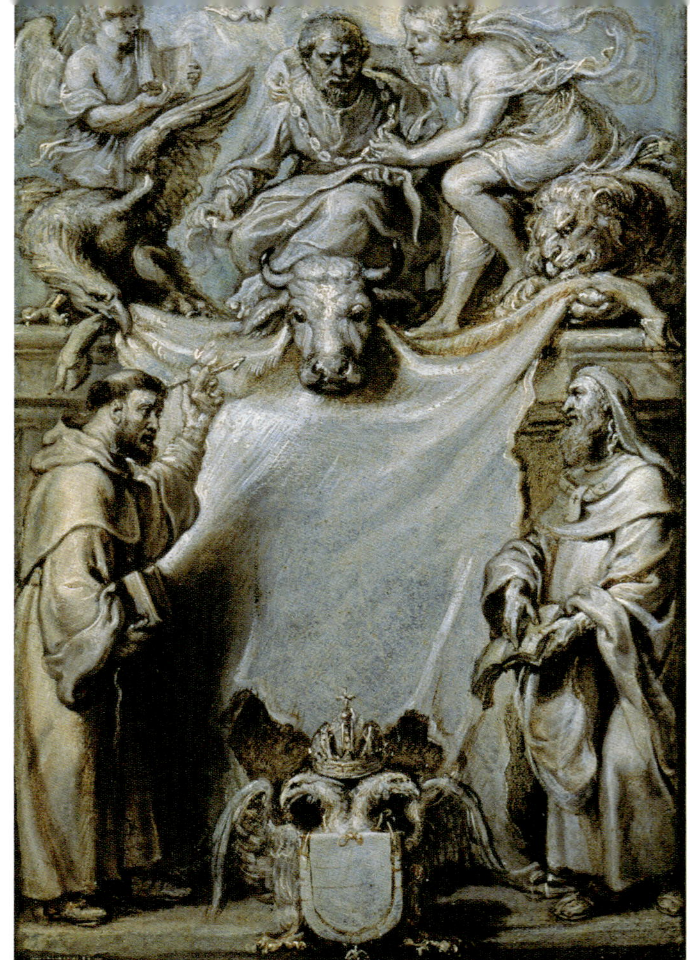

Corderius's Commentaries on Saint Luke, 1628, oil on paper on canvas, 31.6 x 22.1cm (12½ x 8¾in), The Courtauld Gallery, London, UK

This is a modello that Rubens painted for the title page of a book he was illustrating for the Plantin Press. Corderius is the Latinized name used by Mathurin Cordier (c.1479–1574), a theologian, teacher and humanist who wrote the Commentaries on Saint Luke in the 16th century. With strong chiaroscuro, the image resembles a classically designed relief.

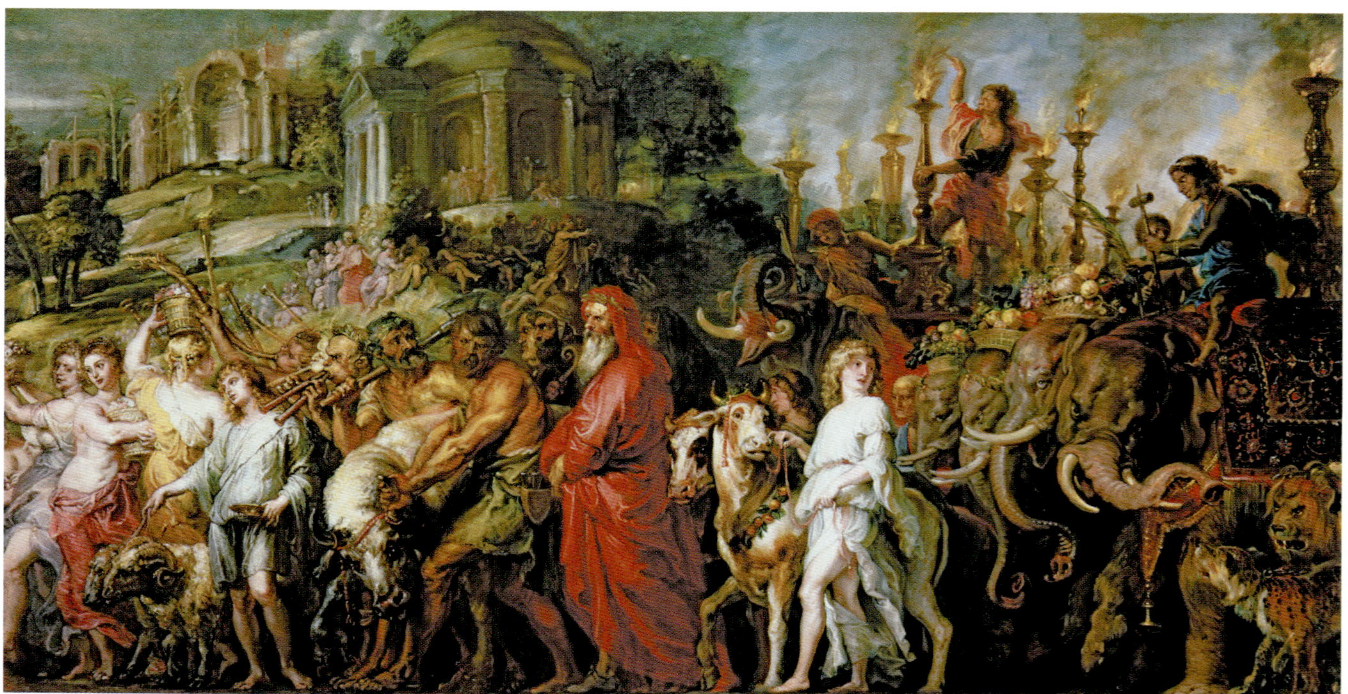

*A Roman Triumph, c.*1630, oil on canvas, stuck down on oak, 86.8 x 163.9cm (34 x 64½in), The National Gallery, London, UK

Partly derived from Andrea Mantegna's *Triumph of Julius Caesar,* this depicts the highest honour that could be bestowed upon a Roman general: the triumphal procession. It commemorates a campaign victory, everyone celebrating as the procession passes through Rome, culminating at the Temple of Jupiter on the Capitoline hill.

Triumphal processions occurred throughout ancient Rome's nearly 1,000-year history. Rubens captures the hustle, bustle, colour and excitement of the event.

The Virgin and Child Venerated by Eight Saints, c.1631–33, oil on panel, 35 x 53cm (13¾ x 20 in), Private Collection

Following the Renaissance idea of a *Sacre Conversazione*, this shows the Virgin and Child sitting on a throne, surrounded by several saints who were alive during different time periods, but all are engaged in conversations or are relating to each other in some way. This is a sketch, but shows many details of the work it was being prepared for, including Mary's crown and the various saints with their characteristic attributes, who include Saints Barbara, Catherine, Elizabeth of Hungary, Augustine, Francis of Assisi and Mary Magdalene. All of these elements would have been recognized by 17th-century viewers.

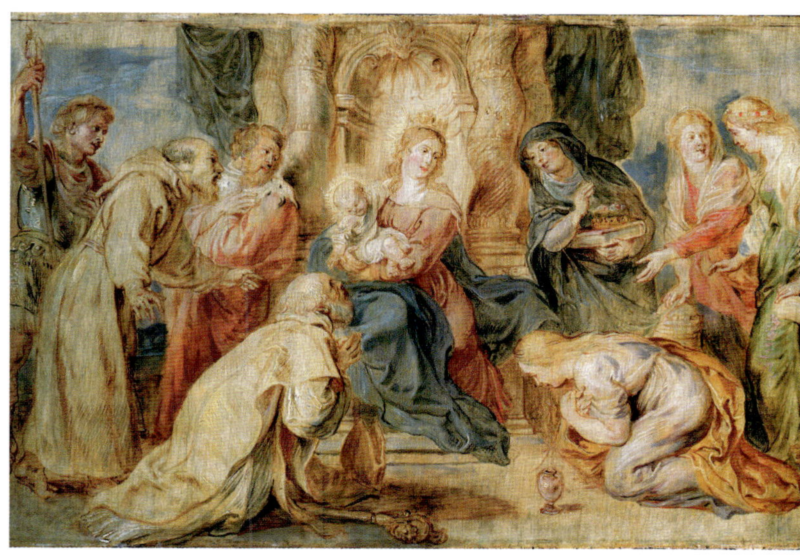

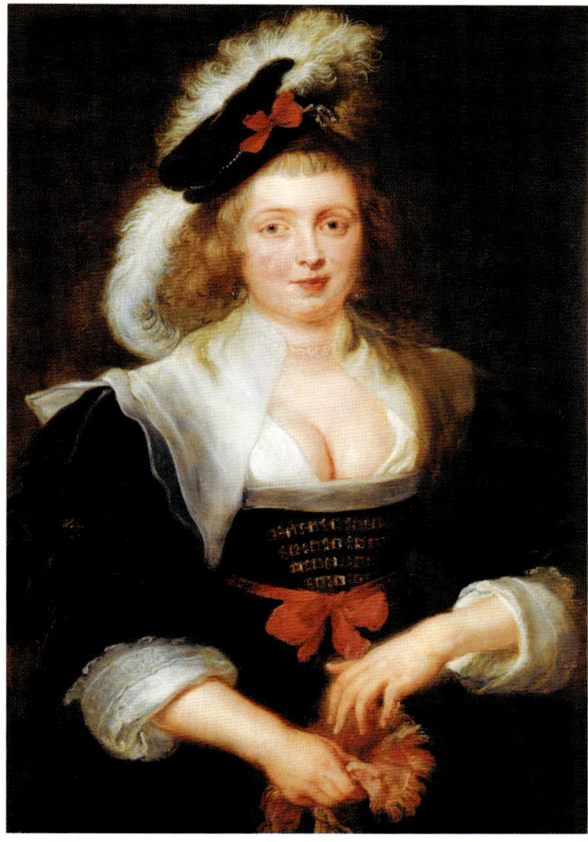

Hélène Fourment Putting on a Glove, c.1630–32, oil on canvas, 97 x 69cm (38 x 27in), Alte Pinakothek, Munich, Germany

It is generally accepted that Rubens's personal portraits were executed solely by himself and not by workshop assistants. This is a painting of his wife Hélène. Several of these paintings were subsequently copied by his students and admirers, which has sometimes caused confusion, but this one has been generally agreed upon to be the work of Rubens alone.

The Holy Family Surrounded by Saints, c.1630, oil on panel, 79.5 x 64cm (31⅓ x 25⅛in), Museo del Prado, Madrid, Spain

The Virgin sits with Jesus in a grand architectural space, surrounded by various saints. Above her, angels prepare to crown her as the Queen of Heaven. This is a fairly small preparatory sketch for the large altar painting that the Infanta Isabella commissioned Rubens to paint for the Augustinians at Antwerp in 1628. The low viewpoint takes into account the position from which viewers would see the painting.

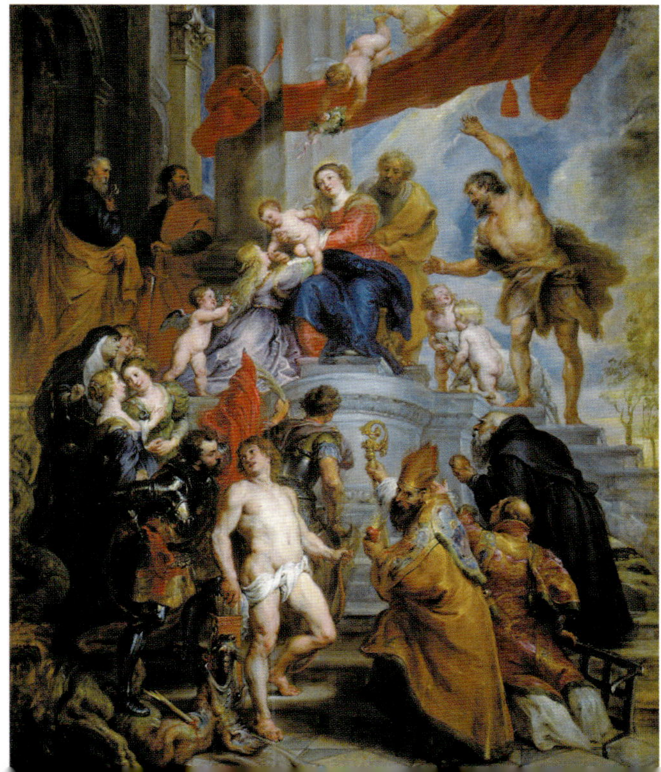

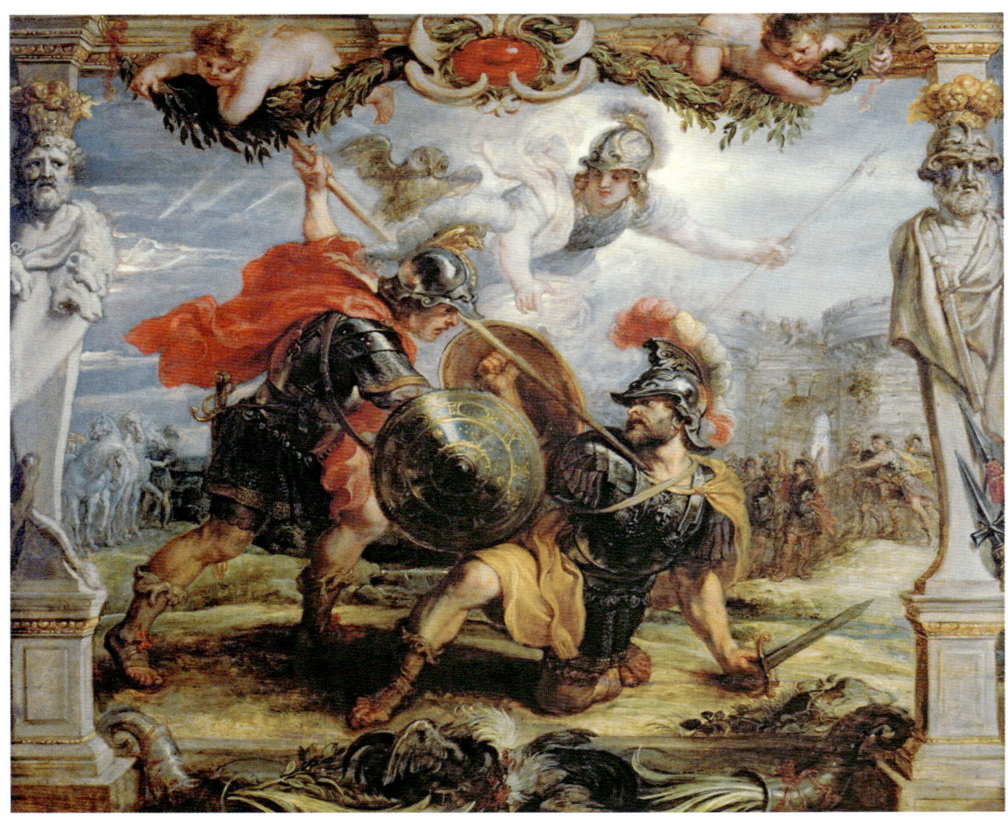

Achilles Defeating Hector,
1630–32, oil on panel,
108 x 127cm (42½ x 50in),
Musée des Beaux-Arts,
Pau, France

In Greek mythology, Achilles
was a hero of the Trojan
War and the greatest
warrior of Homer's Iliad.
His most renowned exploit
during the war was the
slaying of the Trojan hero
Hector outside the gates
of Troy. The Greek tragedian
Aeschylus wrote a trilogy of
plays about Achilles, including
his defeat of Hector. This is
Rubens's interpretation of
the moment as a design
for one of his tapestries.

The Last Supper, 1630–32,
oil on panel, 45.8 x 41cm
(18 x 16in), The State
Pushkin Museum of Fine
Arts, Moscow, Russia

This is one of two studies
for Rubens's completed
work of this subject (see
opposite). Along with Jesus,
the most prominent figure
at the table is Judas, who
has a nervous expression,
while with his yellow halo,
Jesus appears calm. He
is surrounded by all his
apostles and is about to
bless the bread and wine. A
dog can be seen under the
table, probably symbolizing
faith, although its proximity to
Judas could also imply greed.

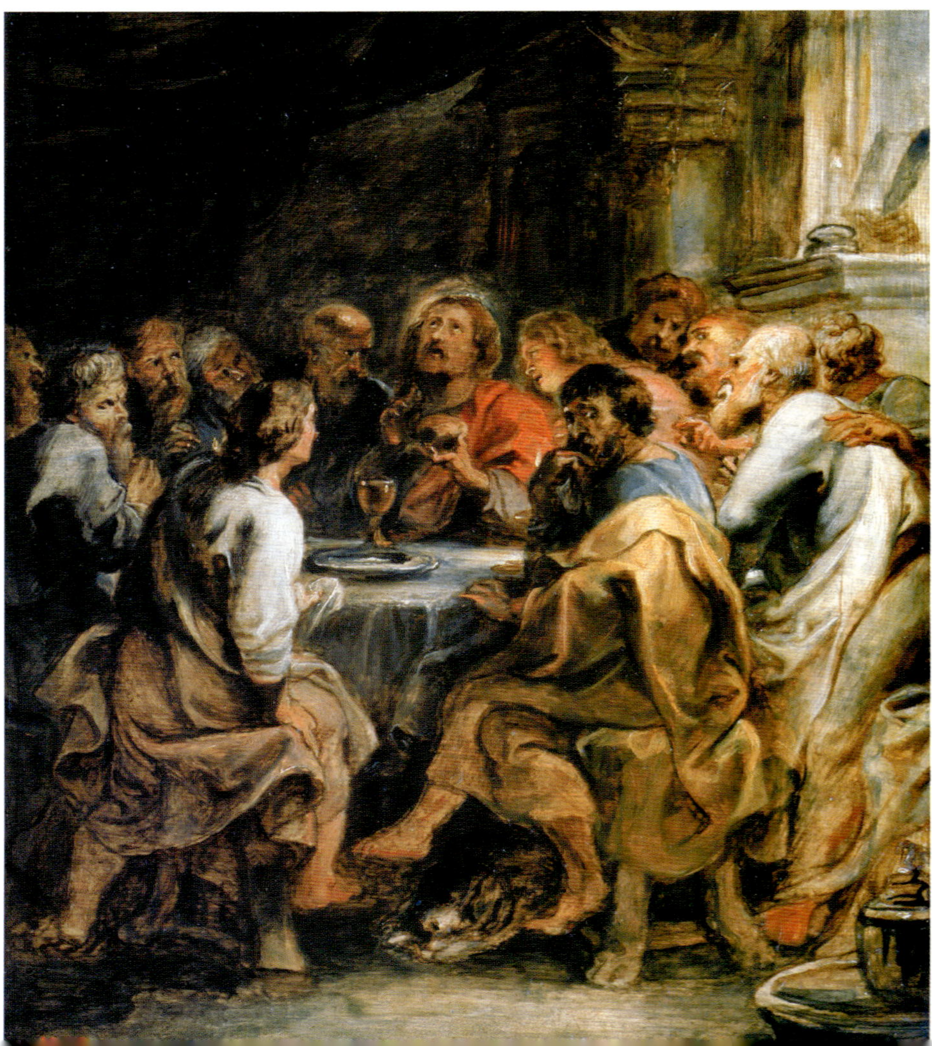

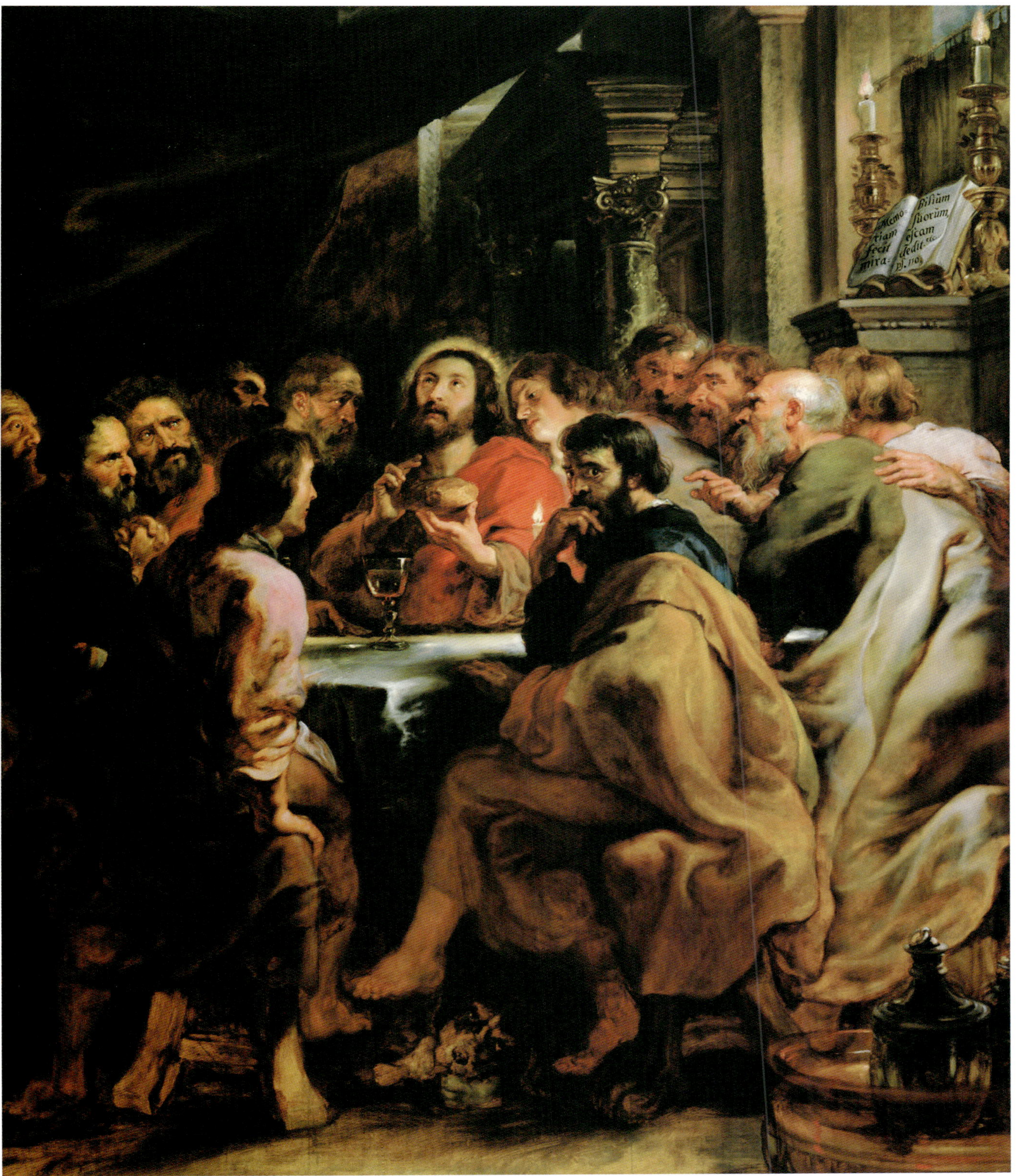

The Last Supper, 1630–31, oil on canvas, 304 x 250cm (120 x 98in), Pinacoteca di Brera, Milan, Italy

Commissioned by Catherine Lescuyer in memory of her father, this was part of an altarpiece in the Church of Saint Rombout in Mechelen. Jesus and the Apostles are at the Last Supper. Judas, in blue, turns away from the table, holding his hand to his mouth. Jesus is dressed in red at the centre, about to bless the loaf and cup of wine.

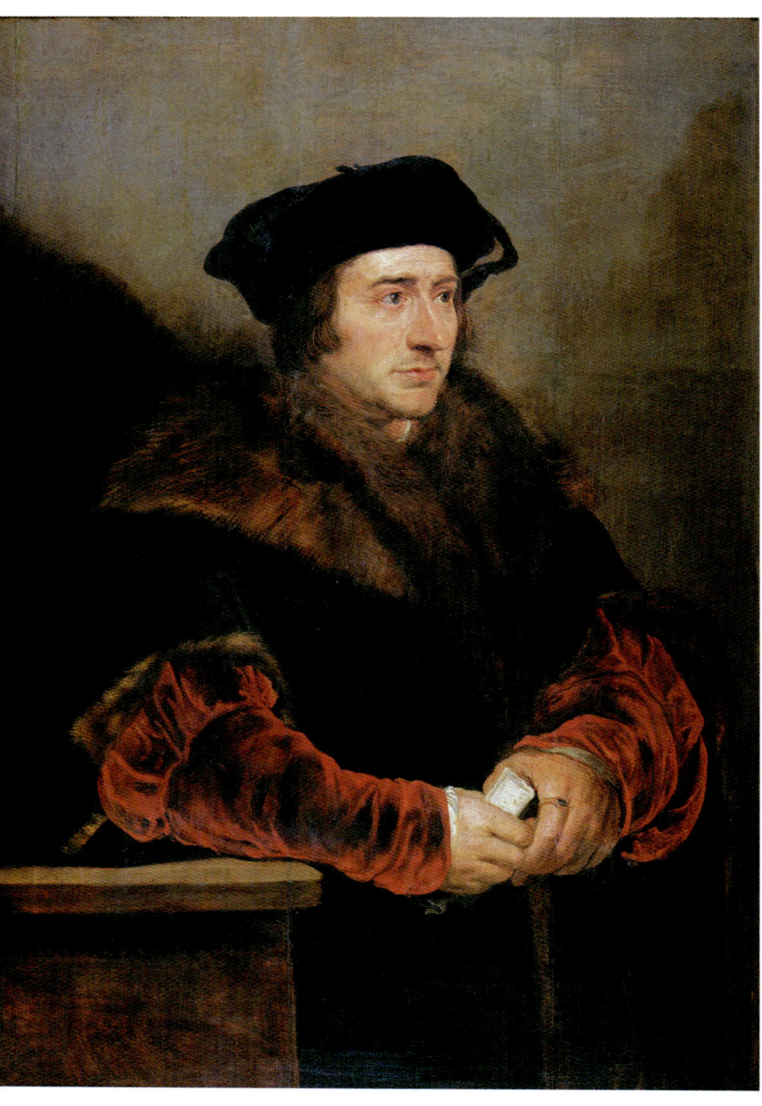

Portrait of Thomas More, 1630–35, oil on panel, 105.6 x 73cm (41½ x 28¾in), Museo Nacional del Prado, Madrid, Spain

As an artist of the Northern Renaissance, Hans Holbein the Younger had always interested Rubens, and this is his 17th-century interpretation of Holbein's 1527 portrait of Thomas More, the English humanist and statesman. Rubens was fascinated by his Northern Renaissance heritage, and particularly by the accuracy and bravado of Holbein's style, and also by the philosophies of Thomas More. Dressed in sumptuous, costly fabrics and a gold ring that all convey his elevated status, More's cape, with its fur collar, magistrate's cap and piece of paper, also allude to his intellectual and scholarly mind.

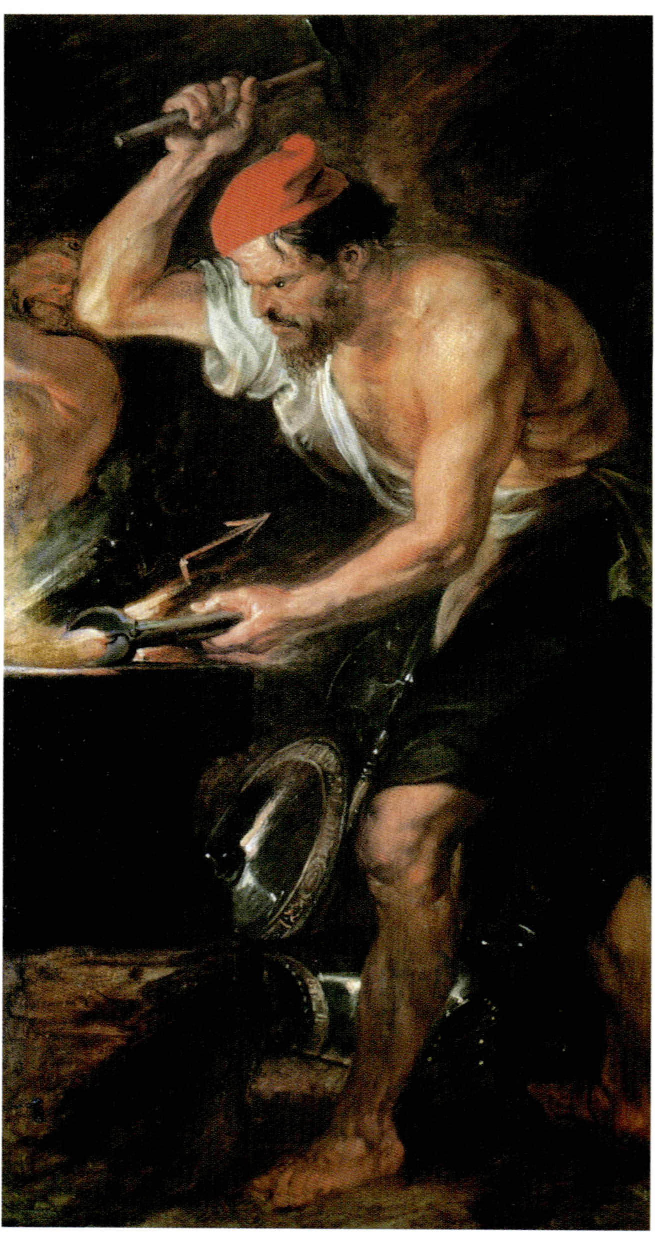

Vulcan Forging the Thunderbolts of Jupiter, 1636–37, oil on 182.5 x 99.5cm (71⅞ x 39⅛in), Museo Nacional del Prado, Madrid, Spain

Vulcan, the son of Jupiter and Juno, was born deformed, and because of this, he was hated by the gods. Exiled to Hades, he became identified with blacksmiths, and Rubens shows him making lightning bolts for Jupiter with the aid of Cyclops, a giant with only one eye. The shield, axe and cuirass on the ground allude to weapons that Vulcan made for Achilles. This is one of Rubens's many paintings made for the Torre de la Parada.

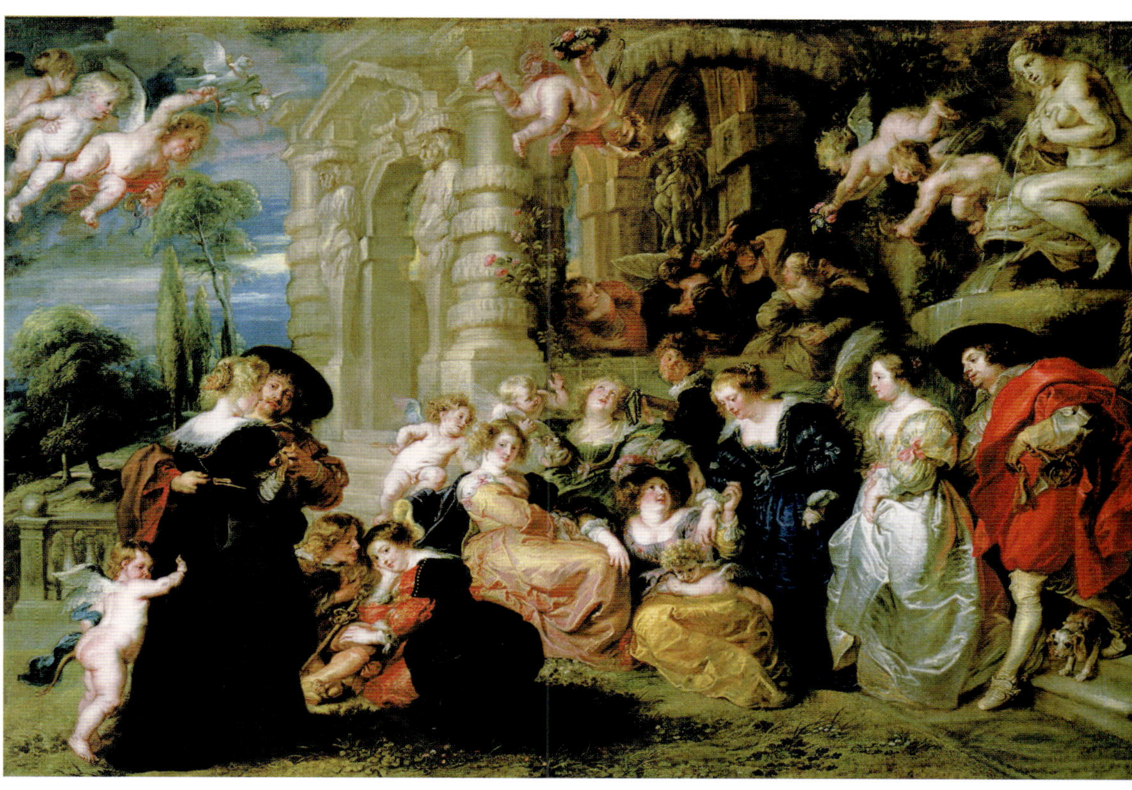

The Garden of Love, 1633–34, oil on canvas, 199 x 286cm (78⅓ x 112½in), Museo Nacional del Prado, Madrid, Spain

A scene from a court feast: a group of figures flirt and relax in an idyllic garden (presaging the Rococo style of the following century). Cupids carry objects that symbolize conjugal love, such as a pair of doves. The sculptures of the three Graces and Venus nursing signify marital bliss, while the peacock represents the goddess Juno, who protects matrimony.

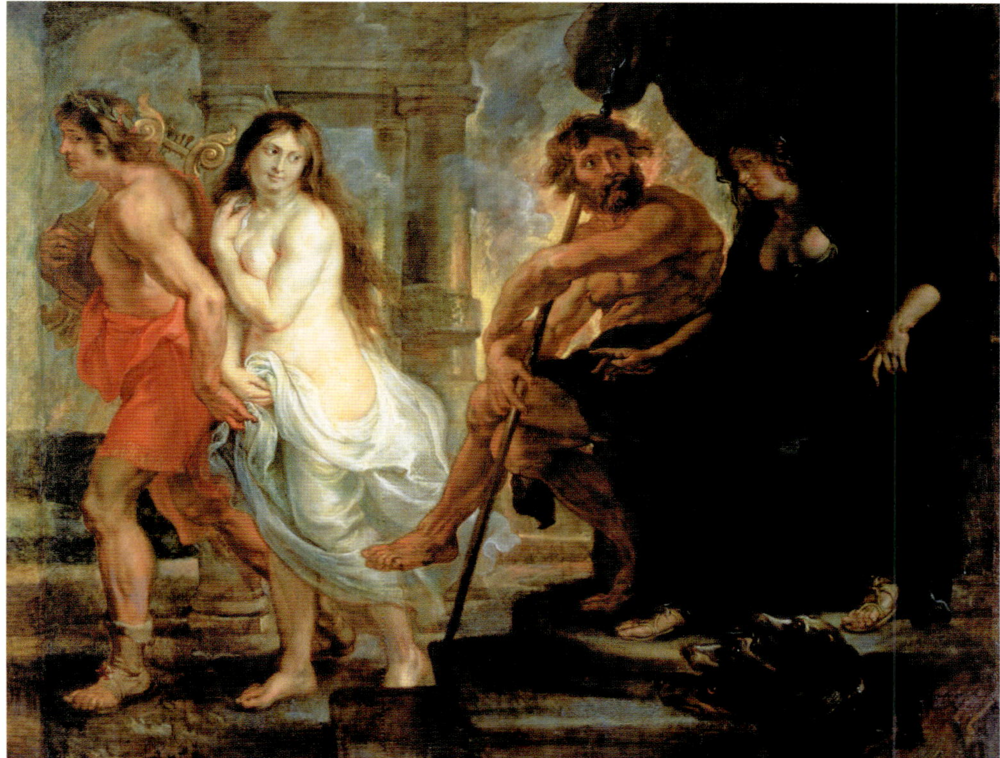

Orpheus and Eurydice, 1636–37, oil on canvas, 196.5 x 247.5cm (77⅓ x 97⅓in), Museo Nacional del Prado, Madrid, Spain

Orpheus descends into the Underworld to recover his wife, Eurydice, who died after being bitten by a serpent. Pluto and Proserpine, the god and goddess of the Underworld, are so moved by the music of Orpheus's lyre that they consent to his request. They impose one condition on him: that he does not look at his beloved until they have both left the Underworld. Here, Rubens has portrayed Orpheus at the moment he is about to look back at his beloved wife.

*Crowning of the Victor, c.1615,
revised in 1630, oil on oak,
47.5 x 65.5cm (18¾ x 25¾in),
Kunsthistorisches, Vienna, Austria*

Rubens first created this painting
in 1615 but then reworked it
15 years later, as much of the
style appears to match his late
approach, with painterly marks
applied with coarse brushstrokes.
Until recently, the work was
believed to be an oil sketch, but
the fact that he made changes
to it has raised questions
about it – as yet unresolved.

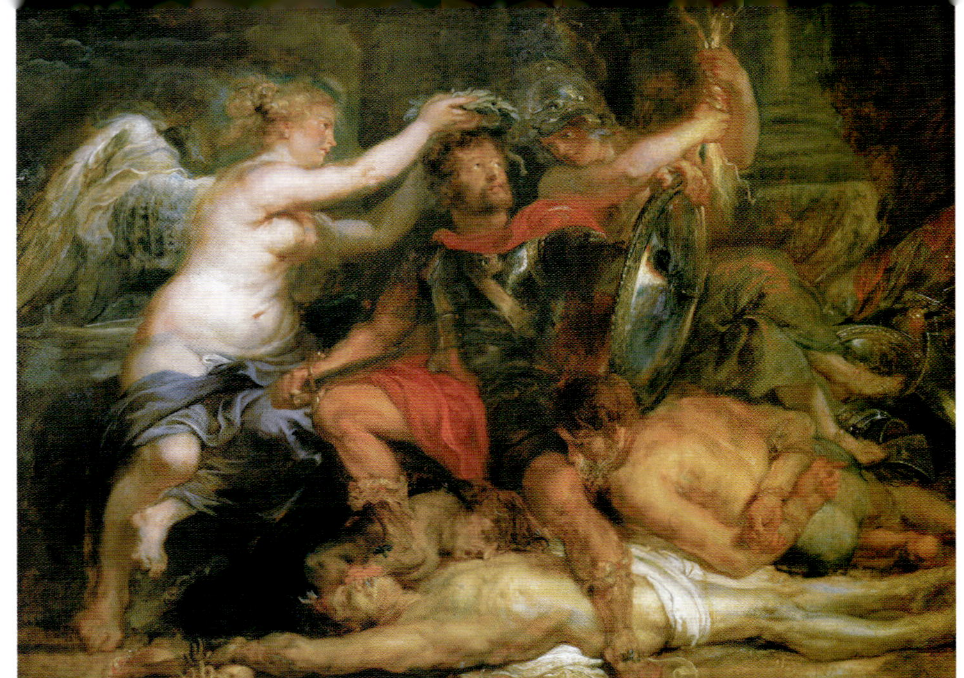

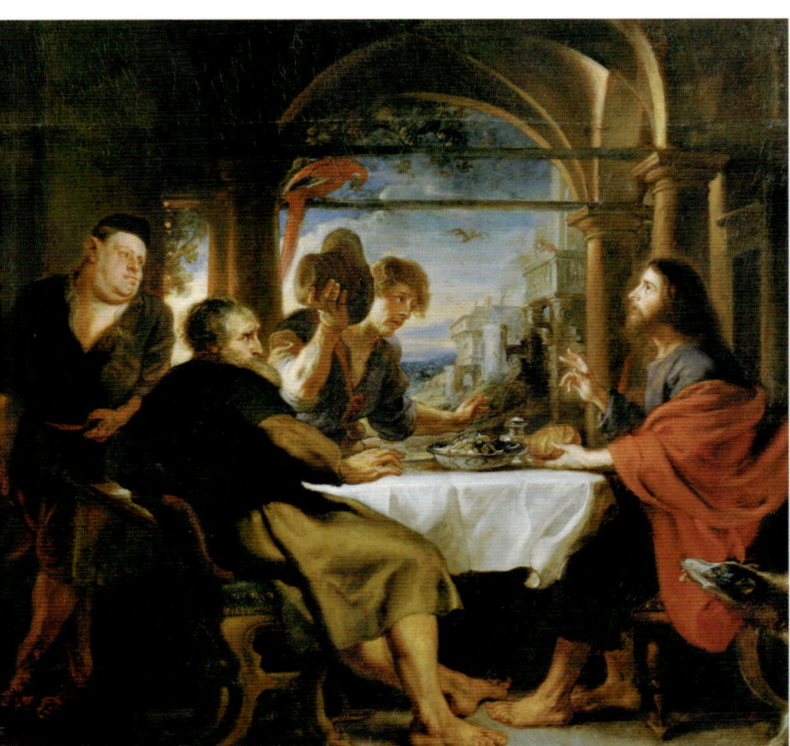

*The Supper at Emmaus,
1635–40, oil on canvas,
144 x 157cm (56⅔ x
61⅞in), Museo Nacional
del Prado, Madrid, Spain*

From the New Testament
story after Christ's
Crucifixion, two pilgrims on
their way to Jerusalem meet
a traveller, whom they invite
to dinner at their friend's
house. At the table, their
unknown guest blesses the
bread, and with shock they
recognize that he is Jesus
resurrected. This painting
was acquired for King
Philip IV at the auction of
Ruben's belongings in 1640.

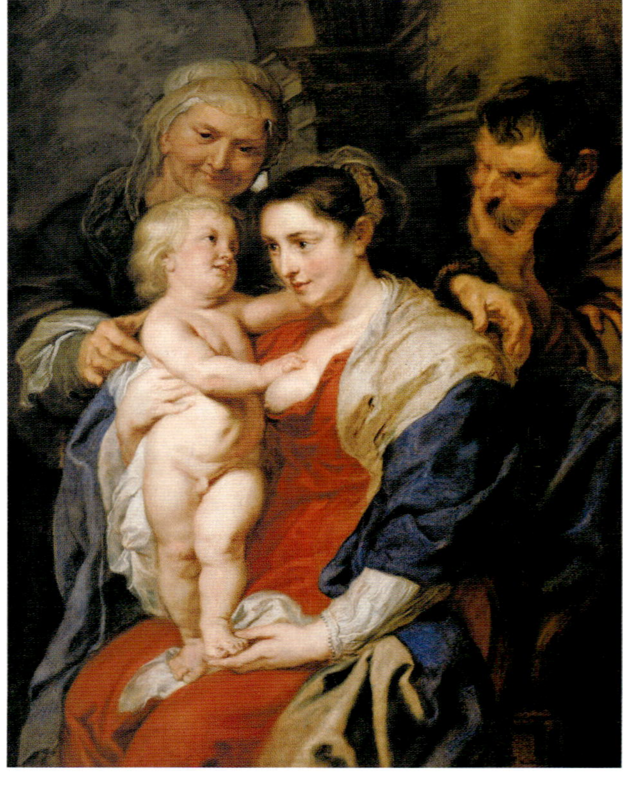

*The Holy Family with Saint
Anne, c.1630, oil on canvas,
116cm x 91cm (45⅔ x
35⅞in), Museo Nacional
del Prado, Madrid, Spain*

Here, Jesus stands on his
mother's lap, clutching her
neck and looking into
her face, and she returns
his gaze. Behind them,
tenderly enclosing the little
group, are Saint Joseph
and Saint Anne, who look
at the child with wonder.
Rubens used his late wife,
Isabella Brant, as the
model for the Virgin in
this painting, clothing her
in his customary red.

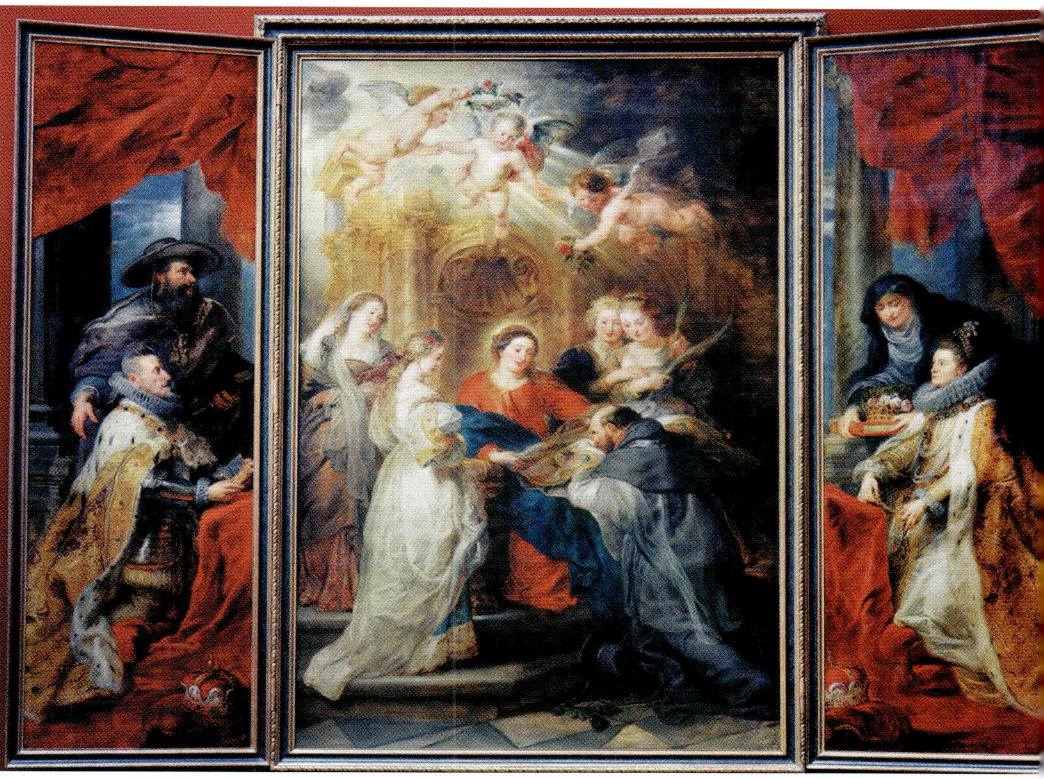

The Ildefonso Altarpiece, 1630–32, oil on panel, central panel: 352 x 236cm (138½ x 93in), side panels: 352 x 109cm (138½ x 43in), Kunsthistorisches, Vienna, Austria

This is a triptych named after the central panel here, which shows Saint Ildefonso's vision of the Virgin Mary, bathed in light, giving him a vestment. The Archduke Albert had founded the Ildefonso Brotherhood in the church of Saint Jacob op de Coudenberg in Brussels, to encourage loyalty to the Habsburg dynasty – and the altarpiece was commissioned for the Brotherhood by the Infanta shortly after her husband's death. On the wings, Albrecht and Isabella kneel as they are presented to the Virgin by their respective patron saints, Saint Albrecht and Saint Elisabeth of Hungary.

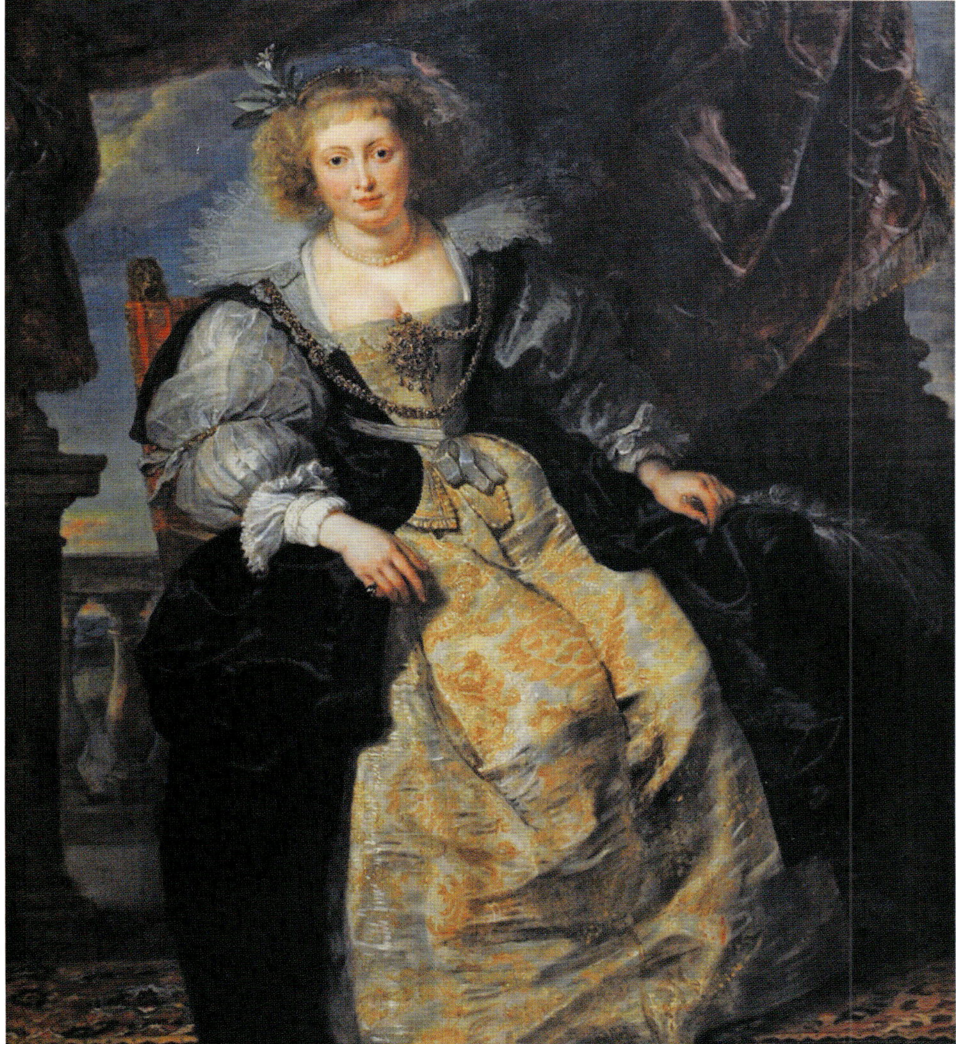

Hélène Fourment in her Bridal Gown, c.1630, oil on oak, 163.5 x 136.9cm (64⅓ x 53⅞in), Alte Pinakothek, Munich, Germany

Four years after the death of his first wife, Rubens married Hélène Fourment, who, at 16 years old, was considered by many to be the prettiest young woman in Flanders. Despite his grief at the death of Isabella, he found happiness with his second wife, and from the start she became his muse. By then, Rubens was extremely wealthy, and here Hélène is dressed for their wedding in an expensive gown and jewels, including a 'Medici' ruff, curled hair, brocade, gold and satin.

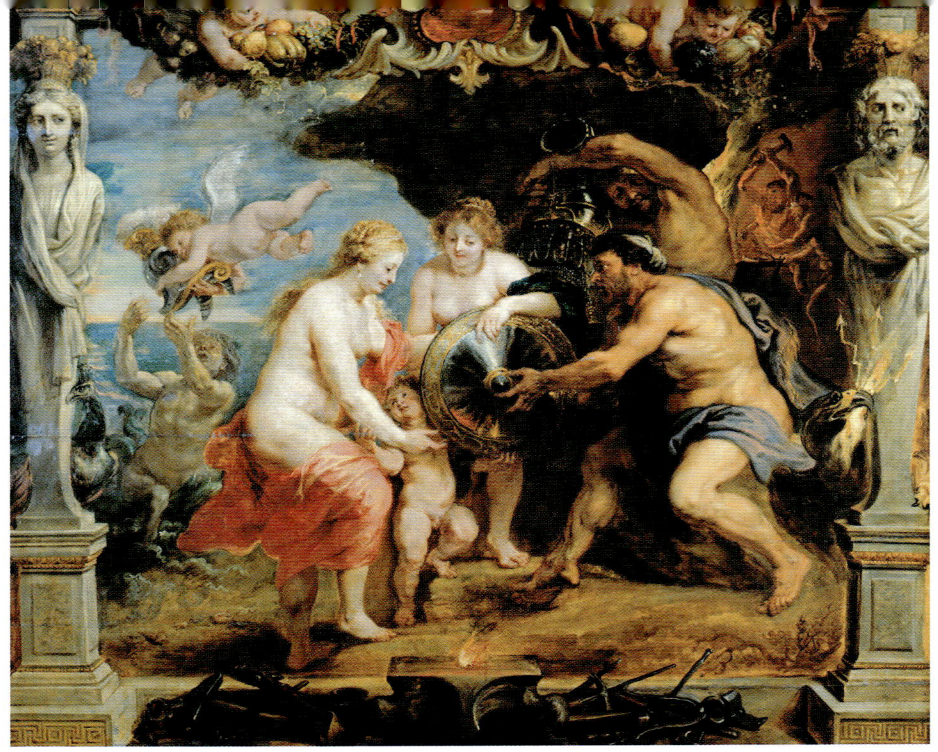

Thetis Receiving the Arms of Achilles from Vulcan, 1630–35, oil on panel, 108 x 126cm (42½ x 49⅔in), Musée des Beaux-Arts, Pau, France

This shows the scene after the Greek hero Achilles had lost his armour. He had lent it to his friend Patroclus, but then decided he should once again participate in the Trojan War. His mother Thetis asked Vulcan, the god of fire, for help. Vulcan set to work forging this new armour, and here, in this oil sketch, the fifth in a series of eight tapestry designs, Vulcan hands a shield to Thetis.

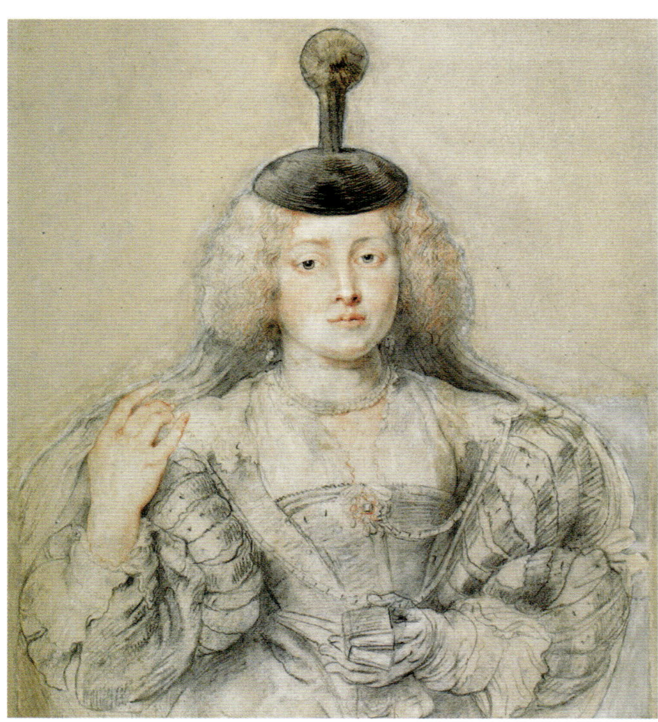

*Hélène Fourment, c.*1630–31, black, red and white chalk on paper, 55 x 61cm (21⅓ x 24in), The Courtauld Gallery, London, UK

This is a drawing of the 16-year-old daughter of an Antwerp silk merchant – the young woman that Rubens married in 1630. Rubens constantly celebrated the beauty of his young wife, including in this large drawing that presents Hélène in a splendid costume while also retaining intimacy and naturalness. Hélène adjusts her veil, which is attached to her headdress. Rubens derived this apparently natural gesture from a classical sculpture of Venus.

The Union of the Crowns, 1630–34, oil on canvas, 64 x 49cm (25 x 19¼ in), The State Hermitage Museum, St Petersburg, Russia

Charles I proposed that the central oval of the Banqueting Hall ceiling at Whitehall should celebrate the union of the crowns of Scotland and England, which was considered to be James I's most notable achievement. This is Rubens's preparatory sketch for the picture, showing James ordering his infant son Charles to be brought to the throne by personifications of England and Scotland, who, with Minerva, hold the two crowns of the kingdoms over his head.

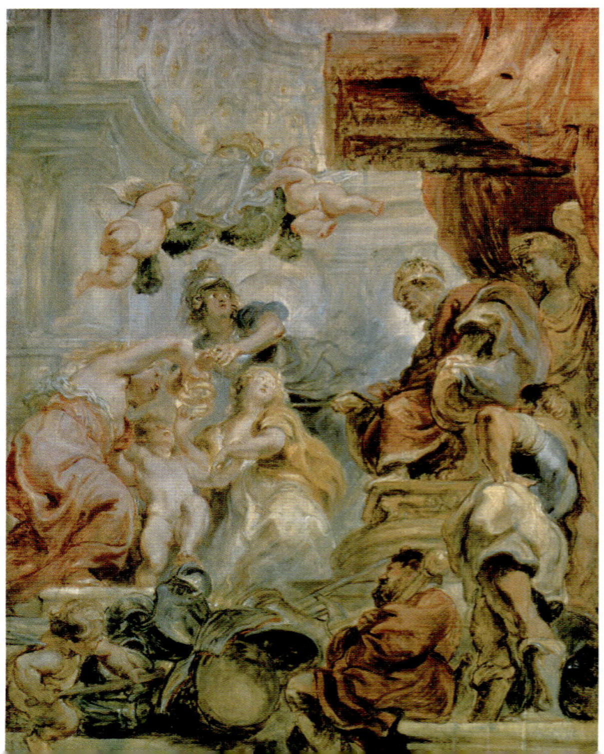

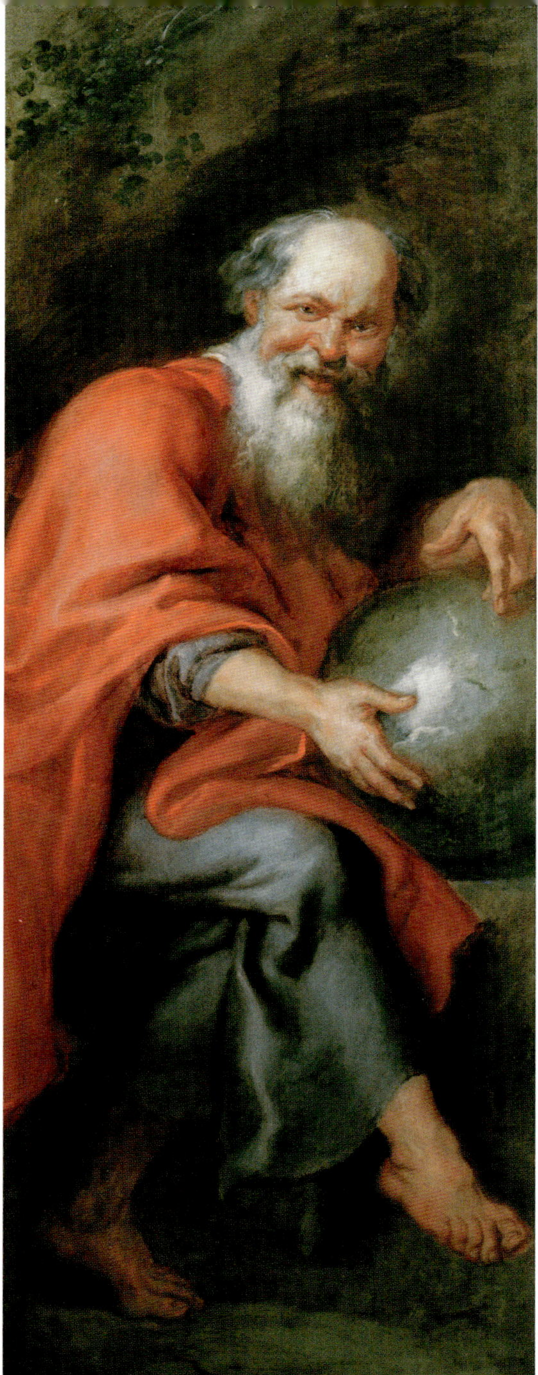

Democritus, the Laughing Philosopher, 1636–38, oil on canvas, 180.5 x 66cm (71 x 26in), Museo del Prado, Madrid, Spain

As the philosophical counterpart of Heraclitus (below), Democritus of Abdera (460–370BCE) laughs while holding a globe of the Earth, showing his amusement over the meaning of life and earthly vanities. Often called 'The Laughing Philosopher' or 'The Mocker', Democritus always laughed about the foolishness he saw around him among his fellow citizens, which makes his personality the antithesis of Heraclitus.

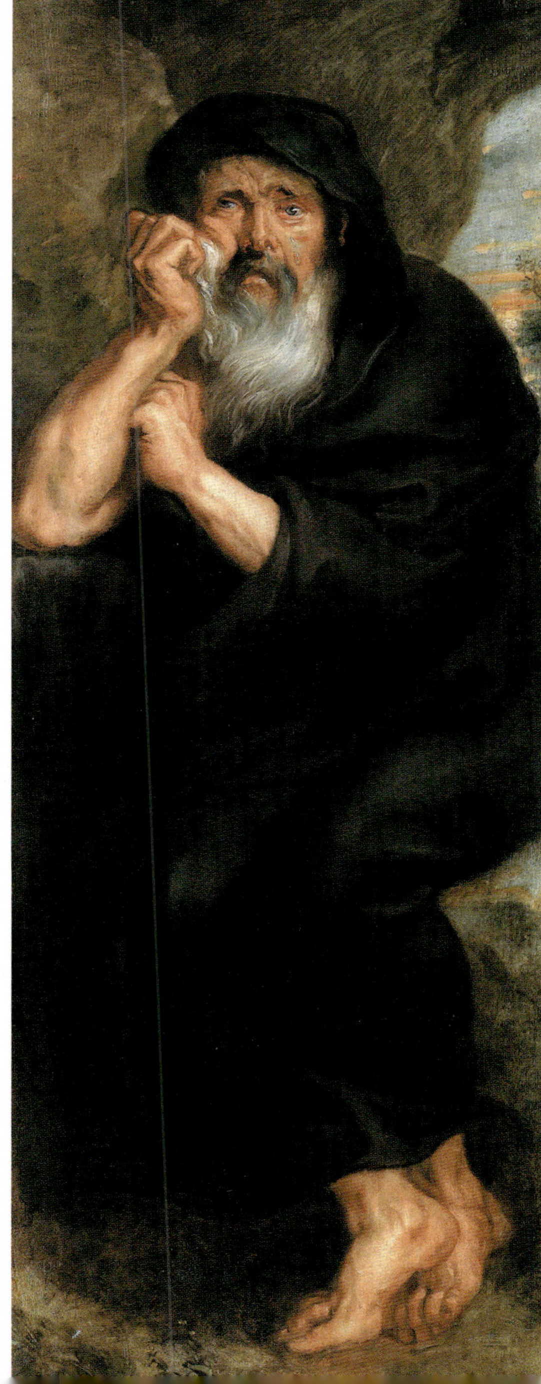

Heraclitus, the Crying Philosopher, 1636–38, oil on canvas, 183 x 64.5cm (72 x 25⅜in), Museo del Prado, Madrid, Spain

In a black tunic, the Greek philosopher Heraclitus of Ephesus (540–470BCE) leans on a stone, weeping. He embodies the idea of a tragic view of life, always perceiving the negatives and considering the future with a lonely and pessimistic attitude. Painted for the Torre de la Parada, this work directly contrasts with the image of Democritus (above) – they were painted as a pair.

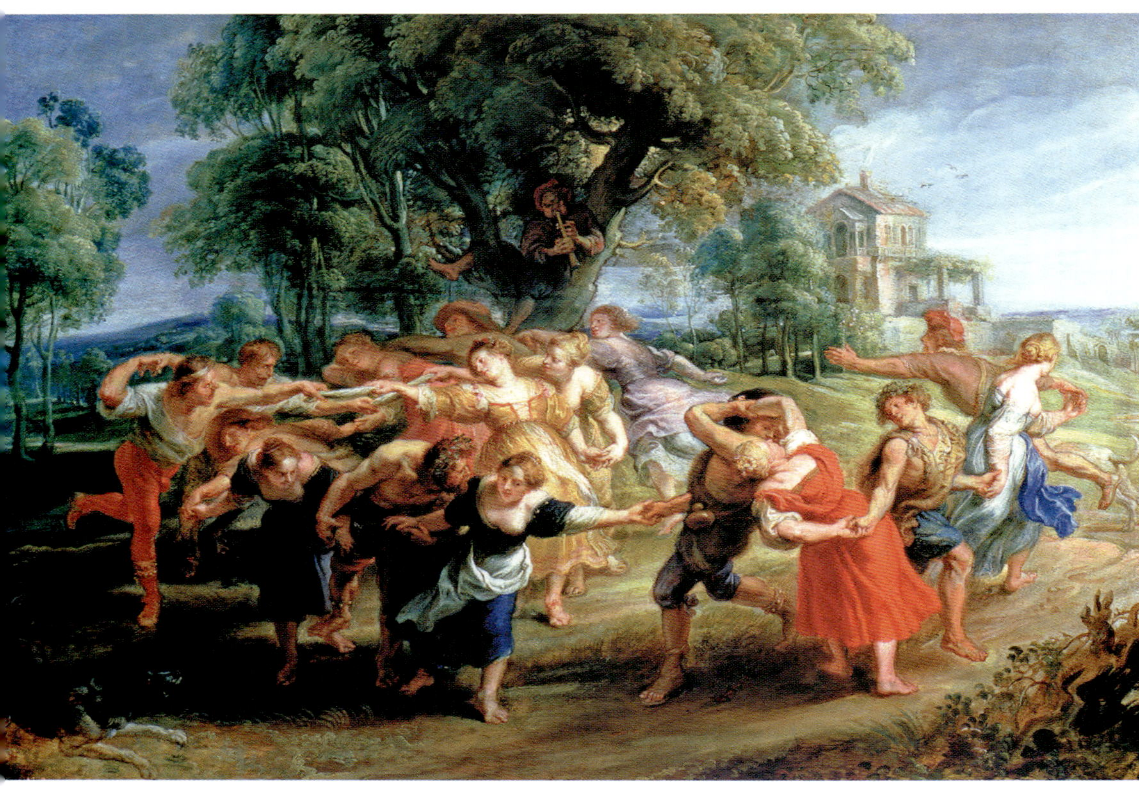

Dance of Mythological Characters and Villagers, 1630–35, oil on panel, 73 x 106cm (28¾ x 41¾in), Museo del Prado, Madrid, Spain

A group of peasants dance in a lively whirl, accompanied by a flautist in a tree. The landscape is Italian, with a Palladian villa in the background. The dynamic composition, colour and frivolity convey a sensation of happiness and freedom, epitomizing Rubens's own happiness in his new marriage. He kept this painting for the rest of his life. It was acquired after his death by Philip IV.

The Education of the Virgin, 1625–26, oil on canvas, 194 x 140cm (76⅓ x 55in), Koninklijk Museum voor Schone Kunsten, Antwerp, Belgium

Several writings by early Christians that give accounts of God, Jesus, his apostles and his teachings, are known as the *Apocrypha*, considered by the Church as useful but not divinely inspired. This illustrates one of these stories, which tells how the Virgin Mary was brought up as a child in the Temple at Jerusalem because her parents Saints Joachim and Anne foretold that she would be chosen by God.

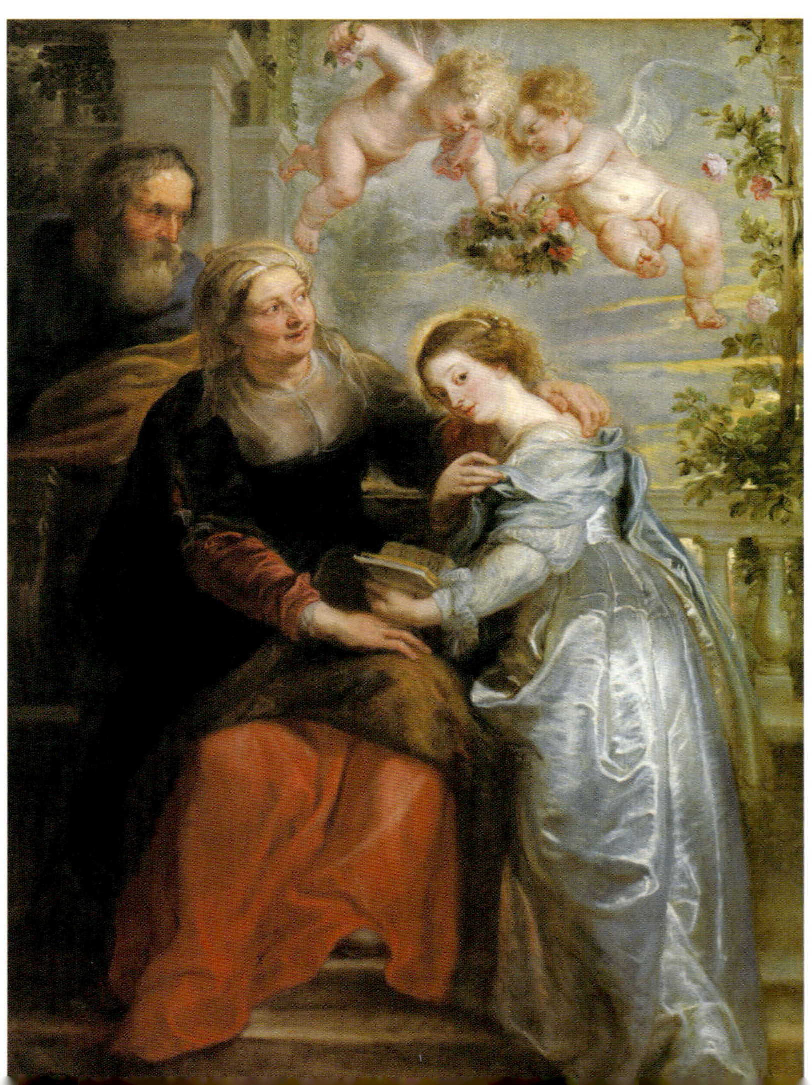

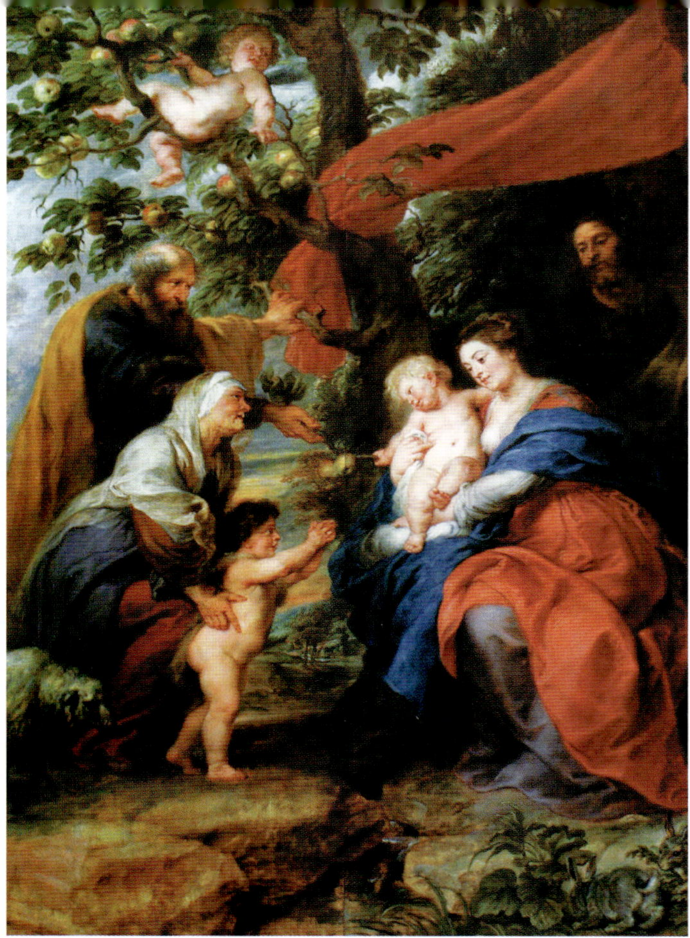

The Holy Family under an Apple Tree, c.1632, oil on panel, 106.9 x 96.5cm (42¹⁄₁₆ x 38in), Sterling and Francine Clark Institute, Massachusetts, USA

Here, Elizabeth kneels to hold her little son John the Baptist, who gestures to Jesus on Mary's lap. John's father Zacharias offers Jesus an apple branch. This gesture symbolizes how Jesus will sacrifice himself to redeem humanity from Adam and Eve's sin. The Virgin Mary, wearing Rubens's customary red and blue, sits beneath the tree, holding the baby, with Joseph behind.

Rubens, his Wife Hélène Fourment and their Son Frans, c.1635, oil on wood, 203.8 x 158.1cm (80¼ x 62¼ in), The Metropolitan Museum of Art, New York, USA

This is a self-portrait with Hélène and one of their five children, walking in a 'Garden of Love.' The little boy shows the work to be a tribute to Hélène as a wife and mother. The parakeet in the top right corner is a symbol of the Virgin Mary, and so of an ideal mother figure. Rubens shows himself as a middle-aged man, his gaze directing viewers to his wife.

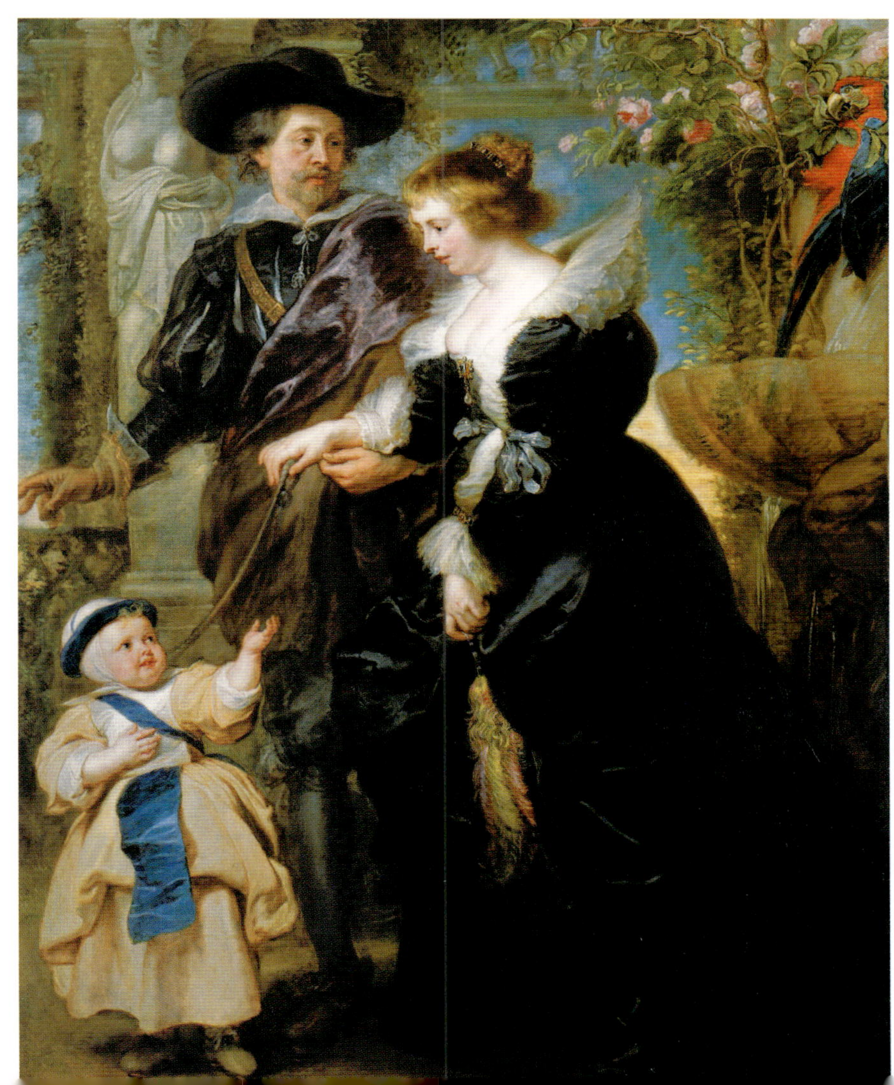

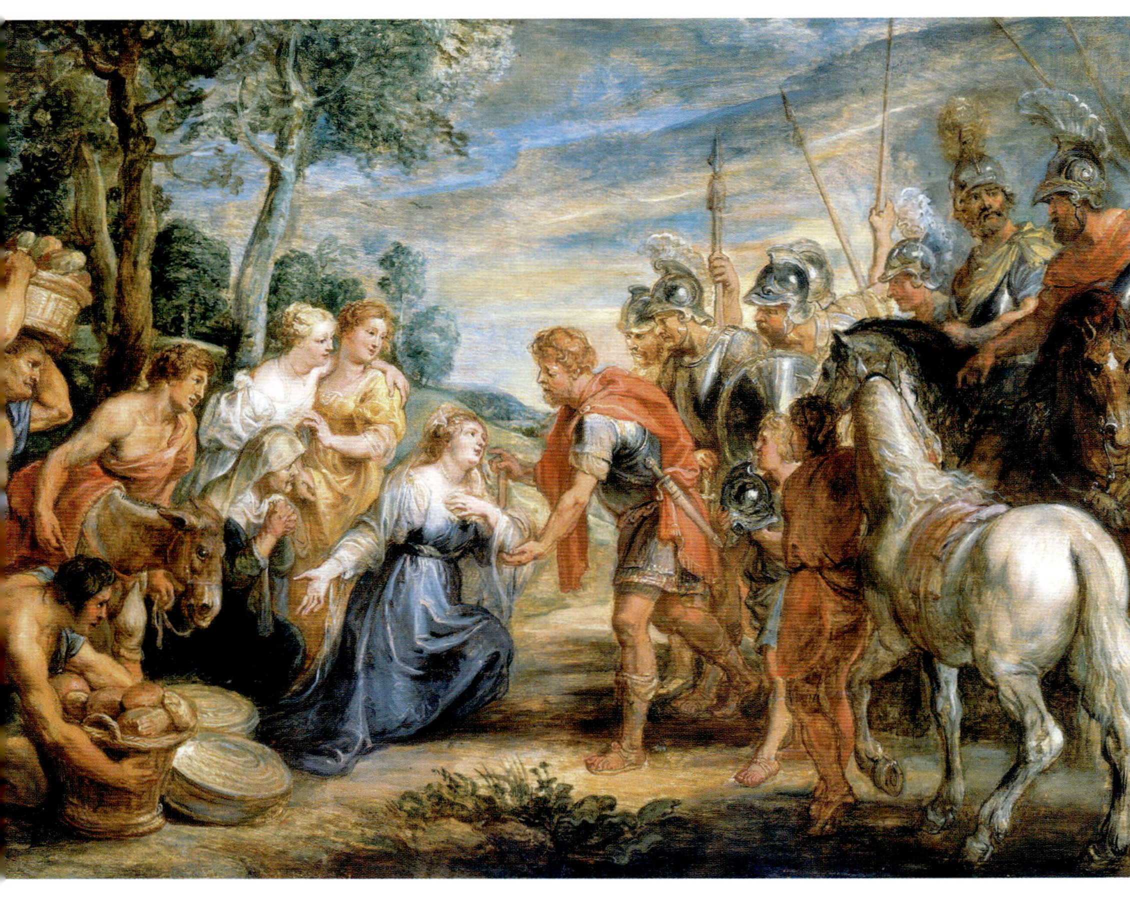

The Meeting of David and Abigail, c.1630, oil on panel, 44.7 x 66.3cm (17⅝ x 26⅛in), National Gallery of Art, Washington DC, USA

This biblical narrative describes an episode during David's exile in the wilderness. David sent some men to ask for food from a wealthy sheep farmer – who refused. Infuriated, David set out with 400 armed men to seek revenge, but the farmer's wife, Abigail, quickly packed provisions, loaded them on donkeys, and set out to intercept David and his men. After she pleaded with him, David retreated.

James I Uniting England and Scotland, c.1632–33, oil on panel, 63.5 x 48.3cm (25 x 19in), Birmingham Museum and Art Gallery, England, UK

This is one of Rubens's dynamic decorations that he painted for the ceiling of Inigo Jones's new building in London. This sketch was almost certainly produced when Rubens returned to Antwerp and planned the ceiling in full. Rubens was always aware of the viewpoints of those who would be observing his work – expressive, dynamic and dramatic foreshortening had become a speciality.

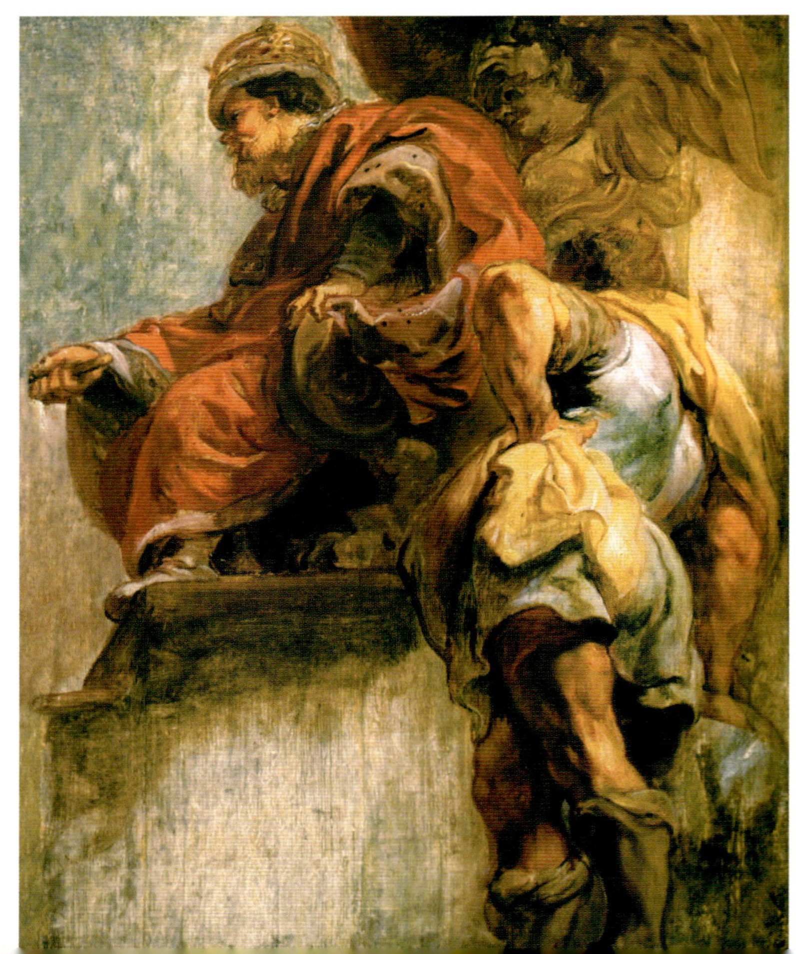

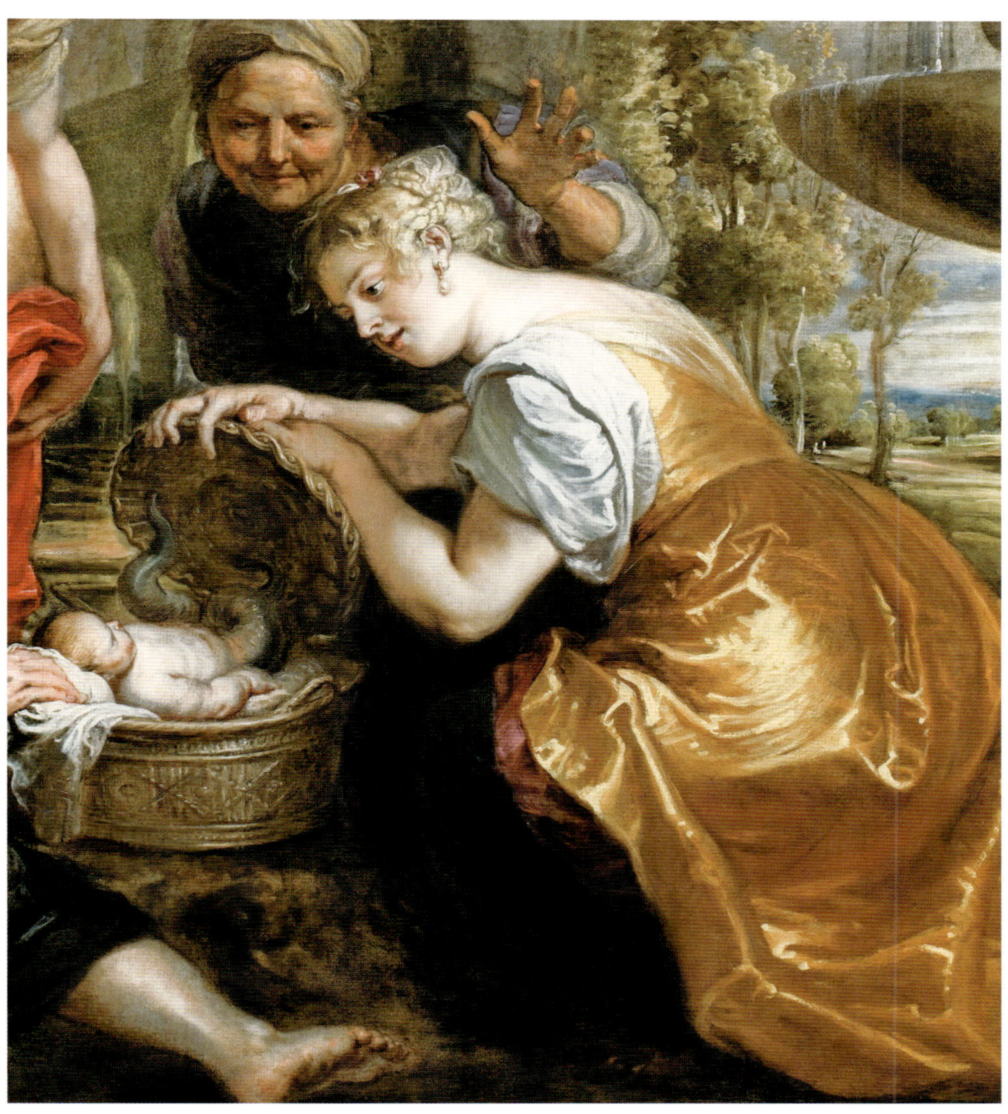

The Finding of Erichthonius,
1632–33, oil on canvas,
109.3 x 103.4cm
(43 x 40⅝in), Allen
Memorial Art Museum,
Oberlin, Ohio, USA

The story of the discovery
of the snake-legged infant
Erichthonius, son of Vulcan
and Gaea, has been related
by several classical authors.
This vivid canvas, with its
robust figures and free
brushstrokes, is the only
surviving fragment of a much
larger composition. Despite
his wide knowledge of all
writers on the subject,
Rubens based this just on
Ovid's narration of the
tale. The execution reflects
Rubens's unfailing admiration
of Titian and Veronese.

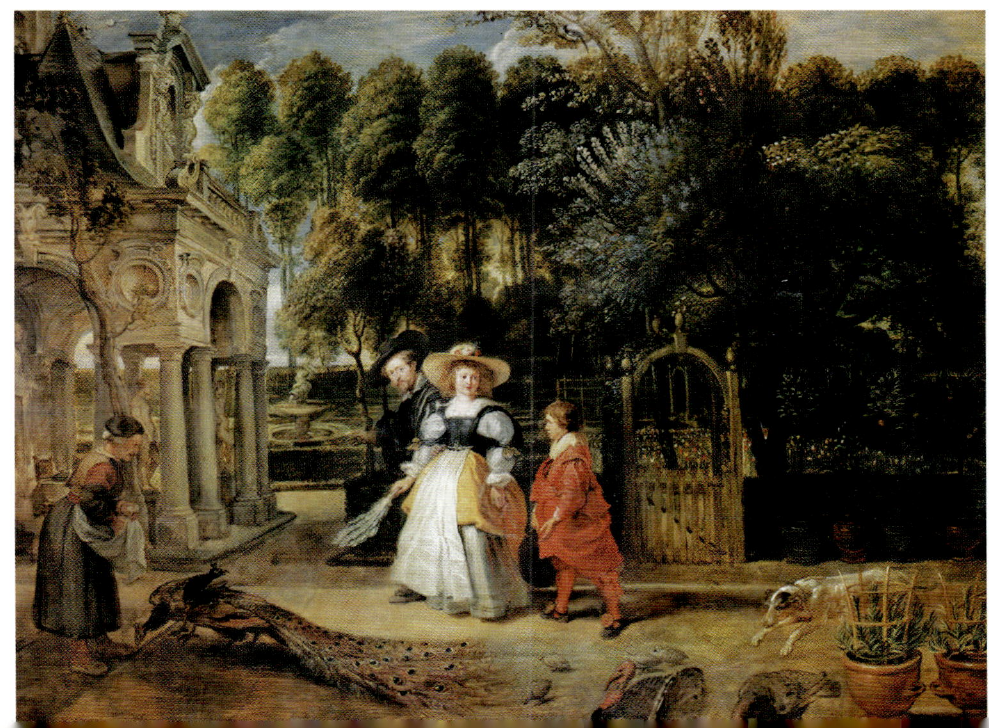

*Rubens in his Garden with
Hélène Fourment, c.*1630–31,
oil on wood, 97.5 x 130.8cm
(38⅓ x 51⅓in), Alte
Pinakothek, Munich, Germany

With Hélène and his son
Nicolaas from his first
marriage, this shows Rubens
in his garden at Antwerp. It
follows a long tradition of
family and marriage portraiture
in the Netherlands, and
gardens represented the
Virgin and love. The dog
is an emblem of fidelity,
and the lush vegetation
suggests fertility.

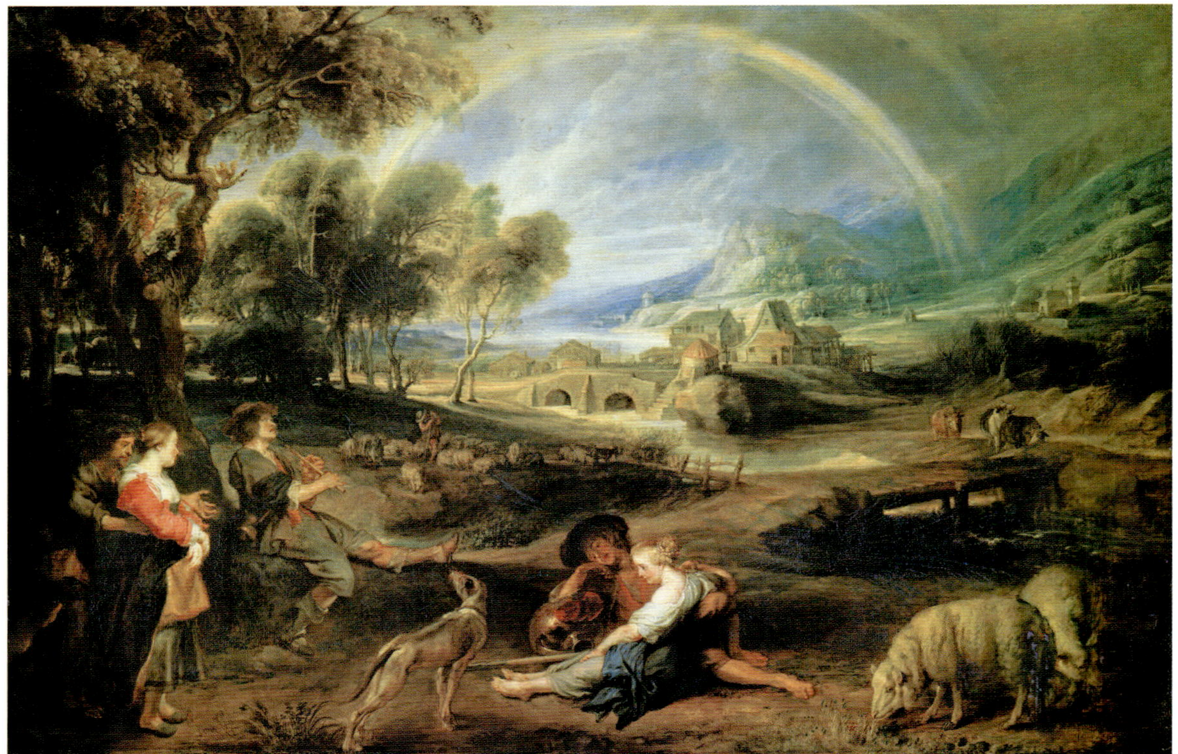

Landscape with a Rainbow,
1632–35, oil on canvas
(transferred from panel),
86 x 130cm (33¾ x 51in),
State Hermitage Museum,
St Petersburg, Russia

Borrowing elements of this
composition from Titian and
Carracci and from his actual
memories of Italian countryside,
Rubens opened up the landscape
and bathed the background with
a soft, atmospheric haze, while
the middle ground is flooded by
light. Although the figures in the
foreground are peasants, this
tranquil and harmonious scene
is a forerunner of the later
French Rococo-style atmosphere
of harmony and tranquillity.

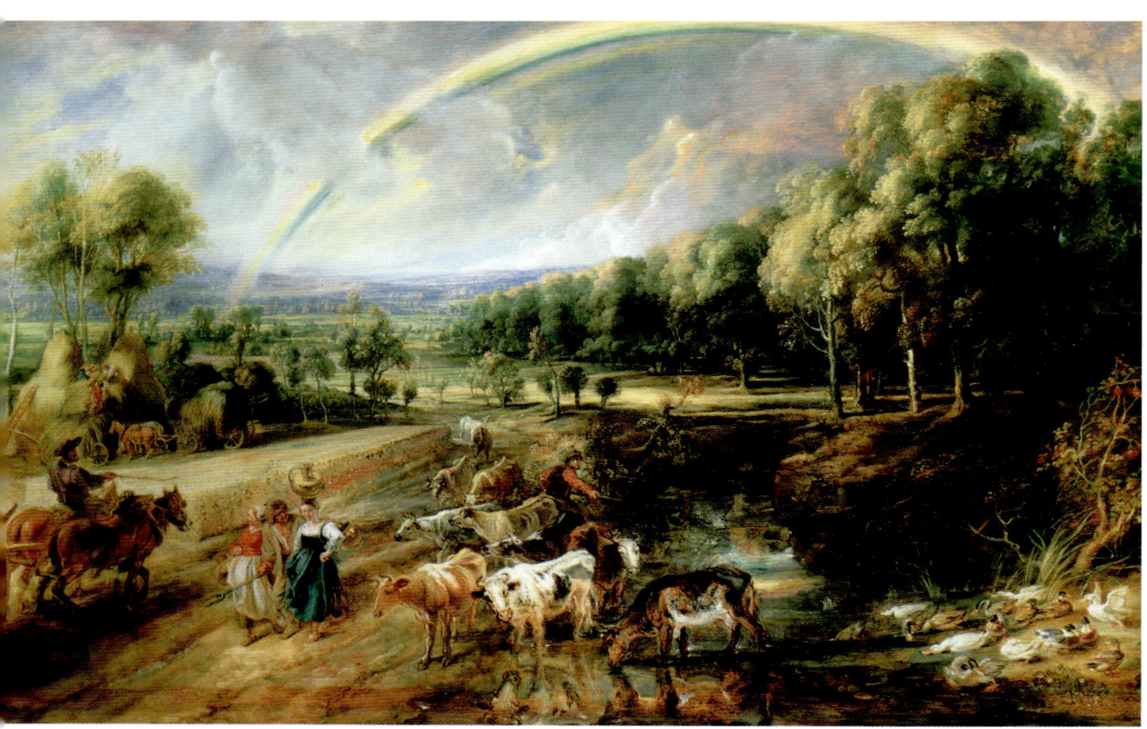

The Rainbow Landscape,
c.1636, oil on oak panel,
135.6 x 235cm (53⅓ x
92½in), The Wallace
Collection, London, UK

A view from Rubens's manor
house, Het Steen, over the
surrounding countryside,
this was painted for pleasure,
and remained in Rubens's
personal collection until his
death. Expressing his love of
the surrounding landscape,
this elevated viewpoint
captures peasants and
milkmaids returning from
the fields, driving home
cattle and gathering hay.
The rainbow represents
the covenant between God
and Man after the flood.

The Feast of Herod, 1635–38, oil on canvas, 208 x 264cm (82 x 104in), Scottish National Gallery, National Galleries of Scotland, Edinburgh, UK

Probably painted for Gaspar de Roomer (c.1596–1674), a Flemish merchant based in Naples, this richly coloured biblical story shows Herod granting the wish of his stepdaughter, Salome, for dancing so beautifully. King Herod had not anticipated that Salome would ask for the head of John the Baptist. Here at a banquet, she presents the head to him, and he shrinks back in horror.

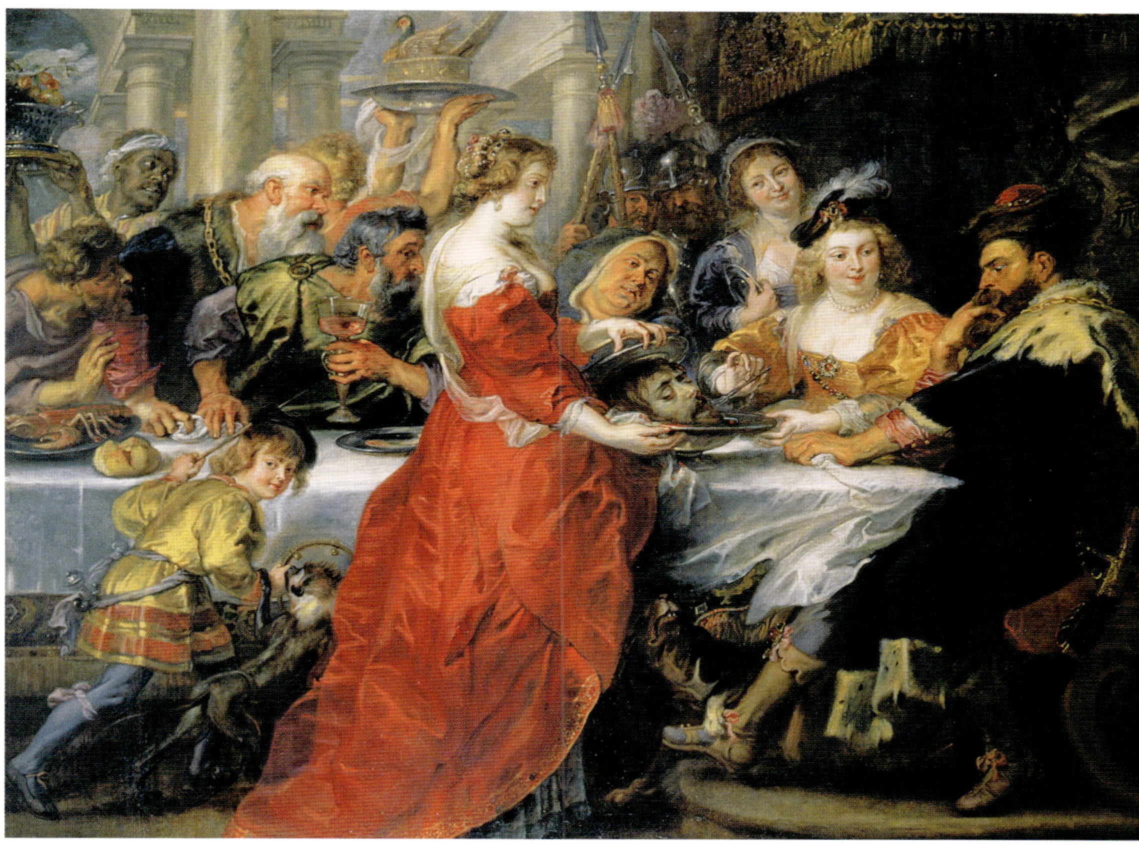

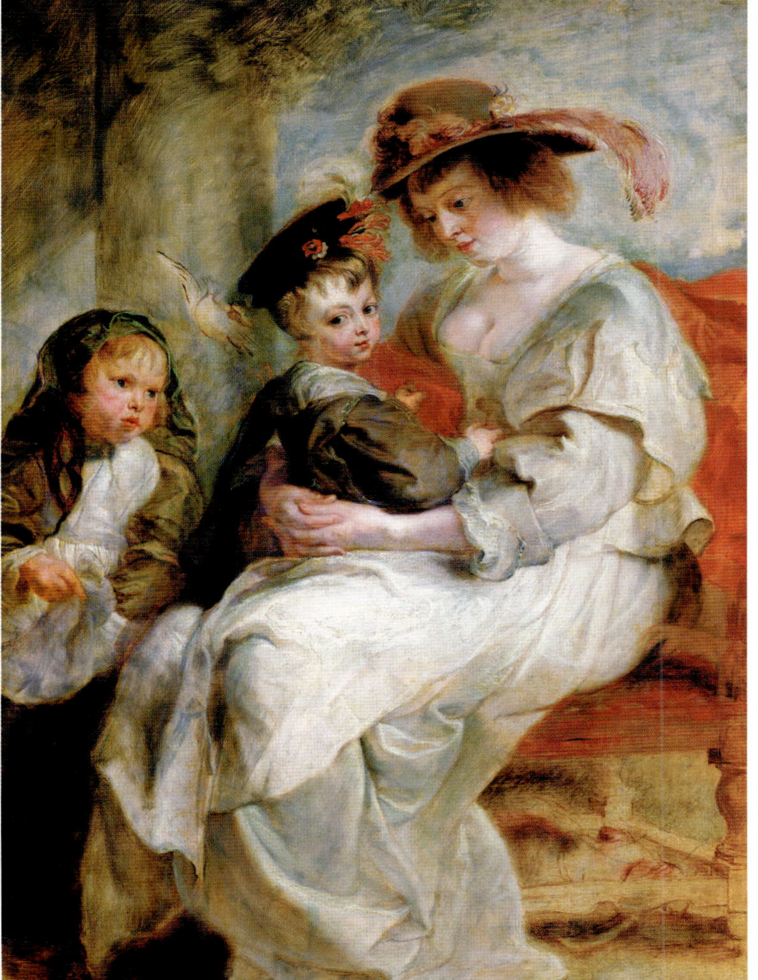

Hélène Fourment and her Children, 1635–36, oil on panel, 115 x 85cm (45¼ x 33½in), Musée du Louvre, Paris, France

Continuously inspired by his young wife, Rubens captures her rosy-cheeked, sitting with two of their children, Clara Johanna and Frans. Rubens had planned to expand this work progressively as their young family grew, but unfortunately, he did not live to do this. Unlike his depictions of Hélène as a goddess, here he portrayed her as a fashionably dressed, serene and affectionate young mother.

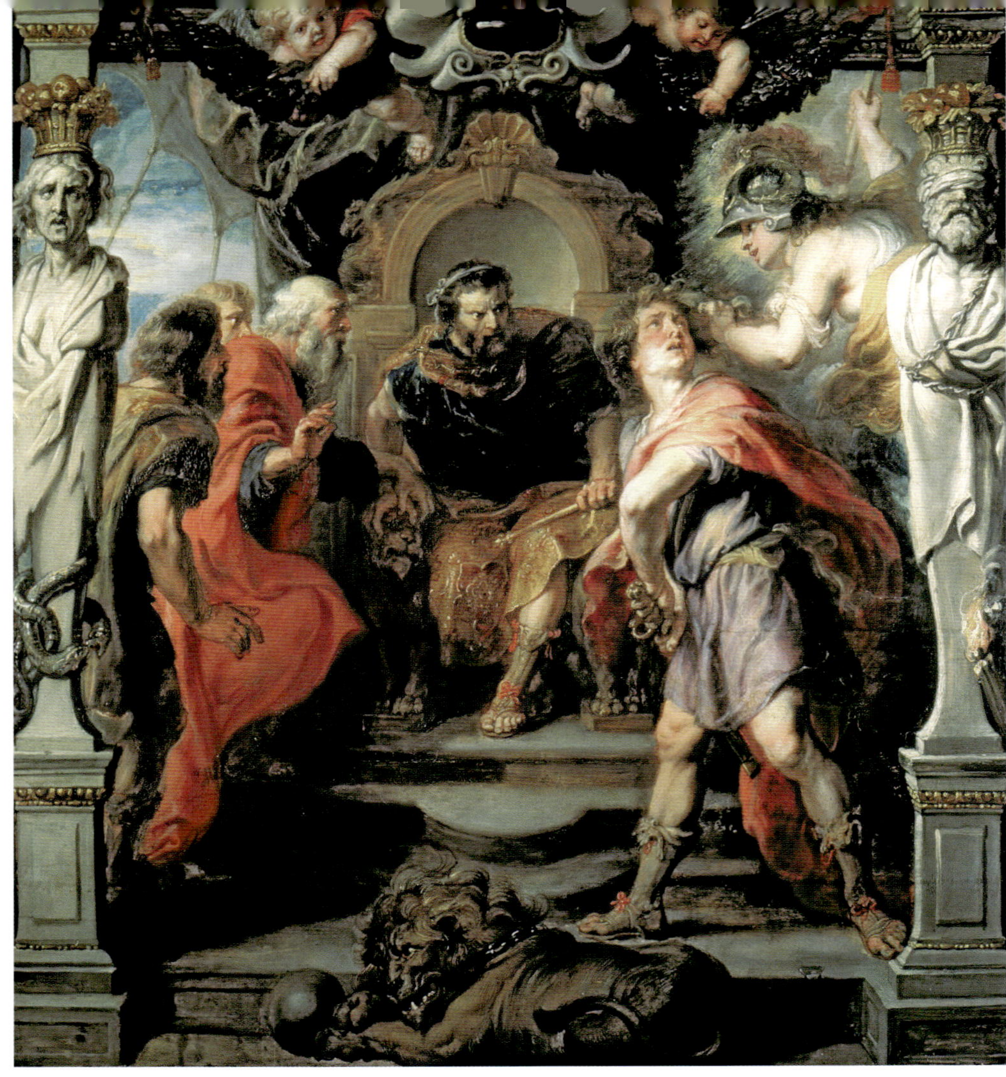

Wrath of Achilles,
*c.*1633, oil on panel,
106.8 x 108.5cm (42 x
42¾in), The Courtauld
Gallery, London, UK

The fourth painting in
Rubens's series of eight on
the stories of Achilles, this
shows King Agamemnon,
who had to give back his
beloved Chryseis to her
father, the priest of Apollo, in
order to stop the plague. In
place of Chryseis, he took
Achilles's beloved Briseis and,
livid, Achilles refused to take
any further part in the
Trojan War. Here, the two
men are being restrained
by Nestor and Minerva.

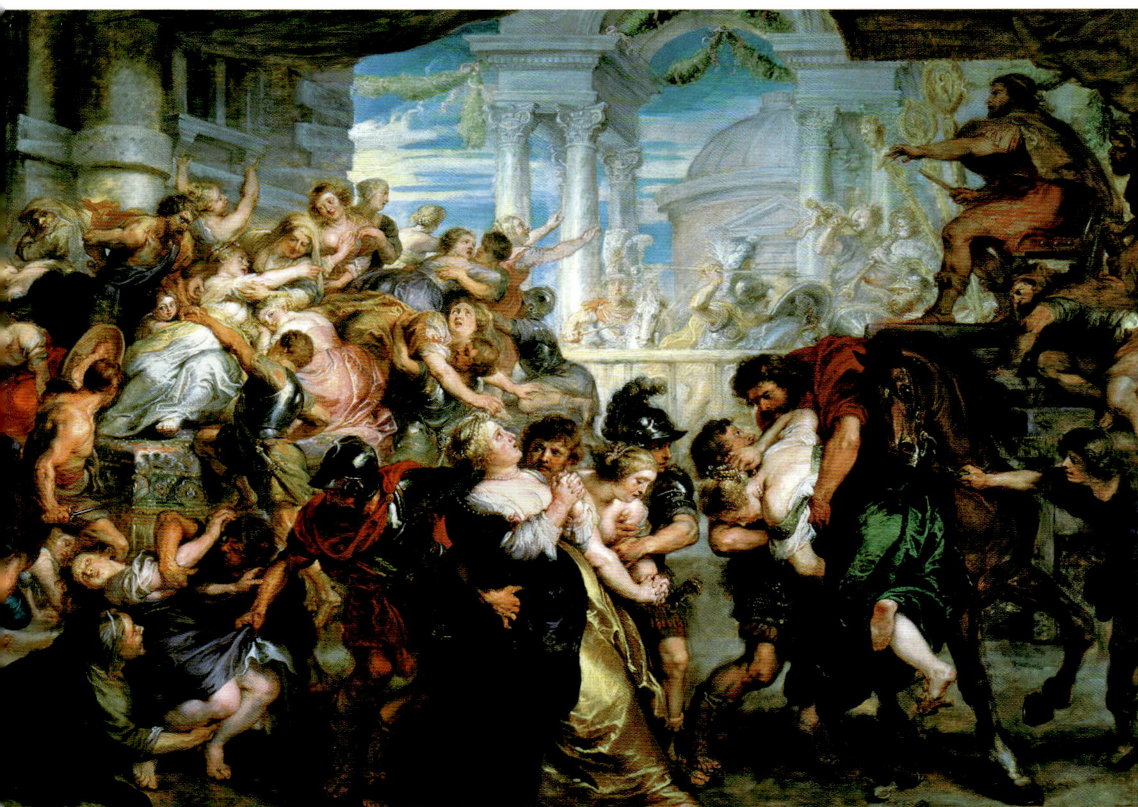

The Rape of the Sabine
*Women, c.*1635–40, oil on
oak, 169.9 x 236.2cm
(66⅞ x 93in), The National
Gallery, London, UK

'Rape' in this context means
abduction. Plutarch wrote
that the Sabine tribe were
invited to games in Rome,
but at a sign from King
Romulus, the Romans carried
the women away. Here,
although the architecture is
classical, the women wear
contemporary Flemish dress.
Rubens shows the heroic,
action-packed struggle by the
women, who ultimately lost
– and the Romans secured
wives for themselves.

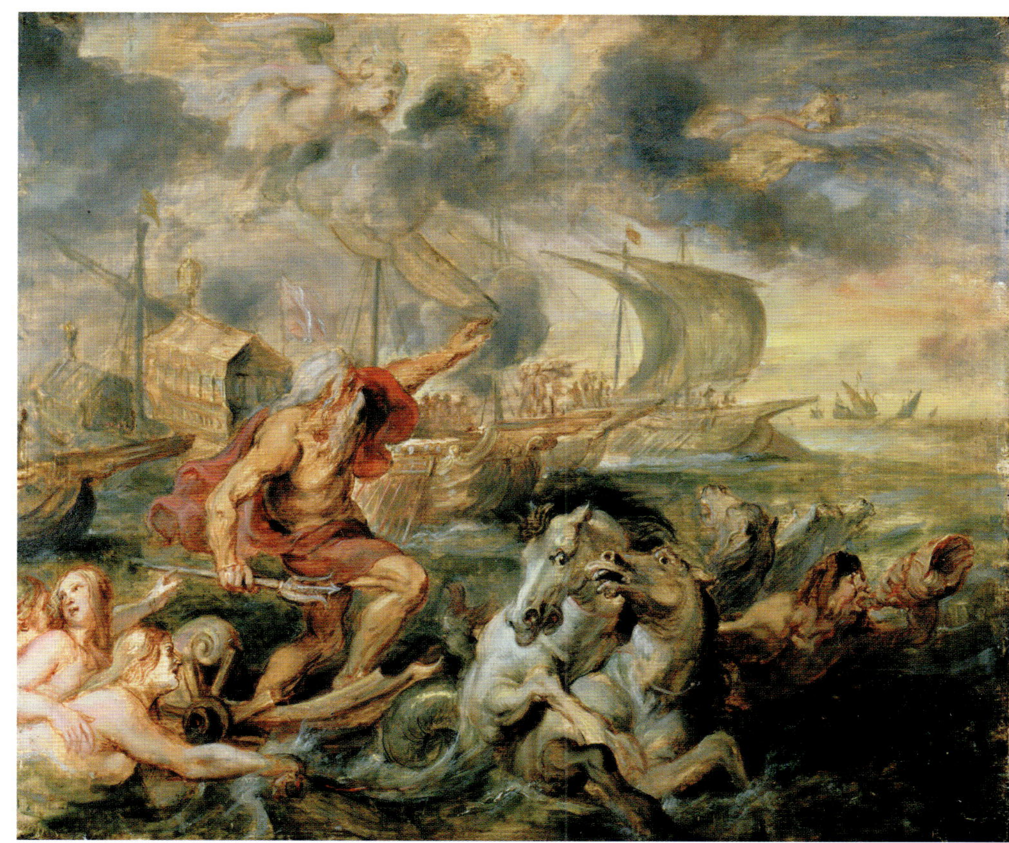

Neptune Calming the Tempest, 1635, oil on panel, 49 x 64.1cm (19¼ x 25¼in), Fogg Art Museum, Harvard Art Museums, Massachusetts, USA

Neptune, the god of the sea, rides over crashing waves in a shell drawn by sea horses, heralded by a triton blowing a large conch shell and attended by three swimming nereids. Neptune gestures at three personifications of the wind above. Beyond him, several ships represent the fleet that the Cardinal Infante Ferdinand took from Barcelona to Genoa in April 1633.

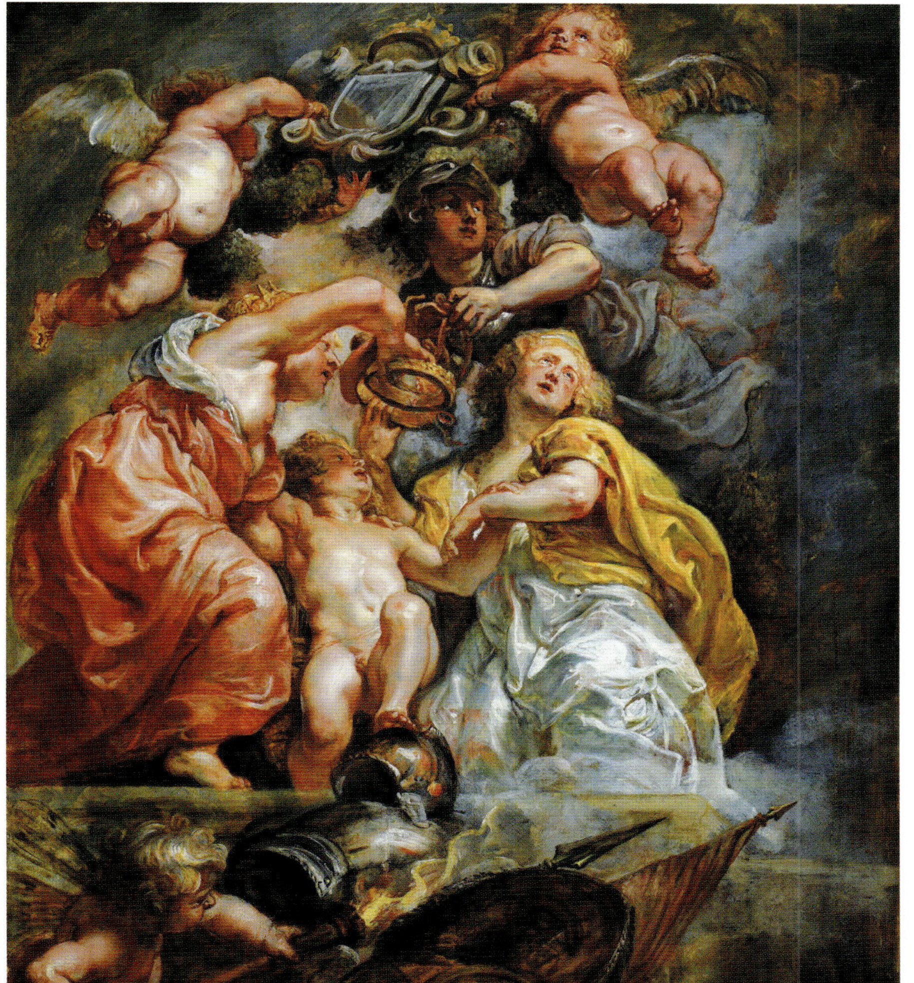

*The Union of England and Scotland, c.*1633–34, oil on oak, 84.4 x 65.7cm (32¼ x 25¾in), Minneapolis Institute of Arts, Minnesota, USA

Along with *The Union of the Crowns* (sketch on page 238) and *The Finding of Erichthonius* (page 243), this is an oil sketch for Charles I of England's commission. Celebrating his father's achievements and the power of the Stuart monarchy, Charles aimed to show the benefits that had come to Britain. In this painting, the child represents young Prince Charles, as the apotheosis of the union between England and Scotland. Three women crown him: the woman in red personifies England; the woman in yellow represents Scotland; and the third is Minerva, goddess of wisdom and war.

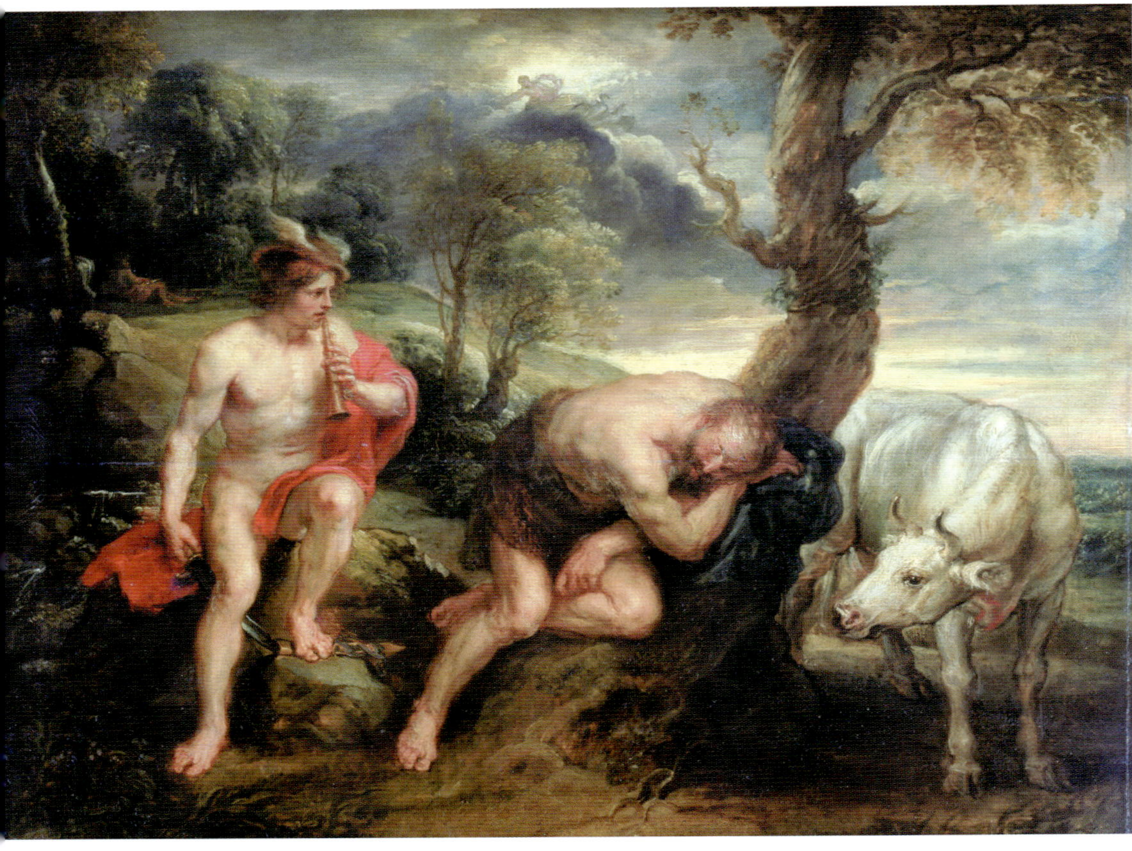

Mercury and Argus,
1635–38, oil on panel,
63 x 87.5cm (24⅞ x
34½in), Gemäldegalerie,
Dresden, Germany

From Ovid's *Metamorphoses*,
this relays the story of Io,
the beautiful daughter of the
river god Inachus, who is
seduced by Jupiter. To hide
Io from his jealous wife,
Jupiter turns her into a
cow, but Juno persuades
her husband to give her
the cow and orders the
hundred-eyed Argus
to guard it. Jupiter asks
Mercury to kill the guard.
Here, Mercury plays music
to make Argus sleep,
before stabbing him.

*The Triumph of Judas
Maccabeus*, 1635, oil on
canvas, 310 x 228cm (122 x
89¾in), Musée des Beaux-
Arts, Nantes, France

Created for the Bishop of
Tournai and paid for with
funds raised by local
residents, this richly coloured
painting was one of several
works by Rubens that was
subsequently seized by
Napoleon's troops and sent
to France in 1794. It depicts
the Old Testament story
of Judas Maccabeus, a
Jewish priest who led the
Maccabean Revolt against
the Seleucid Empire
in 167–160BCE.

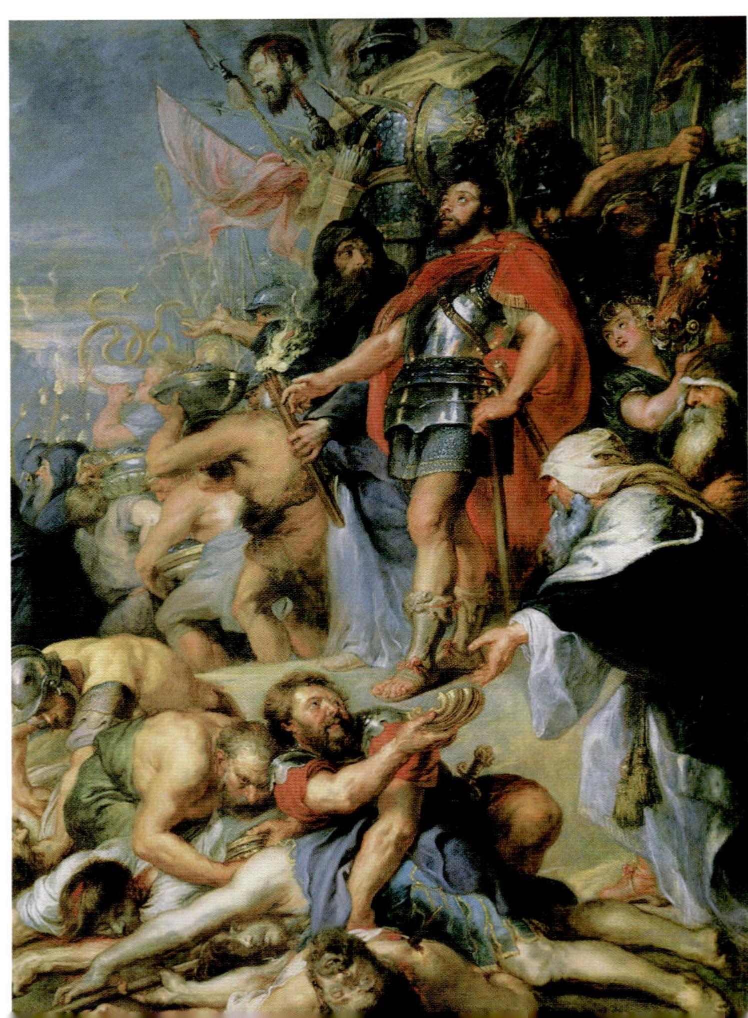

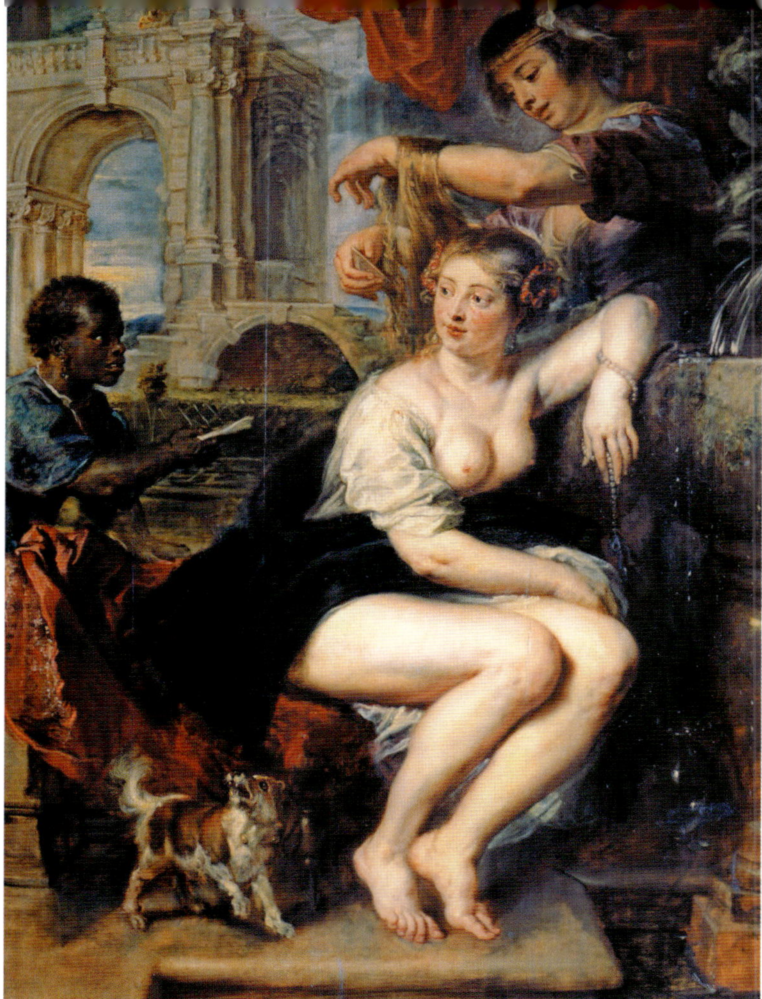

Bathsheba at the Fountain,
*c.*1635, oil on oak,
175 × 126cm (68⅞ ×
49⅔in), Gemäldegalerie,
Dresden, Germany

From the biblical story,
Bathsheba is at her toilet,
here seen by a fountain. A
maid combs her golden hair
as a messenger arrives with
a letter sent by King David,
who can just be seen looking
down on her in the upper
left corner of the painting.
The dog symbolizes
Bathsheba's fidelity to her
husband, who is away fighting
in David's army, while the
king aims to seduce his wife.

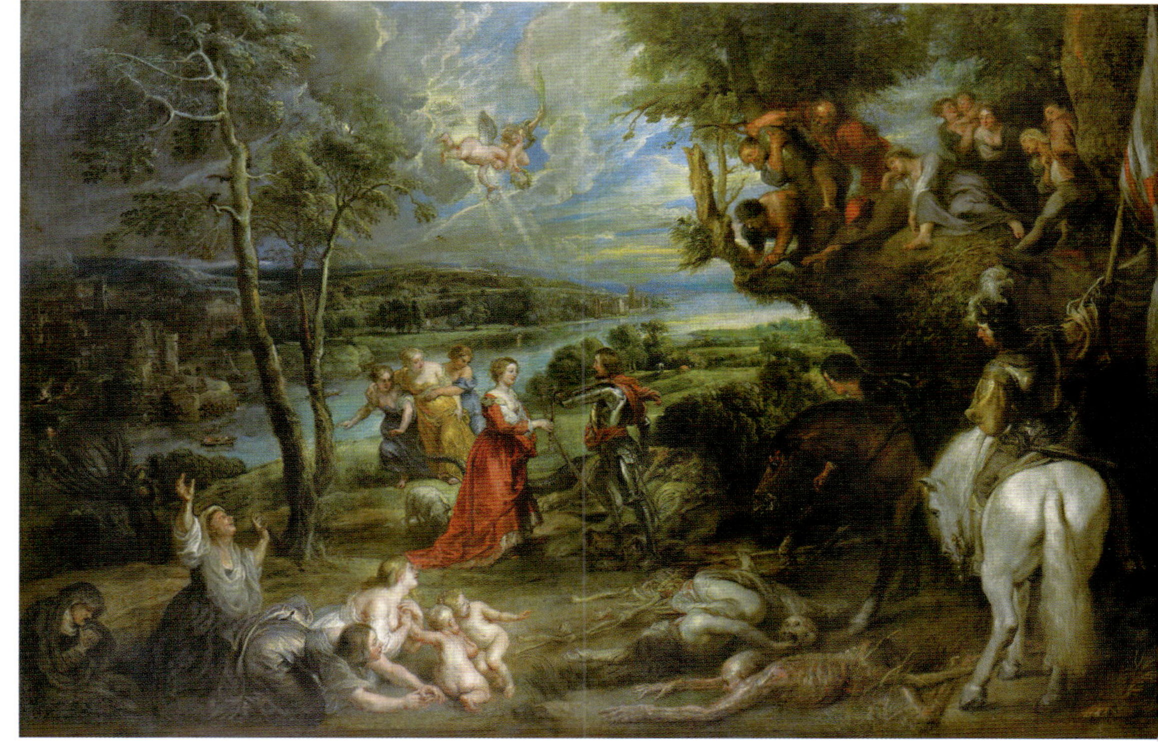

Landscape with Saint George
and the Dragon, 1630–35, oil
on canvas, 152.5 × 226.9cm
(60 × 89⅓in), The Royal
Collection, London, UK

In 1677, the painter, engraver,
art critic and diplomat
Roger de Piles (1635–1709)
noticed that the setting and
characters in this painting are
specifically English. Since then,
it has been generally agreed
that this celebrates England:
the river is the Thames, and
Saint George is an allusion
to Charles I. As with most
of Rubens's landscapes, he
added to it later, enlarging
the canvas as he did so.

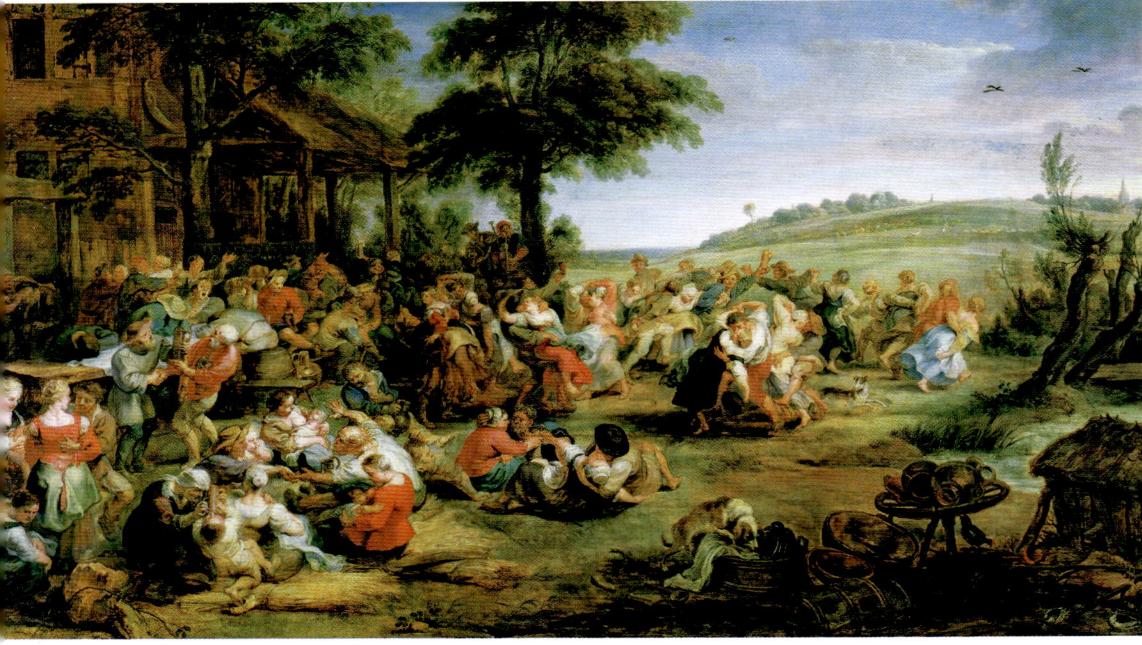

The Kermesse, or *The Village Fête* (detail), c.1635–38, oil on panel, 149 x 261cm (58⅔ x102¾in), Musée du Louvre, Paris, France

Rubens's friend Brueghel was known as 'the painter of peasants', and Rubens owned at least 12 of his works. This is Rubens's view of peasants in the countryside enjoying a festival: dancing, drinking and behaving coarsely. It is a denunciation of humanity's excesses. Expressing the joy of living and the pleasures of the senses, the dog in the foreground is a traditional symbol of gluttony.

Nymphs and Satyrs, 1638–40, oil on canvas, 139.7 x 167cm (55 x 65¾in), Museo del Prado, Madrid, Spain

Under some trees, a group of nymphs and satyrs are shown enjoying themselves. The nymphs personify the abundance of the fields, while the satyrs watch over the woods. Together, they harvest the fruits offered by Nature. A child satyr offers a cluster of grapes to a tiger – an allusion to Bacchus. Some of the figures are based on classical sculptures.

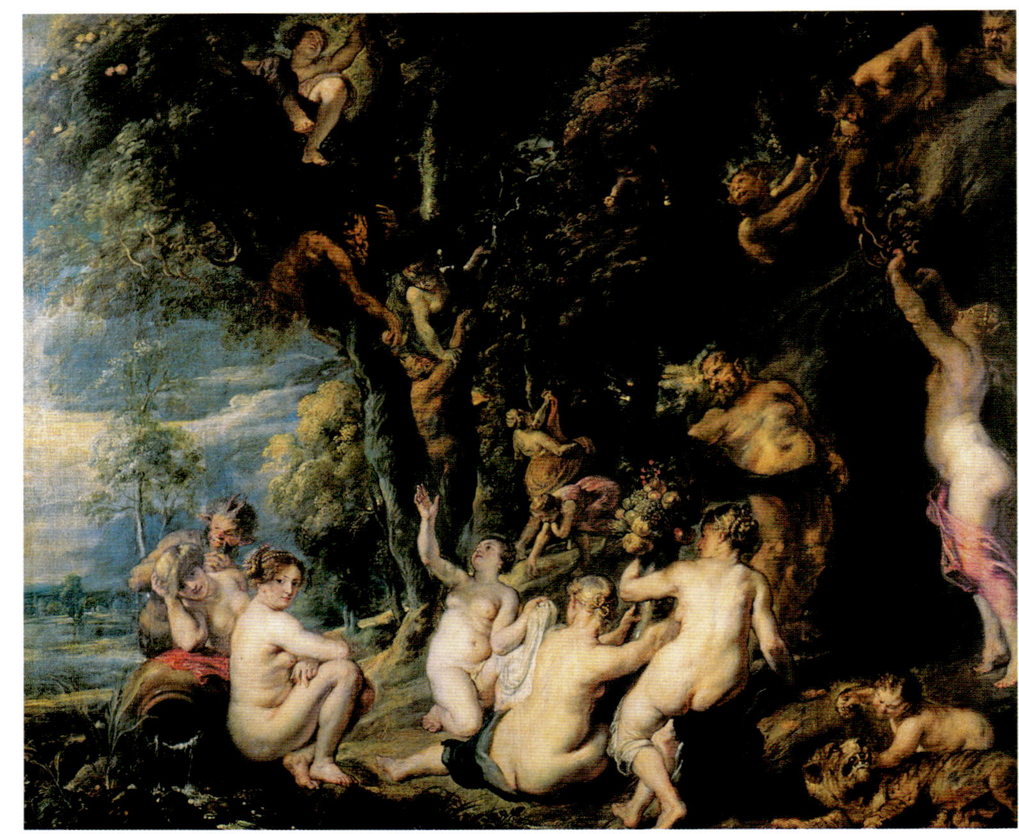

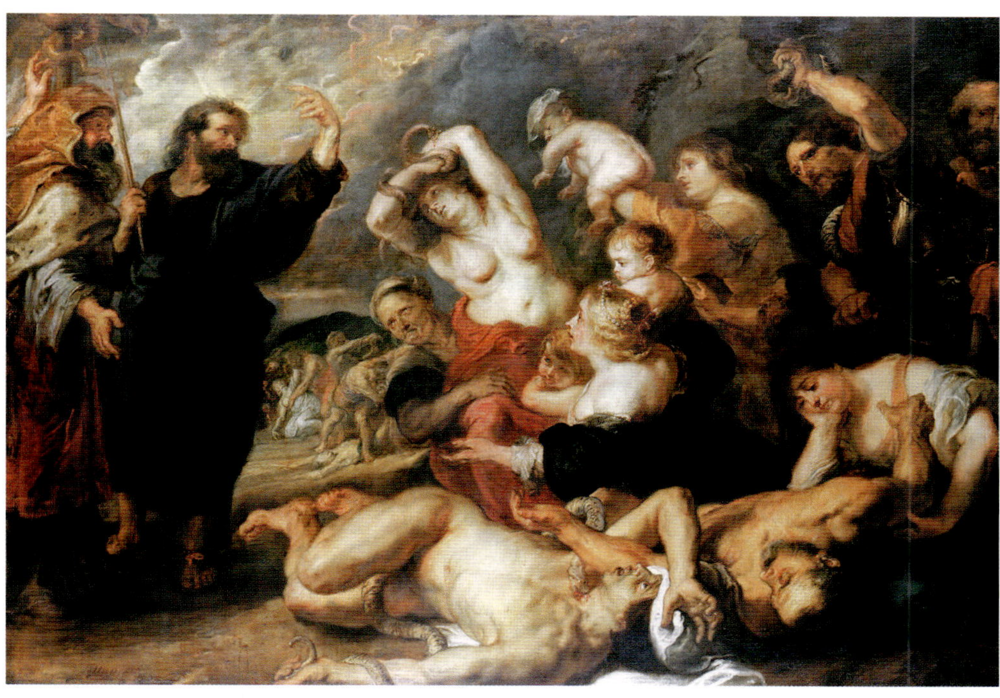

The Brazen Serpent, 1635–40, oil on canvas, 186.4 x 264.5cm (73⅓ x 104in), The National Gallery, London, UK

From the Old Testament, the people of Israel are being attacked by a plague of serpents that God sent to punish them. Moses, at the left, with the hooded Eleazar, calls to them to look at a bronze serpent he has set up on a pole. He says: 'Everyone that is bitten, when he looketh upon it shall live.' Produced with Rubens's studio assistants, some areas of the work have been painted by less accomplished artists.

Massacre of the Innocents, 1635–40, oil on oak, 198.5 x 302.2cm (78 x 119in), Alte Pinakothek, Munich, Germany

This depicts the awful massacre ordered by King Herod, who had been told by the Magi – astrologers from the East – that a King of the Jews had been born, and intended to prevent him from becoming a rival. Mary, Joseph and their newborn child fled. The action revolves around three main groups, all representing murder, despair and ruthless killing, while Herod awaits information about the accomplishment of his orders.

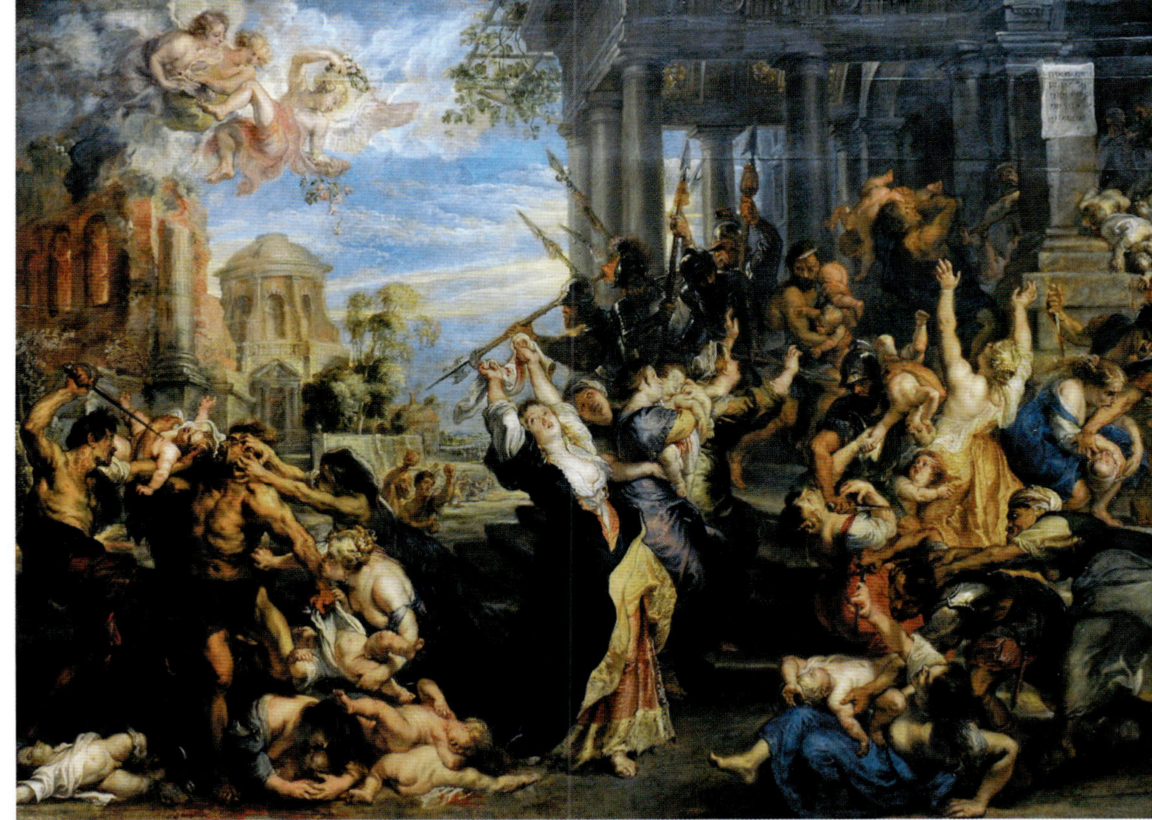

Christ Carrying the Cross,
1634–37, oil on wood,
74 × 55cm (29 × 21¾in),
Rijksmuseum, Amsterdam,
the Netherlands

A preliminary sketch for an
altarpiece, this action-filled
work shows Christ stumbling
beneath the weight of the
cross as he carries it to his
Crucifixion. Simon of Cyrene
and a muscular young man
struggle to help him, the
drama emphasized by
the muscular figure being
portrayed from behind.
Veronica tenderly wipes
Christ's face with her veil,
while Christ's mother and
Saint John watch helplessly.
To arouse even more
stirring emotions, Rubens
has turned Christ's head to
look piercingly out of the
image, directly at the viewer.

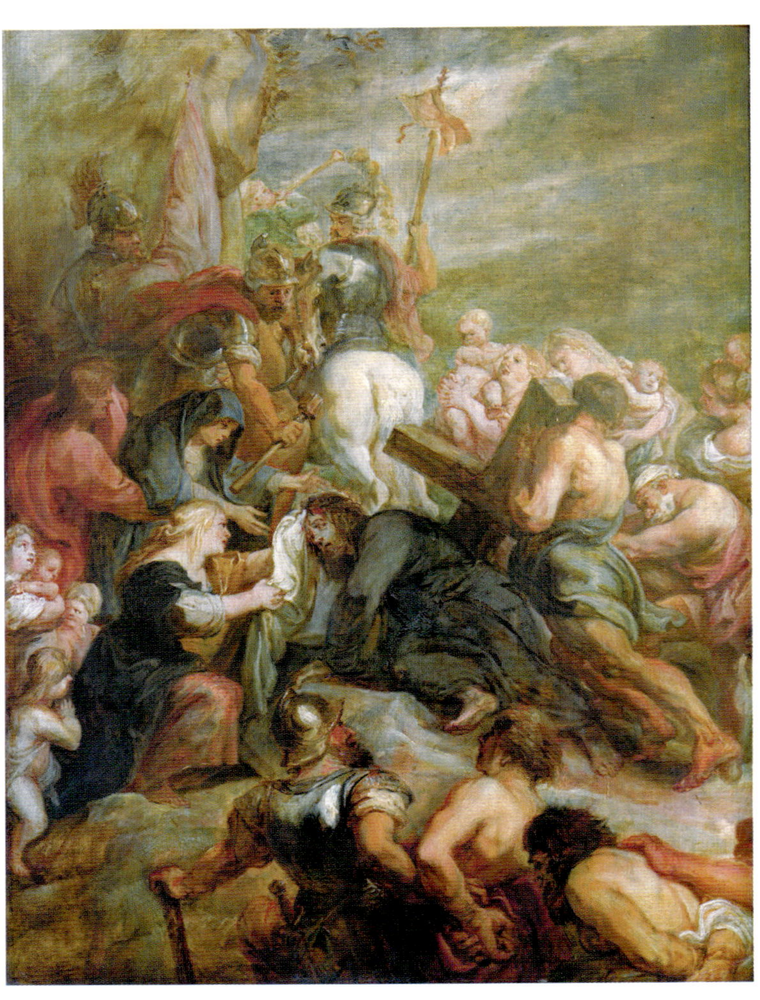

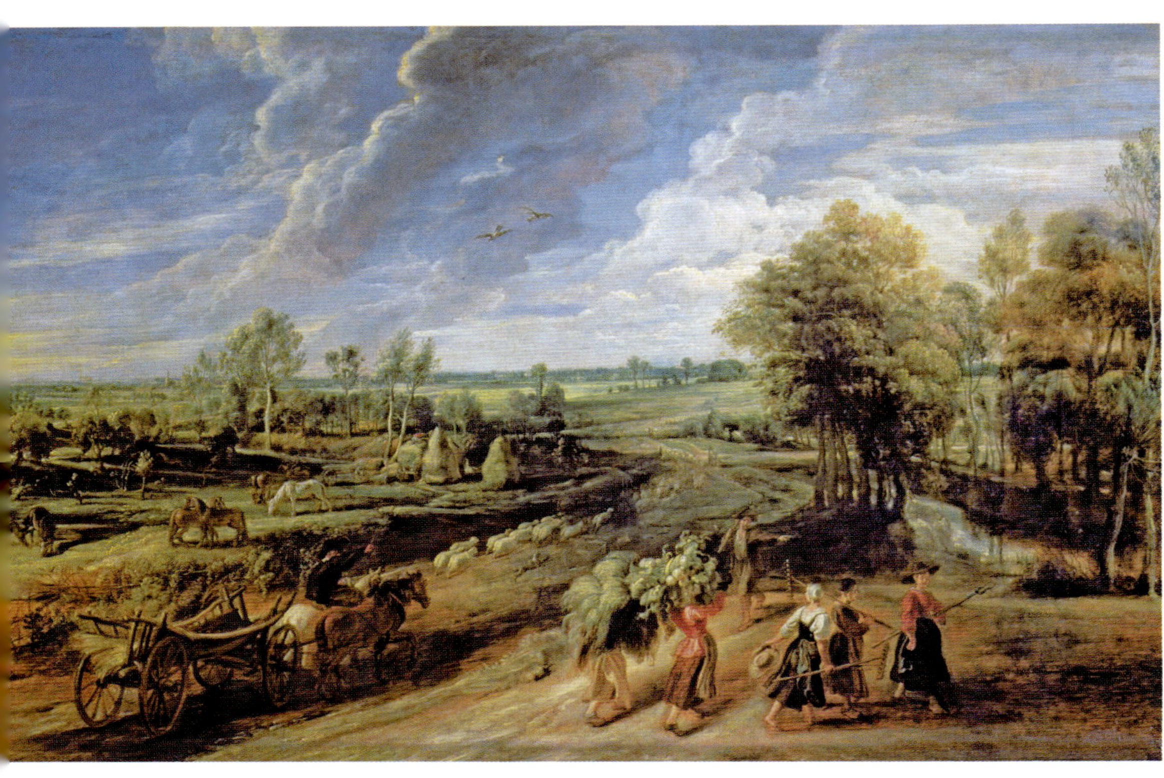

*Return of the Peasants from the
Fields, c.*1632–34, oil on panel,
121 × 194cm (47½ × 76¼in),
Pitti Palace, Florence, Italy

Although Rubens was
absorbed by landscapes and
the natural world in his later
career, he nonetheless
included human elements,
here expressing a story
for all to 'read'. Under an
atmospheric sky, a young girl is
walking to a village and a man
is giving her directions. Their
body language is conveyed in
their gestures as they stand in
the open fields that feature a
stream, trees heavy with fruit,
tired horses resting after a
long day, and women returning
home laden with produce.

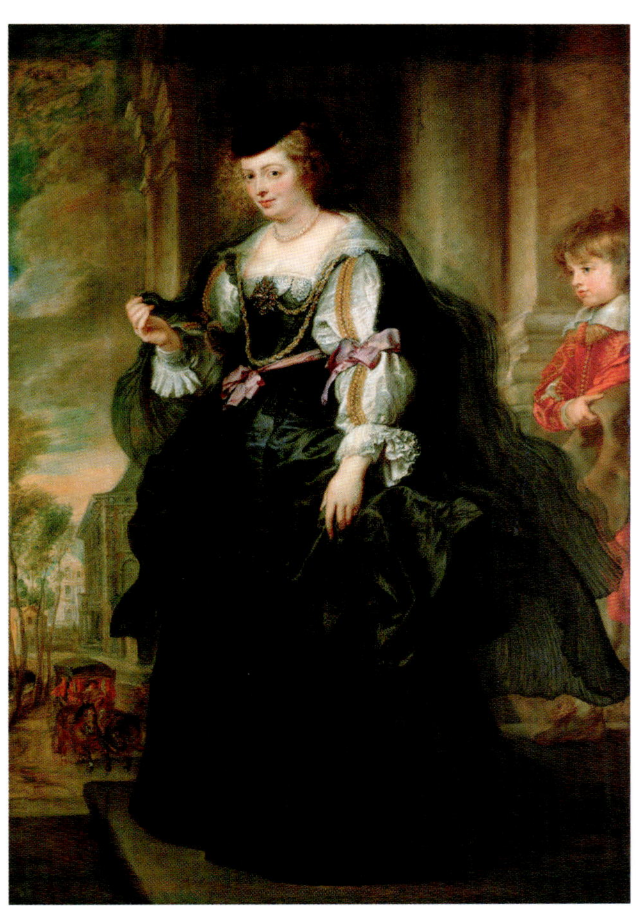

Portrait of Hélène Fourment with a Coach, c.1639, oil on panel, 195 x 132cm (76¾ x 52in), Musée du Louvre, Paris, France

Clearly passionately in love with his young second wife, Rubens painted her leaving their grand home with their son Frans just behind her. Dressed in a fashionable black satin Spanish robe, her hat – also the height of fashion – derived in Flanders. The dark fabrics emphasize her pale alabaster skin tone. The two-horsed carriage symbolizes marital harmony, while her feminine hand gesture suggests modesty. Details such as her pearls are painted in thick impasto. This is believed to be the last portrait of Hélène by Rubens, and expresses his ease with the sumptuous admired Baroque style.

Self-portrait, 1638–40, oil on canvas, 109.5 x 85cm (43 x 33½in), Kunsthistorisches Museum, Vienna, Austria

In later life, Rubens withdrew from almost all his diplomatic duties and concentrated on his art and his family. While the stance of this self-portrait does not differ much from earlier versions, a sense of introspective melancholy can be detected in his eyes. Yet the pose continues to display characteristics of his earlier court portraiture, and his handling shows his continued vigour when painting; Rubens's advancing years and weakening eyesight did not diminish his dexterity.

INDEX

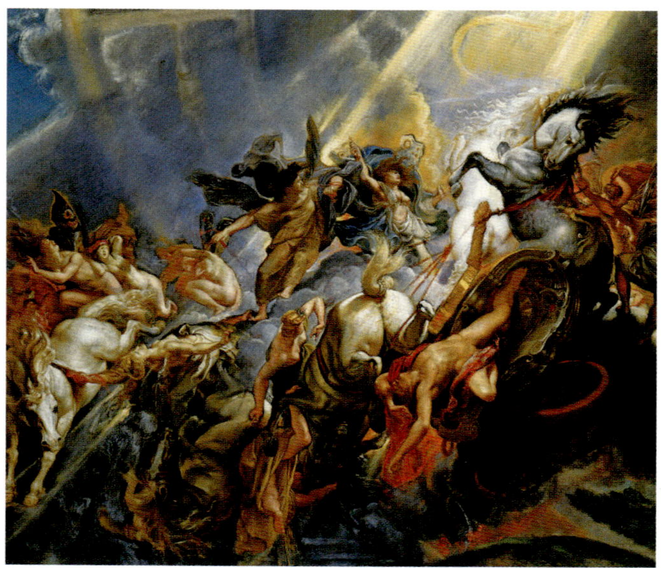

The Fall of Phaeton, 1604–05, oil on canvas.

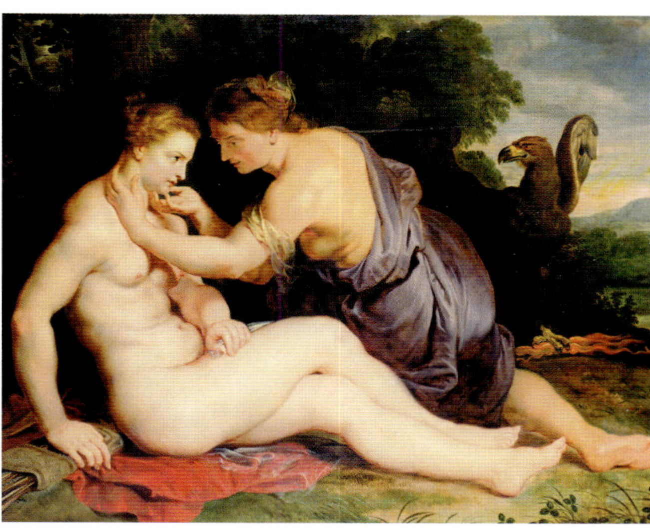

Jupiter and Callisto, 1613, oil on canvas.

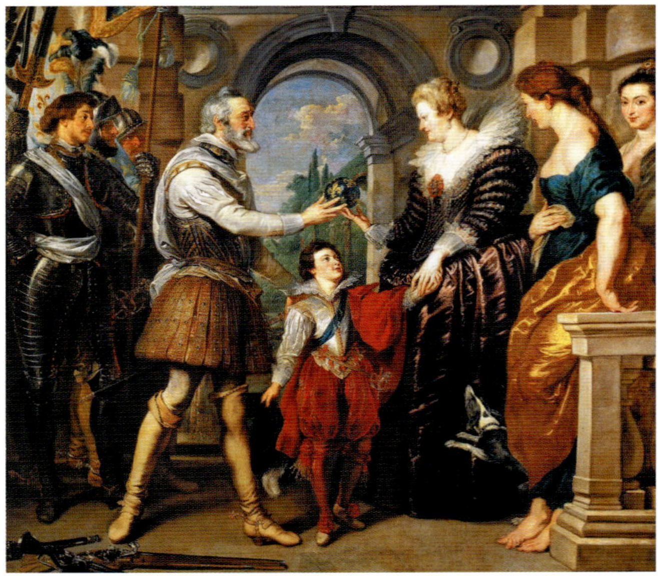

The Consignment of the Regency, c.1622–25, oil on canvas.

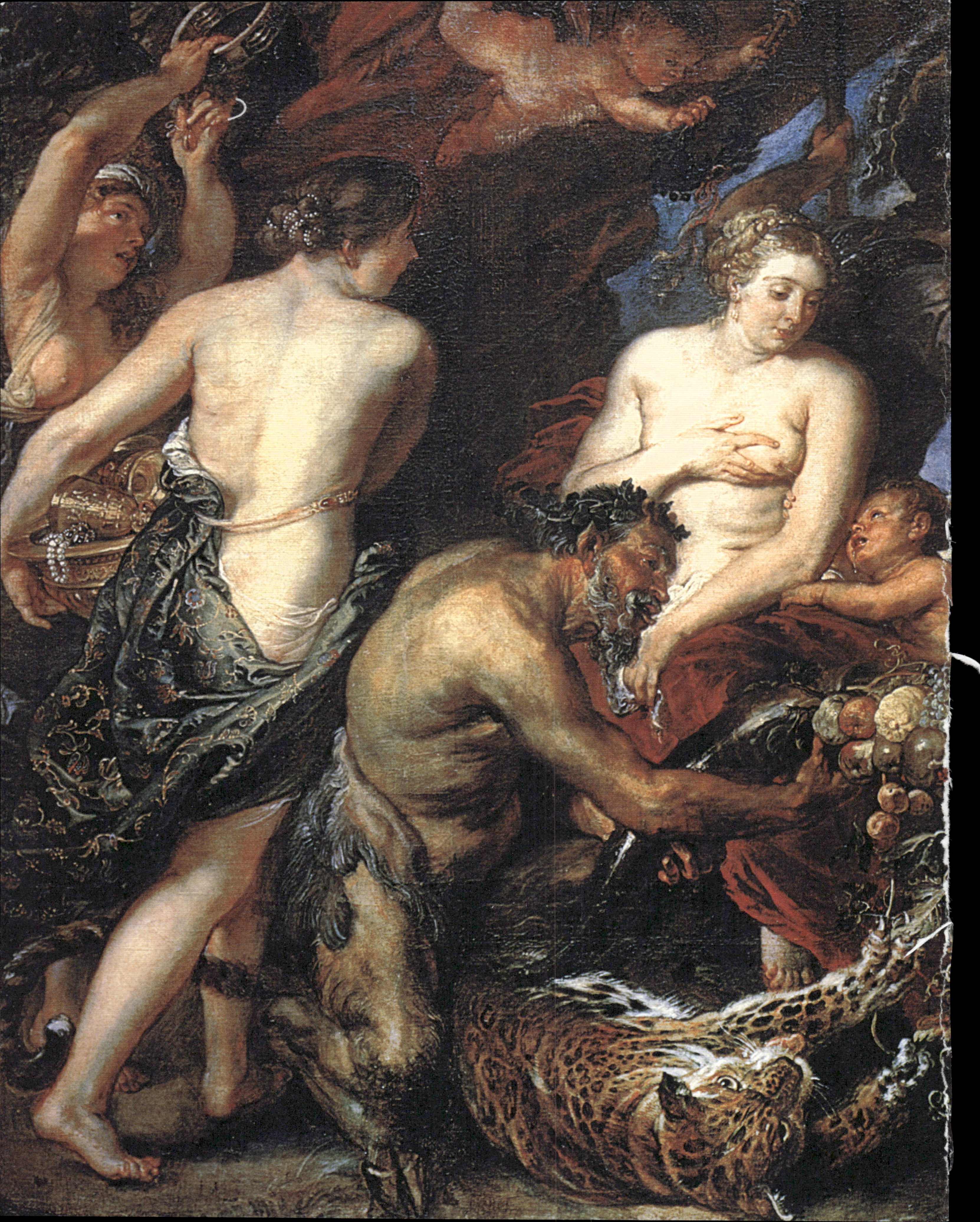